¡ACCIÓN!

- ⚜ Student-centered Learning
- ⚜ Practical Communication Skills
- ⚜ Cultural Relevancy

GLENCOE

Macmillan/McGraw-Hill

Itinerary for Success

¡Acción! presents language in its real-life context— giving teens make friends, and to survive speaking world. The student text features communication-based lessons mental grammar applications that the skills to communicate, in the Spanish-with develop- and real-life encourage...

- Communication
- Divergent thinking
- Cooperative learning

¡Acción! fully supports natural communication. It presents the "living" language of the Spanish-speaking world. Students learn the language as they follow the real-life situations of several teens from contemporary Hispanic cultures in the U.S. to Europe and Latin America.

Success-Oriented Objectives

Each lesson excites curiosity by opening with a colorful *¡A comenzar!* introduction—which sets forth the language functions the student is expected to master by the end of the lesson. Examples of these language functions are found in the dialogues, letters, postcards, brochures, and other language applications that follow.

So Simple!

¡Acción! presents grammar in functional, "how to…" terms, and in manageable amounts to assure student mastery. The *Estructura Actividades* provide students with ample opportunity to exchange information and express themselves meaningfully. No other textbook encourages personalized communication as effectively as *¡Acción!*

Contextualized Vocabulary

Engaging activities give students immediate practice in using new words and idioms within their active contexts. Students learn high-frequency words and phrases in manageable, carefully controlled quantities.

Expressing Ourselves

Situaciones provide an opportunity for students to apply—both in spoken and written formats—the vocabulary, structures, functions, and cultural insights that have been presented in the lesson.

Being There

The *Cultura viva* emphasizes the human, dynamic aspect of Spanish. Students learn appropriate expressions of everyday social courtesy and skills, as well as interesting facts about Hispanic art and music, the richness and variety of regional foods, and the diversity that exists within the Spanish-speaking world.

Putting It All Together

Each chapter ends with a *Repaso* or review of the functions presented throughout the lessons to reinforce language competence.

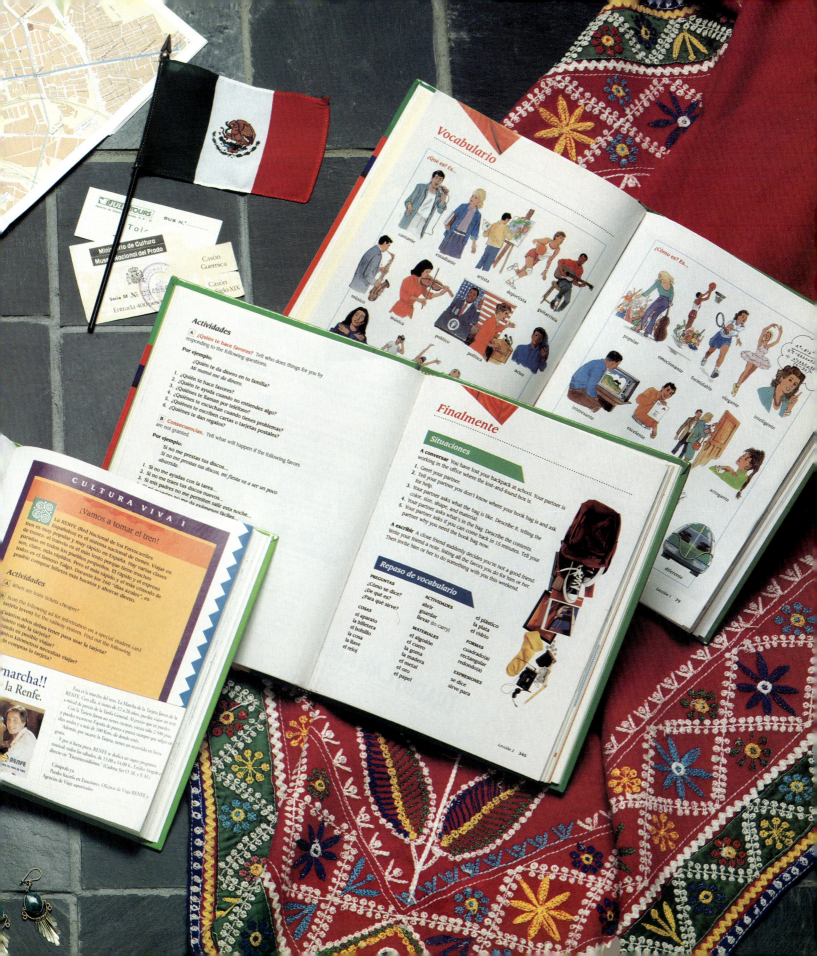

¡Acción!=Options!

The **Teacher's Wraparound Edition** with pages identical to the student edition, plus teaching suggestions and techniques, enriches and expands every page. The **Wraparound** **Edition** includes  alternate teaching approaches that you can adapt to your own style. It provides you with current teaching techniques and language strategies and includes topics such as **Getting Ready For the Lesson**, **Cooperative Learning**, **Total Physical Response**, and **For the Native Speaker**. The **Teacher's Wraparound Edition** is the richest and most supportive Spanish language teaching resource available.

Getting Started

Lesson introductions  and **Bell Ringer** review activities provide you with clearly stated lesson goals, resources, and pupil preparation activities so you can "kick off" with what students already know.

Culture: Yesterday and Today

Share cultural information with your students that directly relates to the ***Cultura viva*** reading through the teacher topic, **Did You Know?**

Critical Thinking Activities ask students to focus on similarities  and differences between the Hispanic culture and their own through thought- provoking questions and observations.

The **Teacher's Wraparound Edition** also emphasizes the practical, everyday applications of language. All activities are designed to encourage a high level of participation and communication through small group and cooperative activities.

Exercising and Applying Language Skills

A major advantage of ***¡Acción!*** is the wealth of alternate activities provided for teachers and students. Conversational and written activities accompany each lesson to reinforce and expand lesson objectives. Highlights of these activities are their contextualized format, meaningful communication and real-world application. Activities **For the Native Speaker** focus on techniques for adapting the text to the needs of native speakers of Spanish.

The Action Never Stops

The comprehensive *¡Acción!* series includes a number of valuable support materials—designed to enrich and enliven classroom and homework activities.

- **Writing Activities Workbook** extends the lesson through the written medium and provides reinforcement for vocabulary and grammar skills.
- **Estructura Masters** activities provide additional student practice on each Estructura topic.
- **Diversiones Masters** support the lesson content in lively, new formats including word puzzles and realia-based activities.
- **Lesson Quizzes** are contextually designed to reinforce student confidence by testing knowledge and skills in *Vocabulario* and *Estructura* sections of each lesson.
- **Testing Program** measures student mastery in all four skills plus culture.
- **Vocabulario Transparencies** offer colorful visual cues to present and practice vocabulary and stimulate classroom conversation.
- **Audio Cassette Program** develops listening comprehension skills through a variety of recorded activities. Accompanied by a **Student Tape Manual** for recording student responses and checking comprehension of spoken Spanish.
- **Video Cassette Program** captures the flavor of the cultural settings in the student text while reinforcing the functions and vocabulary chapter-by-chapter. The video is accompanied by a **Video Activity Booklet** in both Teacher and Pupil versions.
- **Computer Software: Practice and Test Generator** provides additional student practice of vocabulary, grammar, and culture through independent work. Teachers may select items for testing purposes.
- **Teacher's Classroom Resource Box** contains ancillary materials for initiating a variety of classroom activities.

Packaging the Action

To provide you with maximum flexibility, *¡Acción!* materials are available in a number of different ways.

		Level 1	Level 2
■ Student Text	ISBN	0-02-635301-6	*635324-5
■ Teacher Wraparound Edition	ISBN	0-02-635302-4	*635325-3

Ancillaries are available as follows:

		Level 1	Level 2
■ Writing Activities Workbook	ISBN	0-02-635303-2	*635326-1
■ Writing Activities Workbook, TAE	ISBN	0-02-635304-0	*635327-X
■ **Estructura** Masters with Answer Key	ISBN	0-02-635344-X	*635346-6
■ **Diversiones** Masters with Answer Key	ISBN	0-02-635348-2	*635349-0
■ Lesson Quizzes with Answer Key	ISBN	0-02-635313-X	*635336-9
■ Testing Program with Answer Key	ISBN	0-02-635305-9	*635328-8
■ Vocabulario Transparencies	ISBN	0-02-635308-3	*635332-6
■ Situation Cards	ISBN	0-02-635353-9	*635355-5
■ Audio-Cassette Program	ISBN	0-02-635306-7	*635329-6
■ Student Tape Manual, PE	ISBN	0-02-635309-1	*635333-4
■ Student Tape Manual, TAE	ISBN	0-02-635352-0	*635354-7
■ Video Program	ISBN	0-02-635307-5	*635331-8
■ Video Cassette Script	ISBN	0-02-635311-3	*635334-2
■ Video Activity Booklet	ISBN	0-02-635312-1	*635335-0
■ Computer Software: Practice and Test Generator			
IBM Version	ISBN	0-02-635339-3	*635342-3
Apple Version	ISBN	0-02-635341-5	*635343-1
■ Teacher's Classroom Resource Box	ISBN	0-02-635351-2	*635356-3

*When ordering from Level 2, numbers should be preceded by ISBN 0-02-.

¡ACCIÓN!

See the Action for Yourself

To request an examination copy of all basic and ancillary materials, please call or write your nearest area office.

1. **NORTHEAST REGION**
GLENCOE
17 Riverside Drive
Nashua, NH 03062
603-880-4701

2. **MID-ATLANTIC REGION**
GLENCOE
Princeton-Hightstown Road
P.O. Box 409
Hightstown, NJ 08520
609-426-7356

3. **ATLANTIC-SOUTHEAST REGION**
GLENCOE
Brookside Park
One Harbison Way, Suite 101
Columbia, SC 29212
803-732-2365

4. **SOUTHEAST REGION**
GLENCOE
6510 Jimmy Carter Boulevard
Norcross, GA 30071
404-446-7493

5. **MID-AMERICA REGION**
GLENCOE
4635 Hilton Corporate Drive
Columbus, OH 43232
614-759-6600

6. **MID-CONTINENT REGION**
GLENCOE
846 East Algonquin Road
Schaumburg, IL 60173
708-397-8448

7. **SOUTHWEST REGION**
GLENCOE
320 Westway Pl., Suite 550
Arlington, TX 76018
817-784-2100

8. **TEXAS REGION**
GLENCOE
320 Westway Pl., Suite 550
Arlington, TX 76018
817-784-2100

9. **WESTERN REGION**
GLENCOE
610 E. 42nd St., #102
Boise, ID 83714
208-378-4002
Includes Alaska

10. **CALIFORNIA REGION**
GLENCOE
15319 Chatsworth Street
P.O. Box 9609
Mission Hills, CA 91346-9609
818-898-1391

CATHOLIC SCHOOL REGIONS
BENZIGER PUBLISHING

EAST/SOUTHEAST REGION
Joe McKenney
Benziger Publishing Company
25 Crescent Street
Stamford, CT 06906
203-964-9109

MIDWEST/WEST REGION
Tim Downs
Benziger Publishing Company
846 E. Algonquin Road
Schaumburg, IL 60173
708-397-8448

FOR HAWAII
Donald Hosaka, Rep.
Macmillan/McGraw-Hill International
1613 Kanalui Street
Honolulu, HI 96816
Telephone: 808-734-6971
Telefax: 808-735-4590

FOR ALL OVERSEAS K-12 SCHOOLS:
Macmillan/McGraw-Hill International
866 Third Avenue
New York, NY 10022-6299
Telephone: 212-702-3276
Telex: 225925 MACM UR
Telefax: 212-605-9377

FOR CANADIAN ORDERS:
Maxwell Macmillan Canada
1200 Eglinton Ave., East, Suite 200
Don Mills, Ontario M3C 3NI
Telephone: 416-449-6030
Telex: 069.59372
Telefax: 416-449-0068

Inquiries may also be directed to the corporate office:

Glencoe Division
Macmillan/McGraw-Hill
936 Eastwind Drive
Westerville, OH 43081

90170-7

¡Acción!

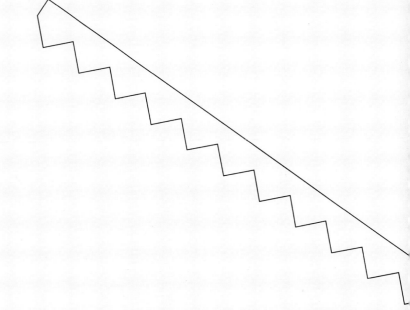

VICKI GALLOWAY

DOROTHY JOBA

ANGELA LABARCA

GLENCOE

Macmillan/McGraw-Hill

Lake Forest, Illinois   Columbus, Ohio   Mission Hills, California   Peoria, Illinois

Send all inquiries to:
Glencoe Division, Macmillan/McGraw-Hill
15319 Chatsworth Street
P.O. Box 9509
Mission Hills, CA 91395-9509

ISBN 0-02-635302-4
ISBN 0-02-635316-4
ISBN 0-02-635321-0

1 2 3 4 5 6 7 8 9   96 95 94 93 92 91

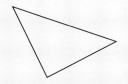

CONTENTS

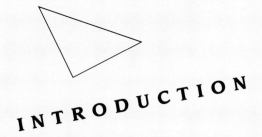

INTRODUCTION

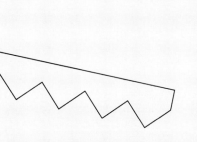

Welcome to the world of *¡Acción!*, the junior high and high school Spanish series by the Glencoe Division of Macmillan/McGraw-Hill School Publishing Company. *¡Acción!* is more than a catchy title. It is a communication-based language program that emphasizes the active involvement of the learner in all stages of instruction. As your students become active partners in gaining proficiency in all four language skills, and in acquiring cultural awareness, you will find that teaching Spanish becomes more rewarding than ever before. And this Teacher's Wraparound Edition provides you with an abundance of practical suggestions and resources to make learning even more successful. *¡Acción!* offers features that will encourage students to become motivated, enthusiastic learners in all phases of instruction. These features include:

- a communication-based curriculum
- contextualized learning
- learner-centered instruction
- cooperative learning
- a developmental approach to grammar
- a contextualized approach to vocabulary
- an integrated, participatory approach to culture

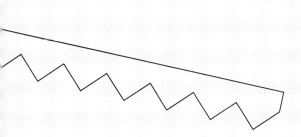

FEATURES AND BENEFITS

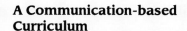

A Communication-based Curriculum

Perhaps the main challenge in the Spanish classroom today is finding ways to engage students in meaningful, communicative activities. The learner-based approach in the *¡Acción!* series maximizes the amount of time students spend in developing language skills and cultural awareness in order to communicate effectively. All aspects of the instructional design—from the presentation of new material, to testing and evaluation—engage learners in the process of communicating in Spanish. Students are actively involved in comprehending and responding appropriately to oral and written messages within authentic cultural contexts.

As you use *¡Acción!* Level 1 in your classroom, you will quickly see how it integrates vocabulary, grammatical structures, and culture to emphasize the main objective: to communicate meaningfully with others in Spanish. *¡Acción!* Language functions uses as the organizing

principle for integrating these linguistic and cultural elements. The activities in this series have been carefully developed to motivate students to socialize, request information, perform specific tasks, and discuss issues and ideas relevant to their personal interests through appropriate listening, speaking, reading, and writing formats. And in each lesson, the wealth of authentic materials and cultural insights encourage communication within real-life contexts that reflect the diversity of the contemporary Spanish-speaking world. This Teacher's Wraparound Edition offers an easy-to-follow, step-by-step guide to using these materials most effectively in order to make your classroom one in which communication in Spanish flows as naturally and spontaneously as possible through all phases of instruction: presentation, practice, evaluation, and reentry.

Contextualized Learning

An essential characteristic of the communication-based classroom is contextualized learning. This means that everything students learn is presented within a context, or set of circumstances, that could actually take place in real life. There are no isolated lists of material, no unrelated sequences of practice items designed solely to focus on grammatical forms. Verb forms are described by the function, or purpose, they fulfill. Vocabulary is presented topically. Culture comes alive through authentic documents, photos, and activities, all of which are integrated into the lesson. All presentation of material is reinforced immediately by practice that immerses students in personalized, youth-oriented contexts. Language becomes a means to an end, rather than an end in and of itself.

This emphasis on contextualized learning engages students both intellectually and psychologically. When learners are actively engaged, they are more successful in achieving the objectives of each lesson. In contextualized learning, success for all learners is assured if they are adequately prepared to engage in the learning activity, carefully guided through it, and positively reinforced for their participation. In the *¡Acción!* series, students are always given clear, concrete instructions for completing each learning activity in the Student Text. The Teacher's Wraparound Edition offers additional, easy-to-follow steps that help to prepare students for specific stages in the learning process. Both the Student Text and the Teacher's Wraparound Edition detail techniques for acknowledging and rewarding students.

Learner-centered Instruction

Today's classroom is comprised of students who not only have diverse learning styles, but who may also, in a collective sense, represent any number of cultural backgrounds. The emphasis on learner-centered instruction in the *¡Acción!* series anticipates this classroom composition and offers ideas for responding positively to such diversity. Specific teaching suggestions accompany each lesson, guiding the teacher in setting up a cooperative learning environment that values diversity and encourages all students to become personally invested in their own learning. The emphasis on meeting and respecting the needs of all learners encourages students to support each other in the process of developing language proficiency and cultural awareness.

The Teacher's Wraparound Edition gives a variety of suggestions and extra activities for students who have special learning needs. Specific ideas in the section called *Reteaching* will help those students who have difficulty mastering the important lesson concepts. The topic *For the Native Speaker* offers activities specifically designed for students who have some native proficiency in Spanish. The learner-centered approach in *¡Acción!* offers each student, regardless of background, learning style, or special need, resources to achieve success in developing proficiency in Spanish.

Cooperative Learning

Another key to the effective development of language skills in the communication-based classroom is cooperative learning. The basic principle of cooperative learning states that all students are active partners not only in their own learning, but in that of their classmates as well.

¡Acción! includes numerous paired and grouped activities, and, as a result, peer interaction becomes an integral part of the learner-centered classroom. Students work with each other to achieve the same objective: meaningful communication in Spanish.

The Teacher's Wraparound Edition assists you in applying cooperative learning strategies. Additional background information on the topic of cooperative learning can be found in this Teacher's Manual on page 19. In this section you will find a complete discussion of suggestions to make your classroom come alive as students actively work together to achieve proficiency.

A Developmental Approach to Grammar

As you become familiar with the instructional design of the *¡Acción!* series, you will notice that it employs a developmental approach to learning grammar. In teaching certain key verbs, this approach means that students become well-acquainted with the function of each verb form, as reflected in a specific verb ending, prior to exposure to the complete verb paradigm. By function, we mean a communication act which serves a particular purpose. For example, in Level 1 (Capítulo 2, Lección 1), the singular forms of the verb **ser** are presented under the functional topic: How to identify and Describe People and Things ("To identify yourself, use **soy** . . . ; to identify someone or something, use **es** . . . ; to question someone you speak to informally, use **eres** . . ."). In this example, and in many other instances, students practice each verb form in a variety of real-life contexts that makes each form meaningful to them.

Why does *¡Acción!* employ a developmental approach to the teaching of grammar? Experience shows that students need time and adequate practice to develop proficiency in using grammatical forms effectively. Research also indicates that what is learned together is stored together, and consequently, retrieved together in active language usage. As an example, when the learner's mind is flooded with all forms of present tense *-ar* verbs in the same lesson, there are two predictable results: there is usually insufficient time to practice all forms for student mastery; and the student tends to confuse the forms on recall.

The developmental approach in the *¡Acción!* series gives students sufficient time to become well-versed in using each specific grammatical form in a context that reinforces its communicative function. In Level 1, the principal structures presented in this approach include present tense and regular preterit tense verb forms, descriptive and possessive adjectives, and *gustar* + indirect object pronouns. Grammar topics are recycled at appropriate intervals. Specific references to lessons in which related forms are treated are given in the Teacher's Wraparound Edition under the topic *Structure Focus*.

A Contextualized Approach to Vocabulary

A key characteristic of the *¡Acción!* series is its contextualized approach to presenting, practicing, testing, and recycling vocabulary. The initial contextualization occurs through the thematic presentation in the **Vocabulario** section of each lesson.

A glance at any **Vocabulario** presentation will indicate the vocabulary theme (greetings; occupations; foods; going places, etc.). In each lesson, the presentation begins with a lead-in introductory phrase, or exchange, that establishes the context (**¿Qué quieres hacer? Quiero ...**) This is followed by a series of individual vocabulary items or phrases that naturally occur within this context (**ir a casa, comprar algo, leer revistas, escuchar discos [Capítulo 1, Lección 2]**). Clear, colorful visuals help to clarify the meaning of each word or phrase, and further establish the context. This system of presenting vocabulary thematically, visually, and with contextualized labeling, helps students to organize and group new words, and relate them to vocabulary from other lessons.

In each lesson, practice activities involve students in tasks that are inherently valuable communication acts. At the same time, these and many other activities promote long-term vocabulary retention by deliberately recycling words into new and different situations and contexts. The end-of-chapter **Repaso** further reenters vocabulary by asking students to use words taught in the chapter lessons at a more integrated, recombined level. For example, in the **Repaso** for Capítulo 2, students are asked to "think of as many words as you can to talk about what you do on Sundays, according to the following categories." The activity is accompanied by a semantic "map" with the phrase, **los domingos** at the center, and the following categories around the perimeter: **¿por qué?, ¿cuándo?, ¿dónde?, ¿qué?** In this way, students are asked to use numerous words and phrases they have learned previously in a new, more consolidated context.

Words presented in each **Vocabulario** are integrated to the fullest extent possible into all other sections of the lesson. For example, they appear as preview in the *¡A comenzar!* section of each lesson. They are reinforced through their natural contextual link to the grammar structures presented later in the lesson. Vocabulary is reentered in the *Cultura viva* section, and further reentered in the closing *Finalmente* section where the lesson's vocabulary is summarized. The *Finalmente* speaking and writing activities (*A conversar* and *A escribir*) recombine vocabulary with the lesson's grammatical structures by asking students to communicate both conversationally and in writing on specific situational topics. In later lessons, vocabulary that was actively introduced at an earlier stage is recycled within new, appropriate contexts in order to ensure that these words are not forgotten. Deliberate and conscientious recyling of active vocabulary is perhaps the best approach to ensure that words and phrases are stored by the learner for long-term retention.

The Teacher's Wraparound Edition provides several support mechanisms to assist teachers in vocabulary presentation and practice. These include reteaching suggestions for students who may require yet another approach to mastering the vocabulary; additional (but optional) words that are related to those taught in the student text under the heading *When Students Ask;* and alternate words that are commonly used in certain areas of the Spanish-speaking world, presented here under the topic *Regionalisms.* The emphasis that *¡Acción!* places on integrating vocabulary learning into all phases of developing proficiency in Spanish is among its most pedagogically-sound features.

Integrated Development of All Four Language Skills

The *¡Acción!* series maximizes its communication-based curriculum by integrating into all phases of instruction the development of the four language skills: listening, speaking, reading, and writing. Students may frequently use reading and listening skills when carrying out speaking or writing activities. For example, in a paired practice format, Students A and B may be asked to fill out an order form for T-shirts. Student A reads the items on the order form to Student B and then writes down Student B's response to each item. At the same time, Student B listens to Student A read the form and then tells Student A his or her preferences. The partners are then asked to reverse roles. In this way, the activity has involved students in all four skills in order to complete the task. Regardless of which skills are being practiced, students may often need to brainstorm on the specific task as an initial, preparatory step. For example, in Capítulo 2, Lección 3, students are asked to "converse with a classmate about your plans for tomorrow. Use the following expressions: **Voy a . . . , Necesito . . . , Quiero . . . , Pienso . . .**" For activities such as this one, students can perform the task more readily if they are given a few minutes to think about the task and rehearse their statements mentally. You may want to encourage students to write down some key words on a sheet of paper before beginning the activity.

A closer look at how the *¡Acción!* series treats the development of each language skill illustrates how they are integrated in both the Student Text and in the ancillary materials.

Listening

In the typical Spanish classroom, the teacher is the primary source for listening to a variety of spoken utterances. Sometimes what the teacher says in Spanish is specifically related to a section in the Student Text. At other times, teachers may wish to speak to students about themselves and their daily activities, as well as to talk to students about their own activities and interests. Above all, we urge you to use as much spoken Spanish in the classroom as possible in order to maximize listening, and to make the study of Spanish a real-life, dynamic experience for your students.

In addition to teacher talk in general, the *¡Acción!* series provides numerous opportunities for developing the listening skill. The opening *¡A comenzar!* of each lesson includes a dialogue, or some other contextualized presentation, which may either be read aloud by the teacher, or listened to using the audio cassette accompanying the lesson. Each lesson includes oral activities, many of which are designed as whole class practice. For these, the teacher may model each practice item in the activity. In the case of paired and small-group activities, the teacher may wish to do these initially as whole class activities so that students have the opportunity to hear the teacher model the practice items.

In the Student Text there is an emphasis on interaction with other classmates where listening to what a classmate says is critical to completing the activity. This is especially true in the case of paired and small-group activities. In this way, students are made responsible for what they hear. The directions to these activities include having students record the information they hear from their classmates by taking notes and reporting back to the class, or at other times, by writing a paragraph summarizing the information they heard.

The vocabulary and grammar structures highlighted in each lesson of *¡Acción!* are further practiced through the Audio Cassette Program. These listening activities are accompanied by a Student Tape Manual containing tasks based on the information they heard from the recording for students to carry out. These contextualized tasks include following directions while looking at a map, writing down telephone numbers and addresses, and summarizing conversations, to name a few. For each section of the lesson, there is a corresponding recorded listening activity of this contextualized nature.

Additional practice in listening comprehension is provided through the Video Cassette Program, which includes a Video Activities Booklet. The Video Cassette Program features a variety of native speakers from various regions of the Spanish-speaking world, highlighted by those from the three main locales of the Student Text: San Antonio, Madrid, and Miami. The Video Activities Booklet offers contextualized activities that combine reading, writing, and speaking with the input students receive through listening. Students learn listening comprehension strategies as they focus on specific tasks each time they hear and see a given video segment.

The Teacher's Wraparound Edition offers many suggestions that promote listening comprehension development. Teachers have access to detailed guidelines as well as scripts of listening-based material. These scripts include presentation, review, reteaching, expansion, and additional practice. Specifically, teachers may wish to use the *Total Physical Response* activities in the Teacher's Wraparound Edition in order to emphasize the listening skill.

Speaking

Critical to the success of this communication-based series is the emphasis on speaking. Within each lesson, from the introduction of new material to the last summary activity, students are encouraged to speak within purposeful, real-life contexts. The speaking topics are both relevant and interesting and will motivate students to want to speak. Throughout the series, students are asked to express their personal likes and dislikes, opinions, and preferences through surveys, interviews, role-playing, and other task-oriented activities. Non-threatening formats that include paired and small-group activities further encourage students to express themselves conversationally in Spanish. All speaking activities are performed within the framework of the vocabulary and grammar structures taught in a particular lesson, plus words and structures that were taught in earlier lessons. The vocabulary and structures students are expected to use in each speaking activity are modeled through one or more examples (**Por ejemplo**) so that students understand how to express themselves. In many instances, students are provided with a group of key vocabulary words from which they may choose in order to express themselves on a personal level.

In Level 1, (Capítulo 5, Lección 2), students learn "how to describe something they don't know the word for" (circumlocution). This valuable technique for communicating a message successfully, even when a key word is not known, or remembered, furthers the students' progress toward learning how to communicate in the real world. Also in Level 1, students learn how to use hesitation words, or space fillers, such as **bueno, pues,** and **a ver,** thereby learning yet another communicative technique for "buying time" while they think of how to express themselves in Spanish. Additional devices that help students to express themselves are **a)** learning how to summarize ideas with expressions such as **entonces** and **por eso;** and **b)** learning how to express ideas in sequence using **primero, después, luego,** and **entonces.** Many of the **Cultura viva** topics guide students in how they should express themselves within an authentic cultural context. These considerations include formal versus informal speech, expressions of courtesy, gestures, and use of diminutives.

Because speaking is such an integral part of the series, Speaking Tests are included as part of the Testing Program accompanying *¡Acción!* Level 1.

Reading

Each lesson in the *¡Acción!* series consistently integrates reading with listening, speaking, and writing. What is unique in this series, however, is the approach it takes in its implicit development of reading strategies that will result in students being able to read authentic Spanish materials. Students are constantly asked to read authentic texts such as telephone listings, advertisements, announcements from newspapers and magazines, invitations, tourist brochures, mail order forms, television listings, weather reports, floor plans of a house, and numerous other real-world documents for the factual information they provide. These documents frequently provide the information necessary for the completion of an activity in the Student Text. In Level 1, (Capítulo 1,

Lección 3) for example, students are asked to read a brochure from San Antonio in order to give the correct telephone number of each place described in the brochure. Authentic texts such as this serve to reinforce, through their content, the lexical and grammatical structures presented in a particular lesson. By their attractive color and design, they not only provide a direct connection to the real world, they also make learning more interesting and enjoyable.

The widespread use of authentic texts in the Student Edition means that learners will not immediately understand everything they read in a given document. Nor are they expected to. However, students are encouraged to guess at the meaning of unknown words. The Teacher's Wraparound Edition topic *Learning from Realia* provides key questions that teachers may wish to use in order to help students derive maximum benefit from these readings. Beginning with Level 1, Chapter 4, the **Cultura viva** readings are accompanied by strategies for reading Spanish texts for greater understanding.

In addition to the authentic documents previously described, there is a longer, more comprehensive **Lectura** in the final lesson of each chapter. Each of these readings has been chosen on the basis of its appealing content, its thematic link to the chapters, and for its level of reading difficulty. The activities that accompany the **Lectura** focus on pre-reading and post-reading strategies and activities that will allow students to read successfully in Spanish. Students are guided to read globally, to work with cognates and word derivation, and to interact with the content of the reading in other meaningful ways. For each **Lectura,** the Teacher's Wraparound Edition gives more suggestions to the teacher for helping students to develop sound reading strategies.

Students are asked to read on many other occasions in each lesson of the *¡Acción!* series. For example, students may begin an activity by first reading a passage, then reacting to it through a speaking or writing format. At times students may need to read a list of items accompanying an activity in order to complete a listening comprehension task in the Audio or Video Programs.

Writing

¡Acción! integrates writing with other skills by asking students to write what they have already learned to read, understand aurally, and say. One of these three language skills often becomes the stimulus for writing. For example, students may be asked to write a response to an invitation. They may be directed to complete a form with information they hear from either the Audio or the Video Program. On other occasions they may be asked to categorize vocabulary they have rehearsed orally by listing activities according to those they want to do, and those they don't want to do. At other times, students may need to write down information they hear from their partner in order to report back to the entire class. In these ways, students are asked to write in contexts where writing is the most natural form of expression. At the same time, these activities allow students to express their own views, reactions, and interests within a writing framework that provides guidance in syntax and sentence structure.

The *A escribir* activity at the end of each lesson provides a more open-ended context for students to express themselves in writing. As students progress through the Level 1 textbook, the writing activities become progressively more open-ended as students acquire more control of Spanish.

Context and purpose help the student to know what to write, as well as how to express the written message. Such guidance saves students from the frustration of writing beyond their knowedge and ability levels. It also saves you, the teacher, from reading and correcting written activities in which students have exceeded their capacity to write successfully.

In addition to those activities that are specifically designed to develop the writing skill, the *¡Acción!* series offers many other opportunities. For example, as a preliminary step for a given activity, students may be asked to write down a list of words that they will want to use in carrying out the main activity. In this way, students are asked to organize their thoughts so that they are better prepared to carry out a communicative task. Many of the speaking activities are easily converted to a writing format. Suggestions for reporting and summarizing oral activities in the Teacher's Wraparound Edition are easily adaptable for writing practice. Finally, the Teacher's Wraparound Edition provides specially designed written activities for students who are native speakers of Spanish, since it is frequently the writing skill that poses the greatest challenge for these learners.

An Integrated and Participatory Approach to Culture

The *¡Acción!* series places great importance on developing student awareness of the culture in which the target language is spoken. Researchers tend to agree that competency in cultural behaviors is inextricably linked to proficiency in a second language. Rather than relegate culture to one isolated section, in the *¡Acción* series it appears throughout the lesson, integrated into the presentation and practice of both vocabulary and structures. There is abundant use of authentic documents that reflect the cultural themes. These authentic materials are often used as a point of departure for communicative activities. Ancillary materials further integrate cultural themes with language practice—most notably in the Audio and Video components. Both of these components present Spanish-speakers in culturally authentic contexts. Moreover, they include interesting and challenging activities based on these real-life, culturally authentic models. Similarly, the lesson's grammatical structures and vocabulary are integrated into activities designed to reinforce the cultural themes of the *Cultura viva.* Students are challenged to perform personalized linguistic tasks within cultural contexts.

The basic organization of the Student Text reflects an emphasis on the integration of culture and language. Each two-chapter sequence features a specific geographic locale. A storyline involving characters who live in each locale unites the language taught in those two chapters. Exploring the lives of people who live in a specific city also brings that locale to life. This approach also minimizes students' tendency to stereotype by encouraging them to distinguish among the various cultures in which Spanish is spoken. In Level 1, San Antonio, Madrid, and Miami serve as points of departure from which students explore the entire Spanish-speaking world. This approach enables the teacher to treat both the cultural and linguistic diversity that characterizes the Hispanic world in a comprehensive, yet systematic way.

In Level 1, two cities that serve as points of departure are located in the United States. This offers several advantages.

1. Students can relate to characters who in many ways live similar lives.

2. Students find that their study of Spanish has a more immediate personal relevance as they learn to appreciate Spanish as an important language in the United States. They may even come to realize that gaining proficiency in Spanish can enhance their own future personal and career opportunities.

3. Students gain a deeper understanding of the role that Hispanics have played in the history of the United States and greater appreciation of the Hispanic influence in this country.

4. Some students may learn to recognize the wealth of Spanish language and Hispanic culture in their immediate environment. As a result, they may become interested in watching local Spanish television, listening to Spanish radio programs, reading Spanish newspapers and magazines, or going to Hispanic restaurants, movies, and museums. They may become motivated to look for everyday signs of Spanish language and culture in offices, buses, or phone books. They may begin speaking Spanish with native speakers in school, at work, or in their neighborhoods. Once students can relate what they learn in the classroom to their own lives, they tend to become avid learners.

The integrated, contextualized approach to learning culture in the *¡Acción!* series may be the key in assisting your students in developing cultural awarenesss and competency. This feature is reinforced by a section called *Critical Thinking Activity* in the Teacher's Wraparound Edition. These activities guide students in analyzing what culture is and how it affects all people. Other approaches often leave students asking themselves and you, "Why do they do (say) it that way?" Too often, teachers are at a loss for a response. The *Critical Thinking Activities* in this Teacher's Wraparound Edition anticipate that question by offering you guidelines and insights to help your students become critical thinkers. The notes encourage students to compare culturally determined behaviors and beliefs with their own. As they compare, they gain a greater understanding and acceptance of cultural differences by focusing as much on what people share as human beings as on the cultural differences that separate them.

SERIES COMPONENTS

In order to adapt the learner-centered, communication-based curriculum in *¡Acción!* to your own teaching style, you may want to become more familiar with the various resources the *¡Acción!* series has to offer. Each level of the series consists of the following components, all of which are described in detail in this Teacher's Wraparound Edition.

- **Student Edition**
- **Teacher's Wraparound Edition**
- **Writing Activities Workbook, Pupil Edition**
- **Writing Activities Workbook, Teacher's Annotated Edition**
- **Lesson Quizzes with Answer Key**
- **Testing Program with Answer Key**
- **Vocabulario Transparencies**
- **Diversiones Masters**
- **Estructura Masters**
- **Audio Cassette Program**
- **Student Tape Manual to accompany the Audio Cassette Program**
- **Student Tape Manual, Teacher's Annotated Edition, to accompany the Audio Cassette Program.**
- **Video Cassette Program**
- **Video Activities Booklet to ac-**

company the Video Cassette Program with Teacher's Manual
- **Computer Software: Practice and Test Generator**

Level 1: Student Edition

¡Acción! Level 1 consists of six chapters, each of which is subdivided into six lessons. Geographically, Level 1 focuses on three specific locales in the Spanish-speaking world, devoting two chapters to each locale as the setting for a storyline involving specific characters who live in that area. The following specific cities are featured:

Capítulos 1–2 San Antonio
Capítulos 3–4 Madrid
Capítulos 5–6 Miami

Organization of the Student Text

The lessons in each chapter contain the following sections:

- **¡A comenzar!**
- **Vocabulario**
- **Cultura viva 1**
- **Estructura 1**
- **Cultura viva 2**
- **Estructura 2**
- **Finalmente**

¡A comenzar! This opening section introduces the lesson's objectives via a concise summary of the language functions that students are expected to perform by the end of the lesson. Examples of these language functions are found in the dialogue (letter, postcard, form, etc.) that follows. This presentation also serves to introduce the recurring characters and develop the storyline that continues over two chapters. *Actividades preliminares* are included as part of the lesson opener, offering students immediate, controlled practice in using one or more of the language functions just introduced.

Vocabulario New words are presented in thematic groups. These words are further arranged under a lead-in phrase that establishes the conversational context. The presentation includes a wide range of colorful, well-designed visuals that further aid in establishing context. The **Actividades** that follow reinforce new words and phrases by engaging students in personalized language tasks that recombine previously learned vocabulary and structures with those new to the lesson.

Cultura viva 1 This is the first of the two culture presentations in each lesson. The *Cultura viva* frequently develops a cultural theme introduced in the opening dialogue. This section includes activities which provide students with an opportunity to use the target language to express cultural insights in real-life contexts.

Estructura 1 This section presents a grammar topic in functional, how-to terms. The focus is on what linguistic structure (verb form, adjective, article) is needed in order to express a specific language function

or task. Contextualized activities immediately practice the grammatical structures by relating them to tasks that students are asked to perform in a variety of formats: alone, with one classmate, in a group, with the entire class.

Cultura viva 2 This section of the lesson serves the same purpose as the first culture presentation by offering additional cultural insights into the Spanish-speaking world. Integrated activities continue to reinforce the language and cultural material presented in the lesson.

Estructura 2 This section presents an additional structure topic in functional, student-centered terms. As in the case of Estructura 1, contextualized practice allows students to immediately use the structure in personalized formats.

Finalmente Each lesson ends with a summary section that serves two purposes. *Situaciones* provide an opportunity for the learner to apply the lesson's vocabulary, structures and even culture points, in two guided, yet open-ended activities. The *A conversar* provides detailed guidelines for students to work in pairs to perform specific oral language tasks. A *escribir* does the same with real-life contexts that elicit a writing task.

The Repaso de vocabulario provides students with a list of the lesson vocabulary, organized by communicative topics (**Preguntas, La familia, Lugares,** etc.). This list offers students easy access to a vocabulary study aid. It also serves as a ready reference as they perform the *Situaciones* activity on this same page of the Student Text.

End of Chapter *Repaso*

The chapter *Repaso* serves several purposes. The *¿Recuerdas?* section asks students to remember, and express in Spanish, the communicative functions that have been taught throughout the six lessons that comprise the chapter. The activities that follow reinforce these communicative functions by asking students to use them at a higher, more integrated level. These activities reinforce the concept that language learning is continuous, and that what is learned today is related to what is learned the next day.

The Teacher's Wraparound Edition

A unique component of this series is the Teacher's Wraparound Edition (TWE) which you are currently reading. It is labeled "wraparound" because its design offers the teacher consistent, specific suggestions in the left, right, and bottom margins that surround or "wrap around" each two-page spread of the Student Text. The Student Text, as it appears in the Teacher's Wraparound Edition, has been slightly reduced in size in order to provide more space for teacher notes. The TWE provides techniques for working with every aspect of the Student Text. It offers, in essence, a complete set of lesson plans, previewing and expansion techniques, and alternatives that you can adapt to your own teaching style and to the learning styles of your students. Its purpose is to save valuable teacher preparation time. A closer look at the various types of support that the notes provide may help you decide how you can most effectively use this Teacher's Wraparound Edition to its fullest advantage.

There are two basic categories of notes provided in the Teacher's Wraparound Edition:

1. primary topics which appear in the left- or right-hand margins relate most directly to the material on the corresponding pupil page,

2. secondary topics (found at the bottom margin) that complement the material on the pupil page by offering additional related strategies. These topics include *Getting Ready for the Lesson; Total Physical Response* activities; *Cooperative Learning;* and activities *For the Native Speaker.*

Description of Primary Teacher's Wraparound Topics

Lesson Objectives At the beginning of each lesson is a list of the communicative functions that students will be able to perform by the end of that lesson. These concise, clearly stated objectives tell in essence the purpose of the lesson and guide you in teaching it most effectively.

Lesson Resources The beginning of each lesson also provides references to all ancillary materials designed to supplement that lesson in the Student Text. These include the Writing Activities Workbook, Vocabulario Transparencies, Audio Cassette Program and accompanying Student Tape Manual, Diversiones Masters, Estructura Masters, Testing Program, Lesson Quizzes, Video Cassette Program with accompanying Activities Booklet, and Computer Software: Practice and Test Generator. As you come to each section within the lesson, the most appropriate of these ancillary components are listed once again for easy reference. Such access to the many resources for presenting, practicing, applying, and testing the material

allows you to plan exciting, varied lessons that efficiently integrate all four language skills with cultural awareness.

Bell Ringer Reviews These activities provide reentry of earlier vocabulary and structures as independent student work at the beginning of the class, when the teacher is frequently engaged in various administrative duties, and when students may otherwise be waiting for teacher direction. They are also designed to assist students in "switching gears" from the previous class. For ease of use, the Bell Ringer Reviews appear consistently in four locations in each lesson:

1. at the beginning of the lesson;

2. with the introduction of vocabulary;

3. with the introduction to Estructura 1;

4. with the introduction to Estructura 2.

Presentation Suggestions and strategies for presenting the material featured in each lesson section (*¡A comenzar!, Vocabulario, Cultura viva 1* and *2, Estructura 1* and *2,* and *Finalmente*) are given in notes at the beginning of that section. These presentation notes include suggestions for what to do and say, as well as ways to involve students actively in the presentation process. These suggestions prepare students to be more receptive to the new material they are about to encounter. The following teacher notes merit a more detailed description.

Presentation to Estructura 1 and 2 The notes in this section are designed to expand the ways in which the teacher can assist students in carrying out the functions in the lesson. They stress practice in all four language skills. These suggestions are also designed to facilitate the developmental approach to presenting and practicing structure.

Structure Focus. These notes highlight which verb forms, or other grammatical structures, are featured in the lesson. In addition, they give the teacher an overview of how the entire grammar strand is presented in the Student Text.

Actividades All sections of each lesson include practice activities for immediate application. Many notes refer to these activities and serve to:

1. provide responses to all practice activities;

2. suggest ways of extending a given activity;

3. suggest additional related activities to supplement those in the Student Text.

When Students Ask This marginal note offers teachers immediate access to vocabulary items that are related by topic to those presented in the **Vocabulario** of each lesson. It enables the teacher to anticipate students' curiosity and be prepared to expand on each lesson's vocabulary as needed. Teachers may elect to include this optional vocabulary in practice activities, as they choose. However this vocabulary is not tested as part of the Testing Program accompanying the series.

Regionalisms The incorporation of regional variations of vocabulary items allows the teacher to maximize the realism of the Student Text by pointing out that there are other, equally appropriate ways of saying the same thing in different regions of the Spanish-speaking world.

Reteaching The emphasis that the *¡Acción!* series places on learner-centered instruction includes options to meet all student needs. Consequently, this note offers teachers an alternate approach for students who experience difficulty in learning the lesson vocabulary or grammar. The topic *Reteaching* also appears at the end of the *Estructura 1* and *Estructura 2* sections of the lesson, providing yet another approach to presenting the grammar topics. The Reteaching suggestions may also be used for reentry and review.

Did You Know? These notes provide additional background information on various aspects of each *Cultura viva* topic. This information may be shared with the class, as the teacher chooses.

Critical Thinking Activities The questions in these notes are designed to encourage students to develop analytical skills. By working with culture within a critical thinking framework, students can focus on both similarities and differences when comparing diverse Hispanic cultures with each other, and with non-Hispanic culture in the United States.

Additional Primary Teacher Wraparound Topics

Classroom Management These are alternate suggestions for grouping students for specific tasks that appear in the Student Text. These notes appear at appropriate times in the lesson and allow for flexibility in adapting the presentation and practice to diverse teaching styles. In addition, suggestions for varying the classroom grouping and seating arrangements by alternating among whole class, small group, and paired activities, offer teachers options for meeting the needs of different learning styles and interests.

Learning from Photos and Realia
These notes highlight special features of the photos and authentic documents that appear on specific pages of the Student Text. They encourage teachers to explore with their students the wealth of language and cultural information that such photos and authentic texts bring to the lesson. These notes also offer specific techniques and activities for integrating these colorful, real-life additions to the text into the lesson, using them to their fullest advantage. The notes include questions, many of which are designed to assist learners in developing both reading and critical thinking skills.

Description of Secondary Teacher Wraparound Topics

Located along the bottom margin, these topics complement the material in the Student Text by offering additional related strategies that will help to meet the objectives of the lesson.

Getting Ready for the Lesson
These explicit suggestions serve to preview the lesson's vocabulary, grammar, and cultural themes before students are asked to open their textbooks. These notes encourage the teacher to maximize the important preview phase of instruction. They are designed to prepare students for success in achieving the lesson objectives, and to motivate them to want to explore the lesson in depth by linking *what they already know* with the new material they are about to learn. The techniques used in this segment, including the use of visual and audio resources, provide comprehensible, contextualized input in order to stimulate students' interest and involvement in the lesson about to be presented.

Total Physical Response Activities
Each *Vocabulario* section is supported by suggestions to reinforce learning of vocabulary items through in-class aural comprehension based on the Total Physical Response Method developed by James J. Asher. The principal objective of the TPR activities is to focus student attention on spoken cues as they perform physical tasks in response to teacher commands. A second objective is to assist learners in developing listening strategies in the target language in a non-threatening and supportive way.

TPR activities relieve students of the need to speak, while nevertheless allowing them to demonstrate their ability to understand spoken Spanish. An additional benefit of TPR is that it provides a change of pace, due to the physical movements required, as students respond to commands in Spanish. Moreover, these activities often apply cooperative learning principles since they tend to involve students in interactive situations as they help each other to accomplish the TPR tasks.

Pronunciation The *¡Acción!* series treats Spanish pronunciation as an integral part of second language learning, offering in both the Audio and Video Cassette Programs many real-life models for students to emulate. These real-life models are presented without conscious discussion of how to pronounce individual sounds or words, thereby eliminating the need to devote long periods of valuable in-class time to such non-communicative activities.

On the other hand, the *¡Acción!* series does offer teachers flexibility and options for adapting the text to their own teaching style. Consequently, teachers who wish to focus more directly on pronunciation practice will find in each lesson short verses that practice one or more of the Spanish sounds that tend to be difficult for native English speakers. Since their content reinforces the *Cultura viva* topics, the pronunciation verses are located on the corresponding page in the Teacher's Wraparound Edition. These same pronunciation verses are also recorded, and appear at the end of each lesson of the Audio Cassette Program.

For the Native Speaker Each Teacher's Wraparound Edition lesson includes activities designed primarily for students who are native speakers of Spanish. These notes offer suggestions for challenging students both to explore their own cultural background and to develop greater fluency in understanding, speaking, reading, and writing Spanish. These notes offer activities that can substitute for, or expand on, those in the Student Text, as the teacher chooses. They also offer suggestions for integrating these activities into the total classroom management. Further discussion on the topic of teaching native Spanish-speakers can be found on page 24.

Cooperative Learning These suggestions provide guidelines for peer interaction in order to carry out specific activities in the Student Text. As discussed earlier, cooperative learning reflects two basic principles:

1. each learner is responsible for his or her learning, and responsible as well at for maintaining a positive classroom environment that

supports the learning process for all students;

2. all members of the class respect each other and the contribution that each individual makes to the learning process.

The cooperative learning notes that appear in the Teacher's Wraparound Edition offer detailed suggestions for maximizing peer interaction through specific grouping techniques. For a more detailed description of Cooperative Learning and suggestions for implementing it in the classroom, see page 19.

The Writing Activities Workbook

This ancillary component provides additional writing practice to reinforce all vocabulary and structures presented in the lesson. As is the case in the Student Text, writing activities are contextualized. The Workbook employs a variety of stimuli to elicit written responses including art, hand-written notes, and authentic documents. The *Repaso* pages, located at the end of each workbook chapter, correspond to each *Repaso* in the Student Text and give additional practice for these cumulative activites. The Writing Activities Workbook is also available in the form of a Teacher's Annotated Edition which includes responses to each activity.

Lesson Quizzes with Answer Key

Individual quizzes, in a contextualized format, are provided for each *Vocabulario, Estructura 1,* and *Estructura 2* section of each lesson. They are designed to quickly tell both student and teacher how well the

content of a specific section of the lesson has been mastered. An Answer Key is included at the back of the Lesson Quizzes booklet.

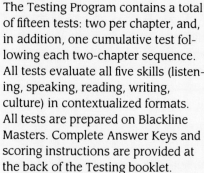

The Testing Program with Answer Key

The Testing Program contains a total of fifteen tests: two per chapter, and, in addition, one cumulative test following each two-chapter sequence. All tests evaluate all five skills (listening, speaking, reading, writing, culture) in contextualized formats. All tests are prepared on Blackline Masters. Complete Answer Keys and scoring instructions are provided at the back of the Testing booklet.

The Speaking Tests have been separated from the listening, reading, writing, and culture tests to allow greater flexibility in their administration. Due to the time-consuming nature of testing the speaking skill, you may wish to test only a few students on any given day while the remainder of the class works independently. The Speaking Tests include two formats: teacher-student, and paired students who are asked to converse on a specific topic. Suggestions for presenting and evaluating the Speaking Tests are given at the front of this section of the Testing Program.

Vocabulario Transparencies

The visuals that appear in the *Vocabulario* section of each lesson have been converted into full-color overhead transparencies to provide additional options to presenting, cueing, and evaluating new words and phrases taught in each lesson. The words and phrases that accompany each visual in the Student Text have been deleted from these transparencies to provide greater flexibility in their use.

Diversiones Masters

These Blackline Masters offer lively, alternate activities that practice lesson vocabulary and structures. Crossword puzzles and other word games, realia-based activities, and a variety of other formats are part of the Diversiones Masters booklet.

Estructura Masters

These activities, on Blackline Masters, further reinforce each *Estructura* topic, lesson by lesson, through contextualized formats. An Answer Key is included at the back of the Estructura Masters booklet.

Audio Cassette Program

The Audio Cassette Program contains the following content designed to reinforce each lesson in the Student Text:

- the dialogue (or other presentation format) found in the opening *¡A comenzar!* of each lesson
- *Vocabulario* activity
- *Estructura 1* activity
- *Estructura 2* activity
- *Situaciones: A conversar* and **A escribir** activities
- *Pronunciación activity*
- *Repaso* activity

Student Tape Manual

The Student Tape Manual contains the follow-up activities to which students respond as they listen to the recorded material in each lesson of the Audio Cassette Program. Many of these activities include visuals as well as authentic documents to create a real-life, contextualized listening experience. With the exception of the opening dialogue (or other contextualized format), all recordings contain new material that has been developed to complement and directly reinforce each section of the Student Text.

Student Tape Manual, Teacher's Annotated Edition

The annotated edition of the Student Tape Manual includes all material found in the Student Edition. Also, the Teacher's Annotated version contains the complete tape script. Answers to each activity are also provided. For teachers who wish to include pronunciation, each lesson of the Student Tape Manual, Teacher's Annotated Edition, includes one or more *Pronunciación* verses. These short rhymes are related in theme and content to the corresponding *Cultura viva* topics in the Student Text. Each verse contains one or more critical sounds for students to listen to and repeat after the model speaker.

Video Cassette Program

The hour-long video cassette program is divided into six major segments that correlate to the six chapters of the Student Text. Each chapter of the video is divided into four components:

- **Chapter Opener**
- **Lecciones**
- **Enfoque cultural**
- **Te toca a ti**

The Chapter Opener sequence captures the flavor of each of the three Spanish-speaking cities featured in Level 1: San Antonio, Madrid, and Miami. Following this introduction is a series of short segments lasting from 30 seconds to 2 minutes each.

These segments feature vocabulary, structure, and culture topics from each lesson in the Student Text. The *Enfoque cultural* brings to life some of the cultural highlights presented in the chapter. *Te toca a ti* serves as a visual or audio presentation designed to elicit active oral or written production on the part of the student. All video segments were shot on location and feature real people in real life situations using authentic, unscripted language.

Video Activities Booklet with Teacher's Manual

The Video Activities Booklet provides follow-up tasks that are directly related to the video segments. All activities are contextualized and offer clear student instructions regarding what to watch and listen for. The Activities Booklet includes a Teacher's Manual, Culture Notes, and a complete transcript of the video soundtrack.

Computer Software: Practice and Test Generator

This three-disk software program offers students additional practice on the vocabulary, structures, and culture topics in each lesson of the Student Text. In addition, this software program allows teachers to select items randomly in order to print them out for testing purposes. The software disks are available for both IBM-compatible machines and the Apple II family.

¡Acción! Level 1 in two volumes

¡Acción! Part A and *¡Acción!* Part B is a two-volume edition of *¡Acción!* Level 1. It is designed primarily for junior high and intermediate programs where the Level 1 material is

normally covered in two years. This split Level 1 edition is also appropriate for other language program configurations. The split edition is available both in Student Editions and Teacher's Wraparound Editions.

¡Acción! Part A consists of Level 1, Chapters 1–3. *¡Acción!* Part B begins with an *Enlace* review, and continues with Level 1, Chapters 4–6. The *Enlace* review contains new, communication-based activities that reenter all material taught in Part A. The Teacher's Wraparound Edition of Part B includes page references indicating where each vocabulary and structure was initially presented in the first volume of the two-volume edition.

¡Acción! Parts A and Part B include the following components: Student Text, Teacher's Wraparound Edition, and Writing Activities Workbook. The Vocabulario Transparencies, Lesson Quizzes, Audio Cassette Program, Video Cassette Program, Diversiones Masters, Estructura Masters, and Computer Software: Practice and Test Generator, are totally compatible with the split edition of Level 1.

COOPERATIVE LEARNING

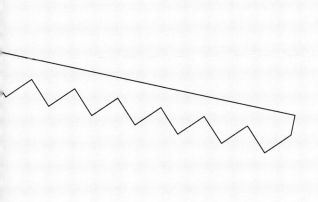

There are numerous benefits to be derived from applying the principles of cooperative learning to the process of learning a second language. For example:

1. Students working together in pairs or groups spend more time actively engaged in communication practice than if each has to wait for his or her turn to communicate directly with the teacher. In a class of thirty students, each student may count on no more than a minute of speaking practice a day if speaking opportunity is limited to interaction with the teacher. This translates to less than three hours of non-continuous practice a year.

2. Cooperative learning activities offer students short, continuous opportunities to communicate in meaningful contexts, whereas isolated short answers are often the norm for verbal interaction between teacher and student in classrooms that rely solely on this type of interaction as the major opportunity for students to practice speaking;

3. by working in pairs or groups, students are personally involved and invested. Activities are designed to hold them directly responsible for completing their parts of the task and providing support necessary for their partner(s) to do the same.

4. Working in pairs or small groups often reduces performance anxiety. Students tend to be less self-conscious performing in the target language for an audience of one or several other classmates rather than in front of the teacher and the entire class.

5. Having the time and opportunity to practice language without constant and direct supervision of the teacher shifts the perspective on making errors in the target language from something "bad" that the teacher must correct, to something that is a necessary and inevitable part of the learning process.

6. Paired and group communication practice more closely parallels the speaking and listening tasks for

which we naturally use language than does speaking in front of the class. Small group communication allows students to practice contextually the various functions of language, including exchanging information, solving problems, asking and answering questions, giving and receiving feedback, and helping each other.

7. Peer interaction promotes a positive social climate for learning in which students begin to see each other as resources for their own learning. By participating in activities that encourage each other to share feelings, opinions, ideas, and experiences, students begin to appreciate the uniqueness of each individual.

8. Dividing the class into smaller units allows the teacher to assess (by "eavesdropping" on various pairs and groups) the degree to which individual students and the class as a whole have understood and assimilated the material just presented.

9. The teacher may use peer interaction to meet more successfully the individual needs of students by designing small units for specific purposes, such as: a) to challenge gifted students, b) to provide extra practice for slower learners, c) to combine gifted students with weaker students in a peer-tutoring situation, d) to group native Spanish-speakers together for special projects, or e) to assign native Spanish-speakers to each group to act as resources.

The success of cooperative learning depends on both the task design of a given activity and the correlation between the objectives of that task and the type of peer interaction best suited to achieve them. The following suggestions for effective grouping may help to implement this approach more easily.

Suggestions for Effective Grouping

Group Composition The initial question in setting up groups is what criteria to use to decide which students will work together? Current research suggests that no major benefits derive from grouping students either homogeneously or heterogeneously according to ability (that is, deliberately putting high achievers with low achievers to "even out" groups, or grouping high achievers together to encourage them to excel). Furthermore, some researchers believe that such grouping practices can actually damage the sense of community in the classroom by creating a hierarchy in the class based on ability.

However, within pairs or small groups, task differentiation appears to be successful in meeting individual students' needs by allowing each student to perform a specific role in the pair or group that maximizes his or her own strength. The teacher can select the task or allow students to choose the specific task that each will carry out. For example, students who are shy about speaking in front of a large group may be best suited to serving as the recorder who writes a summary of what happens in the group. Similarly, a more confident, outgoing student who is comfortable and competent in speaking Spanish may be an excellent choice for the reporter who orally summarizes the group's task for the entire class. Other group roles include the interviewer, who should be confident enough to ask questions and conduct the discussion using only Spanish,

and respondents, the role usually played by all members of the group who contribute the information needed for the activity. These same roles often occur in paired work, and can be divided among the two partners according to the same criteria outlined above.

Another way to individualize grouping is to select specific pairs and groups to carry out variations on the same activity or to work on one of the optional activities provided in the Teacher's Wraparound Edition while other pairs or small groups perform the major activity. In selecting activities to be done during the same time frame, it is helpful for the activities to be related in some way; for example, using similar vocabulary but using different structures, or shifting time references from past to present.

Other possibilities for related but different group activities carried out at the same time can be based on emphasizing different skills, with several groups concentrating on reading a specific passage, while other groups write questions about, or a summary of, the passage. The technique of multiple, related group tasks is particularly effective with large classes, especially if pairs or groups are to report a summary of their task to the entire class. The variation on a major learning theme serves to maintain students' interest by avoiding endless repetition of the same task in the large class context.

Setting Up Groups Several options exist to assist the teacher in setting up groups on a random basis, regardless of ability levels. Whatever the seating arrangement you use in your class, you can have students simply "count off" in Spanish. There are two basic techniques. One is to have students count from **uno** to the number of people in each group, with the last person in the group saying *punto,* indicating where the group ends. Then, the next student begins with *uno,* and so forth. This technique allows for a minimum amount of movement of students and desks, since pairs or groups will be sitting near their partners. If desired, roles can be assigned on the same random basis, for example, *uno* is the interviewer, *dos* is the recorder, *tres* is the reporter. This is also helpful in paired activities, since the teacher can give the instruction that *uno* asks the questions, *dos* replies, and so on. If desired, letters of the alphabet can be used in the same way, with students counting off *A, B, C, CH,* etc.

Another counting-off technique for setting up paired or grouped activities involves having students count up to the number of students present, then pairing at random (for example, *dos, cuatro, seis, y ocho están en el grupo A,* etc.). This technique involves more movement of students, more organizational time, and more attention from the teacher. It is often best effected by writing out the combinations of groups ahead of time and then transferring these to the board.

A third way of randomly assigning students involves preparing letters on small pieces of paper of equal sizes which individual students select from an envelope. Then, any of the matching techniques for pairing or grouping described above can be used. While the amount of movement triggered by these more random methods of selection may seem somewhat excessive, sufficient preparation and practice in setting up the groups prior to class will minimize this effect. The benefits gained from such random grouping techniques include engaging students in listening to the teacher's instructions, and encouraging active language use in the process of students

finding their partners (*"¿Qué número tienes?"*). In addition, the physical movement offers students an energizing break from being seated during most class periods and can be controlled sufficiently by the teacher's preparation in organizing the movement.

Since much valuable class time can be lost in moving students into cooperative learning groups, it is important that you establish routine patterns and clear procedures to minimize the time involved in setting up pairs and groups. Once you have devised specific patterns and procedures for setting up pairs and groups that seem to work well with your classes, you may wish to continue using the same pair and group selection methods for several weeks at a time so that students develop a rapport with several partners before moving on to new pairs or groups. Equally important, however, is to provide all students the opportunity to work with all members of the class in order to avoid setting up cliques and reinforcing competitive tendencies that are at odds with the social climate most conducive to cooperative learning.

Using classroom seating arrangement patterns to determine members of pairs or groups is another option that is more time-efficient and involves the least amount of movement and distraction from the activity. The disadvantage of this option is that students tend to work always with the same partners, with little interpersonal interaction with classmates who sit on the other side of the room, unless the teacher makes an effort to move the class around. This is not as difficult as it may sound. You may wish to experiment with the following alternatives, depending on the way your classroom is organized.

Techniques for Classrooms Arranged with Vertical Rows If your desks are arranged in vertical rows, pairs or groups may cut horizontally across rows. Thus, the first people in rows 1 and 2 form a pair, the same in rows 3 and 4, and so forth. If there are an odd number of rows, the students in the extra row can work in pairs by assigning the first person in the row to work with the person behind him or her. You can achieve variety in paired partners using the seated arrangement by rows by alternating the selection of the odd-row working arrangement to include all rows (row 1 is the odd row, rows 2 and 3, and 4 and 5 work together). You can also have more students in more rows move, so that the first person in row 1 works with the first person in row 4, the same for 2 and 5, with row 3 the odd row. This will involve some extra traveling time.

The same row procedure can work in setting up groups, depending on the number of rows and the desired number of students to work in each group. If the number of students in the group is the same as the number of rows, the first person in each row is assigned to group 1, and the second person in each row joins group 2, and so forth. Groups of 4 can be selected by combining the first two people in each of the two side-by-side rows. In the event of an odd number of rows, students can follow the same procedure as for pairs, with the first four students in the odd-numbered row working together, then the next four. For groups of three or five students, the count-off technique may be used up one row and down the next. This will minimize movement of students and desks.

One technique for maximizing student contact with all members of the class, while still maintaining the seating arrangement in rows, involves applying the count-off technique with the teacher pointing at random to individual students in different areas of the room to give the next number in the series. This random selection process involves more time and movement of students than techniques that employ student location as the principal determinant of group membership.

Techniques for Classrooms with Alternate Seating Arrangements

One alternative to seating students in rows is to seat them in a double semicircle arrangement, which provides greater flexibility in using student seating to determine pair or group partners with a minimum of physical movement. For example, a student sitting in the front semicircle can pair up easily with a student sitting in back of him or her or to his or her left or right. Groups can easily be formed by counting off in different ways, either from left to right in the front semicircle, right to left in the back, or from front row to back. The reverse directions can also be used for counting off, adding more variety to group membership. Also, groups of four can be formed by combining the first two students in the front semicircle with the two students sitting immediately behind them. To vary partners in either pairs or groups, one student at the far end of either semicircle can move to the opposite end, forcing all students in that semicircle to move down one seat.

Other seating arrangements include having students sit in groups of four, facing each other. This classroom design is most appropriate for teachers who wish to make cooperative learning the major source of interaction in the classroom. It allows for student pairs or group practice at any time with little or no movement. The goal of having all

students interact can be achieved by having one or two students trade places with those in another group or simply move the group to the left or right of the original group. Assigning each group a number, with each seat in the four-student grouping arrangement labeled with a letter, allows for easy alteration in the original group formations, with students occupying seat A in group 1 moving to the same seat in group 2, and so on.

Of course, whatever the usual seating arrangement of a given class, it can always be altered for a specific activity prior to students coming to class in order to minimize the movement of desks and students during class. Students can then either be assigned places upon entering the classroom or choose their new seat at random, depending on the teacher's objectives for that particular class period. In addition, any of the random selections described above can also be used to ensure that all students eventually interact with each other in paired or group activities, whatever their usual classroom seating arrangement may be.

Determining Group Size The principal determinant of the size of the group is the objective of the activity. A note suggesting group size is frequently included as part of the *Cooperative Learning* activity in the Teacher's Wraparound Edition. In setting up a cooperative learning situation for which a specific group size is not given, or in redesigning the group process defined in the marginal notes, it is important to determine the exact role that each member of the pair or group is to play in order to achieve the communication objective of the activity. Remember that paired activities are often the

easiest to devise, since they involve only two well-defined roles. In general, the larger the group, the more organization with respect to group roles is needed. A group leader is always needed, and may be given the title of group interviewer or coordinator. This is especially true of groups larger than five. Larger groups offer more distractions from the task at hand unless each student has a clear understanding of his or her role and its importance in completing the group activity.

Special Considerations for Paired Activities Activities best suited for pairs are those designed for students to perform tasks involving one-on-one interaction with specific roles to be played. In most paired activities, it is usually helpful to have students reverse roles at a given point in the time allotted for the activity. Signaled by the teacher, this point should be the time at which most students have completed the task in their original roles and should be announced prior to students beginning the activity.

In dividing the class into pairs, you may encounter an uneven number of students in the class that day. In this event, you have several options:

1. In brief activities, you, the teacher, can serve as one student's partner.

2. If you know in advance that there is an odd number of students, you can select one student to perform a variety of functions such as aiding you in monitoring the performance of several pairs, or working with a specific pair by helping them to work through difficulties they may experience, or by taking notes on what they do and reporting back to the class at the end of the activity.

3. If students are to reverse roles in carrying out the task, the extra student can serve as an observer of a pair until the point of role reversal. At this juncture, the extra student may join the pair and assume one of the roles. The student who has been replaced then serves as observer. The observer's role can be defined as a resource to the pair, contributing words, structures, or instructions with which students need help.

Special Considerations for Grouped Activities While the *Cooperative Learning* notes in the Teacher's Wraparound Edition offer guidelines for some of the choices that you, the teacher, will make in grouping students, you may feel more comfortable with grouping techniques once you have a better understanding of why and how to group in order to achieve specific goals. When all groups of students are working on the same task, all groups should be of the same size whenever possible. When faced with extra students, you may either distribute them to other groups, adding a specific role for them to play (observer, resource person, time-keeper, helper), or you may put them all into a smaller group and redefine the group roles, perhaps having one of the more advanced students in this makeshift group handle the roles of both recorder and reporter.

When various groups are working on different related activities (as described in the Group Composition section above), the size of the individual groups will vary according to the nature of the specific activity in which each group is involved.

Activities for Cooperative Learning In order for students to succeed at cooperative learning, the activities in which they participate without the direct supervision and control of the teacher must be highly engaging. When learners share responsibility for attaining the objectives of a cooperative learning activity, they are more apt to take their responsibility seriously if they have a personal stake in the performance of the group. Most students enjoy the cooperative learning process and become more actively involved precisely because they are "turned on" by the rewards of actually being able to communicate successfully in the target language, in a context that is meaningful to them. Since the activities in *¡Acción!* Level 1 reflect this communication-based, learner-centered approach, they are all adaptable to cooperative learning techniques, even when specific suggestions to do so are not given.

An important factor is that all activities be well-structured. The teacher should tell students precisely what to do, and how to do it. This does not mean that these activities are not openended, that is, allowing for free choice of student output. In most cases, these activities are exactly designed so that students will employ a great deal of creativity in determining the content of the activity. What is defined for them is the purpose of the activity, the goal it is designed to achieve, and the specific steps in the process they are to take in reaching that goal. For example, compare two versions of the same activity:

A. Describe your family to your partner.

B. Describe your immediate family members to your partner, giving the name, the relationship to you, the age, and two physical characteristics of each one. Your partner

will tell you the same about his or her immediate family.

Version A is likely to produce open-ended responses with which students are likely to enter into vocabulary and structure zones for which they are not prepared. Both partner's responses may be of uneven length and quality. If students do not clearly understand what they are expected to do, they cannot be held accountable for doing it. In Version B, students receive more clearly stated objectives and expectations for what each is to do in this paired activity. It is more likely that each student will successfully carry out his or her role with interest, attention, and cooperation.

Efficient Use of Cooperative Learning In general, activities involving peer interaction should be relatively brief. The longer the activity, the greater the chance that students will become distracted from the task. If your objective involves a more complex activity, it is often a good idea to break the activity into shorter, more manageable steps so that students manage their time more carefully and remain focused on what they are expected to do.

Students should be told how much time they will have to carry out the activity. This time allotment should be carefully monitored by you, or a member of the class who is particularly time oriented. It is important from the beginning of the school year not to let students convince you to deviate from the amount of time allotted for a given activity. As your students become more experienced in working with specific time limits for cooperative learning activities, your classroom will flow easily from activity to activity.

Cooperative Learning: Benefits

While much has been said regarding the benefit of cooperative learning for the student, there is also much to be gained by the teacher. Cooperative learning shifts some of the burden of learning from the teacher to the students. In this new role, the teacher is more concerned with setting up the conditons for learning than with being responsible for the learning of all students at all times. Students themselves can share more responsibility for their own learning. This active involvement of all students in the learning process makes your job easier. It also makes the time you spend planning for your classes more rewarding and productive. Although implementing cooperative learning strategies in your classroom may take a little time, the end results are worth the investment.

Native Speakers of Spanish in the Classroom

As the number of Hispanics in the United States continues to grow in nearly all regions of the country, more teachers will be able to benefit from the assets that Spanish-speaking students bring to the classroom. These students are frequently most proficient in understanding and speaking Spanish. For these reasons, they may serve as valuable additional models for students who are not native Spanish speakers. On the other hand, their proficiency may be limited in the following ways.

1. Their speech may include Anglicisms in both vocabulary and grammary (**Voy a chequearlo** instead of **Voy a revisarlo**, or **Te llamo para atrás** rather than **Te llamo de nuevo**).

2. They may also code-switch (mix Spanish and English in the same sentence or stream of speech, often without realizing it). This phenomenon occurs for many different reasons, including a cultural gap, where Spanish does not have an equivalent of an English concept (boyfriend vs. **novio**).

3. Their proficiency may be limited to various home and family-related contexts so that they may seem quite competent in discussing activities but may lack vocabulary and structures to deal with more complex topics such as school activities or world geography.

4. Their familiarity with culture-determined behaviors, values, norms, and beliefs common to Spanish-speaking countries may be limited to those typical of their own background.

5. The range of language proficiency and cultural awareness of an individual student may range from that of a dominant English-speaker who knows a few words of Spanish, to the equivalent of an educated native Spanish speaker well-versed in his or her own culture and its relationship to other Hispanic cultures. Where a given student falls in that range depends on several factors:

   a. whether or not he or she was born in the United States (if so, the birthplace of parents or grandparents can also be a factor);
   b. the number of years of schooling completed in a Spanish-speaking country before coming to the United States;
   c. the language(s) spoken in the home;
   d. socioeconomic details of both the student's experience in a Spanish-speaking country and that of living in the United States (urban, rural, or suburban living situation, educational level of parents, parents' professions);
   e. the individual student's response to peer pressure to speak English or Spanish.

Each of the above factors may be considered in determining the needs of native speakers of Spanish in your classroom.

Meeting the needs of the native Spanish-speaker will help to reduce tension, which may occur between English-dominant and Spanish-dominant students, in two ways:

1. English-dominant students realize that native Spanish-speakers do not "know everything" about Spanish, and, despite apparent fluency, have real needs that are met with activities designed especially for them;

2. The additional activities designed primarily for native Spanish-speakers will avoid possible complaints of boredom, while, at the same time, will maximize their contribution as a whole.

¡Acción!

LEVEL 1

VICKI GALLOWAY

DOROTHY JOBA

ANGELA LABARCA

GLENCOE
Macmillan/McGraw-Hill

Lake Forest, Illinois   Columbus, Ohio   Mission Hills, California   Peoria, Illinois

Send all inquiries to:
Glencoe Division, Macmillan/McGraw-Hill
15319 Chatsworth Street
P.O. Box 9609
Mission Hills, CA 91346-9609

ISBN 0-02-635301-6 (Student Edition)
ISBN 0-02-635302-4 (Teacher's Wraparound Edition)

1 2 3 4 5 6 7 8 9 96 95 94 93 92 91

Acknowledgments

The authors and editors would like to express their deep appreciation to the numerous Spanish teachers throughout the United States who advised us in the development of these teaching materials. Their suggestions and recommendations were invaluable. We wish to give special thanks to the educators whose names appear below.

Program Consultant
C. Ben Christensen
San Diego State University
San Diego, California

Educational Reviewers

Marilyn V.J. Barrueta
Yorktown High School
Arlington, Virginia

D. H. Bell
Nogales Unified School District #1
Nogales, Arizona

Mary M. Carr
Lawrence North High School
Indianapolis, Indiana

Gail B. Heffner Charles
Walnut Ridge High School
Columbus, Ohio

Desa Dawson
Del City Senior High School
Del City, Oklahoma

Irma Díaz de León
San Antonio Independent
   School District
San Antonio, Texas

Linda Erdman
Huntington Beach Union High
   School District
Huntington Beach, California

Janet Ghattas
Weston Public Schools
Weston, Massachusetts

Paula Hirsch
Windward School
Los Angeles, California

Margarita Esparza Hodge
Northern Virginia
   Community College
Alexandria, Virginia

Anne G. Jensen
Campbell Union High
   School District
San Jose, California

Nancy Kilbourn
Simi Valley Unified
Simi Valley, California

María A. Leinenweber
Glendale Unified School District
Glendale, California

Myriam Met
Montgomery County
   Public Schools
Rockville, Maryland

Cheryl Montana-Sosa
Oakdale Bohemia Junior High
Oakdale, New York

VeAnna Morgan
Portland Public Schools
Portland, Oregon

John Nionakis
Hingham Public Schools
Hingham, Massachusetts

Gail R. Pack
McKinney Independent
   School District
McKinney, Texas

Marilynn Pavlik
Lyons Twp. High School
La Grange, Illinois

Carol F. Robison
Hingham High School
Hingham, Massachusetts

Bonnie S. Schuster
Fairfax County
Reston, Virginia

Mary Thomas
Northside Independent
   School District
San Antonio, Texas

María J. Treviño
Northside Independent
   School District
San Antonio, Texas

María Elena Villalba
Miami Palmetto Senior High
Miami, Florida

María Elena Watkins
Edgewood Independent
   School District
San Antonio, Texas

Rosanne Webster
Minerva-DeLand School
Fairport, New York

Rosemary Weddington
Franklin County High School
Frankfort, Kentucky

Janet M. Wohlers
Weston Public Schools
Weston, Massachusetts

Contents

C A P Í T U L O   1

¡Bienvenidos a San Antonio!

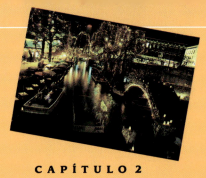

C A P Í T U L O 2

Mis compañeros en San Antonio

••

vi

CAPÍTULO 3

¡Vamos a España!

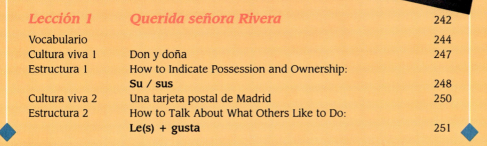

C A P Í T U L O 4

¿Cómo son los españoles?

ix

C A P Í T U L O 5

¡Me gusta vivir en Miami!

xi

xii

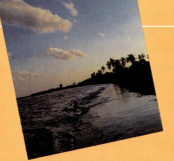

C A P Í T U L O 6

De visita en Miami

xiii

México y La América Central

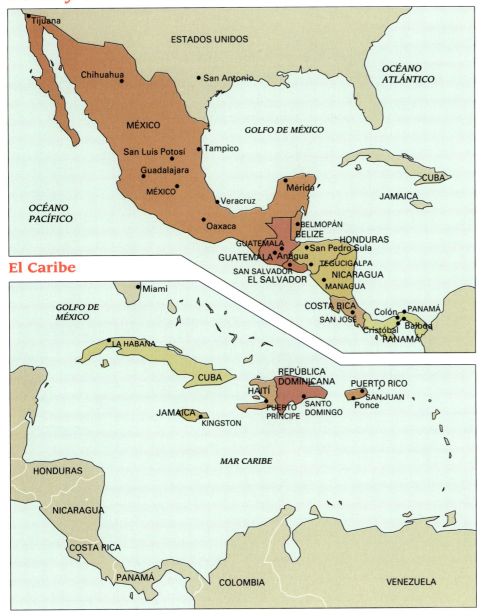

El Caribe

La América del Sur

España

MAR CANTÁBRICO

FRANCIA

San Sebastián

La Coruña   Oviedo   Santander   Bilbao   ANDORRA

CORDILLERA CANTÁBRICA

Santiago de Compostela   León   Pamplona

Vigo

Río Duero

Burgos

SIERRA DE GUADARRAMA

Zaragoza

Valladolid   Barcelona

Salamanca

Ávila   MENORCA

MADRID   Palma de Mallorca

PORTUGAL   *Río Tajo*   MALLORCA

Toledo

Valencia   IBIZA

Río Guadalquivir   Murcia   Alicante

LISBOA   *MAR MEDITERRÁNEO*

Córdoba

Sevilla   Granada   *SIERRA NEVADA*

Cádiz   Málaga

Gibraltar (Reino Unido)

OCÉANO ATLÁNTICO   ARGELIA

MARRUECOS

OCÉANO ATLÁNTICO   ESPAÑA

Islas Baleares

Islas Canarias   ÁFRICA

1

Chapter Overview

Cultural setting

Chapter 1 is set in San Antonio. The storyline revolves around two characters, Chris, a native of San Antonio, and David, an exchange student from Costa Rica.

The main cultural issue appears in Lección 4 and again in Lección 6 regarding confusion over the Hispanic system of **apellidos.**

Rationale

A This chapter focuses primarily on helping students learn the meanings of a large group of infinitives (-**ar** and -**er**) in preparation for their use in conjugated form in Chapter 2. We have done this in order to lessen the overload often experienced by students who must cope with both "what to say" and "how to say it" (the meaning and form of a verb) in attempting to communicate with some spontaneity.

B Since the goal throughout this series is meaningful language use and the establishment of familiarity, confidence, and comfort levels for learners, we have progressed slowly with the following criteria in mind: learner interest, immediacy of need, and widest application of structures presented.

C The main thrust of Chapter 1 is the initial development of listening and speaking skills. Writing skill development at this point is confined to list making and guided sentence composition. Reading skill development utilizes authentic ads and brochures containing predictable, factual information.

D You will notice also that activities are designed to begin to build connected discourse through early entry and use of additive and contrastive devices such as **y** and **pero,** the use of **porque** for stating reasons and substantiat-

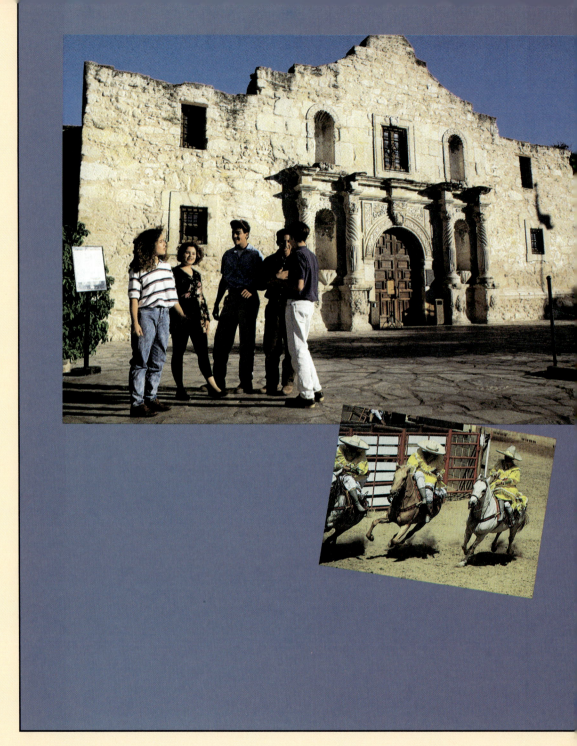

Estructura

This chapter focuses primarily on active use of first and second persons of **ser, llamarse, querer, necesitar, gustar,** and **saber** to talk about where you are from, what your name is, things you want or need to do, like to do, and know how to do.

A complete listing of the language objectives of the chapter appears in the **Repaso,** pages 70–71.

2

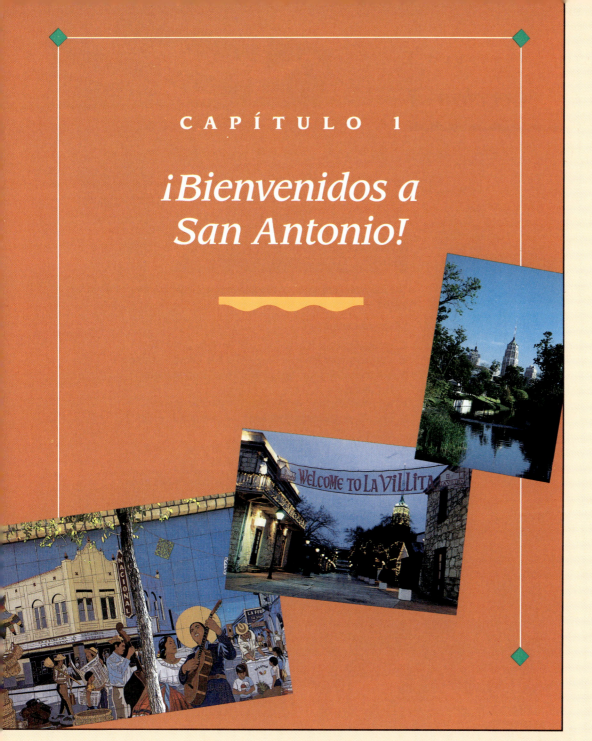

CAPÍTULO 1

¡Bienvenidos a San Antonio!

ing statements, and introduction of common conversational "fillers" such as **bueno, pues,** and **a ver.**

We hope you and your students enjoy this first glimpse of the city of San Antonio!

Lección 1

Objectives

By the end of this lesson, students will be able to:

1. greet friends and family
2. say their name and ask what someone else's name is
3. say where they are from and ask where someone else is from

Lesson 1 Resources

1. Workbook, pp. 1–5
2. Vocabulario Transparency 1.1
3. Cassette 1.1
4. Student Tape Manual, pp. 1–3
5. Lesson Quizzes, pp. 1–2
6. Computer Software, Disk 1
7. Video Cassette
8. Estructura Masters 1.1
9. Diversiones Masters 1.1

¡A comenzar!

Presentation

A. Lead students through each of the seven functions given on page 4, progressing from the English to the Spanish for each function. Then have students find these words and phrases in the dialogue on page 5.

Lección 1

Hola, ¿qué tal?

¡A comenzar!

The following are some of the things you will be learning to do in this lesson.

When you want to . . .	You use . . .
1. greet friends or family	• **Hola, ¿qué tal?**
2. say what your name is	• **Me llamo** + name.
3. ask someone your age his or her name	• **¿Cómo te llamas?**
4. acknowledge an introduction	• **Mucho gusto.**
5. ask where someone your age is from	• **¿De dónde eres?**
6. say where you are from	• **Soy de** + place.
7. answer "yes" to a question	• **Sí.**

Now find examples of the above words and phrases in the following conversation.

Getting Ready for Lesson 1

You may wish to use one or more of the following suggestions to prepare students for Lección 1:

1. Have students keep their books closed. Introduce yourself: **Buenos días (Buenas tardes). Me llamo**... Greet students in the class individually with the phrase **¿Cómo te llamas?**... **Mucho gusto.** Shake hands with each student.
2. Use the map on page 9 of your textbook to familiarize students with the Spanish-speaking world. Write the word **país** on the board. Explain that there are twenty-one countries where Spanish is spoken (write the number 21 on the board). Pronounce the name of each country and have students repeat after you.

In San Antonio, Chris Pearson meets a new exchange student,
David, as they enter school.

CHRIS: **Hola, ¿qué tal?**
DAVID: **Hola.**
CHRIS: **Me llamo Chris Pearson. ¿Cómo te llamas?**
DAVID: **David Vargas. Mucho gusto.**
CHRIS: **¿De dónde eres, David?**
DAVID: **Soy de Costa Rica, de San José. ¿Eres de aquí, de San Antonio?**
CHRIS: **Sí, soy de aquí.**

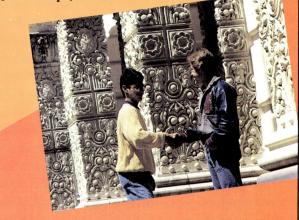

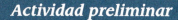

Actividad preliminar

Greet and introduce yourself to a person sitting next to you. Find out his or her name.

Por ejemplo:

ESTUDIANTE A	ESTUDIANTE B
(1) Hola, ¿qué tal?	(2) Hola.
(3) Me llamo Mónica. ¿Cómo te llamas?	(4) Me llamo David. Mucho gusto.
(5) Mucho gusto.	

Lección 1 **5**

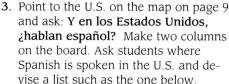

B. Introduce the Lección 1 dialogue by reading it aloud, or by playing the cassette version. Explain to students that they are going to hear a conversation between two people. Have them listen to find out a) if these people know each other well, and b) where each is from.

C. Now have students open their books and look at the dialogue. Ask students to describe:
1. the way questions are written
2. the way exclamations are written
3. the way question words are written (with an accent mark)

D. Lead students through the dialogue. For example: **Cuando Chris dice ''Hola, ¿qué tal?'', ¿qué dice David? ¿Qué dices tú?/Cuando Chris dice: ''Me llamo Chris Pearson. ¿Cómo te llamas?'', ¿qué dice David? ¿Qué dices tú?**, etc.

E. Have students listen to the recorded dialogue again and raise their hands each time they hear a question asked.

Actividad preliminar

Answers
Answers will vary according to each student's name.

3. Point to the U.S. on the map on page 9 and ask: **Y en los Estados Unidos, ¿hablan español?** Make two columns on the board. Ask students where Spanish is spoken in the U.S. and devise a list such as the one below.

ESTADO	CIUDAD
California	Los Ángeles
Texas	El Paso
	San Antonio

4. Tell students the country you are from: **Soy de los Estados Unidos, de Michigan. (Soy de México, de San Luis Potosí.)** Ask students individually where they are from: **¿De dónde eres, Tim?** Allow them to respond with only the name of the state, city, etc. List in columns on the board the countries, states, and cities where students are from.

Bell Ringer Review

Directions to students: Unscramble these words and form four questions in Spanish. Don't forget to punctuate and write accents correctly!

1. llamas te como
2. Antonio de San eres
3. tal que
4. de eres donde

Presentation

1. Lead students through each of the four responses to **¿Qué tal?** on page six.
2. Ask individual students the question **¿Qué tal?** Each student should answer using one of the four responses on page 6. Then have student A ask student B, **¿Qué tal?** Have each student ask this question of the person sitting behind him or her.

Regionalisms

You may wish to tell students that in some parts of the Spanish-speaking world the following words or phrases are alternatives to those presented in the Vocabulario. **Soy de aquí. (Soy de acá).** **¿Eres de aquí? (¿Eres de acá?)**

Vocabulario

¿Qué tal?

muy bien

bien

no muy bien

regular

6   CAPÍTULO 1

Total Physical Response

Getting Ready

If this is the first time you have used the Total Physical Response technique, you may want to explain to students what TPR is. A description of the TPR approach is given in the **¡Acción!** Level 1 Teacher's Manual.

New words for TPR 1
levántense   salten
siéntense   paren
caminen
den vuelta

6

Actividades

A **¿Y tú?** Ask three classmates how they are.

Por ejemplo:

ESTUDIANTE A
Hola, ¿qué tal?

ESTUDIANTE B
Bien (No muy bien, Regular).

B Respond to the following questions in Spanish.

1. Hola, ¿qué tal?
2. ¿Cómo te llamas?
3. ¿Eres de California?
4. ¿De dónde eres?

7

Presentation

1. Read the Cultura viva on page 8. Then have students look at the map on page 9. Pronounce the name of each country and it's capital. Have students repeat after you. Ask students to identify the countries of **América del Norte; América Central;** and **América del Sur.**
2. Refer to the section in the Teacher's Edition called Getting Ready for Lesson 1 (p. 4). If you did not cover steps 2-4 earlier, you may choose to do them now as you teach the Cultura viva.
3. Do the **Actividades** on page 8.

Did You Know?

If you were asked **¿De dónde eres?** outside the U.S., the name of the country would usually be given first. This would be followed by either the city or state. Large cities in the U.S. tend to be more well-known throughout the world than their states, for example, Chicago, rather than Illinois. People from Latin American refer to people from the U.S. as **norteamericanos** or **estadounidenses.**

Critical Thinking Activity
Ask students why Spanish is spoken in all of the countries identified on the map on page 9, including areas of the United States. What two major countries (Brazil and Portugal) are not identified on the map? Why not?

Actividades

Actividad A Answers
Answers will vary according to each student's name and place of origin.

Actividad B Answers
Answers will vary according to the country each student in the group wrote on his or her paper.

8

CULTURA VIVA

Las tres Américas

People from the United States call themselves Americans. However, there are actually three Americas: **América del Norte, América Central,** and **América del Sur.** Spanish is spoken in eighteen countries in the Americas, as well as in Puerto Rico, areas of the United States, and Spain.

Actividades

A Introduce yourself to the class. Tell where you are from originally. If you have always lived in your area, say **Soy de aquí.**

Por ejemplo:

> Me llamo Eva. Soy de los Estados Unidos, de Miami.

B Form groups of three to five students. Each member of the group will write the name of a Spanish-speaking country on a slip of paper and turn it over. The students in your group will try to guess where you are from by asking **sí / no** questions. First, they will ask what general area you are from.

Por ejemplo:

> ¿Eres de América Central?

Then they will guess your country. For each wrong guess, say **No, no soy de...** When they guess correctly, say **¡Sí! Soy de...**

See if your group can guess the country of origin of each group member before the other groups do.

Pronunciation

1. You may wish to play the recorded version of this pronunciation activity located at the end of Cassette 1.1. You may also wish to write the pronunciation activity on the chalkboard, or on an overhead transparency and have students copy it into their notebooks.

A, e, i, o, u.
¿De dónde eres Marilú?
U, o, e, a, i.
¿De dónde eres Mariví?
I, a, u, o, e.
¿De dónde eres, Juan José?

2. Have students repeat in unison. Lead students away from lazy vowel sounds and Anglicized stress patterns.

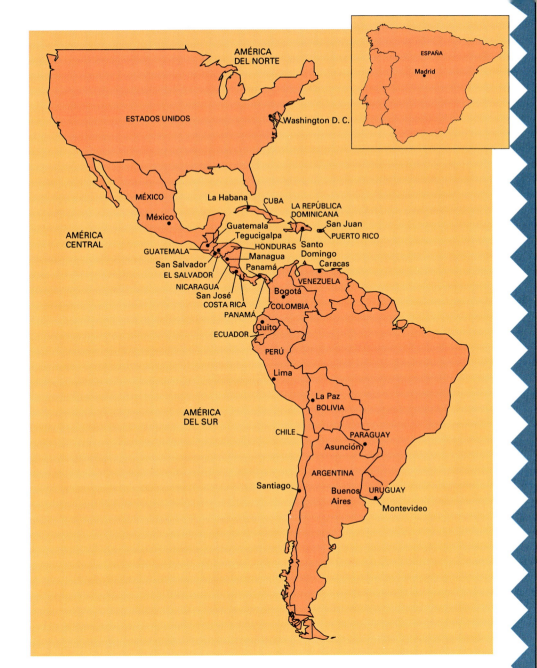

AMÉRICA
DEL NORTE

ESPAÑA

Madrid

ESTADOS UNIDOS

Washington D. C.

MÉXICO

México

La Habana

CUBA

LA REPÚBLICA
DOMINICANA

San Juan

PUERTO RICO

AMÉRICA
CENTRAL

Guatemala
Tegucigalpa

GUATEMALA

HONDURAS

Santo
Domingo

San Salvador
EL SALVADOR

Managua
Panamá

Caracas

NICARAGUA

VENEZUELA

San José
COSTA RICA

Bogotá

PANAMÁ

COLOMBIA

Quito

ECUADOR

PERÚ

Lima

La Paz
BOLIVIA

AMÉRICA
DEL SUR

CHILE

PARAGUAY

Asunción

ARGENTINA

Santiago

Buenos
Aires

URUGUAY

Montevideo

Lección 1 **9**

Additional Practice
After doing Actividades A and B on page 8, give students a blank map of the Americas to fill out. Make sure they include the capital of each country.

Cooperative Learning

1. Give each student an unlabeled map of South America. In pairs, students will try to find out the names of countries, capitals, and geographical features (mountain ranges, rivers, bodies of water) by questioning their partners and filling in the missing information.

2. Have students work in teams of four and "adopt" a South American country. Each group will work independently in the library to find out the following interesting facts about the country: population, main industry, government, currency, etc. Have students draw the flag of the country to display in the classroom.

Actividad C Answers
1. Hola. Me llamo Alicia. Soy de Venezuela.
2. ... Julia... Argentina.
3. ... Juana... Nicaragua.
4. ... Norma... Ecuador.
5. ... Ricardo... Chile.
6. ... Enrique... Costa Rica.

Actividad D Answers
1. Soy de Caracas.
2. ... Buenos Aires.
3. ... Managua.
4. ... Quito.
5. ... Santiago.
6. ... San José.

C Some students from Central and South America are visiting the U.S. How would they introduce themselves and say where they are from?

Por ejemplo:

Carlos / Perú
Hola. Me llamo Carlos.
Soy de Perú.

1. Alicia/Venezuela

2. Julia/Argentina

3. Juana/Nicaragua

4. Norma/Uruguay

5. Ricardo/Chile

6. Enrique/Costa Rica

D The people in activity **C** are from the capital of their countries. What city will each say he or she is from?

Por ejemplo:

Carlos / Perú
Soy de Lima.

For the Native Speaker
1. Have native speakers write a report of at least 100 words on one or more of the countries identified on page 9. The report should include information on history, government, agriculture, and industry.
2. Have native speakers write a report on the country from which their family came. They might wish to compare aspects of life in their native country with life in the U.S.

Finalmente

Situaciones

A conversar Working in groups of four, use the following cues to converse in Spanish.

1. On the first day of school you introduce yourself to three students who are talking together.
2. Find out the name of each of the students and where each is from.
3. They will ask you where you are from.

Repaso de vocabulario

PREGUNTAS (Questions)

¿Cómo te llamas?
¿De dónde eres?
¿Eres de (aquí)?
¿Qué tal?

SALUDOS (Greetings)

Hola.
Me llamo...
Mucho gusto.

OTRAS PALABRAS (Other words)
Y EXPRESIONES

bien
muy bien
no muy bien
regular
Sí.
Soy de (aquí).

Lección 1   **11**

Situaciones

Lesson 1 Evaluation
The A conversar situation on this page is designed to give students the opportunity to use as many language functions as possible listed on page 4 of this lesson. The A conversar is also intended to show how well students are able to meet the lesson objectives listed on page 4.

Presentation

Prior to doing the A conversar on this page, you may wish to play the Situaciones listening activity on Cassette 1.1 as a means of helping students organize the material.

Repaso de vocabulario
The words and phrases in the **Repaso de vocabulario** have been taught for productive use in this lesson. They are summarized here as a resource for both students and teacher. The **Repaso de vocabulario** serves as a convenient resource for the **A conversar** activity on this page. It also gives the teacher a source for writing additional practice or evaluation activies such as quizzes and tests beyond those provided by the publisher.

Have native speakers make a list of greetings, formal and informal, that they use or have heard. They can demonstrate a formal and informal greeting in a minidrama.

Lección 2

Objectives

By the end of this lesson, students will be able to:

1. invite a friend to do something
2. accept an invitation and say thank you
3. say what they want to do and ask a friend what he or she wants to do

---

Lesson 2 Resources
1. Workbook, pp. 6–9
2. Vocabulario Transparencies 1.2
3. Cassette 1.2
4. Student Tape Manual, pp. 4–7
5. Lesson Quizzes, pp. 3–6
6. Computer Software, Disk 1
7. Video Cassette
8. Estructura Masters 1.2
9. Diversiones Masters 1.2

Bell Ringer Review

Directions to students: Copy and complete these sentences by filling in the missing words.

1. **Soy de _____ Rico.**
2. **_____ llamo Carlos Molina.**
3. **¿Eres _____ California?**
4. **_____ gusto.**
5. **Hola. ¿ _____ tal?**

¡A comenzar!

Presentation

A. Lead students through each of the four functions given on page 12, progressing from the English to the Spanish for each function. Then have students find these words and phrases in the dialogue on page 13.

12

Lección 2

¿Qué quieres hacer?

¡A comenzar!

The following are some of the things you will be learning to do in this lesson.

When you want to . . .	You use . . .
1. invite a friend to do something	• **¿Quieres** + activity?
2. say you want to do something	• **Quiero** + activity.
3. accept an invitation	• **Cómo no.**
4. thank someone	• **Gracias.**

Now find examples of the above words and phrases in the following conversation.

Getting Ready for Lesson 2

You may wish to use the following suggestions to prepare students for Lección 2: Have students keep their books closed. Explain in Spanish the kinds of things students will be learning to do in Spanish class. As you talk, list the following on the board: **hablar, conversar, escuchar, leer, practicar, aprender**

español. Illustrate each word with gestures, pictures, or by using the Vocabulario Transparencies 1.2

Chris and David continue their conversation.

DAVID: **¿Quieres hablar inglés o español?**
CHRIS: **Bueno, español. Quiero practicar. ¿Quieres tomar algo?**
DAVID: **¿Dónde?**
CHRIS: **En la cafetería.**
DAVID: **Sí, cómo no. Gracias.**

Actividad preliminar

Ask a classmate if he or she wants to do the following things. He or she will respond **Sí, cómo no** or **No, gracias.**

Por ejemplo:
> practicar el tenis

ESTUDIANTE A	ESTUDIANTE B
¿Quieres practicar el tenis?	Sí, cómo no. (No, gracias).

1. hablar español
2. tomar algo en la cafetería
3. hablar inglés
4. estudiar

B. Introduce the Lesson 2 dialogue by reading it aloud, or by playing the cassette version. Explain to students that they are going to hear another conversation between David and Chris. Have students listen to find out what language Chris wishes to use when speaking to David, and why.

C. Now ask students to open their books and look at the dialogue as you lead them through what is said. Ask the following questions:

1. **Cuando Chris pregunta: "¿Quieres tomar algo?", ¿qué pregunta David?**
2. **Cuando David pregunta: "¿Dónde?", ¿qué dice Chris?**
3. **¿Acepta David la invitación o no?**

D. What other places can you go to get something to drink? Students should respond in English. Write their responses on the board in Spanish: **en el restaurante, en casa, en el café,** etc.

E. Play the cassette tape again. Have students raise their hands when they hear questions asked.

Extension
In pairs, have students practice the dialogue, changing **hablar** and **cafetería** to one of the following words written on the board: **conversar, practicar, aprender, escuchar, leer; en el restaurante, en casa, en el café.**

Actividad preliminar

Answers
1. ¿Quieres hablar español? / Sí, cómo no. (No, gracias.)
2. ¿Quieres tomar...? / Sí... (No,...).
3. ¿Quieres hablar...? / Sí... (No,...)
4. ¿Quieres estudiar?/ Sí... (No,...).

Class Management
The Actividad preliminar may be done as a whole class activity, if preferred. The teacher takes the role of student A, calling on individual students to answer each item.

13

Vocabulario

<table>
<tr><td>

Vocabulary Teaching Resources

1. Vocabulario Transparencies 1.2
2. Workbook, p. 6
3. Cassette 1.2
4. Student Tape Manual, p. 5
5. Lesson Quizzes, pp. 3–4

</td></tr>
</table>

Bell Ringer Review

Directions to students: Write a logical answer to each question below. There may be more than one correct answer.

1. ¿De dónde eres?
2. ¡Hola! ¿Qué tal?
3. ¿Eres de aquí?
4. ¿Eres de la América del Sur?

Presentation

1. Have students open their books to pages 14–15. Model each of the phrases on these pages. Begin each phrase with **Quiero...** Have students repeat each phrase in unison.
2. Ask individual students whether or not they want to do one or more activities on pages 14–15. For example:
   Karla, ¿Quieres ir a casa?
   Sí (No, no) quiero ir a casa.

Quiero...

comprar algo

leer libros

ir a casa

escuchar discos

escuchar la radio

leer revistas

ver la tele

ver películas

ver el partido

hablar con el maestro

hablar por teléfono

hablar con la maestra

14 CAPÍTULO I

Total Physical Response

Getting Ready

Bring to class various objects and magazine pictures that represent the vocabulary taught on pages 14–15. Arrange these on a table in front of the class, or attach the pictures to the board or wall so that they are visible to all students. For TPR 2, model actions that students that students can easily imitate in cases where the objects or pictures will not be used.

New Words

toca	toquen
estudia	estudien
habla	hablen
señala	señalen

estudiar

nadar

comer algo

montar en bicicleta

hacer la tarea

dar un paseo

practicar deportes

jugar béisbol

jugar fútbol

jugar tenis

jugar baloncesto

jugar fútbol americano

bailar

andar en monopatín

jugar videojuegos

correr

visitar amigos

Extension

After teaching the Vocabulario on pages 14–15, you may wish to extend the presentation in the following way: Using the new vocabulary for reference, make up some statements about yourself. Have students respond with **sí** or **no** to indicate whether or not they believe you. For example: **Quiero escuchar música "rock". Quiero ver el programa....** (current TV show). **Quiero ir a casa a descansar.**

Regionalisms

You may wish to tell students that in some parts of the Spanish-speaking world the following words or phrases are alternatives to those presented in the Vocabulario.

hablar con el maestro (hablar con el profesor)
hacer la tarea (hacer los deberes)
jugar baloncesto (jugar básquetbol)
jugar béisbol (jugar a la pelota) (Cuba)
jugar fútbol (jugar balompié) (South America)
videojuegos (juegos electrónicos)
ver películas (ver filmes)
ver el partido (ver el juego)

Note. After extensive surveys and discussions with native speakers, we have opted for omission of **al** after **jugar**. This usage is no longer common among speakers of the majority of Spanish-speaking countries. If you are uncomfortable with its omission, you should use **al** with your students. However, you may wish to allow students the option of using it or not.

TPR 1

(Invite groups of four or five students to the front of the class.)
Toquen las revistas.
Toquen los discos.
Toquen la casa.
Toquen la bicicleta.
Toquen el teléfono.
(Repeat with commands to individual students using **Toca.**)

TPR 2

Estudien las notas.
Estudien el libro de español.
Hablen con el maestro.
Hablen por teléfono.
Estudia el libro de inglés.
Estudia las notas de español.
Habla con_____.
Habla con_____.

15

Actividad A Answers
Answers will vary but may include the following:

1. Quiero leer revistas pero no quiero andar en monopatín.
2. Quiero bailar pero no quiero correr.

Actividad B Answers
Answers will vary but may include the following: **jugar tenis; jugar fútbol; jugar béisbol; jugar baloncesto; nadar; correr**

Actividad C Answers
Answers will vary, but may include the following: **Quiero ir a casa; estudiar; jugar videojuegos; jugar fútbol; comer algo; etc.**

Additional Practice
After doing Actividades A, B, and C, you may wish to reinforce the learning with the following:

1. Ask for a show of hands:
¿Cuántos quieren ver la tele, leer libros, etc.? Tally the responses to determine the popularity of various activities. For example: **leer** = 3; **ver la tele** = 4; etc. Ask: **¿Cuál es más popular? ¿Cuál es menos popular?**
2. Ask students individually what they want to do after school. Encourage them to elaborate by asking: **¿Y...?** For example:
Maestra(o):¿Qué quieres hacer después de las clases?
Estudiante: Quiero ir a casa.
Maestra(o): ¿Y...?
Estudiante: Y hacer la tarea.

Reteaching

Using Vocabulario Transparencies 1.2, lead students through the Vocabulario from pages 14–15. Point to each visual on the overhead and have individual students say or write the corresponding activity.

Actividades

A Quiero... What are your choices for doing things after school? Use the words and expressions in the **Vocabulario** on pages 14 and 15 and write each activity in one of two columns: things you want to do **(Quiero...)** and things you don't want to do **(No quiero...)**. Contrast these with the word **pero** *(but)*. Report back to the class.

Quiero...   No quiero...

Por ejemplo:

   Quiero escuchar discos pero no quiero hacer la tarea.

B Actividades. As a counselor at a summer camp, you are in charge of scheduling the daily activities. List five activities you want your campers to do each day.

C ¿Qué quieres hacer? Ask a classmate what he or she wants to do after school. Your classmate then asks another student the same question.

Por ejemplo:

ESTUDIANTE A   ESTUDIANTE B
¿Qué quieres hacer, Ana?   Quiero jugar baloncesto.

16 CAPÍTULO 1

¡Bienvenidos a San Antonio!

La Villita is a small historic area in the heart of San Antonio. It was originally settled in the 1700's near the mission of **San Antonio de Valero,** known today as **El Álamo.** The Hispanic heritage of San Antonio is evident in the street names of **La Villita,** such as Hidalgo Walk and Guadalupe Walk. Today many citizens of San Antonio are bilingual, that is, they are able to function in two languages: Spanish and English. Over half of greater San Antonio's one million people are Mexican Americans. More than half of the city's state legislative representatives and the city council are Hispanic.

Actividad

Tell one place you want to see in San Antonio.

Por ejemplo:

    Quiero ver El Álamo.

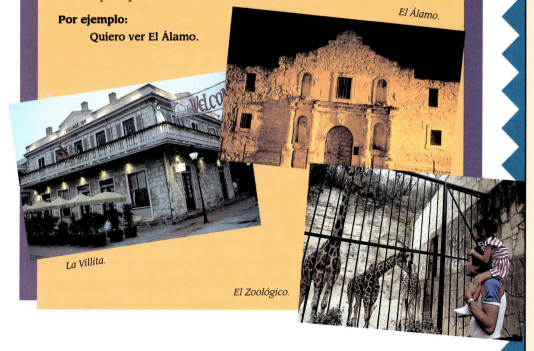

El Álamo.

La Villita.

El Zoológico.

Pronunciation

1. Play the recorded version of this activity, located at the end of Cassette 1.2. You may also wish to write this verse on the board and have students copy it into their notebooks.
 **Bella, bella,
 mi tierra.
 Chiquita, bonita
 La Villita**.

2. Have students repeat words and phrases individually and in unison. You may wish to focus on the /ll/ and /v/ sounds: **Bella; La Villita.**

Cultura viva 1

Presentation

Read the Cultura viva on this page. If possible, bring in additional photos of San Antonio from your school library or from other sources. Using a map of San Antonio, have students identify streets that bear Hispanic names. List these street names on the chalkboard.

Did You Know?

The battle for the Alamo occurred in March 1836, when the Spanish forces, under General Antonio López de Santa Ana, attacked the American forces fighting for Texas independence, under the leadership of William Travis. Travis, Davy Crockett, and Jim Bowie fought and died at the Alamo. In April 1836, Santa Ana surrendered to General Sam Houston. The Lone Star Republic was born.

Actividad

Actividad Answers
Answers will vary but may include the following:

1. **Quiero ver La Villita.**
2. **Quiero dar un paseo.**

Additional Practice
After doing the Actividad on this page, you may wish to reinforce the culture presentation by having students complete the following sentences about San Antonio.

1. An historic area in downtown San Antonio is called _____.
2. People who can speak two languages are _____.
3. More than _____ million people live in greater San Antonio. Half of them are _____ Americans.
4. San Antonio is a city in the state of _____.

Bell Ringer Review

Directions to students: Copy the following activities on your paper and draw an illustration for each one.

1. leer libros
2. andar en monopatín
3. dar un paseo
4. jugar videojuegos
5. correr

Structure Focus

In this lesson, the presentation of the verb **querer** is limited to **quiero/quieres**. Students will learn the other forms of **querer** in Chapter 2, Lessons 4–6.

Presentation

Lead students through steps 1–5 on page 18. If you have taught the Vocabulario on pages 14 and 15, students will already be familiar with these two forms of **querer**.

Actividades

Actividad A Answers

Answers will vary but may include the following:
1. **En el parque quiero jugar tenis. No quiero jugar fútbol.**
2. **En casa quiero hablar por teléfono. No quiero estudiar.**

Estructura

How to Talk about What You Want to Do — **Quiero / quieres**

1. To say that you want to do something, say **Quiero** + activity.

   Quiero tomar algo.

2. To say what you don't want to do, say **No quiero** + activity.

   No quiero nadar.

3. When you want to ask if someone wants to do something, say **¿Quieres** + activity?

   ¿Quieres jugar béisbol?

4. To ask someone what he or she wants to do, say **¿Qué quieres hacer?**

5. If you don't want to do anything, say **No quiero hacer nada.**

Actividades

A Quiero... No quiero... Say what you want to do and what you don't want to do in each of the following places.

Por ejemplo:

   en la biblioteca
   En la biblioteca quiero leer algo.
   No quiero hacer la tarea.

18 CAPÍTULO 1

1. en el parque

2. en casa

3. en la fiesta

4. en la clase

B **No, gracias.** Invite three classmates to do different activities listed in the **Vocabulario** on pages 14 and 15. Your classmates will politely refuse. You then ask what each wants to do instead.

Por ejemplo:

ESTUDIANTE A	ESTUDIANTE B
(1) **Carlos, ¿quieres jugar tenis?**	(2) **No, gracias.**
(3) **Entonces** (then)**, ¿qué quieres hacer?**	(4) **Quiero descansar.**

Actividad A Extension
Have students write down as many activities as they know that are associated with the following places. Set a time limit of one minute.

1. en el parque
2. en casa
3. en la fiesta
4. en la clase

Actividad B Answers
Answers will vary.

Class Management
Actividad B may be done in the following way: First have students turn to the person beside them, then reverse roles. Next have them turn to the person behind or in front of them, then reverse roles. Finally have pairs of students perform for the class.

Reteaching

Use a personal narration to illustrate the Estructura topic on page 18. For example: **Quiero ir a muchos lugares hoy. En el parque quiero..., en la biblioteca, quiero...** You may also wish to use the Vocabulario Transparencies 1.2 as visual cues, or have students refer to pages 14–15 as you narrate.

Presentation

Read the Cultura viva on this page. Using a map of the United States, have students locate cities that are of Spanish origin in the states mentioned in the reading. Make a list of these cities on the chalkboard.

Did You Know?

St. Augustine, Florida is the oldest European settlement in North America. Juan Ponce de León landed there in 1513. Pedro Menéndez de Avilés founded St. Augustine as a permanent settlement in 1565. The Spaniards were the first to introduce the horse, cow, pig, and sheep to North America, as well as wheat, rice, pototoes, grapes, sugar, oranges, and bananas.

Critical Thinking Activity

Discuss the following with your students: 1. Who founded their town or city? 2. What is the ethnic makeup of their town or city? 3. What groups of people settled in their state? 4. Give some reasons why people would leave their country to settle in a foreign country. 5. How were the Spaniards who settled in what is now the United States the same or different from present-day inmigrants? 6. What contributions have different ethnic groups made to our society?

Actividad Answers

Answers will vary. Use a map of the United States to confirm student's responses

---

La herencia española en los Estados Unidos

Many parts of the present-day United States were settled by Spanish speakers who arrived at least a hundred years before the first English settlers. The Europeans who discovered and explored the present-day southern states of Florida, Georgia, North Carolina, South Carolina, Tennessee, Alabama, Mississippi, Arkansas, and Louisiana were Spanish. In the West, the Spanish were the first to explore and settle the states of California, Texas, New Mexico, Colorado, and Arizona.

Actividad

Look at this map of the United States. Your teacher will pronounce the names of the cities shown, which were settled by Spaniards. Listen to how they sound in Spanish, then repeat. Can you think of any other places in the U.S. with Spanish names?

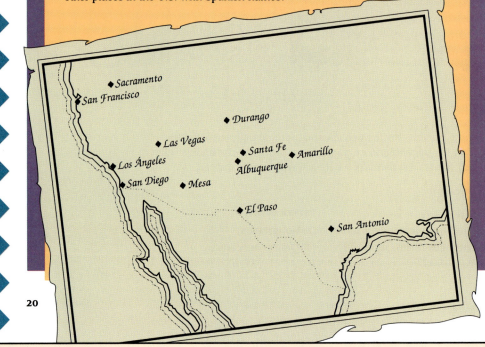

20

Pronunciation

1. You may wish to play the recorded version of this pronunciation activity, located at the end of Cassette 1.2. You may also wish to write these lines on the chalkboard and have students copy them into their notebook.
San José y Santa Fe,
San Diego y Laredo,

El Cerrito y Los Alamitos:
Todos en los Estados Unidos.
2. Have students repeat words and phrases individually and in unison. You may wish to focus on the sound of /d/ in the following words: **Laredo, todos, Estados,** *San* **Diego, Unidos.**

Finalmente

Finalmente

A conversar Use the following cues to converse with a classmate in Spanish.

1. On the first day of school, you introduce yourself to a new student and say "Pleased to meet you." Your classmate will do the same.
2. Find out where each other is from.
3. Invite your classmate to do something. He or she says yes or no and thanks you.

Repaso de vocabulario

PREGUNTAS (Questions)
¿Qué quieres hacer?
¿Quieres...?

ACTIVIDADES Y EXPRESIONES
andar en monopatín
bailar
comer algo
comprar algo
correr
dar un paseo
descansar
escuchar discos
    la radio
estudiar
hablar con el maestro
    con la maestra
    por teléfono
hacer la tarea
ir a casa

jugar baloncesto
    béisbol
    fútbol
    fútbol americano
    tenis
    videojuegos
leer libros
    revistas
montar en bicicleta
nadar
practicar deportes
tomar algo
ver el partido
    películas
    la tele
visitar amigos

OTRAS PALABRAS (other words) **Y EXPRESIONES**
Gracias.
No, gracias.
No quiero hacer nada.
Quiero...
Sí, cómo no.

Lección 2 **21**

Situaciones

Lesson 2 Evaluation
The A conversar situation on this page is designed to give students the opportunity to use as many language functions as possible listed on page 12 of this lesson. The A conversar is also intended to show how well students are able to meet the lesson objectives. These objective are also listed on page 12 of this lesson.

Presentation

Prior to doing the A conversar on this page, you may wish to play the Situcciones listening activity on Cassette 1.2 as a means of helping students organize the material.

Repaso de vocabulario

These words and phrases in the Repaso de vocabulario have been taught for productive use in this lesson. They are summarized here as a resource for both students and teacher. The Repaso de vocabulario also serves as a convenient resource for the A conversar activity on this page. It also gives the teacher a source for writing either additional practice or evaluation activities such as quizzes and tests in addition to those provided by the publisher.

Learning From Photos

Have different students take the parts of the teen-agers in the two photos on this page and role play a conversation in Spanish. What would each person in the photos say? If these were two boys, what would they say?

For the Native Speaker

1. Have native speakers write a brief biography, including interests, personal achievements, etc., incorporating the use of **querer** and the new vocabulary on pages 14–15.
2. Have native speakers write letters to various people using the appropriate style and vocabulary. They might write to their parents explaining some of the activities done in school. For example: **Quiero decirles algunas cosas que hacemos en la escuela diariamente, en clase, etc.**
3. Dictation: Have native speakers listen as you read aloud a Spanish newspaper article about sports. Read it again with pauses so they can write. Have them check their papers for correct spelling.

Lección 3

Objectives

By the end of this lesson, students will be able to:

1. greet someone formally
2. ask how someone is and say how they are
3. ask or tell at what time an event takes place to the nearest hour or half hour
4. use numbers 0–20

Lesson 3 Resources
1. Workbook, pp. 10–15
2. Vocabulario Transparency 1.3
3. Cassette 1.3
4. Student Tape Manual, pp. 8–10
5. Lesson Quizzes, pp. 7–10
6. Test Booklet, pp. 1–5
7. Computer software, Disk 1
8. Video Cassette
9. Estructura Masters 1.3
10 Diversiones Masters 1.3

Bell Ringer Review

Directions to students: Answer the following questions.

1. ¿Quieres tomar algo?
2. ¿Quieres jugar tenis o béisbol? ¿Dónde?
3. ¿Quieres hablar inglés o español?

¡A comenzar!

Presentation

A. Lead students through each of the four functions given on page 22, progressing from the English to the Spanish for each function. Then have students find these words and phrases in the dialogue on page 23. (con'd top of page 23)

Lección 3

¡Buenos días!

¡A comenzar!

The following are some of the things you will be learning to do in this lesson.

When you want to . . .	You use . . .
1. greet someone formally	• Buenos días (Buenas tardes, Buenas noches).
2. ask how someone is: informally formally	• ¿Cómo estás? ¿Cómo está usted?
3. say how you are	• Estoy (No estoy) bien.
4. give the time an event takes place	• a las + hour

Now find examples of the above words and phrases in the following conversation.

THOMAS JEFFERSON HIGH SCHOOL

SAN ANTONIO, TEXAS

COURSE - TITLE	PERIOD	ROOM	INSTRUCTOR
ESTUDIOS SOCIALES			
Historia de los Estados Unidos	9	203	Bradford
Historia europea	10	114	Chávez
Geografía mundial	3	229	Friedman
Gobierno/Economía	1	25	Wong
MÚSICA Y ARTE			
Banda sinfónica			
Orquesta	10	301	
Conjunto instrumental	11	102	Smithers
Conjunto vocal	8	117	Logan
Coro de concierto	4	205	García
Arte	4	61	Jones
	7	224	López
			Jones
IDIOMAS EXTRANJEROS			
Francés I			
Francés II			

Getting Ready for Lesson 3

You may wish to use one or more of the following suggestions to prepare students for this lesson:

1. Ask students individually: ¿Cómo estás? Illustrate possible responses on the board with faces: muy bien, bien, regular, no muy bien. If a student answers no muy bien, follow up with ¿Qué pasa? ¿Problemas? ¿problemas con una clase? ¿la tarea? Respond appropriately to the student's utterance: ¡Qué bueno! or ¡Qué pena!

2. Write your class schedule on the board, giving the name of each class (in Spanish) and the time it meets. Tell the students how many classes you have and what time each one meets. If you have a free period, tell the students: No tengo clase a la(s) _____.

David meets with Señora Kaplan, his guidance counselor, to explain a problem with his schedule.

SRA. KAPLAN: **Buenos días, David. Soy la señora Kaplan.**
DAVID: **Buenos días, señora. ¿Cómo está usted?**
SRA. KAPLAN: **Estoy muy bien, gracias. Y tú, ¿cómo estás?**
DAVID: **Muy bien, pero sólo tengo cinco clases y necesito tomar seis.**
SRA. KAPLAN: **Entonces, quieres otra clase. ¿A qué hora?**
DAVID: **A las diez.**

Actividades preliminares

A To greet the following people in the morning, would you say: **Buenos días, ¿cómo está usted?** or **Hola, ¿cómo estás?**

1. a classmate
2. your Spanish teacher
3. a guidance counselor
4. an exchange student
5. the parent of a classmate

B Greet the person sitting next to you and, using the following as a guide, find out how he or she is.

ESTUDIANTE A	ESTUDIANTE B
Hola, ¿cómo ____?	Muy ____. ¿Y tú?

C Now greet your teacher.

ESTUDIANTE	MAESTRO(A)
Buenos días. ¿Cómo ____?	Buenos días. Muy ____. ¿Y tú?

Lección 3   23

B. Introduce the Lesson 3 dialogue by reading it aloud, or by playing the cassette version. Have students listen for the following information:
   1. Is David talking to someone older or younger than he?
   2. To whom might David be talking?
   3. How can you tell?
   4. Ask students to raise their hands when they hear David state his problem.

C. Now ask students to look at the dialogue as you lead them through what is said. For example, **Cuando la señora dice: "¿... cómo estás?", ¿qué dice David? ¿Y qué dice la señora?,** etc.

Actividades preliminares

Actividad A Answers

1. Hola, ¿cómo estás?
2. Buenos días, ¿cómo está usted?
3. ... está usted?
4. ... estás?
5. ... está usted?

Actividad B Answers
—Hola, ¿cómo estás?
—(No) Muy bien, ¿Y tú?
—(No) Muy bien.

Actividad C Answers
—Buenos días. ¿Cómo está usted?
—Buenos días. (No) Muy bien. ¿Y tú?
—(No) Muy bien.
(Students and teacher will want to use **Buenas tardes** if it's afternoon.)

Additional Practice
After doing Actividades A, B, and C on this page, you may wish to reinforce the learning with the following: Write the following times on the board. Then ask students what they want to do at these times. **Por ejemplo: (10:00)**
A las diez quiero hablar con la maestra.

1. a la una (1:00)
2. a las tres (3:00)
3. a las seis (6:00)

Bell Ringer Review

Directions to students: Write out four questions asking a friend if he or she wants to do fun activities with you on Saturday. Suggest an hour and include whether it is A.M. or P.M. **Por ejemplo: ¿Quieres montar en bicicleta a las ocho de la mañana?**

Presentation

1. Have students find the corresponding player on page 24 as you say each number aloud. Begin with **cero**.
2. In unison, have students repeat after you each number in sequence.
3. Ask individual students to read the numbers in the order they are presented on page 24.
4. Begin the **Actividades** practice, pp. 24–26.

Extension

You may wish to give students the other written forms of 16–19: **dieciséis, diecisiete, dieciocho, diecinueve.** The forms given here are selected to emphasize the additive system and to facilitate use.

Class Management

From now on, to divide students into small groups for various activities, you may wish to have them count themselves off in the following manner: **uno, dos, tres, fuera; cuatro, cinco, seis, fuera; siete, ocho nueve, fuera, etc.**

Vocabulario

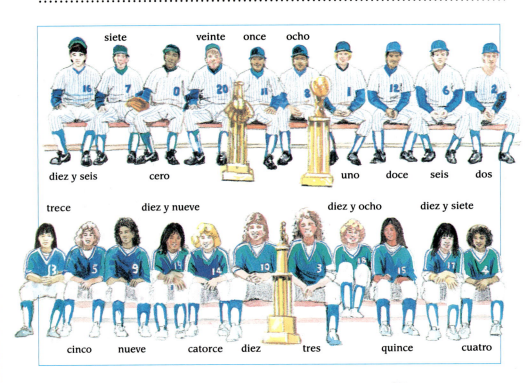

siete   veinte   once   ocho

diez y seis   cero   uno   doce   seis   dos

trece   diez y nueve   diez y ocho   diez y siete

cinco   nueve   catorce   diez   tres   quince   cuatro

Actividades

A **Números de teléfono.** David needs to call the classmates listed here. Tell him what number to dial, based on what he has written in his notebook.

Por ejemplo:
> **Mónica**
> *Cuatro, tres, dos, seis, ocho, cuatro, siete.*

1. **Mark**   2. **Patricia**   3. **Marta**   4. **Robert**

Patricia Acosta
423-9781
Mark Cohen
298-5002
Mónica Ocampo
432-6847
Robert Salinas
597-0564
Marta Varela
238-7013

Total Physical Response

Getting Ready
Write the numerals for 0–20 on separate cards. Attach the cards to the chalkboard.

New Words
dale   escriban
empareja   emparejen

TPR 1
Toca el número 6.
Señala el número 15.
Toca el número 11.
Señala el número 20.
Toca el número _____.
Señala el número _____.
Empareja el número y el número 7.
Empareja el número y el número 14.

B **Quiero comprar algo.** The school's drama club is having a sale to raise money. Below are the items for sale and their prices. To support the club, many teachers have made purchases. You are the cashier. Tell them how much they owe.

periódicos $2.00

libros $6.00

discos $8.00

revistas $3.00

Por ejemplo:

> señorita Díaz / tres libros
> *Diez y ocho dólares, señorita Díaz.*

1. señora Martínez / dos discos
2. señor Pérez / seis revistas
3. señor Olmos / cinco revistas
4. señorita Vargas / diez periódicos
5. señora Camacho / tres libros
6. señorita Vilas / una revista, un libro y un periódico
7. señora Morelos / tres libros y un periódico

Lección 3 **25**

C **En San Antonio.** With a partner, look at the brochure from San Antonio. You want to do several things and need to make phone calls for more information. Your partner will be the operator and give you the number you need.

Por ejemplo:

  ir a La Villita

ESTUDIANTE A	ESTUDIANTE B
Quiero ir a La Villita.	299-8610.

1. comer en la Plaza del Mercado
2. ir a El Álamo
3. escuchar música en el Teatro Arneson del Río

4. ver los animales en el Zoológico
5. ir a la Catedral de San Fernando
6. ver la exhibición en el Instituto Cultural Mexicano

LUGARES DE INTERÉS EN SAN ANTONIO

La Villita

Villita y Álamo. Tel. 299-8610. Tiendas de artesanías, galerías de arte, restaurantes. Abierta todos los días.

El Álamo

Plaza de El Álamo. Tel. 225-1391. La misión más famosa de Texas donde cayeron sus 188 defensores el 6 de marzo de 1836. Abierta diariamente.

La Catedral de San Fernando

115 Main Plaza. Tel. 227-1297. La catedral fue el centro geográfico y social de la ciudad hasta 1900. Abierta todos los días de 9 a 5.

El Zoológico

Más de 3,500 especimenes de 800 especies. Abierto diariamente de 9:00 a 5:00. Tel. 555-7693.

El Zoológico

El Palacio del Gobernador Español

Plaza del Mercado

514 W. Commerce. Tel. 299-8600. Tiendas, restaurantes. Modelo tradicional de los antiguos mercados mexicanos. Abierta diariamente.

El Teatro Arneson del Río

En la Villita. música de jazz, mariachis, "country", flamenco, ópera, bailes folklóricos. Tel. 226-4651.

Instituto Cultural Mexicano

600 Plaza HemisFeria. Tel. 227-0123. Exhibición de arte contemporáneo de artistas mexicanos. Museo que contiene más de 3000 años de la cultura mexicana.

Señor, señora, señorita

In Spanish, you address a person either formally or informally. Generally, you address strangers and people you call by their last names formally. For example, **señor Martín, señora Vargas, señorita Olmos.** You use **señora** for a married woman, and **señorita** for an unmarried woman.

You address informally your friends, people your own age or younger, and other people you call by their first names. To greet someone informally, say **Hola** and **¿Qué tal?** or **¿Cómo estás?**

To greet someone you address formally, you generally do not say **Hola** but rather **Buenos días** (in the morning), **Buenas tardes** (in the afternoon), or **Buenas noches** (in the evening). Then you would ask **¿Cómo está usted?**

FORMAL: **Buenos días, señora Martínez. ¿Cómo está usted?**
INFORMAL: **¡Hola, David! ¿Cómo estás? (¿Qué tal?)**

The titles **señor, señora,** and **señorita** are often abbreviated when followed by the person's last name: **Sr. Vilas, Sra. Kaplan, Srta. Ríos.** These words are capitalized when they are abbreviated but not when written out in full: **Buenos días, señora. ¿Cómo está usted, señorita?**

Actividades

A What do the following abbreviations stand for?
   Sra.   **Srta.**   **Sr.**

B To greet the following people in the morning, would you say **Hola, ¿qué tal?** or **Buenos días. ¿Cómo está usted?**

4.

3.

2.

1.

Pronunciation

A. You may wish to write this verse on the board and have students copy it into their notebook.
   Hola, José. ¿Qué tal?
   Buenas tardes,
   señora Carvajal.

B. Have students repeat words and phrases individually and in unison. You may wish to focus on the following sounds:
   /j/ José Carvajal
   /t/ tal, tardes

Cultura viva 1

Presentation
Read the Cultura viva 1 on this page. You may wish to emphasize the distinction between formal and informal by writing these two lines on the chalkboard: **Buenos días, ¿cómo está usted?** and **Hola, ¿cómo estás? (¿qué tal?)**

Did You Know?
There is not a "Ms." designation in Spanish—all unmarried women are referred to as **señorita.**

In many parts of the Hispanic world, you address your own family members informally, but always show respect to the eldest or the most authoritarian member by addressing that person formally. For example, to your brother or sister, you would say **¿Cómo estás?**, but to your grandmother or grandfather, **¿Cómo está usted?**

Critical Thinking Activity
What reasons can you give for having both a formal and an informal way of addressing people in Spanish? Are there any words or expressions in English that serve a similar purpose?

Actividades

Actividad A Answers
Sra. / señora
Srta. / señorita
Sr. / señor

Actividad B Answers
1. Hola, ¿qué tal?
2. Hola, ¿Qué tal?
3. Buenos días. ¿Cómo está usted?
4. Buenos días. ¿Cómo está usted?

Estructura

Structure Teaching Resources

1. Workbook, pp. 12–15
2. Cassette 1.3
3. Student Tape Manual, pp. 9–10
4. Estructura Masters 1.3
5. Lesson Quizzes, p. 10

Bell Ringer Review

Write the following numbers on the chalkboard. Directions to students: Copy the numbers and fill in the missing ones in each sequence. Watch your spelling!

1. once, _____, trece, _____, quince
2. _____, diez, quince, _____
3. _____, cuatro, _____, ocho, diez
4. diez y nueve, _____, quince, trece, _____

Structure Focus

In this lesson, the presentation of time is limited to the whole and half hour, since that is when most social events (parties, sports events, dances, etc.) begin. As a related grammar topic, students will learn to say and ask the time, **Es la una; Son las dos, etc.** in Chapter 3, Lesson 6.

Presentation

Lead students through steps 1–5 on pages 28 and 29. You may want to give other examples of when various events take place by drawing additional times on the chalkboard.

Extension

After presenting the structure on pages 28–29, you may wish to reinforce the topic of greetings by asking students how they would greet a teacher at the times shown on the clocks in step 5, page 29.

How to Ask at What Time Something Takes Place   ¿A qué hora es...?

1. To ask at what time an event happens, say **¿A qué hora es...?**

   ¿A qué hora es el partido?
   ¿A qué hora es la clase?

2. To say at what time an event happens, say **Es a las...** and give the hour.

   El partido es a las dos.   **La película es a las ocho.**

3. To say that something happens at one o'clock, you say **a la una**.

   El picnic es a la una.

4. To say that something takes place at half past the hour, you add **y media**.

   La clase de español es a la una y media.   **La fiesta es a las siete y media.**

28 CAPÍTULO 1

Cooperative Learning

Have students work in groups of three. Give each student a different-colored index card. Student A will write an activity, for example, **jugar tenis**. Student B will write an hour, for example, **a las ocho**. Student C will write the part of day, for example, **de la noche**. Collect the cards, separate them by color, and redistribute them to the groups. Students will then combine the information and write new, complete sentences.

5. To show the difference between A.M. and P.M., you add **de la mañana** (in the morning), **de la tarde** (in the afternoon), or **de la noche** (after sunset).

El partido es a las diez de la mañana.

La clase es a la una de la tarde.

El baile es a las ocho de la noche.

Actividades

A **¿A qué hora?** Chris and David have a lot of things planned for today. But Chris can't remember at what time each activity is scheduled so he asks David. Play the roles with a classmate.

Por ejemplo:

el picnic

ESTUDIANTE A	ESTUDIANTE B
¿A qué hora es el picnic?	A las dos de la tarde.

1. la fiesta
2. la clase de tenis
3. el programa de español
4. el concierto
5. el partido de fútbol

> 11:30 AM el programa de español
> 1:00 PM la clase de tenis
> 2:00 PM el picnic
> 3:30 PM el partido de fútbol
> 5:30 PM la fiesta
> 9:00 PM el concierto

B **Después de las clases.** Tell six activities you want or need to do after school and say at what time you will do them.

Por ejemplo:

Quiero ver la tele a las cuatro.
Necesito jugar tenis a las cuatro y media.

Cultura viva 2

Presentation

Read the Cultura viva on this page. If possible, bring additional photos of Spanish missions in the U.S. from your school library or from another resource.

Did You Know?

The Spanish missionaries established missions in all the regions they explored, especially in Florida, New Mexico, Arizona, and California. In California, for example, twenty-one missions were founded by Father Junípero Serra and Father Fermín Lausen. They are now maintained by the state as tourist attractions.

Critical Thinking Activity

Compare how the Spaniards established their presence in what is now the American Southwest to the English exploration and settlement of the American colonies on the east coast of the U.S.

Actividad

Answers
Answers will vary but may include the following:
Silencio; No tirar basura; Prohibido jugar; No correr; Prohibido fumar.

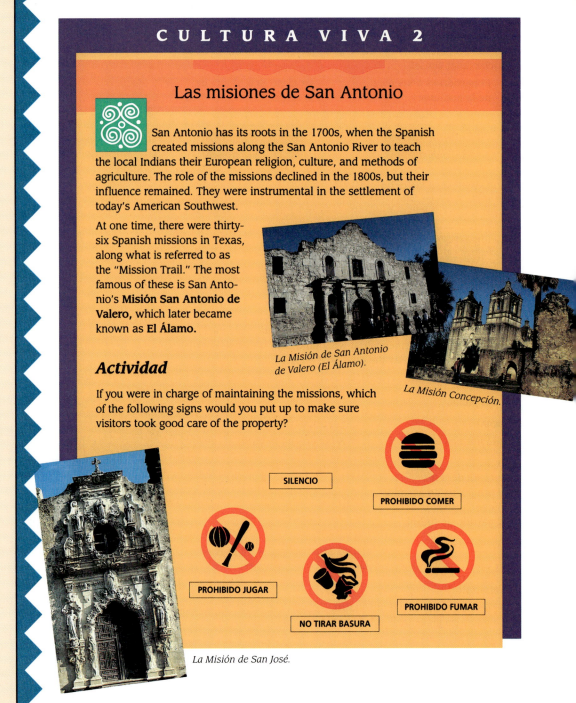

CULTURA VIVA 2

Las misiones de San Antonio

San Antonio has its roots in the 1700s, when the Spanish created missions along the San Antonio River to teach the local Indians their European religion, culture, and methods of agriculture. The role of the missions declined in the 1800s, but their influence remained. They were instrumental in the settlement of today's American Southwest.

At one time, there were thirty-six Spanish missions in Texas, along what is referred to as the "Mission Trail." The most famous of these is San Antonio's **Misión San Antonio de Valero,** which later became known as **El Álamo.**

La Misión de San Antonio de Valero (El Álamo).

La Misión Concepción.

Actividad

If you were in charge of maintaining the missions, which of the following signs would you put up to make sure visitors took good care of the property?

SILENCIO

PROHIBIDO COMER

PROHIBIDO JUGAR

NO TIRAR BASURA

PROHIBIDO FUMAR

La Misión de San José.

Pronunciation

A. You may wish to write the following lines on the chalkboard or show on an overhead transparency. You may also want to have your students copy these lines into their notebook:
**Hay cinco misiones en San Antonio.
Pero la más famosa es El Álamo.**

B. Have students repeat words and phrases individually and in unison. You may wish to focus on the vowel sounds.

Finalmente

Situaciones

A conversar Use the following cues to converse with a classmate in Spanish.

1. You and a friend have decided to spend Saturday together. When you arrive at your friend's home, you greet his or her mother and ask how she is.
2. Your friend asks if you want something to eat or drink.
3. Then the two of you agree upon three things you will do that day and at what time you will do each activity.

Repaso de vocabulario

PREGUNTAS

¿A qué hora es... (la clase)?
¿Cómo está usted?
¿Cómo estás?

SALUDOS

Buenas noches.
Buenas tardes.
Buenos días.

PERSONAS

el señor (Sr.)
la señora (Sra.)
la señorita (Srta.)
usted

DINERO

el dólar
los dólares

LOS NÚMEROS

cero
uno
dos
tres
cuatro
cinco
seis
siete
ocho
nueve
diez
once
doce
trece
catorce
quince
diez y seis
diez y siete

diez y ocho
diez y nueve
veinte

LA HORA

a la(s) + hour
de la mañana
de la noche
de la tarde
y media

Lección 3 **31**

For the Native Speaker

Have native speakers write a paragraph of fifty to seventy-five words telling about various school events. Give the names of the events and their starting and ending times.

Lección 4

Objectives

By the end of this lesson, students will be able to:

1. say what they like to do and find out what a friend likes to do
2. ask a friend what he or she needs to do
3. talk about their classes

Lesson 4 Resources

1. Vocabulario Transparencies 1.4
2. Workbook, pp. 16–21
3. Cassette 1.4
4. Student Tape Manual, pp. 11–14
5. Lesson Quizzes, pp. 11–15
6. Computer Software, Disk 1
7. Video Cassette
8. Estructura Masters 1.4
9. Diversiones Masters 1.4

Bell Ringer Review

Display Vocabulario Transparencies 1.2. Directions to students: Write three activities you want to do. Write two you don't want to do.

¡A comenzar!

Presentation

A. Lead students through each of the eight functions given on page 32, progressing from the English to the Spanish for each function. Then have students find these words and phrases in the dialogue on page 33.
(continued top of page 33)

Lección 4

¿Qué te gusta estudiar más?

¡A comenzar!

The following are some of the things you will be learning to do in this lesson.

When you want to . . .	You use . . .
1. name one of your classes	• **la clase de** + subject
2. find out what a friend likes to do	• **¿Te gusta** + activity?
3. make sure what you said is correct	• **¿no?** at the end of your statement
4. say what you like to do	• **Me gusta** + activity.
5. say good-bye	• **Adiós. Hasta luego.**
6. ask a friend what he or she needs to do	• **¿Necesitas** + activity?
7. indicate that you didn't catch what someone said	• **¿Cómo?**
8. offer a choice	• **... o...**

Now find examples of the above words and phrases in the following conversation.

David Vargas López			0260358	
STUDENT NAME			STUDENT NO.	
PERIOD	DAYS	SEQ.	COURSE TITLE	RO
8:00			inglés	2
9:00			biología	1
10:00				2
11:00			álgebra	
12:00			almuerzo	
1:00			historia	
2:00			educación física	

Getting Ready for Lesson 4

You may wish to use one or more of the following suggestions to prepare students for the lesson:

1. Have students look at David's schedule on page 32 and listen as you make statements about the times his classes meet. Some statements should be true, some false. Have students respond with **sí** or **no,** or simply raise their hands when they hear a false statement. For example: **La clase de inglés es a las dos. La clase de historia es a la una.**

2. Write the following continuum on the board: **me gusta mucho/ me gusta/ no me gusta mucho/ no me gusta.** Illustrate with faces,

Señora Kaplan helps David with his schedule.

SRA. KAPLAN: A ver..., tú eres David López, ¿no?
DAVID: **Bueno, soy David Vargas López.**
SRA. KAPLAN: ¿Cómo? ¿Vargas López?
DAVID: **Sí, señora.**
SRA. KAPLAN: ¡Ay, perdón!... A ver, necesitas tomar otra clase a las diez.
DAVID: **Sí, señora.**
SRA. KAPLAN: ¿Qué te gusta estudiar más, música, drama o geografía?
DAVID: **Pues, música. Me gusta mucho tocar la guitarra.**
SRA. KAPLAN: Entonces, música a las diez.
DAVID: **Gracias, señora.**
SRA. KAPLAN: De nada, David. Adiós. Hasta luego.

Actividades preliminares

A Respond to the following questions. Then ask a classmate the same questions.

1. ¿Qué te gusta más, correr o nadar?
2. ¿Qué te gusta más, bailar o descansar?
3. ¿Qué te gusta más, mirar la tele o estudiar?

B Tell when each of David's classes meets.

Por ejemplo:

   La clase de inglés es a las ocho.

C How well do you know your classmates? Ask a classmate three things you think he or she likes to do.

Por ejemplo:

ESTUDIANTE A
Te gusta correr, ¿no?

ESTUDIANTE B
Sí, me gusta.

Lección 4 **33**

B. Introduce the Lesson 4 dialogue by reading it aloud or by playing the cassette version. Have students raise their hands when they hear a question that asks David to make a choice. Ask students to listen in order to find out what choice is made.

C. Now ask students to open their books and look at the dialogue as you lead them through what is said. For example, **Cuando la señora pregunta: "¿Qué te gusta estudiar más...?", ¿qué dice David? ¿Por qué? ¿Qué dice la señora?**

D. After reading the dialogue with your students, follow up with questions such as: **¿Te gusta estudiar álgebra? ¿A qué hora es tu clase de álgebra? ¿Te gusta estudiar historia?,** etc.

Actividades preliminares

Actividad A Answers
1. Me gusta más correr (nadar).
2. Me gusta más bailar (descansar).
3. Me gusta más ver la tele (estudiar).

Actividad B Answers
La clase de inglés es a las ocho. La clase de biología es a las nueve. La clase de álgebra es a las once. La clase de historia es a la una. La clase de educación física es a las dos.

Actividad C Answers
Answers will vary but may include the following: **Te gusta leer, ¿no? Te gusta nadar, ¿no? Te gusta bailar, ¿no?**

Additional Practice
Have students say two things they want to do but can't because they need to do something else. For example, **Quiero jugar fútbol pero necesito hacer la tarea. Quiero montar en bicicleta pero necesito comer algo.**

---

gestures, and tone of voice the shades of difference between these expressions. Tell the class what you like to do and don't like to do. For example: **Me gusta mucho leer libros de horror pero no me gusta estudiar,** etc.
3. Ask students individually: **¿Te gusta...?** using various infinitives.

4. Ask students to compare the following: **¿Qué te gusta más, leer o ver la tele? ¿correr o bailar? ¿descansar o hacer la tarea?**

Vocabulary Teaching Resources

1. Vocabulario Transparencies 1.4
2. Workbook, pp. 16–17
3. Cassette 1.4
4. Student Tape Manual, p. 12
5. Lesson Quizzes, pp. 11–12

Bell Ringer Review

Directions to students: Complete the following expressions in a logical manner. Begin each sentence with **(No) Quiero...**

1. andar _____   4. jugar _____
2. leer _____   5. comprar _____
3. ver _____

Presentation

A. Have students open their books to page 34.
   1. Model each new word on page 34. Begin each phrase with **Me gusta estudiar...** Have students repeat each phrase in unison.
   2. Ask individual students whether or not they like to study each subject on page 34. For example, **Tim, ¿te gusta estudiar historia?** Encourage students to give a complete response. For example, **Sí, me gusta estudiar historia.**
   3. Ask individual students, **¿qué te gusta estudiar?** Encourage students to give a complete response. For example, **Me gusta estudiar geometría;** etc.

B. Now have students look at the vocabulary presentation on page 35.
   1. Model the question, **¿Qué necesitas hacer para la clase?** Then model each phrase, beginning each time with the word **Necesito...** Have students repeat each phrase in unison.

Vocabulario

¿Qué te gusta estudiar?
Me gusta estudiar...

historia

inglés

francés

español

biología

química

álgebra

geometría

música

arte

educación física

34   CAPÍTULO 1

Total Physical Response

Getting Ready

For TPR activities 1 and 3, use Vocabulario Transparencies 1.4.

New Words

saca   saquen
ve   escribe

TPR 1

Ve al proyector y
... toca el libro de español.
... señala el libro de biología.
... señala la clase de arte.
... toca el libro de inglés.
... señala la clase de música.

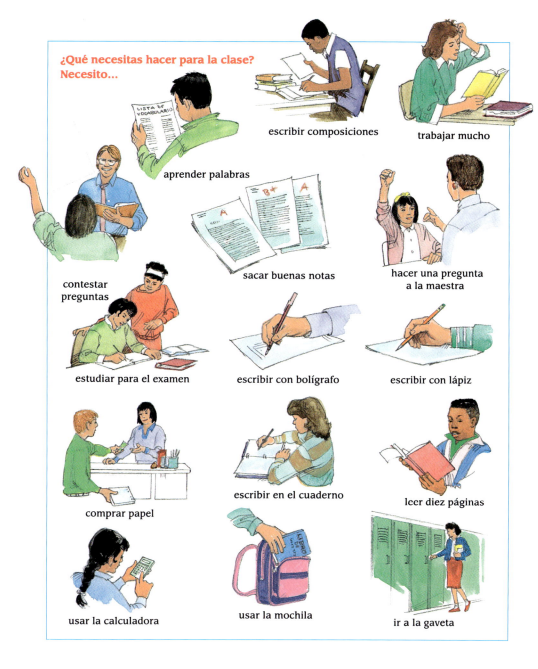

**¿Qué necesitas hacer para la clase?
Necesito...**

escribir composiciones

trabajar mucho

aprender palabras

sacar buenas notas

hacer una pregunta a la maestra

contestar preguntas

estudiar para el examen

escribir con bolígrafo

escribir con lápiz

comprar papel

escribir en el cuaderno

leer diez páginas

usar la calculadora

usar la mochila

ir a la gaveta

Lección 4 **35**

When Students Ask

You may wish to give students the following additional vocabulary to allow them to talk about their individual classes and interests.

el alemán	el japonés
la carpintería	el latín
el chino	la mecánica
la cívica	física
la contabilidad	la orquesta
el coro	el periodismo
la declamación	el portugués
el dibujo técnico	la psicología
el drama	el ruso
la economía	la sociología
doméstica	
la geografía	
el hebreo	
el italiano	
la natación	
el programación de	
computadoras	
la trigonometría	

Regionalisms

You may wish to tell students that in other parts of the Spanish-speaking world the following words or phrases are alternatives to those presented in the Vocabulario:

el bolígrafo (la pluma)
la calculadora (la máquina de calcular)
el cuaderno (la libreta)
el examen (la prueba)
la gaveta (el casillero) (el armario)

TPR 2
Saquen un lápiz.
Muéstrenme un bolígrafo.
Saquen dos cuadernos.
Muéstrenme un lápiz y un bolígrafo.
Levántense si tienen papel.
Siéntense si tienen una calculadora.
Levántense si tienen clase de inglés.
Salten si tienen buenas notas. Caminen si tienen papel.

Sonrían si tienen el libro de español.

TPR 3
Ve al proyector y toca
... el verbo "trabajar".
... señala el verbo "contestar".
... señala el verbo "estudiar".
... escribe la palabra "páginas".
... toca _____.
... señala _____.

Actividades

Actividades

A **Preferencias.** Using the list of classes in the **Vocabulario** on pages 34 and 35, say whether or not you want to study each.

Por ejemplo:
> Quiero estudiar geometría.
> No quiero estudiar química.

Now find out from three of your classmates what their preferences are.

Por ejemplo:

ESTUDIANTE A	ESTUDIANTE B
¿Qué quieres estudiar?	Quiero estudiar español, arte...

B **Las clases.** Write out a schedule of the classes you are taking, using the Spanish names of the subjects. Your teacher will tell you the names in Spanish of any subjects you are taking that do not appear in the **Vocabulario.**

Por ejemplo:
> inglés
> historia

Then you and a classmate will exchange schedules. Ask if your classmate likes to study each subject listed.

Por ejemplo:

ESTUDIANTE A	ESTUDIANTE B
¿Te gusta estudiar inglés?	Sí, me gusta. (No, no me gusta).

C **¿Fácil o difícil?** Tell whether the following are easy (**fácil**) or difficult (**difícil**) for you.

Por ejemplo:
> Es fácil (difícil) _____ en la clase de _____.

1. sacar buenas notas
2. escribir composiciones
3. contestar preguntas
4. aprender palabras
5. estudiar para exámenes
6. leer libros

36 CAPÍTULO 1

Curso de Cultura Norteamericana

Precio: $31.25 (más una cuota de inscripción de $25.00*). Esta cuota cubre un curso de 15 horas de clase. Sin crédito. 1.5 CEU's.
Los estudiantes que se inscriben en un curso de cultura deben tener un nivel correspondiente al curso Advanced English 1, por lo menos.

	Lunes y Miér
CE 751-1 Introduction to American Culture, Part 1 (sesión I)	11:00-12:2
CE 752-2 Introduction to American Culture, Part 2 (sesión II)	11:00-12:2
CE 753-3 Introduction to American Culture, Part 3 (sesión III)	11:00-12:2

Cursos Regulares de Inglés Para Hispanohabla

Precio: $85.00 (más una cuota de inscripción de $25.00* Esta cuota cubre un 45 horas de clase. Sin crédito. 4.5 C

CLASES VESPERTINAS | Lunes y M |
CE 110-1 English for Spanish Speakers I | 6:00-
CE 410-1 English for Spanish Speakers IV | 6:00-
CE 510-2 English for Spanish Speakers V | 7:30-
CE 610-2 English for Spanish Speakers VI | 7:30-
| Martes y |
CE 310-3 English for Spanish Speakers III | 6:00
CE 710-3 Advanced English I | 6:00
CE 750-4 Introduction to American Culture | 7:30
CE 210-4 English for Spanish Speakers II | 7:30
CE 110-4 English for Spanish Speakers I | 7:30

CLASE EN SABADO
Esta clase cubre lo mismo que los cursos regulares, pero en una sola sesión.
CE 210-7 English for Spanish Speakers II | S 9:00

36

D **En la clase.** Which of the following activities do you need to do to get ready for Spanish class? Which do you not need to do?

Por ejemplo:

> hacer la tarea
> *Necesito hacer la tarea.*

1. andar en monopatín
2. estudiar
3. hablar con los compañeros
4. usar la calculadora
5. leer revistas
6. cantar
7. preparar las lecciones
8. ver películas
9. jugar fútbol
10. sacar fotos
11. comprar papel y bolígrafos
12. ir a mi gaveta
13. usar la mochila

E **En las clases.** Tell what you need to do in each of the following classes.

Por ejemplo:

> la clase de historia
> *Necesito escribir composiciones y leer libros.*

1. la clase de español
2. la clase de educación física
3. la clase de matemáticas
4. la clase de inglés
5. la clase de historia

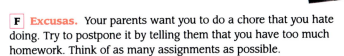

F **Excusas.** Your parents want you to do a chore that you hate doing. Try to postpone it by telling them that you have too much homework. Think of as many assignments as possible.

Por ejemplo:

> Necesito escribir dos composiciones para la clase de inglés. También necesito aprender quince palabras para la clase de español y...

2. Using poster board, prepare a card for each of the classes listed, plus any other classes mentioned by the students (**drama, ciencias, arte, etc.**). As you show each card to the class, students will draw an object that can be used in the class. They will then compare their drawings with those of the other members in their group, and tell each other whether they like the class.

Cultura viva 1

Presentation

Read the Cultura viva on this page. To clarify the concept of **apellidos**, you may wish to write "David Vargas López" on the chalkboard. Point out to students that "Vargas" is his father's family name; "López" is his mother's family name.

Did You Know?

In the Hispanic world women always keep their family name after they marry. Upon her marriage, a woman will add her husband's family name to her own and connect it with **de**. In the Hispanic world, people always maintain their mother's maiden name on all legal documents—driver's license, I.D. card, etc.

You may wish to ask students if they know their mother's maiden name. Have them write their first name followed by their two family names.

Critical Thinking Activity

What advantages are there to using both your mother's and your father's family name?

Actividades

Actividad A Answers
Pedro Cervantes Tejeda.
Alejandro Dávila Monroy.
Hernán Luján Muñoz.
Carmen Morelos Imán.
Julio Ramos Olivera.
María Trujillo Romero.

Actividad B Answers
El amor... / García Márquez, Gabriel.
La guerra... / Vargas Llosa, Mario.
Tiempo... / Martín Santos, Luis.
Cuando... / González Vera, José S.
Las cortes... / García Roldán, Ángela.

C U L T U R A   V I V A   1

Apellidos

In the Spanish-speaking world, people use two family names (**apellidos**): their father's family name followed by their mother's maiden name. In David's case there was confusion on the part of Sra. Kaplan over his family name. Which of David's names is that of his father's family? In the United States, many Spanish-speaking people do as David does and use only one family name, their father's.

Actividades

A In the Hispanic world, since the father's family name is the main one, it is the one used to list people alphabetically. Below are the names of some exchange students from Latin America in Chris's school. Say them in alphabetical order.

Julio Ramos Olivera
Carmen Morelos Imán
Alejandro Dávila Monroy

Hernán Luján Muñoz
María Trujillo Romero
Pedro Cervantes Tejeda

B The librarian has received several best-selling novels by Spanish and Latin American authors. But she doesn't know under what name to catalogue them. Give the name under which each of the following cards should be filed.

TÍTULO	AUTOR
El amor en los tiempos del cólera	Gabriel García Márquez
La guerra del fin del mundo	Mario Vargas Llosa
Tiempo de silencio	Luis Martín Santos
Las cortes de Coquaya	Ángela García Roldán

---

118 CEDILLO - CERVANTES

CEDILLO Eusebio 1855 Burton Dr. 4
  John Eric 2205 IH 35 4
  Joseph 9020 Research Blvd 4
  Maria 5901 Chase Cir 46
  Oscar 1899 Wooten Park Dr 92
  Ruth 4620 Quientte Dr 54
  S C 2331 Highgrove Ter 92
CEDILLOS Reynaldo
  10220 Oak Hollow Dr 748
CEDRONE Alfredo 5140 Hyridge Dr 385
CELBERTI-BARRETT Joya 448-
CELIS Carlos Martinez 634-
  22310 Jollyville Rd ....
  Jorge 8970-C Westover Club Dr 345-1
  Maria Elena 22893 Jollyville Rd 345-3
CENICEROS Jesus A 345-1
  6693 Starstreak Dr ....
CENTENO Raymond 499-48
  5911 Brassiewood Dr ....
CEPEDA Jose 6933 Lovely Ln 458-74
  Luis 2330 Willow Creek Dr 443-384
  Simon 2522 Durwood 550-497
CEPERO Carolyn L 3322 Westrock 443-712
CEPRESS Jerry & Monica 445-943
  13883 Merseyside Dr ....
CERA Saul 3277 Atascosca Dr 889-721
CERCHIONE Emita 4015 Yager Ln 446-019
CERCONE Laura 8909 Leisure Rd 383-552
CERDA Adam 304 Elmwood Pl 446-240
  Alex 703-B Hammack Dr 482-539
  Alfonso J Jr 2021-A Kirksey Dr 354-719
  Bangie & Frank 171 Parker Ln 834-292
  Cynthia 6800 Research Blvd 442-541
  Elisar 8144 Jinx Ave 854-379
  Francisco A Jr 8119 Banister Ln 448-905
  Hector 1200-C W Braker Ln 441-414
  Jesus 1012 Morin Dr 843-013
  John Albert 2006 E 11th St 272-613
  Jose 1322 Inks 747-537
  Leticia 2900-C N Braker Ln 874-431
  Lisa 854-721
  Maria 4402 Willow Creek Dr 443-734
  Maria S 511 Whelsee Ln 558-019
  Martin 1591 Pegasus St 629-472
  Maximino 3803 Haskell St 525-830
  Nora 28055 Morin Dr 585-311
  Sandra 13129 Pegasus St 828-716
  Sylvia 7172-B Salt Springs Dr 522-034
CERRITO Rogelio Avila 828-350
  4166 W 7th ....
CERRONI...

Estructura 1

How to Say What You Like and Don't Like to Do

Me gusta/te gusta

1. When you want to tell someone what you like to do, say **Me gusta** + activity.

   Me gusta jugar béisbol.

2. When you want to tell someone what you don't like to do, say **No me gusta** + activity.

   No me gusta montar en bicicleta.

3. To ask a friend if he or she likes to do something, say **¿Te gusta** + activity?

   ¿Te gusta nadar?

4. Your friend will respond with either **Sí, me gusta** or **No, no me gusta.**

5. To ask a friend what he or she likes to do, say **¿Qué te gusta hacer?**

Actividades

A **¿Qué te gusta hacer?** Write down five of your favorite weekend activities. Then write five things you don't like to do on weekends.

Por ejemplo:

> **Me gusta descansar. No me gusta estudiar.**

Then ask a classmate about his or her list.

ESTUDIANTE A
¿Qué te gusta hacer?

ESTUDIANTE B
Me gusta ver la tele. No me gusta leer revistas.

Estructura 1

Structure Teaching Resources
1. Workbook, pp. 18–19
2. Cassette 2.4
3. Student Tape Manual, p. 13
4. Estructura Masters 1.4
5. Lesson Quizzes, p. 13

Bell Ringer Review

Directions to students: Write down each of the classes you are taking and tell at what time each class meets. Round the time off to the nearest half hour.

Structure Focus

In this lesson, the presentation of **gustar** is limited to **Me gusta / te gusta**. The plural forms, **Me gustan / te gustan** are presented in Chapter 1, Lesson 6.

Presentation

Lead students through steps 1–5 on page 39. You may wish to give additional examples by making statements about your own likes and dislikes. Illustrate with gestures, board drawings, etc. Ask students to indicate whether they think your statements are true or not by responding **sí** or **no**.

Actividades

Actividad A Answers
Answers will vary but will include the following:
Me gusta jugar tenis; comprar algo; ver la tele; ver películas. No me gusta estudiar; hacer la tarea; escribir composiciones.

Class Management

You may want to have students compare their list of activities in groups of two. Then ask several students to read their list for the class.

B **¡Ay, Bruno!** Bruno spends too much time on recreation and not enough time on schoolwork. Ask Bruno if he likes to do the following activities. Your partner will answer for him.

Por ejemplo:

hacer la tarea

ESTUDIANTE A	ESTUDIANTE B (Bruno)
¿Te gusta hacer la tarea?	No, no me gusta.

1. usar la calculadora
2. hablar por teléfono
3. comer
4. descansar
5. escuchar discos
6. trabajar
7. leer diez páginas de tarea
8. jugar béisbol
9. escribir en el cuaderno
10. comprar discos
11. contestar preguntas
12. aprender palabras
13. hacer preguntas en clase

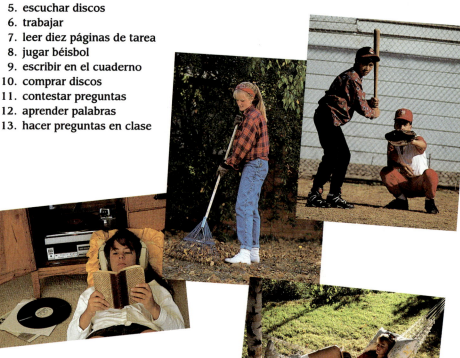

¿Cómo? No entiendo.

If you didn't hear or didn't catch what someone said and you want it repeated, say **¿Cómo?**

If you heard, but you didn't understand, say **No entiendo.**

If someone uses a word you don't understand, you can ask to have it explained by saying **¿Qué quiere decir...?**

Actividad

What would you say in the following situations: **¿Cómo?, No entiendo,** or **¿Qué quiere decir...?**

1.

2.

3.

Hola. ¿Quieres helado?

X + 5A = 21A - ⅗ =

Cultura viva 2

Presentation

1. Read the Cultura viva on this page. You may wish to write these three phrases on the chalkboard for emphasis:
   ¿Cómo?
   No entiendo.
   ¿Qué quiere decir...?
2. Ask students to tell you the words or phrases they use in English when they don't hear something someone said, or if they don't understand something, or when they want something explained. Write these English equivalents on the chalkboard.

Did You Know?
Many Spanish-speaking people also say **¿Qué?** if they didn't hear; **No comprendo** if they didn't understand; and **¿Qué significa...?** if they want an explanation.

Actividad Answers
1. No entiendo.
2. ¿Cómo?
3. ¿Qué quiere decir "helado"?

Additional Practice
After doing the Actividad on this page, you may want to give additional examples that will cue one of the phrases in the Cultura viva reading. For example: **¿Sabes cocinar? ¿Quieres patinar? ¿Quieres ir a la playa?** Write one or more of these questions on the chalkboard so that students can respond with, **¿Qué quiere decir "patinar",** etc.

Pronunciation

A. You may wish to play the recorded version of these lines, located at the end of Cassette 1.4. You may also wish to write the lines on the chalkboard or on an overhead transparency, and ask your students to copy them into their notebooks.

Hay muchas palabras que no entiendo.
Sin embargo, me defiendo.

B. Have students repeat words and phrases individually and in unison. You may wish to focus on the diphthong **ie**.

Additional words that students know are: **h**ola; **h**acer; **h**ablar; **h**ora; **h**istoria;

Structure Teaching Resources
1. Workbook, pp. 20–21
2. Cassette 2.4
3. Student Tape Manual, p. 13
4. Estructura Masters 1.4
5. Lesson Quizzes, pp. 14–15

Bell Ringer Review

Directions to students: Draw a circle on your paper and write the word **clases** inside it. Around the circle write the names of as many classes in Spanish as you can remember. Connect each class name to the circle with a line.

Presentation

A. Lead students through steps 1–7 on pages 42–43. For emphasis, you may wish to write on the chalkboard one or more examples given with each step. You may want to ask students to volunteer additional examples for you to write on the chalkboard.

B. As you lead students through step 5, point out the **z** to **c** spelling change in the plural of **lápiz**. Also point out the changes in accent from singular to plural of **examen** and **composición**.

Extension

After presenting the structure on pages 42–43, you may wish to have students look up the following words in a Spanish dictionary and draw some conclusions about gender.

1. **educación, información, natación**
2. **actividad, contabilidad, habilidad**
3. **sistema, programa, problema, idioma**

Point out to students that even though they may not know the meaning of a word, they can frequently determine whether that word is masculine or feminine by its ending.

42

Estructura 2

How to Talk about One Thing or More Than One　　**El / la los / las**

1. The names for persons and things in Spanish fall into one of two categories: **el** words (often referred to as "masculine" words) or **la** words (often referred to as "feminine" words). In dictionaries these categories are abbreviated as *m.* and *f.*

2. Most names of things or people that end with the letter **-o** are masculine. To talk about one thing or person, use the word **el** before it. To talk about more than one, use **los** and add **-s** to the end of the word.

One person or thing (singular)	Several persons or things (plural)
el maestro	**los maestros**
el partido	**los partidos**
el libro	**los libros**

3. Most names of things or people that end with the letter **-a** are feminine. With these words, to talk about one thing or person, you use the word **la** before it. To talk about more than one, use **las** and add an **-s** to the end of the word.

One person or thing (singular)	Several persons or things (plural)
la señorita	**las señoritas**
la tarea	**las tareas**
la nota	**las notas**

4. Some words don't end in either **-o** or **-a.** For these you must learn if they are **el** words or **la** words the first time you see them.

la clase	**el tenis**
la tele	**el fútbol**

5. If a word does not end in **-a, -o,** or **-e,** you add **-es** when you want to talk about more than one person or thing.

el señor	**los señores**
el papel	**los papeles**
el examen	**los exámenes**
el lápiz	**los lápices**

6. There are some words that are exceptions.

el problema	la foto	el álgebra
el idioma	la radio	el día

7. When you want to refer to something or someone more specifically, use **de**. For example, to say "the Spanish book" instead of just "the book," say **el libro de español**.

the algebra test	el examen de álgebra
the English class	la clase de inglés
the baseball game	el partido de béisbol

Actividades

A **¿Cómo se dice. . .?** Give the Spanish name for the following things.

Por ejemplo:

El cuaderno.

1.
2.
la gaveta
4.
5.
6.
7.
3.
8.
9.
10.
11.
12.
13.
14.

B **¿Qué necesitas?** Your classmate is having trouble getting ready for class. Ask if he or she needs the following items.

Por ejemplo:

ESTUDIANTE A	ESTUDIANTE B
¿Necesitas el lápiz?	Sí, gracias. (No, gracias).

C **En mi escuela.** Give two specific examples of the following.

Por ejemplo:

estudiantes
Estudiantes de español y estudiantes de biología.

1. libros   2. clases   3. partidos

D **El club de español.** The Spanish Club is selling some used items to raise money. Support the club by buying three of the items below. Your partner will play the role of cashier and tell the amount you must pay.

Por ejemplo:

ESTUDIANTE A	ESTUDIANTE B
Quiero comprar los bolígrafos, las revistas y la película.	Entonces, necesitas catorce dólares.

3 dólares   5 dólares   6 dólares   4 dólares

5 dólares   3 dólares   2 dólares   6 dólares

Finalmente

Situaciones

A conversar Use the following cues to converse with a classmate in Spanish.

1. Find out what activities your partner likes to do.
2. Invite your partner to do one of these activities after school **(después de las clases).**
3. Your partner accepts but **(pero)** tells what he or she needs to do for homework first.
4. Ask your partner at what time he or she wants to do the activity you have decided upon.
5. Agree on a time and say good-bye.

Repaso de vocabulario

PREGUNTAS

¿Qué te gusta más?
¿Te gusta...?

CLASES

el álgebra
el arte
la biología
las ciencias
la educación física
el español
el francés
la geometría
la historia
el idioma
el inglés
las matemáticas
la música
la química

COSAS (Things)

la gaveta
el bolígrafo
la calculadora
la clase
la composición
el cuaderno
el examen
    (los exámenes)
el lápiz (los lápices)
la mochila
la nota
la página
la palabra
el papel
la pregunta

ACTIVIDADES

aprender
contestar
escribir
estudiar
hacer una pregunta
sacar buenas notas
trabajar
usar

DESPEDIDAS (Saying Good-bye)

Adiós.
Hasta luego.

OTRAS PALABRAS

¿cómo?
¿no?
o

EXPRESIONES

estudiar para un examen
Me gusta + activity.
Necesito (Necesitas) + activity.

Lección 4 **45**

Finalmente

Situaciones

Lesson 4 Evaluation
The A conversar situation on this page is designed to give students the opportunity to use as many language functions as possible listed on page 32 of this lesson. The A conversar is also intended to show how well students are able to meet the lesson objectives. These objective are also listed on page 32 of this lesson.

Presentation
Prior to doing the A conversar and A escribir on this page, you may wish to play the Situaciones listening activities on Cassette 1.4 as a means of helping students organize the material.

Repaso de vocabulario

The words and phrases in the Repaso de vocabulario have been taught for productive use in this lesson. They are summarized here as a resource for both students and teacher. The Repaso de vocabulario also serves as a convenient resource for the A conversar activity on this page. It also gives the teacher a source for writing either additional practice, or evaluation activities, such as quizzes and tests.

For the Native Speaker
Have native speakers work in pairs to talk about four or five of their weekend activities, choosing the best and the worst. They could share their experiences with the class.

Lección 5

Objectives

By the end of this lesson, students will be able to:

1. talk about what they know how to do and tell or ask a friend what he or she knows how to do
2. say where they want to go and ask a friend where he or she wants to go

---

Lesson 5 Resources
1. Workbook, pp. 22–27
2. Vocabulario Transparencies 1.5
3. Cassette 1.5
4. Student Tape Manual, pp. 15–19
5. Lesson Quizzes, pp. 16–19
6. Computer software, Disk 1
7. Video Cassette
8. Estructura Masters 1.5
9. Diversiones Masters 1.5

Bell Ringer Review

Directions to students: Make a list of at least five school supplies you will need to buy for school this year.

¡A Comenzar!

Presentation

A. Lead students through each of the four functions given on page 46, progressing from the English to the Spanish for each function. Then have the students find these words and phrases in the dialogue on page 47.

B. Introduce the Lesson 5 dialogue by reading it aloud, or by playing the cassette version. Explain that David is trying to decide on an

Lección 5

¿Sabes hablar español?

¡A comenzar!

The following are some of the things you will be learning to do in this lesson.

When you want to . . .	You use . . .
1. describe what you know how to do	• **Sé** + activity.
2. tell a friend what he or she knows how to do	• **Sabes** + activity.
3. ask a friend where he or she wants to go	• **¿Quieres ir** + place?
4. give a reason or explain why	• **porque**

Now find examples of the above words and phrases in the following conversation.

Getting Ready for Lesson 5

You may wish to use the following suggestions to prepare students for the lesson:

1. Make a series of true or false statements about yourself. Have students raise their hands if they agree. For example: **Sé hablar español y francés. Sé jugar fútbol americano. Sé bailar muy bien.**

2. On the chalkboard, list several after-school activities. Use photos or drawings to illustrate any new words as you write and say them. Have students say whether or not they know how to do each activity. Students should respond with **sí** or **no**. For example: **¿Sabes sacar fotos? ¿Sabes dibujar? ¿Sabes cantar?**

David wants to sign up for an after-school activity. Chris Pearson is helping him decide which one.

CHRIS: **Bueno... ¿quieres estudiar fotografía?**
DAVID: **Pues no, porque ya sé sacar fotos.**
CHRIS: **Claro, ya sabes sacar fotos. A ver, entonces... ¿arte?**
DAVID: **Bueno, sí. Me gusta dibujar.**
CHRIS: **Oye, también te gusta el fútbol, ¿no?**
DAVID: **Sí, claro.**
CHRIS: **¿Quieres ir al partido?**
DAVID: **No sé. ¿A qué hora?**
CHRIS: **A las cuatro.**
DAVID: **Sí, cómo no.**

Actividades preliminares

A Say whether you already know how **(Ya sé)** or don't know how **(No sé)** to do the following.

Por ejemplo:
> hablar francés
> *Ya sé (No sé) hablar francés.*

1. nadar
2. jugar tenis
3. hablar español
4. montar en bicicleta
5. jugar baloncesto
6. andar en monopatín

B Tell whether you like to do the following activities.

Por ejemplo:
> dibujar
> *Me gusta (No me gusta) dibujar.*

1. hablar por teléfono
2. jugar fútbol americano
3. estudiar
4. comer en la cafetería

Lección 5 **47**

additional course to take in school. Have students listen to find out:
1. what activities are suggested to him;
2. whether or not he chooses an additional school activity;
3. where he is invited to go.

C. Now ask students to open their books and look at the dialogue on page 47 as you lead them through what is said. You may want to check for understanding by asking students to do the following:
1. name one activity associated with **fotografía (películas)**; **arte (papel, bolígrafo, etc)**.
2. name the activities that David knows how to do or likes to do: **sacar fotos; dibujar; el fútbol.**
3. Have students respond with **sí** or **no** to the following statements about David: **Quiere estudiar fotografía. (no) Quiere estudiar arte. (sí) Quiere ir al partido de fútbol. (sí)**
4 Have students complete what David might say. For example: **No quiero (necesito) estudiar fotografía porque _____. Quiero estudiar arte porque _____. Quiero ir al partido de fútbol porque _____.**

Actividades preliminares

Actividad A Answers
Answers will vary, but students should begin each response with either **ya sé** or **no sé**.

Actividad B Answers
Answers will vary, but students should begin each response with either **me gusta** or **no me gusta**.

Additional Practice
After doing Actividad A on page 47, you may wish to reinforce the learning with the following: In groups of four, have students tally how many in their group know how to do each activity.

Bell Ringer Review

Directions to students: Write **el, la, los,** or **las** in front of the following words:

1. gaveta
2. cuaderno
3. lápices
4. matemáticas
5. tele
6. examen
7. química
8. álgebra
9. página
10. idioma

Presentation

A. Have students open their books to page 48.
   1. Model the question, **¿Qué sabes hacer?** Then model each new word or phrase on this page. Begin each time with **Sé...** Have students repeat each word or phrase in unison.
   2. Ask individual students whether or not they know how to do each activity. Begin by telling students whether or not you know how to do that activity. For example: **No sé patinar. Gloria, ¿sabes patinar?**

B. Now have students look at the vocabulary presentation on page 49.
   1. Model the question, **¿Adónde quieres ir?** Then model each new phrase, beginning each time with the word **Quiero ir...** Have students repeat each phrase in unison.

Vocabulario

¿Qué sabes hacer?
Sé...

Hola, ¿qué tal?

hablar español

cocinar

sacar fotos

tocar la guitarra

patinar

manejar un coche

patinar sobre hielo

usar la computadora

dibujar

cantar

esquiar

montar a caballo

48   CAPÍTULO 1

Total Physical Response

Getting Ready

For TPR 1, photocopy Vocabulario Transparencies 1.5, and distribute a copy for each student. For TPR 2, bring magazine pictures to class for the various locations. Draw a large tick-tack-toe grid on the board and number each square from 1 to 9.

New Words

marca	pizarra	cubran
cubre	marquen	pon
salta		

TPR 1

(Give each student a photocopy of the Vocabulario Transparencies 1.5. Students should work together in pairs.)

¿Adónde quieres ir?
Quiero ir...

al partido

al parque

al cine

al campo

al estadio

al restaurante

al baile

al centro comercial

a la playa

a la cafetería

a la escuela

a la piscina

a la tienda

a la biblioteca

a la ciudad

a la fiesta

Lección 5   49

Actividades

Actividad A Answers
Answers will vary.

Actividad B Answers
Answers will vary but may include the following:
Quiero (Necesito, Me gusta) ir a la playa.
No me gusta (Quiero, Necesito) ir al cine.

Actividad C Answers
Answers will vary.

Actividad D Answers
Answers will vary but may include the following:

1. Si quiero usar la computadora, necesito ir a la escuela (a casa).
2. ... bailar... al baile.
3. ... ver la tele... a casa.
4. ... ver películas... al cine.
5. ... patinar sobre hielo... al centro comercial (al parque).
6. ... hablar español... a la escuela (a la casa de...).
7. ... cocinar... a casa.
8. ... leer libros... a la biblioteca (a casa).
9. ... comprar algo... al centro comercial (a la tienda).
10. .. practicar deportes... al parque (al estadio).
11. .. hacer la tarea... a casa (a la biblioteca).
12. ... nadar... a la piscina (a la playa).

Additional Practice
Have students place each of the activities in the Vocabulario on page 48 on the following continuum: **muy bien, bastante bien, no muy bien, no sé.** Then have them summarize about themselves. For example: **Sé dibujar muy bien. Sé tocar la guitarra bastante bien.**

Reteaching

Ask students to turn to the Vocabulario on pages 48–49. Have students list the activities and things they associate with each item. For example: **la fiesta: bailar,** etc.

Actividades

A **¿Sabes...?** Name four things you know how to do, choosing from the **Vocabulario** on pages 48 and 49. Then name four things you don't know how to do.

Por ejemplo:

> **Sé dibujar. No sé cocinar.**

B **¿Quieres ir?** Tell whether or not you want to, like to, or need to go to each of the places listed in the **Vocabulario.**

Por ejemplo:

> al partido
> *Quiero (Me gusta, Necesito) ir al partido.*

C **El tiempo.** Make a list of five places for you and a friend to go when the weather is good **(si hace buen tiempo).** Then make a list of five other places you can go if the weather is bad **(si hace mal tiempo).** Invite a classmate to do one of the activities from your list, according to what the weather is like today.

Por ejemplo:

Si hace buen tiempo	Si hace mal tiempo
la piscina	el cine

D **Lugares.** Tell where you need to go when you want to do the following activities.

Por ejemplo:

> montar a caballo
> *Si quiero montar a caballo, necesito ir al campo (al parque).*

1. usar la computadora
2. bailar
3. ver la tele
4. ver películas
5. patinar sobre hielo
6. hablar español
7. cocinar
8. leer libros
9. comprar algo
10. practicar deportes
11. hacer la tarea
12. nadar

For the Native Speaker

Have native speakers write a paragraph of at least fifty words explaining how to play their favorite sport (tennis, basketball, etc.). They should mention player positions, equipment, and famous players of that sport.

Las notas

The grading scale varies throughout the Spanish-speaking world. Scales of 1–5, 1–7, 1–10, 1–20 and even 1–100 are used. Generally, students have many required courses (including Spanish and a foreign language) and few electives. Foreign languages are considered important and many students take two. English and French are the most popular languages, followed by German and Italian. Latin and sometimes classical Greek are also usually offered. Here's a typical grading scale from Colombia.

10 = **sobresaliente**
9 = **distinguido**
8 = **bueno**
6–7 = **aprobado**
1–5 = **no aprobado**

Boletín de evaluación

Alumno: Tatiana Blanco Rodríguez

Materias

Biología II	8,7	bueno
Álgebra y Geometría	7,7	aprobado
Educación religiosa	8,6	bueno
Ciencias sociales	9,4	distinguido
Cívica	10	sobresaliente
Geografía	10	sobresaliente
Historia	9,6	distinguido
Español (literatura)	7,2	aprobado
Inglés	7,7	aprobado
Educación estética	8,0	bueno
Ed. fís., rec. y deporte	9,0	distinguido
Actividades vocacionales	8.5	bueno
Hogar	10	sobresaliente
Comercio	6,0	aprobado

Actividades

A Based on Tatiana's grades, would she say she likes or dislikes the following classes?

Por ejemplo:

biología
Me gusta estudiar biología.

1. cívica
2. geografía
3. álgebra y geometría
4. educación física, recreación y deporte
5. inglés

B Rate yourself according to the scale above in the following subjects. Use the ratings of **sobresaliente** to **aprobado.**

1. español
2. educación física
3. ciencias
4. arte y música
5. matemáticas
6. inglés
7. historia

Pronunciation

A. You may wish to play the recorded version of these pronunciation lines, located at the end of Cassette 1.5. You may also wish to write this verse on the board and have students copy it into their notebook.
**Aprobado en biología,
distinguido en geometría,**
**bueno en francés,
¡no aprobado en inglés!**

B. Have students repeat words and phrases individually and in unison. You may wish to focus on the /**g**/ sound as in **biología** and **geometría.**

Cultura viva 1

Presentation

Read the Cultura viva 1 on this page. You may wish to discuss with students the differences between the grading system in the U.S. and that of the Hispanic world. For example, using the grading scale on page 51, what would be the equivalent number or letter grade in your school?

Did You Know?

In the majority of Hispanic countries most students attend six years of elementary school and 5 or 6 years of secondary school. A secondary school is not the equivalent of junior and senior high in the U.S. Some students may attend a technical school, while others attend an **escuela normal** to prepare to become teachers. Still other students attend a **colegio** to prepare to enter a university. In general, students study more subjects per semester than do students in the U.S., and for this reason some classes meet every other day. It's also common to attend classes on Saturdays.

Actividades

Actividad A Answers

1. Me gusta estudiar cívica.
2. Me gusta estudiar geografía.
3. No... álgebra y geometría.
4. ... educación física...
5. No... inglés.

Actividad B Answers
Answers will vary.

Learning From Realia

1. What kind of a student is Tatiana Blanco Rodríguez?
2. What is another word in Spanish for **alumno?**
3. How does this report card differ from yours?

How to Talk about Things **Sé / sabes**
You Know How to Do

1. To say you know how to do something, use **Sé** + activity.
   Sé montar a caballo.

2. To say you don't know how to do something, use **No sé** + activity.
   No sé dibujar.

3. To say you already know how to do something, use **Ya sé** + activity.
   Ya sé usar la computadora.

4. To ask a friend if he or she knows how to do something, you use **¿Sabes** + activity?
   ¿Sabes esquiar?

Actividades

A **¿Quién sabe...?** Make a list of five activities. Survey your classmates and for each activity find at least one person who knows how to do it very well.

Por ejemplo:
   esquiar

ESTUDIANTE A	ESTUDIANTE B
¿Sabes esquiar?	Sí, sé esquiar muy bien. (No, no sé esquiar).

Bell Ringer Review

Directions to students: Draw three circles on your paper, leaving space between them. Write one of these words in each circle: **ciencias, idiomas, matemáticas.** Draw connecting lines out from each circle and write as many school subjects as you can for each of the three topics.

Structure Focus

In this lesson, the presentation of **saber** is limited to **sé / sabes.** Additional forms of **saber** are taught in Chapter 2, Lessons 4, 5, and 6.

Presentation

Lead students through steps 1–4 on page 52. Follow up by telling students things you know how to do. For example: **Ya sé esquiar; tocar la guitarra; manejar un coche, etc.** Ask individual students what they know how to do. **¿Sabes dibujar; patinar sobre hielo; etc.?**

Actividades

Actividad A Answers

Answers will vary, but will include activities from the Vocabulario on page 48 as well as the activities taught in Lesson 2, pp. 14–15.

Class Management

1. Actividad A may be done in groups of two, if preferred. Student A asks student B the questions from his or her list.
2. You may choose to allow students to circulate around the class to collect their information.

Cooperative Learning

After students have completed Actividad A on page 52, collect the list of five activities that each student wrote. Pick one interesting or different activity from each list. On the chalkboard, make a grid with a square for each activity. Have students copy the grid onto a sheet of paper, then walk around the room asking other students if they know how to do these activities. Students should sign the appropriate square if they know how to do the activity. Give prizes to the first five students who turn in their signed sheet.

B **¿No quieres estudiar?** Bruno's guidance counselor is advising him on next semester's classes. He rejects each suggestion and explains why. Play the roles of Bruno and his counselor with a classmate.

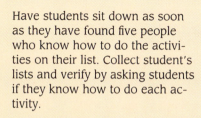

Por ejemplo:

> francés

ESTUDIANTE A

¿Quieres estudiar francés?

ESTUDIANTE B (Bruno)

No, porque ya sé hablar francés. (No, no me gusta estudiar idiomas).

1. arte
2. música
3. fotografía
4. literatura
5. dibujo técnico
6. ciencias domésticas

C **Quiero ser miembro.** Tell whether or not you want to join the following clubs. Be sure to tell why.

el club de esquí

Por ejemplo:

> Sí, quiero ser miembro porque me gusta esquiar. (No, no quiero ser miembro porque no sé esquiar).

4. el club de computadoras

3. el club de fotografía

1. el club de ciclismo

2. el club de español

5. el club de arte

6. el club de música

Lección 5 **53**

Read the Cultura viva on this page. If possible, play a selection of mariachi music in class. Two well-known songs are "Adelita" and "Cielito lindo."

Did You Know?

A mariachi band usually consists of nine to twelve musicians playing the violin, guitar, and trumpet. There are no wind instruments. Everyone in the band participates in the singing, with two or three musicians taking solo responsibilities.

Folk songs called **corridos** have long been popular in Mexico. Many **corridos** tell of the Mexican Revolution of 1910-1921. Several **corridos** have been recorded by Linda Ronstadt on her album "Canciones de Mi Padre."

A mural is a scene or design that decorates the wall of a public building. Three famous Mexican muralists are José Clemente Orozco, considered one of the foremost mural painters of the 20th century, Diego Rivera, and David Alfaro Siqueiros. All three artists have created murals showing scenes from Mexican history and legends.

Critical Thinking Activity

From your knowledge of mariachi music, can you compare it to any other form of music played in the United States? Consider both the kinds of instruments used and the types of songs in making your comparison.

Actividad

Answers

Answers will vary.

CULTURA VIVA 2

Arte y música del suroeste

The Spanish-speaking influence, particularly Mexican, is a principal element of the music and art of San Antonio and other cities in the Southwest, including El Paso, Los Angeles, and San Diego. No festival would be complete, for example, without **mariachis**, musical groups that entertain with traditional songs of Mexico. The **mariachi** tradition of the Southwest is often maintained through the family.

Murals, or wall paintings, are a traditional art form in the Spanish-speaking world. In San Antonio, local artists, as well as internationally known artists like Juan O'Gorman, make vivid statements on buildings in both commercial and residential areas.

Actividad

Ask a classmate if he or she knows how to do the following activities related to art and music.

1. **dibujar**
2. **pintar**
3. **tocar la guitarra (el saxofón, el piano, el clarinete, la trompeta)**
4. **cantar**
5. **bailar**

Pronunciation

A. You may wish to play the recorded version of these pronunciation lines, located at the end of Cassette 1.5 These lines are taken from the refrain of the Mexican song "Cielito lindo." You may wish to write them on the chalkboard or on an overhead transparency and ask your students to copy them into their notebook. **Canta y no llores, porque cantando se alegran, cielito lindo, los corazones.**

B. Have students repeat the words and phrases individually and in unison. You may also wish to sing the song "Cielito Lindo" in class. You may wish to focus on the /**a**/ and /**i**/ sounds. For example, c**a**nt**a**; c**a**nt**a**ndo; **a**le-gr**a**n; ciel**i**to l**i**ndo

Estructura 2

How to Say Where You Want to Go

The infinitive ir

1. To say you want to go somewhere, say **Quiero ir.**

2. To say you don't want to go, say **No quiero ir.**

3. To invite someone to go, say **¿Quieres ir?**

4. To ask a friend where he or she wants to go, say **¿Adónde quieres ir?**

5. To say where you want to go using feminine (**la**) words, you say **Quiero ir a la** + place.

>   **Quiero ir a la fiesta.**   **No quiero ir a la piscina.**

6. To say where you want to go using masculine (**el**) words, you say **Quiero ir al** + place (**a** + **el** = **al**).

>   **¿Quieres ir al partido?**   **No, quiero ir al cine.**

7. To say you want to go home, you simply say **Quiero ir a casa.**

8. To say you don't want to go anywhere, say **No quiero ir a ningún lugar.**

Actividades

A **Después de las clases.** Ask two classmates where each wants to go after school. Each classmate will tell you where and at what time.

Por ejemplo:

ESTUDIANTE A	ESTUDIANTE B
¿Adónde quieres ir?	Quiero ir a la piscina a las tres.

¿Te gusta escuchar discos y bailar?

¿Quieres ir a una fiesta?

La fiesta es mañana a las ocho en mi casa.

¡Hasta pronto!

Margarita Espronceda
Teléfono 686-9021

Lección 5 **55**

Structure Teaching Resources

1. Workbook, pp. 25–27
2. Cassette 1.5
3. Student Tape Manual, p. 18
4. Estructura Masters 1.5
5. Lesson Quizzes, p. 19

Bell Ringer Review

Directions to students: Organize the following list of words under three headings: **lugares, objetos, actividades.**

cuaderno, biblioteca, bolígrafo, bailar, fiesta, dibujar, coche, piscina, cafetería, restaurante, calculadora, ciudad, trabajar, página, cocinar.

Structure Focus

Students will learn to use the infinitive **ir**. The conjugated forms of **ir** are taught in Chapter 2, Lesson 3.

Presentation

Lead students through steps 1–8 on page 55. You may wish to emphasize step 6 by writing examples of **a** + **el** = **al** on the chalkboard.

Actividades

Actividad A Answers
Answers will vary but may include the following:
Quiero ir al parque a las cuatro.
Quiero ir al partido a las siete.
Note. If students need help with vocabulary, have them turn to the Vocabulario, page 49.

Learning From Realia

Ask students to write a response to the party invitation on this page. Their reply should be addressed to Margarita. You may also want your students to write a party invitation, modeled on the one given here.

B **¿Por qué?** Tell why you do or don't want to go to the following places.

Por ejemplo:

> (No)Quiero ir al restaurante porque (no) quiero comer.

1. al parque
2. a la fiesta
3. a la tienda
4. al estadio
5. al campo
6. a la playa
7. a la biblioteca
8. a casa

C **Lugares.** Name the places you like to go in the following situations.

Por ejemplo:

> cuando (when) quieres ver una película
> *Cuando quiero ver una película, me gusta ir al cine "Fox".*

1. cuando quieres comer
2. cuando quieres jugar fútbol
3. cuando quieres leer
4. cuando quieres bailar
5. cuando quieres nadar
6. cuando quieres patinar
7. cuando quieres descansar
8. cuando quieres comprar algo
9. cuando quieres estudiar

D **Invitaciones.** You have met a new student. Find out what this person likes to do, and invite him or her to go to the appropriate place, choosing from the list below.

a casa	al baile	al estadio
a la piscina	al campo	al parque
a la playa	al centro comercial	al restaurante
a la tienda	al cine	

Por ejemplo:

> nadar

ESTUDIANTE A	ESTUDIANTE B
(1) ¿Te gusta nadar?	(2) Sí, me gusta.
(3) ¿Quieres ir a la piscina?	(4) Sí, cómo no.

1. jugar videojuegos
2. ver la tele
3. bailar
4. ver películas
5. comprar discos
6. ver el partido de fútbol
7. nadar

56   CAPÍTULO 1

Cooperative Learning

After students have completed Actividad A on page 52, collect the list of five activities that each student wrote. Pick one interesting or different activity from each list. On the chalkboard, make a grid with a square for each activity. Have students copy the grid onto a sheet of paper, then walk around the room asking other students if they know how to do these activities. Students should sign the appropriate square if they know how to do the activity. Give prizes to the first five students who turn in their signed sheet.

Finalmente

....

A conversar Invite a classmate to go someplace at a specific time after school. He or she will either accept your invitation or politely refuse and give a reason.

A escribir Write a note to a classmate.

1. Introduce yourself.
2. Tell what you like and don't like to do and places you like to go.
3. Say what you know how to do.
4. Then ask your classmate about the same topics.

Repaso de vocabulario

PREGUNTAS

¿Adónde quieres ir?
¿Sabes + activity?

ACTIVIDADES

cantar
cocinar
dibujar
esquiar
manejar un coche
montar a caballo
patinar
patinar sobre hielo
sacar fotos
tocar la guitarra

LUGARES

el baile
la biblioteca
la cafetería
el campo
el centro comercial
el cine
la ciudad
la escuela
el estadio
la fiesta
el parque
la piscina
la playa
el restaurante
la tienda

OTRAS PALABRAS

el coche
la computadora
la foto
porque

EXPRESIONES

No quiero ir a ningún lugar.
Ya sé + activity.

Lección 5 **57**

For the Native Speaker

Have native speakers write a letter to a relative in their native country. They may describe some places they like and dislike to go.

Finalmente

Situaciones

Lesson 5 Evaluation
The A conversar and A escribir situations on this page are designed to give students the opportunity to use as many language functions as possible listed on page 46 of this lesson. The A conversar and A escribir are also intended to show how well students are able to meet the lesson objectives, also listed on page 46 of this lesson.

Presentation
Prior to doing the A conversar and A escribir on this page, you may wish to play the Situaciones listening activities on Cassette 1.5 as a means of helping students organize the material.

Repaso de vocabulario
The words and phrases in the Repaso de vocabulario have been taught for productive use in this lesson. They are summarized here as a resource for both students and teacher. The Repaso de vocabulario also serves as a convenient resource for the A conversar and A escribir activities on this page. It also gives the teacher a source for writing either additional practice or evaluation activities such as quizzes and tests, in addition to those provided by the publisher.

Learning From Photos
In the photo on page 57 what might these two people be saying to each other? Write a dialogue about what they are saying.

Lesson 6

Objectives

By the end of this lesson, students will be able to:

1. talk about what they like and dislike, and ask a friend what he or she likes or dislikes
2. express reactions to situations
3. use connecting words to link similar or different ideas
4. name the letters of the Spanish alphabet and spell in Spanish

Lesson 6 Resources

1. Workbook, pp. 28–32
2. Vocabulario Transparency 1.6
3. Cassette 1.6
4. Student Tape Manual, pp. 20–23
5. Lesson Quizzes, pp. 20–23
6. Test Booklet, pp. 7–14
7. Computer software, Disk 1
8. Video cassette
9. Estructura Masters 1.6
10. Diversiones Masters 1.6

Bell Ringer Review

Directions to students: Write three statements about what you want to do at various times today. **Por ejemplo: A las tres quiero...**

¡A comenzar!

Presentation

A. Lead students through each of the five functions given on page 58, progressing from the English to the Spanish for each function. Then have the students find these words and phrases in the dialogue on page 59.

Lección 6

Me gusta San Antonio

¡A comenzar!

The following are some of the things you will be learning to do in this lesson.

When you want to . . .	You use . . .
1. give your likes and dislikes	• **(No) me gusta(n)** + object(s).
2. ask the likes and dislikes of a friend	• **¿Te gusta(n)** + object(s)?
3. express reactions	• **¡Qué** + descriptive word!
4. express contrast or difference	• **pero**
5. express similarity	• **y también**

Now find examples of the above words and phrases in the following conversation.

Getting Ready for Lesson 6

You may wish to use one or more of the following suggestions to prepare students for the lesson.

1. Have students volunteer their own preferences from the following categories. List their preferences on the board along with their articles.

a. Las clases que me gustan más.
b. Los deportes que me gustan más.
c. Las películas que me gustan más.
d. Los restaurantes que me gustan más.
e. Las ciudades que me gustan más.

Graciela, a friend of Chris Pearson's, has heard about David and introduces herself.

GRACIELA: ¡Hola! Me llamo Graciela. Soy amiga de Chris.
DAVID: Hola. Mucho gusto. Me llamo David Vargas.
GRACIELA: ¿Vargas? ¿No eres David López?
DAVID: Bueno, me llamo David Vargas López pero...
GRACIELA: Pero aquí eres David Vargas, claro.
DAVID: Pues, sí.
GRACIELA: ¿Te gustan las clases de aquí, David?
DAVID: Sí, me gustan mucho. Y también me gusta San Antonio.
GRACIELA: ¡Qué bueno!

Actividad preliminar

Compare two of your classes. If you like both of them, connect them with **y también.** If you like one but not the other, connect them with **pero.**

Por ejemplo:

la clase de historia / la clase de inglés
Me gusta la clase de historia y también me gusta la clase de inglés.

la clase de ciencias / la clase de álgebra
Me gusta la clase de ciencias pero no me gusta la clase de álgebra.

Tally the number of times a particular item is mentioned. Have students count aloud with you. Rank the top ten according to class preference.

2. Write the following list of names on the board and ask students to say the names in alphabetical order.

Ramón Pérez Guzmán
Olivia Vargas Ramos
Vicente Olivares Fernández
Javier Benavides Martínez
María Sánchez Moreno

Ask students to imagine that Ramón Pérez Guzmán married Olivia Vargas Ramos and they had a son named Juan. What would Juan's complete name be?

B. Introduce the Lesson 6 dialogue by reading it aloud, or by playing the cassette version. Ask students to listen for the following information:
   1. David's complete name
   2. the name David is known by at school (in San Antonio)

C. Now ask students to open their books and look at the dialogue as you lead them through what is said. For example, **Cuando Graciela pregunta: ''¿No eres David López?'', ¿qué dice David? Cuando Graciela pregunta: ''¿Te gustan las clases de aquí...?, ¿qué dice David?**

D. Remind students about the Spanish use of **apellidos.** You may want to refer them to the Lesson 4 Cultura viva, page 38.

Actividad preliminar

Actividad Answer
Answers will vary but may include the following: **Me gusta la clase de arte y también la clase de dibujo técnico. Me gusta la clase de cívica pero no me gusta la clase de matemáticas.**

Additional Practice
After doing the Actividad preliminar on page 59, you may wish to reinforce the learning with the following:

1. In pairs, have students find out if their partner likes the following. **Por ejemplo: las clases de aquí** *¿Te gustan las clases de aquí? —Sí. Me gustan mucho. (No. No me gustan).*

a. los exámenes de matemáticas
b. los partidos de fútbol americano
c. las revistas de deportes
d. las películas de Tom Cruise
e. los discos de Janet Jackson

2. Have students name two things they like about school. **Me gusta(n) _____ y también me gusta(n) _____.**

Vocabulario

Vocabulario

Vocabulary Teaching Resources

1. Vocabulario Transparency 1.6
2. Workbook, p. 28
3. Cassette 1.6
4. Student Tape Manual, p. 20
5. Lesson Quizzes, p. 20

Bell Ringer Review

Directions to students: Draw a picture to represent each of the following expressions.

1. ir a la gaveta
2. la educación física
3. sacar fotos
4. el bolígrafo
5. leer revistas
6. escuchar discos
7. correr
8. la calculadora

Presentation

A. Have students open their books to page 60.
1. Model each new expression on this page. Help convey to students the meaning of each phrase by the tone of your voice, and by using appropriate facial expressions. Have students repeat each phrase in unison.
2. Call out each expression once again. This time, ask students how they would express each reaction in English.

When Students Ask

You may want to give students the following expressions related to this vocabulary.
¡Qué estupendo!
¡Qué maravilloso!
¡Qué miedo!
¡Qué barbaridad!

¡Qué raro!

¡Qué divertido!

¡Qué aburrido!

¡Qué difícil!

¡Qué fácil!

¡Qué suerte!

¡Qué pena!

¡No me digas!

¡Qué horror!
¡Qué desastre!

¡Qué bueno!

¡Qué va!

60 CAPÍTULO 1

Total Physical Response

Getting Ready

For TPR 1, model different facial and/or body expressions that represent the pictures. For TPR 2, photocopy and enlarge the images on the Vocabulario transparency. Attach these enlarged visuals to the board.

New Words

toma   quita   devuelve

TPR 1

Muéstrenme "¡Qué difícil!"
Muéstrenme "¡Qué raro!"
Muéstrenme "¡Qué suerte!"
Muéstrenme "¡Qué aburrido!"
Muéstrale a _____ "¡Qué bueno!"
Muéstrale a _____ "¡Qué horror!"

Actividades

A ¡Qué raro! Respond to the following situations using an expression from the **Vocabulario**.

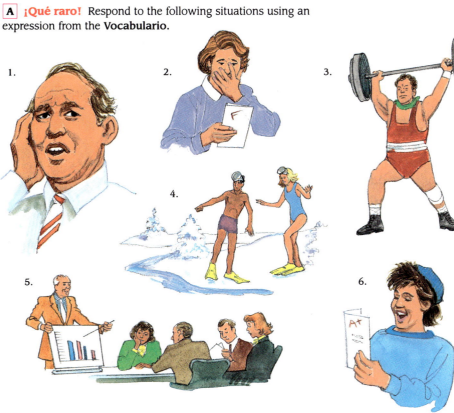

1.
2.
3.
4.
5.
6.

B ¡No me digas! Several of Graciela's classmates say the following things. How would you react to what they say?

Por ejemplo:

> No me gustan las fiestas.
> *¡Qué pena! (¡Qué raro!)*

1. No sé nadar.
2. Quiero estudiar biología avanzada.
3. No quiero estudiar.
4. Ya sé hablar español.
5. Necesito leer dos páginas de historia.
6. No sé leer francés.
7. Necesito escribir tres composiciones.
8. Quiero ir a la fiesta de Mariví.
9. Sé bailar muy bien.
10. Me gusta usar la computadora.

Lección 6 **61**

Actividades

Actividad A Answers

1. ¡Qué pena!
2. ¡Qué horror! (¡Qué desastre!)
3. ¡Qué difícil!
4. ¡Qué raro!
5. ¡Que aburrido!
6. ¡Qué bueno! (¡Qué suerte!)

Actividad B Answers
Answers will vary but may include the following:

1. ¡Qué pena! (¡Qué raro!)
2. ¡Qué díficil! (¡Qué bueno!) (¡Qué horror!)
3. ¡Qué pena! (¡Qué bueno!)
4. ¡Qué bueno! (¡Qué suerte!)
5. ¡Qué fácil! (¡Qué aburrido!)
6. ¡Qué pena!
7. ¡Qué desastre! (¡Qué horror!)
8. ¡Qué bueno! (¡Qué divertido!)
9. ¡Qué suerte! (¡Qué bueno!) (¡Qué va!)
10. ¡Qué raro! (¡Qué bueno!)

Additional Practice
After doing Actividades A and B, you may wish to reinforce the lesson by doing the following activities:

1. Have students react to classes. For example: **la clase de inglés: ¡qué fácil!**
2. Have students react to activities. For example: **dibujar: ¡qué dificil!**

Reteaching

Have students react to your statements. For example:

1. **Soy maestro(a) pero no me gustan los estudiantes.** (Show stern facial expression.)
2. **Me gustan los exámenes difíciles.**
3. **Me gusta dar buenas notas a mis estudiantes.**
4. **Me gusta la música clásica.**
5. **Me gusta montar a caballo en casa.**
6. **Sé esquiar.**
7. **No sé hablar español.**

61

Cultura viva 1

Presentation

Read the Cultura viva 1 on this page. Model the three hesitation expressions and have students repeat after you. Encourage students to use these expressions in their speech.

Did You Know?

Pues and **bueno** both have the same connotation when used as "hesitation words." They mean "well." **A ver** is used frequently when someone says "let's see."

Critical Thinking Activity

What does the Cultura viva reading tell us about languages? Can you make a generalization?

Actividad

Actividad Answer

1. b
2. d
3. c
4. a

Learning From Photos

What do you think the people in the photos on this page might be saying? Can you create a short dialogue in Spanish for each photo? Try to include some hesitation words from the Cultura viva reading on this page.

Pues, bueno, a ver

In several lessons in this chapter, you have seen a few words like **pues, bueno,** and **a ver.** Spanish-speaking people use these words as "hesitation words" or "space fillers," the way we in English might say "well," "then," or "OK."

Actividad

Match each question below with the best response.

1. ¿Quieres tomar algo?
2. ¿A qué hora es el programa?
3. Hola, ¿cómo estás?
4. ¿Qué quieres hacer?

a. Bueno, ¿quieres dar un paseo?
b. Sí, cómo no.
c. Pues, no muy bien.
d. A ver... a las cinco o a las cinco y media.

"Bueno, ¿qué te gusta hacer?"

A ver, ¿adónde quieres ir?

Pronunciation

A. You may wish to play the recorded version of these pronunciation lines, located at the end of Cassette 1.6. You may also wish to write this verse on the board and have students copy it into their notebook.
Pues...
bueno... a ver,
¿qué quieres hacer?

B. Have students repeat words and phrases individually and in unison. You may wish to focus on the /r/ sound as in **ver** and **hacer**.

Estructura 1

....

How to Talk about What You Like or Dislike   **Gusta / gustan + object(s)**

1. To say you like something, say **Me gusta + el / la +** object.
   Me gusta el fútbol.   **Me gusta la playa.**

2. To say you don't like something, say **No me gusta + el / la +** object.
   No me gusta la clase de arte.

3. To say you like more than one thing, say **Me gustan + los / las** + objects.
   Me gustan los discos.

4. To say you don't like more than one thing, say **No me gustan + los / las** + objects.
   No me gustan las revistas.

5. To ask a friend if he or she likes one thing or more than one thing, say **¿Te gusta + el / la +** object? or **¿Te gustan + los / las** + objects?
   ¿Te gusta el álgebra?   **¿Te gustan las fiestas?**

Actividades

A **Preferencias.** Which of the following do you like more?

Por ejemplo:

> **Si quieres nadar, ¿qué te gusta más, la playa o la piscina?**
> *Me gusta más la playa. (Me gusta más la piscina).*

1. Si quieres leer algo, ¿qué te gustan más, las revistas o los libros?
2. ¿Qué te gusta más, la tele o el cine?
3. En la escuela, ¿qué te gustan más, las clases o los deportes?
4. ¿Qué te gustan más, las ciencias o las matemáticas?
5. ¿Qué te gustan más, los bailes o las fiestas en casa?
6. ¿Qué te gustan más, los conciertos o los partidos?

Lección 6 **63**

Estructura 1

Structure Teaching Resources
1. Workbook, pp. 29–31
2. Cassette 1.6
3. Student Tape Manual, p.21
4. Estructura Masters 1.6
5. Lesson Quizzes, pp. 21–22

Bell Ringer Review

Directions to students: Copy the following words and expressions, and write the opposite of each one.

1. ¡Qué fácil!   3. ¡Hola!
2. Me gusta.   4. ¡Qué divertido!

Structure Focus

In this lesson, the presentation of **gustar** is limited to **gusta / gustan + object(s)**. **Le(s) gusta +** infinitive is taught in Chapter 4, Lesson 1. **Le(s) gusta(n)** + object(s) is taught in Chapter 4, Lesson 3. **Nos gusta(n)** is taught in Chapter 6, Lesson 2.

Presentation

Lead students through steps 1–5 on page 63. For additional examples, you may wish to place visuals or other items around the classroom. Point to the item(s) using the expression **Me gusta(n)...** For example, **Me gustan las revistas. No me gusta el fútbol americano, etc.**

Actividades

Actividad A Answers
1. Me gustan las revistas (los libros).
2. Me gusta la tele (el cine).
3. Me gustan las clases (los deportes).
4. Me gustan las ciencias (las matemáticas).
5. Me gustan los bailes (las fiestas en casa).
6. Me gustan los conciertos (los partidos).

63

Actividad B Answers

Actividad B Answers

Answers will vary but may include the following:

Me gustan los maestros pero no me gustan las tareas.

Me gustan las fiestas pero no me gusta la cafetería.

Me gusta el tenis pero no me gusta el fútbol americano.

Me gustan las clases pero no me gustan los exámenes.

Extension

After doing Actividad B, you may wish to extend it in the following way: Ask students what David might say he likes and dislikes about San Antonio.

Reteaching

Tell students some things you like. Then ask them what they like. For example: **Me gusta la música rock. ¿Te gusta la música rock? Me gustan las películas. ¿Te gustan las películas?**

B **Me gusta la escuela, pero...** David likes some things about school, but he doesn't like other things. Following is his list of likes and dislikes.

sí, ...	pero	no, ...
1. la clase de inglés		los exámenes
2. los maestros		las tareas
3. las clases		la historia
4. el tenis		el fútbol americano
5. las fiestas		la cafetería

How would David say what he likes and dislikes? Make four statements.

Por ejemplo:

> **Me gusta la clase de inglés, pero no me gustan los exámenes.**

Saludos y despedidas

In countries where Spanish is spoken, people usually shake hands when they greet and say good-bye to each other. Men often greet each other by shaking right hands and placing their left hands on each other's upper arms. Men who are good friends or relatives will give each other a hug, **un abrazo**. Men sometimes kiss women on the cheek, and two women will often kiss each other on the cheek or simply touch cheeks.

Actividad

How would you greet the following people?

1. your good friend Graciela
2. your good friend Carlos
3. your uncle
4. your favorite cousin David

con la mano

con un abrazo

con un beso

Lección 6 **65**

Cultura viva 2

Presentation

Read the Cultura viva on this page. Students may feel shy or awkward about demonstrating these greetings in class. You may want to bring additional photos instead.

Did you Know?

Generally, Spanish-speaking people are very outwardly affectionate and demonstrative upon meeting each other. **Un abrazo** is given freely, especially to intimate friends of the family who are considered part of the extended family.

You may wish to illustrate the phenomenon of conversational distance. Have students form two lines, back to back. For twenty to thirty seconds, have them introduce and greet the person in back of them. After the allotted time, have them turn and have the two lines face each other, maintaining the same distance. Explain that this is a comfortable speaking distance in many countries—not just the Spanish-speaking world. Have students compare this to their own "comfort zone." Have them stand at a distance that makes them comfortable.

Critical Thinking Activity
Compare and contrast the way people in Hispanic countries greet and say good-bye with the way people in the U.S. do.

Actividad

Actividad Answer
Answers will vary depending on the student's gender.

Pronunciation

A. You may wish to play the recorded version of these pronunciation lines, located at the end of Cassette 1.6. You may also wish to write these lines on the chalkboard or on an overhead transparency and ask your students to copy them into their notebooks.
¡Hola, hola,
pajarito sin cola!

B. Have students repeat the words and phrases individually and in unison. You may wish to focus on the /o/ and /a/ sounds as well as the /h/ and /j/ sounds.

Bell Ringer Review

Directions to students: Work with a partner. Partner A: dictate three sentences to Partner B; then let him or her check your paper to see if all words are spelled correctly. Partner B will dictate three sentences to Partner A and check for correct spelling.

Partner A:

1. Me gusta nadar en la piscina.
2. Necesito leer las revistas en la biblioteca.
3. Quiero hablar con el maestro de historia.

Partner B:

1. ¿Te gusta más jugar tenis o béisbol?
2. Eres de San Antonio,¿no?
3. A ver. El partido es a las seis.

Presentation

The pronunciation of the letters of the alphabet is as follows:

a	*a*	n	*ene*
b	*be*	ñ	*eñe*
c	*c*	o	*o*
ch	*che*	p	*pe*
d	*de*	q	*cu*
e	*e*	r	*ere*
f	*efe*	rr	*erre*
g	*ge*	s	*ese*
h	*hache*	t	*te*
i	*i*	u	*u*
j	*jota*	v	*uve*
k	*ca*	w	*doble u*
l	*ele*	x	*equis*
ll	*elle*	y	*i griega*
m	*eme*	z	*zeta*

Estructura 2

How to Spell in Spanish   **The Spanish alphabet**

The Spanish alphabet contains thirty letters. It includes four letters that are not found in English: **ch, ll, ñ,** and **rr.** The letters **k** and **w** are used only to spell words from other languages, such as **kilo** and **Washington.**

To learn the names of the letters and their order, do as Spanish-speaking students do and chant them in rhythm. Say the name of the last letter on each line louder than the others.

¡a, b, c, ch;	ñ, o, p, q;
d, e, f, g;	r, rr, s, t;
h, i, j, k;	u, v, w;
l, ll, m, n;	x, y, z!

Actividades

A **El examen.** How good are your eyes? Can you read the letters from this eye chart?

B **¿Cómo? No entiendo.** Ask four classmates their names. When each answers, say you don't understand. Then they will spell their last name out for you.

Por ejemplo:

ESTUDIANTE A	ESTUDIANTE B
(1) ¿Cómo te llamas?	(2) Me llamo Enrique Gómez.
(3) ¿Cómo?	(4) Enrique Gómez. G-ó-m-e-z.

C **Nombre y número.** You want to talk with David Vargas, but no one is home and the answering machine is on. Leave a message so he can return your call.

1. Identify yourself.
2. Spell your last name.
3. Give your phone number. (**Mi número de teléfono es...**)

66 CAPÍTULO 1

Note. Names for the letters *b, v,* and *w* vary from country to country. Have your students use the locally accepted ones.

Actividades

Actividad A Answers
A / ce, e / i, ele, jota / u, zeta, eme, pe / cu, ge, eñe, erre, o.

Actividades B and C Answers
Answers will vary.

Reteaching

Choose a letter from the Spanish alphabet on this page. Ask individual students what three letters follow it.

Finalmente

Finalmente

Situaciones

A conversar Use the following cues to converse with a partner in Spanish.

1. You and your partner are going to spend Saturday together. Ask your partner where he or she wants to go. Your partner responds that he or she doesn't know.
2. Find out what your partner likes to do. Then invite him or her to go someplace or do something.
3. Your partner accepts your invitation and asks at what time you want to do the activity. Give the time you will meet.
4. Thank your partner and say good-bye.

A escribir Your friends have been wondering what to buy you for your birthday. Write down your likes and dislikes (**Me gusta[n]... pero no me gusta[n]...**). Include sports, leisure activities, places, classes, and school activities.

Repaso de vocabulario

PREGUNTA	pena!
¿Te gusta(n)...?	raro!
	suerte!
REACCIONES	va!
¡No me digas!	
¡Qué...	**OTRAS PALABRAS**
aburrido!	a ver
bueno!	bueno
desastre!	pero
difícil!	pues
divertido!	también
fácil!	y
horror!	

Situaciones

Lesson 6 Evaluation
The A conversar and A escribir situations on this page are designed to give students the opportunity to use as many language functions as possible listed on page 58 of this lesson. The A conversar and A escribir are also intended to show how well students are able to meet the lesson objectives, also listed on page 58 of this lesson.

Presentation

Prior to doing the A conversar and A escribir on this page, you may wish to play the Situaciones listening activities on Cassette 1.6 as a means of helping students organize the material.

Repaso de vocabulario

The words and phrases in the Repaso de vocabulario have been taught for productive use in this lesson. They are summarized here as a resource for both students and teacher. The Repaso de vocabulario also serves as a convenient resource for the A conversar and A escribir activities on this page. It also gives the teacher a source for writing either additional practice, or evaluation activities such as quizzes and tests in addition to those provided by the publisher.

For the Native Speaker
Have native speakers make a list of exclamations used in their native countries that are different from those presented in the lesson. They can make a list comparing the Spanish expressions to English equivalents.

Lectura

Presentation

A. Before reading the Lectura, you may wish to have students discuss the Lectura topic by answering the following questions:

1. What are the ads about?
2. Can you find any words that look the same as or similar to English words?

B. Now have students scan the Lectura silently to themselves, or work with a partner. Have them answer the Actividad on page 69.

Actividad

Answers

1. Productos GARCIS
   14-06-33
   Deportes Apolo
   12-25-87
   Deportes Corral
   12-1182; 12-1202
2. Productos GARCIS
   14-06-33
   Deportes Apolo
   12-25-87

Lectura

Look at the telephone book advertisements below. You will be able to figure out many of the words from the context in which they appear or because they look like English words that have similar meanings.

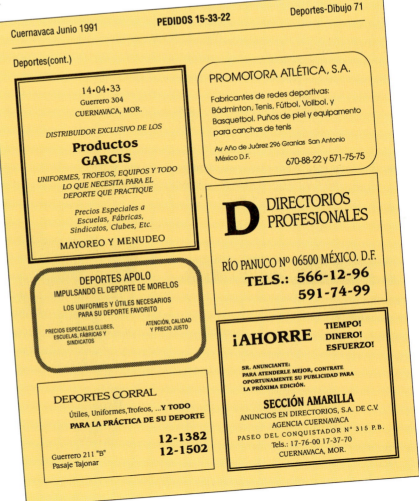

Getting Ready for Reading

You may want to discuss the following keys to successful reading with your students before asking them to read the Lectura on page 68:

1. Look for cognates. For example: **productos, uniformes directorios**.

2. When reading, you may encounter words that have similar forms in English and in Spanish but have different meanings. These words are called false cognates. For example: **lectura** = reading, **librería** = bookstore. Context will usually help you determine whether or not the word is a true cognate or a false cognate.

Actividad

Chris Pearson's Mexican pen pal is in charge of ordering trophies for her school's sports banquet.

1. Tell her the name and number of the stores in the phone book on page 68 that sell trophies.

2. Then tell the name and number of those stores that might give special rates to schools.

Bell Ringer Review

Directions to students: Write out in Spanish your own telephone number and the telephone numbers of three friends or family members.

¿Recuerdas?

Presentation

To review Chapter 1, call on individual students to give an example for each communicative function listed for Lecciones 1–3 and Lecciones 4–6, pages 70–71. The numbers in parentheses on pages 70–71 refer to the page(s) in Chapter 1 where each function was presented. You may wish to have your students go back to these pages for additional review and practice before continuing on to the Actividades, pages 71-73.

Lecciones 1–3 Answers

The following words and phrases are examples for each of the 16 functions listed under Lecciones 1-3. These words and phrases should be included in the students' response to each function listed.

1. **¿Cómo está usted? Hola. ¿Qué tal?**
2. **¿Cómo te llamas?**
3. **¿Qué tal? (¿Cómo estás?)**
4. **Me llamo ...**
5. **Soy de ...**
6. **¿De dónde eres?**
7. **Mucho gusto.**
8. **¿Quieres...?**
9. **Cómo no.(No, gracias.)**

Capítulo 1   Repaso

¿Recuerdas?

Do you remember how to do the following things, which you learned in **Capítulo 1**?

LECCIONES 1 a 3

1. greet people formally and informally (pp. 4, 22)
2. ask someone's name (p. 4)
3. say how you feel (p. 6)
4. say who you are (p. 4)
5. say where you are from (p. 4)
6. ask where someone is from (p. 4)
7. acknowledge an introduction (p. 4)
8. invite a friend to do something (p. 12)
9. accept or decline an invitation (pp. 12, 18)
10. thank someone (p. 12)
11. say what you want and do not want to do (p. 18)
12. greet someone formally (pp. 22, 27)
13. ask someone to whom you speak formally how he or she is (pp. 22, 27)
14. ask a friend how he or she is (p. 22)
15. use numbers 0 to 20 (p. 24)
16. ask and tell the time something takes place (p. 28)

LECCIONES 4 a 6

1. say good-bye (p. 32)
2. say what you need to do (p. 35)
3. say what you like and don't like to do (p. 39)
4. ask a friend what he or she likes to do (p. 39)
5. indicate that you don't understand (p. 41)
6. talk about one thing or more than one (pp. 42, 43)
7. explain why (p. 46)
8. say what you know how and don't know how to do (p. 52)
9. ask someone what he or she knows how to do (p. 52)

10. say where you want to go (p. 55)
11. invite someone to go somewhere (p. 55)
12. say what things you like and dislike (p. 63)
13. ask someone what he or she likes and dislikes (p. 63)
14. spell your name in Spanish (p. 66)

Actividades

A **El vocabulario de la escuela.** On a sheet of paper, list all the words or phrases you can think of related to school, based on the following questions.

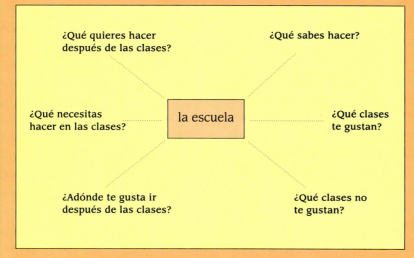

¿Qué quieres hacer después de las clases?

¿Qué sabes hacer?

¿Qué necesitas hacer en las clases?

la escuela

¿Qué clases te gustan?

¿Adónde te gusta ir después de las clases?

¿Qué clases no te gustan?

B **Presentaciones.** In three sentences, tell who you are, where you are from, and what you like to do.

C **El periódico de la escuela.** As a reporter for the school newspaper, you want to interview David. Prepare five questions to ask him about his background and his reaction to his new school in San Antonio.

10. Gracias.
11. Quiero... (No quiero...)
12. Buenos días (Buenas tardes; Buenas noches.)
13. ¿Cómo está usted?
14. ¿Cómo estás?
15. Uno, dos, tres, etc.
16. ¿A qué hora...?
    A las...

Lecciones 4-6 Answers

The following words and phrases are examples of each of the 14 functions listed under Lecciones 4-6. These words and phrases should be included in the students' response to each function listed.

1. Adiós. (Hasta luego).
2. Necesito...
3. Me gusta...
   No me gusta...
4. ¿Te gusta...?
5. ¿Cómo? No entiendo.
6. El (Los) libro(s)
   La (Las) muchacha(s)
7. ... porque...
8. Sé... (No sé)...
9. ¿Sabes...?
10. Quiero ir a la (al)...
11. ¿Quieres ir a la (al)...?
12. Me gusta(n)...
    No me gusta(n)...
13. ¿Te gusta(n)...?
14. a, b, c, ch, etc.

Actividades

Actividad A Answers
Answers will vary according to each student.

Actividad B Answers
Answers should begin with the following phrases:
Me llamo...
Soy...
Me gusta...

Actividad C Answers
Answers will vary, but may include the following:
¿Cómo te llamas?
¿De dónde eres?
¿Te gustan las clases aquí?
etc.

Actividad D Answers
Answers will vary, but may include the following:
¿Quieres escuchar discos?
¿Quieres jugar tenis?
¿Quieres tomar algo?
etc.

Actividad E Answers
Answers will vary but may include the following:
Me gusta correr. También me gusta nadar.
No me gusta montar a caballo ni montar en bicicleta, pero me gusta andar en monopatín.

D **Reacciones.** A classmate invites you to do six things. Accept or reject them, and give an explanation.

Por ejemplo:

ESTUDIANTE A

¿Quieres jugar béisbol?

ESTUDIANTE B

Sí, cómo no. Me gusta jugar béisbol. (No, gracias. ¡Qué aburrido!)

E **Me gusta porque...** Tell whether you like or want to do the following things, and explain why.

Por ejemplo:

Me gustan las fiestas porque me gusta bailar y comer. También me gusta escuchar discos. Pero no sé cantar y no me gustan los videojuegos.

LA MÚSICA
tocar instrumentos
cantar
escuchar música de _____

EL ARTE
dibujar
ir a museos

LOS DEPORTES
correr
nadar
jugar _____
montar a caballo
montar en bicicleta
andar en monopatín

LAS FIESTAS
bailar
comer
cantar
escuchar discos
hablar
jugar videojuegos

LA ESCUELA
la clase de _____
el maestro de _____
la maestra de _____
leer _____
estudiar _____
aprender _____

F **Nuevos amigos.** At a Spanish Club meeting, you were asked to take down names of new members. Arrange the names on the top of page 73 alphabetically by family name.

1. **Aurelio Casas Torres**
2. **Mónica Esquivel Lema**
3. **José Manzanares Villa**
4. **Maricarmen Llorens Parga**
5. **Arturo Rodríguez Zepeda**
6. **Miguel Olivares Río**
7. **Estela Díaz Álvarez**
8. **Ángela Chávez Hernández**
9. **María Herrera Pinto**
10. **Enrique Colón García**

G La nota. Bruno and Alicia were caught exchanging a note during class and their teacher tore it up. Reconstruct the message by putting the pieces in order.

H ¡Prohibido! Below are some signs from San Antonio. Match each sign with a place you would probably find it.

Por ejemplo:

en la ciudad

NO ESTACIONAR

NO CORRER

PROHIBIDO JUGAR

PROHIBIDO ENTRAR

PROHIBIDO COMER

NO TIRAR BASURA

Bienvenidos a San Antonio

PROHIBIDO FUMAR

SILENCIO

1. en el museo
2. en la tienda
3. en la cafetería
4. en la piscina
5. en la escuela
6. en el parque
7. en el cine
8. en la playa
9. en la biblioteca
10. en el restaurante
11. en la ciudad

Note pieces (handwritten):
- No, gracias. Quiero descansar en casa.
- ¿Qué tal? ¿Quieres ir al partido?
- Bueno, ¿a qué hora es la fiesta?
- Entonces, ¿quieres ir a la fiesta de Chris?
- No sé cuándo es, pero sé que te gusta bailar.

Actividad F Answers
1. Casa Torres, Aurelio.
2. Colón García, Enrique.
3. Chávez Hernández, Ángela.
4. Díaz Álvarez, Estela.
5. Esquivel Lema, Mónica
6. Herrera Pinto, María
7. Llorens Parga, Maricarmen
8. Manzanares Villa, José
9. Olivares Río, Miguel
10. Rodríguez Zepeda, Arturo

Actividad G Answers
1. ¿Qué tal? ¿Quieres ir al partido?
2. No, gracias. Quiero descansar en casa.
3. Entonces, ¿quieres ir a la fiesta de Chris?
4. Bueno, ¿a qué hora es la fiesta?
5. No sé cuando es pero sé que te gusta bailar.

Actividad H Answers
Answers will vary.

Chapter Overview

Cultural setting

Chapter 2 continues with the characters of Chris and David in San Antonio. The main cultural issue revolves around conflicting concepts of time—earliness and lateness.

Rationale

A You will notice in this chapter that verb conjugations are presented without the subject pronouns. Experience has shown that students tend to lean very heavily on these subject pronouns, with the following consequences:

- Inappropriate speech patterns, especially the **yo**-studded response.
- Weak internalization of the endings. Students will typically allow the subject pronoun to carry the weight of the message and be less concerned (in spontaneous situations) with the verb ending.
- Students interpret the subject pronouns as optional and are less likely to know when their message warrants the use of these pronouns.

Subject pronouns are presented for active use in Chapter 3 where their functions are explained and practiced: emphasis, contrast, and clarification.

B In this chapter, the irregular verbs **ir** and **ser** are presented before the regular present tense conjugation. Because of their irregularity and high frequency, **ir** and **ser** lend themselves to "spotlighting." This approach also allows for a concentration on some difficult concepts in foreign language learning:

- the concept of person
- the concept of number
- the concept of **tú / usted**
- the concept of present tense descripton.

By presenting the verbs **ir** and **ser** before the regular present tense

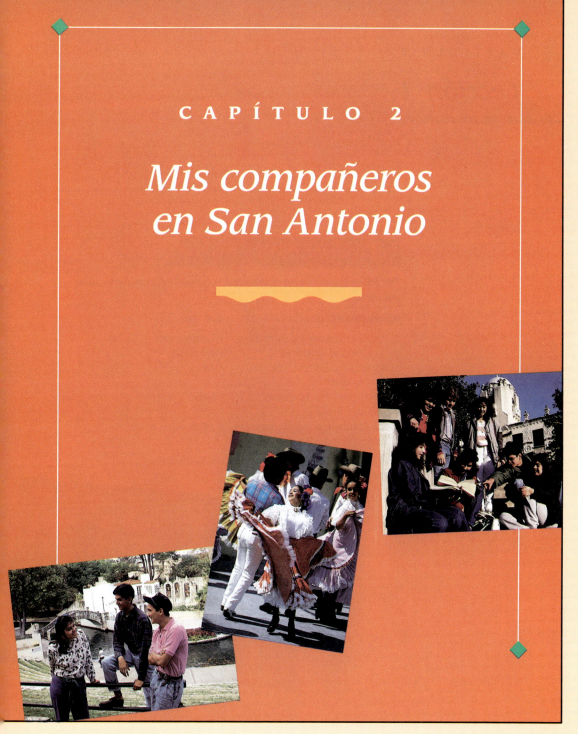

CAPÍTULO 2

Mis compañeros en San Antonio

conjugations, the concepts above can be presented and practiced without students' having to cope with a variety of verbs and a variety of meanings.

C Regular present tense conjugation is presented through the functions the verb endings perform. For example, to talk about myself, I use **-o.** Each function is presented separately, followed by practice and integration. Because of this functional presentation, we have opted not to separate **-ar** and **-er** verbs, but rather to present them together to display their similarities:

- the **-o** for talking about myself; the **-s** for talking to a friend
- the single vowel (**-a** or **-e**) for reporting about someone
- the **-mos** for "we"; and the **-n** for reporting about people and for talking to a group.

Having just completed a chapter using infinitives, students should have some of the **-a** or **-e** barrier removed by this time. The ability to describe in the present will probably still move slowly, but our experience has shown that spontaneity and student comfort and reward will be achieved much earlier, and the language skills will be more stable and enduring.

D In the presentation of **-ar** and **-er** verbs, the singular **usted** form has been temporarily omitted from presentation and practice in order to:

- more fully consolidate the reporting function of the third person singular endings
- remove an added communicative decision from students as they are trying to cope with the concept of morphology.

E The **tú/usted** distinction will be brought back in Chapter 3.
We hope you and your students enjoy the remainder of your stay in San Antonio!

Estructura

This chapter focuses primarily on

- use of **pensar** for talking about plans
- use of **ser** in all its forms for identifying, describing, and telling where people are from
- use of **ir** in all its conjugated present-tense forms for saying where people go
- present tense conjugations of **-ar** and **-er** verbs to talk about what one generally does or is doing.

A complete listing of the language objectives of the chapter appears on pages 154–155.

Lección 1

Objectives

By the end of this lesson, students will be able to:

1. thank someone and say "You're welcome"
2. identify or describe people and things
3. find out where people are from

Lesson 1 Resources
1. Workbook, pp. 35–40
2. Vocabulario Transparencies 2.1
3. Cassette 2.1
4. Student Tape Manual, pp. 26–31
5. Lesson Quizzes, pp. 24–27
6. Computer Software, Disk 1
7. Video Cassette
8. Estructura Masters 2.1
9. Diversiones Masters 2.1

Bell Ringer Review

Directions to students: On a sheet of paper, write down all the words you know that are associated with the following topics.
la clase
la composición
el partido

¡A comenzar!

Presentation

A. Lead students through each of the five functions on page 76, progressing from the English to the Spanish for each function. Then have students find these words and phrases in the dialogue on page 77.

Lección 1

Los compañeros de clase

¡A comenzar!

The following are some of the things you will be learning to do in this lesson.

When you want to . . .	You use . . .
1. thank someone for something	• **Gracias por** + object.
2. say "You're welcome"	• **De nada.**
3. identify or describe one person or thing	• **Es...**
4. identify or describe several persons or things	• **Son...**
5. find out where people are from	• **¿Son de** + place?

Now find examples of the above words and phrases in the following conversation.

Invitación

¿A qué? a un picnic

¿Dónde? en el parque Olmos

¿Qué día? el domingo, cinco de octubre

¿A qué hora? a las dos de la tarde

76 CAPÍTULO 2

Getting Ready for Lesson 1

You may wish to use one or more of the following suggestions to prepare students for the lesson:

Display pictures from newspapers, magazines, album covers, etc. of various well-known personalities. Select several pictures to talk about. Give your own opinion, saying, for example: **Me gusta mucho Madonna. Es sensa-** cional. No me gustan _____. **¡Son horribles!** Use gestures and tone of voice to convey positive or negative aspects of each personality. Have students agree or disagree using **Sí** or **No.** If they disagree ask: **¿Cómo es, en tu opinión, entonces?** and help them select a word they would use to describe the person. List these words on the board and use them to describe the people in

Chris has invited some exchange students from several schools to a picnic. Mariví is from Caracas, Venezuela.

MARIVÍ: **¡Hola, Chris! ¡El picnic es sensacional! Gracias por la invitación.**

CHRIS: **De nada.**

MARIVÍ: **¡Qué amables son los muchachos! ¿Son de tu escuela?**

CHRIS: **Sí, son compañeros de clase.**

Actividades preliminares

A Thank a classmate for the following.

Por ejemplo:
  el libro

ESTUDIANTE A	ESTUDIANTE B
Gracias por el libro.	**De nada.**

1. **el lápiz**
2. **la invitación**
3. **el videojuego**
4. **las fotos**

B Describe your classmates, using the following words.

Por ejemplo:
  puntuales
  Mis compañeros de clase (no) son puntuales.

1. **elegantes**
2. **inteligentes**
3. **populares**
4. **impacientes**
5. **puntuales**
6. **sociables**

the pictures. Compare and contrast your opinion with students' opinions: **Para mí es ____. Para ti es ____.**

amable
diferente
elegante
excelente
fenomenal
horrible
importante
independiente
inteligente
interesante
paciente
responsable
sensacional

You may wish to accompany these words with an intensifier (**muy** or **super**). Confine your descriptions to cognates ending in -**e,** or a consonant at this point.

B. Introduce the Lesson 1 dialogue by reading it aloud, or by playing the cassette version. Tell students they are going to hear a conversation between two people. Have them listen to find out the following information:

1. Do the two people know each other?
2. Are they at school, at the library, at a game, or at a party of some sort?
3. Does the girl like the event and the people who are there?

C. Now ask students to open their books and look at the dialogue as you lead them through what is said. For example,

3. ¿De dónde es Mariví? Chris? David? Y tú, ¿de dónde eres? ¿De dónde soy yo?
2. ¿Cómo es el picnic?
3. Cuando Mariví dice: "Gracias por la invitación", ¿qué dice Chris?
4. ¿Cómo son los muchachos del picnic?
5. ¿De dónde son los muchachos?
6. ¿Quiénes son?

D. You may wish to point out the use of the masculine forms **muchachos** and **compañeros** when talking about males and females in the same group.

Actividades preliminares

Actividad A Answers
1. Gracias por el lápiz./De nada.
2. ... la invitación...
3. ... el videojuego...
4. ... las fotos...

Actividad B Answers
Answers will vary but may include the following:
Mis compañeros de clase (no) son elegantes.
Mis compañeros de clase son inteligentes y populares. Etc.

Bell Ringer Review

Directions to students: Copy these two columns on a sheet of paper; then decide how you would match them. Draw a line to connect each pair.

1.	la piscina	a.	montar a caballo
2.	el estadio	b.	manejar
3.	la guitarra	c.	ver el partido
4.	el campo	d.	tocar
5.	un coche	e.	nadar

Presentation

A. Have students open their books to pages 78 and 79. Begin by modeling each new word on page 78. Begin each time with **Es...** Have students repeat each phrase in unison.
Call students' attention to the difference between **músico** and **música**. Ask them to point out other examples of masculine vs. feminine forms on this page. You may also wish to point out that the **-ante** and **-ista** endings remain the same for masculine and feminine.

B. Ask students to take the role of the person in each illustration on page 78 and make a statement about what he or she likes, or knows how to do. For example, **Soy artista. Me gusta (Sé) pintar, dibujar, estudiar arte. Soy político(a). Me gusta (Sé) hablar bien, estudiar historia. Soy escritor. Me gusta leer y escribir. Me gustan los libros.**

Vocabulario

¿Qué es? Es...

cantante   estudiante   artista   deportista   guitarrista

músico   música   político   política   actor

actriz   bailarín   bailarina   escritor   escritora

78 CAPÍTULO 2

Total Physical Response

Getting Ready
For **TPR 1**, bring to class magazine pictures of famous people whose professions are known to the students. Or borrow photos from the journalism teacher that represent the vocabulary words. Display the pictures on the bulletin board. For **TPR 2**, select a student for every picture used in **TPR 1**. Have the student hold the picture up in front of the class. Give commands to the students who are in their seats.

New Words
esconde	ve	salúdalo
pon	retrato	

Pre-activity
Set the scene by discussing the people and professions illustrated.

¿Cómo es? Es...

popular   emocionante   formidable   elegante   inteligente

interesante   excelente   amable   arrogante

horrible   deprimente   increíble   diferente

Lección 1 **79**

C. Have students look at the new words on page 79. Begin by modeling the question, **¿Cómo es?** Then model each new word on page 79, beginning each time with **Es...** Use facial expressions and tone of voice to help convey the meaning of each adjective. Have students repeat each phrase in unison.

When Students Ask

You may want to give students the following additional vocabulary in order to talk about what they want to be.

ingeniero(a)	contador/a
arquitecto(a)	mecánico(a)
plomero(a)	electricista
cocinero(a)	bombero(a)
sastre	

Regionalisms

You may wish to tell students that in some parts of the Spanish-speaking world the following words or phrases are alternatives to those presented in the Vocabulario.

**el/la estudiante
(el/la alumno[a]);
de nada (no hay de qué);
formidable (chévere)** (Caribbean, Colombia)

TPR 1

Dale la foto del bailarín a una chica.
Dale la foto del actor a _____.
Pon el retrato de la escritora en la mesa.
Esconde la foto del político en tu mochila.
Esconde la foto de la estudiante en tu libro.
Toma la foto del guitarrista y dámela.
Toma el retrato del músico y dámelo.

TPR 2

Camina hacia el artista y salúdalo.
Camina hacia el bailarín y dile: "Eres increíble".
Ve hacia el actor y dile: "Eres excelente".
Ve al político y dile: "Eres inteligente".
Salta hacia el artista y dile: "Eres interesante".
Ve al artista y dile: "Eres diferente".

Actividades

Actividad A Answers

1. i	4. b	7. e
2. g	5. a	8. d
3. f	6. h	9. c

Actividad B Answers

Answers will vary but may include the following: **Quiero ser deportista. No quiero ser político(a). Etc.**

Actividad C Answers

Answers will vary.

Extension

After doing Actividad C, you may wish to extend it in the following way: Have students think of statements they would make about themselves. For example, **Quiero ser _____ porque me gusta _____.** You may want to teach the expression **¿Cómo se dice _____?** in order to find out any words they need to complete their statements.

Then ask them to read their statements to the class. Make a tally on the board to find the popularity of certain professions.

Actividad D

1. Quiero ser guitarrista porque me gusta tocar la guitarra.
2. ... bailarina... bailar.
3. ... escritora... escribir.
4. ... bailarín... bailar.
5. ... músico... escuchar música.
6. ... deportista... practicar deportes (jugar béisbol).
7. ... actriz... estudiar drama.
8. ... deportista... jugar tenis.
9. ... cantante... cantar.

Actividades

A **¿Qué hacen?** Your guidance counselor wants to make sure you understand what people with the following occupations do. Choose from the list of activities on the right.

Por ejemplo:

> cantantes: cantar

1. estudiantes	a. hablar en público
2. guitarristas	b. practicar deportes
3. bailarines	c. actuar en dramas
4. deportistas	d. escribir libros y artículos
5. políticos	e. dibujar y pintar
6. músicos	f. bailar
7. artistas	g. tocar la guitarra
8. escritores	h. tocar instrumentos
9. actores	i. leer y aprender

B **Quiero ser...** Choosing from the professions in the **Vocabulario,** tell your guidance counselor what you want to be and not like to be.

Por ejemplo:

> **Quiero ser cantante. No quiero ser político.**

C **¿Qué quieres ser?** Choosing from the professions in the **Vocabulario** on pages 78 and 79, ask three classmates what they would like to be.

Por ejemplo:

ESTUDIANTE A	ESTUDIANTE B
(1) **Anita, ¿qué quieres ser?**	(2) **Quiero ser bailarina. Y tú, Juan, ¿qué quieres ser?**

D **Porque me gusta.** The following students have decided what they want to be and they explain why. Tell what they say, using the suggestions below.

bailar	escribir	leer
cantar	escuchar música	practicar deportes
dibujar	estudiar drama	tocar la guitarra

Cooperative Learning

Actividades B-D: For **B,** have students work in pairs with the people across from them. For **C,** ask students to work with the people behind them in their teams, asking and answering questions. Then they can share their answers with the team. For **D,** have students pantomime the actions with each other in a round-robin activity. Moving in a clockwise direction, they may pantomime what he or she likes and the other students will write down their guess. Then they can share their responses.

Por ejemplo:

> Quiero ser artista porque me
> gusta dibujar.

1.

2.

3.

4.

5.

6.

8.

9.

7.

E **¿Cómo es?** David Vargas wants to know your opinions of the
following. Write down your responses.

Por ejemplo:

> la música "rock"
> *La música "rock" es formidable.*

1. la música clásica
2. la playa
3. la tarea
4. el fútbol americano
5. la música de (singer / group)

6. la escuela
7. la televisión
8. el amigo ideal
9. mi actor favorito
10. mi actriz favorita

Actividad E
Answers will vary.

Additional Practice
After doing Actividades A, B, C, D,
and E, you may wish to reinforce the
learning with one of the following:

1. Ask students individually to
   choose one occupation from the
   Vocabulario. Ask individual students **¿Qué quieres ser?** Focus
   on the use of correct gender
   (**escritor** vs. **escritora**). Follow
   this activity with personal questions. For example, **¿Por qué
   quieres ser deportista, Mary?
   ¿Te gusta jugar tenis? ¿Te gusta
   jugar baloncesto? Etc.**
2. Conduct a student survey to find
   out which well-known public personalities are the most popular in
   each category. For example, **cantantes: El/La cantante más
   popular es _____. Etc.** Ask about
   other categories as well, for
   example:
   a. **el deporte más popular**
   b. **la ciudad más interesante**
   c. **el restaurante más diferente**
   d. **la clase más interesante**
   e. **el/la estudiante más amable**

Reteaching

Ask individual students to volunteer
to act out one of the professions in
the Vocabulario on page 78. Call on
other students to tell what profession
is being imitated. Then ask students
to rate the imitation using one of the
adjectives on page 79.

For the Native Speaker

Have native speakers select one of the
occupations from the Vocabulario and describe the necessary training and the duties of someone who has that occupation.

Presentation

A. Before reading the Cultura viva, you may want to ask students for the most popular names for girls. Write the name or names on the chalkboard. Ask students to tell you the name of the girl in the dialogue in page 77. Write **Mariví** on the chalkboard. Tell students: **La muchacha del picnic se llama Mariví. Su nombre es realmente María Victoria.**

B. Now read the Cultura viva selection and proceed to Actividades A and B on this page.

Did You Know?

In Hispanic countries, many boys are also named after the Virgin Mary, since there is great devotion to her in most Hispanic countries. Boys are named **Mario.**

Actividades

Actividad A Answers

1. e	4. f	7. c
2. a	5. i	8. d
3. h	6. g	9. b

Actividad B Answers

Answers may include the following: John Paul; Tommy Lee; Mary Elizabeth; etc.

Learning From Realia

Ask students to look at the addresses on the two letters on page 82. You may want to ask students to guess what these two people might be called by their friends.

CULTURA VIVA 1

María

Chris's friend is named **Mariví**. The most common girl's name in Hispanic countries is **María**, which is often combined with another name. A shortened form of these combined names is commonly used.

Actividades

A Below, on the left are some popular combinations with **María.** Match them with their shortened forms on the right.

1. **María del Pilar**	a. **Mariluz, Marilú**
2. **María de la Luz**	b. **Mariví**
3. **María de los Ángeles**	c. **Marité, Maité**
4. **María Isabel**	d. **Marisol**
5. **María Elena**	e. **Maripili**
6. **María del Carmen**	f. **Maribel, Marisa**
7. **María Teresa**	g. **Maricarmen**
8. **María Soledad**	h. **Mariángel**
9. **María Victoria**	i. **Malena, Manena**

B Do you know anyone with a combined first name? Does he or she also use a shortened form?

Srta. María Isabel Ramos
3021 Sepúlveda Blvd.
Los Ángeles, CA 91342

Sra. María Elena Godoy de Peña
25 Río Grande Avenue
El Paso, TX 79905

Pronunciation

A. You may wish to play the recorded version of these pronunciation lines, located at the end of Cassette 2.1. You may also wish to write this verse on the board and have students copy it into their notebook:
**El nombre de María
cinco letras tiene.
La M, la A, la R,**

**La I, la A,
¡Ma—rí—a!**

B. Have students repeat words and phrases individually and in unison. You may wish to focus on the /r/ sound in the following words: **nombre; María; ere.**

Estructura 1

How to Identify and Describe People and Things

Soy / eres / es

To identify people, places, and things, use forms of the verb **ser,** "to be."

1. To identify yourself, use **soy** to say:
   - who you are   **Soy Maribel.**
   - what you are   **Soy estudiante.**
   - where you are from   **Soy de Costa Rica.**

2. To identify someone or something, use **es.**

   Chris es estudiante también. Es de San Antonio. San Antonio es muy divertido.

3. To question someone you speak to informally, use **eres.**

   Eres David, ¿no?
   ¿Eres estudiante?
   ¿De dónde eres?

   Remember that you speak informally to a friend, someone you call by his or her first name, or someone your age or younger.

4. When speaking to someone who is older, or whom you don't know very well, or to whom you must show respect, use the formal **¿Es usted...?** or **Usted es.... Usted** can be abbreviated in written form as **Ud.**

¿Eres Joaquín? / Sí, soy Joaquín Ramos. / ¿Es usted el señor Ramos? / Sí, soy el papá de Joaquín. / Es guitarrista, ¿no? / No, soy cantante.

Lección 1   **83**

Structure Teaching Resources
1. Workbook, pp. 37–38
2. Cassette 2.1
3. Student Tape Manual, p. 28
4. Estructura Masters 2.1
5. Lesson Quizzes, p. 26

Bell Ringer Review

Directions to students: Use each of the following words to express an idea. **Por ejemplo: hablar _____ hablar por teléfono.**

1. andar_____
2. escribir_____
3. contestar_____
4. trabajar_____
5. leer_____
6. ver_____
7. jugar_____
8. aprender_____
9. comprar_____
10. estudiar_____

Structure Focus
In Estructura 1, the presentation of **ser** is limited to **soy/eres/es**. The other forms of **ser** are taught in Estructura 2 of this lesson, page 87.

Presentation

A. Lead students through steps 1–6 on pages 83 and 84. You may wish to write additional examples of each form of **ser** on the chalkboard as you proceed through steps 1–6. For example, **Soy maestro(a); soy de aquí.** Then ask individual students to use this form of **ser** by asking, **Y tú, Mark, ¿de dónde eres? ¿Eres maestro? Etc.**

B. You may want to emphasize the difference between informal and formal by having students role-play the dialogue at the bottom of page 83.

Actividad A Answers
Answers should include the following:

1. álgebra: horrible, importante, difícil
2. la tarea: increíble
3. Bruno: no es (soy) paciente, inteligente, responsable
4. la clase de arte: formidable
5. el maestro: sensacional, muy amable

Extension
After doing Actividad A, you may wish to extend it in the following ways:

1. Check students' written responses as a whole class activity. Ask students to identify the five things or people as you list them on the chalkboard. Then have students volunteer the words Bruno uses to describe each.
2. For reading development, ask students to take turns reading Bruno's note.
3. Using Bruno's note as a model, you may want to ask students to write a note of their own to their guidance counselor describing the classes they are taking.

Actividad B Answers

1. (1) ¿Es usted cantante, señora García? (2) Sí, soy cantante. ¿Y tú? (3) Soy estudiante. ¿De dónde es usted? (4) Soy de Guatemala. ¿Y tú? (5) Soy de aquí.
2. ¿ ... músico, señor Pérez? / ... Soy de Argentina...
3. ¿ ... deportista, señorita del Valle?/ ... España...
4. ¿ ... escritora, señora Nieves? / ... México...
5. ¿ ... político, señor Morales?/ ... Venezuela...
6. ¿ ... bailarín, señor Martínez? / ... Costa Rica...

Notice that in the third illustration **usted** is not used with **es.** Although **es** can mean "he is, she is, it is," or "you are," you don't need to use **usted** in this case because **es** clearly means "you are."

5. When you speak about someone whom you call **señor, señora,** or **señorita,** you must include an **el** or **la.** When you talk directly to that person, you omit the **el** or **la.**

> La señora Olmos es cantante. El señor Vilas es artista.
>
> Señora Olmos, ¿cómo está usted? Y usted, señor Vilas, ¿cómo está?

6. When you want to ask what someone or something is like, you say ¿Cómo es?

> ¿Cómo es Mariví?   Es muy popular.
>
> ¿Cómo es el picnic?   Es sensacional.

Actividades

A **Estimada señora Kaplan.** Read the following note Bruno has written to Mrs. Kaplan, his guidance counselor.

> Estimada Sra. Kaplan:
>
> No me gusta la clase de álgebra. ¡Es horrible! Sé que el álgebra es importante, pero es muy difícil. La tarea es increíble. No soy paciente ni inteligente y no me gusta estudiar. Tampoco soy muy responsable. Pero en la clase de arte soy diferente. Para mí, la clase de arte es formidable. El maestro es sensacional, muy amable. Sé que no soy artista, pero me gusta dibujar.
>
> Bruno

Now write down five things or people Bruno describes in his note. Then list the words Bruno uses to describe each one.

Por ejemplo:

> álgebra: *horrible, importante...*

B **Las familias.** Relatives of several exchange students are visiting in the U.S. Ask them what they do and where they are from, using the information below. Play the roles with a classmate.

El señor López
Perú

Por ejemplo:

El señor López / Perú

ESTUDIANTE A

(1) ¿Es usted artista, señor López?

(3) Soy estudiante. ¿De dónde es usted?

(5) Soy de aquí.

ESTUDIANTE B

(2) Sí, soy artista. ¿Y tú?

(4) Soy de Perú. ¿Y tú?

1. La señora García
Guatemala

2. El señor Pérez
Argentina

3. La señorita del Valle
España

4. La señora Nieves
México

5. El señor Morales
Venezuela

6. El señor Martínez
Costa Rica

C **Para mí, es fácil.** Use the example below to make a chart in which you rate at least eight activities from easiest to hardest. Then report to the class about yourself.

muy fácil	*fácil*	*difícil*	*muy difícil*
nadar	hablar español	esquiar	escribir libros

Por ejemplo:

Para mí, es muy fácil nadar. Es fácil hablar español. Es difícil esquiar. Es muy difícil escribir libros.

Presentation

Read the Cultura viva selection on this page. Explain to students the accomplishments of each individual on page 86. For example, Nancy López, golfer; Julio Iglesias, singer; María Conchita Alonso, singer, actress (starred in *Moscow on the Hudson*); Gloria Estefan, singer, composer; Jimmy Smits, actor in award-winning program *L.A. Law;* Mary Jo Fernández, tennis player; Gabriel García Márquez, writer, Nobel prize winner in literature; Keith Hernández, baseball player for the Mets; Emilio Estévez, actor and son of actor Martin Sheen.

Did You Know?

There are numerous other prominent Hispanics including the following: Roberto Goizueta, president of Coca-Cola; Plácido Domingo, internationally known opera star; Linda Ronstadt, singer; Franklin Chang Díaz, NASA astronaut; Carolina Herrera, fashion designer.

Actividad Answers

Nancy López es deportista.
Julio Iglesias es cantante.
María Conchita Alonso es actriz y cantante.
Gloria Estefan es cantante.
Jimmy Smits es actor.
Mary Jo Fernández es deportista.
Gabriel García Márquez es escritor.
Keith Hernández es deportista.

Extension

After doing the Actividad on this page, you may wish to extend it in the following way: Ask students to name other prominent Hispanics they know. Write the list of names on the chalkboard. Discuss their accomplishments.

CULTURA VIVA 2

Hispanos famosos

Spanish-speaking countries have produced leaders in many fields including government, entertainment, athletics, and the arts. There are also many well-known Hispanic-Americans in this country. How many of the following prominent Hispanics do you know?

Nancy López

Julio Iglesias

María Conchita Alonso

Jimmy Smits

Mary Jo Fernández

Gloria Estefan

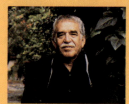

Gabriel García Márquez

Keith Hernández

Actividad

Identify the people above by their occupations.

Por ejemplo:
   Emilio Estévez
   Emilio Estévez es actor.

Emilio Estévez

Pronunciation

A. You may wish to play the recorded version of these pronunciation lines, located at the end of Cassette 2.1. You may also wish to write this verse on the board and have students copy it into their notebook:
   **Nombres hispanos
   en todo el mundo:
   Santiago y San Diego,
   Santa Fe y San José,
   El Dorado y Colorado.
   Presencia hispana,
   cultura hermana.**

B. Have students repeat words and phrases individually and in unison. You may wish to focus on the /a/ and /o/ sounds in the following words: **Santiago; San Diego; Santa; Dorado; Colorado; hermana.**

Estructura 2

How to Identify and Describe People and Things — Son/somos

The following are forms of **ser** to use when you want to talk about more than one person or thing.

1. To identify yourself and someone else ("we"), use **somos**.

   Marité y yo somos estudiantes. Somos de aquí.
   Soy escritor y mi amiga es actriz. Somos de Miami.

2. To identify more than one person or thing ("they"), use **son**.

   Chris y Graciela son fenomenales. Son de San Antonio.

3. To tell or ask the identity of more than one person you are talking to ("both of you" or "you all"), use **ustedes son** or **¿son ustedes? Ustedes** can be abbreviated in written form as **Uds.**

Son can mean "they are" or "you are." If the meaning is clearly "you are," you do not need to add **ustedes**.

   ¿De dónde son ustedes?   **Somos de Nueva York.**
   Son estudiantes, ¿no?   **Pues, sí. También somos músicos.**

4. You can use **ser** following **quiero, me gusta,** and **necesito** to tell what you want, like, and need to be.

   Quiero ser músico.
   Me gusta ser popular.
   Necesito ser muy paciente.

5. The following is a summary of all the forms of the verb **ser.**

SINGULAR	PLURAL
soy	somos
eres	sois*
es	son

*This form is rarely used in the Spanish-speaking world, except for Spain.

For the Native Speaker

Have native speakers write a short biography of one of the famous Hispanics pictured on page 86. They should mention the person's background, personal accomplishments, and importance to the Hispanic community and, if the Hispanic is from this country, to the U.S.

Structure Teaching Resources
1. Workbook, pp. 39–40
2. Cassette 2.1
3. Student Tape Manual, p. 28
4. Estructura Masters 2.1
5. Lesson Quizzes, p. 27

Bell Ringer Review

Directions to students: Write down the names of the classes you are taking this year. Beside the name of each class, write two words that describe it. If possible, use different words to describe each class.

Structure Focus

In Estructura 2, the presentation of **ser** is limited to **son/somos.** The other forms of **ser** were taught in Estructura 1 of this lesson. All forms of **ser** are summarized at the bottom of page 87.

Presentation

A. Lead students through steps 1–6 on pages 87 and 88. You may want to give additional examples including yourself and several students. For example, **El señor Martínez y yo somos maestros. Sonia y Karen son estudiantes. También son deportistas. _____ y _____ son de aquí, pero _____ es de Chicago.**

B. In step 3, you may want to point out that when asking a question, the verb usually comes first, as in **¿Son ustedes de aquí?**

C. In step 4, you may want to have students say what they want to be. For example, **Quiero ser _____. Me gusta ser _____. Necesito ser _____.**

   Note. The **vosotros** form is included whenever the entire verb pardigm is presented in chart form. It is not practiced for active use in this program, nor is it tested.

6. To ask what people or things are like, say **¿Cómo son?**

> **¿Cómo son los deportistas?** **Son fenomenales.**

Notice that to describe more than one person or thing, you must change the descriptive word. If it ends in **-e**, you add **-s**. If it ends in a consonant, you add **-es**.

> **Mariví es muy paciente.**
> **Chris y David son pacientes también.**
> **La clase de inglés es fácil.**
> **Las clases de español y álgebra son fáciles también.**

Actividades

A **¡Qué amables!** David admires many of the people he has met in San Antonio. What would he say to the following individuals?

Por ejemplo:

> el Sr. López / inteligente
> *Señor López, ¡qué inteligente es usted!*

1. la Sra. Kaplan / paciente
2. Bárbara y Carmen / interesantes
3. la Sra. Pérez / inteligente
4. Julia y Javier / amables
5. la Srta. Fernández / responsable

B **¿Cómo son?** A new student in your school asks your opinions about the following. Tell him what you think.

Por ejemplo:

> mi escuela / las escuelas en general
> *Mi escuela es excelente. Las escuelas en general son difíciles.*

1. la clase de español / las clases en general
2. mi amigo (amiga) / los compañeros de clase
3. el coche Porsche / los coches en general
4. el presidente de los Estados Unidos / los políticos en general

C **Los compañeros y yo.** What do you and your friends have in common? Make five statements about yourselves.

Por ejemplo:

> **Somos deportistas. También somos muy amables...**

Finalmente

Finalmente

Situaciones

Situaciones

A conversar

1. Invite a classmate to see a movie.
2. Your classmate asks what the movie is like.
3. Describe it. Include in your description something about the actors, actresses, dancers, or singers.
4. Your classmate will react to your choice of movie or program and accept or decline your invitation.

A escribir Write a note to a classmate about your impressions of the school year so far.

1. Tell which classes and teachers you like. Add an exclamation indicating your reaction to each (**¡Qué...!**).
2. Also tell which classes you dislike. Add appropriate exclamations.
3. Finally, ask your classmate what classes he or she likes and what the teachers are like.

Eduardo James Olmos

Julie Carmen

Repaso de vocabulario

PREGUNTAS

¿Qué eres / es / son?
¿Es usted...?
¿Cómo es / son?

PERSONAS

el actor
la actriz
el / la artista
el bailarín
la bailarina
el / la cantante

el compañero de clase
la compañera de clase
el / la deportista
el escritor
la escritora
el / la estudiante
el / la guitarrista
la música
el músico
la política
el político
ustedes (Uds.)

CORTESÍA

De nada.
Gracias por...

DESCRIPCIONES

ser +
  amable
  arrogante
  deprimente
  diferente
  elegante
  emocionante

excelente
formidable
horrible
increíble
inteligente
interesante
popular

Lección 1 **89**

Lección 2

Objectives

By the end of this lesson, students will be able to:

1. describe someone or something using appropriate gender endings
2. describe a mixed group of people
3. say what they plan to do
4. ask who someone is

Lesson 2 Resources

1. Workbook, pp. 41–46
2. Vocabulario Transparencies 2.2
3. Cassette 2.2
4. Student Tape Manual, pp. 32–35
5. Lesson Quizzes, pp. 28–31
6. Computer Software, Disk 1
7. Video Cassette
8. Estructura Masters 2.3
9. Diversiones Masters 2.3

Bell Ringer Review

Directions to students: Copy these sentences, then rewrite them in the plural. Follow the model.
Por ejemplo: El actor es fenomenal. *Los actores son fenomenales.*

1. **El político es arrogante.**
2. **La guitarrista es amable.**
3. **El artista es excelente.**
4. **Me gusta la película emocionante.**
5. **No me gusta el libro deprimente.**
6. **Usted es muy puntual.**

¡A comenzar!

Presentation

A. Lead students through each of the four functions on page 90, progressing from the English to the Spanish for each function. Then have students find these words and phrases in the dialogue on page 91.

Lección 2

¿Cómo es David?

¡A comenzar!

The following are some of the things you will be learning to do in this lesson.

When you want to . . .	You use . . .
1. describe what someone or something is like	• **es** + adjective ending in **-o** (masculine) or **-a** (feminine)
2. describe what a mixed group of people is like	• **son** + adjective ending in **-os**
3. say what you plan to do	• **Pienso** + activity.
4. When you want to ask who someone is	• **¿Quién es?**

Now find examples of the above words and phrases in the following conversation.

Getting Ready for Lesson 2

You may wish to use one or more of the following suggestions to prepare students for the lesson:

1. Have students keep their books closed. To familiarize students with descriptors, use a fictitious character as a foil, especially when practicing negative descriptors. You might either invent your own character, or use ''Bruno,'' the re-curring character in the practice activities in these lessons, whose image appears on page 53. For example: **Quiero presentarles a mi amigo Bruno. El pobrecito es feo. No es guapo.** (Use facial expressions, gestures, and tone of voice to convey meaning.) **También es muy gordo** (gesture) **y un poco tonto** (use gesture on page 95). **Dicen que también es ta-**

At Chris's picnic, Mariví asks Graciela about David, who has not yet arrived.

GRACIELA: **¡Hola, Mariví! La fiesta es muy divertida, ¿no?**

MARIVÍ: **Sí, los compañeros de Chris son simpáticos. Y el muchacho de Costa Rica, ¿quién es?**

GRACIELA: **David. Es fantástico... muy listo y ¡qué guapo!**

MARIVÍ: **¿Está aquí?**

GRACIELA: **Todavía no, no sé por qué.**

MARIVÍ: **Pues, ya es tarde. Son casi las cuatro y media.**

GRACIELA: **Ya sé. Pienso ir a casa a las cinco. David es muy simpático pero necesita ser más puntual.**

Actividad preliminar

Describe the following people or things using the descriptive word that follows each.

Por ejemplo:

Tom Cruise /¿guapo?
Sí. Tom Cruise es guapo. (No, no es guapo).

1. Janet Jackson /¿guapa?
2. el director de la escuela /¿listo?
3. la clase de español /¿divertida?
4. los compañeros de clase /¿simpáticos?
5. los partidos de béisbol (fútbol americano, baloncesto, etc.) / ¿fantásticos?
6. las muchachas de la escuela /¿simpáticas?
7. los muchachos de la escuela /¿divertidos?

Lección 2   **91**

caño—necesita ser más generoso. Bruno no es muy aplicado—no saca buenas notas. Si quiere sacar buenas notas, necesita ser más responsable. También necesita ser más aplicado. Necesita ser más puntual y más independiente. Etc.

2. Use the photos of famous personalities on page 86, and make comments about each. Use facial expressions, gestures, and tone of voice to communicate positive and negative qualities. For example: _____ **es un cantante bueno (malo) pero (y) es muy feo.** Have students respond with **sí** or **no** to indicate agreement or disagreement.

B. Introduce the Lesson 2 dialogue by reading it aloud, or by playing the cassette version. Tell students they are going to hear a conversation between two people. Have them listen to find out the following information:
  1. Whom are Mariví and Graciela talking about?
  2. Are their comments positive or negative?

C. After students have answered the questions above, have them listen to the dialogue again. This time ask them to raise their hands when they hear one thing that one of the girls thinks David needs to improve.

D. Now ask students to open their books and look at the dialogue as you lead them through what is said. For example, **Cuando Graciela dice: "La fiesta es muy divertida, ¿no?", ¿qué dice Mariví? Etc.**
Note. Está, used here to express location, is not introduced for active use at this time. It will be formally introduced in Capítulo 3, Lesson 2.

Actividad preliminar

Actividad preliminar Answers
1. Sí. (No) Janet Jackson (no) es guapa.
2. Sí. (No) El director de la escuela (no) es listo.
3. Sí. (No) La clase de español (no) es divertida.
4. Sí. (No) Los compañeros de clase (no) son simpáticos.
5. Sí. (No) Los partidos de béisbol (no) son fantásticos.
6. Sí. (No) Las muchachas de la escuela (no) son simpáticas.
7. Sí. (No) Los muchachos de la escuela (no) son divertidos.

Vocabulary Teaching Resources
1. Vocabulario Transparencies 2.2
2. Workbook, pp. 41–42
3. Cassette 2.2
4. Student Tape Manual, p. 32
5. Lesson Quizzes, p. 28

Bell Ringer Review

Directions to students: Imagine you are an active member of each club below. How would you say you like each club subject?

1. el club de matemáticas
2. el club de música
3. el club de francés
4. el club de ciencias
5. el club de deportes

Presentation

1. Have students open their books to pages 92 and 93. Ask them to look at these pages as you model each new word. Begin by modeling the question **¿Cómo es?** Then introduce each new word with **Es...** Use facial gestures and tone of voice to help convey meaning. Have students repeat each phrase in unison.

2. You may wish to use "Bruno," the recurring character in the practice activities (see page 53) to help teach the Vocabulario. For example: **Quiero presentarles a mi amigo Bruno. El pobrecito es feo, ¿no? No es guapo.** (Use facial expressions, gestures, and tone of voice to convey meaning.) **También es muy gordo** (gesture) **y un poco tonto** (use gesture on page 95). **Dicen que también es tacaño—necesita ser más generoso. Bruno no es muy aplicado—no saca buenas notas. Si quiere sacar buenas notas, ne-**

Vocabulario

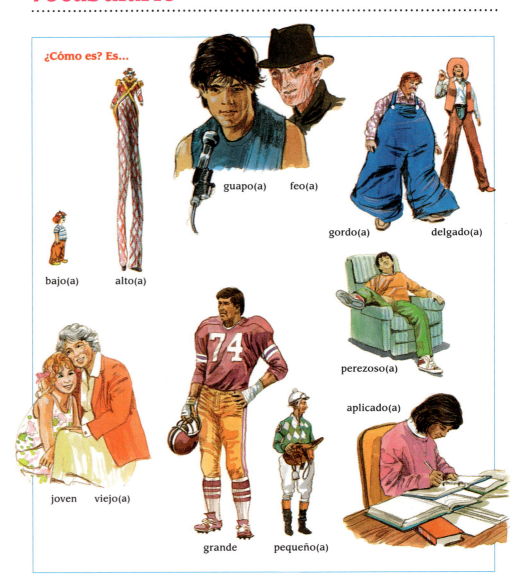

¿Cómo es? Es...

guapo(a) feo(a)

gordo(a) delgado(a)

bajo(a) alto(a)

perezoso(a)

aplicado(a)

joven viejo(a)

grande pequeño(a)

92 CAPÍTULO 2

Total Physical Response

Getting Ready
Draw arrows on the board pointing **atrás** and **adelante**. Label them.

New Words
Levanten la mano derecha.	atrás
Levanten la mano izquierda.	adelante
Levanten las manos.	hacia

TPR 1

Levántense.	Den vuelta.
Siéntense.	Caminen adelante.
Levántense.	Caminen atrás.
Salten.	Siéntense.

Las personas altas, levántense.
Las personas simpáticas, siéntense.
Los chicos altos, levántense y salten.
Las personas generosas, levanten la mano derecha.

antipático(a) simpático(a)

malo(a) bueno(a)

divertido(a) aburrido(a)

listo(a) tonto(a)

generoso(a) tacaño(a)

Es un poco gordo. Es bastante gordo. ¡Es muy gordo! ¡Es demasiado gordo!

Lección 2 **93**

cesita ser más responsable. También necesita ser más aplicado. Necesita ser más puntual y más independiente. Etc.

When Students Ask

You may wish to give students the following additional words to allow them to describe people.

moreno(a) **nuevo(a)**
rubio(a) **pelirrojo(a)**

Additional Practice

Have students select the words they would use to describe David and Chris. Have students select from the list the three adjectives they would most want used to describe themselves and the three they would least want used.

Las personas buenas, levanten la mano izquierda.
Las personas tacañas, levanten las manos.
Las personas aplicadas, levanten la mano derecha.

TPR 2
(Call on individual students.)
Camina hacia un estudiante bajo.

Salta hacia una estudiante buena.
Ve a un chico joven.
Sonríe a una chica alta.
Dale el libro a una muchacha aplicada.
Dale el lápiz a un muchacho divertido.
Dale el bolígrafo a una muchacha simpática.
Escribe el nombre de un muchacho aplicado.

Actividades

Actividad A Answers
1. ¡Qué alto!
2. ¡Qué aplicado!
3. ¡Qué malo!
4. ¡Qué divertido!
5. ¡Qué aburrido!
6. ¡Qué guapo!
7. ¡Qué perezoso!

Actividad B Answers
Answers will vary but may include the following:

1. El libro de matemáticas es aburrido (interesante; difícil).
2. El Presidente de los Estados Unidos es bueno (listo; aburrido).
3. El señor Scrooge es tacaño.
4. Freddy es feo.
5. Chris es guapo (alto; simpático).
6. Frankenstein es malo (feo).
7. Mi disco favorito es divertido.

Actividad C Answers
1. Yolanda, necesitas hablar con los amigos…
2. Bruno, … estudiar y hacer la tarea.
3. Anita, … prestar revistas…
4. Miguel, … correr o jugar tenis.
5. Carlos, … comer más.

Extension
After doing Actividades A, B, and C, you may wish to extend the lesson as follows: Provide students with your own statements and have them react simply with ¡Qué bueno/malo/interesante/aburrido/tonto, etc.! For example:

1. No quiero dar más exámenes.
2. Me gusta la ópera.
3. No me gustan los estudiantes aplicados, etc.

Reteaching
Ask each student to bring in several illustrations from magazines or newspapers. Hold each one up for the class to see, or place them around the classroom. Ask students to describe each illustration using words from the Vocabulario.

Actividades

A **¿Cómo son?** React to the following illustrations using the expression ¡Qué…!

B **Descripciones.** David wants to know what you think of the following. Describe each item.

Por ejemplo:

> Nueva York
> *Nueva York es grande.*

1. el libro de matemáticas
2. el presidente de los Estados Unidos
3. el señor Scrooge
4. Freddy (de la calle Elm)
5. Chris
6. Frankenstein
7. mi disco favorito

C **¿Qué necesito hacer?** Tell what some of Chris's friends need to do to improve themselves. Choose your suggestions from the column on the right.

Por ejemplo:

> Eva: un poco gorda.
> *Eva, necesitas nadar o practicar deportes.*

1. Yolanda: Quiero ser más divertida.
2. Bruno: No soy muy aplicado.
3. Anita: Quiero ser más generosa.
4. Miguel: Soy bastante perezoso.
5. Carlos: Soy demasiado delgado.

a. comer más
b. prestar (lend) revistas y discos a los amigos
c. estudiar y hacer la tarea
d. correr o jugar tenis
e. hablar con los amigos de algo cómico

For the Native Speaker
Have native speakers write a descriptive paragraph of at least fifty words describing a classmate or a celebrity.

Cooperative Learning
The members of each team will write down positive comments about their team members. They will also write down suggestions for improving themselves. For example: **Jane es simpática. Necesito estudiar más.** Collect the papers and read a few to the class. Students can agree or disagree with the statements. (Make sure students are nice to each other.)

Los ademanes

Gestures, like words, differ from culture to culture. The following are some common gestures that accompany conversations in Spanish.

tacaño(a)

tonto(a)

adiós

no

listo(a)

Actividad

Make one of the above gestures. Your classmates will guess the word you are illustrating.

Lección 2   **95**

Cultura viva 1

Presentation

A. Before reading the Cultura viva, you may want to ask students to demonstrate some common gestures used in the U.S. Have two students model these for the class.

B. Read the Cultura viva selection. Model each gesture shown on page 95, and have students imitate your gestures.

Did You Know?
Hispanics can be rather animated in conversation. Hand movements and gestures are a natural part of their conversation.

Critical Thinking Activity
How do gestures help people to communicate?

Actividad Answers
Gestures and answers will vary according to each student.

Extension
You may want to encourage students to use appropriate gestures and facial expressions from now on.

Pronunciation

A. You may wish to play the recorded version of these pronunciation lines, located at the end of Cassette 2.2. You may also wish to write this verse on the board and have students copy it into their notebook:
Ni tonto ni tacaño,
ni aburrido ni inteligente.

**Yo soy un muchacho
común y corriente.**

B. Have students repeat words and phrases individually and in unison. You may wish to focus on the /**r**/ sound as in **aburrido** and **corriente**.

Bell Ringer Review

Directions to students: Whom do you admire and respect most? Least? Write down the names and describe the two people.

Presentation

Lead students through steps 1–3 on page 96. You may wish to demonstrate the concepts of singular vs. plural; masculine vs. feminine by talking about male and female students. For example, **Larry es aplicado. Kelly es aplicada. Larry y Kelly son aplicados. Etc.**

Actividades

Actividad A Answers
Es: aburrido, feo, gordo, paciente, popular.
No es: responsable, aplicado.

Extension
You may wish to extend Actividad A as follows: Have students make recommendations to Bruno. For example: **Bruno, necesitas estudiar, (ser) más interesante, etc.**

Actividad B Answers
Alicia es divertida, guapa y delgada. Es responsable pero es impaciente y no es popular. Es muy aplicada. Sabe hablar inglés muy bien porque quiere practicar y estudiar.

Estructura 1

How to Describe People and Things　　　*Adjectives ending in -o/-a*

You have already used some descriptive words (adjectives) in Spanish.

> **David es interesante. Mariví es interesante también.**
> **David no es puntual. Mariví y Graciela son puntuales.**
> **David es amable. Los compañeros de clase son amables también.**

1. Many adjectives end in **-o** or **-a,** depending on the person or thing you are describing. If you want to describe a male or a masculine word (**el** words), the adjective ends in **-o.** If you want to describe a female or a feminine word, the adjective ends in **-a.**

   > **David es simpático.**
   > **Graciela es guapa.**
   > **El deportista es simpático.**
   > **La deportista es demasiado delgada.**
   > **El libro es muy bueno.**
   > **La fiesta es bastante aburrida.**

2. To describe more than one person or thing, add **-s** to the adjective.

   > **Los libros son aburridos.**
   > **Las fiestas son divertidas.**

3. When you want to describe more than one person or thing, but some of them are masculine and some are feminine, use the masculine plural form of the noun and the adjective ending **-os.**

   > **Mis compañeros de clase son simpáticos.**
   > **¡Qué generosos son mis amigos!**
   > **David y Graciela son muy aplicados.**

Actividades

A **Mi amigo Bruno.** Below is a description of Bruno. Make two lists, **Es** and **No es.** Place words that describe him in the **Es** list and those that don't in the **No es** list.

> Bruno es aburrido, un poco feo y demasiado gordo. No es muy responsable pero es paciente y bastante popular. Y no es muy aplicado. Por ejemplo, no sabe hablar inglés muy bien porque no quiere practicar ni estudiar.

B **La amiga de Bruno.** Bruno's girlfriend Alicia is not like Bruno at all. She's just the opposite. List her characteristics.

Por ejemplo:

> Alicia es divertida. (No es aburrida)...

C **Los estudiantes de intercambio.** The photos on the right are of next year's two exchange students. Say at least four things to describe each of them.

D **¿Cómo eres?** Rate yourself based on the following characteristics. Answer on a scale of: **un poco, bastante, muy,** or **demasiado.**

Por ejemplo:

> ¿Eres perezoso(a)?
> Carlos: *Soy un poco perezoso.*
> María: *Soy muy perezosa.*

1. ¿Eres simpático(a)?
2. ¿Eres listo(a)?
3. ¿Eres generoso(a)?
4. ¿Eres aplicado(a)?
5. ¿Eres alto(a)?
6. ¿Eres divertido(a)?
7. ¿Eres viejo(a)?
8. ¿Eres bueno(a)?

E **Gente.** List two people who fit each of the following categories.

Por ejemplo:

> actores viejos
> *Paul Newman es viejo.*

1. escritores interesantes
2. cantantes buenos
3. maestros simpáticos
4. deportistas altos

Adela, la muchacha de Peru

Carlos, el muchacho de España

Lección 2 **97**

Actividad C Answers
Answers will vary but may include the following:
Adela: Es de Perú. Es simpática; joven; lista.
Carlos: Es de España. Es delgado; aplicado; joven.

Actividad D Answers
Answers will vary, but should always include one of the following: **un poco, bastante, muy, demasiado.**

Actividad E Answers
Answers will vary, but should include names that the teachers will recognize.

Additional Practice
After doing Actividades A, B, C, D, and E on page 97, you may wish to reinforce the learning with the following:

1. List five characteristics that you and a good friend share. For example: **Los dos somos bajos, muy simpáticos... (Las dos somos bajas, muy simpáticas...)**
2. Interview two classmates to get their opinions of the following topics. Record their opinions and report back to the class. If their opinions are similar, connect them with **y.** If they are different, connect them with **pero.** For example: **las clases de ciencias**
Estudiante A: ¿Cómo son las clases de ciencias?
Estudiante B: Son horribles.
Estudiante C: ¡Qué va! Son muy buenas.
(A la clase:) **Según Ken, las clases de ciencias son horribles, pero según Ann son muy buenas.**
    1. la cafetería de la escuela
    2. el fútbol americano
    3. la muñeca "rock"
    4. el álgebra
    5. los maestros
    6. los muchachos de la escuela

Reteaching
Describe the following people using the descriptive words in the Vocabulario on pages 92 and 93:
los compañeros de clase
Bruno
las amigas

97

Cultura viva 2

Presentation
Read the Cultura viva selection on this page. Based on the reading, you may want to ask students to name some of the benefits an exchange student would experience from living in another country. You may want to write these on the chalkboard.

Did you know?
Most exchange students who come to the U.S. will return to their own country after living with a family for approximately a year, and attending a local high school. Most foreign students have already studied English and are very proficient when they arrive in the U.S. There are also many exchange students from the U.S. who stay with families in various countries in Latin America, especially in Mexico.

Critical Thinking
After reading the Cultura viva, can you think of any additional benefits of being a foreign exchange student? What might be some disadvantages to living abroad for a year?

Actividad Answers
Answers will vary, but students should use active vocabulary and structures learned in earlier lessons, as well as in Lesson 2.

Extension
After doing the Actividad, you may wish to extend the lesson by inviting an exchange student in your school to speak to the class.

Learning from Photos
You may want to ask students to name as many verbs as they can think of that are associated with the photos on page 98. For example, **hablar, correr, jugar, visitar, aprender, contestar, escribir, trabajar, hacer una pregunta, bailar.**

Los estudiantes de intercambio

David is a student from Costa Rica studying for a school year in the United States. He is one of many thousands of high school students throughout the world who have chosen to study in a foreign country. Many high schools across the United States have programs in which American students study abroad, and students from abroad come to study in American schools.

Many new experiences await David during his year in the United States. All his classes are in English; he learns to play American sports that are not played commonly in his native land—baseball and football, for example; he lives with an American family who treats him as a son and brother. And in addition to learning English, he also learns how to live in another culture—skills that will be of invaluable use throughout his entire life.

Actividad

Imagine that you are an exchange student in Costa Rica. Answer the following questions that a Costa Rican classmate asks you.

1. **¿De dónde eres?**
2. **¿Qué clases te gustan más?**
3. **¿Cómo es la escuela en los Estados Unidos?**
4. **¿Cómo son tus compañeros de clase?**
5. **¿Qué te gusta hacer?**

Now ask your classmate two questions about life in Costa Rica.

98 CAPÍTULO 2

Pronunciation
A. You may wish to play the recorded version of these pronunciation lines, located at the end of Cassette 2.2. You may also wish to write this verse on the board and have students copy it into their notebook:
Ser estudiante de intercambio
es una gran aventura:
aprendes otro idioma,
vives otra cultura.

Sea España, México, Perú o Bolivia—
sabes que en ese país
tienes familia.

B. Have students repeat words and phrases individually and in unison. You may wish to focus on the /v/ sound as in **aventura; vives; Bolivia.**

Estructura 2

How to Say What You Plan to Do

Pienso / piensas + the infinitive

To say what you want or need to do, you have used **Quiero** and **Necesito** + activity.

> **Quiero ver la tele pero necesito hacer la tarea.**

To ask a friend if he or she wants or needs to do something, you have used **¿Quieres?** and **¿Necesitas?** + activity.

> **¿Quieres ir a casa?**
> **¿Necesitas comprar algo?**

1. To say what you plan to do, say **Pienso** + activity.
   > **Pienso ir al cine.**

2. To ask a friend if he or she plans to do something, say **¿Piensas + activity?**
   > **¿Piensas estudiar?**

3. To ask a friend what he or she plans to do, say **¿Qué piensas hacer?**

4. To say you don't plan to do anything, say **No pienso hacer nada.**

5. In the examples above, the word that names the activity is called an "infinitive" (to do, to buy, to be, to go). Infinitives end in **-ar, -er,** or **-ir.** So far, you have used infinitives to ask and say several things. Find the infinitives in the following sentences.

> **¿Qué quieres hacer?**   **Quiero tomar algo.**
> **¿Te gusta jugar fútbol?**   **No, me gusta jugar baloncesto.**
> **¿Sabes esquiar?**   **Ya sé esquiar muy bien.**
> **¿Necesitas hacer la tarea?** **Sí, necesito estudiar álgebra.**
> **¿Qué piensas hacer?**   **Pienso comprar discos.**

> **Structure Teaching Resources**
> 1. Workbook, p. 46
> 2. Cassette 2.2
> 3. Student Tape Manual, p. 34
> 4. Estructura Masters 2.2
> 5. Lesson Quizzes, p. 31

Bell Ringer Review

Directions to students: Draw a "happy face" and a "grumpy face" on your paper. Write down as many words as you can think of that describe each face.

Structure Focus

In this lesson the presentation of **pensar** is limited to **pienso/piensas** + infinitive. The other forms of **pensar** will be taught in Chapter 2, Lessons 4, 5, and 6.

Presentation

A. Lead students through steps 1–5 on page 99. You may wish to reinforce steps 3 and 4 by having each student turn to his or her partner and asking the question **¿Qué piensas hacer hoy?** Following the response, reverse roles: **Y tú, ¿qué piensas hacer?** Set a time limit of thirty seconds. Then have each pair perform for the class.

B. In step 5, point out that the infinitive form of the verb consists of two words in English, but only one word in Spanish. Ask students to give additional examples of infinitives in Spanish. You may want them to look for them in the Repaso de vocabulario of each earlier lesson.

Actividades

Actividad A Answers
Answers will vary but may include the following:
Si no necesito ir a la escuela, pienso jugar tenis y hablar con amigos. También pienso estudiar, escuchar música y descansar.

Actividad B Answers
Answers will vary but may include the following:
Quiero ir a casa porque necesito ver el partido de fútbol. Quiero ir a casa porque necesito practicar tenis. Etc.

Actividad C Answers
Answers will vary, but students should use a form of the verb **pensar** in each utterance.

Actividad D Answers
Answers will vary.

Additional Practice
After doing Actividades A, B, C, and D on page 100, you may wish to reinforce the learning with the following: Have students invite their partners to go somewhere or do something. Partners will refuse and tell something they need to do or plan on doing instead. **Por ejemplo:**
Estudiante A: ¿Quieres ir al cine?
Estudiante B: No, gracias. Necesito (Pienso) estudiar.
Estudiante A: ¿Quieres ir a la biblioteca?
Estudiante B: No, gracias. No me gusta estudiar en la biblioteca.
Rehearsal time: one minute. Then have pairs perform for the class. Have students tell what they need to do every day but one thing they plan to do tomorrow that is different. **Por ejemplo: Todos los días necesito _____ pero mañana pienso**

Reteaching
Ask students personalized questions using **piensas.** For example: **¿Piensas leer revistas?** Have students answer in complete sentences.

Actividades

A **¿Qué piensas hacer?** School is canceled for tomorrow. What five things do you plan to do?

Por ejemplo:

> Si no necesito ir a la escuela, pienso ver películas...

B **Quiero ir a casa.** You're at a boring party and you want to leave. Give five reasons why you need to go home.

Por ejemplo:

> Quiero ir a casa porque necesito hacer la tarea.

C **¿Y tus compañeros?** Find out what three classmates plan to do this weekend.

Por ejemplo:

ESTUDIANTE A	ESTUDIANTE B
(1) ¿Qué piensas hacer?	(2) **Pienso descansar y hablar por teléfono. ¿Y tú?**
(3) **Pienso comprar discos.**	

D **El fin de semana.** Complete the following sentences to write about your plans for the weekend.

Por ejemplo:

> Quiero...
> *Quiero jugar videojuegos, andar en monopatín y ver la tele.*

1. Pienso...
2. No pienso...
3. Necesito...
4. No necesito...
5. Quiero...
6. No quiero...

Cooperative Learning
Prepare an interview form and provide a copy for each student in the class. Students should then interview students from another Spanish class, if possible (if not, from their own class). Then each student should share the interview results with his or her teammates and the class.

Finalmente

Situaciones

A conversar Use the following cues to converse with a classmate about plans for Saturday.

1. Ask your partner what he or she plans to do.
2. Your partner will say that he or she is planning to go to the movies and will say with whom (**con Carlos, con Mónica, etc.**).
3. Ask what that person is like. Your partner will respond saying three or four things.
4. Ask what movie your partner is going to see.
5. Give your reaction to the movie. (**¡Qué...!**).

A escribir Write a letter of introduction to a new pen pal.

1. Start with **Estimado(a)...** Tell who you are and where you are from.
2. Describe your appearance and personality. Use the words **muy, bastante, un poco,** and **demasiado.**
3. Then tell what you like to do and where you like to go in your spare time. Finish your letter **Tu amigo(a),** and your name.

Repaso de vocabulario

PREGUNTA

¿Qué piensas hacer?
¿Quién es?

DESCRIPCIONES

ser +
   aburrido(a)
   alto(a)
   antipático(a)
   aplicado(a)
   bajo(a)
   bueno(a)

delgado(a)
divertido(a)
feo(a)
generoso(a)
gordo(a)
grande
guapo(a)
joven
listo(a)
malo(a)
pequeño(a)

perezoso(a)
simpático(a)
tacaño(a)
tonto(a)
viejo(a)

PERSONAS

la muchacha
el muchacho

OTRAS PALABRAS

bastante
demasiado
un poco

EXPRESIÓN

Pienso (Piensas)
+ activity.

Lección 2 **101**

Finalmente

Situaciones

Lesson 2 Evaluation
The A conversar and A escribir situations on this page are designed to give students the opportunity to use as many language functions as possible listed on page 90 of this lesson. The A conversar and A escribir are also intended to show how well students are able to meet the lesson objectives, also listed on page 90.

Presentation
Prior to doing the A conversar and A escribir on this page, you may wish to play the Situaciones listening activities on Cassette 2.2 as a means of helping students organize the material.

Repaso de vocabulario
The words and phrases in the Repaso de vocabulario have been taught for the active use in this lesson. They are summarized here as a resource for both students and teacher. The Repaso de vocabulario also serves as a convenient resource for the A conversar and A escribir activity on this page.

Lección 3

Objectives

By the end of this lesson, students will be able to:

1. ask where a friend is going and tell where they are going
2. ask what a friend is going to do and tell what they are going to do
3. tell about events in sequence
4. talk about what belongs to someone

Lesson 3 Resources
1. Workbook, pp. 47–52
2. Vocabulario Transparencies 2.3
3. Cassette 2.3
4. Student Tape Manual, pp. 36–39
5. Lesson Quizzes, pp. 32–36
6. Test Booklet, pp. 15–22
7. Computer Software, Disk 1
8. Video Cassette
9. Estructura Masters 2.3
10. Diversiones Masters 2.3

Bell Ringer Review

Directions to students: Copy the following words and write the opposite of each one.
alto, listo, guapo, viejo, tacaño, antipático, paciente, grande, aplicado.

¡A comenzar!

Presentation

A. Lead students through each of the seven functions given on page 102, progressing from the English to the Spanish for each function. Then have the students find these words and phrases in the dialogue on page 103.

Lección 3

¿Tarde o temprano?

¡A comenzar!

The following are some of the things you will be learning to do in this lesson.

When you want to . . .	You use . . .
1. find out where a friend is going	• **¿Adónde vas?**
2. say where you are going	• **Voy a** + place.
3. explain what you are going to do	• **Voy a** + activity.
4. find out what a friend is going to do	• **¿Qué vas a hacer?**
5. put events in sequence: now, then, afterward	• **ahora, luego, después**
6. talk about what belongs to someone	• object + **de** + person
7. excuse yourself	• **Con permiso.**

Now find examples of the above words and phrases in the following conversation.

Getting Ready for Lesson 3

You may wish to use one or more of the following suggestions to prepare students for the lesson.

1. Have students keep their books closed. Tell students about your schedule for today and the rest of this week. Say where you're going, what you plan to do, and why. Distribute to each student a list of places people go, for example: **al parque, al partido, a la reunión, a la fiesta, a casa, al gimnasio, a la tienda, a la biblioteca, al hospital, a la casa de un amigo, etc.** As they listen to your plans, have them check off the places they hear. For example: **Necesito hacer muchas cosas hoy. Después de las clases voy a ir a una reunión de los maestros en la cafetería. Luego voy a la tienda porque ne-**

David finally arrives at the picnic. He sees Graciela, who is about to leave.

DAVID: **¡Hola, Graciela! ¿Qué tal?**

GRACIELA: **David, ¡por fin! ¡Qué elegante!**

DAVID: **¿Yo? ¿Elegante?**

GRACIELA: **Bueno, David, hasta luego.**

DAVID: **Pero, ¿adónde vas?**

GRACIELA: **Pues, ahora voy a casa. Voy a comer.**

DAVID: **Pero es muy temprano. Y ¿qué vas a hacer después de comer?**

GRACIELA: **Luego voy a la casa de Mariví. Bueno, ya es tarde. Con permiso.**

DAVID: **Pero, Graciela...**

GRACIELA: **Adiós, David.**

DAVID: **Ay, ¡qué mala suerte!**

Actividad preliminar

It's 3:00 P.M. on a school day. Tell three places that you are going, choosing from the list on the right. Use **ahora, luego,** and **después** to tell the order in which you are going to the three places.

Por ejemplo:

Ahora voy al gimnasio. Luego... Después...

Ahora...	**voy a la biblioteca.**
Luego...	**voy al gimnasio.**
Después...	**voy a casa.**
	voy al centro comercial.
	voy al cine.
	voy a la casa de mi amigo(a).

cesito comprar casetes. Después voy a la biblioteca porque necesito un libro y entonces voy a casa a cocinar.

2. **Now ask students: ¿Adónde voy?** Allow them to answer with **a la tienda, al parque,** etc.

3. Ask students individually, **¿Adónde vas hoy?**

4. Make some statements about where you are going and for what reasons.

Some should be logical, others illogical. Have students respond with **Sí** or **No** or simply raise their hands or say **¡Qué va!** in response to your illogical statements. For example: **Voy a a cafetería. Allí voy a montar a caballo. Luego voy al gimnasio. Voy a hacer ejercicio. Voy al centro también. Voy a cocinar. Voy a casa. Voy a comprar un libro,** etc.

B. Introduce the Lesson 3 dialogue by reading it aloud, or by playing the cassette version. Have students listen for the following information:
   1. who are the people talking?
   2. who is leaving?

C. Now ask students to open their books and look at the dialogue as you lead them through what is said. For example: **¿Qué le dice Graciela a David? Cuando David dice: "¿adónde vas?", ¿qué dice Graciela? Para David, ¿es tarde o temprano? Cuando David dice: "Y ¿qué vas a hacer después?", ¿qué dice Graciela? ¿Adónde vas tú después de las clases?**

D. You may wish to read the dialogue or play the cassette version again. Have students raise their hands when they hear the questions about where someone is going and what someone is going to do. When students raise their hands, stop and have them respond individually to the question. For example, **¿Adónde vas?** They should not be required to use a verb **(Voy)** in their response, simply **a la, al, a** + place.

Actividad preliminar

Actividad Answers
Answers will vary, but students should use **ahora, luego, después** in their response.

Additional Practice
After doing the Actividad preliminar on page 103, you may wish to reinforce the learning with the following: Have students turn to their partners and find out where they are going today. When their partner tells them, they will give a reaction such as **¡Qué bueno/interesante/aburrido!** For example:
Estudiante A: ¿Adónde vas?
Estudiante B: Voy a la biblioteca. Voy a estudiar.
Estudiante A: ¡Qué aburrido!
Then reverse roles. Allow one minute rehearsal time.

Bell Ringer Review

Directions to students: Write on your paper all the words you can think of that are associated with the following words:

estudiante
deportista
músico(a)

Presentation

1. Have students open their books to pages 104 and 105. Ask them to look at these pages as you model each new phrase. Begin by modeling the questions **¿Adónde vas ahora?** and **¿Qué vas a hacer?** Then introduce each new phrase. Make sure students understand the distinction between going somewhere, and doing something once they arrive at their destination. Have students repeat each Vocabulario phrase in unison.

2. To emphasize time sequence, you may want to write **primero, luego, después, entonces, también** on the chalkboard. Have students practice saying this sequence, adding activities after each.

3. The Vocabulario for Lesson 3 contains the following new infinitives: **ganar, buscar, limpiar.** Have students make some associations with these words through the following types of questions: **ganar: Si quieres ganar dinero, ¿qué necesitas hacer? limpiar: ¿A qué hora necesitas limpiar tu habitación todos los días? Etc.**

Vocabulario

¿Adónde vas ahora?

Primero voy al gimnasio.

Luego voy a la cafetería.

Después voy al trabajo.

Entonces voy al centro.

¿Qué vas a hacer?

Voy a hacer ejercicio.

Voy a hablar con los amigos.

Voy a ganar dinero.

Voy a buscar un regalo.

104   CAPÍTULO 2

Total Physical Response

Getting Ready

On posterboards, draw or glue illustrations of the following places: **el centro, el gimnasio, la habitación, la playa, la cafetería, el parque.** Place the posters in different areas of the room. For **TPR 2,** you will need a newspaper and a box wrapped as a gift.

New Words

haz	hagan
lee	lean
vayan	

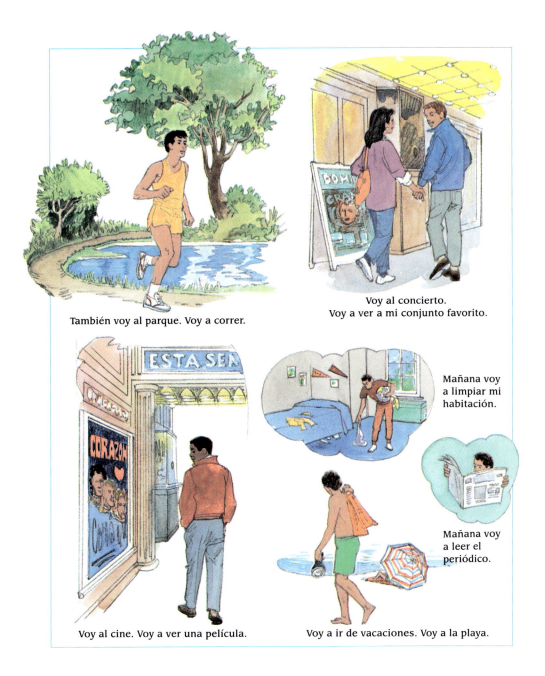

También voy al parque. Voy a correr.

Voy al concierto.
Voy a ver a mi conjunto favorito.

Mañana voy a limpiar mi habitación.

Mañana voy a leer el periódico.

Voy al cine. Voy a ver una película.

Voy a ir de vacaciones. Voy a la playa.

TPR 1

Primero levántese.
Siéntese.
Ahora, hagan ejercicio.
Levánten las manos y hagan ejercicio.
Apunten a la playa.
Apunten al _____.
Levántense y vayan al parque.
Caminen al cine.
Vayan a la cafetería.

TPR 2

(to individual students)
Ve a la playa.
Haz ejercicio en el gimnasio.
Toma el periódico y lee en la habitación.
Dale el regalo a _____.
Ve con _____ al cine.

Actividad A Answers
Answers will vary,

Actividad B Answers
Answers will vary but may include the following:

1. (No) Voy al parque. Voy a montar bicicleta.
2. (No) Voy al cine... ver la película...
3. (No) Voy al centro... comprar revistas.
4. (No) Voy al centro comercial... , hablar con amigos.
5. (No) Voy al trabajo... ganar dinero.
6. (No) Voy a la casa de... hacer la tarea.
7. (No) Voy al gimnasio... mirar el partido de baloncesto.
8. (No) Voy a la piscina... nadar.
9. (No) Voy a la playa... nadar.
10. (No) Voy al campo... montar en bicicleta (trabajar) (descansar).
11. (No) Voy al concierto... ver a mi conjunto favorito.

Actividad C Answers
Answers will vary.

Class Management
Actividad C may be done as a whole class activity, if preferred. The teacher takes the role of Student A, calling on individual students to answer for Student B.

Reteaching

Tell students to write down five answers for each of the following questions: **¿Adónde vas ahora? ¿Qué vas a hacer?**

Actividades

A **Después de las clases.** Tell five things you plan to do after school and the order in which you're going to do them.

Por ejemplo:

> Primero voy a buscar un regalo. Luego voy a hacer ejercicio. Después...

B **¿Adónde vas?** Write down whether you're going to go to the following places. Then list what you're going to do in each place. Report back to the class.

Por ejemplo:

> la biblioteca
> *Voy a la biblioteca. Voy a hacer la tarea.*
> *(Voy a leer el periódico, etc.). (No voy a la biblioteca).*

1. el parque
2. el cine
3. el centro
4. el centro comercial
5. el trabajo
6. la casa de (nombre de un amigo)
7. el gimnasio
8. la piscina
9. la playa
10. el campo
11. el concierto

C **Mañana.** Converse with a classmate about your plans for tomorrow. Use the following expressions: **Voy a..., Necesito..., Quiero..., Pienso...**

Por ejemplo:

ESTUDIANTE A	ESTUDIANTE B
(1) **¿Adónde vas mañana?**	(2) **Primero voy a la biblioteca.**
(3) **¿Qué vas a hacer?**	(4) **Necesito escribir una composición. Y tú, ¿qué piensas hacer?**
(5) **Voy al trabajo. Necesito ganar dinero.**	

For the Native Speaker

In a paragraph of at least 50 words, tell where you are going and what you are going to do on your next school holiday.

Cooperative Learning

1. Pick four places of interest to the class (**cine, centro,** etc.). Have students choose one of these places and give reasons why they will go there. Then students will move to the four corners of the classroom and interview each other about why they're going there.
2. Have teams of students brainstorm about what activities they can do on a typical day or weekend. Then have them categorize the activities according to those they can do together, and those they can't. They should give a reason for the activities they cannot do together.

¡Qué elegante!

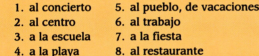

In Hispanic countries, people dress up to go out in public, especially if they expect to meet someone or be introduced. In a restaurant or at a party, people of all ages tend to dress more formally than people in the U.S. Casual clothing is worn only at home, for working outdoors, or for recreation.

Actividad

Tell how you would dress to go to each of the following places, using:

a) muy elegante
b) bastante elegante
c) un poco elegante
d) nada elegante

Por ejemplo:

al estadio: nada elegante

1. al concierto
2. al centro
3. a la escuela
4. a la playa
5. al pueblo, de vacaciones
6. al trabajo
7. a la fiesta
8. al restaurante

Pronunciation

A. You may wish to play the recorded version of these pronunciation lines, located at the end of Cassette 2.3. You may also wish to write this verse on the board and have students copy it into their notebook.

¡Hola! ¿Qué tal?
¿Cómo estás?
Dime preciosa,
¿adónde vas?

B. Have students repeat words and phrases individually and in unison. You may wish to focus on the /v/ sound as in ¿Adónde vas?

Cultura viva 1

Presentation

Read the Cultura viva selection on this page. Then you may wish to read the Lesson 3 dialogue again on page 103. Why does Graciela say to David, **¿Qué elegante?** Why does David respond the way he does?

Did you know?

Although clothing and styles of clothing worn by Hispanics are very similar to what is worn in the U.S., Hispanics in general tend to dress more formally and in a more conservative manner. For example, pants, which are common for women to wear in the U.S., are not worn on formal occasions. On the other hand, American teenage styles are very popular among young people in other countries.

Actividades

Actividad Answers
1. a or b
2. b or c
3. c
4. d
5. d
6. b or c
7. a or b
8. a, b, or c

Critical Thinking Activity
Ask students to imagine they are in a Hispanic country. How would they answer the Actividad? Compare both sets of answers.

Learning From Photos
You may want to ask students how the people are dressed in each photo on page 107: **muy elegante; bastante elegante; un poco elegante; nada elegante.**
Then ask students to say where the people are in each photo **(en la biblioteca; en la fiesta; en el restaurante).**

Bell Ringer Review

Directions to students: Write down the following names of places, then draw a picture which represents each one. Put a star by your favorite. **el gimnasio, el centro comercial, el cine, la habitación, el parque, el campo**

Structure Focus

In this lesson students will learn all forms of the verb **ir**. Students have used the infinitive form only prior to this lesson.

Presentation

Lead students through steps 1–7 on pages 108 and 109. If you have taught the Vocabulario for Lesson 3, students will already be familiar with the **voy** and **vas** forms.

Estructura 1

How to Say or Ask Where Someone Is Going or What Someone Is Going to Do   *The verb* **ir**

1. To talk about going someplace, use the verb **ir**.

SINGULAR	PLURAL
voy	vamos
vas	vais*
va	van

*This form is rarely used in the Spanish-speaking world, except for Spain.

2. To ask people where they are going, use **adónde** and the appropriate form of **ir**.
   - To ask where a friend is going:
     ¿Adónde vas, Anita?   **Voy al trabajo.**
   - To ask more than one friend:
     ¿Adónde van ustedes?   **Vamos a la piscina.**
   - To ask about other people:
     ¿Adónde van Chris y David?   **Van al centro.**

3. To suggest to a friend that you both go somewhere, say **¿Por qué no vamos a** + place?
   ¿Por qué no vamos al cine?

4. To say that you are not going anywhere, say **No voy a ningún lugar.**

5. To talk about what you or others are going to do, use a form of **ir** + **a** + infinitive.

   ¿Vas a limpiar la habitación?   **No, ahora voy a correr.**
   ¿Qué van a hacer ustedes?   **Vamos a trabajar.**

6. To say that you aren't going to do anything, say **No voy a hacer nada.**

108   CAPÍTULO 2

7. You don't need to make separate statements to tell where you are going and what you are going to do there. You may combine the two thoughts in one sentence in the following way.

> **Vamos al centro a buscar un regalo.**
> **¿Vas a la piscina a nadar?**
> **José va a casa a limpiar la habitación.**

Actividades

A **Lugares.** The following are things you like, want, need, or plan to do. Tell where you go to do them.

Por ejemplo:

> **Me gusta correr.**
> *Voy al parque (al campo, a la playa, etc.).*

1. **Me gusta ganar dinero.**
2. **Pienso jugar fútbol.**
3. **Necesito limpiar la habitación.**
4. **Quiero tomar algo.**
5. **Quiero comer.**
6. **Quiero ver una película.**
7. **Pienso andar en monopatín.**
8. **Me gusta montar a caballo.**
9. **Necesito buscar un libro.**

Lección 3 **109**

Actividades

Actividad A Answers
1. Voy al trabajo.
2. ... al estadio (al parque).
3. ... a casa.
4. ... a la cafetería (al restaurante).
5. ... a la cafetería (al restaurante; a casa).
6. ... al cine (a casa).
7. ... al parque.
8. ... al campo (al parque).
9. ... a la biblioteca (a la tienda; al centro).

Additional Practice
After doing Actividad A on page 109, you may wish to reinforce the learning with the following:
1. Ask students to invite you to go somewhere with them based on your interests. For example, you say: **Necesito estudiar.** Students respond: **¿Por qué no vamos a la biblioteca?**
   a. **Me gustan las películas.**
   b. **Quiero correr.**
   c. **Me gusta bailar.**
   d. **Sé nadar muy bien.**
   e. **Me gustan los partidos de _____.**
   f. **Necesito ir de compras.**
   g. **Quiero descansar.**
2. Have students suggest specific places to go in your area for the following. For example, you say: **Quiero comer. ¿Adónde voy?** Students respond: **¿Por qué no va a _____(name of restaurant)?**
   a. **bailar**
   b. **jugar baloncesto**
   c. **leer**
   d. **comprar libros**
   e. **nadar**
   f. **descansar**
   g. **comer bien**

Actividad B Answers
Answers will vary, however students should use the sequence of **primero, luego, después, etc.** in listing the places they will go.

Actividad C Answers
Answers will vary according to each student's list from **B.**

Actividad D Answers
Answers will vary. To encourage students to make comparisons and contrasts, you may want to write the words **y** and **pero** on the chalkboard as a reminder.

Actividad E Answers
1. ¿Por qué no vamos al centro (al centro comercial) entonces?
2. ¿ ... al parque (a la playa, al campo)...?
3. ¿ ... al gimnasio (al parque, a la playa)...?
4. ¿ ... a la playa (a la piscina)...?
5. ¿ ... al estadio (al parque)...
6. ¿ ... al baile (a la fiesta)...?
7. ¿ ... al cine...?
8. ¿ ... al restaurante (a la cafetería)...?

B **Un fin de semana muy ocupado.** Plan a busy and exciting weekend. Make two columns: in one column write the places you will go; in the other write the things you will do there. Report back to the class.

Por ejemplo:

Primero voy al centro comercial.	**Voy a buscar un regalo.**
Después voy al gimnasio.	**Voy a hacer ejercicio.**

C **Preguntas.** A classmate will ask you about your weekend in activity **B.**

ESTUDIANTE A	ESTUDIANTE B
(1) ¿Adónde vas?	(2) **Primero voy a la casa de Todd.**
(3) ¿Qué vas a hacer?	(4) **Vamos a escuchar discos.**

D **Entre todos.** Compare your plans with those of a classmate. First tell what you are going to do, then tell your classmate's plans. If both of you have similar plans, compare them using **y.** If your plans are different, contrast them with **pero.**

Por ejemplo:

> **Voy al campo y Anita va al campo también.**
> **(Voy al campo pero Anita va a la ciudad).**

E **¿Por qué no vamos?** A classmate drops some hints about things to do. For each, make an appropriate invitation.

Por ejemplo:

ESTUDIANTE A	ESTUDIANTE B
Necesito estudiar.	**¿Por qué no vamos a la biblioteca entonces?**

1. **Necesito comprar algo.**
2. **Quiero dar un paseo.**
3. **Necesito hacer ejercicio.**
4. **Sé nadar muy bien.**
5. **Me gustan los partidos de fútbol.**
6. **Me gusta bailar.**

7. Me gustan las películas de terror.

8. Quiero comer algo.

F **Excusas.** Suggest four different places to which you and a classmate can go. Your classmate will say no to each and give a reason.

Por ejemplo:

ESTUDIANTE A	ESTUDIANTE B
¿Por qué no vamos al parque a jugar béisbol?	No, gracias. El béisbol es muy aburrido. (No me gusta jugar béisbol. Necesito limpiar la habitación, etc.).

G **¿Y ustedes?** Ask two classmates the following questions about their after-school plans. Take notes. Report back to the class.

1. ¿Adónde van?
2. ¿A qué hora?
3. ¿Qué van a hacer?

Por ejemplo:

> Matt y Meg van al gimnasio. Matt va a hacer ejercicio pero Meg va a ver el partido de baloncesto. Meg va a las dos y media. Matt va a las cuatro.

H **¿Adónde van?** Tell where you and your friends go on a typical day. Then tell a place you don't go.

1. Primero vamos a...
2. Luego vamos a...
3. Después...
4. Entonces...
5. También...
6. No vamos a...

Actividad F Answers
Answers will vary but may include the following:
¿Por qué no vamos al baile?/No, gracias. No sé bailar.

Actividad G Answers
Answers will vary.

Class Management
You may wish to do Actividad G as a small group activity. Students can work in groups of three. Each student in the group will ask the other two the questions in G. When all three students in the group have finished questioning the others, each one will report back to the whole class.

Actividad H Answers
Answers will vary according to each student.

Additional Practice
After doing the Actividades on this page, you may wish to reinforce the lesson with the following:
1. Have students practice inviting their partners somewhere using **¿Por qué no vamos a _____?** The partner will accept with **Gracias, muy amable** and then tell something he or she needs to do first. Then reverse roles. For example:
   Student A: **¿Por qué no vamos al parque?**
   Student B: **Gracias, muy amable, pero necesito estudiar.**
   Allow 30 seconds for partner practice before performing for class.
2. You may want to have students guess where you go after school (**Ud. va a _____.**) or where the following people go: **el director de la escuela, los amigos, el maestro de inglés, álgebra, etc.**

Reteaching

In groups of four, have students ask each other the following questions: **¿Adónde van después de las clases? ¿Qué van a hacer?** A recorder for the group will write down the answers, and a reporter will relate the results to the class.

Presentation

Read the Cultura viva selection on this page. For emphasis, you may wish to write the following two expressions on the chalkboard: **perdón; con permiso.** You may wish to demonstrate these expressions to the class by reaching over a student's desk, or lightly bumping into a student, followed by the appropriate expression.

Did you know?

Con permiso and **perdón** may be used before the fact, as when asking a person to allow you to go by or when asking for a person's attention. However, only **perdón** is used after the fact, as when you have bumped into someone. **Con permiso** is also a polite way to ask for something you need. Moreover, if you're going to ask for help or clarification, or if you accidentally hit someone, you may say **discúlpeme.** This means, "Excuse me, I'm sorry." If you are interrupting someone, you may also say **dispénseme.**

Critical Thinking

Write the following **expresiones de cortesía** on the chalkboard: **por favor, gracias, de nada, perdón.** In groups of three, have students prepare skits in which they will use these expressions. Then have students perform in front of the class.

Actividad Answers

1. Perdón.
2. Con permiso.
3. Con permiso.
4. Perdón.

Ay, perdón

When you want to excuse yourself for something you said or did (such as bumping into someone), say **Perdón.** If you need to excuse yourself for something you are going to do (such as interrupt or walk in front of someone), say **Con permiso.**

Actividad

What should you say in each of the following situations?

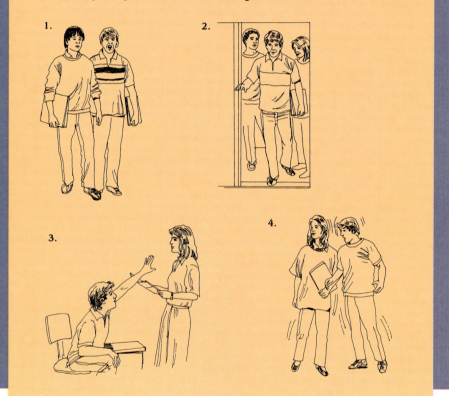

1.
2.
3.
4.

Pronunciation

A. You may wish to play the recorded version of these pronunciation lines, located at the end of Cassette 2.3. You may also wish to write this verse on the chalkboard and have students copy it into their notebook.
   Cuando empujas a alguien en el camión, necesitas decir: —Ay, perdón.

Si el ascensor está lleno y quieres bajar en cierto piso, debes decir: —Con permiso.

B. Have students repeat words and phrases individually and in unison. You may wish to focus on the /j/ sound as in **empujas; bajar.**

Estructura 2

How to Talk about What Belongs to Others

De *for possession*

1. To talk about other people's things, use the word **de** + person.

   La habitación de Mariví es grande y bonita.
   Las fiestas de David son muy divertidas.
   ¿Son difíciles los exámenes de la maestra de español?

2. When **de** is followed by the word **el**, the contraction **del** is formed (**de** + **el** = **del**).

   Es el coche del maestro de historia.
   Las tareas del señor López son bastante fáciles.

3. To ask to whom something belongs, say **¿De quién es?** To ask to whom more than one object belongs, say **¿De quién son?**

   ¿De quién es el dinero?   **Es del señor Varela.**
   Y ¿de quién son las fotos?   **Son de Jaime.**

Actividades

A **En San Antonio.** Name several things or persons for each of the following categories.

Por ejemplo:

   las clases de David Vargas
   Música, inglés, historia...

1. **las clases de tu amigo(a)**
2. **los amigos de Chris Pearson**
3. **los cantantes favoritos de tu mamá (papá)**
4. **los discos favoritos de tus amigos**

Estructura 2

Structure Teaching Resources
1. Workbook, pp. 51–52
2. Cassette 2.3
3. Student Tape Manual, p. 37
4. Estructura Masters 2.3
5.. Lesson Quizzes, pp. 35–36

Bell Ringer Review

Directions to students: Dictation: Partner A will dictate three sentences to Partner B, then let him or her check Partner B's written work against Partner A's paper. Reverse, and B will dictate to A.

A. 1. **Me gustan los partidos de fútbol porque son muy emocionantes.**
   2. **¿Por qué no vamos al campo esta tarde?**
   3. **¿Qué van a hacer Uds. el sábado por la noche?**

B. 1. **Voy a la biblioteca a estudiar.**
   2. **David es buen estudiante de idiomas.**
   3. **La habitación de Malena es pequeña pero bonita.**

Presentation

Lead students through steps 1–3 on page 113. You may wish to emphasize step 2 by writing several examples of **de** + **el** = **del** on the chalkboard.

Actividades

Actividad A Answers
Answers will vary.

B **¿Cómo es?** Identify each item below by saying that it belongs to either one of your classmates or a teacher. Then describe the item.

Por ejemplo:

> el coche
> *El coche del señor Vilas es nuevo. (El coche de Kim es muy viejo).*

1. la clase
2. el libro
3. los exámenes
4. los discos
5. la tarea

C **¿De quién es?** The people below have lost things at school. Ask your classmate to whom each of the following objects belongs. Your classmate will guess, based on the person's talents.

Por ejemplo:

> el libro de química / el Sr. Arias: maestro de ciencias

ESTUDIANTE A
¿De quién es el libro de química?

ESTUDIANTE B
Es de Sr. Arias. Es maestro de ciencias.

1. la guitarra
2. los lápices de colores
3. la composición de francés
4. la calculadora
5. las cámaras
6. la raqueta de tenis

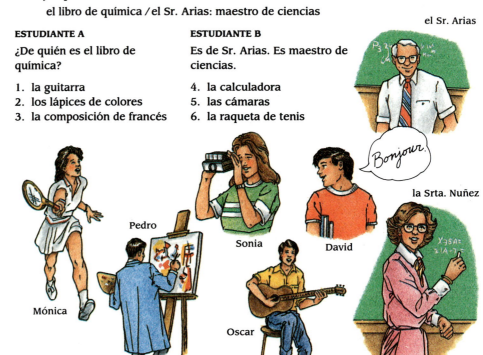

el Sr. Arias

la Srta. Nuñez

Pedro

Mónica

Sonia

David

Oscar

Bonjour.

Finalmente

Finalmente

Situaciones

Situaciones

Lesson 3 Evaluation
The A conversar and A escribir situations on this page are designed to give students the opportunity to use as many language functions as possible listed on page 102 of this lesson. The A conversar and A escribir are also intended to show how well students are able to meet the lesson objectives, also listed on page 102.

A conversar Your parent is lending you the car for the first time. Play the roles with a classmate.

1. Your parent asks where you are going.
2. Tell three places you plan to go (**Ahora..., luego..., después...**). Also tell what you are going to do in each place.
3. Finally, your parent asks at what time you plan to return home **(regresar).**
4. Be sure to thank your parent for the car.

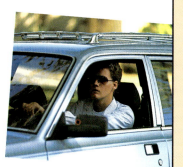

A escribir Someone you hardly know invites you to go to his or her house on Saturday. You don't care to go, but you don't want to be rude.

1. Write a note thanking him or her for the invitation **(la invitación).**
2. Say how busy you will be, telling all the places you need to go on Saturday.
3. Tell what time you need to go to each place.
4. Then tell the things you're going to do in each place.

Presentation
Prior to doing the A conversar and A escribir on this page, you may wish to play the Situaciones listening activities on Cassette 2.3 as a means of helping students organize the material.

Repaso de vocabulario

Repaso de vocabulario
These words and phrases in the Repaso de vocabulario have been taught for the active use in this lesson. They are summarized here as a resource for both students and teacher. The Repaso de vocabulario also serves as a convenient resource for the A conversar and A escribir activities on this page.

LUGARES
el centro
el gimnasio
la habitación
el pueblo
el trabajo

ACTIVIDADES
buscar
ir
ir de vacaciones

ganar
hacer ejercicio
limpiar

COSAS
el concierto
el conjunto
el dinero
el ejercicio
el periódico
el regalo

las vacaciones

OTRAS PALABRAS Y EXPRESIONES
ahora
el / la amigo(a)
con permiso
de
del
después
entonces

favorito(a)
luego
mañana
primero

PREGUNTAS
¿Adónde vas?
¿De quién es / son...?
¿Por qué no vamos al (a la)...
¿Qué vas a hacer?

Learning From Photos
You may want to ask students to look at the photo on page 115 and answer the following question: **¿Cómo es el muchacho?** Ask students what the person in the photo might say about himself.

Lección 3 **115**

For the Native Speaker
Describe your father's car or that of another relative.

Lección 4

Objectives

By the end of this lesson, students will be able to:

1. ask about a friend's routine actions and tell about their own
2. use expressions of time and frequency
3. say that something doesn't matter
4. get a friend's attention

Lesson 4 Resources

1. Workbook, pp. 53–57
2. Vocabulario Transparency 2.4
3. Cassette 2.4
4. Student Tape Manual, pp. 40–43
5. Lesson Quizzes, pp. 37–40
6. Computer Software, Disk 1
7. Video Cassette
8. Estructura Masters 2.4
9. Diversiones Masters 2.4

Bell Ringer Review

Directions to students: Write three things you plan to do after school using **pienso**.

¡A comenzar!

Presentation

A. Lead students through each of the four functions given on page 116, progressing from the English to the Spanish for each function. Then have the students find these words and phrases in the dialogue on page 117.

B. Introduce the Lesson 4 dialogue by reading it aloud, or by playing the cassette version. Ask students to listen for the following information:
   1. What time does David finally arrive at the picnic?

Lección 4

¿Qué pasa?

¡A comenzar!

The following are some of the things you will be learning to do in this lesson.

When you want to . . .	You use . . .
1. inquire about a friend's routine actions	• **-as** on the end of **-ar** verbs; **-es** on the end of **-er** verbs
2. talk about your routine actions	• **-o** on the end of verbs
3. say it doesn't matter	• **No importa.**
4. get a friend's attention	• **Oye.**

Now find examples of the above words and phrases in the following conversation.

Graciela García
20 San Pedro
San Antonio
555-4830

Getting Ready for Lesson 4

You may wish to use one or more of the following suggestions to prepare students for the lesson.

1. Tell students some things you routinely do and don't do. For example:
   Llego temprano a la escuela.
   No llego tarde.
   Como en la cafetería.
   No como en un restaurante.
   En el parque juego tenis.
   No juego béisbol.
   Leo *Newsweek.*
   No leo *Time.*

2. Ask students to recall as many of the things you do and don't do as they can. List infinitives on the board under the words **Sí** and **No**. For example:

Chris finally sees David and wants to know what happened.

CHRIS: **David... ¡Por fin! Son las cinco de la tarde. ¿Qué pasa?**
DAVID: **Pues, nada. ¿Por qué?**
CHRIS: **¿No llegas un poco tarde?**
DAVID: **¿Tarde? ¿A las cinco? ¡Qué va!**
CHRIS: **Bueno, no importa. ¿Juegas béisbol?**
DAVID: **Pues, no juego muy bien pero me gusta.**
CHRIS: **¿Vamos a jugar entonces?**
DAVID: **Bueno. Oye, necesito hablar con Graciela esta noche. ¿Sabes su número de teléfono?**

Actividades preliminares

A Tell which sports you play. Then tell one sport you don't like to play.

Por ejemplo:

> **Juego béisbol y baloncesto pero no me gusta jugar fútbol americano.**

B Answer the following questions about whether you're punctual or not. You might wish to use **a veces** *(sometimes)* to answer.

Por ejemplo:

> **¿Llegas tarde o temprano a la escuela?**
> *A veces llego tarde.*

1. **¿Llegas tarde o temprano a las fiestas?**
2. **¿Llegas tarde o temprano a la clase de español?**
3. **¿Llegas tarde o temprano al cine?**
4. **¿Llegas tarde o temprano a los partidos?**

Lección 4 **117**

---

2. Where does Chris invite David to go?

C. Now ask students to open their books to page 117 and look at the dialogue as you lead them through what is said. For example:
1. **Cuando Chris pregunta: "¿Qué pasa?", ¿qué dice David?**
2. **Cuando Chris dice: "¿No llegas un poco tarde?", ¿qué dice David?**
3. **Cuando Chris dice: "¿Juegas béisbol?", ¿qué dice David?**
4. **¿A qué hora llega David?**
5. **Si el picnic es a las dos, ¿llega tarde David, en tu opinión?**

D. Have students consider their concepts of early and late. Make the following statements and have students answer the question, **¿Llegas tarde o temprano?** for each one.
1. **La fiesta es a las siete. Llegas a las seis.**
2. **La clase es a la una. Llegas a la una y media.**
3. **El partido es a las cuatro de la tarde. Llegas a las cinco.**
4. **La película es a las nueve. Llegas a las ocho y media.**
5. **El baile es a las ocho. Llegas a las nueve.**

Actividades preliminares

Actividad A Answers
Answers will vary, however students should use **juego** in their response.

Actividad B Answers
1. (A veces) Llego tarde (temprano) a las fiestas.
2. (A veces) Llego tarde (temprano) a la clase de español.
3. (A veces) Llego tarde (temprano) al cine.
4. (A veces) Llego tarde (temprano) a los partidos.

Sí	No
llegar	llegar
temprano	tarde
comer en la	comer en un
cafetería	restaurante
jugar tenis	jugar béisbol
leer *Newsweek*	leer *Time*

a. **¿Juegas fútbol (baloncesto, etc.)?**
b. **¿Lees el periódico?**
c. **¿Haces la tarea?**
d. **¿Llegas tarde a casa?**

3. Ask students individually about things they do. Allow them to respond with **Sí** or **No.** For example:

4. Follow up with questions using **llegar:**
a. **Llego a la escuela a las ocho. ¿A qué hora llegas tú?**
b. **Llego a casa las cinco. ¿A qué hora llegas tú?**
   Have students respond with only the time.

Bell Ringer Review

Directions to students: Somebody left the following items on your desk: **radio, discos, calculadora, periódico, guitarra.** Tell to whom they belong.

Presentation

1. Have students open their books to page 118. Ask them to look at this page as you model the question **¿Cuándo?** Ask students to imagine today is October 15.
2. You may want to begin by modeling **hoy** vs. **mañana.** Then model each new word or phrase and have students repeat in unison. Lead students through the words and phrases, pausing to give examples of **esta mañana; esta tarde; esta noche.** For example, **Esta mañana necesito trabajar. Esta tarde, voy al centro comercial a las cuatro. Esta noche voy al partido de fútbol. Etc.** Repeat this presentation for the phrases **(mañana) por la mañana; por la tarde; por la noche.**

When Students Ask

You may wish to give students the following additional vocabulary to allow them to talk about their activities.
**esta semana
el fin de semana
a menudo
la semana que viene**

Vocabulario

¿Cuándo?

15 de octubre

esta mañana — 8 9 10 11 12

esta tarde — 1 2 3 4 5 6 ← Hoy

esta noche — 7 8 9 10 11

16 de octubre

(mañana) por la mañana — 8 9 10 11 12

(mañana) por la tarde — 1 2 3 4 5 6 ← Mañana

(mañana) por la noche — 7 8 9 10 11

Total Physical Response

Getting Ready

On four posters, draw a rising sun, full sun, setting sun, and a half moon. Attach the posters to the chalkboard. Draw curved arrows between the posters. The arrows stand for **por la mañana, por la tarde, por la noche.** When the teacher gives a command, students will go to the chalkboard and stand in front of the appropriate poster.

New Words

asiste	asistan
sal	lleguen
regresen	salgan

Actividades

A **Hoy y mañana.** Tell three things you want, plan, or need to do today. Then tell the same for tomorrow.

Por ejemplo:

> Hoy quiero (pienso, necesito)... Mañana...

B **¿Qué vas a hacer?** Tell two things you are going to do today for each of the time categories below.

esta mañana   **esta tarde**   **esta noche**

Por ejemplo:

> **esta mañana**
> *Esta mañana voy a ir a la biblioteca.*

C **¿Cuándo?** Tell whether you do the following activities **por la mañana, por la tarde,** or **por la noche.**

Por ejemplo:

> Nado...
> *Nado por la tarde.*

1. Hago la tarea...
2. Hago ejercicio...
3. Juego béisbol (fútbol, etc.)...
4. Llego a la escuela...
5. Estudio español...
6. Estudio matemáticas...
7. Como en la cafetería...
8. Hablo por teléfono...
9. Veo películas...
10. Limpio la habitación...
11. Voy al concierto...

Actividades

Actividad A Answers
Answers will vary but may include the following: **Hoy pienso estudiar química. Mañana voy a descansar y nadar.** For all responses, students should use either **quiero, pienso,** or **necesito.**

Actividades B and C Answers
Answers will vary.

TPR 1

(Call on pairs of students.)
Asistan al concierto.
Vayan al centro.
Caminen al gimansio esta tarde.
Lleguen temprano a la playa.
Regresen de la escuela a las cuatro.
Vayan a jugar fútbol.
Salgan de la biblioteca a las 7.
Regresen del cine por la tarde.

TPR 2

Ve al cine esta noche.
Ve al partido de fútbol.
Compra algo en el centro.
Sal de la escuela temprano.
Regresa del restaurante tarde.
Ve al parque a montar a caballo.
Asiste a la clase de español.

Actividad D Answers

1. (1) ¿Qué haces por la mañana?
(2) Necesito (Voy a, Quiero, Pienso) correr. (3) Entonces, vas al parque (al estadio, al gimnasio), ¿no?
2. ¿ ... luego?/ ... leer revistas / ... a la biblioteca (a casa)...?
3. ¿ ... por la tarde? / ... nadar / ... a la playa (a la piscina)...?
4. ¿ ... después? / ... jugar baloncesto / ... al gimnasio...?
5. ¿ ... entonces? / ... comprar algo / ... al centro comercial (a la tienda)...?
6. ¿ ... por la noche?/ ... comer algo / ... al restaurante (a casa)...?
7. ¿ ... luego? / ... ver una película / ... al cine...?

Class Management

You may wish to do Actividad D as a whole class activity initially. The teacher takes the role of Student A, calling on individual students to answer for Student B. You may then want to do Actividad D again, this time in a paired group format.

Learning From Photos

1. You may want students to use the three photos on page 120 as cues for conversation. For example, ask students to role-play a person in the photos. How would that person say what they were going to do **por la mañana, por la tarde, por la noche?**
2. Have students describe the people shown in each photo by asking, **¿Cómo son los muchachos; las muchachas?** Etc.

Reteaching

Using the Vocabulario on page 118, or Vocabulario Transparency 2.4, ask individual students to say where they are going **esta mañana; esta tarde; esta noche.** Begin by asking, **¿Adónde vas...?**

D **¿Qué haces hoy?** It's Saturday and you have many plans for the day. Your partner asks about your plans for the following times. Then he or she guesses where you will go.

Por ejemplo:

ahora / hacer ejercicio

ESTUDIANTE A

(1) ¿Qué haces ahora?

(3) Entonces, vas al gimnasio, ¿no?

1. por la mañana / correr
2. luego / leer revistas
3. por la tarde / nadar
4. después / jugar baloncesto
5. entonces / comprar algo
6. por la noche / comer algo
7. luego / ver una película

ESTUDIANTE B

(2) Quiero (Voy a, Necesito, Pienso) hacer ejercicio.

Cooperative Learning

Write different activities on separate slips of paper. Put them in an envelope. Give each team an envelope containing these slips. Each team will distribute the activities in the envelope among the members of the team. Each member takes turns reading the strips out loud. The team must then decide the sequence of the activities according to **por la mañana; por la tarde; por la noche.** With the help of the team members, the team's recorder writes the list in the proper sequence.

CULTURA VIVA 1

Puntualidad

All cultures have different ideas of late and early. How late you can be without being considered rude depends on the activity. In David's culture, it is not considered poor manners to arrive two or three hours after the announced time for a party.

Actividad

How late can you be to the following events in the United States without being impolite? (**¿Cinco minutos, quince minutos, media hora, una hora?**)

1. **una fiesta**
2. **una cita** (appointment)
3. **una clase**
4. **un partido**
5. **una película**

GRAN FIESTA
DE FIN DE AÑO
1990 - 1991
CON
Los Ramblers

LUNES 31 DE DICIEMBRE
Hora: 7:00 pm. Valor: $35.00

Local: Saint John Parish Hall

Cupo Limitado

Información: 826-6700 • 252-0859

*Mariano Santana Quiñones
Lilia Rodríguez de Santana
tienen el honor de invitarle
a la boda de su hija
Olga Lilia Santana
con
Carlos Adalberto Román
el sábado, veintitrés de junio
a las dos y media de la tarde
Capilla de San Judas Tadeo
130 S. San Augustine
San Antonio, Texas*

Cultura viva 1

Presentation

Read the Cultura viva on this page. You may want to refer students to the Lesson 4 dialogue on page 117. Why does David say, **¿Tarde? ¿A las cinco? ¡Qué va!**?

Did you Know?

When you are invited to a party at an Hispanic home, you are never expected to arrive at the time given. It is acceptable to be more than an hour late in arriving. On the other hand, it is not considered polite to arrive before the time mentioned in the invitation. In other words, it is better to arrive late than to arrive early. In general, it is common to drop in on friends without calling ahead of time, or to call an hour or so before you arrive at their house.

Critical Thinking Activity

When is it critical to arrive on time for an event? When is it permissible to be late?

Actividad Answers

Answers will vary.

Learning From Realia

You may wish to ask students the following questions about the realia on page 121.
1. What do you think this invitation is for? What words help you to determine this? At what time is the event? What will be Olga Lilia Santana's complete name after she is married?
2. What is the ticket for? Where is the event going to take place? What telephone numbers would you call for more information?

Bell Ringer Review

Directions to students: Turn a piece of notebook paper sideways, then write these three headings across the top of your paper, leaving space between each word: **siempre, a veces, nunca.** Read the statements below and decide how often you do each. Write each one in the appropriate column.

Soy puntual. Esquío en las montañas. Juego tenis. Como en la cafetería. Limpio la casa. Manejo un coche. Veo películas de terror. Escucho música clásica. Soy paciente. Compro regalos. Monto a caballo. Soy generoso(a). Hago la tarea. Gano mucho dinero.

Structure Focus

In Estructura 1 of this lesson, the presentation of **-ar** and **-er** verbs is limited to the **yo** form. Students should begin to associate the **-o** ending with self description.

The **tú** forms of **-ar** and **-er** verbs are presented in Estructura 2 of this lesson. Third person singular and plural forms are presented in Lesson 5; and the **nosotros** forms are presented in Lesson 6.

Presentation

Lead students through steps 1–4 on page 122. Explain to students that there are several English equivalents of the present tense. For example, **juego** can mean many things according to context: I play, I'm playing, I do play, I'm playing (tomorrow).

Estructura 1

How to Talk about Routines   *"Yo" form of* **-ar** *and* **-er** *verbs*

1. To say that you generally or typically do something, replace the **-ar** or **-er** ending of most infinitives with **-o**. The **-o** indicates "I" **(yo)**.

trabajar	**Trabajo mucho en las clases.**
comer	**Como en la cafetería con mis amigos.**

2. Some verbs are formed differently.

ver	veo	**Veo la tele por la noche.**
hacer	hago	**No hago nada.**
saber	sé	**Ya sé esquiar.**
ir	voy	**No voy a la cafetería hoy.**
ser	soy	**Soy bastante alta.**
dar	doy	**Doy un paseo por el campo.**

3. Other verbs are also formed differently. The part of the verb that is left when you remove **-ar** or **-er,** (that is, the "stem" of the verb) changes spelling from **e** to **ie** (as in **querer** and **pensar**) or **u** to **ue** (as in **jugar**). These are called "stem-changing verbs."

querer	quiero	**Quiero ir al cine.**
pensar	pienso	**No pienso hacer nada**
jugar	juego	**Juego tenis por la tarde.**

In the future, when you see stem-changing verbs, the infinitive will be followed by the letters that indicate the stem change.

pensar (ie)	entender (ie)
jugar (ue)	querer (ie)

4. To talk about when you do various activities, you may use the words **siempre** *(always)*, **a veces** *(sometimes)*, and **nunca** *(never)*.

> **Siempre hago mi tarea por la noche.**
> **A veces me gusta escuchar música cuando estudio.**
> **Nunca estudio en la biblioteca.**

122   CAPÍTULO 2

Cooperative Learning

Using the chart below, have each team member graph the Actividad B on page 123. Each member will share his or her list. The recorder for the team will keep track. Then the team will draw a graph to depict their activities. (see below)

S = **siempre**
AV = **a veces**
N = **nunca**

Actividades

A **¿Sí o no?** Which of the following things do you do? Which don't you do?

Por ejemplo:

> Comprar muchos discos.
> *(No) Compro muchos discos.*

1. descansar por la noche
2. jugar fútbol
3. escuchar música clásica
4. hablar español en casa
5. ganar dinero
6. leer el periódico
7. hacer ejercicio
8. ver películas de terror
9. dar paseos
10. hacer la tarea por la tarde

B **Autobiografía.** Tell how often you do each of the activities below, using **siempre, a veces,** or **nunca.**

Por ejemplo:

> cantar
> *A veces canto.*

1. nadar
2. bailar
3. limpiar mi habitación
4. escuchar música
5. jugar béisbol
6. ir al cine

C **Cuando voy al centro.** Tell what you do when you go to the following places.

Por ejemplo:

> al centro
> *Cuando voy al centro compro regalos.*

1. a la escuela
2. a casa
3. al campo
4. a la playa
5. a la biblioteca
6. al gimnasio
7. a la casa de mi amigo (amiga)

D **Me gusta pero...** Name six things you like to do but don't do very often.

Por ejemplo:

> nadar
> *Me gusta nadar pero no nado mucho.*

Actividades

Actividad A Answers
1. (No) Descanso...
2. (No) Juego...
3. (No) Escucho...
4. (No) Hablo...
5. (No) Gano...
6. (No) Leo...
7. (No) Hago...
8. (No) Veo...
9. (No) Doy...
10. (No) Hago...

Actividad B Answers
Answers will vary, however students should always use **siempre, a veces,** or **nunca** in their response.

Actividad C Answers
1. Cuando voy a la escuela...
2. Cuando voy a casa...
3. Cuando voy al campo...
4. Cuando voy a la playa...
5. Cuando voy a la biblioteca...
6. Cuando voy al gimnasio...
7. Cuando voy a la casa de mi amigo(a)...

Actividad D Answers
Answers will vary, however each response should include **Me gusta... pero no... mucho.**

Additional Practice
After doing Actividades A, B, C, and D, you may wish to reinforce the lesson by doing the following activities:

1. Have students tell what they do at various times during a school day. For example:
   a. a las diez de la mañana
   b. a las dos de la tarde
   c. a las cuatro de la tarde
   d. a las ocho de la noche
2. Ask students to list in order things they are doing tomorrow: **Primero voy a la escuela. Luego juego tenis con mis amigos. Entonces _____.**

Reteaching
Ask students how they would say they do the following: **trabajar en casa; comer en la cafetería; ver la tele; hacer ejercicio; saber sacar fotos; ir a la playa; dar un paseo.**

123

Cultura viva 2

Presentation

A. Read the Cultura viva on this page. You may wish to lead students through the list of baseball teams. Ask students how many teams they can identify.

B. To reinforce the presentation, you may want to bring in baseball cards of Hispanic baseball stars who are playing or have played in the major leagues.

Did You Know?

Although soccer is the dominant sport in Spanish-speaking countries, baseball enjoys a large following, especially in the Caribbean, Venezuela, Mexico, and some Central American countries. Many Hispanic players are drafted by the major leagues in the United States. Many major league stars have come from Latin America, including Mexico's Fernando Valenzuela, the Dominican Republic's Pedro Guerrero, Panama's Rod Carew, and the late Roberto Clemente from Puerto Rico.

Critical Thinking Activity

Can you think of some reasons why baseball players from Mexico and the Caribbean nations have become stars in the major leagues in the United States?

Actividad Answers

Answers will vary.

El béisbol

At the picnic, Chris asks David if he plays baseball. Although baseball is not commonly played in many Spanish-speaking countries, it is the most popular sport in the Caribbean nations and players of Hispanic descent have made major contributions to the sport.

La República Dominicana, for example, has contributed more players to U.S. teams than any other country of its size in the world. When the World Series is over in the United States, baseball season begins in the Caribbean, and Latin American players on U.S. teams return to their home countries for the winter baseball season. A popular gift for children there is **el bate, el guante y la pelota** (bat, glove, and ball).

Actividad

On the right are the U.S. major league teams as they are known in Spanish. Which is your favorite baseball team? Describe it.

Por ejemplo:

> Mi equipo favorito: los Dodgers de Los Ángeles. Son formidables.

LIGA AMERICANA

División del este	División del oeste
Orioles de Baltimore	Ángeles de California
Medias Rojas de Boston	Medias Blancas de Chicago
Indios de Cleveland	Reales de Kansas City
Tigres de Detroit	Mellizos de Minnesota
Cerveceros de Milwaukee	Atléticos de Oakland
Yanquis de Nueva York	Marineros de Seattle
Azulejos de Toronto	Rangers de Texas

LIGA NACIONAL

División del este	División del oeste
Cachorros de Chicago	Bravos de Atlanta
Expos de Montreal	Rojos de Cincinnati
Mets de Nueva York	Astros de Houston
Filis de Filadelfia	Dodgers de Los Ángeles
Piratas de Pittsburgh	Padres de San Diego
Cardenales de San Luis	Gigantes de San Francisco

Pronunciation

A. You may wish to play the recorded version of these pronunciation lines, located at the end of Cassette 2.4. You may also wish to write the following lines on the chalkboard or an overhead transparency and ask your students to copy them into their notebook:
Medias Rojas y Reales,
Medias Blancas, Cardenales, Cerveceros y Mellizos son mis equipos favoritos.

B. Have students repeat words and phrases individually and in unison. You may wish to focus on the /d/ sound as in **Medias.**

Estructura 2

How to Ask about a Friend's Routine

"Tú" forms of -ar and -er verbs

1. To ask a friend what he or she does or is currently doing, replace the **-ar** or **-er** ending of the infinitive with either **-as** (for infinitives ending in **-ar**) or **-es** (for infinitives ending in **-er**). The **-as** and **-es** endings indicate "you" when speaking to someone your age or a relative.

   Oye, ¿tocas la guitarra?　　**No, toco el saxofón.**
   ¿Qué lees, Miguel?　　**Leo una revista.**

2. You have seen that **ser** and **ir** are formed differently.

   Eres David Vargas, ¿no?
   ¿Adónde vas esta noche?

3. Remeber that certain verbs have a spelling change in the part of the verb that remains when you remove **-ar** and **-er** (the "stem" of the verb).

pensar	piensas	**¿Qué piensas hacer hoy?**
querer	quieres	**¿Quieres practicar deportes?**
jugar	juegas	**¿Juegas tenis?**

4. When you want to ask a friend what he or she is doing, say **¿Qué haces?**

   ¿Qué haces?　　**Pues, no hago nada.**

For the Native Speaker

1. Write a paragraph of about 75 words describing a sport that is played in your native country, (or a Spanish-speaking country) but not in the U.S.

2. Prepare a report about your favorite sport star. Present it in front of the class.

Structure Teaching Resources
1. Workbook, pp. 56–57
2. Cassette 2.4
3. Student Tape Manual, p. 41
4. Estructura Masters 2.4
5. Lesson Quizzes, pp. 39–40

Bell Ringer Review

Directions to students: Copy these sentencês and put the verbs into their proper places.
veo, hago, soy, sé, voy

1. _____ bastante baja.
2. Siempre _____ mis tareas por la noche.
3. No _____ al concierto el sábado.
4. Esta noche _____ mi programa favorito.
5. Ya _____ montar en bicicleta.

Structure Focus
In Estructura 2 of this lesson, the presentation of **-ar** and **-er** verbs is limited to the **tú** form. Third person singular and plural forms are presented in Lesson 5; and the **nosotros** forms are presented in Lesson 6.

Presentation

A. Lead students through steps 1–4 on page 125. You may want to explain to students that **das, haces,** and **sabes** are regular in form.

B. You may want to follow up the presentation on page 125 by asking students individually whether or not they do the following things. They may respond simply with **Sí** or **No.**
   1. **¿Bailas?**
   2. **¿Estudias en la biblioteca a veces?**
   3. **¿Ves la tele por la tarde o por la noche?**

4. ¿Cocinas esta noche?
5. ¿Practicas español en casa?
6. ¿Juegas deportes?
7. ¿Hablas por teléfono por la noche?
8. ¿Comes en el restaurante a veces?
9. ¿Ves películas?
10. ¿Haces la tarea por la tarde o por la noche?

Actividades

Actividad A Answers
1. ¿Cantas? / Sí, canto. (No, no canto).
2. ¿Practicas...? / Sí, (No, no) practico...
3. ¿Bailas? / Sí, (No, no) bailo...
4. ¿Corres? / Sí, (No, no) corro...
5. ¿Dibujas? / Sí, (No, no) dibujo...
6. ¿Lees...? / Sí, (No, no) leo...
7. ¿Estudias...? / Sí, (No, no) estudio...
8. ¿Ves...? / Sí, (No, no) veo...
9. ¿Juegas...? / Sí, (No, no) juego...
10. ¿Haces...? / Sí, (No, no) hago...

Actividad B Answers
Answers will vary but may include the following:
1. ¿Qué haces en casa? En casa descanso.
2. ¿ ... En el cine veo películas.
3. ¿ ... En la clase de español hablo español.
4. ¿ ... En el gimnasio juego deportes.
5. ¿ ... En el centro comercial hablo con amigos.
6. ¿ ... En la playa nado.
7. ¿ ... En el campo monto a caballo.
8. ¿ ... En la biblioteca leo libros y revistas.

Actividad C Answers
Answers will vary.

Actividades

A **¿Sí o no?** Ask a classmate if he or she does the following activities.

Por ejemplo:

cocinar

ESTUDIANTE A	ESTUDIANTE B
¿Cocinas?	Sí, cocino. (No, no cocino).

1. cantar
2. practicar deportes
3. bailar
4. correr
5. dibujar
6. leer muchas revistas

7. estudiar álgebra
8. ver muchas películas
9. jugar (tenis, béisbol, fútbol, etc.)
10. hacer ejercicio

B **Por todas partes.** Ask a classmate what he or she does at the following places.

Por ejemplo:

en el parque

ESTUDIANTE A	ESTUDIANTE B
¿Qué haces en el parque?	En el parque corro.

1. en casa
2. en el cine
3. en la clase de español
4. en el gimnasio

5. en el centro comercial
6. en la playa
7. en el campo
8. en la biblioteca

C **Quiero saber.** Write a list of questions to ask a classmate about himself or herself using the following question words.

Por ejemplo:

¿qué?
¿Qué haces por la noche? (¿Qué lees? ¿Qué estudias? etc.)

1. ¿qué?
2. ¿cuándo?
3. ¿a qué hora?
4. ¿adónde?

126   CAPÍTULO 2

Finalmente

Finalmente

Situaciones

A conversar Converse with a classmate using the following cues.

1. Greet your partner and ask what sports he or she plays.
2. Invite your partner to an appropriate sports event tomorrow night. Your partner says he or she wants to go, but mentions all the things he or she needs to do.
3. Say something terrific about the team.
4. Your partner accepts the invitation and tells you what time he or she needs to return home **(regresar).**

A escribir An exchange student from Chile, Antonio, is going to spend his first weekend in the U.S. at your house. He writes to you, asking how you spend your weekends. Write back telling him all the things you usually do and places you usually go on Saturdays **(los sábados)** and Sundays **(los domingos).** Divide your activities into the categories of morning, afternoon, and evening. Start your letter **"Estimado Antonio,"** and end with **"Tu amigo(a),"** and your name.

Repaso de vocabulario

PREGUNTA
¿Cuándo?
¿Qué haces?

EXPRESIONES DE TIEMPO
a veces
esta mañana
esta noche
esta tarde
hoy
nunca

por la mañana
por la noche
por la tarde
siempre
tarde
temprano

ACTIVIDAD
llegar (a)

OTRAS EXPRESIONES
No importa.
oye

Lección 4 **127**

Situaciones

Lesson 4 Evaluation
The A conversar and A escribir situations on this page are designed to give students the opportunity to use as many language functions as possible listed on page 116 of this lesson. The A conversar and A escribir are also intended to show how well students are able to meet the lesson objectives, also listed on page 116.

Presentation

Prior to doing the A conversar and A escribir on this page, you may wish to play the Situaciones listening activities on Cassette 2.4 as a means of helping students organize the material.

Repaso de vocabulario

These words and phrases in the Repaso de vocabulario have been taught for productive use in this lesson. They are summarized here as a resource for both students and teacher. The Repaso de vocabulario also serves as a convenient resource for the A conversar and A escribir activities on this page. It also gives the teacher a source for writing either additional practice or evaluation activities such as quizzes and tests in addition to those provided by the publisher.

Learning From Photos

You may want to ask your students to think of five questions in Spanish they would ask the person in the photo on page 127. Then ask students how this person might answer their questions.

Lección 5

Objectives

By the end of this lesson, students will be able to:

1. report or ask about routine actions of one or more people
2. ask if what they've said is correct
3. suggest that a friend do something
4. ask why

Lesson 5 Resources
1. Workbook, pp. 58–63
2. Vocabulario Transparencies 2.5
3. Cassette 2.5
4. Student Tape Manual, pp. 44–48
5. Lesson Quizzes, pp. 41–44
6. Computer Software, Disk 1
7. Video Cassette
8. Estructura Masters 2.5
9. Diversiones Masters 2.5

Bell Ringer Review

Directions to students: You are the reporter for the sports section of your hometown newspaper. You are going to interview your favorite player from your favorite baseball team. Write down lots of questions to ask him about what he does in his spare time. Use the **tú** form in your questions.

¡A comenzar!

Presentation

A. Lead students through each of the five functions given on page 128, progressing from the English to the Spanish for each function. Then have the students find these words and phrases in the dialogue on page 129.

Lección 5

El Día de la Raza

¡A comenzar!

The following are some of the things you will be learning to do in this lesson.

When you want to . . .	You use . . .
1. report or ask about routine actions of someone else	• -a on the end of -ar verbs -e on the end of -er verbs
2. report or ask about routine actions of others	• -an on the end of -ar verbs -en on the end of -er verbs
3. ask if what you've said is correct	• ¿verdad?
4. ask why	• ¿Por qué?
5. suggest that a friend do something	• ¿Por qué no + activity?

Now find examples of the above words and phrases in the following conversation.

Getting Ready for Lesson 5

You may wish to use the following suggestions to prepare students for the lesson:

1. Talk to the class about the ways we celebrate holidays in the U.S., focusing on a recent or upcoming holiday. Some possibilities are Columbus Day **(el Día de la Raza)**, Veteran's Day **(el Día de los Veteranos)**, Thanksgiving **(el Día de Acción de Gracias)**, Christmas **(la Navidad)**, or some other holiday or celebration that is special in your area. For example: **Mañana es el Día de los Veteranos. ¿Qué hacemos este día? Pues, no vamos a la escuela. Practicamos deportes con los amigos, visitamos a la familia o vemos una película. En las ciudades hay desfiles por la tarde: los soldados en uniforme y la gente de la ciudad**

David and Graciela are talking on the way home from school.

DAVID: **Oye, Graciela, el domingo celebran el Día de la Raza aquí en San Antonio, ¿verdad?**

GRACIELA: **Sí, ¿por qué?**

DAVID: **Pues, ¿qué hacen?**

GRACIELA: **Bueno, depende. Muchas personas visitan a los amigos o hacen un picnic.**

DAVID: **Y tú, ¿qué haces?**

GRACIELA: **Pues, en mi casa mi mamá prepara una comida especial. ¿Quieres venir?**

DAVID: **Gracias, pero por la tarde voy con Chris al parque a jugar fútbol.**

GRACIELA: **Bueno, primero van al parque, pero después, ¿por qué no celebras el día en mi casa con mi familia? ¿Quieres?**

DAVID: **¡Qué buena idea! Gracias.**

Actividades preliminares

A Do people in your area do the following things to celebrate Thanksgiving? Answer **sí** or **no**.

1. **Celebran el día en casa.**
2. **Hacen un picnic.**
3. **Van al restaurante por la noche.**
4. **Comen con la familia.**
5. **Ven la tele por la tarde.**
6. **Ven una película por la mañana.**

B How well do you know your classmates? Make guesses about what three classmates like to do, using **¿verdad?** to ask if you're right.

Por ejemplo:

ESTUDIANTE A

Amy, te gusta cocinar, ¿verdad?

ESTUDIANTE B

Sí, es verdad. (No, ¡qué va!)

Lección 5 **129**

B. Introduce the Lesson 5 dialogue by reading it aloud, or by playing the cassette version. Have students listen to the dialogue twice to see how many activities and places they can hear being discussed.

C. Now ask students to open their books to page 129. Lead students through what is said. For example,

1. ¿Qué día celebran?
2. ¿Qué hacen para celebrar el día?
3. Graciela y su familia preparan una comida especial. ¿Qué hacen Chris y David?
4. ¿Qué hacen Graciela y David el Día de la Raza?

Actividades preliminares

Actividad A Answers
Students will answer **sí** or **no** to all items.

Actividad B Answers
Answers will vary, however students should use **¿verdad?** with each question they ask.

Class Management
Actividad B may be done as a whole class activity, if preferred. The teacher takes the role of Student A, calling on individual students to answer each time.

Additional Practice
After doing Actividad B on page 129, you may wish to reinforce the learning with the following: Invite a classmate to do four things. If your classmate refuses an invitation, ask him or her for a reason. For example:
(1) **¿Por qué no vamos al gimnasio?**
(2) **No, gracias**
(3) **¿Por qué?**
(4) **Necesito trabajar (Quiero ir a la casa de David, etc.).**

---

pasan por las calles, y escuchamos la música de las bandas, etc.
You may wish to have students refer to the photos of festivals on page 133 while you describe festival celebrations.

2. Choose a holiday and ask for a show of hands regarding activities: **¿Qué hacen ustedes?**
   a ¿Visitan a los does amigos?
   b. ¿Van a bailes?
   c. ¿Hacen un picnic?
   d. ¿Celebran en casa?
   e. ¿Ven el desfile?
   f. ¿Comen demasiado?, etc.

Bell Ringer Review

Directions to students: From the list below choose five activities and say that you like to do them, but you don't do them very often.

jugar tenis
ver películas
montar a caballo
hablar por teléfono
montar en bicicleta
leer el periódico
comer en restaurantes
bailar
esquiar
ver la tele
estudiar
cocinar

Presentation

1. Have students open their books to pages 130 and 131. Ask them to look at these pages as you model the foods in each group. Begin with the phrase, **Para el desayuno, ¿qué comidas te gustan?** Then model each food item. Have students repeat each item in unison.
2. Say whether or not you like each food in the Vocabulario. For example, **Me gusta el cereal. Connie, ¿te gusta el cereal? Etc.**

Actividades

Actividad A Answers
Answers will vary.

130

Vocabulario

Para el desayuno, ¿qué comidas te gustan?   ¿Y para el almuerzo?

las papas fritas
el cereal
la mantequilla
la hamburguesa
la ensalada de lechuga y tomate
la mermelada
los huevos
el pan tostado
el sandwich de jamón y queso

Actividades

A **¿Te gusta?** Tell five things you like to eat or drink. Then tell five you don't like.

Por ejemplo:

> Me gusta el pollo, la ensalada...
> No me gusta el café...

B **¿Qué sabes preparar?** Tell three things you know how to make. Then tell two things you'd like to learn how to (**aprender a**) make.

Por ejemplo:

> Sé preparar ensaladas.
> Quiero aprender a preparar pasteles.

130 CAPÍTULO 2

Total Physical Response

Getting Ready
Bring to class real, plastic, or illustrations of food items in the Vocabulario. Arrange these on a table by food groups.

New Words
come   coman
compra   compren
tomen   cubran

TPR 1

(Call on two students.)
Toquen el cereal.
Señalen el pan tostado.
Coman la hamburguesa.
Cubran la fruta.
Tomen un refresco.
Muéstrenme el pescado.
Apunten a los pasteles.
Compren papas fritas.

Y ¿qué vas a preparar para la cena?

la sopa de legumbres

el pollo

la carne

el arroz con frijoles

el pescado

Para el postre me gusta(n)...

los pasteles

el helado

la fruta

¿Qué bebidas te gustan?

la gaseosa

la leche   el té   el jugo   el agua   el café   el refresco

C **¿Adónde vamos?** Suggest to a classmate a good place to get the following foods or drinks in your area. Your classmate agrees or disagrees.

Por ejemplo:

pizza

ESTUDIANTE A

Si quieres comer pizza, ¿por qué no vamos a Tony's?

ESTUDIANTE B

Buena idea. (No, vamos a Sal's).

1. desayuno
2. ensaladas
3. hamburguesas
4. sandwiches
5. pollo
6. helado
7. papas fritas
8. pasteles
9. pescado

Tomen café.
(Repeat with individual students and interchange the commands with different foods.)
Toma té.   Compra fruta.   Come pollo.

TPR 2

(Hand out all the food items so that each student has one.)
Levántense si tienen comida para el desayuno.
Levanten las manos si tienen comida para el almuerzo.
Levanten la mano derecha si tienen comida para la cena.
Levanten la mano izquierda si tienen bebidas.
Sonrían si tienen postres.
Las personas con pan tostado y cereal, párense.

D **Recomendaciones.** Working in pairs or small groups, rate four items served at a local eating place. It could be a restaurant, pizza parlor, fast food chain, or even the school cafeteria. Rank the items using the following scale.

5 **exquisito:**
4 **delicioso:**
3 **bueno:**
2 **tolerable:**
1 **malo:**
0 **horrible:**

Share your ratings with the class.

Por ejemplo:

> En el restaurante Olympia las ensaladas son exquisitas (5). Las hamburguesas son deliciosas (4). Los postres son buenos (3). Las papas fritas son tolerables (2). ...Entonces, el total es 14.

E **El picnic.** Chris and Héctor are discussing plans for another picnic. Chris has a list of what everyone is supposed to do. First, tell what he puts down for himself. Then fill in the rest of the list.

CHRIS: **A ver, vas a comprar los refrescos, ¿verdad? Jim compra la pizza y Graciela lleva el helado.**

HÉCTOR: **Bueno. Y ¿quién cocina?**

CHRIS: **Mi mamá. Y Mariví prepara el pollo frito.**

HÉCTOR: **Y tú, ¿qué haces?**

CHRIS: **¿Yo? Pues, nada. Descanso.**

Por ejemplo:

> **Héctor**
> *Comprar los refrescos.*

1. yo
2. Jim
3. Graciela
4. Mamá
5. Mariví

Más recomendado

	COMA MAS	COMA MENOS
Carnes	Pescado, Pollo o pavo (sin pellejo)	Carne roja (res, p ternera) Vísceras tocino, salchicha
Huevos	Claras o sustitutos de huevos sin colesterol	Yemas
Productos Lácteos	Leche descremada (non-fat), Yogurt descremado, Queso cottage descremado, Quesos descremados, Nieves	Leche entera, condensada, ev Yogurt entero Crema Queso cottage, Quesos entero Helados
Frutas y Verduras	Frescas	Fritas o con cre
Panes y Cereales	Cereales y panes de trigo, avena, centeno, arroz integral, Pastas	Pasteles y gall Panes en los q huevo es un i importante
Grasas	No saturadas (aceites vegetales de maíz, de soya, de ajonjolí), Aderezos sin grasas o con grasas no saturadas, Margarina con grasas no saturadas	Saturadas (ac coco, de palm no, de grasa, Aderezos de ladas con ye (mayonesa) Mantequilla

✓ Se recomienda una dieta con un máximo de 300 mg de coleste
✗ Una yema de huevo contiene 274 mg. de colesterol.

Festivales

One of the most important Hispanic holidays is October 12, **El Día de la Raza.** On this date, Spanish-speaking people around the world celebrate the arrival of Spaniards in the Americas (that is, South, Central, and North America) and the beginning of a new American people.

People in San Antonio celebrate many other occasions that honor its Mexican-American community and its rich Mexican heritage. The following are major festivals that draw tourists from around the country.

marzo	**Paseo de marzo** honoring its Mexican-American veterans
abril	**Fiesta San Antonio:** nine days of parades, festivals, sporting events, band concerts, and art shows
mayo	**Cinco de mayo:** Mexico's defeat of French invasion
junio	**Fiesta Noche del Río:** Hispanic musical revue
julio	Hispanic State Fair: performing artists from Texas and Mexico
agosto	**Semana de las Misiones,** special events celebrating the history of the missions
septiembre	**La Feria del Río** and **Diez y seis de septiembre:** Mexican independence
diciembre	Christmas Mexican-style: **Las posadas,** a musical enactment of the story of Mary's and Joseph's search for shelter in Bethlehem, and **Fiesta de las Luminarias,** a festival of lights
enero	**Los Pastores,** a Christmas miracle play

Actividad

Tell what month you want to go to San Antonio and why.

Por ejemplo:

> Quiero ir en marzo porque quiero ver el Paseo de marzo.

Lección 5 **133**

Cultura viva 1

Presentation

Read the Cultura viva on this page. You may want to ask students what holiday is celebrated in the U.S. on or about October 12. Lead students through the festivals listed on this page.

Did You Know?

Three additional holidays are celebrated by many Mexican/Hispanics. They are:
1. **10 de mayo, el Día de las Madres.**
2. **2 de noviembre, el Día de los Muertos** (All Soul's Day), honoring the memories of departed family members. Elaborate picnics are held in the cemeteries, special offerings are given, special altars are made, and special breads and candies in the shape of skulls and skeletons are prepared.
3. **6 de enero, el Día de los Reyes Magos** (The Epiphany). Special cakes are prepared. Children place food under their bed as treats for the Three Wise Men's camels. The following morning when they awake they receive their gifts left by the Wise Men.

Critical Thinking Activity

Compare and contrast the celebration and meaning of **el Día de la Raza** with the Columbus Day holiday in the U.S.

Actividad Answers

Answers will vary, however students should give a reason with their response using **porque.**

Learning From Photos

You may want to ask students to tell in what month the top photo was taken. On what occasions might the other two photos have been taken?

Pronunciation

A. You may wish to play the recorded version of these pronunciation lines, located at the end of Cassette 2.5. You may also wish to write this verse on the board and have students copy it into their notebook:
**A Castilla y a León
nuevo mundo dio Colón.**

B. Have students repeat words and phrases individually and in unison. You may wish to focus on all of the vowel sounds in this verse.

For the Native Speaker

Describe your family celebration of Christmas, Cinco de mayo, or some other important holiday in at least 100 words.

Bell Ringer Review

Directions to students: You have invited a friend over for dinner tonight. You are aware that he is trying to lose weight. Write down what you will serve that will be healthy for both of you. Then draw a picture of your table as you will set it.

Structure Focus

In Estructura 1 of this lesson, the presentation of -**ar** and -**er** verbs is limited to the third person singular. Third person plural forms are presented in Estructura 2 of this lesson. The **yo** and **tú** forms of -**ar** and -**er** verbs were presented in Lesson 4. The **nosotros** forms will be presented in Lesson 6.

Presentation

A. Lead students through steps 1–3 on page 134. For step 1 you may want to write examples of -**ar** and -**er** verbs on the chalkboard to show students how to drop the endings and replace them with the third person endings.

B. In order to familiarize students with the third person forms, you may wish to ask for a show of hands in response to the following questions:
1. ¿Quién monta a caballo?
2. ¿Quién canta bien?
3. ¿Quíen toca el piano?
4. ¿Quién trabaja demasiado?
5. ¿Quién come mucho?
6. ¿Quién ve películas de terror?
7. ¿Quién llega tarde a clases?
8. ¿Quién corre todos los días?
9. ¿Quién lee revistas de deportes? Etc.

Estructura 1

How to Report on the Routine Actions of Someone Else *Third person singular, -ar and -er verbs*

You have learned how to say what you do, and to tell or ask a friend what he or she does.

> **A veces corro en la playa. Nado un poco también.**
> **Y después de nadar, ¿qué haces?**

1. To tell what someone else does or is doing, replace the -**ar** ending with -**a**. Replace the -**er** ending with -**e**. The endings -**a** and -**e** indicate "he," "she," or "it."

bailar	Graciela baila bien.
cantar	También canta muy bien.
hacer	¿Qué hace Chris?
comer	Come con Graciela en la cafetería.

2. The following verbs are formed differently.

| ser | es | David es simpático. |
| ir | va | ¿Adónde va Mariví? |

3. Remember that the following verbs have changes in their stems.

pensar	piensa	¿Qué piensa hacer hoy Graciela?
querer	quiere	Quiere ir al cine.
jugar	juega	Entonces, ¿no juega tenis?

Actividades

A **Un día muy ocupado.** David has planned the following for tomorrow. Write down what he does at the following times: **por la mañana, por la tarde, por la noche.**

Por ejemplo:

> por la mañana
> *Por la mañana, primero nada. Luego... Después...*

Pienso nadar a las ocho de la mañana, desayunar a las nueve y media, estudiar a las diez, dar un paseo con Graciela a la una de la tarde, jugar baloncesto con los muchachos a las dos y media, y descansar a las cuatro. A las seis de la tarde voy a comprar discos para la fiesta. A las siete, quiero ir a casa a ver el partido de fútbol con Chris. Después del partido pienso comer algo y leer un poco.

B **Un sábado típico.** Tell a classmate what you do on a typical Saturday in the order you do each activity, using **primero, luego, después, entonces.** Your partner takes notes. Then you reverse roles. Each of you reports to the class.

Por ejemplo:

> Primero como. Luego voy al parque. Después...
> (A la clase): Primero Ana come. Luego va al parque.

C **¿Cómo es?** Interview a classmate. Use the following questions as a guide. Report your findings back to the class.

Por ejemplo:

> ¿Qué deportes practica?

ESTUDIANTE A	ESTUDIANTE B
¿Qué deportes practicas?	Juego tenis. También nado.

(A la clase:) Tom practica tenis y también nada.

1. ¿Qué hace los fines de semana (weekends)?
2. ¿Qué revistas lee?
3. ¿Qué come esta noche?
4. ¿Qué hace después de las clases hoy?
5. ¿Qué programas ve en la tele?

Cooperative Learning

In teams of four have students plan what they would bring to a class picnic. They should discuss their likes and dislikes and agree on a menu. One member of the team reads the menu to the class.

Actividades

Actividad A Answers
Por la mañana, primero nada. Luego desayuna. Después estudia. Por la tarde: da un paseo, juega baloncesto, descansa, va a comprar discos. Por la noche: va a casa, ve el partido, come, lee.

Actividades B and C Answers
Answers will vary, however students should remember to use the third person verb forms when reporting back to the class.

Class Management
Actividades B and C may be done as a whole class activity initially. The teacher will take the role of Student A, asking individual students to respond for Student B. In Activity B, have all students write down what each individual student says. Then have various students read a summary of the activities they have written down on their paper.

Learning From Photos

You may wish to have students look at the photo on this page and respond to the following questions: **¿Qué hace la muchacha? ¿Qué piensa comer? ¿Qué piensas comer tú?**

Additional Practice
After doing Actividades A, B, and C, you may wish to reinforce the lesson by doing the following activities: Have students make up some sayings, using the following phrases. For example: *El que termina primero, ayuda a su compañero.*
1. El que habla mucho, _____.
2. El que no practica, _____.
3. El que siempre juega, _____.
4. El que no descansa, _____.

Reteaching

How would you say your mother or father does the following activities? **trabajar en casa; comer muy poco; ver la tele; hacer ejercicio; saber manejar un coche; ir al centro comercial; dar un paseo.**

Cultura viva 2

Presentation
Read the Cultura viva selection on this page. Ask students what ingredients are common to each of the dishes shown in the photos. Point out that the **tortilla** is included in some form with each dish.

Did You Know?
Thousands of years ago, the people in what is now Mexico discovered how to grow corn. It became their most important food. The Aztecs used corn to prepare the **maza** for **tortillas.** Many people to this day prepare them in a traditional manner: The corn is softened in hot limewater, boiled and ground into a meal or **masa.** The **masa** is formed into a 2" ball and then rolled on a flat stone called a **metate.** The **tortillas** are then flipped back and forth with the hands until they are thin and about 6" in diameter. They are then baked on an ungreased griddle until golden brown and blistered. **Tortillas** can also be fried crisp and lightly salted (like chips), or served as snacks called **antojitos.** They can be filled and rolled up as **enchiladas,** which means "chillied up."

Critical Thinking Activity
Give some reasons why the basic foods consumed in different parts of the world vary. Why are traditional diets changing in many parts of the world?

Actividades

Actividad A Answers
Answers will vary.

Actividad B Answers
Queso, tomate, carne, pollo, lechuga.

CULTURA VIVA 2

La cocina mexicana del suroeste

Mexican cooking is deeply rooted in the American Southwest, from Texas to Colorado, from New Mexico to California. Some of the most basic ingredients are corn, beans, a great variety of **chiles** (hot peppers), and tomatoes.

The **tortilla,** usually made from corn, is to Mexicans what bread is to other cultures. It is used in a great many ways. It can be eaten by itself, served warm and soft, or it can be filled with a variety of ingredients—including beef or chicken, avocado, beans, cheese, or vegetables—to form **tacos, enchiladas, burritos, tostadas,** or **quesadillas.**

Actividades

A Are there any Mexican restaurants in your area? Which of the dishes listed above do you like?

Por ejemplo:

> Me gusta comer enchiladas de pollo.

B Which of the following ingredients would you use to make a taco?

queso	carne	pollo	papas
tomate	pescado	frijoles	lechuga
frutas	huevos	legumbres	mermelada

136   CAPÍTULO 2

Pronunciation

A. You may wish to play the recorded version of these pronunciation lines, located at the end of Cassette 2.5. You may also wish to write this verse on the board and have students copy it into their notebook:
De Monterrey a Santa Fe,
de Saltillo a Amarillo:
la comida mexicana
cruza la frontera norteamericana.

B. Have students repeat words and phrases individually and in unison. You may wish to focus on the /ll/ sound as in **Saltillo; Amarillo.**

136

Estructura 2

How to Describe the Routine Actions of Others

Third person plural -ar, -er verbs

You have learned to report what activities another person does.

> **Después de las clases, Ana juega baloncesto, Emilio trabaja y la Señora Ruiz lee.**

1. To report on what more than one person does or is doing, replace the **-ar** with **-an** and the **-er** with **-en**. The endings **-an** and **-en** indicate "they."

   > **¿Descansan José y Víctor?   No, corren con María.**

2. You have seen that the following verbs are formed differently.

ir	**van**
ser	**son**

3. Remember that the three stem-changing verbs you have used have special forms.

jugar	**juegan**
querer	**quieren**
pensar	**piensan**

4. The same endings used to describe other people's actions are used to talk to people **(ustedes)** about their activities. Since the endings **-an** and **-en** can refer to "they" as well as "you" (plural), it is sometimes necessary to use the word **ustedes** to avoid confusion.

¿José y Alicia hablan inglés?

Sí, hablan muy bien.

¿Hablan ustedes inglés?

Sí, un poco.

Lección 5 **137**

Structure Teaching Resources
1. Workbook, pp. 62–63
2. Cassette 2.5
3. Student Tape Manual, p. 46
4. Estructura Masters 2.5
5. Lesson Quizzes, p. 44

Bell Ringer Review

Display Vocabulario Transparencies 2.5. Directions to students: Look at the illustration and decide what is being served. Write sentences describing the foods that you see and giving your reactions to each one.

Structure Focus

In Estructura 2, the presentation of **-ar** and **-er** verbs is limited to the third person plural. The **nosotros** forms will be presented in Lesson 6.

Presentation

A. Lead students through steps 1–4 on page 137. For step 1 you may want to write examples of **-ar** and **-er** verbs on the chalkboard to show students how to drop the endings and replace them with the third person plural endings.

B. In order to familiarize students with the third person plural forms, you may wish to have students react to your statements below, using one of the following: **¡Qué raro / interesante / bueno / malo / aburrido!** Etc.
Cuando invito a mis amigos a mi casa, siempre...
1. **limpian mi habitación**
2. **ven la tele**
3. **preparan la comida**
4. **hablan español**
5. **sacan fotos**
6. **juegan fútbol**
7. **comen demasiado**

Actividades

Actividad A Answers

1. Hablan.
2. Escriben.
3. Corren.
4. Dan un paseo.
5. Trabajan.

Actividad B Answers

Answers will vary.

Additional Practice

After doing Actividades A and B on page 138, you may wish to reinforce the learning with the following: Compliment the people below on the things they do well. For example: **Andrea, nadas muy bien.**

1. dos compañeras de tu clase
2. dos compañeros de tu clase
3. dos maestros
4. una amiga especial
5. un amigo muy bueno
6. el maestro (la maestra) de español

Extension

You may wish to restrict Actividad B to school or after school activities. Allow students to appoint a "recorder" in the group or select one yourself. The recorder will simply listen and take notes as the two or three classmates interview each other. For example: **¿Qué estudias? ¿Qué haces por la tarde después de las clases? Etc.**

For variety, you may want to have partners interview each other in front of the class. Have the class serve as recorders, first volunteering the similarities, then the differences.

Reteaching

How would you say your friends do the following activities?

trabajar en casa; comer mucho; ver la tele; hacer ejercicio; no saber manejar un coche; ir al centro comercial; dar un paseo.

Actividades

A ¿Qué hacen? Describe what the people below are doing.

Por ejemplo:

    Comen.

1.

2.

3.

4.

5.

B ¿Qué hacen los compañeros? Divide into groups of three or four and ask your classmates the questions below. After you have asked all of your questions, give a tally of the results.

Por ejemplo:

    Dos compañeros saben esquiar. Uno sabe andar en monopatín. Tres saben montar a caballo.

1. ¿Qué saben hacer?
2. ¿Qué deportes practican?
3. ¿Qué deportes miran?
4. ¿Qué leen?
5. ¿Qué programas ven en la tele?
6. ¿Adónde van después de las clases?
7. ¿Qué comen después de las clases?
8. ¿Qué hacen durante las vacaciones?

138 CAPÍTULO 2

Finalmente

Finalmente

Situaciones

A conversar Your parent has asked you to fix dinner tonight because you've invited a classmate over. Offer choices to your classmate to find out what he or she likes to eat. Include items such as salad, soup, meat, fish, vegetables, dessert, and beverage. Decide on a meal that both you and your classmate will like.

A escribir Write a note to a new student in class about the food in your school cafeteria.

1. Tell what you usually eat and drink and whether you like those foods and beverages.
2. Then tell where the best places to eat are in your area according to the following categories: pizza, hamburgers and fries, chicken, tacos, desserts, etc. **(Por ejemplo: Cuando quieres comer pizza, necesitas ir a...).**

Repaso de vocabulario

PREGUNTAS
¿Por qué?
¿Por qué no...?
¿verdad?

LAS COMIDAS DEL DÍA
el almuerzo
la cena
el desayuno

LA COMIDA
el arroz
la carne

el cereal
la ensalada
los frijoles
la hamburguesa
el huevo
el jamón
la lechuga
la legumbre
la mantequilla
la mermelada
el pan
el pan tostado
las papas fritas

el pescado
el pollo
el queso
el sandwich
la sopa
el tomate

LAS BEBIDAS
el agua (f.)
el café
la gaseosa
el jugo
la leche

el refresco
el té

LOS POSTRES
la fruta
el helado
el pastel

ACTIVIDAD
preparar

Lección 5 **139**

Lección 6

Objectives

By the end of this lesson, students will be able to:

1. say what day of the week they'll see someone
2. say what usually happens on certain days of the week
3. agree and say that they understand
4. say what they and someone else have in common

Lesson 6 Resources

1. Workbook, pp. 64–69
2. Vocabulario Transparencies 2.6
3. Cassette 2.6
4. Student Tape Manual, pp. 49–53
5. Lesson Quizzes, pp. 45–47
6. Test Booklet, pp. 23–30
7. Computer Software, Disk 1
8. Video Cassette
9. Estructura Masters 2.6
10. Diversiones Masters 2.6

Bell Ringer Review

Directions to students: Write a note to your friend telling him or her what you eat **por la mañana, por la tarde, por la noche.**

¡A comenzar!

Presentation

A. Lead students through each of the five functions given on page 140, progressing from the English to the Spanish for each function. Then have students find these words and phrases in the dialogue on page 141.

Lección 6

sábado

domingo *comer en casa de Graciela, ¡ a las siete en punto!*

¡Hasta el domingo!

¡A comenzar!

The following are some of the things you will be learning to do in this lesson.

When you want to . . .	You use . . .
1. say what day of the week you'll see someone	• **Hasta el** + day.
2. say what customarily happens on certain days of the week	• **los** + day (plural)
3. agree to something	• **De acuerdo.**
4. say that you understand something	• **Entiendo.**
5. say what you and someone else have in common	• **-amos** on the end of **-ar** verbs; **-emos** on the end of **-er** verbs

Now find examples of the above words and phrases in the following conversation.

Getting Ready for Lesson 6

You may wish to use one or more of the following suggestions to prepare students for the lesson:

1. Begin by talking about the school schedule for the week, in terms of what happens on each day: **el lunes, el martes,** etc.

2. Next describe the routines in your school schedule, using **los lunes, los martes,** etc.

3. Then describe your plans for the weekend: **El fin de semana es diferente: Los sábados no vamos a la escuela y no necesitamos estudiar. Los sábados descansamos y visitamos a los amigos.** Then ask individual students: **¿Qué haces tú el fin de semana?**

GRACIELA: **Bueno, ¡hasta el domingo! Los domingos comemos a las siete.**

DAVID: **De acuerdo.**

GRACIELA: **Pero a las siete en punto, ¿eh?**

DAVID: **Sí, entiendo. Parece que aquí en los Estados Unidos todo es "en punto".**

GRACIELA: **Bueno, depende.**

DAVID: **Entonces, hasta el domingo... ¡a las siete en punto!**

Actividad preliminar

Invite a classmate to go to the movies this weekend. Complete the following dialogue, using the words below.

bien	cómo no	de acuerdo
el	el sábado	en punto

ESTUDIANTE A

(1) ¿Quieres ir al cine _____ sábado?

(3) No, es a las siete _____.

(5) _____. Entonces, hasta _____.

ESTUDIANTE B

(2) Sí, _____. La película es a las siete y media, ¿verdad?

(4) Muy _____. ¿Quieres comer algo después?

B. Introduce the Lesson 6 dialogue by reading it aloud, or by playing the cassette version. Tell students that they are going to hear a conversation between David and Graciela, and that they are making plans for their date. Have students listen for the following information:

1. What day of the week is their date?
2. At what time is their date?
3. What are they going to do?

C. Now ask students to open their books and look at the dialogue as you lead them through what is said. For example,

1. ¿A qué hora comen los domingos en casa de Graciela?
2. Graciela dice: "a las siete en punto". ¿Por qué? ¿Es porque David siempre llega tarde o porque siempre llega temprano?

Actividad preliminar

Actividad preliminar Answers
1. el
2. cómo no
3. en punto
4. bien
5. de acuerdo (cómo no)/el sábado

Additional Practice
After doing the Actividad preliminar on page 141, you may wish to reinforce the learning with the following: Tell whether you always, sometimes, or never understand the following.
Por ejemplo:
el libro de inglés
Siempre (A veces, Nunca) entiendo el libro de inglés.

1. las tareas de español
2. los exámenes de historia
3. las lecciones del maestro (de la maestra) de matemáticas
4. las preguntas del maestro (de la maestra) de ciencias

Bell Ringer Review

Directions to students: Poor Luis is home sick. It's Saturday, and from his window he can see all his neighborhood friends as they begin their favorite weekend activities. Imagine what Luis sees and write down what everyone is doing. Think of as many activities as you can.

Presentation

1. Have students open their books to pages 142 and 143. Ask them to look at these pages as you model the days of the week and additional expressions. Begin with the phrase, **Los días de la semana son...** Then model each day. Have students repeat each word or phrase in unison.
2. You may want to ask students what they notice about how months and days are written in Spanish (not capitalized). On what day does the Hispanic week begin?
3. Model the phrases at the bottom of page 142 and have students repeat both in unison and individually. Have individual students repeat after you, **¡Hasta mañana! ¡Hasta el jueves! Etc.**

Vocabulario

Los días de la semana

OCTUBRE					el fin de semana	
lunes	martes	miércoles	jueves	viernes	sábado	domingo
		1	2	3	4	5
6	7	8	9	10	11	12

¡Hasta mañana!

¡Hasta el jueves!

¡Hasta el sábado!

¡Hasta el martes!

¡Hasta el fin de semana!

142 CAPÍTULO 2

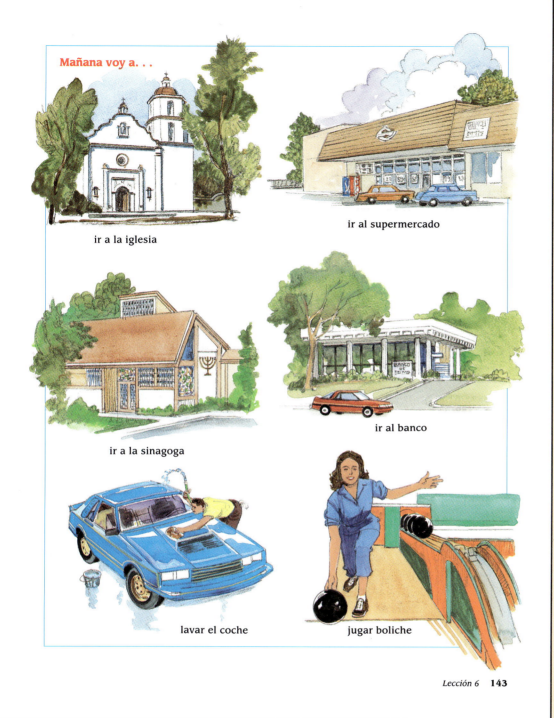

Mañana voy a. . .

ir a la iglesia

ir al supermercado

ir a la sinagoga

ir al banco

lavar el coche

jugar boliche

Lección 6 **143**

TPR 2

(Command students to do something on a particular day. They will write the activity in one of the squares below the correct day.)

Ve a la "playa" el sábado.
Entrega la "tarea" el martes.
Camina a la "escuela" el miércoles.
Ve a "lavar el coche" el lunes.
Diviértete en el "parque" el viernes.
Compra un "libro" el jueves.
Ve a la "iglesia" el domingo.
Asiste al partido de "fútbol" el viernes.
Regresa de "Los Ángeles" el sábado.
Ve al "supermercado" el lunes.
Toma "fotos" de la clase el martes.
Diviértete en la "fiesta" el domingo.
Ve a "jugar boliche" el jueves.

Actividades

Actividades

A **El calendario.** Here is a week from Graciela's calendar. Tell what she has planned for each day of the week and what time of day she is doing each activity. The first one is done as an example.

Por ejemplo:

lunes
El lunes por la tarde come con Chris.

B **El fin de semana.** Tell five things you are doing this weekend. Be sure to give the day and the time.

Por ejemplo:

El sábado por la mañana corro. Voy a correr a las siete.

C **Una semana de vacaciones.** Think of your next vacation. Write down your plans for each day of your week.

Por ejemplo:

el lunes
El lunes descanso.

D **¡Hasta mañana!** Make plans with a classmate to get together this week. Agree on what you want to do and set a date.

Por ejemplo:

ESTUDIANTE A	ESTUDIANTE B
(1) **¿Quieres ir al centro?**	(2) **No, gracias. No me gusta. ¿No quieres jugar boliche?**
(3) **De acuerdo. ¿Cuándo?**	(4) **¿El viernes por la tarde, a las tres?**
(5) **Bueno. ¡Hasta el viernes!**	(6) **¡Hasta el viernes!**

144 CAPÍTULO 2

Palabras e imágenes

Depending on our culture, we associate different things with different words. In the United States, for example, the word "time" is often associated with actions: "wasting time," "saving time," "spending your time wisely."

Every word in your language has images and feelings that you have attached to it because of your culture. But these associations will not necessarily be shared by people from other cultures. Even though you and someone from another culture may recognize each other's words, the ideas you gather from them may not be the same.

Actividad

Think for a moment and give a quick description (or make a quick sketch) of the following: *family, breakfast, bread, house.* Now compare your descriptions or drawings with David's. What differences do you notice?

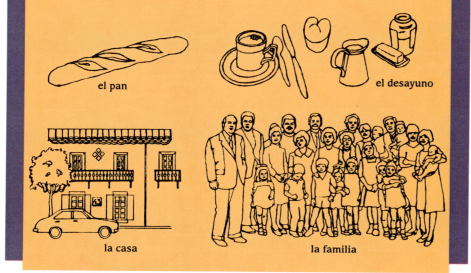

el pan

el desayuno

la casa

la familia

Lección 6 **145**

Cultura viva 1

Presentation
Read the Cultura viva on this page. Then have students do a simple word association. Give them the word "meal" or "car," for example. Have them list in no more than 20 seconds all the words in English that come to mind. Ask students to share their responses and compare the differences between students' images.

Critical Thinking Activity
To do the Actividad on this page, you may want to do the following activity with books closed. Give each student a blank piece of paper. Have students fold their paper in half, lengthwise, and then in thirds. This gives them 6 squares in which to draw. After students finish their sketches have them compare with each other and with David's images on page 145. Working in groups, discuss the differences and similarities.

Actividad Answers
Answers will vary.

Pronunciation
A. You may wish to play the recorded version of these pronunciation lines, located at the end of Cassette 2.6. You may also wish to write this verse on the board and have students copy it into their notebooks:
**Haces, produces, corres como loco
y andas preocupado.
Pienso, contemplo, observo y toco
y así estoy ocupado.**

B. Have students repeat words and phrases individually and in unison. You may wish to focus on the vowel sounds.

Bell Ringer Review

Directions to students: Write these three days on your paper: **sábado, lunes, domingo,** leaving space between them. Then write down every word you can think of associated with that day. It may be a general opinion held by people, your own opinion, and/or things you do on that day.

Structure Focus

In Estructura 1 of this lesson, the presentation of **-ar** and **-er** verbs is limited to the **nosotros** form. The **yo** and **tú** forms of **-ar** and **-er** verbs were presented in Lesson 4. Third person singular and plural forms were presented in Lesson 5.

Presentation

A. Lead students through steps 1–3 on page 146. For step 1 you may want to write examples of **-ar** and **-er** verbs on the chalkboard to show students how to drop the endings, and replace them with the **nosotros** endings.

B. You may want to remind students that they have already learned the **quiero/quieres** forms of the verb **querer;** and the **pienso/piensas** forms of the verb **pensar.**

Estructura 1

How to Describe Routine Actions You Have in Common with Others

"Nosotros" forms of -ar and -er verbs

You have already learned to say what you and others ("we") are like, where you're from, and where you go.

> **Mis amigos y yo somos deportistas. Somos de San Antonio. Vamos al gimnasio esta noche.**

1. To describe other actions that you and others do, use the following endings.

-ar verbs	-amos
-er verbs	-emos

   Hablamos español con David. También vemos los partidos de fútbol cuando David juega.

2. You also use the "we" form to suggest to someone that the two of you do something.

   > **¿Por qué no damos un paseo?**
   > **¿Por qué no comemos algo luego?**

3. In the following stem-changing verbs, note that there is *no* stem change in the form that expresses what you and others ("we") do.

querer		entender	
quiero	queremos	entiendo	entendemos
quieres	queréis*	entiendes	entendéis*
quiere	quieren	entiende	entienden

pensar		jugar	
pienso	pensamos	juego	jugamos
piensas	pensáis*	juegas	jugáis*
piensa	piensan	juega	juegan

*This form is rarely used in the Spanish-speaking world, except for Spain.

Actividades

A En común. Think of what you and a good friend have in common. Complete the following sentences.

1. Nunca queremos...
2. Mañana pensamos...
3. Los fines de semana jugamos...
4. Somos...
5. A veces vamos...

B ¿Cómo son los norteamericanos? Answer David's questions about life in the U.S.

1. ¿Cuándo llegan ustedes a la escuela?
2. ¿A qué hora comen ustedes aquí?
3. ¿Qué deportes practican?
4. ¿Qué clases necesitan tomar?
5. ¿Qué hacen después de las clases?
6. ¿Adónde van los fines de semana?
7. ¿Siempre entienden las lecciones?

C Estudiante de intercambio. You are a student living in a foreign country. A classmate acts as your host and asks you the following questions about what you and your friends do back home.

1. ¿A qué hora van a la escuela?
2. ¿Qué estudian?
3. ¿Juegan fútbol americano?
4. ¿Qué comen en la escuela?
5. ¿Qué tareas no entienden bien?
6. ¿Adónde van los fines de semana?

D Mis compañeros y yo. The Spanish students in your school are comparing themselves with the French students. Form groups of three or four. Ask your classmates the following questions, then report back to the class.

Por ejemplo:

> ¿Qué hacen después de las clases hoy?
>
> (A la clase:) Mark y yo vamos al banco. Bill quiere lavar el coche.

1. ¿Qué deportes juegan?
2. ¿Qué tareas no entienden bien?
3. ¿Qué piensan hacer el fin de semana?
4. ¿Adónde quieren ir durante las vacaciones?
5. ¿A qué hora hacen las tareas por la noche?

Lección 6 **147**

147

Cultura viva 2

Presentation

Read the Cultura viva selection on this page. You may wish to write on the chalkboard a list of activities that are typically done on Sundays in Hispanic countries, according to the reading. Then ask students what they typically do on Sundays and compare the two lists.

Did You Know?

Sunday is also a day for religious celebration. Families frequently attend Mass in the morning.

Critical Thinking Activity

Have students compare and contrast the activities they do on Sunday with those mentioned in the reading.

Actividades

Actividades A and B Answers
Answers will vary according to each student.

¡Por fin el domingo!

In Spanish-speaking countries, Sunday is a special day. In addition to being market day during the morning hours, Sunday is a day to be spent outdoors. It is also a family day. Families, including infants, children, grandparents, aunts, and uncles, go to parks and plazas to enjoy the sunshine and fresh air as well as each other's company. Others visit friends or relatives. Many people enjoy picnics in the country, while others prefer to go to a movie and then to a restaurant for supper.

Actividades

A Tell what you generally do on Sunday by completing the following sentences.

> Los domingos mi familia y yo _____. Mis amigos y yo _____.

B Rate the days of the week from your most favorite (1) to your least favorite (7). Tell what you do on each day.

Por ejemplo:

> (1) El sábado. Juego boliche con los amigos.

148   CAPÍTULO 2

Pronunciation

A. You may wish to play the recorded version of these pronunciation lines, located at the end of Cassette 2.6. You may also wish to write this verse on the chalkboard and have students copy it into their notebook:

De lunes a sábado
pura tensión.
¡No hay como el domingo
para la diversión!

B. Have students repeat words and phrases individually and in unison. You may wish to focus on the /-sión/ ending of **tensión** and **diversión**.

148

Estructura 2

How to Say or Ask When Something Takes Place — Los días de la semana

1. When you want to ask when something takes place, you say
    ¿Cuándo es...?

    > **¿Cuándo es el partido de béisbol?**

2. To express plans in terms of days of the week, use **el** + day.

    > **El martes necesito ir al supermercado.**
    > **El sábado vamos al cine.**

3. To express routines in terms of days of the week, use **los** + day.

    > **Los lunes la clase de inglés es a las nueve y media.**
    > **Los domingos por la mañana vamos a la iglesia.**

    Notice that you must add **-s** to **sábado** and **domingo** to say that something takes place every Saturday or Sunday.

    > **Los sábados y los domingos siempre vamos al parque.**

4. To say that you do something every day, say **todos los días.**

    > **Todos los días Enrique y yo corremos en el parque.**

5. To say what you do on weekends, say **los fines de semana.**

    > **Los fines de semana descanso y veo la tele.**

Actividades

A **Esta semana.** Tell what you plan, want, or need to do on four days next week.

Por ejemplo:

> **El miércoles por la noche pienso ir al cine.**

Estructura 2

Structure Teaching Resources
1. Workbook, pp. 68–69
2. Cassette 2.6
3. Student Tape Manual, p. 51
4. Estructura Masters 2.6
5. Lesson Quizzes, p. 47

Bell Ringer Review

Directions to students: Complete the following sentence with three different endings:
El fin de semana yo...

Presentation

Lead students through steps 1–5 on page 149. You may wish to emphasize step 2 by giving more examples, such as, **el lunes voy a la biblioteca; el martes quiero ir al partido;** etc.

Actividades

Actividad A Answers
Answers will vary.

OCTUBRE						
lunes	martes	miércoles	jueves	viernes	sábado	domingo
		1	2 clase de computadoras 6:00	3	4 nadar 9:00	5
6 club de arte 3:00	7 clase de guitarra 4:00	8	9 clase de computadoras 6:00	10	11 nadar 9:00	12 Día de la Raza Graciela en punto 7:00
13 club de arte 3:00	14 clase de guitarra 4:00	15	16 clase de computadoras 6:00	17	18 nadar 9:00	19
20 club de arte 3:00	21 clase de guitarra 4:00	22	23 clase de computadoras 6:00	24	25 nadar 9:00	26
27	28 clase de guitarra 4:00	29	30	31		

B **¿Adónde va David?** Tell what David does on certain days of the week based on his calendar. Tell what time he does each activity.

Por ejemplo:

> Va a la clase de guitarra los martes. La clase es a las cuatro.

C **Todos los días.** List what you typically do each day of the week.

D **Lugares favoritos.** What special places do you like to go? Say when and where you go and what you do.

Por ejemplo

> Los sábados
> *Los sábados voy a la playa porque me gusta nadar. También doy un paseo con mis amigos y después jugamos boliche.*

150 CAPÍTULO 2

Cooperative Learning
In pairs, write each other a letter describing what you do on the various day of the week, including school days and weekends. Tell whether you do the activities in the morning, afternoon, or evening.

Finalmente

Situaciones

A conversar Use the following cues to converse with a partner.

1. Invite him or her to go somewhere and do something on Saturday night.
2. Your partner will politely refuse your invitation, saying all the things he or she is doing on that night.
3. Insist by describing how great your plan is **(Por ejemplo: ¡Pero la película es fantástica!).**
4. Your partner suggests another time and another place. Agree and give the time to meet.
5. Your partner accepts and confirms the time and day.

A escribir Write a note to your Spanish-speaking pen pal. Describe what you and your friends or classmates ("we") do on the various days of the week, including school days and weekends. Be sure to tell whether you do the activities in the morning, afternoon, or evening. Then ask what your pen pal does with friends at various times.

Repaso de vocabulario

LOS DÍAS DE LA SEMANA
el lunes
el martes
el miércoles
el jueves
el viernes
el sábado
el domingo

OTRAS PALABRAS Y EXPRESIONES
entender (ie)
de acuerdo
el fin de semana
hasta
todos los días

ACTIVIDADES
jugar boliche
lavar

LUGARES
el banco
la iglesia
la sinagoga
el supermercado

Lección 6   **151**

For the Native Speaker

Interview a relative to find out what activities he or she used to do on Sundays in his or her native country. Report to the class.

Finalmente

Situaciones

Lesson 6 Evaluation
The A conversar and A escribir situations on this page are designed to give students the opportunity to use as many language functions as possible listed on page 140 of this lesson. The A conversar and A escribir are also intended to show how well students are able to meet the lesson objectives. These objectives are also listed on page 140 of this lesson.

Presentation
Prior to doing the A conversar and A escribir on this page, you may wish to play the Situaciones listening activities on Cassette 2.6 as a means of helping students organize the material.

Repaso de vocabulario
These words and phrases in the Repaso de vocabulario have been taught for active use in this lesson. They are summarized here as a resource for both students and teacher. The Repaso de vocabulario also serves as a convenient resource for the A conversar and A escribir activities on this page. It also gives the teacher a source for writing either additional practice or evaluation activities such as quizzes and tests in addition to those provided by the publisher.

A. Before reading the Lectura, you may wish to have students discuss in groups the following questions related to the reading topic:
  1. In their opinion, what is the biggest problem caused by listening to a Walkman?
  2. Why do people like to listen to a Walkman?

B. Have one student from each group report back to the class. Discussing the above questions will help students think about the theme of the Lectura.

C. Now have students read the Lectura silently to themselves, or work with a partner. Then have them answer the Actividades questions on page 153.

Lectura

You will be able to figure out many of the words in the following reading from the context in which they appear or because they look like English words that have similar meanings. First, look over the article below, then do the activities on the following page.

¡Llena tu cabeza de rock!

Los jóvenes de todo el mundo, que pueden tener un "Walkman" con audífonos y todo, tienden cada vez más a escuchar su música favorita, que por lo general es rock o pop, a todo volumen, cuando van por la calle, mientras estudian, durante un partido de fútbol, en fin, a toda hora.

Algunos se alarman; piensan que eso puede afectar el sistema auditivo. Pero los expertos dicen que esto no es cierto, que usted puede escuchar su música favorita, al máximo que le dé su equipo, con audífonos o no, y en todo caso el efecto es menor que el experimentado por trabajadores de una fábrica estridente.

152 CAPÍTULO 2

Getting Ready for Reading

You may want to discuss the following keys to successful reading with your students before having them read the Lectura on page 152:
1. Begin by asking students what they do when they run across a word they don't know in English. List on the board or on an overhead transparency the techniques students use.

2. Some of these techniques may be skipping over the word, guessing the meaning from context, relating the unknown word to a similar word, etc. Tell students they can use the same techniques when they are reading in Spanish.

3. Tell students that when they read the Lectura they should write down on a sheet of paper any key words they don't understand. Then they should read the

Actividades

A Find all the words you know or think you can recognize. Write them down in the order in which they appear.

B Find the lines that tell you:

1. when people listen to their favorite music
2. whether listening at a high volume, with or without earphones, can damage your hearing
3. which is worse, loud music or noise in a factory

C Chris Pearson goes everywhere with his Walkman. According to the following article, will this affect his hearing? Read the words you think answer this question.

D Find the Spanish words for:

1. factory workers
2. earphones
3. hearing

E The words **cuando, mientras, durante, a toda hora** relate to:

1. place
2. time
3. people

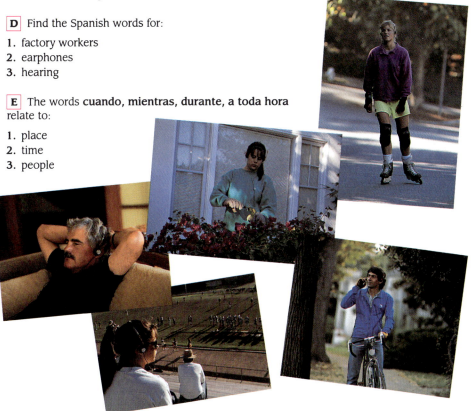

Lectura   **153**

Lectura again and make an educated guess about the meaning of the unknown words, trying to make a global sense of the reading instead of a word-for-word English meaning.
4. Look for cognates. For example: **volumen, expertos, estridente.**

Bell Ringer Review

Directions to students: Ask your friend three things he or she plans to do this weekend.

¿Recuerdas?

Presentation

To review Chapter 2, call on individual students to give an example for each communicative function listed on pages 154–155. The numbers in parentheses on pages 154–155 refer to the actual page(s) in Chapter 2 where each function was presented and practiced. You may wish to have your students go back to these pages for additional review and practice before continuing on to the Actividades, pages 155–157.

Lecciones 1–3 Answers

The following words and phrases are examples for each of the 12 functions listed under Lecciones 1–3.

1. Gracias por...
2. De nada.
3. ¿Son de...?
4. Soy... (eres, es, etc.)
5. ¿Es...? ¿Son...?
6. ¿Quién es?
7. Pienso... ¿Piensas...?
8. ahora, luego, después
9. Voy... (vas, va, etc.)
10. Voy a... (vas a, etc.)
11. Perdón. Con permiso.
12. de (del)

Capítulo 2   Repaso

¿Recuerdas?

Do you remember how to do the following things, which you learned in **Capítulo 2**?

LECCIONES 1–3

1. thank someone for something (p. 76)
2. say "You're welcome" (p. 76)
3. ask where people are from (p. 76)
4. identify and describe people and things in terms of occupations, appearance, and characteristics (pp. 78–79, 83, 87)
5. ask what people or things are like (pp. 83, 87)
6. ask who someone is (p. 90)
7. say what you are planning to do and ask what a friend is planning to do (p. 99)
8. put events in sequence (p. 102)
9. ask and say where people are going (p. 108)
10. ask and say what people are going to do (pp. 108, 109)
11. excuse yourself (p. 112)
12. tell what belongs to others (p. 113)

LECCIONES 4–6

1. say that it doesn't matter (p. 116)
2. get a friend's attention (p. 116)
3. describe your routine actions (p. 122)
4. inquire about a friend's routine actions (p. 125)
5. ask whether what you've said is correct (p. 128)
6. ask why (p. 128)
7. tell what you want to eat or drink (pp. 130, 131)
8. describe or ask about the routine actions of others (pp. 134, 137)
9. indicate that you understand something (p. 140)
10. agree to something (p. 140)
11. tell what day of the week something happens (p. 142)

12. suggest that you and a friend do something (p. 146)
13. tell about routine actions you and others share (p. 146)
14. express routines in terms of days of the week (p. 149)

Actividades

A **Los domingos.** Think of as many words as you can to talk about what you do on Sundays, according to the following categories.

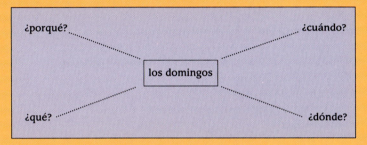

¿porqué?   ¿cuándo?

los domingos

¿qué?   ¿dónde?

B **¿Somos compatibles?** Use the following questions to interview a classmate. Write down your classmate's answers.

1. ¿Te gustan las ciudades grandes o pequeñas?
2. ¿Quieres ser famoso(a) / popular / importante?
3. ¿Es importante ser aplicado(a) / generoso(a) / simpático(a)?
4. ¿Te gusta ir a los partidos / las fiestas / los museos / los restaurantes elegantes / la playa?
5. ¿Te gusta bailar / cantar / cocinar / comer / estudiar?
6. ¿Sabes esquiar / usar computadoras / montar a caballo?
7. ¿Qué clases te gustan más?

Actividad D Answers

Answers will vary but may include the following:

¿Cómo te llamas?
¿De dónde eres?
¿Te gustan los deportes?
¿Te gusta la música o el arte?
¿Tocas un instrumento?
¿Qué haces los fines de semana?

Actividad E Answers

Answers will vary but should include the following:

1. Estudio...
2. (no) Me gusta...
3. Sé...
4. Sé...
5. Soy miembro de...
6. Me gustan...
7. Hago (or other appropriate verb)...
8. Quiero... / Pienso...

Actividad F Answers

Answers will vary. After rehearsing in pairs, you may wish to have students perform in front of the class.

D **El estudiante nuevo.** You must introduce a new student to your Spanish class. Choose a classmate who will pretend to be the new student.

1. Prepare five questions to ask the student to get the following information: name, where he or she is from, interests, talents, and routine activities.
2. Use these questions to interview the student, taking notes as you do.
3. Using your notes, introduce the student to the class. The class may ask more questions if they wish.

E **Quiero ir a Costa Rica.** You are to be interviewed for a scholarship to spend six months with a Costa Rican family. Use the following questions as a guide to prepare an outline of things you want to say during the interview.

1. ¿Qué estudias en la escuela?
2. ¿Qué te gusta hacer? ¿Qué no te gusta hacer?
3. ¿Qué idiomas sabes?
4. ¿Qué sabes hacer?
5. ¿De qué clubes eres miembro?
6. ¿Qué clases te gustan más en la escuela? ¿Por qué?
7. ¿Qué haces después de las clases y los fines de semana?
8. ¿Por qué quieres ir a Costa Rica? ¿Qué piensas hacer allí?

F **Invitaciones.** A classmate insists on inviting you out, but you don't feel like going and explain why. Your classmate keeps on insisting and suggests four more activities or places. Offer an excuse for each.

Por ejemplo:

ESTUDIANTE A
¿Quieres ir al cine?

ESTUDIANTE B
No, gracias. Necesito hacer algo importante. (No me gusta el cine).

G **Inventario de palabras.** List five words or phrases for each category below.

1. palabras fáciles
2. palabras difíciles
3. palabras útiles (useful)
4. palabras elegantes
5. palabras horribles

H **No sé por qué somos amigos.** Make a list of what you and your best friend have in common—personal characteristics, classes, interests, sports, abilities. Then list the differences. Put your lists into sentences to describe your friendship.

Por ejemplo:

> Roberto y yo somos amigos. Roberto estudia francés, pero yo estudio español...

I **Queridísima mamá.** David wrote this letter to his mother in San José, Costa Rica. However, the letter was smudged in the rain. What words would you use to complete the letter?

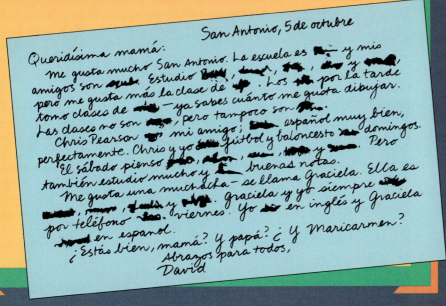

San Antonio, 5 de octubre

Queridísima mamá:

Me gusta mucho San Antonio. La escuela es ▮▮ y mis amigos son ▮▮. Estudio ▮▮, ▮▮, ▮▮ y ▮▮, pero me gusta más la clase de ▮▮. Los ▮▮ por la tarde tomo clases de ▮▮ —ya sabes cuánto me gusta dibujar. Las clases no son ▮▮, pero tampoco son ▮▮.

Chris Pearson ▮▮ mi amigo; ▮▮ español muy bien, perfectamente. Chris y yo ▮▮ fútbol y baloncesto ▮▮ domingos. El sábado pienso ▮▮, ▮▮, ▮▮ y ▮▮. Pero también estudio mucho y ▮▮ buenas notas.

Me gusta una muchacha—se llama Graciela. Ella es ▮▮, ▮▮, ▮▮ y ▮▮. Graciela y yo siempre ▮▮ por teléfono ▮▮ viernes. Yo ▮▮ en inglés y Graciela ▮▮ en español.

¿Estás bien, mamá? Y papá? ¿Y Maricarmen? Abrazos para todos,
David

Actividades G and H Answers
Answers will vary.

Actividad I Answers
Answers will vary but may include the following:

1. grande / amables / química, álgebra, inglés, historia, francés / lunes / arte / difíciles, fáciles
2. es / habla / jugamos / los
3. correr, lavar el coche, dibujar, nadar, bailar / saco
4. amable, bonita, lista, popular / hablamos / los / hablo / habla

Chapter Overview

Cultural setting

In this chapter you will meet two new characters: Kim, a high school student from Los Angeles, and her friend Pilar, who lives in Madrid. Many aspects of daily life in Madrid are presented; however, the primary cultural problem revolves around Kim's confusion in trying to locate Pilar's apartment on **"el primer piso."** Kim has a frustrating conversation with **"el portero"** and discovers she is not on the first floor, but rather **"la planta baja."**

Rationale

A Activities are designed to practice present tense conjugation to foster the "feel" for a) narration with sequencing devices such as **primero, entonces, después,** and b) frequency using **siempre, a veces, nunca.**

B The initial presentation and practice with **estar** has been purposely distanced from the verb **ser.** Any joint appearance of the two is purely coincidental and the result of normal language use. We strongly recommend that you not try to contrast their usage through an activity that asks students to select one or the other. **Ser** should be well anchored in context, at least conceptually, and the context should pull out the form. Contrasting **ser** and **estar** at this point may only complicate and confuse. Indeed, it is our experience that the two verbs are rarely confused when the context is clear.

C The modifiers **un/una** and **mi(s)/tu(s)** are presented here for productive control, although students have seen them frequently and used them in manipulative fashion prior to this chapter.

D Another aspect of language which is presented in more gradual fashion in this text is numbers. This is because num-

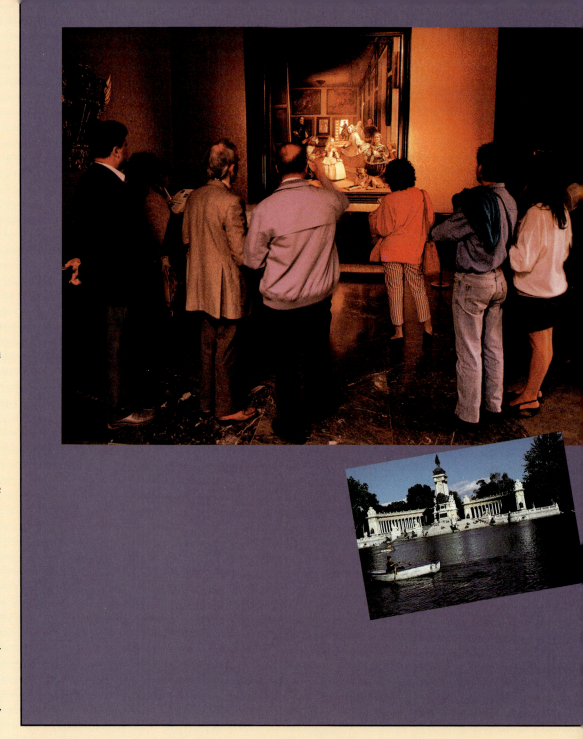

Estructura

The following structures are presented in this chapter:

- the verb **deber** for giving advice
- the present tense of **-ir** verbs as well as a summary of all previously taught present tense forms
- the **tú/usted** distinction
- the ordinal numbers for sequencing
- the numbers from 20–100
- the verb **estar** for locations and for describing feelings
- the verb **hay** and the question word **¿cuántos?**
- the verb **tener**
- the indefinite articles
- the possessive pronouns **mi(s)** and **tu(s)**
- **Es/Son** + hour and minutes to tell time

A complete listing of the language objectives of the chapter appears on page 236.

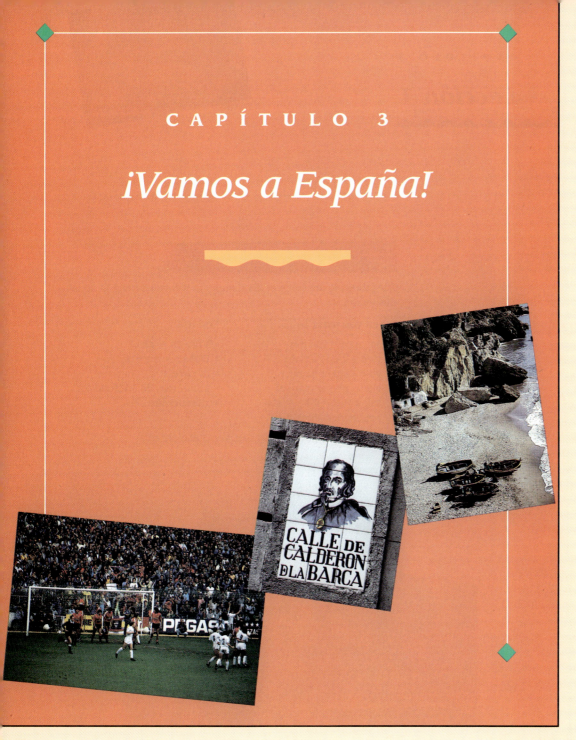

CAPÍTULO 3

¡Vamos a España!

bers, as they are used in real life, are difficult. In real life speech, numbers are delivered rapidly: prices are quoted, addresses and phone numbers given. While certainly students can memorize numbers from 1–100 for short-term uses such as quizzes, real skill at using and comprehending them takes time. Presentation of numbers is therefore broken into segments to allow longer familiarization periods with a particular grouping focus.

E There is a heavier emphasis on "noun vocabulary" in this chapter: names of objects, rooms and articles in houses. It is truly impossible to predict a universal and generic vocabulary that will relate to the needs and interests (and trends) of all learners.

We hope you and your classes enjoy your stay in Madrid. *¡Bienvenidos a España!*

Lección 1

Objectives

By the end of this lesson, students will be able to:

1. talk about routine actions
2. compare, contrast, emphasize, and clarify using subject pronouns
3. give addresses and phone numbers
4. give advice

Lesson 1 Resources

1. Workbook, pp. 72–77
2. Vocabulario Transparencies 3.1
3. Cassette 3.1
4. Student Tape Manual, pp. 56–60
5. Lesson Quizzes, pp. 48–52
6. Computer Software, Disk 1
7. Video Cassette
8. Estructura Masters 3.1
9. Diversiones Masters 3.1

Bell Ringer Review

Directions to students: Turn a piece of paper sideways. Across the top write the names of the seven days of the week. (Did you remember that the Spanish calendar begins with **lunes**?) Now write down your activities for this week in columns under the days.

¡A comenzar!

Presentation

A. Lead students through each of the five functions given on page 160, progressing from the English to the Spanish for each function. Then have students find these words and phrases in the letter on page 161.

Lección 1

El Palacio Real

Una carta de Madrid

¡A comenzar!

The following are some of the things you will be learning to do in this lesson.

When you want to . . .	You use . . .
1. say where you live	• **Vivo en** + place.
2. give a friend advice	• **Debes** + activity.
3. give a street name	• **la calle...**
4. give a phone number	• **El número de teléfono es...**
5. ask a friend if he or she remembers something	• **¿Recuerdas...?**

Now find examples of the above words and phrases in the following note.

Kim Robbins
279 La Brea Ave.
Los Angeles, CA
91306
USA

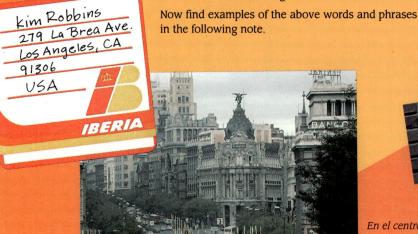

En el centro de Madrid

160

Getting Ready for Lesson 1

You may wish to use one or more of the following suggestions to prepare students for the lesson:

1. Begin by telling students that in this lesson they will be traveling to Spain. Describe where Spain is located (use map) and what countries border it: **Hoy hacemos un viaje a España. España está en Europa. Está al sur de** Francia, al norte de Africa y al este de Portugal.

2. Explain who the characters are in this chapter:
Viajamos con Kim Robbins, una estudiante de Los Ángeles, California, que visita a su amiga Pilar. Pilar vive en Madrid con su familia. Madrid es la capital de España, y por eso es una ciudad muy importante.

Kim Robbins, from Los Angeles, is in Madrid with a group of her classmates. She plans to visit Pilar Mestre, a former exchange student in her high school. Kim is reading a letter from Pilar.

...Y debes saber la dirección. Vivo en el barrio Salamanca, en la calle Goya:

Srta. Pilar Mestre Fernández
C/Goya, 85 1° B, izqda.
28010 Madrid
España

Un fuerte abrazo de

Pilar

P.D. Debes llamar primero por teléfono. Recuerdas el número, ¿verdad? Es 276-45-83.

Actividades preliminares

A Tell where you live, first the town and state, and then the street.

Por ejemplo:

Vivo en _____, en la calle _____.

B Give your telephone number in Spanish.

Por ejemplo:

Mi número de teléfono es _____.

B. Introduce the Lesson 1 letter by reading it aloud or by playing the cassette version.

C. Now ask students to open their books and look at the letter as you lead them through what is said. Have students find the names of the following places:
1. **el país**
2. **la ciudad**
3. **la calle**
4. **el barrio** (Explain **barrio: Una sección de la ciudad.**)

D. You may want to follow up by asking students:
1. **¿Dónde vives tú?**
2. **¿Cuál es tu dirección?**
3. **¿En qué barrio vives?**
   You may want to illustrate the difference between **Soy de _____,** and **Vivo en _____.**
   For example: **Soy de Nueva York pero ahora vivo en Houston.**

E. Call students' attention to the way Pilar ends her letter: **un fuerte abrazo.** You may want to give students other ways to end letters: **tu amigo(a), con cariño, besos y abrazos.**

F. Tell students: **Pilar dice que Kim debe llamar primero. ¿Qué número debe marcar?**

Actividades preliminares

Actividad A and B Answers
Answers will vary.

Additional Practice
After doing Actividades A and B, you may want to reinforce the learning by explaining to students that "a classmate wants to get better grades. What advice would you give your classmate regarding the following?" For example:
comer en la clase
No debes comer en la clase.

1. llegar tarde a las clases
2. recordar el día del examen
3. escuchar música cuando estudias
4. hacer la tarea todos los días
5. ser antipático(a) con el maestro(a)

---

3. Refer students to the photos on pages 165, 168, and 169, and describe some of the things to be seen in Madrid. For example: **En Madrid, la capital de España, hay muchos lugares interesantes. El Museo del Prado es un museo de arte muy famoso. Tiene cuadros de pintores de muchos países, etc.**

4. You may wish to have students come up with some words of their own to describe the city of Madrid. For example: **Es grande/importante/interesante, etc.**

Bell Ringer Review

Directions to students: Unscramble the following sentences to find out when we do things.

1. nadar los voy playa a sábados gusta porque me la
2. familia los boliche jugamos yo amigos y mi miércoles con los
3. a supermercado necesito el comprar ir jueves al leche

Presentation

A. Have students open their books to the Vocabulario on pages 162 and 163. Ask them to look at page 162 as you model the introductory lines: **Si voy a España, ¿qué debo hacer? Antes de viajar, debes...** Then model each new phrase and have students repeat in unison. Lead students through the words and phrases, pausing to ask related questions. For example, **Paula, ¿qué idioma aprendes, inglés o español? Roberto, ¿escribes cartas a tus amigos?** Etc.

Vocabulario

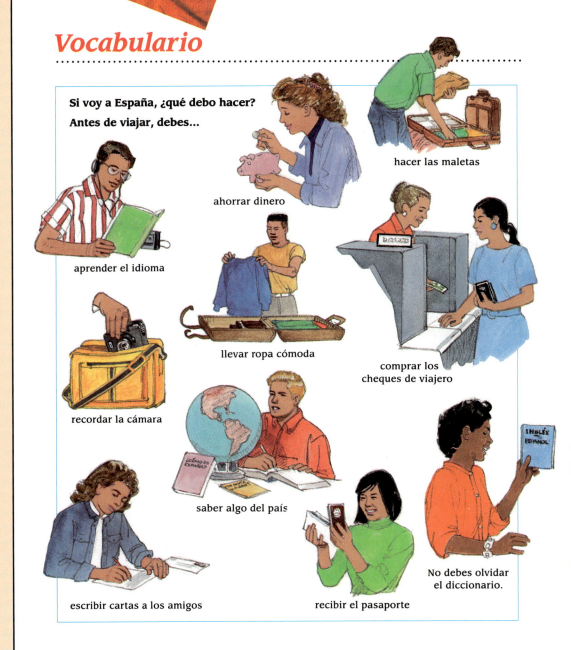

Si voy a España, ¿qué debo hacer?

Antes de viajar, debes...

ahorrar dinero

hacer las maletas

aprender el idioma

llevar ropa cómoda

comprar los cheques de viajero

recordar la cámara

saber algo del país

No debes olvidar el diccionario.

escribir cartas a los amigos

recibir el pasaporte

Total Physical Response

Getting Ready

Draw lines on a sheet of paper dividing it into 10 squares. In each square draw or paste an illustration of one of the objects listed in the Vocabulario. Make copies and give one sheet of illustrations to each student. Have students cut up their sheet and place each illustration in an envelope. On a separate sheet, draw 10 squares as above, and number 1–10. Make copies and give one copy to each student. Students will now remove their illustrations from their envelope and lay them face up on their desk, next to the numbered sheet.

TPR 1

**Pongan la cámara en el número 10.
Pongan el mapa en el número 2.**

Después de llegar, debes...

cambiar dinero

llamar a los amigos

estudiar el mapa

comprar regalos

dormir

vivir en casa de una familia española

salir por la noche

Actividades

A El viaje. You're going to spend two weeks with a cousin in Chicago. Tell whether or not you should do the following.

Por ejemplo:

> saber el número de teléfono
> *Debo saber el número de teléfono.*
> llevar el pasaporte
> *No debo llevar el pasaporte.*

1. saber algo de la ciudad
2. cambiar dinero
3. sacar fotos
4. salir por la noche con la familia
5. comprar regalos
6. escribir cartas a los amigos
7. comprar cheques de viajero
8. ahorrar dinero
9. llevar ropa cómoda
10. comprar un mapa
11. hacer las maletas
12. aprender el idioma

Lección 1 **163**

Pongan el pasaporte en el número 8.
Pongan la ropa en el número 1.
Pongan el cheque de viajero en el número 6.
Pongan la carta en el número 4.
Pongan la calle en el número 3.
Pongan el diccionario en el número 9.
Pongan la maleta en el número 5.
Pongan el país en el número 7.

(Follow with an oral activity to check correct placement. **¿Dónde está _____?**)

TPR 2
Repeat the above, calling on individual students to give one command to the class. Write the command on the board. ''Pongan _____ en el número _____''.

Actividad B Answers

1. d
2. f
3. a
4. e
5. b
6. c
7. g

Actividad C Answers

1. Quiero visitar un museo importante. / Si quieres visitar..., debes ir al Museo del Prado.
2. ... comprar regalos. / ..., debes ir al almacén el Corte Inglés.
3. ... ver una película... / ... al cine El Palacio de la Música.
4. ... dar un paseo... / ... al Parque del Retiro.
5. ... ver un partido ... / ... al Estadio Bernabéu.
6. ... tomar un refresco. / ... a la cafetería Manila.

Additional Practice

After doing Actividades A, B, and C on pages 163 and 164, you may wish to reinforce the learning with the following:

1. What advice would you give a friend who is going to visit the home of a Spanish family? Write down what your friend should or should not do. **Por ejemplo:** comer demasiado
   No debes comer demasiado.
   a. ver demasiado la tele
   b. hablar inglés
   c. recordar las costumbres
   d. llamar a los amigos en los Estados Unidos
   e. ser simpático(a)
   f. llegar muy temprano
   g. ser tacaño(a)
   h. llevar un regalo
   i. dormir en el sofá
   j. leer las cartas personales de la familia
2. Have students tell what the perfect guest always does and never does, using the following infinitives: **ver, hablar, recordar, leer, llamar, ser, llegar, llevar, dormir, leer.** For example: **Nunca ve demasiado la tele.**

164

B **Consejos.** Tell Kim what she should do in each of the following cases in the left-hand column. Choose your answers from the column on the right.

Por ejemplo:

   viajar a España / recibir el pasaporte
   Si quieres viajar a España, debes recibir el pasaporte.

1. comprar ropa
2. saber algo del país
3. saber el idioma
4. sacar fotos
5. cambiar dinero
6. escribir a Pilar
7. llamar a los amigos

a. estudiar
b. ir al banco
c. saber la dirección
d. ir a las tiendas
e. llevar la cámara
f. leer libros y estudiar el mapa
g. saber el número de teléfono

C **En Madrid.** The following are some things Kim wants to do during her visit to Madrid. Use the photos to suggest where she might go. Play the roles with a classmate.

Por ejemplo:

   comer algo bueno

El Restaurante El Cuchi

ESTUDIANTE A
Quiero comer algo bueno.

1. visitar un museo importante
2. comprar regalos
3. ver una película en español

ESTUDIANTE B
Si quieres comer algo bueno, debes ir al restaurante El Cuchi.

4. dar un paseo con los amigos
5. ver un partido de fútbol
6. tomar un refresco

164   CAPÍTULO 3

For the Native Speaker

Imagine that you have a relative coming from either your hometown (or any Latin American country you desire) to stay with you for the summer. Write a short compostion describing where you plan to take your relative and what you plan as entertainment for him or her. Do some research on your city's landmarks, historical places, museums, shopping malls, etc., by writing to your city's Chamber of Commerce. From the information they send, you can choose different sites to visit.

El Parque del Retiro

El almacén El Corte Inglés

El Estadio Bernabéu

El Museo del Prado

El Cine Gran Vía

La Cafetería Manila

D **¡Buen viaje!** Before Kim left for Spain, Tony, a Spanish-speaking classmate, called her to wish her a good trip. Match Kim's replies to the questions he asked.

Tony

1. ¿Cuándo sales para Madrid?
2. ¿Y cuándo llegas?
3. ¿Es la primera vez que visitas España?
4. ¿Sabes algo de Madrid?
5. ¡Qué bueno que sabes el idioma!
6. ¿Recibes muchas cartas de Pilar?
7. ¿Y dónde vive Pilar?

Kim

a. No muchas. Pilar no escribe mucho.
b. En la calle Goya.
c. Pues sí, un poco, lo que leo en los libros, pero Madrid es una ciudad muy grande.
d. Sí. Es la primera vez que salgo de los Estados Unidos.
e. Sí, pero pienso practicar mucho. Quiero aprender más.
f. El domingo. Salgo a las siete de la tarde.
g. Llego a las once de la mañana.

165

3. Have students give their own list of things they always do or never do when they visit someone's home. For example: **Cuando visito la casa de un amigo, nunca hablo demasiado y siempre soy simpático(a).**

Actividad D Answers
1. f
2. g
3. d
4. c
5. e
6. a
7. b

Additional Practice
After doing Actividad D on this page, you may wish to reinforce the lesson with the following activities:

1. Tell students individually what they should and shouldn't do. If a students always does something, he or she responds with **siempre.** If he or she never does that thing, he or she responds with **nunca.**
   Por ejemplo: estudiar
   Siempre estudio.
   a. ser simpático(a)
   b. ahorrar dinero
   c. limpiar la habitación
   d. regresar temprano a casa
   e. trabajar en las clases
   f. saber las lecciones

2. Have students tell what advice their parents give them, that is, what their parents say they should or should not do. For example: **Debes estudiar más. No debes salir por la noche los lunes.**

Reteaching

Place the following items (or pictures of them) in a bag: camara, dictionary, passport, record, map, math book, calculator, skateboard, telephone, comfortable clothing, travelers checks, book, pencil, pen. Ask individual students whether or not the item he or she takes out of the bag should be included in a trip to Spain. **¿Debo llevar... a España?** Have students respond with a complete sentence.

Cultura viva 1

Presentation

Read the Cultura viva on this page. You may wish to bring to class additional photos of Spanish landmarks, to supplement those on page 166. You may also wish to share reproductions of works painted by the four Spanish artists named in the reading.

Did You Know?

Spain is the third largest country in Europe. Only the Soviet Union and France are larger. Spain is also the second most mountainous country in all of Europe (after Switzerland). In addition to many other attractions, Spain is known for two extensive beaches that span the Mediterranean. The painters mentioned in the reading are famous for different reasons: El Greco—for his surrealistic paintings depicting saints and martyrs. One of his most famous paintings is the one on page 166. Diego Velázquez was a court painter best known for *Las Meninas*, a portrait of the royal family with Velázquez himself in the foreground. Francisco Goya, a court painter of the 1800's, is famous for *El Tres de Mayo*, a depiction of the French invasion of Spain. Pablo Picasso developed a style (cubism) that became known for its bold inventiveness and sharp, delineated lines (see page 235).

Critical Thinking Activity

Based on both the reading and the photos on this page, make some general comparisons between the United States and Spain.

Actividad

Actividad Answer
Answers will vary.

¡España me encanta!

Spain is an ancient country of great beauty and variety with many monuments to mark its long history. Tourists marvel at its Roman ruins, its Moorish palaces, its medieval castles.

Spain has provided some of the world's greatest artists—El Greco, Velázquez, Goya, and Picasso. No tourist should leave Spain without spending at least one day in Madrid at the Museo del Prado to see some of the best works of these artists as well as artists from many other European countries.

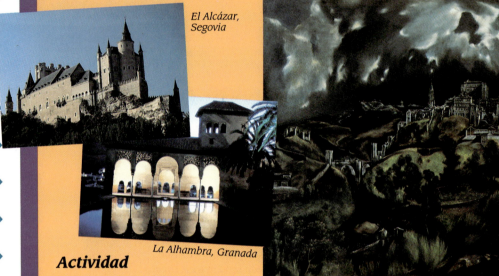

El Alcázar, Segovia

La Alhambra, Granada

Vista de Toledo, de El Greco

Actividad

You are going to Spain. Tell whether or not you want to do the following activities while you are there.

1. esquiar
2. comprar regalos
3. ir a la playa
4. visitar el Museo del Prado
5. comer comida española
6. ver un partido de fútbol
7. hablar español
8. hacer nuevos amigos

166

Pronunciation

A. You may wish to play the recorded version of these pronunciation lines, located at the end of Cassette 3.1. You may also wish to write this verse on the chalkboard and have students copy it into their notebook:
Quien no ha visto Sevilla
no ha visto maravilla.

Quien no ha visto Granada
no ha visto nada.

B. Have students repeat words and phrases individually and in unison. You may wish to focus on the following sounds:
/ll/ Sevilla; maravilla
/d/ Granada; nada

Estructura 1

How to Describe Routines   *Verbs ending in* -ir

To describe people's actions, you have used different forms of **-ar** and **-er** verbs.

> **Pablo, ¿estudias inglés?**
> **Elena, ¿quieres ir al cine?**
> **Pilar y Roberto no piensan hacer nada hoy.**
> **En mi casa comemos a las siete y media.**

1. There is a third category of verbs, which end in **-ir**. You have already used five of them.

> **escribir**
> **recibir**
> **salir**
> **vivir**
> **dormir (ue)**

To describe people's actions with these verbs, you use the same endings as for **-er** verbs.

> **¿Escriben ustedes muchas cartas?**
> **Miguel no escribe mucho pero yo escribo cartas a los amigos que viven en España. Recibo muchas también.**

2. The exception is the "we" form. It ends in **-imos.**

> **vivir**   **Vivimos en la calle Montero.**
> **salir**   **Los viernes salimos por la noche.**
> **escribir**   **No escribimos composiciones en la clase de álgebra.**

3. **Salir** is an **-ir** verb you will use often. It has one special form: when you want to say "I go out," say **salgo.**

> **Salgo con mis compañeros los sábados por la noche.**
> **Siempre salimos a las ocho.**

¿Te gusta salir por la noche?

Estructura 1

Structure Teaching Resources
1. Workbook, p. 73
2. Cassette 3.1
3. Student Tape Manual, p. 57
4. Estructura Masters 3.1
5. Lesson Quizzes, pp. 49–50

Bell Ringer Review

Directions to students: You are preparing for a trip to Spain. You will be gone for two weeks. Draw your suitcase and "pack" it. Then label in Spanish the items inside.

Presentation

Lead students through steps 1–3 on page 167. For step 2, you may want to give students additional examples of **-ir** verbs to demonstrate that, with the exception of the **nosotros** form, they already know these verb endings.

Actividades

Actividad A Answers
1. Vive en Madrid.
2. Viven en San Antonio.
3. Answers will vary.
4. Answers will vary.

Actividad B Answers
Answers will vary but should include the following:
1. Salgo por la noche los.../Salgo con...
2. Salimos a las...
3. Vamos a...
4. Hacemos... (or other appropriate verb)
5. Duermo hasta las...

Actividad C Answers
Answers will vary, however students should respond with at least five activities for each item.

Reteaching
A. Ask students how they would say they do the following: **recibir regalos; vivir en la ciudad; salir temprano; dormir mucho; escribir cartas**
B. Ask students how they would say that they and their friends do each of the activities in A.

Learning From Photos
You may want to ask students to identify the two figures represented in the statue.

Actividades

A **¿Dónde viven?** Tell where the following people live.

Por ejemplo:

> el presidente de los Estados Unidos
> *Vive en Washington.*

1. Pilar Mestre (la amiga de Kim)
2. David Vargas y Chris Pearson
3. tú y los compañeros
4. el /la maestro(a) de español

B **¿Te gusta salir?** Interview a classmate, asking the following questions. Write down your classmate's responses and report back to the class.

1. En general, ¿cuándo sales por la noche? ¿Con quién sales?
2. ¿A qué hora salen Uds.?
3. ¿Adónde van?
4. ¿Qué hacen?
5. Si sales el viernes por la noche, ¿hasta (until) qué hora duermes el sábado?

C **Todos los días.** Think of as many activities as possible that you and your classmates do in terms of the following categories.

Por ejemplo:

> en casa
> *En casa dormimos, hablamos por teléfono, vemos la tele, comemos, hacemos la tarea...*

1. después de las clases
2. en las clases
3. los fines de semana
4. en las vacaciones
5. por la noche
6. antes de los exámenes

En la Plaza de España.
¿Qué hacen los muchachos?

168 CAPÍTULO 3

Madrid

Madrid is Spain's capital and largest city. It is a metropolis of over four million people. People from Madrid (called **madrileños**) enjoy being outdoors year round, taking walks, window-shopping, or meeting in the many **plazas** throughout the city. **Plazas** are found at the intersection of several streets. Here **madrileños** can gather at outdoor **cafés,** buy newspapers and magazines at **quioscos** (stands), or sit and talk on park benches.

¿Qué quieres comprar?

¿Qué piensan comprar?

PLAZA DE CANALEJAS

La Plaza Mayor

Actividad

Give the names of the plazas shown on the map.

PLAZA DE ESPAÑA
PLAZA DE COLÓN
PLAZA DEL CARMEN
PLAZA DE CALLAO
PLAZA VÁSQUEZ DE MELLA
PLAZA DE SAN MARTÍN
PLAZA DE ISABEL II
PLAZA DE ORIENTE
PLAZA DE CIBELES
PLAZA DE SAN MIGUEL
PLAZA CANALEJAS
PUERTA DEL SOL
PLAZA MAYOR
PLAZA JACINTO BENAVENTE
PLAZA DE SANTA ANA
PLAZA TIRSO DE MOLINA

Lección 1 **169**

Pronunciation

A. You may wish to play the recorded version of these pronunciation lines, located at the end of Cassette 3.1. You may also wish to write this verse on the chalkboard and have students copy it into their notebook:
**No hay nada mejor
que pasar la tarde
en la Plaza Mayor.**

B. Have students repeat words and phrases individually and in unison. You may wish to focus on the /z/ sound as in **plaza.**

Cultura viva 2

Presentation

Read the Cultura viva on this page. You may wish to bring to class additional photos of Madrid landmarks, to supplement those on page 169.

Did You Know?

Madrid is located on a plateau about 2,150 feet above sea level. It is one of the highest capitals in Europe. Madrid became the capital of Spain in 1561 largely because of its location near the exact geographic center of Spain. One of Madrid's most famous plazas is **la Plaza de España** with its large statues of Don Quijote and Sancho Panza (see opposite page). Another important plaza is the large, crescent-shaped **Puerta del Sol** which marks the center of downtown Madrid.

An important building in Madrid is **el Palacio Real**, built in the 1700's. The Spanish royal family lived in the palace until 1931. The present king of Spain, Juan Carlos, lives with his family in the **Palacio Zarzuela**, located on the outskirts of the city. Madrid is also known for a huge park called **el Parque del Retiro**, which covers more than 350 acres.

Critical Thinking Activity
Based on both the reading and the photos on this page, make some comparisons between your city or town and Madrid.

Actividad Answers
Answers are given on the map on this page.

Learning From Photos
You may want to ask students to make one statement in Spanish about each photo on this page.

169

Structure Teaching Resources

1. Workbook, pp. 74–77
2. Cassette 3.1
3. Student Tape Manual, p. 58
4. Estructura Masters 3.1
5. Lesson Quizzes, pp. 51–52

Bell Ringer Review

Directions to students: Draw three circles on your paper and write one of the following words in each: **dinero, pasaporte,** and **vivir.** Around each circle write all the words or expressions you can think of related to the principal word. Connect each word to the circle with a straight line.

Structure Focus

Estructura 2 provides a summary and review of **-ar, -er,** and **-ir** verbs. Estructura 2 also presents subject pronouns.

Presentation

Lead students through steps 1–5 on pages 170 and 171. You may wish to stress to your students that subject pronouns are normally used only for emphasis or clarification.

Estructura 2

How to Talk about What People Generally Do

How to Compare and Contrast, and to Emphasize and Clarify

Summary of -ar, -er, and -ir verbs

Subject pronouns

1. The verb endings you have been using express what people generally do or are currently doing. By changing the endings, you indicate the subject of the verb (the person doing the action). The following are the endings for regular **-ar, -er,** and **-ir** verbs.

hablar		comer	
SINGULAR	PLURAL	SINGULAR	PLURAL
hablo	hablamos	como	comemos
hablas	habláis*	comes	coméis*
habla	hablan	come	comen

escribir	
SINGULAR	PLURAL
escribo	escribimos
escribes	escribís*
escribe	escriben

*This form is rarely used in the Spanish-speaking world, except for Spain.

2. Sometimes you will want to make a comparison between what you and someone else want to do. In English, we make these comparisons by stressing such words as "I" and "he."

   I am going to watch this, but *she* wants to watch that.

In Spanish you make this kind of emphasis by adding words such as **yo** (I) and **tú** (you). These words are called pronouns.

Yo voy a ver la tele pero ella va a escuchar música.

I'm going to watch TV, but *she's* going to listen to music.

Cooperative Learning

Each member of each team will write down his or her daily activities under the categories **a veces, siempre,** or **nunca.** Each team will then prepare a graph of their combined daily activities. As a whole class project, combine the team graphs into one class graph.

3. The following are the people you can talk about.

SINGULAR		PLURAL	
yo	I	**nosotros(as)**	we
tú	you	**vosotros(as)***	you
usted	you	**ustedes**	you
él	he	**ellos**	they
ella	she	**ellas**	they

*This form is rarely used in the Spanish-speaking world, except for Spain.

4. As you have seen before, you can also use these words when it would otherwise not be clear whom you were talking about.

> **Mi papá y mi mamá quieren ver un programa de deportes en la tele pero él prefiere el fútbol y ella prefiere el baloncesto.**

5. These pronouns can also stand alone.

> **¿Quién toca la guitarra?**   **Yo.**
> **¿Quién va al partido?**   **Ella.**

Since the words "I, you, he, she" and so on are already indicated by the verb ending in Spanish, use these pronouns only when you want to emphasize or clarify.

Actividades

A ¡Qué va! Bruno says that he no longer (ya no) does certain things. How would his girlfriend Alicia contradict him? Play the roles with a classmate.

¿Qué revistas lees?

Por ejemplo:

> comer mucho

ESTUDIANTE A	ESTUDIANTE B
Ya no como mucho.	¡Qué va! Siempre comes mucho.

1. leer revistas
2. ver programas tontos
3. salir con amigos tacaños
4. llamar a los amigos a las once de la noche
5. tomar Coca-Cola de desayuno
6. dormir en la clase de historia

Lección 1 **171**

Actividades

Actividad A Answers
1. Ya no leo revistas. / ¡Qué va! Siempre lees revistas.
2. ... veo programas tontos./ ... ves...
3. ... salgo con amigos tacaños. / ... sales...
4. ... llamo a los amigos... / ... llamas...
5. ... tomo Coca-Cola... / ... tomas...
6. ... duermo en la clase de historia. / ... duermes...

Answers will vary but should include the following:

1. Llegamos...
2. Estudiamos...
3. Comemos...
4. Salimos...
5. Hacemos...(or other appropriate verb)
6. Vemos...
7. (No) Necesitamos...
8. Vamos... /Comemos
9. (No) Llamamos...
10. (No) Trabajamos... /
    (No) Ahorramos...

Extension

After doing Actividad B, you may wish to reinforce the learning by doing this activity once again in an interview format. Have one or two students ask these questions of two classmates. The two classmates can agree, disagree, or correct each other. For example,

Estudiante A: Salimos a las siete y media.

Estudiante B: No es verdad. Mi amiga y yo salimos a las siete y cuarto.

Actividad C Answers

Answers will vary, however students should use the subject pronouns **yo** and **él/ella** in each statement.

Actividad D Answers

Answers will vary.

Reteaching

Ask students to give the corresponding subject pronoun for each of the following verb forms: **vivo, corren, vemos, trabajan, escribes, llega, compro, hacemos, leen, escribimos, aprendes, baila, voy, gana.**

B **¿Cómo son los norteamericanos?** Some students from Spain want to know what a typical school day is like in the United States. Answer their questions.

Por ejemplo:

> ¿A qué hora salen Uds. de casa?
> *Salimos a las siete y media.*

1. ¿A qué hora llegan a la escuela?
2. ¿Qué estudian?
3. ¿Dónde comen?
4. ¿A qué hora salen de la escuela?
5. ¿Qué hacen después de las clases?
6. ¿Qué ven en la tele?
7. ¿Necesitan estudiar todas las noches?
8. Cuando salen por la noche, ¿adónde van? ¿Qué comen?
9. Por la noche, ¿llaman a los amigos?
10. ¿Trabajan? ¿Ahorran dinero?

C **Somos diferentes.** Write down six statements comparing what you and your best friend do.

Por ejemplo:

> Yo estudio mucho, pero él (ella) nunca estudia.

D **Encuesta.** Working in groups of three, answer the following questions. Appoint a reporter to take notes. Respond with: **yo / él y yo / ella y yo / él / ella / ellos / ellas.** Your teacher will ask the reporter for the results of the survey.

Por ejemplo:

MAESTRO(A)	REPORTERO(A)
¿Quién va a trabajar después de las clases?	Yo (Ella y yo, ellos, etc.).

1. ¿Quién va a ver la tele esta noche?
2. ¿Quién piensa practicar deportes esta tarde?
3. ¿Quién va a estudiar español el año que viene (next year)?
4. ¿Quién va a leer un libro esta noche?
5. ¿Quién quiere visitar España?
6. ¿Quién va a hablar por teléfono hoy?

172 CAPÍTULO 3

Finalmente

Finalmente

Situaciones

A conversar Converse with a classmate on the topic of travel.

1. Find out if your classmate likes to travel.
2. Ask where he or she wants to go on vacation.
3. Ask what he or she does to get ready for the trip **(antes de viajar).**
4. Ask what items he or she takes along.
5. Find out what your classmate likes to do there.
6. Reverse roles.

A escribir You are writing a travel article for the school newspaper.

1. Name a place that you think your classmates would enjoy visiting. **(Deben visitar...).**
2. Tell what they should do or see there.
3. List items that they should take with them.

Repaso de vocabulario

COSAS	PERSONAS	ACTIVIDADES
la calle	él	ahorrar
la cámara	ella	cambiar
la carta	ellas	deber
el cheque de viajero	ellos	dormir (ue)
el diccionario	la familia	hacer las maletas
la maleta	nosotros(as)	llamar
el mapa	tú	llevar
el número de teléfono	ustedes	olvidar
el país	vosotros(as)*	recibir
el pasaporte	yo	recordar (ue)
la ropa		salir

viajar
vivir

OTRAS PALABRAS Y EXPRESIONES

antes de
cómodo(a)
después de
si

*This form is rarely used in the Spanish-speaking world, except for Spain.

Situaciones

Lesson 1 Evaluation
The A conversar and A escribir situations on this page are designed to give students the opportunity to use as many language functions as possible listed on page 160 of this lesson. The A conversar and A escribir are also intended to show how well students are able to meet the lesson objectives, also listed on page 160 of this lesson.

Presentation

Prior to doing the A conversar and A escribir on this page, you may wish to play the Situaciones listening activities on Cassette 3.1 as a means of helping students organize the material.

Repaso de vocabulario

The words and phrases in the Repaso de vocabulario have been taught for productive use in this lesson. They are summarized here as a resource for both students and teacher. The Repaso de vocabulario also serves as a convenient resource for the A conversar and A escribir activities on this page. It also gives the teacher a source for writing either additional practice or evaluation activities such as quizzes and tests in addition to those provided by the publisher.

For the Native Speaker

Imagine you are a travel agent. A customer calls you and requests a written description of a trip to a certain locale in a Hispanic country. Include in your travel description a list of items the traveler must take along, and how he or she must prepare before his or her trip.

Lección 2

Objectives

By the end of this lesson, students will be able to:

1. talk about where people and things are located
2. list things in order
3. identify the floors of a building

Lesson 2 Resources

1. Workbook, pp. 78–83
2. Vocabulario Transparency 3.2
3. Cassette 3.2
4. Student Tape Manual, pp. 61–65
5. Lesson Quizzes, pp. 53–56
6. Computer Software, Disk 1
7. Video Cassette
8. Estructura Masters 3.2
9. Diversiones Masters 3.2

Bell Ringer Review

Directions to students: Your friend doesn't know how to have fun. Write a list of at least ten things he or she should do.

¡A comenzar!

Presentation

A. Lead students through each of the five functions given on page 174, progressing from the English to the Spanish for each function. Then have students find these words and phrases in the dialogue on page 175.

B. Introduce the Lesson 2 dialogue by reading it aloud or by playing the cassette version. Tell students that they are going to hear a telephone conversation. Ask them to listen for the following information:
    1. Where Kim says she is.

Lección 2

¡Todos esperamos tu visita!

¡A comenzar!

The following are some of the things you will be learning to do in this lesson.

When you want to . . .	You use . . .
1. say where you are	• **Estoy en** + place.
2. ask a friend where he or she is	• **¿Dónde estás?**
3. say where something is located	• **Está en** + place.
4. tell where you and someone else (we) are	• **Estamos en** + place.
5. refer to the floor of a building	• **el** + ordinal number + **piso**

Now find examples of the above words and phrases in the following conversation.

174

Getting Ready for Lesson 2

You may wish to use one or more of the following suggestions to prepare students for the lesson.

1. Have students look at the map of Madrid on page 177 as you describe the location of various things in the city using **está**. For example:
Madrid es una ciudad muy grande e interesante. Vamos a ver algunos edificios importantes. Por ejemplo, el **Museo del Prado está en el Paseo del Prado.**

2. Ask students to name the streets and plazas where certain places can be found. For example: **¿Dónde está la Biblioteca Nacional?** Allow students to respond with only the street name.

3. Ask students individually if they live in a house or apartment: **¿Vives en una**

In Madrid Kim leaves her hotel and calls Pilar.

KIM: **A ver… ¿dónde está el número de teléfono de Pilar? Ah, claro. Está en la carta. (*Marca el número*). ¡Hola, Pilar! ¡Ya estoy en Madrid!**

PILAR: **¡Kim! ¡Ya estás aquí? ¡Qué bueno! ¿Dónde estás?**

KIM: **Estoy en la calle Princesa.**

PILAR: **Ah, bueno. Entonces, debes tomar el Metro. Estamos en Colón, línea 4. Recuerdas mi dirección, ¿no?**

KIM: **Sí, la calle Goya, 85.**

PILAR: **Exacto. Estamos en el primer piso. ¡Todos esperamos tu visita!**

KIM: **Bueno, adiós, hasta pronto.**

Actividad preliminar

Tell where the following places are located.

Por ejemplo:
> tu escuela
> *Mi escuela está en la calle Balboa.*

1. tu casa
2. San Antonio
3. Madrid
4. el apartamento de Pilar
5. tu restaurante favorito

Lección 2 **175**

2. How Pilar says Kim can get to her home
3. Pilar's address
4. What floor Pilar lives on

C. Now ask students to open their books and look at the dialogue as you lead them through what is said. As you lead students through the dialogue, alternate between questions about Pilar, and personalized questions to the class. For example:

1. **Cuando quieres ir de compras, ¿cómo llegas al centro? ¿Tomas el autobús? ¿Vas en coche? ¿Vas en bicicleta? Pues, en Madrid, muchos van de un lugar a otro en metro.**
2. **El metro es un sistema de transporte muy rápido. ¿Cuántas líneas hay?** (Have students look at the metro map on page 178.)
3. **Si quieres visitar a Pilar y estás en la Puerta del Sol. ¿qué línea necesitas tomar?**
4. **¿Vive Pilar en una casa o en un apartamento? ¿En qué piso vive?**
5. **¿Cuántos de ustedes viven en apartamento? ¿En qué piso está tu apartamento, _____?**
6. **¿Cuántos de ustedes viven en casa particular?**
7. **¿Cuántos pisos hay en tu casa, Sue? ¿uno? ¿dos? ¿tres? ¿En qué piso está tu habitación?**
8. **¿Cuál es el número de teléfono de Pilar? ¿Qué número debemos marcar para saber si tú estás en casa, _____?**

Actividad preliminar

Actividad preliminar Answers

1. Answers will vary.
2. San Antonio está en Texas.
3. Madrid está en España.
4. El apartamento de Pilar está en la calle Goya, 85.
5. Answers will vary.

casa o en un apartamento? Have them tell where their homes are. For example: **¿Dónde está tu casa (apartamento)?**

4. You may wish to play a geography game and have students guess whether or not you are right as you give real or fictitous locations of cities and countries. Students should respond with **sí** or **no**. Allow five seconds for students to consult with classmates. For example:

1. **Argentina está en la América Central.**
2. **España está en Europa.**
3. **Bogotá está en México.**
4. **Costa Rica está en la América del Sur. Etc.**

Bell Ringer Review

Directions to students: List five of your favorite television shows and tell what day of the week and what time they are on.
Por ejemplo: Los jueves veo el Cosby Show a las ocho de la noche.

Presentation

A. Have students open their books to page 176. Model the question, **¿Dónde está el apartmento?** Then model each new phrase. Begin each time with the phrase **Está en...** Have students repeat each phrase in unison.

B. Tell students that if they wish to go beyond **décimo**, they should use the cardinal system: **el piso once/doce, etc.**
Note. The word **piso** (floor or story) is often used in Spain to indicate apartment. The word **apartamento** has been used throughout this series, however, because it is more universal. **Departamento** is another regionalism of **apartamento.**

When Students Ask

You may wish to give students the following additional vocabulary to allow them to talk about their city or neighborhood.

el bulevar	el barrio
la cuadra	las afueras

Vocabulario

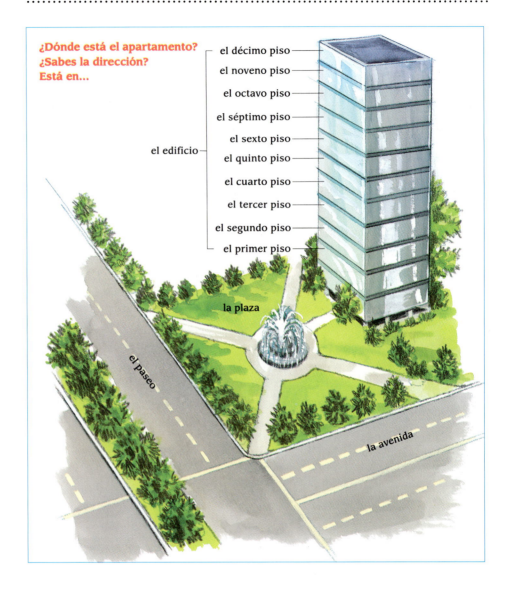

¿Dónde está el apartamento?
¿Sabes la dirección?
Está en...

el décimo piso
el noveno piso
el octavo piso
el séptimo piso
el sexto piso
el quinto piso
el cuarto piso
el tercer piso
el segundo piso
el primer piso

el edificio

la plaza

el paseo

la avenida

176 CAPÍTULO 3

Total Physical Response

Getting Ready
On butcher paper, draw a building and label the floors using numbers (1°, 2°, ...10°). Staple envelopes to each floor so that items may be placed in them. Place the objects for **TPR 1** on a table in front of the class. For **TPR 2**, make copies of the metro map on page 178. Delete the numbers next to the stations, and make one copy per student. Model the vocabulary prior to doing the activity.

New Words

lleva	prepara
sigan	continúen

TPR 1

Pon el "bolígrafo" en el tercer piso.
Lleva el "lápiz" al sexto piso.
Esconde el "papel" en el primer piso.

Actividades

A **¿Dónde están?** Use the map of Madrid to tell where each of the following places is located.

Por ejemplo:

El Corte Inglés
El Corte Inglés está en el Paseo de la Castellana.

1. el Museo del Prado
2. la Biblioteca Nacional
3. la Estación de Atocha
4. el Estadio Bernabéu
5. el Palacio Real

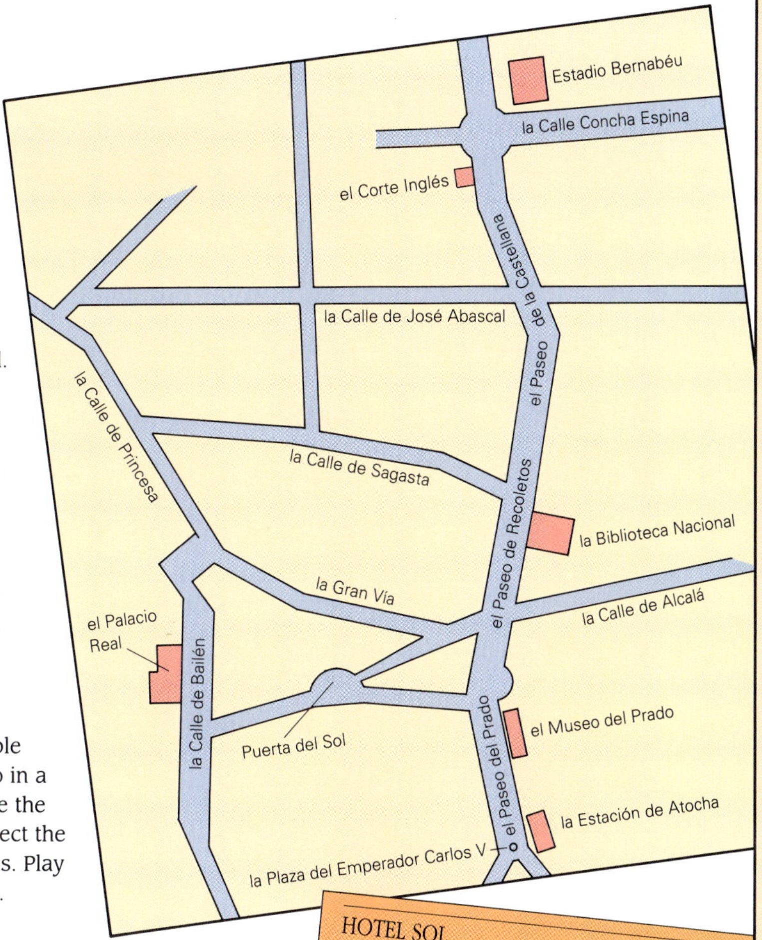

Estadio Bernabéu
la Calle Concha Espina
el Corte Inglés
el Paseo de la Castellana
la Calle de José Abascal
la Calle de Princesa
la Calle de Sagasta
el Paseo de Recoletos
la Biblioteca Nacional
la Gran Vía
la Calle de Alcalá
el Palacio Real
la Calle de Bailén
Puerta del Sol
el Museo del Prado
el Paseo del Prado
la Estación de Atocha
la Plaza del Emperador Carlos V

B **El edificio.** The people below have business to do in a building in Madrid. You are the building's receptionist. Direct the people to their destinations. Play the roles with a classmate.

Por ejemplo:

Sra. Durán / el Hotel Sol

ESTUDIANTE A	ESTUDIANTE B
¿Dónde está el Hotel Sol, por favor?	Está en el tercer piso, señora.

1. Sr. López / la Agencia de Viajes Mundotur
2. Srta. Sabio / la Escuela de Idiomas Serrat
3. Srta. Zayas / la Óptica Unilens
4. Sr. Camacho / la Librería Costas
5. Srta. Larra / el Restaurante Sevilla

HOTEL SOL	3ER PISO
RESTAURANTE SEVILLA	1ER PISO
LIBRERÍA COSTAS	6º PISO
AGENCIA DE VIAJES MUNDOTUR	2º PISO
ESCUELA DE IDIOMAS SERRAT	5º PISO
ÓPTICA UNILENS	7º PISO

Actividades

Actividad A Answers

1. El Museo del Prado está en el Paseo del Prado.
2. La Biblioteca Nacional... el Paseo de Recoletos.
3. La Estación de Atocha... la Plaza del Emperador Carlos V.
4. El Estadio de Bernabéu... Concha Espina.
5. El Palacio Real... la Calle de Bailén.

Actividad B Answers

1. ¿Dónde está la Agencia de Viajes Mundotur, por favor?/ Está en el segundo piso, señor.
2. ¿... la Escuela de Idiomas Serrat,...?/... quinto piso, señorita.
3. ¿... la Óptica Unilens,...?/ ... séptimo piso, señorita.
4. ¿... la Librería Costas,...?/ ... sexto piso, señor.
5. ¿... el Restaurante Sevilla,...?/ ... primer piso, señorita.

Additional Practice

After doing Actividades A and B, you may wish to reinforce the learning by doing the following activity: Write down eight things that you like to do, in order of preference. **Por ejemplo: Primero: Me gusta comer. Segundo: Me gusta ir al cine.** After allowing for preparation time, have students report to the class.

Reteaching

Have students list their recommendations for someone trying to learn Spanish, in order of importance. For example: **Primero: practicar mucho, etc.**

Learning From Realia

A. You may want to have several students read the directory on this page in proper sequence.
B. You may want to make several statements and have students say where you should go. For example, **Necesito un hotel en Madrid. Usted debe ir al Hotel Sol. Está en el 3er piso.**

Lee la "carta" en el noveno piso.
Haz la "maleta" en el segundo piso.
Prepara el "sandwich" en el séptimo piso.
Busca el "número" en el cuarto piso.
Escribe la "carta" en el octavo piso.
Prepara la "lección" en el quinto piso.

TPR 2

(Using the metro map on page 178, tell students where they are to go. They are to write the ordinal number next to the location and draw arrows in the direction they are told to move.)
Primero, vayan a Esperanza.
Segundo, vayan a Ventas.
Tercero, sigan a Avenida América.
Cuarto, vayan a Cuatro Caminos.
Quinto, vayan a Ópera.
Sexto, continúen a Laguna.
Séptimo, regresen a Ópera.

Cultura viva 1

Presentation

Read the Cultura viva on this page. Then proceed to the Actividad. You may wish to discuss the subway system of some major cities in the U.S.

Did You Know?

The metro is a popular means of transportation in many major cities around the world—London, Paris, Mexico City, as well as Madrid.

Note. In Spain **coger el metro** is more commonly used than **tomar**. In many Latin American countries the word used is **tomar**.

Critical Thinking Activity

A. What advantages does the metro system offer compared to other transportation systems? Why are metros more common in larger cities?

B. Working in teams, have students ''build'' a Metro for their town or city. Where would they build the stations, stops, special ''attractions'' and sights? Have them draw their blueprints and compare them with the other teams.

Actividad

Actividad Answers

1. 4
2. 8
3. 3
4. 9
5. 5

Extension

After doing the Actividad, you may wish to extend the learning by giving students additional places on the map. Have students volunteer their own trips on the metro. For example, **Estoy en Oporto. Quiero ir a Sol.**

C U L T U R A   V I V A   1

El Metro de Madrid

In addition to many buses and taxis, Madrid has an efficient and inexpensive subway system called **el Metro**. There are ten lines with connections to all parts of the city.

Actividad

Tell what line you and a friend should take to get to the following places.

Por ejemplo:

> El hotel de Kim está en Ventura Rodríguez. *Debemos tomar la línea 3.*

1. La casa de Pilar está en Colón.
2. La estación de trenes está en Chamartín.
3. El parque zoológico está en Batán.
4. El Estadio Bernabéu está en Concha Espina.
5. Muchos cines están en Callao.

178   CAPÍTULO 3

Pronunciation

A. You may wish to play the recorded version of these pronunciation lines, located at the end of Cassette 3.2. You may also wish to write this verse on the board and have students copy it into their notebook:

Parada primera,
Manuel Becerra.
Luego, Sevilla.

Después la Gran Vía.
Ahora llego a Prosperidad.
¡Y así recorro la ciudad!

B. Have students repeat words and phrases individually and in unison. You may wish to focus on the /r/ and /rr/ sounds as in **primera; Prosperidad; Becerra; recorro.**

178

Estructura 1

....

How to List Things in Order   ***Ordinal numbers***

1. The words **primero, segundo, tercero,** etc. are called ordinal numbers because they tell the order of things. When you use them to describe a masculine (**el**) word, they end in **-o.** When you use them to describe a feminine (**la**) word, they end in **-a.**

    el segundo partido   **la tercera clase**

2. However, when you use **primero** or **tercero** before a masculine singular word, you drop the final **-o.**

    Mañana es el primer día de clases.
    La gaveta de Luis está en el tercer piso.

3. The following abbreviations are commonly used:
    a. when the ordinals end in **-o:**   **2° piso, 4° examen**
    b. when the ordinals end in **-a:**   **3ª clase, 5ª lección**
    c. when the ordinals end in **-er:**   **1ᵉʳ piso, 3ᵉʳ piso**

Actividades

A **Mis clases.** List your classes in order (first, second, etc.).

Por ejemplo:

    La primera clase es álgebra.

B **Está en...** Use the information below to say where the following people are.

Por ejemplo:

    la familia Mestre: 1ᵉʳ piso
    La familia Mestre está en el primer piso.

1. Linda: 2° curso de inglés
2. Marisol: 8° grado
3. Javier: 3ª clase del día
4. José Luis: 4ª clase del día
5. Juana: 5ª avenida de Nueva York
6. Paco: 1ᵉʳ piso
7. la familia Morán: 3ᵉʳ piso
8. la familia Centeno: 10° piso

For the Native Speaker
You have just earned enough money to go on a trip. List which countries you would like to visit and what objects you would need to take along. Then list some countries where you would not like to visit.

Structure Teaching Resources
1. Workbook, pp. 79–81
2. Cassette 3.2
3. Student Tape Manual, p. 62
4. Estructura Masters 3.2
5. Lesson Quizzes, p. 54

Bell Ringer Review
Directions to students: Tell how often you do each of the following activities, using **siempre, a veces,** or **nunca.**
1. **dormir en la clase**
2. **comer bien**
3. **entender las tareas**
4. **salir con amigos antipáticos**
5. **llegar tarde a la escuela**

Presentation
Lead students through steps 1–3 on page 179. For step 2 you may want to refer students to the lesson Vocabulario, page 176, for additional examples. For step 3, you may wish to write these examples on the chalkboard for emphasis.

Actividades
Actividad A Answers
Answers will vary.

Actividad B Answers
1. Linda está en el segundo curso de inglés.
2. Marisol... el octavo grado.
3. Javier... la tercera clase del día.
4. José Luis... la cuarta clase del día.
5. Juana... la quinta avenida de Nueva York.
6. Paco... el primer piso.
7. La familia Morán... el tercer piso.
8. La familia Centeno... el décimo piso.

C **En el hotel.** A student tour group is staying at a hotel in Madrid. You are looking for the following students. Your classmate will tell you what floor each person's room is on, according to the directory below.

Susana Acevedo	312
Héctor Ayala	420
Amalia Bell	521
Julia Malaret	605
Jorge Menéndez	710
Ángela Romero	802
Felipe Santos	120
Marisol Serrat	918
Andrés Velázquez	216

Por ejemplo:

ESTUDIANTE A

(1) **Por favor, ¿en qué piso está la habitación de Susana Acevedo?**

(3) **Gracias.**

1. Felipe Santos
2. Marisol Serrat
3. Jorge Menéndez
4. Julia Malaret
5. Héctor Ayala
6. Ángela Romero
7. Andrés Velázquez

ESTUDIANTE B

(2) **Está en el tercer piso.**

(4) **De nada.**

La Plaza de la Cibeles

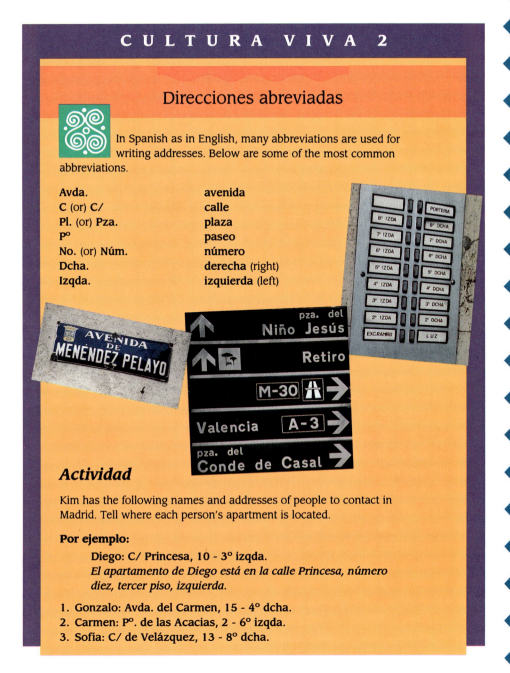

CULTURA VIVA 2

Direcciones abreviadas

In Spanish as in English, many abbreviations are used for writing addresses. Below are some of the most common abbreviations.

Avda.	**avenida**
C (or) **C/**	**calle**
Pl. (or) **Pza.**	**plaza**
Pº	**paseo**
No. (or) **Núm.**	**número**
Dcha.	**derecha** (right)
Izqda.	**izquierda** (left)

Actividad

Kim has the following names and addresses of people to contact in Madrid. Tell where each person's apartment is located.

Por ejemplo:

> Diego: C/ Princesa, 10 - 3º izqda.
> *El apartamento de Diego está en la calle Princesa, número diez, tercer piso, izquierda.*

1. Gonzalo: Avda. del Carmen, 15 - 4º dcha.
2. Carmen: Pº. de las Acacias, 2 - 6º izqda.
3. Sofía: C/ de Velázquez, 13 - 8º dcha.

Presentation

Read the Cultura viva on this page. Lead students through the abbreviations following the reading. Then have students cover the column on the right. Find out whether they can guess the meaning of the abbreviation.

Learning From Photos

You may want to ask students to look at the photos in the Cultura viva and ask them to find all the abbreviations used.

Critical Thinking Activity

Draw a simple map of the street where you live. Locate your house or apartment on the map and write down the directions for finding it. Use as many of the abbreviations on page 181 as possible.

Actividad Answers

1. **El apartamento de Gonzalo está en la Avenida del Carmen, número quince, cuarto piso, derecha.**
2. **... Carmen... Paseo de las Acacias, número dos, sexto piso, izquierda.**
3. **... Sofía... Calle de Velázquez, número trece, octavo piso, derecha.**

Pronunciation

A. You may wish to play the recorded version of these pronunciation lines, located at the end of Cassette 3.2. You may also wish to write this verse on the chalkboard and have students copy it into their notebook:

**Calle del Carmen,
número uno,
vive mi amiga,
piso segundo.**

B. Have students repeat words and phrases individually and in unison. You may wish to focus on the /c/ sound as in **Calle, Carmen.**

Bell Ringer Review

Directions to students: Do you remember gifts from past birthdays? Write down a list of birthday gifts you have received in the past. Follow the model. Draw a picture if you don't know the vocabulary word. **Por ejemplo:**
mi primer regalo: un libro

Presentation

A. Lead students through steps 1–3 on page 182. In step 1, model each form of **estar** for familiarity.
B. There is no attempt to compare and contrast **ser** and **estar** in this presentation. This comparison is made in Level 2.

Learning From Realia

A. You may want to ask your students to look at the advertisement for **Cafeterías California S.A.** and say where each **cafetería** is located, using **estar**. You may also want to review numbers by asking students to tell the various telephone numbers given. Have them give each number separately.
B. You may wish to explain that the abbreviation **S.A.** is equivalent to *Inc.* in English.

Estructura 2

How to Say Where People and Things Are Located　　*The verb* estar

1. You have already practiced saying where someone or something is located by using **está**, as in **La casa de Pilar está en la calle Goya.** Here are the forms of the verb **estar.**

SINGULAR	PLURAL
estoy	estamos
estás	estáis*
está	están

*This form is rarely used in the Spanish-speaking world, except for Spain.

2. The word **en** usually follows the form of **estar** to indicate "at," "in," or "on."

   Miguel está en casa.
   Pilar está en la clase de inglés.
   Mi apartamento está en la calle Segovia.

3. If you want to ask where someone or something is located, use the word **¿dónde?**

   ¿Dónde estás?
   ¿Dónde están los libros de Pilar?

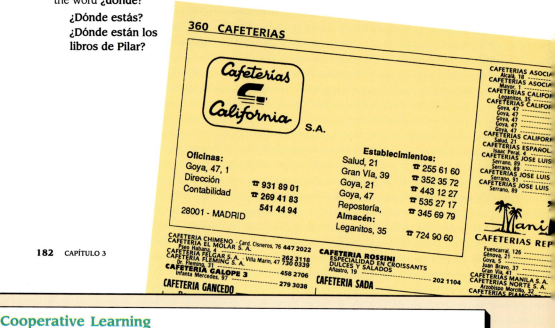

182 CAPÍTULO 3

Cooperative Learning

Give each pair of students a blank floor plan of your school. Students will take turns dictating information about room numbers to each other. Hint: Alternate floors.

Actividades

A **Todo el día.** Take notes while you ask where a classmate generally is at various times during the day. Report back to the class.

Por ejemplo:

> a las ocho de la mañana

ESTUDIANTE A

¿Dónde estás a las ocho de la mañana?

ESTUDIANTE B

A las ocho de la mañana estoy en la clase de historia.

(A la clase:) A las ocho de la mañana, Roberto está en la escuela, en la clase de historia.

1. a las siete de la mañana
2. a las nueve y media de la mañana
3. a las doce de la tarde
4. a la una y media de la tarde
5. a las tres y media de la tarde
6. a las seis de la tarde
7. a las nueve de la noche

B **El horario.** Kim needs to be at certain places at certain times. Tell where she is at the following times, according to her schedule.

Por ejemplo:

> A las nueve está en la clase de español.

9:00 la clase de español
10:30 el Museo del Prado con los compañeros de clase
1:00 la casa de Pilar
5:30 la cafetería California con Jorge
8:00 el cine Goya con Pilar
10:00 el hotel Gran Vía

Actividades

Actividad A Answers

Answers will vary, however students should use the correct form of **estar** in each question and response.

Class Management

Actividad A may be done as a whole class activity initially, if preferred. The teacher takes the role of Student A, calling on individual students to respond for Student B. This activity may be done a second time in pairs.

Actividad B Answers

1. A las diez y media, Kim está en el Museo del Prado con los compañeros de clase.
2. A la una,... la casa de Pilar.
3. A las cinco y media,... la Cafetería California con Jorge.
4. A las ocho,... el cine Goya con Pilar.
5. A las diez,... el hotel Gran Vía.

C **¿Dónde están?** At various times during the day, Pilar's mother wonders where Pilar and Kim are. Respond according to the photos. Then guess what the two girls are probably doing in each place.

Por ejemplo:

> Están en el parque. Dan un paseo (Montan en bicicleta, etc.).

1.

2.

3.

4.

5.

D **Debemos tomar el Metro.** You and a classmate are in Madrid. Tell where the two of you are and where you want to go. Your classmate tells which **Metro** line to take to reach your destination. Use the map on page 178.

Por ejemplo:

> Moncloa / Bilbao

ESTUDIANTE A	ESTUDIANTE B
Estamos en Moncloa y queremos ir a Bilbao.	Debemos tomar la línea 3. Debemos cambiar a la línea 4 en Argüelles.

1. Atocha / la Gran Vía
2. Retiro / Quevedo
3. Lago / Ríos Rosas

4. Serrano / Ventas
5. Chamartín / Concha Espina

Finalmente

Finalmente

Situaciones

A conversar Converse with a classmate about a party.

1. Ask your partner if he or she wants to go to a party at a classmate's house.
2. Your partner asks what day the party is.
3. Respond and also tell what time the party is.
4. Your partner asks where your classmate's home is.
5. Give the full address and phone number.

A escribir The Chamber of Commerce has asked you to write a brochure about the points of interest in your area for Spanish-speaking visitors.

1. Write about the five most important places visitors to your area should see **(Primero deben..., segundo...).**
2. Then write where each of the above attractions is located.

Repaso de vocabulario

PREGUNTAS

¿Dónde está?
¿En qué piso está?

DIRECCIONES

el apartamento
la avenida
la dirección
el edificio
el paseo
el piso
la plaza

NÚMEROS ORDINALES

primero(a)
segundo(a)
tercero(a)
cuarto(a)
quinto(a)
sexto(a)
séptimo(a)
octavo(a)
noveno(a)
décimo(a)

ACTIVIDAD

tomar (to take)

EXPRESIÓN

estar en

Lección 2 **185**

Situaciones

Lesson 2 Evaluation
The A conversar and A escribir situations on this page are designed to give students the opportunity to use as many language functions as possible listed on page 174 of this lesson. The A conversar and A escribir are also intended to show how well students are able to meet the lesson objectives, also listed on page 174 of this lesson.

Presentation
Prior to doing the A conversar and A escribir on this page, you may wish to play the Situaciones listening activities on Cassette 3.2 as a means of helping students organize the material.

Repaso de vocabulario

The words and phrases in the Repaso de vocabulario have been taught for productive use in this lesson. They are summarized here as a resource for both students and teacher. The Repaso de vocabulario also serves as a convenient resource for the A conversar and A escribir activities on this page. It also gives the teacher a source for writing either additional practice or evaluation activities such as quizzes and tests in addition to those provided by the publisher.

For the Native Speaker
Ask native speakers to draw a layout an imaginary building with 5–10 floors (apartment, department store, library, museum, and hotel and restaurant). They will label each floor and add details such as people, furniture, and addressses, using vocabulary from Chapter 3, Lesson 2.

Lección 3

Objectives

By the end of this lesson, students will be able to:

1. tell where people and things are located
2. use numbers from 20 to 100
3. say what there is around them

Lesson 3 Resources

1. Workbook, pp. 84–88
2. Vocabulario Transparency 3.3
3. Cassette 3.3
4. Student Tape Manual, pp. 66–71
5. Lesson Quizzes, pp. 56–59
6. Test Booklet, pp. 41–46
7. Computer Software, Disk 1
8. Video Cassette
9. Estructura Masters 3.3
10. Diversiones Masters 3.3

Bell Ringer Review

Directions to students:
In Spanish give the abbreviations for the following: avenue/street / left/right.

¡A comenzar!

Presentation

A. Lead students through each of the three functions given on page 186, progressing from the English to the Spanish for each function. Then have students find these words and phrases in the dialogue on page 187.

Lección 3

¿Dónde está la calle Goya?

¡A comenzar!

The following are some of the things you will be learning to do in this lesson.

When you want to . . .	You use . . .
1. indicate something to the left / right	• **a la izquierda / a la derecha**
2. say what there is around you	• **Hay** + object(s).
3. point out someone or something in the distance	• **Allí está.**

Now find examples of the above words and phrases in the following conversation.

186 CAPÍTULO 3

Getting Ready for Lesson 3

You may wish to use one or more of the following suggestions to prepare students for the lesson:

1. Have students listen as you give simple directions for finding buildings in your city or town. Write on the board **a la izquierda** and **a la derecha**. Point in the appropriate direction as you talk. For example:

La biblioteca está en la calle Arlington, número 90. A la derecha hay una tienda. El cine Apollo está en la avenida Lincoln. A la izquierda hay un centro comercial.

2. Ask either/or questions about the directions you have just given. For example:
¿Está la biblioteca en la calle Arlington o en la avenida Lincoln?

Kim gets off the **Metro** and asks a police officer for directions.

KIM: **Con permiso, señor. ¿Dónde está la calle Goya?**
POLICÍA: **Estamos en la calle Goya, señorita.**
KIM: **Ah, bueno. A ver, busco el número 85.**
POLICÍA: **¿El 85? Pues... mire, allí está. A la izquierda hay una plaza. ¿No ve usted?**
KIM: **¡Ah, sí! Muchas gracias, señor. Muy amable.**
POLICÍA: **De nada, señorita.**

Actividades preliminares

A Tell what things there are in your locker, using **hay.**

Por ejemplo:
   Hay libros.

B Tell who is seated to the left **(a la izquierda)** and to the right **(a la derecha)** of your desk.

Por ejemplo:
   Carmen está a la izquierda.

Lección 3 **187**

B. Introduce the Lesson 3 dialogue by reading it aloud or by playing the cassette version. Have students listen for the following information:
   1. the address Kim is looking for
   2. the directions the police officer gives Kim

C. Now ask students to open their books and look at the dialogue as you lead them through what is said. For example, the police officer asks Kim if she sees Pilar's building. **(¿No ve usted?** instead of **¿No ves?)** Why? Have them look for the expressions of politeness that Kim uses when addressing the police officer. **(Con permiso, Muchas gracias, Muy amable)**

Actividades preliminares

Actividad A Answers
Answers will vary but may include the following: **Hay bolígrafos, lápices, papel, el libro de...**

Actividad B Answers
Answers will vary.

Bell Ringer Review

Directions to students: Write down for a new student the streets where the following places are located: library, park, your house or apartment, swimming pool, movie theater, gym. **Por ejemplo: La biblioteca está en la calle Elm.**

Presentation

A. Have students open their books to page 188. Model the question, **¿Dónde está...?** Then model each new phrase on this page. Have students repeat each phrase in unison.

As you lead students through the Vocabulario, you may want to pause to ask questions about different locations. For example: **Si estás en el sótano, ¿dónde están los servicios? ¿dónde está el vestíbulo? Etc.**

B. You may wish to name some activities and have students respond with **adentro or afuera** depending on whether they are done in or out of doors.
1. **Jugamos fútbol.**
2. **Montamos a caballo.**
3. **Jugamos videojuegos.**
4. **Vemos la tele.**
5. **Vemos películas.**

Vocabulario

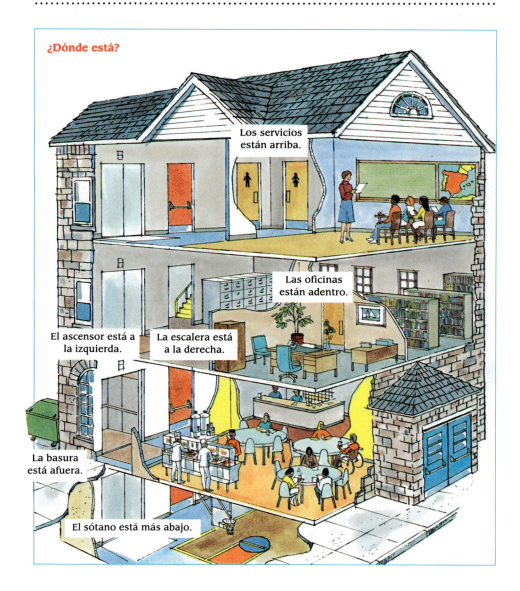

¿Dónde está?

Los servicios están arriba.

Las oficinas están adentro.

El ascensor está a la izquierda.

La escalera está a la derecha.

La basura está afuera.

El sótano está más abajo.

188 CAPÍTULO 3

Total Physical Response

Getting Ready
On the floor of the classroom, outline four spaces that show a cross section of a building (with masking tape). Label each area appropriately with **sótano, vestíbulo, servicio (1° piso),** and **oficina (2° piso).** To the right, outline the stairway, and to the left, outline the elevator.

Areas should be large enough for two students to stand in the squares.

New Words

entra	entren
sube	suban
baja	bajen
espera	esperen

Actividades

A **En el hotel.** Tell Kim where each of the following places in her hotel in Madrid is located.

Por ejemplo:

> el restaurante
> *El restaurante está arriba.*

1. la piscina
2. la recepción
3. la cafetería
4. el gimnasio
5. la basura
6. el ascensor
7. las tiendas

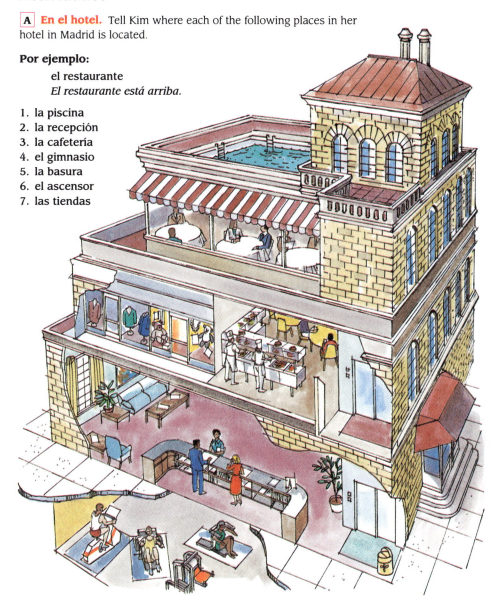

Answers will vary according to the layout of your school building.

Class Management
Actividad B may be done as a whole class activity initially. The teacher takes the role of Student A, calling on individual students to take the role of Student B. Actividad B may be done a second time as a paired activity.

Reteaching
Using Vocabulario Transparency 3.3, or an illustration from a magazine or newspaper, ask students to locate the places taught in the Vocabulario.

Learning From Realia
Ask students to give as much information about the advertisement on this page as possible. For example, the address, telephone number, type of business, hours of business, etc.

B **En mi escuela.** As you arrive at the main entrance of your school, a new student asks you where the following are. Play the roles with a classmate. If your school doesn't have any of the following, say **No hay** (for example, **No hay piscina**).

Por ejemplo:

la cafetería

ESTUDIANTE A
Por favor, ¿dónde está la cafetería?

ESTUDIANTE B
La cafetería está a la derecha (abajo, etc.).

1. las oficinas
2. la biblioteca
3. el gimnasio
4. el auditorio
5. la piscina
6. el servicio de muchachas
7. el servicio de muchachos
8. los autobuses

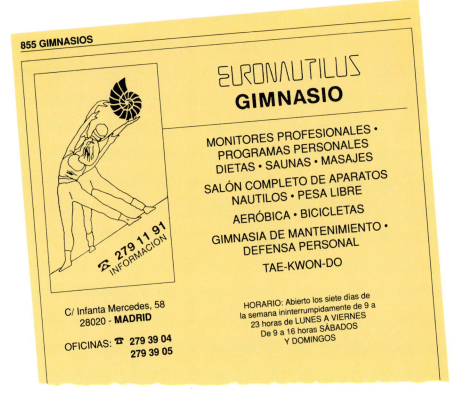

855 GIMNASIOS

EURONAUTILUS
GIMNASIO

MONITORES PROFESIONALES •
PROGRAMAS PERSONALES •
DIETAS • SAUNAS • MASAJES

SALÓN COMPLETO DE APARATOS
NAUTILOS • PESA LIBRE

AERÓBICA • BICICLETAS

GIMNASIA DE MANTENIMIENTO •
DEFENSA PERSONAL

TAE-KWON-DO

☎ 279 11 91
INFORMACION

C/ Infanta Mercedes, 58
28020 - **MADRID**

OFICINAS: ☎ **279 39 04**
279 39 05

HORARIO: Abierto los siete días de la semana ininterrumpidamente de 9 a 23 horas de LUNES A VIERNES De 9 a 16 horas SÁBADOS Y DOMINGOS

Cooperative Learning
In pairs play **¿Qué cuarto es?** Each person picks a room from the following list: **las oficinas, la biblioteca, el gimnasio, la piscina, la clase de historia, de francés, etc.** Describe the room to your partner (location, objects in the room, people, etc.). The other partner must draw the room and identify it.

For the Native Speaker
Choose a partner and make a list of the most desirable places tourists would like to visit within your city. Put the name of each place on a different index card. Choose one place and pretend to tell a tourist (your partner) how to reach that destination.

¿Dónde viven y trabajan los españoles?

Most people in Spain live in and around cities, and the most common form of housing is the apartment. Apartments may be rented or owned, and range in size from one room to two or more whole floors. In smaller apartments, it is common for children to share bedrooms. Apartment addresses often contain the abbreviations **izqda.** and **dcha.,** which indicate that the apartment is either to the left or to the right of the elevator.

As in many large cities, business and office space is at a premium in Madrid. This is especially true in the center of the city, where many different businesses may be located in one building. For example, there may be a store on the street level, a restaurant on the next level, a small hotel on the next level, and offices on other levels.

Actividad

Describe where you live, choosing from the words below.

un apartamento	la ciudad
un condominio	las afueras (suburbs)
una casa	el campo

Por ejemplo:

Vivo en un apartamento, en la ciudad.

Lección 3 **191**

Cultura viva 1

Presentation
Read the Cultura viva on this page. You may wish to have students read the selection silently to themselves, then discuss as a whole class activity. Ask students how each of the three photos on this page reinforces the reading.

Did You Know?
Houses in Spain are different from those in the United States. Most rooms in a house face an inner courtyard instead of opening to a surrounding lawn and garden as in the United States. Houses are generally built of bricks or blocks. It is not unusual to find houses in Spain that have been inhabited for the last two or even three centuries.
Recently, the population in the larger cities has spread to new suburban areas. Although many of these new developments (called **urbanizaciones**) contain separate houses (**casas** or **chalets),** most housing in Spain consists of apartment buildings.

Critical Thinking Activity

Based on the Cultura viva reading compare the types of housing in Spain to where you live. What similarities and differences are there?

Actividad Answer
Answers will vary according to each student.

Pronunciation

A. You may wish to play the recorded version of these pronunciation lines, located at the end of Cassette 3.3. You may also wish to write this verse on the chalkboard and have students copy it into their notebook:
Me llamo Ana María.
Soy hija de los García.

Vivo en la Avenida Torero,
tres, cero, cero, cero
Cerca de la Gran Vía.

B. Have students repeat words and phrases individually and in unison. You may wish to focus on the /v/ sound as in **Vivo; Avenida; Gran Vía.**

Bell Ringer Review

Directions to students: Ask the classmates seated around you where their houses are: **¿Dónde está tu casa?** Write down the information. **Por ejemplo:**
Mi casa está en la calle Green.

Structure Focus

In this lesson, the presentation of numbers is limited to 20–100. The numbers 100–500 are taught in Chapter 4, Lesson 2; the numbers 600 and higher are taught in Chapter 4, Lesson 3.

Presentation

A. Lead students through steps 1–5 on page 192. For step 1, you may wish to model the numbers from 20 to 30, having students repeat each number in unison. Then do the same for step 2, by tens. For emphasis, you may want to write these numbers on the chalkboard.

B. For step 5, you may want to practice giving numbers in pairs by asking students individually, **¿Cuál es tu número de teléfono?**

Actividades

Actividad A Answers
Segovia está a veinte y ocho kilómetros.
Madrid... ochenta y cuatro.
Aranjuez... ochenta y cinco.
El Escorial... treinta y uno.
Ávila... noventa y siete.
Toledo... sesenta y seis.

192

Estructura 1

How to Count from 20 to 100
How to Give Telephone Numbers

1. To count from 21 to 29, you add **y uno, y dos, y tres** and so forth to the word **veinte**.

20	veinte	24	veinte y cuatro	28	veinte y ocho
21	veinte y uno	25	veinte y cinco	29	veinte y nueve
22	veinte y dos	26	veinte y seis		
23	veinte y tres	27	veinte y siete		

When pronouncing the numbers 21 to 29, the **-e** on the end of **veinte** becomes silent, so that these numbers are pronounced **veintiuno, veintidós, veintitrés,** etc. In fact, they are often spelled this way.

2. Below are the words for 30, 40, 50, 60, 70, 80, 90, and 100.

30	treinta	70	setenta
40	cuarenta	80	ochenta
50	cincuenta	90	noventa
60	sesenta	100	cien

3. To count from 30 to 100, do the same as you did for **veinte**, adding **y** and the single-digit numbers.

33	treinta y tres	56	cincuenta y seis
44	cuarenta y cuatro	69	sesenta y nueve

4. In most Hispanic countries, people tend to give their phone numbers by reading them in pairs.

    26-22-14 = veinte y seis / veinte y dos / catorce

In large cities, where phone numbers have seven digits as in the United States, numbers are written and read as follows.

    441-48-13
    cuatro / cuarenta y uno / cuarenta y ocho / trece
    234-61-09
    dos / treinta y cuatro / sesenta y uno / cero nueve

5. To ask what a friend's phone number is, say **¿Cuál es tu número de teléfono?**

Actividades

A **¿A cuántos kilómetros?** In Spain, distance is measured in **kilómetros**, not miles. Tell how far the following cities are in **kilómetros**, according to the road signs.

Por ejemplo:

| ZARAGOZA | 56 |

Zaragoza está a cincuenta y seis kilómetros.

| SEGOVIA | 28 | | ARANJUEZ | 85 | | ÁVILA | 97 |
| MADRID | 84 | | EL ESCORIAL | 31 | | TOLEDO | 66 |

B **¿Sabes el número?** Below are some useful telephone numbers in Madrid. Give each number to a classmate, who then tells you what it is for.

Por ejemplo:

información: 003

ESTUDIANTE A
Cero, cero, tres.

ESTUDIANTE B
Es el número de información.

TELÉFONOS ÚTILES EN MADRID

el aeropuerto 205-43-72

urgencia médica 222-22-22

aerolíneas TWA 205-49-53

información 003

la policía 091

información deportes 197

la Estación de Atocha 228-52-37

el Cine Avenida 221-75-71

Extension
After doing Actividad A, you may wish to extend it by showing students a map of central Spain, including all of the towns above.

Actividad B Answers
Dos, cero cinco, cuarenta y tres, setenta y dos. / Es el número del aeropuerto.
Dos, veinte y dos, veinte y dos, veinte y dos. / Es el número de urgencia médica.
Dos, cero cinco, cuarenta y nueve, cincuenta y tres. / Es el número de aerolíneas TWA.
Cero, noventa y uno. / Es el número de la policía.
Uno, noventa y siete. / Es el número de información deportes.
Dos, veinte y ocho, cincuenta y dos, treinta y siete. / Es el número de la Estación de Atocha.
Dos, veinte y uno, setenta y cinco, setenta y uno. / Es el número del cine Avenida.

Reteaching
Using poster cards, lead students through the numbers 20–30, and then by tens to 100. Have individual students call out each number you show. Then have students write out the number on each card in Spanish.

Additional Practice
After doing Actividades A and B on page 193, you may wish to reinforce the learning with the following:
Have students tell how much money they should spend for the following, giving just the amount in dollars and cents. **Por ejemplo: un disco: $8.50 (ocho cincuenta)**

1. un bolígrafo
2. una revista
3. una cámara
4. una habitación en un hotel elegante, etc.

Cultura viva 2

Presentation

Read the Cultura viva on this page. You may wish to bring to class several **peseta** notes and coins to share with the class.

Did You Know?

To find the current rate of exchange for the **peseta**, look in the financial section of your newspaper for international currencies.

Critical Thinking Activity

Show illustrations of several inexpensive retail items with the price marked in dollars. Give students the current exchange rate. How many **pesetas** would they need to buy each item? (To do this activity, you may wish to teach numbers up to one thousand, found in Chapter 4, Lessons 2 and 3.)

Actividad

Answers
1. Recibo veinte y cinco pesetas.
2. ... sesenta y cinco...
3. ... ochenta...
4. ... treinta y seis...

Learning From Photos

A. You may wish to ask students to read the denominations on the coins shown in the first photo on this page. If they were carrying all of these coins, how much money would they have in U.S. dollars?

B. In the second photo, which of the four words on the sign is in Spanish? Can students identify the other three words by nationality?

C. In the third photo, how much money is this in U.S. dollars?

La peseta española

The **peseta** (abbreviated **pta.**) is the Spanish currency. The **peseta** exchange rate in relation to the dollar can vary. You may buy foreign currency in many U.S. banks, in international airports, and at banks in Spain that display the exchange sign below.

¿Dónde cambian dinero?

Actividad

How much change would you receive from a 100-peseta coin for the following purchases?

Por ejemplo:

> 60 ptas.
> *Recibo cuarenta pesetas.*

1. 75 ptas.
2. 35 ptas.
3. 20 ptas.
4. 64 ptas.

Pronunciation

A. You may wish to play the recorded version of these pronunciation lines, located at the end of Cassette 3.3. You may also wish to write these lines on the chalkboard and have students copy them into their notebook:
¿Vas a España?
Bueno, antes de viajar, hay varias cosas que debes recordar: recibir el pasaporte, hacer las maletas e ir al banco a comprar pesetas.

B. Have students repeat words and phrases individually and in unison. You may wish to focus on the /h/ sound as in **hay; hacer.**

Estructura 2

How to Say What There Is Around You   The verb hay

1. A very useful word in Spanish is **hay**, which means "there is" or "there are."

   ¿Que hay en la ciudad?   **Hay tiendas, oficinas, cines y calles grandes.**

2. Note that **hay** is used to talk about one or more than one thing.

   Hay un lápiz en la mochila. También hay dos bolígrafos.

3. To ask how many there are of something, use **¿cuántos?** (with masculine words) or **¿cuántas?** (with feminine words).

   ¿Cuántos muchachos hay en la clase?
   ¿Cuántas muchachas hay en la clase?
   ¿Cuántos maestros hay en la escuela?
   ¿Cuántas oficinas hay en el edificio?

Actividades

A **¿Qué hay en tu escuela?** Which of the following things does your school have?

Por ejemplo:

   ascensores
   Hay (No hay) ascensores en mi escuela.

1. piscina
2. gimnasio
3. escaleras
4. cafetería
5. oficinas
6. sótano
7. canchas de tenis
8. patios
9. laboratorios
10. auditorio

Hay muchos cafés en Madrid.

Estructura 2

Structure Teaching Resources
1. Workbook, p. 88
2. Cassette 3.3
3. Student Tape Manual, p. 69
4. Estructura Masters 3.3
5. Lesson Quizzes, p. 59

Bell Ringer Review

Directions to students: Tell a new student where the following places in your school are located: library, office, elevator, stairs, bathrooms, gym. Follow the model.
La biblioteca está a la derecha de la oficina.

Presentation

A. Lead students through steps 1–3 on page 195. In step 2, you may want to hold up one item, and then two or more of the same, to demonstrate the use of **hay** for both singular and plural. Hold up one pen and say, **Hay un bolígrafo.** Hold up two pens and say, **Hay dos bolígrafos.**

B. You may wish to demonstrate step 3 by placing two pieces of paper inside a book. Ask students, **¿Cuántos papeles hay en el libro?** Place two calculators or another feminine item on the table. Ask students, **¿Cuántas calculadoras hay?** Repeat with several additional examples. You may also want to have students answer the questions in the examples given in step 3.

Actividades

Actividad A Answers
Answers will vary according to each school building.

196

Learning From Photos

You may want to ask students to identify as much information as possible in the photo on page 195, by asking, **¿Qué hay en la foto?**

Actividad B Answers
Answers will vary.

Actividad C Answers
1. Cien.
2. Veinte y cuatro.
3. Catorce.
4. Veinte.
5. Noventa.
6. Dos.

Additional Practice
Bring a jar of M & M's or other small candies (no more than 100) to class. Place the jar on your desk and have students guess the number by asking, **¿Cuántos dulces hay?** Have each student in the class guess, using the phrase, **Hay...** The one who comes closest gets the candy.

Reteaching

In pairs, have students ask each other what items there are in their house/apartment, or in their own room. For example: **¿Hay videojuegos? ¿Hay radios?, etc.**

B **En mi ciudad.** Tell two things your city or neighborhood has that you like. Then tell two things that it doesn't have that you miss.

Por ejemplo:

> **Hay tiendas y restaurantes pero no hay piscinas y no hay cines.**

C **Problemas.** Solve the following word problems.

1. Si hay veinte muchachos en cada (each) clase de español y hay cinco clases, ¿cuántos muchachos estudian español en tu escuela?
2. Si hay doce personas y cada persona come dos hamburguesas, ¿cuántas hamburguesas comen?
3. Hay veinte personas en la fiesta. Seis van al cine. ¿Cuántas hay en la fiesta entonces?
4. Si hay cinco muchachas en un equipo (team) de baloncesto y hay cuatro equipos, ¿cuántas muchachas juegan?
5. Si hay quince casas y en cada casa hay seis habitaciones, ¿cuántas habitaciones hay?
6. Hay cincuenta estudiantes en el club de español y el club debe ganar 100 dólares. ¿Cuántos dólares debe ganar cada estudiante?

Finalmente

Finalmente

Situaciones

A conversar Play the role of a new student in your school and ask a classmate what there is in your area. Your classmate mentions two or three interesting places. Invite him or her to do something in one of the places this weekend. Set a date.

A escribir While you are visiting Madrid, you write a postcard to a friend.

1. Describe the city.
2. Tell what there is to do in Madrid, and tell two or three activities you plan to do tomorrow.
3. Add any additional information to describe your stay so far.

Repaso de vocabulario

NÚMEROS
treinta
cuarenta
cincuenta
sesenta
setenta
ochenta
noventa
cien

COSAS
el ascensor
la basura
la escalera
la oficina
la peseta

el servicio
el sótano

PREGUNTAS
¿Cuál es tu número de teléfono?
¿Cuántos(as) hay?
¿Qué hay?

INDICACIONES
a la derecha
a la izquierda
abajo
adentro
afuera
allí
arriba

Lección 3   **197**

For the Native Speaker

Write a description of at least 100 words about your house or apartment. Be sure to tell what objects are in each room, and where each room is located in your house or apartment.

Situaciones

Lesson 3 Evaluation
The A conversar and A escribir situations on this page are designed to give students the opportunity to use as many language functions as possible listed on page 186 of this lesson. The A conversar and A escribir are also intended to show how well students are able to meet the lesson objectives, also listed on page 186.

Presentation
Prior to doing the A conversar and A escribir on this page, you may wish to play the Situaciones listening activities on Cassette 3.3 as a means of helping students organize the material.

Repaso de vocabulario

The words and phrases in the Repaso de vocabulario have been taught for productive use in this lesson. They are summarized here as a resource for both students and teacher. The Repaso de vocabulario also serves as a convenient resource for the A conversar and A escribir activities on this page. It also gives the teacher a source for writing either additional practice or evaluation activities such as quizzes and tests in addition to those provided by the publisher.

Lección 4

Objectives

By the end of this lesson, students will be able to:

1. describe feelings and emotions
2. talk to someone formally

Lesson 4 Resources

1. Workbook, pp. 89–94
2. Vocabulario Transparency 3.4
3. Cassette 3.4
4. Student Tape Manual, pp. 72–75
5. Lesson Quizzes, pp. 60–64
6. Computer Software, Disk 1
7. Video Cassette
8. Estructura Masters 3.4
9. Diversiones Masters 3.4

Bell Ringer Review

Directions to students: Have students imagine they are facing the front of the school. Have them tell what is **a la derecha** and **a la izquierda**. For example: **A la derecha hay un parque.** Have them do the same for their house or apartment building.

¡A comenzar!

Presentation

A. Lead students through each of the three functions given on page 198, progressing from the English to the Spanish for each function. Then have students find these words and phrases in the dialogue on page 199.

B. Introduce the Lesson 4 dialogue by reading it aloud or by playing the cassette version. Tell students: **Kim llega al edificio donde vive Pilar, y habla con**

Lección 4

¿En qué piso estamos?

¡A comenzar!

The following are some of the things you will be learning to do in this lesson.

When you want to . . .	You use . . .
1. tell someone you speak to formally that he or she is mistaken	• **Está equivocado(a).**
2. say that you are sure that something is so	• **Estoy seguro(a) que...**
3. describe feelings and emotions	• **Estoy** + feeling.

Now find examples of the above words and phrases in the following conversation.

Getting Ready for Lesson 4

You may wish to do the following to prepare students for the lesson: Ask students in English if they like big cities. Do they get nervous about getting lost, not finding a place, etc.? Tell students that Kim is having difficulties in Madrid.

Kim arrives at Pilar's apartment building but can't seem to find Pilar's apartment. She sees the building's **portero** and asks him.

KIM: **Buenas tardes, señor. ¿Está Pilar Mestre?**

PORTERO: **No, señorita, aquí no.**

KIM: **Pero aquí está la dirección. Dice Goya, 85, primero B, izquierda. Estoy segura que el apartamento está aquí en el primer piso.**

PORTERO: **Pero señorita, usted está equivocada. La familia Mestre vive arriba.**

KIM: **Pues, no sé qué pasa.**

PORTERO: **Ni yo tampoco. Con permiso, señorita, estoy muy ocupado. El apartamento de los Mestre está en el primer piso.**

KIM: **Pero, ¿no estamos en el primer piso?**

PORTERO: **No, señorita, ¡estamos en la planta baja!**

Actividades preliminares

A Based on the conversation above, decide how the **portero** would respond to Kim's statements. Would he say **Sí, señorita,** or **Señorita, usted está equivocada?**

1. **La familia Mestre vive en la calle Goya, 85.**
2. **La familia Mestre vive en el primer piso.**
3. **Estamos en el primer piso.**
4. **Estamos en la planta baja.**

B What are you certain of? Make three different sentences, each one beginning with **Estoy seguro(a) que...**

Por ejemplo:

> **Estoy seguro(a) que mañana es sábado.**

Lección 4 **199**

un señor. Have students listen to find out whether Kim is talking to **el señor Mestre, el papá de Pilar, otro señor.**

C. Now ask students to open their books and look at the dialogue as you lead them through what is said. For example, **Cuando Kim dice: "¿Está Pilar Mestre?", ¿qué dice el portero? ¿Vive Pilar en este edificio? ¿Cómo sabemos? ¿Qué dice el portero? ¿Dónde vive Pilar? ¿Cuál es su dirección?**

D. Have students try to discover which of the following is the cause of Kim's problem:
1. Kim has the wrong address.
2. Kim is not on the first floor.
3. The Mestre family has moved.

E. Have students look at the dialogue again as you ask the following:
1. Kim dice: "Estoy segura...". El portero dice: "Pero, señorita, Ud. está equivocada." ¿Quién está equivocado, el portero o Kim?
2. Cuando Kim dice que no sabe qué pasa, ¿qué dice el portero?
3. Cuando Kim pregunta: "Pero, ¿no estamos en el primer piso?", ¿qué dice el portero?
4. ¿Qué es la planta baja?

Note. In the dialogue, **los Mestre** is the same as **la familia Mestre.**

Actividades preliminares

Actividad A Answers
1. Sí, señorita.
2. Sí, señorita.
3. Señorita, usted está equivocada.
4. Sí, señorita.

Actividad B Answers
Answers will vary.

Bell Ringer Review

Directions to students: Check your backpack, purse, and/or pockets. Then make a list of contents using **hay**.

Presentation

A. Have students open their books to the Vocabulario on page 200. Model the question, **¿Cómo estás?** Then model each word in the Vocabulario, beginning each time with **Estoy...** Use facial expressions and tone of voice to help convey meaning. Have students repeat each phrase in unison.

B. You may wish to give descriptions of situations and have students tell how they feel using expressions from the Vocabulario. Students should focus on agreement of gender for describing themselves. For example:

1. cuando hay exámenes: Cuando hay exámenes, estoy deprimido(a).
2. cuando escuchas música de _____
3. cuando sacas buenas notas
4. cuando estás en un partido de _____
5. cuando no hay clase
6. cuando estás con tus amigos
7. cuando no ahorras dinero
8. cuando trabajas mucho
9. cuando no comes bien y no descansas
10. cuando no haces la tarea

Vocabulario

¿Cómo estás? Estoy...

Mi número de teléfono es 535-9862.

Barcelona es la capital de España.

seguro(a)
equivocado(a)
contento(a)
enojado(a)
triste
emocionado(a)
deprimido(a)
ocupado(a)
aburrido(a)
tranquilo(a)
nervioso(a)
preocupado(a)
EXAMEN FINAL
cansado(a)
enfermo(a)
enamorado(a)

200 CAPÍTULO 3

Total Physical Response

Getting Ready
Use Vocabulario Transparency 3.4. In addition, model different facial expressions and body language to represent the different emotions for **TPR 1** and **2**.

New Words
aplaudan
párense
pies

TPR 1

(Call 3–4 students to the overhead projector, but ask each to perform individually.)
Toca "seguro".
Indica "nervioso".
Cubre "contento".
Marca "aburrido".
Apunta a "emocionado".

Actividades

A **¿Cómo estás?** Tell how you feel in the following situations.

Por ejemplo:

> Hay examen de matemáticas mañana.
> *Estoy nervioso(a) y preocupado(a).*

1. Voy al partido de fútbol americano esta noche.
2. Estoy en la clase de biología.
3. Siempre saco una A en los exámenes de español.
4. Tengo muchas tareas esta noche y mis amigos van al cine.
5. Recibo un cheque de cincuenta dólares.
6. Corro y luego hago ejercicio. Después juego tenis y entonces nado.
7. Vivo en el octavo piso y el ascensor no funciona.
8. Estoy seguro(a) que Buenos Aires es la capital de México.
9. Tengo una temperatura de 100 grados.
10. Necesito leer cincuenta páginas para la clase de historia. También debo escribir una composición para la clase de inglés. También necesito limpiar mi habitación.

B **Lugares.** Make a list of places or circumstances where you never feel the following.

Por ejemplo:

> triste
> *Nunca estoy triste en las fiestas cuando estoy con amigos.*

1. aburrido(a)
2. preocupado(a)
3. contento(a)
4. nervioso(a)
5. equivocado(a)
6. tranquilo(a)
7. deprimido(a)

C **Entonces, ¿qué haces?** What do you do when you're in the following moods?

Por ejemplo:

> triste
> *Cuando estoy triste, hablo con mi amiga Laura.*

1. aburrido(a)
2. preocupado(a)
3. enfermo(a)
4. nervioso(a)
5. deprimido(a)
6. enojado(a)

Presentation

Read the Cultura viva on this page. You may want to refer students back to pages 188 and 189 and ask them to identify what is located on the **planta baja, primer piso, etc.** in each of these drawings.

Did You Know?

In some apartment buildings in large cities there is a doorman who performs many of the same services as the **portero.** However a doorman does not live in the building where he works. Part of his duties may be to let a tenant know he or she has a visitor, pick up the mail, the laundry, and give messages.

Critical Thinking Activity

Imagine the house or apartment you live in is an apartment in Spain. Now tell what is on the **planta baja,** and what is on the **primer piso** of your building.

Actividad Answers

En la planta baja está la Agencia de Viajes Pasaporte.
En el primer piso está el Restaurante Tierra-Mar.
En el segundo piso está el Hostal González.
En el tercer piso está la Academia de Idiomas Hemisferio.
En el cuarto piso está la Casa de Cambio López.
En el quinto piso está la Papelería El Colegial.

La planta baja y la portería

In Spain and elsewhere in Europe, the floor directly above the ground floor is considered the first floor. The ground floor (called **la planta baja** in Spain and indicated in elevators as **PB**) is not usually residential. To find an apartment on the first floor, you must go up one level.

In Pilar's apartment building, Kim mistook the **planta baja** for the first floor and spoke to the **portero.** Many older buildings in Spain still have the traditional **portero,** who serves as custodian and door attendant and whose apartment opens onto the entrance of the building. From there, **el portero** or his wife **(la portera)** can watch who comes and goes, collect packages and mail, and take messages.

Actividad

What is on the **planta baja** according to this directory? What is on each floor of this building?

PB	Agencia de Viajes Pasaporte
1°	Restaurante Tierra-Mar
2°	Hostal González
3°	Academia de Idiomas Hemisferio
4°	Casa de Cambio López
5°	Papelería El Colegial

Pronunciation

A. You may wish to play the recorded version of these pronunciation lines, located at the end of Cassette 3.4. You may also wish to write this verse on the chalkboard and have students copy it into their notebook:
**Subo y bajo en ascensor
del piso primero al tercero
donde está mi amor.**

B. Have students repeat words and phrases individually and in unison. You may wish to focus on the /r/ sound as in **ascensor; amor**

Estructura 1

How to Describe How You and Others Feel   **Estar + *adjectives***

1. To describe moods and feelings, use **estar** with a descriptive word.

    Estoy enojado con Ana. Está ocupada y no quiere salir.

2. Remember that if the descriptive word ends in **-o**, change it to **-a** when describing females. When describing more than one person, add **-s**.

    Alicia está equivocada.
    Eva y Rosa están equivocadas.
    Raúl y Miguel están equivocados.

Remember that if you are describing two or more people—some male and some female—use the ending **-os**.

    Paco y Laura están enamorados.

Actividades

A **¿Cómo reaccionan?** Finish the following phrases, indicating how you and others feel in certain situations.

1. **Cuando no estudio para mi examen y saco una nota mala, mi maestro(a) está...**
2. **Si no regreso** (return home) **hasta la una de la noche, mi mamá y papá...**
3. **Si saco buenas notas en todas mis clases, mis maestros...**
4. **Si no llamo por teléfono a mis amigos, mis amigos...**
5. **El primer partido de baloncesto es hoy y voy al partido con mi papá. Mi papá y yo...**
6. **Tom Cruise visita la escuela hoy. Todas las muchachas...**
7. **Hay examen de historia hoy y María está muy bien preparada. Está...**

Structure Teaching Resources
1. Workbook, pp. 91–92
2. Cassette 3.4
3. Student Tape Manual, p. 73
4. Estructura Masters 3.4
5. Lesson Quizzes, p. 62

Bell Ringer Review
Directions to students: Draw faces that represent the following emotions:
1. **deprimido**
2. **enojado**
3. **enamorado**
4. **preocupado**
5. **emocionado**
6. **enfermo**

Presentation
Lead students through steps 1–2 on page 203. To further illustrate step 2, you may want to refer students to the Vocabulario on page 200. Give each person on this page a name. Then have students make statements about each person, using the correct adjective ending.

Actividades
Actividad A Answers
Answers will vary but may include the following:
1. triste (enojado[a])
2. están enojados (preocupados)
3. están contentos
4. están preocupados (tristes)
5. estamos contentos (emocionados)
6. están emocionadas
7. está contenta (segura)

204

B **¿Cómo están?** Tell how Señorita West and her students are feeling today.

Por ejemplo:

Víctor
Víctor está contento.

2. la señorita West, Víctor
5. Carmen
9. Tony, Raquel
1. Romeo, Julieta
6. Juan, Ignacio
3. Anita
8. Cristóbal
7. Dolores
4. Yolanda, Enrique

C **Situaciones.** Indicate situations when you or others have the following feelings.

Por ejemplo:

Estoy aburrido(a) cuando veo la tele.

1. Mi maestro(a) está aburrido(a) cuando...
2. Mis amigos están nerviosos cuando...
3. Estoy deprimido(a) cuando...
4. Estoy triste cuando...
5. Estoy enojado(a) cuando...
6. Mi maestro(a) está contento(a) cuando...

CULTURA VIVA 2

Así hablan en España

Each region in the Spanish-speaking world has variations in pronunciation. For example, Mexicans sound a little different from Venezuelans, and Argentines sound different from Cubans.

In most areas of Spain, there is a difference in pronunciation that is unique. It is the way the letter **z** (or the letter **c** when it is followed by an **e** or an **i**) is pronounced. The sound is very much like the "th" sound in English.

Actividad

A Pronounce the words below with the pronunciation used in Spain.

la plaza
cinco
quince
la cena
los García
Graciela
el almuerzo
los Sánchez
Barcelona

205

Bell Ringer Review

Directions to students: Copy these three adjectives on your paper. Write two places you associate with them.

1. aburrido
2. contento
3. cansado

Structure Focus

Formality vs. informality was discussed as a culture topic in Cultura viva 1, Chapter 1, Lesson 3 (page 27). In the presentation on this page, the topic of formality vs. informality is discussed in the context of usted vs. tú, and the corresponding form of the verb.

Presentation

Lead students through steps 1–2 on page 206. Remind students they have learned how to talk to a friend, someone their own age, or a family member, using the tú form, which ends in -as with -ar verbs, or -es with -er and -ir verbs. You may wish to make a comparison between the usted and tú forms of verbs by writing the examples on page 206 in the tú form on the chalkboard.

Actividades

Actividad A Answers

1. Señora, ¿habla inglés? / Miguel, ¿hablas inglés?
2. ... ¿juega tenis? / ... ¿juegas tenis?
3. ... ¿quiere visitar los Estados Unidos? / ... ¿quieres... ?

Estructura 2

How to Talk to Someone Formally   Usted / tú

1. In Spanish, remember that when talking to someone about himself or herself, you have to decide which form of "you" to use, **tú** or **usted.** When you address people who (a) are older than you, (b) whom you do not know well, and (c) to whom you must show respect, use forms of the verb that correspond to **usted.** These are the same forms you use to indicate "he" or "she."

2. To express your needs politely, use **quisiera** *(I would like).*

   Perdón, señor, quisiera saber a qué hora sale el tren.

Actividades

A **La señora Ruiz y su hijo.** The guide for Kim's student group in Madrid has brought her teenage son with her. How does Kim ask both the guide and her son **(Miguel),** the following questions?

Por ejemplo:

> vivir en Madrid
> *Señora, ¿vive en Madrid? Miguel, ¿vives en Madrid?*

1. hablar inglés
2. jugar tenis
3. querer visitar los Estados Unidos
4. ir mucho al cine
5. salir esta noche
6. pensar comer con los estudiantes esta noche

B **Preguntas.** Write five questions you would like to ask your teacher about what he or she does every day. Your teacher will then ask you the same questions.

Por ejemplo:

ESTUDIANTE	MAESTRO(A)
Señora, quisiera saber qué deportes practica usted.	Juego tenis. Y tú, ¿qué deportes practicas?

For the Native Speaker

Hand out newspaper comic strips with the speech bubbles cut out. Have native speakers write their own dialogue using vocabulary from this lesson.

Finalmente

A conversar Use the following cues to converse with a classmate.

1. A classmate calls you on the phone. He or she says hi and asks how you are.
2. Respond and ask how he or she is.
3. Your classmate responds and invites you to do something.
4. Accept the invitation but say that you have to do a chore first (wash the car, clean your room, etc.). Say how you feel about it.
5. Your classmate tells you to do the chore first and suggests a specific time to do the activity agreed upon.

A escribir Write an anonymous note to your Spanish teacher (**Estimado[a]...**) explaining why the class is being uncooperative today. Describe how several students are feeling and why. (**Carlos está nervioso porque..., Raquel está enojada porque...**).

Repaso de vocabulario

SENTIMIENTOS

estar +
  aburrido(a)
  cansado(a)
  contento(a)
  deprimido(a)
  emocionado(a)
  enamorado(a)
  enfermo(a)
  enojado(a)
  equivocado(a)

nervioso(a)
ocupado(a)
preocupado(a)
seguro(a)
tranquilo(a)
triste

OTRA PALABRA
quisiera

Lección 4 **207**

---

4. ... ¿va mucho al cine? /
... ¿vas... ?
5. ... ¿sale esta noche? /
... ¿sales... ?
6. ... ¿piensa comer con los estudiantes esta noche? /
... ¿piensas... ?

Actividad B Answers
Answers will vary, however students should use the **usted** form of the verb in each question.

Finalmente

Situaciones

Lesson 4 Evaluation
The A conversar and A escribir situations on this page are designed to give students the opportunity to use as many language functions as possible listed on page 198 of this lesson. The A conversar and A escribir are also intended to show how well students are able to meet the lesson objectives, also listed on page 198.

Presentation

Prior to doing the A conversar and A escribir on this page, you may wish to play the Situaciones listening activities on Cassette 3.4 as a means of helping students organize the material.

Repaso de vocabulario

The words and phrases in the Repaso de vocabulario have been taught for productive use in this lesson. They are summarized here as a resource for both students and teacher. The Repaso de vocabulario also serves as a convenient resource for the A conversar and A escribir activities on this page. It also gives the teacher a source for writing either additional practice or evaluation activities such as quizzes and tests in addition to those provided by the publisher.

Cooperative Learning

Have students assume the role of a living person, perhaps a favorite singer, musician, athlete, actor, etc. of their own gender. Two students will interview the personality to determine his or her identity. Students should prepare ten basic questions to ask the personality. For example:

1. ¿De dónde es usted?
2. ¿Dónde vive usted?
3. ¿Es uste cantante (deportista, etc.)? Or: ¿Qué hace usted?
4. ¿Es muy popular en los Estados Unidos?
5. ¿Viaja mucho?
6. ¿Está en la tele mucho?

Lección 5

Objectives

By the end of this lesson, students will be able to:

1. talk about what they and others have
2. describe objects using **un, una, unos, unas**

Lesson 5 Resources

1. Workbook, pp. 95–99
2. Vocabulario Transparencies 3.5
3. Cassette 3.5
4. Student Tape Manual, pp. 76–80
5. Lesson Quizzes, pp. 65–67
6. Computer Software Disk 1
7. Video Cassette
8. Estructura Masters 3.5
9. Diversiones Masters 3.5

Bell Ringer Review

Directions to students: Write three questions you would like to ask the school principal about his job.

¡A comenzar!

Presentation

A. Lead students through each of the three functions given on page 208, progressing from the English to the Spanish for each function. Then have students find these words and phrases in the dialogue on page 209.

Lección 5

En casa de Pilar

¡A comenzar!

The following are some of the things you will be learning to do in this lesson.

When you want to . . .	You use . . .
1. say what you have	• **Tengo...**
2. ask a friend or relative what he or she has	• **¿Tienes...?**
3. describe objects	• **un / una / unos / unas**

Now find examples of the above words and phrases in the following conversation.

Getting Ready for Lesson 5

You may wish to use one or more of the following suggestions to prepare students for the lesson:

1. Tell students you are writing your wish list for your birthday (or Christmas). Compare what you have to what you want or need. For example: ¿Me pueden ayudar, por favor? Hay tantas cosas que necesito y no sé qué pedir. ¿Qué debo pedir para mi cumpleaños (para la Navidad)? Necesito un coche. Tengo un coche pero es bastante viejo y muy feo. ¿Debo pedir un coche? Quiero un estéreo nuevo. Ya tengo estéreo pero es muy malo. No tengo computadora y quiero una de marca IBM. Tengo cámara pero no funciona bien y me gusta mucho

Kim finally finds Pilar's apartment.

PILAR: ¡Kim! ¡Por fin llegas, guapa! ¡Oye, mamá, ya está aquí Kim!

KIM: ¡Ay, Pilar! ¡Qué cansada estoy! Y ¡qué problema abajo!

PILAR: ¿Abajo? ¿En la planta baja? Pero, ¿por qué? Abajo sólo vive el portero.

KIM: Sí, ya sé. ¡Qué lío!

PILAR: ¿Y no tienes maletas?

KIM: Sí, tengo una maleta grande. Está abajo.

PILAR: Bueno, pasa, pasa. Mi hermano José Luis baja luego.

Actividad preliminar

Ask a classmate if he or she has the following items.

Por ejemplo:
calculadora

ESTUDIANTE A
(1) ¿Tienes calculadora?

ESTUDIANTE B
(2) Sí, tengo calculadora. (No, no tengo calculadora). ¿Y tú?

(3) Sí,... (No,...).

1. pasaporte
2. computadora
3. cámara
4. guitarra
5. dinero
6. monopatín
7. coche
8. estéreo

B. Introduce the Lesson 5 dialogue by reading it aloud or by playing the cassette version. Have students listen to determine the following:

1. ¿Dónde está Kim ahora?
2. ¿Está todavía en la planta baja?
3. ¿Con quién está Kim?

C. Now ask students to open their books and look at the dialogue as you lead them through what is said. For example,

1. ¿Qué dice Pilar cuando llega Kim? (Explain that the word **guapa** is an expression of endearment and friendship among girls in Spain.)
2. Pilar llama a su mamá. ¿Qué dice?
3. ¿Cómo está Kim? ¿Por qué está cansada?
4. Cuando Pilar dice que abajo sólo vive el portero, ¿qué dice Kim?
5. Cuando Pilar pregunta: "¿Y no tienes maletas?", ¿qué dice Kim?
6. Pilar invita a entrar a Kim. ¿Qué dice?
7. ¿Quién va por las maletas?

D. Have students look at the dialogue once again and quickly find the following:

1. dos miembros de la familia de Pilar
2. la ocupación del señor que vive en la planta baja
3. cuántas maletas tiene Kim
4. dónde están sus maletas
5. quién va a buscar las maletas

Actividad preliminar

Actividad preliminar Answers
Answers will vary but should include the following:

1. ¿Tienes pasaporte?/ Sí, (No, no) tengo pasaporte...
2. ¿Tienes computadora? Sí, (No, no) tengo computadora... etc.

---

sacar fotos. No necesito televisor. Ya tengo un televisor estupendo, etc.

2. Ask for a show of hands for questions such as:

   a. ¿Cuántos tienen televisor en casa? ¿Cuántos televisores tienes, Alberto?
   b. ¿Cuántos tienen computadora (guitarra, estéreo, bicicleta, maletas, etc.)?

c. ¿Cuántos teléfonos tienes en tu casa, Ana?

Vocabulario

Bell Ringer Review

Directions to students: Write one sentence for each of the following words, telling when you feel that way.

cansado(a)
enojado(a)
triste
nervioso(a)
ocupado(a)

Presentation

A. Have students open their books to pages 210 and 211. Model the question, **¿Tienes... ?** Then model each new word, beginning each time with **¿Tienes... ?** Have students repeat each question in unison.

B. Model the phrase on page 210, **Sí, y también tengo una colección de...** Then model the new words as in **A.** above.

C. Find out how many "coleccionistas" there are in the class. Go through the list provided in the Vocabulario, asking, for example: **¿Quién tiene una colección de sellos?** Then help students describe their own collections, asking questions such as:
¿Cuántas camisetas tienes?
¿Qué tipo de casetes tienes?
¿Qué tipo de música te gusta más? ¿Cuántos trofeos tienes? ¿Para qué son? ¿Ganas muchos partidos?
Note. el radio = the set; **la radio** = the medium.

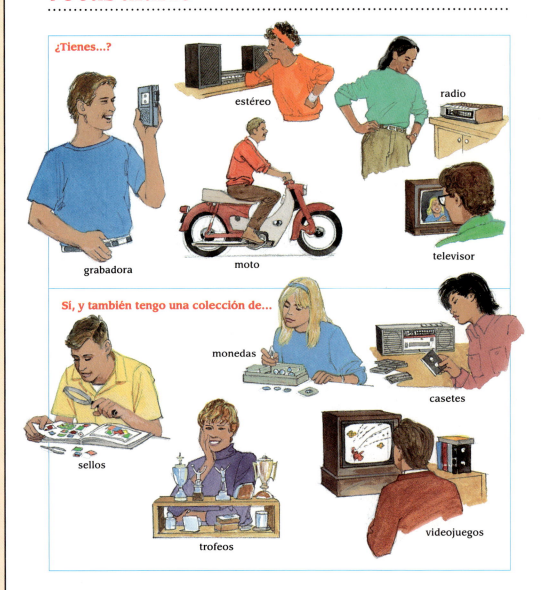

¿Tienes...?

estéreo

radio

grabadora

moto

televisor

Sí, y también tengo una colección de...

monedas

casetes

sellos

trofeos

videojuegos

When Students Ask

You may wish to give students the following additional vocabulary to allow them to talk about their collections.

las miniaturas	las botellas
las piedras	los insectos
la ropa antigua	las conchas
los juguetes	las mariposas
las muñecas	los animales de felpa
las cajas	

Regionalisms

You may wish to tell students that in other parts of the Spanish-speaking world the following words or phrases are alternatives to those presented in the Vocabulario.

el estéreo (el fonógrafo);
la grabadora (el magnetófono) (Spain);
el sello (la estampilla) (Mex.), (timbre)

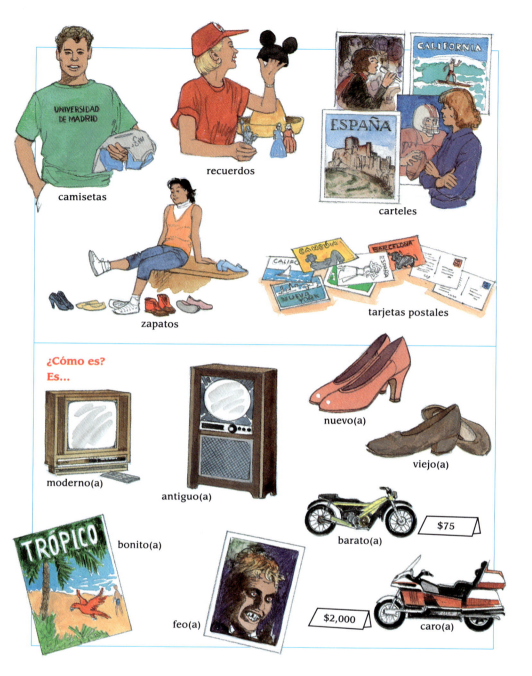

camisetas

recuerdos

carteles

zapatos

tarjetas postales

¿Cómo es?
Es...

moderno(a)

antiguo(a)

nuevo(a)

viejo(a)

bonito(a)

barato(a) $75

feo(a) $2,000   caro(a)

Lección 5 **211**

Total Physical Response

Getting Ready
On a sheet of paper, draw lines, dividing the paper into 16 squares. In each square, draw or paste a picture of one of the "posesiones" in the Vocabulario. Photocopy a set of these for each student and have students cut up the squares and place them in an envelope.

New Word
entreguen

Muéstrenme el televisor.
Muéstrenme la moto.
Toquen los zapatos.
Muéstrenme los casetes.
Cubran las tarjetas postales.
Muéstrenme las camisetas.
Muéstrenme la grabadora.
Entreguen el estéreo a su compañero.

Actividades

Actividades

A ¿Qué tienes? Tell four things you have that are listed in the **Vocabulario.** Then tell four things you don't have.

Por ejemplo:

> Tengo grabadora...
> Pero no tengo moto...

B Mis cosas. Say whether or not you have the following items. A classmate will then guess what activities you like or don't like to do, based on your possessions.

Por ejemplo:

> estéreo

ESTUDIANTE A	ESTUDIANTE B
Tengo estéreo.	Entonces, te gusta escuchar música, ¿verdad?

1. cámara
2. televisor
3. una colección de recuerdos
4. una colección de trofeos
5. una colección de casetes
6. una colección de vídeos

C ¿Qué te gusta más? If you had to choose between the following pairs of items, which one would you choose in each case?

Por ejemplo:

> una calculadora cara o un teléfono barato
> *Quisiera tener un teléfono barato.*

1. un estéreo viejo o una cámara nueva
2. un coche feo o una moto bonita
3. un televisor barato o una grabadora buena
4. una colección de videojuegos nuevos o una colección de monedas antiguas
5. un coche de marca Ford o un coche de marca Mazda
6. una colección de camisetas nuevas o una colección de trofeos grandes
7. una colección de vídeos nuevos o un monopatín barato

For the Native Speaker

1. Write a 75-word paragraph entitled **"Quisiera tener..."** telling about some item you would like to have, why you want it, what you would do with it, etc.
2. Using the items taught in the Vocabulario of this lesson, describe several of your favorite possessions in detail.

Read your description to the class, letting students guess the item you are describing.

Nombres

Pilar's older brother is named **José Luis**. As you have seen with the name **María** in **Capítulo 2**, double first names are very common in Hispanic countries. For example, the following are common names for men.

José Luis   **José Antonio**   **Juan Carlos**   **Jorge Luis**

Men may also have names with religious reference.

Jesús María   **José María Ángel**   **Juan Bautista**

Jesús is a common name and its use is not considered blasphemous or disrespectful. The name **María** is a common second name for men, as well as a first name for women.

Actividad

The following very common Spanish first and last names are often abbreviated. Match the name to the abbreviation.

1. Fdo.   a. José María
2. J. Ma.   b. García
3. Fco.   c. José Antonio
4. Ga.   d. Francisco
5. J.A.   e. Fernando

141 CEREZO - ESCALADA

CEREZO, L. - Núñez Balboa, 98 .... 257 4725
CERÓN VIVANCOS, J.A. - J. Bravo, 78 ...... 474 7375
CERRÓN PARRILLA, F. - E. Polar, s/n 490 1787
CIANCAS MARTÍNEZ, J.A. - Fe, 9 .... 486 4457
CID HARGUINDEY, J.C.
Av. Alberto Alcocer, 41 ....
CONEJO ORTEGA, F. L. - Pl. S. Miguel, 1 ... 250 1793
CORDERO PEINADO, J. M. - B. Granizo, 12 .. 266 8990
(Pozuelo)
CÓRDOBA, DURÁN, A 215 1560
Príncipe Vergara, 757
CORNAGO FERNÁNDEZ, A. - Cdes Val, 18 .... 259 6464
CORONA MUNOS, J. A. - Maiquez, 18 ...455 0582
CORRAL SALETA, F.J. - H. Eslava, 33 ......274 3738
CORRAL SALETA, F.J. - Libra, 21 ....234 4025
CORREDERA ZAMBRANA, J. - A. Cano, 87 ...207 1848
CORTIJO CAMARA, J.L. - Coya, 63 ...443 1191
CULEBRAS FERNANDEZ, J.M. 267 2875
Serrano, 432
CURIEL PANIAGUA, V. - Rguez Marin, 75 ..475 8490
CHOZA FERRER, J.A. 475 9539
P. Reina Cristina, 29
CHUECA DE LAS HERAS, M. 252 2749
Av. Manzanares, 201
DAMOS SEBASTIÁN, J. M. DE - Orense, 28 ...477 5729
DELCÁN DOMÍNGUEZ, J. L. ...465 1934
Ardemans, 38
DIEZ CUERVO, A. - Av. Pablo Iglesias, 54 ...264 7626
DIEZ GÓMEZ, J. M. - Españoleto, 10 ...244 6010
DIEZ YANGUAS, J. - Ecija, 2 ....419 6090

DOMÍNGUEZ DELGADO, J. A.
Bocangel, 68 ....
DOMÍNGUEZ LAZARO, A.R. - Orense, 63 ...
DOMÍNGUEZ MONTERO, P. L.
Av. Ferrol del Caudillo, 10 ....
DOMÍNGUEZ PIEDRAHITA, J. M.
M. Lafuente, 12 ....
DOPICO VILLAR, J. M.
Pl. Cde. V. Suchil, 40 ....
DUQUE AYUSO, R. - Postas, 19 ....
DURÁN SACRISTÁN, M. - Pedro Teixeira, 4...
ECHEVERRÍA BARRIERA, J. M.
D. Octubre, 24 ....
EDO BOLOS, E. J. - S. Trinidad, 16 2
EIZARCH ANTOLI, J. M. 44
Cam Vinateros, 65 ....
ELIO MEMBRADO, F. J. DE 34
Isaac Peral, 60 ....
ELÓSEGUI GRASSET, A. 243
Príncipe Vergara, 99 ....
ELSO QUÍLEZ, E. - Pº Castellana, 420 411
ENCISO PÁEZ, J. C. - Dr. Esquerdo, 272 733
ESCALADA RUIZ - FALCO, J. L. 409
Hermosilla, 301 ....
ESCALADA RUIZ FALCO, J. L. 453 1
Sanchidrian, s/n (Pozuelo) 413 56

Pronunciation

A. You may wish to play the recorded version of these pronunciation lines, located at the end of Cassette 3.5. You may also wish to write these lines on the chalkboard and have students copy them into their notebook:

Juan Horacio,
María Cecilia,
Jaime Ignacio,
Joaquín y Emilia,
Jorge Luis y José María.
¿Ves que hay muchos
en mi familia?

B. Have students repeat words and phrases individually and in unison. You may wish to focus on the /**j**/ and /**h**/ sounds:

/**j**/ Juan; Jaime; Joaquín; Jorge; José.
/**h**/ Horacio; hay.

Cultura viva 1

Presentation

Read the Cultura viva selection on this page. Model the double names in the reading and have students repeat after you. You may want to refer students back to Chapter 2, page 82, to review the examples of double first names for girls.

Did You Know?

In Spanish-speaking countries names selected for children are usually related to the Bible (**Jesús, Ángel, José**), national heroes, a revered family member, or to a saint (**San José, Santa Bárbara, San Antonio**). **El día del santo** is just as important as the birthday, and is celebrated like a birthday. For example, anyone named after San Antonio would celebrate on June 13, as well as on his birthday.

Critical Thinking Activity

Ask students what abbreviation each would use for his or her real name. Have students write it down on a piece of paper and hand it to the teacher. Collect the abbreviations and hand each paper back to a student other than the owner. Now have students figure out to whom their abbreviation belongs.

Actividad

Actividad Answers
1. e   3. d   5. c
2. a   4. b

Learning From Realia

A. You may want students to find the abbreviated double first names in this telephone directory. Ask them to say the names these abbreviations stand for.
B. This directory can be used as a review of numbers.

Bell Ringer Review

Directions to students: Organize this list into two columns according to what you have or don't have: **tengo** and **no tengo**.
teléfono, coche, estéreo, trofeos, monopatín, camisetas, casetes, una colección de tarjetas postales, carteles, muchos discos, videojuegos

Structure Focus

In Estructura 1, the presentation of **tener** is limited to **tengo/tienes**. The remaining forms of **tener** are taught in Estructura 2 of this lesson.

Presentation

Lead students through steps 1–5 on page 214. For steps 3 and 4, you may want to add descriptive words after each possession in the Bell Ringer Review on this page. Then add the appropriate indefinite article. For example, **un teléfono moderno; unas camisetas nuevas,** etc.
Note. **unos** and **unas** can also mean "some."

Estructura 1

How to Say What You Have   Tengo / tienes
Un / una / unos / unas

1. To say that you have or own something, you have used **tengo** followed by the name of the object.

   Tengo discos. Claro, también tengo estéreo.

2. To ask a friend if he or she has something, you use **¿Tienes...?** followed by the name of the object.

   ¿Tienes computadora en casa?

3. When you want to add words describing your possession, you use the word **un** (before masculine words) or **una** (before feminine words). Note that the descriptive word goes after the possession.

   Tengo un libro nuevo.
   Tengo una bicicleta cara.

4. To describe more than one possession, use **unos** for masculine words and **unas** for feminine words.

SINGULAR	PLURAL
Tengo una cámara nueva.	**Tengo unas revistas nuevas.**
Tengo una calculadora vieja.	**Tengo unos discos viejos.**
Tengo un cartel bonito.	**Tengo unos sellos bonitos.**

Remember that descriptive words that do not end in **-o** have only one form in the singular and one form in the plural.

   Tengo un cartel formidable.
   Tengo dos monedas formidables.

5. To ask what brand name a possession is, you say **¿De qué marca?**

   ¿De qué marca es la cámara?   **Es una cámara de marca Kodak.**

Actividades

A **¿Qué quieres?** Ask a classmate if he or she wants the following kinds of things. Then reverse roles.

Por ejemplo:

cámara / nuevo

ESTUDIANTE A

¿Quieres una cámara nueva?

ESTUDIANTE B

Sí. (No, ya tengo una cámara nueva).

1. estéreo / nuevo
2. moto / grande
3. computadora / caro
4. televisor / pequeño
5. videojuegos / divertido
6. carteles / bonito
7. trofeos / grande
8. casetes / barato
9. bicicleta / caro
10. sellos / viejo

B **Más grande y mejor.** Sometimes we want something bigger and better than what we now have. List at least three things you now have and tell whether you would like to replace them with new items.

Por ejemplo:

una computadora
Tengo una computadora vieja. Quisiera tener una computadora nueva. (No necesito una computadora nueva).

C **Mis cosas favoritas.** Write down three favorite possessions. Then tell something about them, for example: why you like them, what you do with them, or what they are like.

Por ejemplo:

Tengo un estéreo de marca... Escucho mis discos todas las noches.
Tengo una colección de camisetas. Tengo quince camisetas. Son de Nueva York, Disneyworld...

Lección 5 **215**

Cultura viva 2

Presentation

Read the Cultura viva on this page. You may wish to ask students to find additional examples of the **vosotros** form from the verb charts in earlier lessons. Write these additional examples on the chalkboard. Ask students to give the infinitive form of these verbs.

Did You Know?

A Spaniard using **vosotros** and a Latin-American using the **ustedes** form have no difficulty understanding each other.

Critical Thinking Activity

Write a short dialogue between you and several friends using the **vosotros** form instead of the **ustedes** form.

Actividad

Actividad Answers

1. ... escribir a Juan José Herrera, a C/ Relojero Losada, 17, 4º B, 24009 León.
2. Same answer as **1**.
3. ... llamar a David Álvarez, al (924) 31–23–79. (... escribir a Ángel Muñoz, a C/ Alboraya, 18, 46010 Valencia).
4. Same answer as **1**.
5. ... escribir a Ignacio Ruiz Pérez, a C/ La Unión, 22, 2º 3A, 29006 Málaga.
6. ... llamar a Ramón Berrueco, al (942) 86–14–28.

Learning from Realia

Have students find examples of the **vosotros** form in this realia piece.

Vosotros

You have probably noticed that when verbs have been explained in the **Estructura** sections of this book, there is one form that is rarely used. This form, called the **vosotros** form, is used only in some areas of Spain between friends and family. Spaniards use it instead of the **ustedes** form to talk to more than one family member or friend.

En España (vosotros)	En Hispanoamérica (ustedes)
compráis	compran
coméis	comen
escribís	escriben
sois	son

Actividad

Using the information on the right, give the names and phone numbers of the people you would contact to buy the following items.

Por ejemplo:

Si quiero comprar videojuegos debo llamar a David Álvarez, al (924) 31-23-79.

1. sellos
2. revistas
3. videojuegos
4. tarjetas postales
5. monedas
6. cámaras

Si queréis **comprar tres video - juegos** (International Karate, Pole Position y Hyperstars) con instrucciones y originales por 1.950 pesetas, debéis llamar a David Álvarez al (924) 31 23 79.

Juan José Herrera **cambia sellos,** postales o revistas. Debéis escribir a C/ Relojero Losada, 17, 4º B. 24009 León.

Dos cartuchos de videojuegos Atari/Human, Cannonball y Video Chec! Kers pueden ser tuyos por sólo 2.000 pesetas. Escribe a Ángel Muñoz. C/ Amargura, 64. Puerto Real. 11510 Cádiz.

Para cambiar postales debéis escribir a Vicente Giner Bosch. C/ Alboraya, 18. 46010 Valencia.

Las monedas de todos los tiempos y países le interesan a Ignacio Ruiz Pérez. C/ La Unión, 22, 2º 3.a 29006 Málaga.

Ramón Berrueco **compra un Átlas Universal usado y un equipo fotográfico con amplificadora.** Su teléfono es (924) 86 14 28.

216   CAPÍTULO 3

Pronunciation

A. You may wish to play the recorded version of these pronunciation lines, located at the end of Cassette 3.5. You may also wish to write these lines on the chalkboard and have students copy them into their notebook:
"Hola, chicos, ¿cómo estáis
¿Qué tal, chicas? ¿Adónde vais?"
Así hablan en Madrid,
también en Toledo y Valladolid.

B. Have students repeat words and phrases individually and in unison. You may wish to focus on the **vosotros** forms: /estáis/ /vais/.

Estructura 2

How to Talk about What You and Others Have
The verb tener

You already know how to say that you have something (**Tengo...**) and to ask a friend what he or she has (**¿Tienes...?**).

To talk about what other people have, use the other forms of the verb **tener**.

SINGULAR	PLURAL
tengo	tenemos
tienes	tenéis*
tiene	tienen

*This form is rarely used in the Spanish-speaking world, except for Spain.

Actividades

A **Las cosas favoritas.** List a favorite possession belonging to the following people.

Por ejemplo:

> una maestra
> *La señorita Cole tiene un coche de marca Ford.*

1. un amigo
2. una amiga
3. tu mamá (Mi mamá...)
4. tu papá
5. tú y tu familia
6. tú y tus amigos
7. los maestros

Si busca un hotel amable para reunirse, descansar, hacer un buen negocio, y no perder el avión, tenemos su hotel.

novotel. Para vivirlo **novotel**

NOVOTEL MADRID
Albacete.1. 28027 MADRID
Tel (91) 405 46 00. Telex 41862 NOVMD
TELEFAX (91) 404 11 05

Estructura 2

Structure Teaching Resources

1. Workbook, pp. 98–99
2. Cassette 3.5
3. Student Tape Manual, p. 78
4. Estructura Masters 3.5
5. Lesson Quizzes, p. 67

Bell Ringer Review

Directions to students: Without looking in your book, can you list the vocabulary words that name things you might possess? The first letter of the word is given, and the number indicates how many words you should have that begin with that letter.
c (4), m (2), r (2), t (2), z (1)

Presentation

Lead students through the presentation on page 217. Model each form of **tener** and have students repeat in unison. You may want to go back to the Vocabulario in Lesson 5 and ask students how they would say a friend has each of these possessions. How would they say two friends have each of these possessions?

Actividades

Actividad A Answers

1. Mi amigo tiene...
2. Mi amiga tiene...
3. Mi mamá tiene...
4. Mi papá tiene...
5. Mi familia y yo tenemos...
6. Mis amigos y yo tenemos...
7. Los maestros tienen...

218

Learning From Realia

A. You may want to ask students to list all the words they recognize in the advertisement on this page. What is this advertisement for?

B. You may want to ask the following questions in Spanish: **¿Dónde está el hotel? ¿Cuál es el número de teléfono? ¿Cuál es la dirección?**

Actividad B Answers

Answers will vary.

Class Management

After forming in small groups, make sure each group has appointed a recorder to take notes, and a reporter to read the notes to the class at the end of this activity. Then begin.

Additional Practice

After completing Actividades A and B, you may wish to reinforce the lesson by doing the following: Ask two classmates whether they have the following things. Then write a sentence telling the things your classmates have. For example: **unos libros de geometría. Estudiante A: Mark y Joe, ¿tienen ustedes unos libros de geometría? Estudiantes B y C: Sí, (No, no) tenemos unos libros de geometría.**

1. calculadoras
2. mochilas
3. caballos
4. computadoras
5. fotos
6. tarjetas postales
7. muchos amigos(as)

Reteaching

Using the items in the Vocabulario on pages 210 and 211, ask individual students whether or not they, their friends, their parents, etc. have these possessions. Use all forms of the verb **tener**.

B **Mis cosas, tus cosas.** Working in small groups, list your prized possessions. Appoint a recorder to take notes and a reporter to read the notes.

Por ejemplo:

> **Tengo una colección de monedas y un estéreo nuevo.**

The reporter will report back to the class on the most interesting thing each person owns and on what people have in common.

Por ejemplo:

> **Tengo unos carteles de España.**
> **Susan tiene una colección de monedas.**
> **Mark y Brian tienen una colección de trofeos.**
> **Todos tenemos discos nuevos.**

Finalmente

Finalmente

Situaciones

A conversar Converse with a classmate about music.

1. Find out what kind of **(qué clase de...)** music your classmate likes. Also ask about his or her dislikes. Give your reactions.
2. Find out what records, videos, and cassettes he or she has. Your classmate will invite you to listen to one recording in particular. Accept or decline the invitation.
3. Reverse roles.

A escribir Write a note to a friend about your gift list for your birthday **(mi cumpleaños)** or Christmas **(la Navidad).**

1. Tell what you already have so you don't receive duplicates.
2. Identify three or four items you want. Describe each item in detail.

Repaso de vocabulario

DESCRIPCIONES	POSESIONES	
antiguo(a)	tener +	el recuerdo
barato(a)	la camiseta	el sello
bonito(a)	el cartel	la tarjeta postal
caro(a)	el casete	el televisor
de marca...	la colección	el trofeo
moderno(a)	el estéreo	el vídeo
nuevo(a)	la grabadora	los zapatos
	la moneda	
PREGUNTA	la moto	
¿De qué marca es?	el radio	

Situaciones

Lesson 5 Evaluation
The A conversar and A escribir situations on this page are designed to give students the opportunity to use as many language functions as possible listed on page 208 of this lesson. The A conversar and A escribir are also intended to show how well students are able to meet the lesson objectives, also listed on page 208.

Presentation

Prior to doing the A conversar and A escribir on this page, you may wish to play the Situaciones listening activities on Cassette 3.5 as a means of helping students organize the material.

Repaso de vocabulario

The words and phrases in the Repaso de vocabulario have been taught for productive use in this lesson. They are summarized here as a resource for both students and teacher. The Repaso de vocabulario also serves as a convenient resource for the A conversar and A escribir activities on this page. It also gives the teacher a source for writing either additional practice or evaluation activities such as quizzes and tests in addition to those provided by the publisher.

For the Native Speaker

Imagine you are a radio disc jockey. Write promotional ads for three new songs in Spanish. Comment on the singers, lyrics, rhythm, etc.

Lección 6

Objectives

By the end of this lesson, students will be able to:

1. describe ownership
2. say and ask the time of day
3. identify rooms of a house
4. describe color preferences

Lesson 6 Resources
1. Workbook, pp. 100–105
2. Vocabulario Transparencies 3.6
3. Cassette 3.6
4. Student Tape Manual, pp. 81–84
5. Lesson Quizzes, pp. 68–72
6. Test Booklet, pp. 47–53
7. Computer Software, Disk 1
8. Video Cassette
9. Estructura Masters 3.6
10. Diversiones Masters 3.6

Bell Ringer Review

Directions to students: Copy the words in Columns A and B. Then pick out the word in Column B that is related to the one in A and underline it.

A	B
1. moneda	videojuegos, dinero
2. cámara	película, cartel
3. colección	sellos, grabadora
4. revistas	recuerdos, fotos
5. viejos	caro, antiguo
6. música	camiseta, estéreo

Lección 6

¡Estás en tu casa!

¡A comenzar!

The following are some of the things you will be learning to do in this lesson.

When you want to . . .	You use . . .

1. describe ownership:
  "my"
  "your" (a friend)
	• mi
	• tu

2. say what time it is	• Son las + hour.
3. identify rooms of a house	• la habitación, el baño, etc.

Now find examples of the above words and phrases in the following conversation.

Getting Ready for Lesson 6

You may wish to use one or more of the following suggestions to prepare students for the lesson:

1. Draw a floor plan of your house or apartment, showing the rooms and the major articles of furniture. Name the rooms and talk about what you do in each place.
2. You may wish to use Colorforms (purchased in a toy store) to illustrate the different rooms of the house and articles in each room. (This technique is very versatile because it allows you to move the pieces of furniture and characters to different rooms.) Tell students that you are planning to buy this house but you are not sure how to decorate it. Describe what you have in mind. For example:

After Pilar's brother brings Kim her suitcase, Pilar shows Kim around her home.

KIM: **Me encanta tu casa, Pilar.**

PILAR: **Bueno, no es muy grande, pero es cómoda. Aquí está tu habitación y el baño está a la derecha. La habitación de mi hermano está a la izquierda.**

KIM: **¡Qué bonita es mi habitación, Pilar!**

PILAR: **Bueno, ¡estás en tu casa! Oye, ya son las seis y media. ¿No quieres salir a tomar unas tapas?**

KIM: **Sí, ¡qué buena idea!**

Actividades preliminares

A The following statements can be made about Pilar's apartment: **La casa no es muy grande. La casa es cómoda. La habitación de Pilar es bonita.** Using **grande, cómodo,** and **bonito,** make as many statements as you can about your home.

B Invite a classmate to do something at the following times.

Por ejemplo:

> **Son las tres.**

ESTUDIANTE A

Son las tres. ¿Por qué no tomamos algo?

1. **Son las cuatro y media.**
2. **Son las seis.**

ESTUDIANTE B

Sí, ¡qué buena idea! (No, gracias, necesito ir a casa).

3. **Son las siete y media.**
4. **Son las nueve.**

Lección 6 **221**

¡A comenzar!

Presentation

A. Lead students through each of the functions given on page 220, progressing from the English to the Spanish for each function. Then have students find these words and phrases in the dialogue on page 221.

B. Introduce the Lesson 6 dialogue by reading it aloud or by playing the cassette version. Have students raise their hands when they hear Pilar mention a room of the apartment where she lives.

C. Now ask students to open their books and look at the dialogue as you lead them through what is said. For example:
1. **Kim dice que le gusta mucho la casa de Pilar. ¿Qué dice?**
2. **¿Cómo es la casa de Pilar?**
3. **¿Dónde está el baño?**
4. **¿Dónde está la habitación del hermano de Pilar?**
5. **¿Cómo dice Pilar "bienvenida"?**

Actividades preliminares

Actividad A Answers
Answers will vary but may include the following: **Mi casa es grande y bonita pero no es muy cómoda. Mi habitación es grande. La habitación de mi hermano es muy grande.**

Actividad B Answers
Answers will vary.

Class Management
Actividad B may be done initially as a whole class activity, if preferred. The teacher takes the role of Student A, calling on individual students to answer each item. Activity B may be done a second time with students working in pairs.

Vocabulario

Bell Ringer Review

Directions to students: Write in words the number that is missing from each sequence.

a. 22, 25, 28, _____.
b. 34, 37, _____.
c. 43, _____, 45 _____.
d. 50, 55, _____.
e. 61, 62, _____.
f. 73, 76, _____.
g. 78, _____, 82.

Presentation

A. Have students open their books to the Vocabulario on pages 222 and 223. Model each new word on page 222. Begin by modeling the phrase, **Los cuartos de la casa son...** Have students repeat each new word in unison. Ask students to name the rooms in their house or apartment by asking, **¿Qué cuartos hay en tu casa? ¿Cuántos cuartos hay en tu casa?**

B. Have students look at the Vocabulario on page 223 as you model the phrase, **Los muebles son...,** and **Los aparatos son...** then model each new word.

C. Model the new words under the introductory phrase, **Mi color favorito es...,** and **¿De qué color es (son)... ?** Ask students which colors they would put in the following categories:
   1. colores aburridos
   2. colores tristes
   3. colores alegres

222

Vocabulario

Los cuartos de la casa son...

el comedor

el baño

la sala

la cocina

la habitación

Total Physical Response

Getting Ready

Outline a house on the classroom floor with masking tape, and leave openings for windows and doors for each room. Label the five rooms. Bring doll furniture to class, or pictures of the furniture and appliances in the Vocabulario.

New Words

mira   cerca de

TPR 1

Pon el armario en la habitación.
Pon la lámpara en la sala.
Pon la mesa en el comedor.
Pon el refrigerador en la cocina.
Pon el escritorio en la habitación cerca de la ventana.
Pon la estufa en la cocina.
Pon la silla en la sala cerca de la puerta.

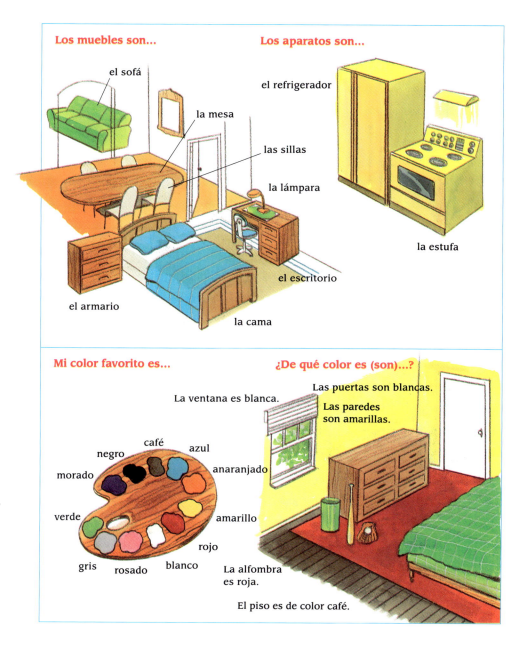

Los muebles son...

el sofá
la mesa
las sillas
el armario
la cama

Los aparatos son...

el refrigerador
la lámpara
el escritorio
la estufa

Mi color favorito es...

café
negro
azul
morado
anaranjado
verde
amarillo
rojo
gris
rosado
blanco

¿De qué color es (son)...?

Las puertas son blancas.
La ventana es blanca.
Las paredes son amarillas.
La alfombra es roja.
El piso es de color café.

Pon el espejo en el baño.
Entra en la cocina.
Mira por la ventana de la sala.
Ve a tu habitación y siéntate en el piso.
Entra en el comedor.
Mira en el espejo.
Siéntate en el piso.
Entra en el comedor.
Mira en el espejo.
Siéntate en la silla.

Párate en la puerta de la cocina.

TPR 2
Levanten las manos si tienen una habitación blanca.
Aplaudan si tienen una cocina verde.
Párense a mi derecha si tienen un baño azul.
Párense a mi izquierda si tienen una sala morada.

Actividades

Actividad A Answers

Answers will vary but may include the following:

1. **Si quiero descansar, voy a mi habitación (la sala).**
2. **...leer,... habitación (sala) (biblioteca).**
3. **...estudiar,... habitación (comedor) (sala) (biblioteca).**
4. **...cocinar,... cocina.**
5. **...hablar por teléfono, ...sala (habitación).**
6. **...escuchar casetes,... habitación (sala).**
7. **...ver la tele,... sala (habitación).**
8. **...comer,... comedor (cocina).**

Actividad B Answers

Answers will vary but should include the following:

El sofá está en el baño. Debe estar en la sala.
La cama está en la cocina. Debe estar en una habitación.
La estufa y el refrigerador están en la habitación. Deben estar en la cocina.
El comedor está en el sótano. Debe estar arriba.
La basura está en la sala. Debe estar afuera.

Actividad C Answers

Answers will vary.

Class Management

A. Actividad C may be done initially as a whole class activity, if preferred. The teacher takes the role of Student A, calling on individual students to take the role of Student B.

B. After doing Actividad C as a small group activity, you may wish to have pairs of students perform in front of the class.

224

Actividades

A **¿Adónde vas?** To which room do you go to do the following activities?

Por ejemplo:

> escuchar música
> *Si quiero escuchar música, voy a mi habitación.*

1. descansar
2. leer
3. estudiar
4. cocinar

5. hablar por teléfono
6. escuchar casetes
7. ver la tele
8. comer

B **Pero, ¿qué pasa?** Bruno is having a strange dream. Tell what is wrong with what he is dreaming and tell how things should be. Make ten statements.

Por ejemplo:

> La cocina está afuera.
> Debe estar adentro.

C **Colores.** What colors do you wear (**llevar**) when you're in the following moods?

Por ejemplo:

> contento(a)
> *Cuando estoy contento(a), llevo ropa roja.*

1. deprimido(a)
2. contento(a)
3. tranquilo(a)

4. enojado(a)
5. triste
6. emocionado(a)

224 CAPÍTULO 3

For the Native Speaker

Have native speakers design a dream-house using felt cutouts (supplied by the teacher). Then they will show the house to the class and explain what is in each room.

Cooperative Learning

Supply each student with a blank floor plan of a two-story house. In pairs, one student will make statements about a room of the house and the other student will try to identify it, writing in the name of the room.

D **El teléfono portátil.** Your family has just bought a portable phone. Several friends call you to ask what you're doing. Then they guess where you are, according to your activities. Play the roles with a classmate.

Por ejemplo:

comer un sandwich

ESTUDIANTE A	ESTUDIANTE B
(1) ¿Qué haces?	(2) **Como un sandwich.**
(3) ¿Estás en la cocina?	(4) **Sí. (No, estoy en el comedor).**

1. descansar un poco
2. tomar un refresco
3. ver un vídeo
4. leer el periódico
5. escuchar discos
6. hacer la tarea
7. jugar videojuegos
8. ver la tele
9. lavar una camiseta

E **La casa de mis sueños.** Describe your dream house, answering the following questions.

1. ¿Cuántas habitaciones hay?
2. ¿Qué cuartos tiene la casa?
3. ¿Cuántos pisos tiene?
4. ¿Qué cuartos están arriba?
5. ¿Qué cuartos están abajo?
6. ¿De qué color es la casa?
7. ¿De qué colores son los cuartos?
8. ¿Son todos los cuartos muy grandes?
9. ¿Cuántos baños hay?
10. ¿De qué colores son los aparatos de la cocina?
11. ¿Qué muebles hay en la sala? ¿y en tu habitación?
12. ¿Todos los cuartos tienen alfombra?

Now describe your house to a classmate, who will draw it and then report back to the class.

Por ejemplo:

La casa de Chris tiene tres habitaciones...

AHORA MÁS VENTAJAS
El Corte Inglés

EL MES DEL MUEBLE

SERIE OSAKA
Librería apilable 3,30 m., con estructura
metálica, lacada en color blanco y gris,
117-175 ... 94.900
Mesa rectangular con tapa cristal, 1,60 × 0,85
m., 25.700 ... 29.900
Silla armadura metálica, asiento y respaldo
tapizada, 9.900 ... 8.690

COLECCIÓN TRÉBOL
Mesa centro, 28.910 ...
Mesa rincón, 24.900 ...
Mesa TV, 36.550 ...
Consola, 35.690 ...
Espejo, 14.400 ...
Estantería, 24.900 ...
Carro tv, 42.650 ...
Mesa teléfono, 18.300 ...
Mueble Hi-Fi, 44.500 ...

Presentation

A. Read the Cultura viva on this page. You may want to make sure students recognize the various **tapas** illustrated on this page by matching them with the food items mentioned in the reading. Then model the Spanish name of each **tapa** plate in the drawing and have students repeat in unison.

B. You may want to ask students which of these **tapas** might be served either in a restaurant or someone's home in the U.S.

Did You Know?

Tapas are appetizers that are served before meals. It is believed the word **tapas,** which means ''lid,'' refers to the complimentary plate of appetizers many bars place like a cover on top of one's wineglass. You may want to point out to students that Spanish cooking is very different from Mexican and other Latin American cooking. It is not hot and spicy, and it does not include tamales, tacos, enchiladas, and burritos.

Critical Thinking Activity

Using your knowledge of Spain, and its geography, can you explain why the **tapas** displayed on this page are typically Spanish?

Actividad

Actividad Answers

Answers will vary, however students should use the polite **quisiera** form in their response, as though they were ordering **tapas** in a restaurant or bar.

Las tapas

Pilar invited Kim to go out for some **tapas.** In Madrid and other Spanish cities, during late afternoon and early evening hours Spaniards of all ages—business people, shoppers, mothers and fathers with their children, grandparents, young people and their friends—begin to fill the many **cafeterías** and eating places that serve **tapas.** People have coffee, soft drinks, or other beverages along with a variety of **tapas,** which include cheese, olives, sausage, pieces of potato omelet **(tortilla),** potato chips, sardines, shrimp, and other shellfish.

Actividad

Below are some typical **tapas** and their names in Spanish. Say what you'd like to eat.

Por ejemplo:

    Quisiera comer...

sardinas

pan y queso

gambas a la plancha

patatas

aceitunas

tortilla española

chorizo

Pronunciation

A. You may wish to play the recorded version of these pronunciation lines, located at the end of Cassette 3.6. You may also wish to write this verse on the board and have students copy it into their notebooks.:
Por la tarde siesta.
Por la noche fiesta.

B. Have students repeat words and phrases individually and in unison. You may wish to focus on the /r/ sound as in **por.**

Estructura 1

How to Talk About What You and Others Have   **Mi(s) / tu(s)**

You have already learned to talk about what belongs to someone else by using **de, de la,** or **del.**

> **El coche de Miguel es fantástico.**
> **Me gusta mucho la clase de la señorita Pérez.**
> **La casa del señor Vargas no es grande pero es cómoda.**

1. To talk about what is yours or a friend's, use **mi** and **tu.**

> **¿Dónde está mi libro?**
> **¿Dónde está tu casa?**

2. To talk about more than one thing, add **-s** to form **mis** and **tus.**

> **Mis libros están en mi habitación.**
> **¿Tus bolígrafos son nuevos?**

Actividades

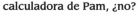

A **Cosas.** In small groups, pass around a large container such as a grocery bag to each member of the group. Each person puts at least one item that everyone knows how to name in Spanish into the bag. Each person then takes a turn removing an item from the bag and tries to guess to whom it belongs.

Por ejemplo:

> **Es mi libro de español... Es tu lápiz, Mark, ¿verdad?... Es la calculadora de Pam, ¿no?**

En el Paseo del Prado

Lección 6 **227**

Estructura 1

Structure Teaching Resources
1. Workbook, pp. 102–103
2. Cassette 3.6
3. Student Tape Manual, p. 82
4. Estructura Masters 3.6
5. Lesson Quizzes, p. 71

Bell Ringer Review

Directions to students: Some gremlins have broken into your friend's house, and have scrambled all the furniture and appliances. Help your friend sort everything out. Label four columns: **sala, comedor, cocina,** and **habitación**, and put each item in its proper place.
armario, estufa, lámparas, mesa y seis sillas, refrigerador, sofá, cama, carteles de cantantes populares, escritorio, alfombra, silla del escritorio, estéreo, televisor

Structure Focus

In this lesson, the presentation of possessive adjectives is limited to **mi(s)** and **tu(s)**. Other forms of possessive adjectives are taught in Chapter 4, Lesson 1, and Chapter 5, Lesson 4.

Presentation

Lead students through steps 1–2 on page 227. Then proceed to the Actividades practice on this page.

Actividades

Actividad A Answers
Answers will vary.

227

Answers will vary, however encourage students to use the photos on this page as cues for making statements.

Additional Practice
After doing Actividades A, B, and C on pages 227 and 228, you may wish to reinforce the learning with the following: With a classmate, put some of your possessions (books, pens, paper, money, notebooks, etc.) together in a pile. Take turns going through the pile and saying to whom each item belongs. For example: **Es mi libro, es tu bolígrafo.**

Reteaching

Have each student write or tape his or her name to one small item. Collect all items in a bag, then redistribute them to the class. Next, each student will say **¿Dónde está mi... ?** The student who has the item with that person's name on it will say, **Aquí está tu...**

Learning From Photos

You may want to have students make statements in Spanish about the photos depicting Madrid life on this page. Ask students to describe what they see in each photo, giving as many details as possible. Finally, you may want to have students say what they see that is different in these photos, compared to similar scenes in the U.S.

B **Una carta a Pilar.** Outline a letter to Pilar, completing the following sentences. Tell her about yourself, your city, your house, and your room, and tell what teenagers do in your country.

Por ejemplo:
> Mi casa está en la avenida Robles, en la ciudad de Stockton.

1. Mi ciudad es...
2. En mi ciudad hay...
3. Mi casa está...
4. En mi casa hay...
5. En mi habitación hay...
6. Los jóvenes de mi país...

C **¿Y tú?** Now ask Pilar about the same topics you described in activity **B**.

Por ejemplo:
> ¿Dónde está tu casa? ¿Dónde está tu ciudad?

El horario español

Mealtimes are not the same in Spain as they are in the United States. The major meal (**el almuerzo**) is between 2:00 and 4:00, when many stores close so that employees can eat at home.

Stores are open again from about 5:00 until 8:00 or 9:00. During these hours—or even somewhat later—streets and **cafés** are filled with people enjoying the **paseo** and having **tapas**. The final meal of the day (**la cena**) is between 9:00 and 11:00, and it is much lighter than dinner in the U.S. At 10:30 or 11:00, night life in Madrid and other major cities begins with movies, plays, and clubs.

Schedules and timetables often state times on the basis of twenty-four hours, beginning at midnight, rather than using A.M. and P.M. For example, 3:00 P.M. would be listed as 15:00 (fifteen hours after midnight). This system is also called "international" or "military" time. For example:

> las tres de la tarde = las quince horas (15,00)
> las ocho de la noche = las veinte horas (20,00)

Actividades

A Give the following times in "international" time.

Por ejemplo:

> 14,00
> Son las dos (de la tarde).

1. 3,00	3. 10,00	5. 17,30
2. 6,00	4. 13,00	6. 23,30

B Compare the scenes of Madrid on page 228 with your city or town.

Por ejemplo:

> Los madrileños... pero en mi pueblo (ciudad)...

TV EL PAIS

sábado 14

Martin Sheen protagoniza *Apocalypse now*, un violento fresco sobre Vietnam que hipotecó de por vida a Francis Ford Coppola. **Sábado, 22.15. TVE-1.**

Cultura viva 2

Presentation

Read the Cultura viva on this page. You may want to write the names of the meals, and the times they are served, on the chalkboard for emphasis. You may also want to explain the word **paseo** (**dar un paseo**). It may be beneficial for students to make a chart comparing international time with the conventional system.

Critical Thinking Activity

Write out your daily schedule using international time. Then give your schedule to a classmate who will change it to regular time.

Actividades

Actividad A Answers

1. Son las tres.
2. Son las seis.
3. Son las diez.
4. Son las trece.
5. Son las diez y siete y media.
6. Son las veinte y tres y media.

Actividad B Answers
Answers will vary.

Learning From Realia

Ask students to look at the T.V. guide and make statements about what programs they could see at various times of the day and night. For example, ¿A qué hora es la película *Apocalypse Now*?

Did You Know?

In Spain, the **almuerzo** is the biggest meal of the day. Typically it includes soup or salad, a main dish of fish or meat, and dessert. Very often the dessert is some type of fruit. Spaniards peel and eat their fruit with a fork and knife. Wine is usually served with the meal, and coffee is served after the meal.

Bell Ringer Review

Directions to students: Draw a picture of your room and label everything in it. Include the colors of your room.

Structure Focus

In Chapter 1, Lesson 3, students learned to say at what time an event takes place to the nearest hour or half hour. The remaining elements of telling time are now presented in this lesson.

Presentation

Lead students through steps 1–6 on page 230. You may want to use a cardboard clock, or draw a series of clocks on the chalkboard, to illustrate telling time.

Learning From Realia

You may want students to tell the times this company is open for business. You may also want to take this opportunity to review the days of the week, and the expressions, **por la mañana; por la tarde; por la noche.**

230

Estructura 2

How to Say and Ask the Time   **La hora**

You have already learned to say what time something takes place.

> **El partido de baloncesto es a las ocho de la noche.**
> **El picnic es a la una y media de la tarde.**
> **Mi clase favorita es a las diez de la mañana.**

1. To say what time it is, use **Son las...** and then give the hour.
   > **Son las cuatro.**
   > **Son las ocho y media.**

2. To ask what time it is, you say **¿Qué hora es?**

3. You express time before the half hour by giving the hour and then adding the minutes, using **y** as a connector.
   > **Son las tres y cinco. (3:05)**
   > **Son las nueve y veinte. (9:20)**

4. You express time after the half hour by giving the approaching hour and subtracting the minutes, using **menos** as a connector.
   > **Son las cuatro menos diez. (3:50)**
   > **Son las cinco menos veinte y cinco. (4:35)**

5. If it is 1:00, after 1:00, or approaching 1:00, you say the following.
   > **Es la una. (1:00)**
   > **Es la una y doce. (1:12)**
   > **Es la una menos diez. (12:50)**

6. Remember that a half hour is **media**. A quarter hour is **cuarto**.
   > **Es la una y media. (1:30)**
   > **Son las nueve y cuarto. (9:15)**
   > **Son las once menos cuarto. (10:45)**

COLEGIO OFICIAL DE FARMACEUTICOS DE MADRID

HORARIO:
De LUNES a VIERNES:
Mañana: 9,30 a 1,45
Tarde: 5 a 8

SABADOS:
Mañana: 10 a 1,45

LA JUNTA DE GOBIERNO

¿Te gusta el horario español?

Cooperative Learning

A. Working in groups, everyone in the class will make a clock (using paper plates, pipe filters, markers). The teacher will then state a time. Everyone will set their clocks accordingly. Each person in the group will confirm the time on his or her clock with the other members of the group.

B. Each member of the group will take turns stating a time. The other members of the group will set their clocks accordingly.

Actividades

A **¿Qué hora es?** Bruno has taken Lulú to a movie. She needs to be home early and keeps asking Bruno the time. What does he tell her at the following times?

Por ejemplo:

> 1:10
> *Es la una y diez.*

1. 1:30
2. 1:45
3. 1:55
4. 2:10
5. 2:22
6. 2:35
7. 2:56

B **Son las tres. ¿Dónde estás?** For the following give the time. Then say where you usually are and what you usually do at that time on a typical school day.

Por ejemplo:

Son las dos menos diez. Estoy en la clase de inglés. Leo el libro y estudio.

1.
2.
3.

4.
5.

6.
7.

Lección 6 **231**

Actividades

Actividad A Answers

1. Es la una y media.
2. Son las dos menos cuarto.
3. Son las dos menos cinco.
4. Son las dos y diez.
5. Son las dos y veinte y dos.
6. Son las tres menos veinte y cinco.
7. Son las tres menos cuatro.

Actividad B Answers

Answers will vary but should include the following:

1. Son las ocho menos cuarto...
2. Son las nueve y veinte...
3. Son las once menos diez...
4. Son las once y cuarto...
5. Es la una menos cuarto...
6. Son las tres y cinco...
7. Son las nueve menos cuarto...

Extension

After doing Actividad B, you may wish to extend the learning by having students say what they do at these times on a typical evening and night; then on a Friday or Saturday night.

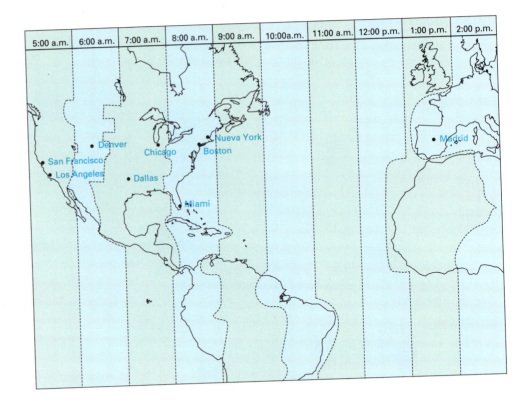

C **Larga distancia.** Pilar's uncle is a pilot for Iberia Airlines and travels frequently to the U.S. When he calls Madrid from the cities below, he must calculate the differences in time zones. What does he say in each case?

Por ejemplo:

Boston / 3:15
Si son las tres y cuarto en Boston, son las nueve y cuarto en Madrid.

1. Chicago / 7:00
2. Dallas / 1:30
3. Denver / 6:10
4. Miami / 2:45
5. San Francisco / 1:20
6. Los Ángeles / 9:30
7. Nueva York / 11: 40

232 CAPÍTULO 3

232

Finalmente

Finalmente

Situaciones

A conversar Your parents are letting you redecorate your room. Converse with a classmate about your plans.

1. Your classmate asks what your room is like now and what you don't like about it.
2. Your classmate wants to know how you're going to change **(cambiar)** your room. Describe your plans, including furnishings, placement, and colors. Your classmate will react to your design.
3. Reverse roles.

A escribir You and your family are moving. Write a for-sale ad for the classified section of your newspaper. Begin your ad with **Se vende casa.**

1. Describe your house in terms of size and appearance.
2. Describe other items in the house that are for sale **(Se venden...).**
3. Give information where buyers may go or call for additional information.

Repaso de vocabulario

POSESIÓN
mi(s)
tu(s)

MUEBLES
el armario
la cama
el escritorio
la mesa
la silla
el sofá

COLORES
amarillo(a)
anaranjado(a)
azul
blanco(a)
gris
morado(a)
negro(a)
café
rojo(a)
rosado(a)
verde

APARATOS
la estufa
la lámpara
el refrigerador

PARTES DE LA CASA
la pared
el piso
la puerta
la ventana

CUARTOS
el baño
la cocina
el comedor
la sala

OTRAS COSAS
la alfombra
el espejo

PREGUNTA
¿De qué color es (son)...?

Lección 6   **233**

Finalmente

Situaciones

Lesson 6 Evaluation
The A conversar and A escribir situations on this page are designed to give students the opportunity to use as many language functions as possible listed on page 220 of this lesson. The A conversar and A escribir are also intended to show how well students are able to meet the lesson objectives, also listed on page 220.

Presentation

Prior to doing the A conversar and A escribir on this page, you may wish to play the Situaciones listening activities on Cassette 3.6 as a means of helping students organize the material.

Repaso de vocabulario

The words and phrases in the Repaso de vocabulario have been taught for productive use in this lesson. They are summarized here as a resource for both students and teacher. The Repaso de vocabulario also serves as a convenient resource for the A conversar and A escribir activities on this page. It also gives the teacher a source for writing either additional practice or evaluation activities such as quizzes and tests in addition to those provided by the publisher.

Presentation

A. Before reading the Lectura, you may wish to have students work in groups to discuss the following questions. These questions are intended to help students think about the theme of the Lectura.

1. Is it true that the colors a person likes tell the personality of that person? Why or why not?

2. Can the colors a person is wearing tell the mood of that person on that particular day? Explain.

B. Have one student from each group report back to the class.

C. Now have students read the Lectura silently to themselves, or work with a partner. Have them answer the Actividades questions on page 235.

Lectura

You will be able to figure out many of the words in the following reading from the context in which they appear or because they look like English words that have similar meanings. First, look over the article below, then complete the activities on the following page.

¿Qué revelan los colores?

Los estudios realizados indican que la gente hace asociaciones entre los colores y ciertas cualidades, y también que su preferencia por un color revela su personalidad...

Naranja (Anaranjado): Es el alma de la fiesta y se lleva bien con todo el mundo, desde el más famoso hasta el de más mala fama.

Rosado: Consentido y mimado, le gusta hacerse concesiones, tiene buen gusto ¡y le falta el valor para vestirse de rojo!

Púrpura (Morado): Tiene temperamento artístico, es sofisticado, le gusta luchar por las causas nobles.

Café: Es realista y práctico, una persona sensata y cuerda que probablemente debería vivir en el campo.

Rojo: Si tiene predilección por este color, usted es una persona communicativa, con una tendencia a cambiar de humor frecuentemente.

Amarillo: Usted posee una gran inteligencia. Le encanta lo nuevo y siempre está a la caza de algo diferente.

Verde: Sociable y activo, le gusta participar en actividades comunitarias.

Azul: Es una persona conservadora, diligente, ¡con un don muy especial para hacer dinero!

234

Getting Ready for Reading

You may want to discuss the following keys to successful reading with your students before having them read the Lectura on page 234:

1. It is not necessary to understand every word, just try to get the general meaning.

2. Look for cognates. For example: **preferencia, inteligencia.**

3. If you see a word you don't understand try to figure out its meaning from context, that is, from the words that come before it and those that follow it.

4. Concentrate on what you understand instead of what you don't understand.

Actividades

A What is this article about?

1. The best colors to paint various rooms in a house.
2. The relationship between one's color preferences and personality.
3. This year's most popular colors in clothing.

B List the cognates (words that look similar to English words and have similar meanings) that you see in this article.

C Which of the words in activity **B** describes you best? Your best friend? A relative?

D Give your five favorite colors in order, using **primero, segundo, tercero,** etc.

Por ejemplo:

> **Primero, me gusta el azul. Segundo,...**

E Do you agree or disagree with the observations made in the above article? Read the personality description for your favorite color and tell whether that description fits you or not.

Por ejemplo:

> **Me gusta el rojo. Soy (No soy) una persona comunicativa...**

The Three Musicians, *de Picasso*

Actividades

Actividad A Answers
2: The relationship between one's color preferences and personality.

Actividad B Answers
estudios, realizados, indican, asociaciones, color (-es), ciertas, cualidades, preferencia, revela, personalidad, predilección, persona, comunicativa, tendencia, humor, frecuentemente, posee, inteligencia, encanta, diferente, sociable, activo, participar, actividades, comunitarias, conservadora, diligente, especial, famoso, fama, concesiones, valor, temperamento, artístico, sofisticado, causas, nobles, realista, práctica, probablemente.

Actividades C, D, and E Answers
Answers will vary.

Learning From Photos
You may want to have students make some statements about the author of this painting, Pablo Picasso, based on the article in the Lectura on page 234.

For the Native Speaker
Have native speakers write a paper on the difference between the meaning of colors in the Hispanic culture and the non-Hispanic culture. (What do colors mean, how are they used, etc.?).

Repaso 3 Resources

1. Workbook, pp. 106–107
2. Cassette 3.6
3. Student Tape Manual, pp. 84–86.
4. Video Cassette

Bell Ringer Review

Directions to students: Say where you are, where you live, and what your phone number is.

¿Recuerdas?

Presentation

To review Chapter 3, call on individual students to give an example for each communicative function listed for Lessons 1–3 and Lessons 4–6, page 236. The numbers in parentheses on page 236 refer to the actual page(s) in Chapter 3 where each function was presented and practiced. You may wish to have your students go back to these pages for additional review and practice before continuing on to the Actividades, pages 236–239.

Lessons 1–3 Answers

The following words and phrases are examples for each of the nine functions listed under Lessons 1–3. These words and phrases should be included in the students' response to each function listed below.

1. Vivo en...
2. Debes...
3. La calle... / El número de teléfono es...
4. escribir, recibir, etc.
5. Yo, tú, usted, él, ella, nosotros(as), ustedes, ellos, ellas
6. Primero, segundo, etc.
7. estar
8. Veinte, treinta, cuarenta, etc....
9. Hay...

Capítulo 3 Repaso

¿Recuerdas?

Do you remember how to do the following things, which you learned in **Capítulo 3**?

LECCIONES 1–3

1. say where you live (p. 160)
2. give a friend advice (p. 160)
3. give and get addresses and phone numbers (pp. 160, 192)
4. describe routine actions (p. 167)
5. compare and contrast, clarify and emphasize (pp. 170, 171)
6. list things in order (pp. 176, 179)
7. say where people, places, and things are located (p. 182)
8. use numbers from 20 to 100 (p. 192)
9. say what there is around you (p. 195)

LECCIONES 4–6

1. describe feelings and emotions (pp. 200, 203)
2. talk to someone formally (p. 206)
3. talk about things you and others have (pp. 210, 211, 217)
4. describe your home in terms of objects and colors (pp. 222, 223)
5. describe ownership (p. 227)
6. tell time (p. 230)

Actividades

[A] **En mi escuela.** Make a list of your school or classroom rules. Post them on the bulletin board.

Por ejemplo:

> Debemos llegar a la escuela a las ocho.

B **Venta de propiedades.** A friend of Pilar's family, Sr. Hernández, has come to the U.S. and needs an apartment for his family of five. Using the ads below, describe to him what is available. A classmate plays the part of Sr. Hernández and asks questions, tells you what he likes and dislikes about each apartment, then selects the one he likes best and tells you why. Tell him the phone number he needs to call for more information.

JEFFERSON PARK Sunny 3 BR-2 bths, with park vu. K,LR, DR, study, d/w, 24 hour doorman, parking avail. $1,450   549-8131

80s E OFF OAK AVE BEAUT STREET ELEV BLDG THE ENTIRE FLOOR IS YOURS A MAMMOTH SIZE APT! CAN YOU AFFORD THE $2,000? IF SO, CALL SINKIN 702-4762

BELLAIRE EAST   Large! Newly renovated 1900 sq ft apart. 3 bedrooms, sep kit, dishwasher. $940 COSMO   18 W. 21 St   714-1929

80s E-off the PARK, charming 3BR Condo, enormous space, $1,075 234 E 81   CITYVIEW   512-4444

Por ejemplo:

ESTUDIANTE A
Hay un apartamento de tres habitaciones.

ESTUDIANTE B
¿En qué calle está? (¿Cuánto es?, ¿Es muy grande?, etc.)

C **Un viaje imaginario.** You are at a famous landmark or tourist attraction, writing a postcard to a friend. Without revealing the name of the place, tell what you are going to visit and see. Your partner will try to guess where you are. Then read your postcard to other classmates and see if they can guess where you are.

Por ejemplo:

ESTUDIANTE A
Querida Pam:
¿Qué tal? Mañana voy al Paseo del Río. También pienso visitar El Álamo. ¡Hasta pronto! Tu amigo, Bo.

ESTUDIANTE B
Estás en San Antonio, ¿verdad?

Lessons 4–6 Answers

The following words and phrases are examples for each of the six functions listed under Lessons 4–6. These words and phrases should be included in the students' response to each function listed below.

1. estar + descriptive word
2. Usted...
3. tener
4. En mi casa hay...
5. Mi(s)... Tú(s)....
6. Es la una. Son las dos, etc.

Actividades

Presentation

Each practice activity in Chapter 3 reviews several of the language functions listed on page 236. Students are asked to use the language they have learned at a higher, more integrated level, compared to the individual practice activities in Lessons 1–6 of Chapter 3.

Actividad A Answers
Answers will vary.

Class Management
This activity may be done in small groups initially, if preferred. After students have come up with their group list of class or school rules, the entire class can decide which of these will be included for display on the bulletin board.

Actividad B Answers
Answers will vary somewhat. Students should concentrate on describing the rooms and size of each apartment. They should also make one or two favorable comments about each apartment in general. You may wish to give students the Spanish equivalents of certain words, and also make sure they understand the meaning of the abbreviated English in these ads.

Actividades C Answers
Answers will vary.

238

Class Management
You may wish to assign Actividad C as homework in order to give students time to choose a tourist attraction, and to organize their thoughts. Then have students read their postcard to their partner, etc.

Actividad D Answers
Answers will vary.

Actividad E Answers
Answers will vary. However you may want to encourage students to look again at the photos of Madrid in this chapter as reminders of places they might go, sights they could see, etc.

Actividad F Answers
Answers will vary.

Additional Practice
After doing the Repaso Actividades on this page, you may wish to reinforce the review with the following: Form small groups. Each student writes on a slip of paper a dream gift he or she would like to receive, and provides the following information about it: (a) description, (b) brand name, (c) why he or she wants it. The spokesperson for each group collects the slips and reads them to the rest of the group. Can the group identify what each person wrote, based on that person's interests?
Por ejemplo: Un(a) estudiante escribe: **Quiero tener una cámara nueva y cara, de marca Pentax. Necesito la cámara porque quiero sacar fotos cuando voy a Colorado.**
Un(a) compañero(a) de clase pregunta: **¿Es el regalo de Lynn?**

Actividad G Answers
Answers will vary.

Class Management
The teacher may want to demonstrate Actividad G for the entire class by taking the role of the **Compradores** and role-playing with one group of **Vendedores.** Once students are familiar with the routine, all groups should be able to perform.

D **¡Buen viaje!** You've decided to send your teacher on a trip. In groups of two or three, describe your plans for him or her by answering the questions below. The class votes on which group's travel plans are best.

1. **¿Adónde va?**
2. **¿Va a estar muy ocupado(a)?**
3. **¿Dónde va a vivir, en un hotel o en un apartamento?**
4. **¿Qué debe hacer antes de salir?**
5. **¿Qué va a hacer allí?**
6. **¿Qué debe llevar?**

E **Imagínate.** Imagine that you are in Madrid for the first time. Write a letter to a parent, friend, or teacher. Use the following questions as a guide in writing your letter.

1. **¿Adónde vas?**
2. **¿Qué ves?**
3. **¿Qué haces?**
4. **¿Qué cosas te gustan?**
5. **¿Qué cosas no te gustan?**
6. **¿Cómo estás? ¿Estás cansado(a)? ¿Por qué? ¿Estás contento(a)? ¿Por qué?**

Por ejemplo:

> Querida Gina:
> ¡Estoy en Madrid! Voy a... También veo... Esta noche pienso...

F **En mi ciudad.** A new student in your school asks about what he or she should do to have a good time in your area. Tell the student what to see, what to take pictures of, what to buy, and where the best places are to eat. The new student asks at least five questions. Play the roles with a classmate.

Por ejemplo:

ESTUDIANTE A	ESTUDIANTE B
¿Adónde voy si quiero comer algo bueno?	Si quieres comer algo bueno, debes ir al restaurante La Boca.

G **En la tienda.** Write the name of a common object (in Spanish) on a piece of paper. The class then forms teams: sellers **(vendedores)** and buyers **(compradores)**. Each group of five **vendedores** forms a store containing only the objects written on their papers. Each group of five **compradores** tries to purchase the objects on their lists.

COMPRADORES	**VENDEDORES**
Give an appropriate greeting.	Respond with an appropriate greeting.
Ask if they have the object you have on your paper.	If you don't have it, say "What a shame. We don't have _____."
	If you do, say "What luck, we have _____."
If they don't have any, ask for another object.	Repeat with the other objects.
Continue until you have asked about everything you have on your lists.	Before your customer gets away, try to sell him or her some of the things you have. Ask "Don't you want _____?"
Every time the clerk tries to sell you something that is not on your list, answer, "What a shame. I already have one."	Say thank you and good-bye.
Say thank you and good-bye.	

Chapter Overview

Cultural setting

Chapter 4 continues with the characters Kim and Pilar in Madrid. The main cultural issues are: the role of the grandmother in the Spanish family; and the conflict between tradition and rapid, revolutionary change in lifestyles. This latter concept is crucial to an understanding of today's Spain.

Rationale

A This chapter serves to consolidate, recombine, and transfer various structural elements previously learned and to expand their concepts into the learning of new yet similar structures. For example:

- the function of expressing likes and dislikes using **gustar,** familiar in terms of concept, and practiced in terms of first and second persons, is now expanded to third person
- the function of third person reporting is elaborated by summative, concluding, and paraphrasing devices (**Parece que... , Dice que... ,Creo que...)**

B You will notice that, beginning in this chapter, each **Cultura viva** is written in Spanish. These readings, accompanied by authentic documents, and the **Lectura** at the end of each chapter, provide opportunities for students to develop reading strategies through magazine and newspaper articles, advertisements, and TV and movie schedules.

C The concept of past time is developed (specifically, the preterit of the verb **ir**) in a non-disruptive fashion, as an undercurrent, via the **Cultura viva 2** in odd-numbered lessons. The preterit will by formally and systematically introduced in Chapters 5 and 6.

Estructura

This chapter focuses on the following structure topics:

- the possessive adjectives **su** and **sus** to talk about what belongs to others;
- the **gustar** construction with **le** and **les** to talk about likes and dislikes of others;
- the verb **tener** for age and personal physical description;
- the adjectives of quantity **todo(s), mucho(s), and poco(s);**
- counting from 100 to 500;
- counting from 600 to the thousands;
- the use of the personal **a;**
- the use of **tener que** + infinitive to talk about obligation;
- the verb **preferir** for stating and asking preferences and the use of **otro;**
- a summary of interrogative words

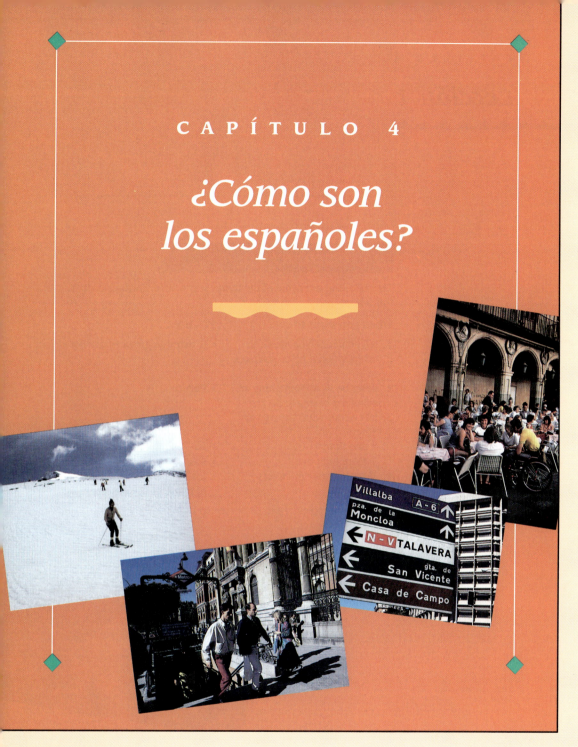

CAPÍTULO 4

¿Cómo son los españoles?

D A summary of question words is presented to consolidate students' ability to request information.

We hope you enjoy the remainder of your stay in Spain!

- the use of **poder** + infinitive to talk about people's abilities.

A complete listing of the language functions of this chapter appears in the Repaso section on page 316.

Lección 1

Objectives

By the end of this lesson, students will be able to:

1. talk about what others like to do
2. talk about what belongs to others
3. identify family members
4. describe what someone or something seems to be like

Lesson 1 Resources

1. Workbook, pp. 108–113
2. Vocabulario Transparency 4.1
3. Cassette 4.1
4. Student Tape Manual, pp. 87–90
5. Lesson Quizzes, pp. 73–75
6. Computer Software, Disk 2
7. Video Cassette
8. Estructura Masters 4.1
9. Diversiones Masters 4.1

Bell Ringer Review

Directions to students: Draw a clock face that represents each of the following times.

1. **Son las diez menos diez y seis.**
2. **Son las doce y cinco.**
3. **Es la una y veinte y cinco.**
4. **Son las cuatro y cuarto.**
5. **Son las siete menos quince.**

¡A comenzar!

Presentation

A. Lead students through each of the four functions given on page 242, progressing from the English to the Spanish for each function. Then have students find these words and phrases in the letter on page 243.

B. Introduce the Lesson 1 letter by reading it aloud or by playing the cassette version. Tell students

242

Lección 1

Querida señora Rivera

¡A comenzar!

The following are some of the things you will be learning to do in this lesson.

When you want to . . .	You use . . .
1. tell someone you speak to formally what he or she likes to do	• **A usted le gusta** + activity.
2. describe what something or someone seems to be like	• **Parece...**
3. talk about what belongs to others	
one thing	• **su**
more than one	• **sus**
4. identify family members	• **los hermanos, la mamá, el papá, la abuela, etc.**

Now find examples of the above words and phrases in the following letter.

Getting Ready for Lesson 1

You may wish to use one or more of the following suggestions to prepare students for the lesson:

1. Talk to students about your family. Bring in photos if you have them. As you name each family member, tell what each likes to do, what his or her interests are, where each lives, and what each does. For example:

Aquí tengo una foto de mi hermana. Se llama Rachel. Le gusta nadar, jugar tenis y esquiar. También le gusta leer novelas policiales de viajar. Rachel es de aquí pero ahora vive en Houston. Es agente de viajes. Trabaja en una agencia muy grande.

2. Describe what students in your class like to do, giving some statements that are not correct. For example:

Kim le escribe una carta a su maestra de español que vive en Los Ángeles.

Madrid
10 de julio

Querida señora Rivera:

Sé que a usted le gusta recibir cartas de sus estudiantes. Pues, aquí estoy en Madrid con Pilar. No tengo tiempo para contar toda mi confusión con la planta baja y el primer piso. ¡Qué lío! Pero por fin estoy aquí en casa de los Mestre. ¡Qué simpáticos son! Pilar manda abrazos para todos.

El apartamento parece bastante pequeño para toda la gente que vive aquí. Son Pilar y sus tres hermanos, su mamá y su papá, y la abuela doña Beatriz. La abuela es del campo, pero no sé cuándo regresa a su pueblo.

Saludos afectuosos de

Kim

Actividades preliminares

A Ask your teacher three questions about what he or she likes to do.

Por ejemplo:

> ¿A usted le gusta jugar tenis?

B Your family has agreed to host Javier, a foreign exchange student from Argentina. On a separate sheet of paper, complete the following letter to Javier. Use Kim's letter to Sra. Rivera as a guide.

> _____ Javier:
>
> ¡Hola! Me llamo _____. Vivo en _____. Mi casa (apartamento) es bastante _____ y (no) me gusta porque _____.
> En mi familia somos _____, _____ y yo. A mi familia le gusta _____ pero no le gusta _____. ¿Qué te gusta hacer a ti? Todos esperamos tu visita.
>
> Tu amigo(a) _____

Lección 1 **243**

---

they are going to hear Kim read a letter she has written from Madrid. Have them listen for the following information:

1. ¿Cómo es la familia Mestre?
2. ¿Cómo es el apartamento de los Mestre?
3. ¿Quiénes viven en el apartamento?

C. Now ask students to open their books and look at the letter as you review it with them, guiding them with the following questions:

1. ¿A quién escribe Kim?
2. ¿Cómo empieza la carta?
3. Kim dice: "Sé que a usted le gusta recibir cartas de sus estudiantes". ¿A ti te gusta recibir cartas? ¿De quién?
4. Kim no va a contar toda la confusión con la planta baja. ¿Por qué?
5. ¿Cómo es la familia Mestre?
6. Según Kim, ¿cómo es el apartamento?
7. ¿Cuántos viven en el apartamento? ¿Quiénes son?
8. La abuela es la mamá del papá de Pilar. ¿Cómo se llama la abuela?
9. ¿De dónde es la abuela?
10. ¿Dónde vive la maestra de Kim?

Note. The family is a sensitive topic for some students, as some families may be single parent, some parents may be unemployed, some may be deceased, some children may live with grandparents. You may want to handle with discretion a student's unwillingness to share in this topic or to talk in class.

Querido(a) is used as a salutation if you know the person you are writing to well. **Estimado(a)** is used either if you don't know the person well, or in business correspondence.

Actividades preliminares

Actividades A and B Answers
Answers will vary.

Maestro(a): A Miguel le gusta correr todos los días.
Estudiante: Sí, es verdad. (No, no es verdad.)
3. Describe members of the class without giving names. Tell what certain students like to do and what their favorite things are. Have the class guess which student is being described.

Bell Ringer Review

Directions to students: Unscramble the following sentences:

1. maleta aquí mi está
2. en escritorio tu habitación tu está
3. mis mochila están en libros la
4. nuevos son bolígrafos tus

Presentation

Have students open their books to the Vocabulario on page 244. Begin introducing the new vocabulary on this page by modeling the phrase, **Los parientes son . . .** Then model each member of the family. For example: **la tía, el tío, los tíos; la prima, el primo, los primos; etc.** Have students repeat after you in unison. For each person in the Vocabulario, you may want to ask students, **¿Cómo es?** Have students describe their brothers and sisters by asking **¿Cómo es tu hermano(a)? ¿Tienes un/a hermano(a) mayor? ¿menor?** Ask individual students if he or she is an only child (**hijo[a] único[a]**).

Vocabulario

Los parientes

los tíos — la tía, el tío
los primos — la prima, el primo
los padres — la madre (la mamá), el padre (el papá)
los hijos — la hija, el hijo

el hermano mayor — la hermana menor — el abuelo, la abuela
los hermanos — los abuelos

Total Physical Response

Getting Ready

Make twelve individual poster strips and label as follows: **Sr. Gómez, Sra. Gómez, Jorge-17 años, Estela-11 años, el abuelo, la abuela, el tío, la tía, la prima, el primo, la hija, el hijo.** Hand out one poster strip each to twelve different students, all of whom will stand up in front of the class.

New Words

señala   señalen
saluda   saluden
dile

Pre-Activity

Make up a short story using the names of the students on the strips and tell how they are related to each other.

A **¿Dónde viven tus parientes?** Make a list of six of your relatives and tell where each one lives.

B **La familia de mi compañero(a) de clase.** Ask a classmate the following questions and take notes. The class will then exchange notes and read the descriptions. See if you can guess who is being described.

1. ¿Dónde está tu casa? ¿Cómo es?
2. ¿Cuántas personas son en tu familia?
3. ¿Cuántos hermanos tienes?
4. ¿Quién es el (la) mayor de la familia?
5. ¿Quién es el (la) menor de la familia?
6. ¿Tienes muchos primos? ¿Quién es tu primo(a) favorito(a)? ¿Cómo es?

Lección 1 **245**

When Students Ask

You may want to give students the following additional vocabulary to allow them to talk about their families.

la madrastra
el padrastro
el/la hijastro(a)
el/la hermanastro(a)
el/la hijo(a) único(a)
Es soltero(a).
Está casado(a).
Está muerto(a).
Está(n) separado(s).
Está(n) divorciado(s).

Actividades

Actividades A and B Answers
Answers will vary.

Additional Practice
After doing Actividad B, you may wish to reinforce the learning with the following:
As a written assignment, have students describe the things each person in their family does. For example: **Mi mamá trabaja todo el día. Luego regresa a casa y prepara la comida y limpia la casa. Mi hermano menor va a la escuela y después juega con sus amigos o ve la tele.**

Learning From Realia

You may want to have students look at the greeting cards on page 245 and have them guess what occasion the cards celebrate. You may also want to have them guess what the word **"querida"** means.

TPR 1

Señalen al padre.
Señalen a la abuela.
Saluden al abuelo.
Señalen a los hijos.
Escriban el nombre del hijo del Sr. Gómez.
Saluden al tío.
Escriban el nombre de la prima de Jorge.
Saluden a los padres.

TPR 2

(Distribute the poster strips to a new group of students.)

Señala al primo de Estela.
Indica a la abuela de los hijos.
Camina hacia el tío.
Saluda a la abuela de _____.
Habla con la madre de Estela.
Mira a los tíos de _____.
Ve al abuelo y dile "Buenos días".

Actividad C Answers
Answers will vary.

Class Management
You may want to have students work in pairs when doing Actividad C. Partners can take turns asking each question and writing down their partner's response.

Actividad D Answers
Answers will vary.

Additional Practice
After doing Actividades A, B , C, and D, you may wish to reinforce the learning with the following activities:

1. Your assignment for Spanish class is to write a brief composition about a favorite relative. Use the questions below as a guide.
   a. **¿Quién es tu pariente favorito?**
   b. **¿Dónde vive?**
   c. **¿Cómo son ustedes similares?**
   d. **¿Cómo son diferentes?**
   e. **¿Qué hacen ustedes?**
2. Have students think of a person (either famous or local) whose family would be familiar to classmates. Have them identify this person only in terms of a relative. Classmates will guess who the person is. For example: **Su hermana mayor está en el equipo de baloncesto de la escuela.** Or: **Su abuelo es el señor X.**

Reteaching

Have students tell one piece of advice they would give to each member of their family. For example: **A mi mamá: Debes descansar más.**

C **Tengo mucha familia.** Talk about three of your favorite relatives, using the questions below as a guide.

1. **¿Cómo son?**
2. **¿Dónde viven?**
3. **¿Qué hacen durante las vacaciones?**
4. **¿Vas a su casa a veces?**
   ¿Cuándo? ¿Qué hacen ustedes?

D **La familia de Pilar.** Describe what each member of Pilar's family seems like to you, based on their appearance in the photo below.

1. **La madre de Pilar parece _____.**
2. **El padre de Pilar parece _____.**
3. **El hermano mayor parece _____.**
4. **Los hermanos menores parecen _____.**
5. **La abuela parece _____.**

For the Native Speaker

Write a character sketch (50–75 words) of one of your relatives. You may want to talk about where your relative lives, his or her immediate family, where they live, occupation, interests, etc. Include information on that person's good and bad qualities.

Cooperative Learning

Have students bring photos of their favorite relative to class. In pairs, have them share information about their relative. As a whole class activity, have each student tell what he or she found out about their partner's relative. Students should also describe the relative to the class, and show the photo, in order for the class to verify that the description is correct.

Don y doña

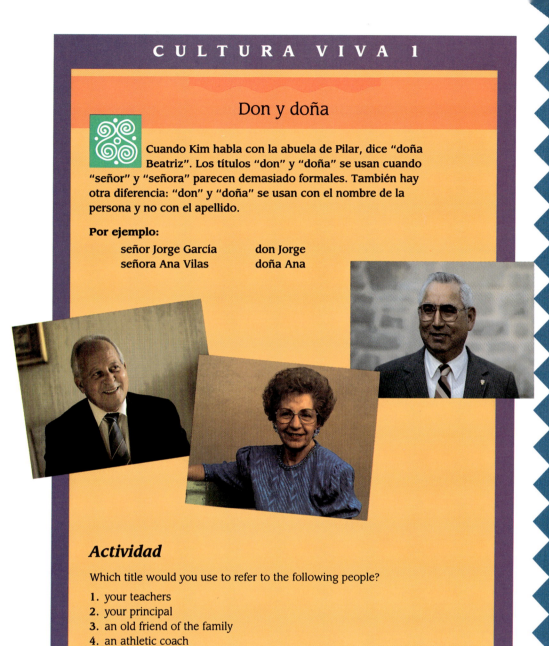

Cuando Kim habla con la abuela de Pilar, dice "doña Beatriz". Los títulos "don" y "doña" se usan cuando "señor" y "señora" parecen demasiado formales. También hay otra diferencia: "don" y "doña" se usan con el nombre de la persona y no con el apellido.

Por ejemplo:

señor Jorge García	don Jorge
señora Ana Vilas	doña Ana

Actividad

Which title would you use to refer to the following people?

1. your teachers
2. your principal
3. an old friend of the family
4. an athletic coach

Cultura viva 1

Presentation

Read the Cultura viva on this page. As a class activity, you may want to have students identify the cognates in this reading and write them on the chalkboard.

Did You Know?

Don and **doña** were originally titles of nobility. Now they are used to show respect to someone of higher social position or to an older person. The titles are capitalized only at the beginning of a sentence.

They are also used with the first and last name together (**don Mario Escobar, doña Tomasa Rivera**). The abbreviations for **don** and **doña** are **D.** and **Da.**

Critical Thinking Activity

What are some titles of respect in English? When do you use these titles and to whom might you say them?

Actividad

Actividad Answers
1. Señor/señora/señorita.
2. Señor/señora/señorita.
3. Don/doña.
4. title choice would depend on the coach/athlete relationship.

Pronunciation

A. You may wish to play the recorded version of these pronunciation lines, located at the end of Cassette 4.1. You may also wish to write this verse on the chalkboard and have students copy it into their notebook:
Don Zacarías Tudela
viene del pueblo Morela.
Es buen zapatero
calzado de cuero.
Su mujer doña Nora
es de Zamora
y goza de la zarzuela.

B. Have students repeat words and phrases individually and in unison. You may wish to focus on the /z/ sound as in **Zacarías; zapatero; calzado; Zamora; goza; zarzuela**

Bell Ringer Review

Directions to students: Draw a tree on your paper with several branches. Each branch represents a part of your family. Draw leaves on the branches and write one person's name on each leaf and what relation that person is to you. Write these words in Spanish.

Structure Focus

In this lesson, the presentation of possessive adjectives is limited to **su** and **sus**. The possessive adjectives **mi(s)** and **tu(s)** were taught in Chapter 3, Lesson 6. The possessive adjective **nuestro** will be presented in Chapter 5, Lesson 4.

Presentation

Lead students through steps 1–2 on page 248. For additional examples, you may want to use the photo of the Mestre family on page 246. Point to each individual and tell how he or she is related to someone else. For example, **Doña Beatriz es la abuela de Pilar. Es su abuela.**

Estructura 1

How to Indicate Possession and Ownership   **Su / sus**

You have already learned to say the following things about what people have.

- To talk about what you own, using **mi** and **mis**.

    Tengo mi libro y mis lápices.

- To talk to a friend about what he or she has, using **tu** and **tus**.

    Maricarmen, ¿tienes tu libro y tus lápices?

- To talk about what someone else has, using **de**.

    Es el libro de Jaime. Son los libros del maestro.

1. To talk about what someone else owns or what other people own, you will use **su** or **sus**. **Su** or **sus** can mean "his," "her," or "their." Use **su** with one thing owned and **sus** with more than one.

    Pilar y su familia viven en un apartamento. Su apartamento es bonito y cómodo.

    José Luis tiene una colección de trofeos. Sus trofeos son muy grandes.

2. You also use **su** or **sus** to mean "your" when talking to one person formally or to more than one person both formally and informally (**usted** or **ustedes**).

    Señor Mestre, su casa está en la calle Goya, ¿verdad?
    Señora Mestre, sus abuelos son del campo, ¿no?
    José Luis y Pilar, ¿tienen su tarea para la clase de inglés?

"¿Son sus maletas, señora?"

A **¡Qué mala memoria!** Bruno is so forgetful in the morning that his sister must make sure he has everything. What are the things she checks?

Por ejemplo:

> lápices
> *Quiere saber si tiene sus lápices.*

1. libros
2. bolígrafos
3. dinero
4. papel
5. cuaderno
6. tareas
7. mochila

B **¿Quién está preparado?** Check to see what a classmate has brought—or not brought—to class today. Make a list of five items to ask about. Reverse roles. Then report back to the class.

Por ejemplo:

el libro | sí ✓ | no

ESTUDIANTE A
John, ¿tienes tu libro?
(A la clase:) John tiene su libro.

ESTUDIANTE B
Sí.

C **¿Y usted, maestro?** Ask your teacher about the following. Use the suggestions below or think of some of your own. Your teacher will then ask you about the same things.

Por ejemplo:

> coche
> *¿Cómo es su coche? (Su coche es nuevo, ¿verdad?, Su coche es grande, ¿no?)*

casa o apartamento
ciudad
calle
familia
amigos

Actividades

Actividad A Answers
1. Quiere saber si tiene sus libros.
2. ... sus bolígrafos.
3. ... su dinero.
4. ... su papel.
5. ... su cuaderno.
6. ... sus tareas.
7. ... su mochila.

Actividad B Answers
Answers will vary, however Student A should use the possessive adjectives **tu** and **su** in his or her responses.

Actividad C Answers
Answers will vary, however if students use the suggestions given, they will say, ¿Como es su casa (apartamento)? ¿Cómo es su ciudad? ¿Cómo es su calle? ¿Cómo es su familia? ¿Cómo son sus amigos?

Extension
After doing Actividad C, you may wish to extend it in the following way. Have students think of additional questions they could ask for each of these topics. You may wish to divide students into groups of three to four and assign each group one of the topics. Provide five minutes for groups to think of as many questions as they can on their topic. As you respond to the questions, have students take notes. For homework, have students prepare a description of "**Mi maestro(a).**"

Reteaching
Hold some of your personal items up for the class to see (pen, paper, pencils, books, etc.) Have individual students identify each object using **Es su...** or **Son sus...**

Cultura viva 2

Presentation

Read the letter from Kim to her Spanish teacher in Los Angeles. You may wish to have each student read one line from the letter.

Did You Know?

The Museo del Prado in Madrid contains one of the finest art collections in the world. It was founded by the royal Spanish family over two centuries ago.

El Escorial is a combination church, monastery, palace, and burial place. It is located about 30 miles northwest of Madrid. It was built by King Felipe II between 1563 and 1584 and contains 300 rooms, 88 fountains, and 86 staircases. King Felipe dedicated El Escorial to Saint Lawrence because Felipe's soldiers defeated the French on Saint Lawrence's Day. Many Spanish monarchs are buried in El Escorial.

Critical Thinking Activity

The Museo del Prado in Madrid contains one of the finest art collections in the world. Do you know of any similar museum in the U.S. or in another country? Why do you think Spaniards are proud of the Museo del Prado? Give some reasons.

Actividad

Actividad Answers
1. **Fui.**
2. **Vi.**
3. Answers will vary but should use **fui** and **vi.**

CULTURA VIVA 2

Una tarjeta postal de Madrid

> Madrid
> 23 de julio
>
> Querida señora Rivera:
> ¡Hola! ¿Cómo está usted? ¡Madrid es estupendo!
> El jueves pasado fui con Pilar al Museo del
> Prado donde vi las pinturas que estudiamos en
> clase. Anoche fui al cine donde vi una película
> en español. Para mí todavía es un poco difícil
> entender las películas en español, pero
> practico el idioma todos los días y ahora
> creo que hablo bastante bien. Mañana
> pensamos visitar El Escorial. Adiós y
> hasta luego.
>
> Saludos de
> Kim

Las Meninas *de Velázquez.*

Actividad

Answer the following questions about what happened in the past.

1. What word does Kim use to say she went somewhere?
2. What word does she use to say that she saw something?
3. Use these two words to tell a place you went last week (**la semana pasada**) and something you saw there.

Por ejemplo:

La semana pasada _____ a (a la, al) _____ y vi _____.

Estructura 2

....

How to Talk about What   **Le(s) + gusta**
Others Like to Do

You have already learned to say what you like to do and to ask a friend or family member if he or she likes to do something.

> **Me gusta ir a España. ¿Te gusta viajar?**

1. To say what someone else likes to do, use **le gusta** + activity.

> **A Jorge le gusta ahorrar dinero.**

2. To say what someone to whom you speak formally likes to do, you also use **le gusta** + activity.

> **A usted le gusta jugar tenis, ¿verdad?**

3. To say what more than one person likes to do, use **les gusta** + activity.

> **A los estudiantes les gusta hablar español.**

4. When speaking to more than one person about what they like to do, also use **les gusta** + activity.

> **¿A ustedes les gusta escuchar discos?**

Notice that in each case, when you are talking about what people like to do, the word **gusta** does not change.

5. In the above examples, the words **a Jorge, a usted, a los estudiantes,** and **a ustedes** clarify who the **le** or **les** is in each case. These words are not necessary if the meaning of **le** or **les** is already clear.

> **Mi hermano favorito es José Luis. Le gusta bailar.**

6. When you want to emphasize what you like to do or contrast it with what a friend likes to do, use **a mí** and **a ti**.

> **Tú y yo somos diferentes. A mí me gusta ir a la playa y a ti te gusta dar paseos por el campo.**

You may also use the phrases **a mí** and **a ti** by themselves.

> **A Pilar le gusta jugar tenis. A mí no. ¿Y a ti?**

Structure Teaching Resources
1. Workbook, pp. 112–113
2. Cassette 4.1
3. Student Tape Manual, p. 89
4. Estructura Masters 4.1
5. Lesson Quizzes, p. 75

Bell Ringer Review

Directions to students: Across the top of your paper, list the towns or cities where your relatives live. Then, under each town, list which relative(s) live(s) there. Exchange lists and discuss yours in Spanish with a partner. For example: **Mi tío Glenn vive en Chicago.**

Structure Focus

In this lesson, the presentation of **gustar** is limited to **Le(s) + gusta**. Students learned to use **Me gusta** and **Te gusta** in Chapter 1, Lesson 4; and **Me gustan** and **Te gustan** in Chapter 1, Lesson 6. **Le(s) gusta(n)** will be taught in Lesson 3 of this chapter.

Presentation

Lead students through steps 1–6 on page 251. As additional examples, and also to review earlier uses of **gustar,** you may want to ask the following kinds of questions of individual students. For example, **¿Te gusta esquiar?** Then repeat the student's answer to the class: **A ____ le gusta esquiar.** Ask another student the same question. Tell the class, **A ____ y a ____ les gusta esquiar. Note.** The verb **gusta** remains singular even if it is followed by more than one infinitive. For example: **A mis amigos les gusta correr y esquiar.**

A **La maleta.** Judging from the contents of Kim's suitcase, what do you think she likes to do? Say six things.

Por ejemplo:

A Kim le gusta escuchar música.

B **¿Qué les gusta?** What do the following people like to do?

Por ejemplo:

tus compañeros de clase
A mis compañeros de clase les gusta hablar español.

1. tus amigos
2. tus padres
3. los deportistas
4. tus hermanos
5. los actores
6. los maestros

Now compare what you like to do with each of the above groups.

Por ejemplo:

A mis amigos les gusta correr pero a mí no.
(A mis amigos les gusta correr y a mí también).

C **Mis compañeros y yo.** Interview a classmate to find out if he or she likes to do the following. Reverse roles. A third classmate **(Estudiante C)** takes notes and reports back to the class about your similarities and differences.

Por ejemplo:

¿Le gusta escribir? ¿Qué escribe?

ESTUDIANTE A
(1) **¿Te gusta escribir?**
(3) **¿Qué escribes?**

ESTUDIANTE B
(2) **Sí, me gusta.**
(4) **Escribo cartas.**

ESTUDIANTE C
A Bill le gusta escribir. Escribe cartas.

1. ¿Le gusta leer? ¿Qué lee?
2. ¿Le gusta ver películas? ¿Qué películas ve?
3. ¿Le gusta ver la tele? ¿Qué programas ve?
4. ¿Le gusta practicar deportes? ¿Qué deportes practica?
5. ¿Le gusta salir por la noche? ¿Adónde va?

252 CAPÍTULO 4

Cooperative Learning

Each team selects someone from the team to write about. Like investigative reporters, they divide up the research topics: classes, family, after-school activities, address, etc. Students compile their notes and write one composition. Each team member is responsible for writing what he or she discovered. The final copies are posted on the bulletin board.

Finalmente

....

A conversar

1. Choose a musician, musical group, actor, actress, or athlete whom you admire. Describe him or her to a classmate. Reverse roles.
2. What else do you know about the celebrity? Describe his or her likes and dislikes. Describe his or her family.

A escribir You have been asked to write an article for the Spanish Club newspaper about a member of your Spanish class. Choose someone you know well.

1. Include the person's name **(Se llama...)** and address.
2. Tell what grade **(el...grado)** the person is in.
3. Describe the person by telling what he or she likes and doesn't like to do.
4. Also describe his or her family.

Repaso de vocabulario

PREGUNTAS	LA FAMILIA	los padres (los papás)
¿Le gusta?	los abuelos	la madre (la mamá)
¿Les gusta?	la abuela	el padre (el papá)
	el abuelo	el/la pariente
POSESIÓN	los hermanos (mayores / menores)	los primos
su	la hermana (mayor / menor)	la prima
sus	el hermano (mayor / menor)	el primo
	los hijos	los tíos
OTRAS PALABRAS Y EXPRESIONES	la hija	la tía
	el hijo	el tío
a mí		
a ti		
parece		

Finalmente

Situaciones

Lesson 1 Evaluation
The A conversar and A escribir situations on this page are designed to give students the opportunity to use as many language functions and as much vocabulary from this lesson as possible. The A conversar and A escribir are also intended to show how well students are able to meet the lesson objectives.

Presentation
Prior to doing the A conversar and A escribir on this page, you may wish to play the Situaciones listening activities on Cassette 4.1 as a means of helping students organize the material.

For the Native Speaker

Pretend you're a reporter for the school newspaper assigned to write an article about a new student in your school. Ask him or her questions such as the following and write the article:
What are your favorite colors? What are your favorite foods? What do you do every day? Which are your favorite classes? What did you do last weekend? What music do you like? What do you like to do in your free time? How many people are there in your family?

Lección 2

Objectives

By the end of this lesson, students will be able to:

1. tell how much something costs
2. tell how old someone is
3. identify people's professions
4. use numbers from 100 to 500
5. express an opinion

Lesson 2 Resources
1. Workbook, pp. 114–119
2. Vocabulario Transparencies 4.2
3. Cassette 4.2
4. Student Tape Manual, pp. 91–95
5. Lesson Quizzes, pp. 76–79
6. Computer Software, Disk 2
7. Video Cassette
8. Estructura Masters 4.2
9. Diversiones Masters 4.2

Bell Ringer Review

Directions to students: Fill in each category below with the names of your own relatives.

hermanos:
primos:
abuelos:
padres:
tíos:

¡A comenzar!

Presentation

A. Lead students through each of the five functions given on page 254, progressing from the English to the Spanish for each function. Then have students find these words and phrases in the dialogue on page 255.

B. Introduce the Lesson 2 dialogue by reading it aloud or by playing

---

Lección 2

¿Cuántos años tiene José Luis?

¡A comenzar!

The following are some of the things you will be learning to do in this lesson.

When you want to . . .	You use . . .
1. ask how much something costs	• ¿Cuánto vale?
2. ask about someone's age	• ¿Cuántos años tiene?
3. say what someone is studying to be	• Estudia para + profession.
4. express an opinion	• Creo que...
5. give someone's profession	• Es ingeniero(a) / empleado(a) de banco, etc.

Now find examples of the above words and phrases in the following conversation.

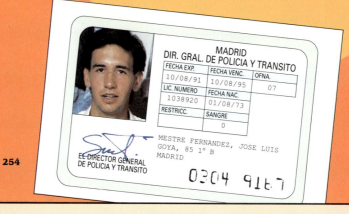

MADRID
DIR. GRAL. DE POLICIA Y TRANSITO

FECHA EXP.	FECHA VENC.	OFNA.
10/08/91	10/08/95	07

LIC. NUMERO	FECHA NAC.
1038920	01/08/73

RESTRICC.	SANGRE
	0

EL DIRECTOR GENERAL
DE POLICIA Y TRANSITO

MESTRE FERNANDEZ, JOSE LUIS
GOYA, 85 1° B
MADRID

0304 9167

254

Getting Ready for Lesson 2

You may wish to use one or more of the following suggestions to prepare students for the lesson:

1. Tell students that you need to buy a gift for a friend or relative's birthday. Tell something the person likes to do. Mention an appropriate gift, and ask how much it costs. For example: **Necesito comprar un regalo para mi hermana.** El lunes es su cumpleaños. Sé que le gusta escuchar música. ¿Debo comprar unos casetes? ¿Cuánto vale un casete? Write some possible prices on the board, including some that are outrageously high or low. Ask students to choose an appropriate price.

2. Show illustrations of items students might wish to buy. Ask individual students ¿Cuánto vale? Allow students to

Pilar y Kim están en un almacén en el centro de Madrid.

PILAR: Necesito comprar un regalo para mi hermano mayor. El jueves es su cumpleaños. Sé que le gusta jugar tenis. ¿Te gusta esta raqueta de tenis?

KIM: Sí, mucho. ¿Cuánto vale?

PILAR: No sé. Creo que no es muy cara.

KIM: ¿Cuántos años tiene José Luis?

PILAR: El jueves cumple diez y nueve años.

KIM: ¿Y qué estudia en la universidad?

PILAR: Estudia para ingeniero.

KIM: Tu papá es ingeniero también, ¿no?

PILAR: Sí, trabaja para la RENFE.

KIM: ¿Y tu mamá?

PILAR: Mi madre es empleada de banco.

Actividad preliminar

Give the age of each of the following people. Then tell if each is younger or older than you.

Por ejemplo:

tu hermano
Mi hermano tiene once años. Es menor que yo.

1. tu amigo(a) favorito(a)
2. tu hermano(a)
3. un(a) vecino(a) (neighbor)
4. un(a) compañero(a) de clase

Lección 2 **255**

---

the cassette version. Tell students they are going to hear a conversation between Kim and Pilar. Have them listen to find out the following information:

1. ¿Dónde están Kim y Pilar?
2. ¿Qué hacen allí?
3. ¿Qué regalo piensa comprar Pilar?

C. Now ask students to open their books and look at the dialogue as you lead them through what is said. Have students find the following information:

1. ¿Cuántos años tiene José Luis?
2. En la familia de Pilar, ¿quiénes trabajan?
3. ¿Dónde trabaja el papá de Pilar?
4. ¿Dónde trabaja la mamá de Pilar?

D. As students look at the dialogue, you may wish to give the following commentary to explain some of the lesson concepts and vocabulary:

José Luis estudia para ingeniero, es decir, estudia ciencias y matemáticas. La mamá de Pilar es empleada de banco y también es agente de propiedades, es decir, vende casas y apartamentos. El papá de Pilar trabaja para la RENFE, que es la compañía de trenes en España. Es como la Amtrak en los Estados Unidos.

Actividad preliminar

Actividad preliminar Answers
Answers will vary but may include the following:

1. Mi amiga favorita tiene quince años. Es mayor.
2. Mi hermano tiene seis años. Es menor.

---

respond with only the suggested price.

3. Give the ages of various students in the class. For example:
John tiene catorce años.
Susan tiene quince años.
Michael también tiene quince años.
Then ask the class ¿Cuántos años tiene John/Susan/Michael? Allow them to respond with only the age.

4. Ask students individually: ¿Dónde trabaja tu papá? ¿tu mamá? Students may answer by naming the place, or you may wish to have them answer in sentences. For example: Mi papá trabaja en IBM. Mi mamá trabaja en el hospital Mercy. Mi papá (mamá) no trabaja.

Vocabulario

Vocabulary Teaching Resources

1. Vocabulario Transparencies 4.2
2. Workbook, pp. 114–115
3. Cassette 4.2
4. Student Tape Manual, p. 92
5. Lesson Quizzes, p. 76

Bell Ringer Review

Directions to students: Copy the following relatives on your paper. Beside each person write three words that best describe that person. Then write down that person's favorite activity. If the person listed below is not in your family, choose someone else to describe. Follow the model.

Mamá: simpática, amable, bonita. Le gusta esquiar.

1. **tu tío favorito**
2. **tu papá**
3. **tu hermano(a)**
4. **tu primo(a)**

Presentation

A. Have students open their books to the Vocabulario on pages 256 and 257. Model each new word, beginning each time with the phrase **Quiero estudiar para...** Have students repeat each phrase in unison. Ask individual students whether or not they want to be one of the professionals listed in the Vocabulario. For example, **Tom, ¿quieres ser periodista?** Encourage students to give a complete response. For example, **Sí, quiero ser periodista.**

B. Ask individual students, **¿Para qué quieres estudiar?** Encourage them to give a complete response. For example, **¿Quiero estudiar para dentista.**

Quiero ser...
Quiero estudiar para...

dentista periodista electricista enfermero(a)

policía mujer policía arquitecto(a) carpintero(a)

bombero(a) mecánico(a) abogado(a)

256 CAPÍTULO 4

Total Physical Response

Getting Ready
Use Vocabulario Transparencies 4.2 and color transparency pens.

New Words
| rectángulo | cuadro |
| triángulo | círculo |

TPR

(Pairs of students.)

Toquen al mecánico.
Escriban el número 20 sobre el supervisor.
Hagan dos círculos azules en el bombero.
Indiquen al dentista con un círculo negro.
Cubran al agricultor.

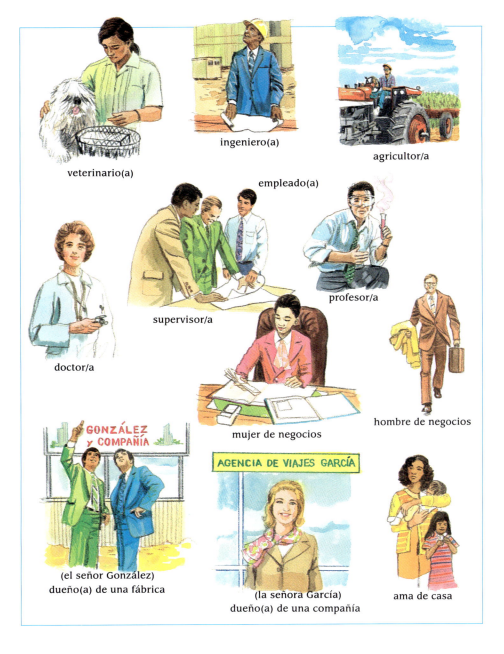

veterinario(a)

ingeniero(a)

agricultor/a

empleado(a)

doctor/a

supervisor/a

profesor/a

mujer de negocios

hombre de negocios

GONZÁLEZ y COMPAÑÍA

(el señor González)
dueño(a) de una fábrica

AGENCIA DE VIAJES GARCÍA

(la señora García)
dueño(a) de una compañía

ama de casa

C. Point to the art in the Vocabulario and ask individual students, **¿Es doctor o doctora?**, etc.

D. Have students identify the professions of some currently well-known people. You may also wish to provide names of local people or TV characters.

E. Have students rank five professions that interest them: **Primero... Segundo... Tercero... Etc.**

When Students Ask

You may wish to give students the following additional vocabulary to allow them to talk about professions:
el/la camarero(a)
el/la agente de viajes
el/la vendedor/a
el/la plomero(a)
el/la cocinero(a)
el/la secretario(a)
el/la programador/a
el/la cartero(a)
el/la fotógrafo(a)
el/la banquero(a)
el/la agente de bienes raíces
el/la peluquero(a)

Regionalisms

You may wish to tell students that in some parts of the Spanish-speaking world the following word is an alternative to the one presented in the Vocabulario.
la fábrica (la factoría) (Puerto Rico)

Pongan dos triángulos verdes en el doctor.
Muéstrenme el veterinario.
Hagan dos cuadros negros en el electricista.
Pongan dos rectángulos anaranjados en el policía.
Escriban el número 16 sobre el ingeniero.
(Repeat with **tú**.)

Actividades

Actividades

A **Ocupaciones.** Using the **Vocabulario** on pages 256 and 257, make a list of the occupations that appeal to you and another list of those that don't. Use the following headings.

Las ocupaciones que me gustan   **Las ocupaciones que no me gustan**

B **¿Qué le gusta hacer?** A classmate describes what various people like to do. Decide what profession each is preparing for, based on these descriptions.

Por ejemplo:

Marta / estudiar biología y zoología, jugar con animales

ESTUDIANTE A
A Marta le gusta estudiar biología y zoología y jugar con animales.

ESTUDIANTE B
Creo que estudia para veterinaria.

1. Enrique / dibujar casas y edificios, estudiar matemáticas
2. Inés / cuidar (care for) niños, leer libros y aprender cosas nuevas
3. Dolores / estudiar matemáticas y trabajar con computadoras
4. Luis y Raúl / estudiar mecánica, trabajar con coches y motores
5. Mauricio / escribir, sacar fotos, saber qué pasa
6. Anita / ganar dinero, ahorrar dinero, tomar decisiones, trabajar en una oficina

C **Cien por ciento.** The people below are describing what percentage of their time they spend doing different activities related to their jobs. For each, tell what you think his or her profession is.

Por ejemplo:

> Juan: Trabajo cincuenta por ciento del tiempo con una computadora. El treinta por ciento del tiempo contesto el teléfono.
> *Creo que es empleado de oficina (de banco, etc.).*

1. **Víctor: Paso sesenta por ciento del día en el hospital y veinte por ciento en la oficina donde veo a mis pacientes. Por la noche descanso y leo libros de medicina.**
2. **Roberto: Paso setenta por ciento de mi tiempo afuera. Saco fotos en la calle y escribo artículos para el periódico.**
3. **Gloria: Paso noventa por ciento del día en casa. Es un trabajo muy difícil y no gano dinero. Limpio, cocino, voy de compras y trabajo todo el día.**
4. **Alicia: Paso todo el día afuera en el campo donde manejo un tractor.**
5. **Yolanda: Paso ochenta por ciento de mi tiempo en mi oficina y veinte por ciento afuera donde visito a los animales.**

D **¿Por qué?** Choosing from the list of professions in the **Vocabulario**, tell two things you would like to be and two you would not like to be. Tell why, using reasons such as those below.

trabajar afuera	hacer trabajos manuales
trabajar adentro	trabajar con animales
trabajar con la gente (people)	ganar mucho dinero
trabajar con los números	reparar cosas

Por ejemplo:

> bombero
> *Quiero ser bombero porque me gusta trabajar afuera, hacer trabajos manuales y trabajar con la gente.*

Actividad C Answers
1. Creo que es doctor.
2. ... periodista.
3. ... ama de casa.
4. ... agricultora.
5. ... veterinaria.

Actividad D Answers
Answers will vary.

Additional Practice
After doing Actividades A, B, C, and D, you may wish to reinforce the learning with the following activity: Have students select occupations from the Vocabulario list that they would not want to have, and tell why. For example: **No quiero ser doctor/a porque no me gusta estudiar ciencias. No quiero ser ama de casa porque no me gusta limpiar la casa.**
Have students identify professions, based on the following questions:
1. **¿A quién visitas si te duelen las muelas?** (Point to your jaw.)
2. **¿A quién visitas si estás enfermo?**
3. **¿Quién escribe artículos para el periódico?**
4. **¿Quién enseña a los estudiantes?**
5. **¿Quién construye casas y edificios?**
6. **¿Quién trabaja afuera en el campo?**
7. **¿A quién llamas si las lámparas no funcionan?**
8. **¿A quién llamas si hay emergencias?**
9. **¿A quién visitas si tienes problemas con el coche?**
10. **¿A quién visitas si tu gato o tu perro está enfermo?**

Reteaching
Ask students to open their books to the Vocabulario on pages 256 and 257 and tell which of the following two categories each occupation falls under: **los que trabajan adentro; los que trabajan afuera.** You may want to write these categories on the chalkboard.

Actividad

¿Quieres comprar algo?

En Madrid y en otras ciudades españolas hay muchas tiendas pequeñas, pero mucha gente prefiere comprar en los grandes almacenes. Hay dos almacenes principales en Madrid con sucursales en otras ciudades grandes. Son El Corte Inglés y Galerías Preciados. Venden una gran variedad de productos y también ofrecen muchos servicios para sus clientes. Por ejemplo, allí puedes comprar muebles, alimentos y ropa, y también puedes cambiar dinero y hacer reservaciones para viajes.

Actividad

You are at the information desk on the **planta baja** of **El Corte Inglés**. Your friend asks where the following items can be purchased. Use the directory to tell which floor each item is on and whether it is up or down.

Por ejemplo:

    zapatos

ESTUDIANTE A

Perdón, señorita (señor), quisiera comprar zapatos.

ESTUDIANTE B

Están arriba en la cuarta planta.

1. discos
2. libros y revistas
3. una cámara
4. una maleta
5. un sandwich y un refresco
6. perfume

EDIFICIO MODA

1° SÓTANO Imagen y Sonido. Discos. Microinformática. Fotografía. Fumador. Papelería. Librería. Tienda de la Naturaleza. Turismo.

B PLANTA BAJA Complementos de Moda. Perfumería y Cosmética. Joyería. Bisutería. Bolsos. Relojería. Marroquinería. Stand Dunhill. Cartier. Bombonería Godiva.

1ª PLANTA Señoras. Confección. Punto. Peletería. Boutiques Internacionales. Lencería y Corsetería. Futura Mamá. Tallas Especiales. Complementos de Moda.

2ª PLANTA Caballeros. Confección. Ante y Piel. Boutiques. Ropa Interior. Sastrería a Medida. C. Gourmet. Artículos de Viajes. Complementos de Moda.

3ª PLANTA Infantil: Niños/as (4 a 10 años). Confección. Boutique. Complementos Bebés. Carrocería. Canastillas. Confección Bebé. Zapatería Bebé. **Chicos/as (11 a 14 años).** **Confección** Boutique Agua Viva. Complementos. **Juguetería.**

4ª PLANTA Zapatería. Señoras, Caballeros y Niños. Deportes. Confección. **Deportiva.** Zapatería Deportiva Armería. Marcas Internacionales. Complementos.

5ª PLANTA Juventud. Confección. Tienda Vaquera. Lencería y Corsetería.

6ª PLANTA Promociones y Ferias. Cosas (regalos juventud). **Servicios:** Cafetería. Restaurante. Pizzería. Bufé.

De compras por Europa.

Pronunciation

A. You may wish to play the recorded version of these pronunciation lines, located at the end of Cassette 4.2.

Hay dos empleados
detrás del mostrador.
Vienen diez clientes,
cada uno comprador.
El primero paga quince
porque es un gran señor.

Y cinco pagan cinco y
dos pagan tres
y uno paga dos
y otro paga seis.
¿Cuánto pagan los diez?

B. Have students repeat words and phrases individually and in unison. You may wish to focus on the -or sound, as in **mostrador, comprador, señor.**

Estructura 1

How to Say How Much or How Many

Adjectives of quantity

To ask how much or how many, you have used **¿cuántos?** or **¿cuántas?**

> **¿Cuántos discos quieres comprar?**
> **¿Cuántas muchachas hay en tu clase?**

1. You can also use the singular form of these words.
   > **¿Cuánto dinero necesitas?**
   > **¿Cuánta leche debo comprar?**

2. When you want to ask how much one thing costs, you say **¿Cuánto vale?** for one thing and **¿Cuánto valen?** for more than one.
   > **¿Cuánto vale el disco?**
   > **¿Cuánto valen las camisetas?**

3. When you want to ask someone's age, you say **¿cuántos años?** and the appropriate form of **tener**.
   > **¿Cuántos años tienes?**
   > **¿Cuántos años tienen tus hermanos?**

¿Cuántos casetes tienes?

4. To tell how much or how many, you can use a specific number or the following words. Note that these words can be used to describe one thing or more than one.

poco / poca / pocos / pocas	a little, few
mucho / mucha / muchos / muchas	a lot, many
todo / toda / todos / todas	every, all

   ¿Tienes muchas camisetas? No, tengo pocas.

   Luis está enfermo. Debe pasar toda la semana en casa.

   En mi escuela, muchos estudiantes estudian español. Pocos estudian latín.

   Mañana Ana va a estudiar todo el día. Todas sus clases son difíciles.

Lección 2   **261**

Actividades

Actividad A Answers
Answers will vary.

Extension
After doing Actividad A, you may wish to extend the learning by having students ask each other how old the following are. For example: **tu casa**

ESTUDIANTE A	ESTUDIANTE B
¿Cuántos años tiene tu casa?	Tiene diez años.

1. la escuela
2. los Estados Unidos
3. el coche de tus padres
4. un libro viejo en la biblioteca

Actividad B Answers
Answers will vary but must include the **yo** form of the verb.

Actividad C Answers
Answers will vary, however students should use **poco, mucho,** and **todo** when they report to the class.

Additional Practice
After doing Actividades A, B, and C, you may wish to reinforce the lesson by doing the following:
A new exchange student asks you questions about your school and city. Play the roles with a classmate. **Por ejemplo: cines en la ciudad**

ESTUDIANTE A	ESTUDIANTE B
¿Hay muchos cines en la ciudad?	Hay pocos. (Hay muchos, No hay muchos).

1. piscinas en la ciudad
2. restaurantes buenos
3. exámenes en la clase de inglés
4. fiestas en la clase de español
5. bailes en la escuela
6. partidos de baloncesto
7. estudiantes aplicados
8. deportistas buenos
9. tarea en las clases

Reteaching
Ask students questions about what there is in the classroom using **poco, mucho, todo.**

Actividades

A **Mis hermanos.** Ask if your classmate has brothers or sisters. Also find out how old they are. Report back to the class about who's older and younger in your classmate's family.

Por ejemplo:

ESTUDIANTE A	ESTUDIANTE B
(1) ¿Tienes hermanos?	(2) **Sí, tengo una hermana.**
(3) ¿Y cuántos años tiene?	(4) **Bueno, mi hermana tiene diez y nueve años.**

(A la clase:) **Sara tiene una hermana mayor.**

B **¿Todos los días?** Describe your routine by completing the following sentences.

1. **Todos los sábados...**
2. **Todos los domingos...**
3. **En muchas clases...**
4. **Muchas veces...**
5. **Pocas veces...**
6. **Todas las noches...**

C **Mis compañeros.** Working in groups of three or four, poll your classmates using the following questions. Report back to the class.

Por ejemplo:

¿Cuántos piensan comer en la cafetería hoy?

(A la clase:) **Todos pensamos comer en la cafetería hoy. (Muchos estudiantes piensan comer afuera. Pocos piensan comer en la cafetería. Nadie** (nobody) **piensa comer en la cafetería hoy, etc.).**

¿Cuántos...

1. ... quieren ser doctores? ¿abogados? ¿ingenieros?
2. ... tienen una familia grande?
3. ... tienen abuelos en casa?
4. ... viven en un apartamento? ¿en una casa?
5. ... tienen una colección en casa?
6. ... practican deportes?

La lotería

¿Qué es una lotería? Pues, compras un billete que lleva un número. Si seleccionan tu número, ganas mucho dinero. En España hay muchas loterías. En una lotería, el ganador recibe cincuenta por ciento del dinero y el otro cincuenta por ciento es para el estado, o el gobierno. Las ganancias del estado pagan muchos servicios. Por ejemplo, se usan para los niños que no tienen padres y para las viudas (señoras que ya no tienen esposos). Una de las loterías más grandes es la de la ONCE (Organización Nacional de Ciegos). Con las ganancias de esta lotería se pagan los salarios de los vendedores de billetes y también se mantienen escuelas para los ciegos (personas que no pueden ver).

Actividades

A The above tells about the Spanish lottery. What do you know about how a lottery works? In the paragraph above, find five people or groups of people who benefit from the lottery system. Which one receives the most money?

B Complete the following sentence:
Si gano la lotería, pienso comprar _____, _____ **y** _____.

JUGAR A LA LOTERIA TRAE SUERTE

lotería nacional
La Lotería

Presentation
Read the Cultura viva on this page. On the chalkboard, you may wish to write several key words that are used in this reading: **billete, ganar, ganador, ganancias.** You may want to give students the meaning of these words.

Did You Know?
Spain is not the only Spanish-speaking country that has a lottery. Many other countries have some type of lottery system, including Mexico, and Colombia.

Critical Thinking Activity
Is there a lottery in your state? What are some advantages and disadvantages of a lottery?

Actividades

Actividad A Answers
1. el estado o el gobierno
2. los niños que no tienen padres
3. las señoras que ya no tienen esposos (viudas).
4. los vendedores de billetes
5. los ciegos
Los ciegos ganan más dinero.

Actividad B Answers
Answers will vary.

Structure Teaching Resources
1. Workbook, p. 119
2. Cassette 4.2
3. Student Tape Manual, p. 93
4. Estructura Masters 4.2
5. Lesson Quizzes, pp. 78–79

Bell Ringer Review

Directions to students: On your paper, draw a picture that represents the following professions:

1. bombero
2. ama de casa
3. agricultor
4. periodista
5. carpintero
6. abogada

Structure Focus

The numbers from 100 to 500 are presented in this lesson. Numbers 600 and on will be taught in Chapter 4, Lesson 3.

Presentation

Lead students through steps 1–3 on page 264. You may first want to review numbers by tens. For step 2, you may wish to model the numbers from 200 to 500, having students repeat each number in unison.

Actividad

Actividad Answers

Las tarjetas postales valen trescientas sesenta y cinco pesetas.
El bolígrafo vale ciento ochenta pesetas.
El cartel vale cuatrocientas pesetas.
La camiseta vale quinientas cincuenta pesetas.
El refresco vale sesenta y cinco pesetas, y el pastel vale ciento sesenta pesetas. El total es doscientas veinte y cinco pesetas.

Estructura 2

How to Count from 100 to 500

You have learned that the word **cien** is used for 100.

> **Necesito cien pesetas, por favor.**

1. For numbers between 101 and 199, use **ciento**.

> **El televisor vale ciento cincuenta dólares.**

2. Below are the words for 200, 300, 400, and 500.

doscientos(as)	**cuatrocientos(as)**
trescientos(as)	**quinientos(as)**

Notice that the ending you use for 200 to 500 (**-os** or **-as**) depends on whether you are describing masculine or feminine words.

> **¿Cuántos discos tiene José? ¡Tiene doscientos!**
>
> **¿Cuántas páginas tiene el libro? Tiene trescientas páginas.**

3. Follow the hundreds with single- and double-digit numbers.

105	**ciento cinco**
240	**doscientos cuarenta**
590	**quinientos noventa**

Actividad

¿Cuánto vale? Pilar has just purchased the items below. Tell how much each one costs.

```
PZA.DEL.ANGEL,16
ART. INFORMATICA
TELEFONO 4692230


TARJETAS
POSTALES
IVA INCLUIDO----  365
TOTAL
              365
```

```
PZA.DEL.ANGEL,16
ART. INFORMATICA
TELEFONO 4692230


BOLÍGRAFO    180
IVA INCLUIDO----
TOTAL        180
```

```
kG    PT/kG    61
CARTEL       PTAS
               400
A  *  TOTAL
             400
```

```
CIF A/78668751
  IVA INCLUIDO

CAMISETA
TOTAL
           550
           550
001CAJERA

     39001
```

```
CIF A/78668751
  IVA INCLUIDO

REFRESCO
PASTEL
TOTAL
            65
           160
           225
001CAJERA

     39001
```

Cooperative Learning

Have students bring or draw pictures of what they want to purchase. They should write the price of the item on the back. In teams, they will take turns showing their picture and asking teammates for the price. The one who is closest to the correct price gets to hold the picture. At the end, the member with the most pictures wins a prize.

Finalmente

Finalmente

Situaciones

A conversar It's the year after your graduation and you happen to see a former classmate. Greet each other and converse about the following.

1. where each of you lives and what your home is like
2. your possessions
3. your daily activities

A escribir You are preparing to interview a local Hispanic professional. Write down questions you will ask this person to obtain the following information.

1. name and profession
2. name and address of his or her company
3. what he or she dislikes about the job
4. what a student must do to prepare for this kind of work

Repaso de vocabulario

PREGUNTAS

¿Cuánto vale?
¿Cuántos años tiene(s)?

OCUPACIONES

el/la abogado(a)
el/la agricultor/a
el ama de casa (f.)
el/la arquitecto(a)
el/la bombero(a)
el/la carpintero(a)
el/la dentista
el/la doctor/a

el/la dueño(a)
el/la electricista
el/la empleado(a)
el/la enfermero(a)
el hombre de negocios
el/la ingeniero(a)
el/la mecánico(a)
la mujer de negocios
la mujer policía
el/la periodista
el policía
el/la profesor/a
el/la supervisor/a
el/la veterinario(a)

NÚMEROS

ciento
doscientos(as)
trescientos(as)
cuatrocientos(as)
quinientos(as)

CANTIDADES

mucho(a)
poco(a)
todo(a)

LUGARES

la compañía
la fábrica

EXPRESIONES

Creo que...
estudiar para

Lección 2 **265**

Situaciones

Lesson 2 Evaluation
The A conversar and A escribir situations on this page are designed to give students the opportunity to use as many language functions and as much vocabulary from this lesson as possible. The A conversar and A escribir are also intended to show how well students are able to meet the lesson objectives.

Presentation
Prior to doing A conversar and A escribir on this page, you may wish to play the Situaciones listening activities on Cassette 4.2 as a means of helping students organize the material.

For the Native Speaker

Native speakers will write 2–3 sentences describing a profession without naming it. For example: **Mi trabajo a veces es peligroso pero al mismo tiempo me da mucha satisfacción. Pongo mi vida siempre en peligro para que el público común tenga tranquilidad.** The class guesses the profession (**policía**).

265

Lección 3

Objectives

By the end of this lesson, students will be able to:

1. talk about what others like and dislike
2. tell how something or someone appears to be
3. identify household pets and common zoo animals
4. use numbers from 600 to the thousands

Lesson 3 Resources
1. Workbook, pp. 120–125
2. Vocabulario Transparencies 4.3
3. Cassette 4.3
4. Student Tape Manual, pp. 96–100
5. Lesson Quizzes, pp. 80–84
6. Test Booklet, pp. 55–63
7. Computer Software, Disk 2
8. Video Cassette
9. Estructura Masters 4.3
10. Diversiones Masters 4.3

Bell Ringer Review

Directions to students: List the people in your immediate family according to their ages.
Por ejemplo: Mi mamá tiene treinta y cinco años. Mi hermano mayor tiene diez y nueve años.

Lección 3

No comprendo a la abuela

¡A comenzar!

The following are some of the things you will be learning to do in this lesson.

When you want to . . .	You use . . .
1. talk about one thing that someone likes	• A + person + **le gusta** + thing.
2. talk about several things that someone likes	• A + person + **le gustan** + things.
3. say how something or someone appears to be	• **Parece que...**

Now find examples of the above words and phrases in the following postcard.

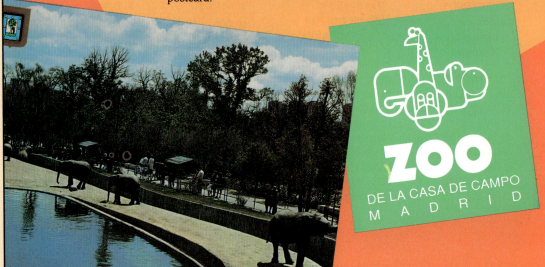

ZOO
DE LA CASA DE CAMPO
M A D R I D

Getting Ready for Lesson 3

You may wish to use one or more of the following suggestions to prepare students for the lesson:

1. Tell students that you are trying to decide on a pet to buy and are having difficulty making a decision. Use the first Vocabulario Transparency 4.3 or some other source to talk about various types of pets. Weigh the pros and cons of each. For example:
Quisiera tener un animal en casa pero no sé qué animal comprar. Quizás un perro (show picture). **Dicen que los perros son muy buenos, pero si tengo un perro, no puedo viajar. Quizás un gato** (show picture). **Dicen que los gatos son muy independientes y que no les gustan las personas.**

Kim le escribe una tarjeta postal a la señora Rivera.

Madrid
26 de julio

Querida señora Rivera:
   Aquí estamos Pilar, sus hermanos menores Felipe y Miguel Ángel, la abuela y yo en el parque zoológico de Madrid. Felipe es simpático, pero creo que Miguel Ángel está demasiado mimado (claro, la abuela cree que es el niño perfecto).
   No comprendo a la abuela. Creo que a ella no le gustan los jóvenes. Pasa los días en casa con Miguel Ángel. Parece que la abuela no está en Madrid de visita. Creo que vive aquí con la familia. ¡Hasta luego!
                        Un saludo
                        afectuoso de
                        Kim

Ms. Sonia Rivera

17 Dover Place

Los Ángeles, CA

91600   E.E.U.U.

Actividad preliminar

Say whether you know that the following statements are true or whether you're not entirely sure. Begin each statement with **Sé que...** or **Parece que...**

Por ejemplo:
   Madrid es una ciudad divertida.
   Parece que Madrid es una ciudad divertida.

1. José Luis es hermano de Pilar.
2. Madrid es la capital de España.
3. Pilar vive en Madrid.
4. José Luis saca buenas notas en la universidad.
5. Kim y Pilar son buenas amigas.

Lección 3   **267**

¡A comenzar!

Presentation

A. Lead students through each of the three functions given on page 266, progressing from the English to the Spanish for each function. Then have students find these words and phrases in the post-card on page 267.

B. Introduce the Lesson 3 postcard by reading it aloud or by playing the cassette version. Have students listen for the following information:

1. ¿Quién está con Kim?
2. ¿Quiénes son Felipe y Miguel Ángel?
3. Según Kim, ¿a la abuela le gustan los jóvenes?

C. Now ask students to open their books and look at the postcard as you lead them through what is said. For example:

1. ¿Dónde está Kim?
2. ¿Cómo es Felipe?
3. ¿A Kim le gusta Miguel Ángel?
4. ¿Dónde pasa la abuela los días?
5. ¿Dónde vive la abuela?

D. Ask students whether Kim mentions any zoo animals in her postcard. (No) Ask students to respond with **Sí** or **No** to tell whether they think Kim and Pilar might have seen each of the following animals at the zoo:

1. canarios
2. pingüinos
3. elefantes
4. leones
5. gatos
6. tigres

Actividad preliminar

Actividad preliminar Answers
1. Sé que José Luis es hermano de Pilar.
2. Sé que...
3. Sé que...
4. Parece que...
5. Parece que...

   You might wish to continue with... **un canario. A los canarios les gusta cantar... unos peces dorados... les gusta nadar, etc.** Show pictures of each animal as you mention it.
2. Ask for a show of hands for the following, asking students: **¿Qué animales les gustan a ustedes? Para la casa, ¿a quiénes les gustan los perros/los gatos/los canarios/los peces dorados, etc.?**

3. Continue to talk about animals, including animals that could be found in a zoo. Show pictures of each new animal as you name it. For example: **Los perros, los gatos, los canarios y los peces dorados pueden vivir en la casa. Pero los pingüinos, los monos, los leones, los tigres, los elefantes, etc. no pueden vivir en la casa. Estos animales pueden vivir en el parque zoológico.**

Vocabulario

Bell Ringer Review

Directions to students: Write down three occupations you would like to have and three you would not like to have. Give reasons for your choices.

Presentation

A. Have students open their books to the Vocabulario on pages 268 and 269. Model each new word on these pages. Begin each phrase on page 268 with **Tengo...** Have students repeat each phrase in unison. Then model each new word on page 269, beginning with the phrase, **En el parque zoológico cuidan...**

B. You may wish to survey the class to find out the most popular pets in the Vocabulario. Rank them using **primero, segundo, tercero, etc.** Do the same for the zoo animals.

C. You may wish to call attention to where descriptive words are placed. For example, **gato negro y blanco, peces dorados, perro pequeño.** Have students add their own descriptions to these animals. For example, **un gato independiente, peces dorados aburridos, un caballo perezoso, un perro gordo, una serpiente verde, un conejo blanco, etc.**

Tengo...

un canario amarillo

un caballo viejo

una tortuga

un ratoncito blanco

unos peces dorados

un periquito azul

un gato negro

un conejo blanco

un perro pequeño

268 CAPÍTULO 4

Total Physical Response

Getting Ready

For **TPR 1,** make three to five copies of the Vocabulario Transparencies. Cut out the animals and distribute one to each student. There should be enough illustrations so that every student has one or two. For **TPR 2,** have one set of illustrations on the front table.

New Words

lleven   dame   denme

TPR 1

(After each command, say **Muéstrenmelos(las)** in order to check for accuracy.)
Pongan los conejos blancos en el piso.
Denme los monos.
Levanten las manos si tienen un ratoncito blanco.

En el parque zoológico cuidan...

los pingüinos

los leones

los elefantes

los monos

los tigres

los osos

los gorilas

las llamas

los camellos

las serpientes

D. You may want to have students describe the zoo animals on page 269. For example: **Los pingüinos son blancos y negros. Son muy divertidos.**

When Students Ask

You may wish to give students the following additional vocabulary to allow them to talk about other animals:

la vaca	el burro
la pantera	el cerdo
el toro	la oveja
el rinoceronte	el chivo
el gallo	el cocodrilo
el hipopótamo	la vicuña
la gallina	la cebra
el caimán	el ciervo
el pato	la girafa
la mariposa	el lobo
la rana	el zorro

Regionalisms

You may wish to tell students that in some parts of the Spanish-speaking world the following words or phrases are alternatives to those presented in the Vocabulario.
el mono (el chango) (Mex. and Central Am.) **(el mico);**
la serpiente (la culebra)

Lleven los elefantes a mi escritorio.
Levanten los pies si tienen un perro.
Denme los caballos viejos.
Lleven los pingüinos a la ventana.
Pongan los camellos debajo de la mesa.
Lleven los peces dorados a la pared.
Denme los osos.
Lleven los gatos negros a la puerta.
(Repeat with different animals.)

TPR 2

Dale el oso a _____.
Dame el periquito azul.
Lleva las llamas a la pared.
Escribe "leones" en la pizarra.
Esconde los gorilas en tu libro.
Pon el conejillo de indias en tu mesa.
Entrega los tigres a _____.
Toca las serpientes y camina a la puerta.
(Repeat commands with other animals.)

Actividades

Actividades

A **Preferencias.** Ask a classmate which animals presented in the **Vocabulario** he or she likes. Then report to the class.

Por ejemplo:

ESTUDIANTE A   **ESTUDIANTE B**

¿Te gustan los gatos?   Sí, (No, no) me gustan.

(A la clase:) A Mary (no) le gustan los gatos.

B **¿Cómo son los animales?** Use the following traits to describe the animals listed below.

bonito   misterioso
divertido   paciente
feo   peligroso (dangerous)
grande   pequeño
independiente   perezoso
inteligente   simpático
listo   tímido

Por ejemplo:

> los gatos
> *Los gatos son (parecen) independientes y misteriosos.*

1. los perros
2. las serpientes
3. los caballos
4. los conejos
5. los leones
6. los osos
7. los pingüinos
8. los monos
9. los gorilas
10. los canarios
11. las tortugas
12. los ratoncitos
13. los camellos
14. las llamas

C **De vacaciones.** Write a note to your neighbor thanking him or her for agreeing to take care of your pet while you're on vacation. Answer the following questions to provide information about your pet. If you don't have a pet, think of a friend's or relative's pet.

1. ¿Cómo es?
2. ¿Cuándo come?
3. ¿Qué le gusta hacer?
4. ¿Qué no le gusta hacer?
5. ¿Dónde duerme?
6. ¿Qué más necesita?

Here is the first line of your letter.

Querido(a) _____:

Gracias por cuidar a *(nombre del animal)...*

For the Native Speaker

Write a letter of application for a job in an animal hospital. Give complete autobiographical data, explain why you want the job, your qualifications, your available work hours, etc.

Cooperative Learning

Teams will brainstorm and make a complete list of animals and their traits. They will then place a star next to the animal they like the most and write a sentence stating why. Compile the lists from each team to see how many of the same animals were chosen in the class.

Los abuelos

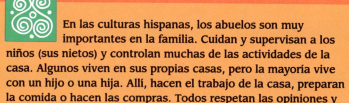

En las culturas hispanas, los abuelos son muy importantes en la familia. Cuidan y supervisan a los niños (sus nietos) y controlan muchas de las actividades de la casa. Algunos viven en sus propias casas, pero la mayoría vive con un hijo o una hija. Allí, hacen el trabajo de la casa, preparan la comida o hacen las compras. Todos respetan las opiniones y recomendaciones de los abuelos.

Actividades

A According to the above reading, which of the following activities do many Hispanic grandparents do?

Por ejemplo:

limpiar la casa
Sí, limpian la casa.

1. cocinar
2. cuidar a los niños
3. ir de compras
4. descansar todo el día
5. expresar sus opiniones
6. ven la tele todo el día
7. jugar con los niños
8. ir a discotecas
9. ganar dinero
10. vivir con sus hijos
11. dar recomendaciones

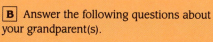

B Answer the following questions about your grandparent(s).

1. ¿Dónde viven tus abuelos?
2. ¿Hablas por teléfono con ellos?
3. ¿A tus abuelos les gustan los jóvenes? ¿Les gustan tus amigos?
4. ¿Les gusta tu música? ¿Les gusta tu ropa?

Lección 3   **271**

Pronunciation

You may wish to play the recorded version of these pronunciation lines, located at the end of Cassette 4.3. You may also wish to write this verse on the chalkboard and have students copy it into their notebook:

Basta de jugar,   Arrorró, mi niño,
basta de correr.   arrorró, mi sol,
Cierra ya tus ojos,   arrorró, pedazo
sol de mi querer.   de mi corazón.

The above are two traditional lullabyes grandmothers sing to children. Take them slowly. If students cannot produce the **rr**, focus on the other elements of pronunciation here. For some students the **rr** will come easily and they will enjoy using it. You may find it helpful to tell students that even Spanish-speaking children have difficulty with it.

Cultura viva 1

Presentation

Read the Cultura viva on this page. You may wish to read it aloud to the class, or have students read silently to themselves. Then do the Actividades.

Did You Know?

From an early age, children in Hispanic cultures are taught to respect and help the elderly.

Critical Thinking Activity

Imagine that your grandparents were living with you. How would your life change? Is it a good idea for grandparents to live with their children and grandchildren?

Actividades

Actividad A Answers
1. Sí, cocinan.
2. Sí, cuidan a los niños.
3. Sí, van de compras.
4. No, no descansan todo el día.
5. Sí, expresan sus opiniones.
6. No, no ven la tele todo el día.
7. Sí, juegan con los niños.
8. No, no van a discotecas.
9. No, no ganan dinero.
10. Sí, viven con sus hijos.
11. Sí, dan recomendaciones.

Actividad B Answers
Answers will vary.

Additional Practice

Ask students what advice Pilar's grandmother would give to the following members of her family.
Por ejemplo:
Pilar va a las discotecas todos los fines de semana.
No debes ir a las discotecas todos los fines de semana.
1. Los hermanos menores no sacan buenas notas.
2. José Luis sale todas las noches con una chica diferente.
3. Pilar nunca ahorra dinero.

Bell Ringer Review

Directions to students: What do animals eat? Make two headings on your paper: **carnivores** and **herbivores.** Then look at the animals shown on pages 268 and 269 in your text. List the meat eaters and the plant eaters in the appropriate columns on your paper.

Structure Focus

In this lesson, the presentation of **gustar** is limited to **Le gusta(n)** and **Les gusta(n). Le(s) gusta** + infinitive was taught in Chapter 4, Lesson 1. Students learned to use **me gusta** and **te gusta** in Chapter 1, Lesson 4; and **me gustan** and **te gustan** in Chapter 1, Lesson 6.

Presentation

Lead students through steps 1–3 on page 272. For additional examples you may want to make statements about students in the class. For example, **A José le gusta estudiar. A Luisa le gusta nadar. A Janey y Paula les gustan los deportes. A Julio no le gustan las tareas. Etc.** Have students react to the above statements.

Estructura 1

How to Describe Other People's Likes and Dislikes   **Le gusta(n) / Les gusta(n)**

You have already learned to say what another person likes and doesn't like to do.

> **A Kim le gusta viajar. También le gusta sacar fotos.**

You have also learned to say what two or more people like and don't like to do.

> **A mis compañeros les gusta bailar. No les gusta cantar.**

1. To say that someone likes one thing, use **le gusta** + object.
   > **A Pilar le gusta el parque zoológico.**
   > **A Kim le gusta Madrid.**

2. To say that someone likes more than one thing, use **le gustan** + objects.
   > **A José Luis le gustan sus clases.**
   > **A Miguel Ángel le gustan las serpientes.**

3. To say what more than one person likes or does not like, use **les gusta** or **les gustan.**
   > **A los estudiantes les gusta la señora Rivera.**
   > **A los hermanos de Pilar les gustan las vacaciones.**
   > **¿A ustedes les gustan los bailes de la escuela?**
   > **A mis padres no les gusta la tele.**

Actividades

A **¿Qué le gusta?** List at least two likes and dislikes for the following people.

Por ejemplo:

> un amigo
> *A mi amigo Tom le gustan los videojuegos.*
> *No le gustan los exámenes de historia.*

1. tu amigo(a)
2. tu mamá o tu papá
3. tu primo(a)
4. tu maestro(a) de español
5. tu hermano(a)
6. un(a) compañero(a) de clase

B **¿Qué les gusta?** Complete the sentences below to describe differences in the interests of the following groups of people.

1. A los niños les gusta(n)...
2. A los jóvenes les gusta(n)...
3. A los padres les gusta(n)...
4. A los abuelos les gusta(n)...
5. A los maestros les gusta(n)...

C **Animales.** List two animals you like and two you don't like.

Por ejemplo:

> **Me gustan los perros pero no me**
> **gustan los gatos.**

Then compare the results in a small group, announcing the similarities and differences to the class.

Por ejemplo:

> **A Mark y a Chris les gustan los osos**
> **pero no les gustan los elefantes.**

Lección 3   **273**

Actividades

Actividad A Answers
Answers will vary, however students should use **le gusta(n)** in each response.

Actividad B Answers
Answers will vary but may include the following:

1. ... comer, estar con sus familias
2. ... hablar con amigos, jugar deportes
3. ... leer, trabajar, ver la tele
4. ... cuidar a sus nietos, hablar con sus familias
5. ... leer, hablar, trabajar con los estudiantes

Actividad C Answers
Answers will vary, however when reporting back to the class, students should use **les gustan** in each statement.

Additional Practice
After doing Actividades A, B, and C, you may wish to reinforce the lesson by doing the following activity:
In pairs, find out which of the following your partner's family members like. For example: **fútbol o fútbol americano.**
A mi hermano le gusta el fútbol.
1. *Julio Iglesias o Whitney Houston*
2. **San Francisco o Los Ángeles**
3. **Kevin Costner o Mel Gibson**
4. **la tele o el estéreo**
5. **leer un libro o escuchar la radio**

Reteaching

Using the Estructura 1 presentation on page 272 as a reference, have students write down five things their friends or family members like.

Learning from Realia

You may wish to have students look at the cartoon on page 273 and have them say as much as they can about it.

273

Presentation
Read the Cultura viva on this page. You may wish to have students guess what **diario** means, given the context. Then do the Actividades.

Did You Know?
La calle Serrano is probably the most expensive shopping area of Madrid. One can find many fashionable stores there.
The Plaza Mayor is in the heart of old Madrid. It is surrounded by 136 houses built in the 17th century. Most of the houses have remained in the same family, generation after generation.
Paella is a Valencian rice dish with a variety of seafood.

Critical Thinking Activity
What regional dishes do you associate with various parts of the United States?

Actividades

Actividad A Answers
Sola: ir a un concierto en la Plaza Mayor.
Acompañada: ir a la casa de Maura, ir de compras en la calle Serrano, a comer paella.
Fui. Fuimos.

Actividad B Answers
La semana pasada, luego, ayer, después del concierto.
All refer to times in the past.

Actividad C Answers
En la calle Serrano: vi gente elegante y cosas demasiado caras en las tiendas.
En la Plaza Mayor: vi un concierto y un grupo de estudiantes norteamericanos.

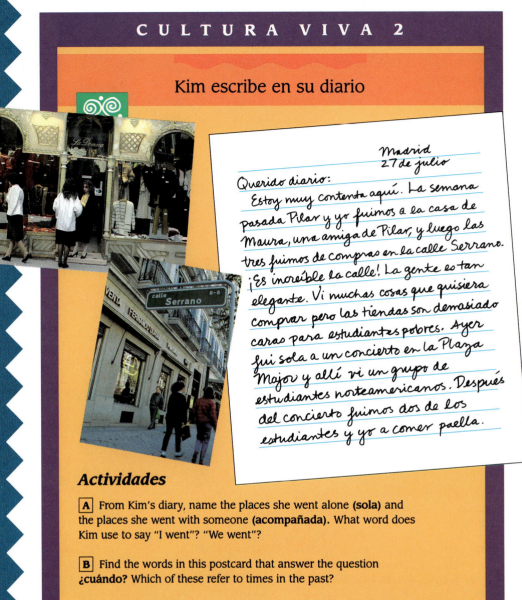

CULTURA VIVA 2

Kim escribe en su diario

> Madrid
> 27 de julio
>
> Querido diario:
> Estoy muy contenta aquí. La semana pasada Pilar y yo fuimos a la casa de Maura, una amiga de Pilar, y luego las tres fuimos de compras en la calle Serrano. ¡Es increíble la calle! La gente es tan elegante. Vi muchas cosas que quisiera comprar pero las tiendas son demasiado caras para estudiantes pobres. Ayer fui sola a un concierto en la Plaza Mayor y allí vi un grupo de estudiantes norteamericanos. Después del concierto fuimos dos de los estudiantes y yo a comer paella.

Actividades

A From Kim's diary, name the places she went alone **(sola)** and the places she went with someone **(acompañada).** What word does Kim use to say "I went"? "We went"?

B Find the words in this postcard that answer the question **¿cuándo?** Which of these refer to times in the past?

C What would Kim say she saw in each of the following places?
En la calle Serrano vi _____. En la Plaza Mayor vi _____.

Estructura 2

How to Count from 600 to the Thousands

You have learned that the numbers for 200, 300, 400, and 500 end either in **-os** or **-as,** depending on what you are describing.

> **El televisor vale trescientos dólares.**
> **Hay doscientas personas en el estadio.**

1. The numbers from 600 to 900 work the same way. They are:

600	**seiscientos(as)**
700	**setecientos(as)**
800	**ochocientos(as)**
900	**novecientos(as)**

2. The word for 1,000 is **mil.** To say 2,000, 3,000, 4,000, and so on, you say:

> **dos mil, tres mil, cuatro mil, etc.**

3. Notice how numbers are combined. To give numbers in the thousands in Spanish, use a period instead of a comma, as in the last three examples.

115	**ciento quince**
231	**doscientos treinta y uno**
355	**trescientos cincuenta y cinco**
1.400	**mil cuatrocientos**
2.800	**dos mil ochocientos**
3.335	**tres mil trescientos treinta y cinco**

4. When you combine numbers, as in the examples above, only the numbers that indicate "hundreds" (200, 300, 400, etc.) change endings, depending on whether you are describing masculine or feminine nouns.

> **Hay doscientas quince muchachas en la escuela.**
> **Y hay doscientos veinte y dos muchachos.**
>
> **El coche vale nueve mil quinientos dólares.**
> **El trofeo vale tres mil cuatrocientas pesetas.**

Estructura 2

Structure Teaching Resources
1. Workbook, pp. 124–125
2. Cassette 4.3
3. Student Tape Manual, p. 98
4. Estructura Masters 4.3
5. Lesson Quizzes, pp. 83–84

Bell Ringer Review
Directions to students: Write five sentences that show the likes and dislikes of your grandparents. You may list your grandmother and grandfather separately, if you prefer. Be sure to use **le** or **les** with a form of **gustar.**

Structure Focus
Numbers 600 and up are taught in this lesson. The numbers from 100 to 500 were taught in Chapter 4, Lesson 3. The numbers 0–20 were taught in Chapter 1, Lesson 3; the numbers 21–100 were taught in Chapter 3, Lesson 3.

Presentation
A. Lead students through steps 1–4 on page 275.

B. Have students give dates from history or from events in their lives. Write the dates on the board using period and commas and read them to the students. Draw their attention to the commas and periods and to the spelling of 700 and 900.

Cooperative Learning
Have students bring in magazines or newspapers that have ads for items on sale. Teams cut out the ads and make a collage of the bargains. Make sure they show the price of the item. Each team presents their collage to the class as if it were an ad for a particular store.

Actividad

¡Qué suerte! On a TV game show, you have won $6,500 and now you must decide how to spend the money. Choose from the selection of prizes below.

Por ejemplo:

Quiero la bicicleta. Vale quinientos treinta y cinco dólares. También quiero _____. Vale _____.

el teléfono
portátil $750

el estéreo $695

el viaje a Miami $1400

la videocasetera $620

la bicicleta $535

la moto $1100

el viaje a España $3225

Finalmente

Situaciones

A conversar You want to buy a pet at the mall. A classmate will play the role of the salesclerk.

1. Ask the salesclerk what pets the store has.
2. Ask about the age, colors, and other characteristics of three pets the salesclerk has mentioned.
3. Ask about the cost of each one.
4. Make a selection.

A escribir On a separate sheet of paper, complete the application for part-time work at the local veterinary clinic.

¿Cómo se llama? _____
¿Cuál es su dirección? _____
¿Cuál es su número de teléfono? _____
¿Cuántos años tiene? _____
¿Por qué quiere trabajar en la clínica? _____
¿Qué animales le gustan más? _____
¿Hay animales que no le gustan? _____
¿Cuántas horas quiere trabajar? _____ ¿Qué días? _____
¿Tiene experiencia? _____ ¿Dónde? _____

Repaso de vocabulario

ANIMALES
el caballo
el camello
el canario
el conejillo de Indias
el conejo
el elefante
el gato
el gorila

el león
la llama
el mono
el oso
el periquito
el perro
el pez dorado
    (pl. los peces dorados)
el pingüino
el ratoncito

la serpiente
el tigre
la tortuga

NÚMEROS
seiscientos(as)
setecientos(as)
ochocientos(as)
novecientos(as)
mil

PERSONAS
los/las jóvenes
el/la niño(a)

OTRAS PALABRAS Y EXPRESIONES
cuidar
Parece que...
el parque zoológico

Lección 3 **277**

Finalmente

Situaciones

Lesson 3 Evaluation
The A conversar and A escribir situations on this page are designed to give students the opportunity to use as many language functions and as much vocabulary from this lesson as possible. The A conversar and A escribir are also intended to show how well students are able to meet the lesson objectives.

Presentation
Prior to doing the A conversar and A escribir on this page, you may wish to play the Situaciones listening activities on Cassette 4.3 as a means of helping students organize the material.

For the Native Speaker

Directions to students: Set up an imaginary zoo using either stuffed animals or pictures from magazines. Choose several animals and give descriptions of each, pretending you are a guide taking tourists through the zoo. The descriptions can be done in writing and orally.

Lección 4

Objectives

By the end of this lesson, students will be able to:

1. describe someone's physical characteristics
2. say what they and others have to or must do
3. talk about specific people using the personal **a**

Lesson 4 Resources
1. Workbook, pp. 126–129
2. Vocabulario Transparency 4.4
3. Cassette 4.4
4. Student Tape Manual, pp. 101–104
5. Lesson Quizzes, pp. 85–87
6. Computer Software, Disk 2
7. Video Cassette
8. Estructura Masters 4.4
9. Diversiones Masters 4.4

Bell Ringer Review

Directions to students: Practice the following numbers in Spanish. Write them out in words on your paper and pronounce them out loud. 600, 700, 800, 900, 1.000

¡A comenzar!

Presentation

A. Lead students through each of the four functions given on page 278, progressing from the English to the Spanish for each function. Then have students find these words and phrases in the dialogue on page 279.

B. Introduce the Lesson 4 dialogue by reading it aloud or by playing the cassette version. Tell students they are going to hear Pilar describe other members of her family to Kim.

Lección 4

El álbum de familia

¡A comenzar!

The following are some of the things you will be learning to do in this lesson.

When you want to . . .	You use . . .
1. describe someone's characteristics	• pelirrojo(a), rubio(a), etc.
2. talk about someone's features	• ojos azules, pelo negro, frenos en los dientes, bigote, etc.
3. say what someone must do	• **Tiene que** + activity.
4. talk about specific people	• ... **a** + person

Now find examples of the above words and phrases in the following conversation.

Getting Ready for Lesson 4

You may wish to use the following suggestion to prepare students for the lesson: Bring to class photos of your family that you may have used in Lesson 1 of this chapter (or use the Vocabulario Transparency). Show the photos (or transparency) as you describe what the people look like. As you describe hair color, eye color, etc., you may wish to have students raise their hands if these descriptions also apply to them.

Kim y Pilar miran fotos de la familia de Pilar.

PILAR: Mira, Kim, aquí hay una foto de mis tíos. A la derecha está mi tía Elena. Es periodista. Es muy divertida. Ya ves que es muy guapa. Tiene pelo negro y ojos azules.

KIM: ¿Y quién es el niño con frenos en los dientes?

PILAR: Es José Antonio, el hijo de tía Elena. A ver... ¿ves a la pelirroja con anteojos? Es mi otra tía, Lidia, que trabaja en la RENFE. Siempre está muy ocupada. Tiene que trabajar mucho, incluso los fines de semana. Ahora, ¿ves al hombre con bigote?

KIM: ¿El señor alto que está a la izquierda?

PILAR: Sí. Es Juan Ignacio, el esposo de mi tía Lidia. Enseña historia en la universidad y escribe novelas policiales.

KIM: ¿Y quién es la niña rubia?

PILAR: Es Paloma, la hija de Lidia y Juan Ignacio.

Actividades preliminares

A The following relatives appear in the photo Pilar shows Kim.

Elena   José Antonio   Lidia   Paloma   Juan   Ignacio

Based on Pilar's explanation, tell who is being described.

1. Es el esposo de Lidia.
2. Es periodista.
3. Son los primos de Pilar.
4. Es la hija de Lidia.
5. Es el hijo de Elena.
6. Es profesor y escritor.
7. Es pelirroja y tiene anteojos.
8. Tiene pelo negro y ojos azules.
9. Tiene frenos en los dientes.

B Think of four people you enjoy seeing. Tell when or where you usually see them.

Por ejemplo:

Veo a mi prima Inés los fines de semana.

Lección 4 **279**

C. Now ask students to open their books and look at the dialogue. Ask them to give the names of the following members of Pilar's family:

1. la periodista
2. la tía de José Antonio
3. la esposa de Juan Ignacio
4. el profesor de historia
5. la mamá de Paloma
6. el papá de Paloma

D. Have students say how the following people would complete these statements:

1. Me llamo Juan Ignacio. Enseño _____. Escribo _____.
2. Me llamo Elena. Soy _____.
3. Me llamo Lidia. Trabajo en _____.

E. Which of the following questions does Pilar answer for at least one of her relatives? Have students raise their hands for questions answered.

1. ¿De dónde es?
2. ¿Cuántos años tiene?
3. ¿Qué es?
4. ¿Cómo es?
5. ¿Cómo se llama?
6. ¿Quién es?
7. ¿Dónde está en la foto?
8. ¿Dónde trabaja?
9. ¿Adónde va?
10. ¿Qué le gusta hacer?

Note. The definite article may be used with **pelo, ojos,** etc. For example: **Tiene el pelo negro y los ojos azules.**

Actividades Preliminares

Actividad A Answers
1. Juan Ignacio.
2. Elena.
3. José Antonio, Paloma.
4. Paloma.
5. José Antonio.
6. Juan Ignacio.
7. Lidia.
8. Elena.
9. José Antonio.

Actividad B Answers
Answers will vary.

Bell Ringer Review

Directions to students: Write a note to a friend telling him or her what kind of new pet you want and some qualities it should have.

Presentation

Have students open their books to the Vocabulario on page 280. Model each new word beginning each phrase with **Tiene...** Have students repeat each phrase in unison. Ask students to name someone in the class who has one of the physical characteristics in the Vocabulario. For example, **¿Quién tiene pelo lacio? ¿Quién tiene pelo corto? Etc.**

When Students Ask

The following additional vocabulary may be provided to allow students to describe people's hair or skin color:
moreno(a)
trigueño(a)
castaño(a)

Vocabulario

¿Cómo es? Tiene...

pelo lacio • pelo negro • pelo rizado • ojos azules • Usa anteojos. • barba • ojos verdes • pelo largo • pelo corto • ojos negros • frenos en los dientes • Es pelirroja. • Usa lentes de contacto. • Es rubio. • ojos de color café • bigote

Total Physical Response

Getting Ready
For **TPR 1,** give students construction paper to cut out a blue circle, a green rectangle, a black square, and a brown triangle.

New Word
la figura

TPR 1

Si tienen ojos azules, levanten el círculo azul.
Si tienen ojos negros, muéstrenme el cuadro negro.
Si tienen ojos verdes, muéstrenme el rectángulo verde.
Miren a la persona a su derecha o izquierda.
Levanten la figura del color de sus ojos.

Actividades

A **Mis compañeros de clase.** Give the name of at least one classmate who has the following characteristics.

Por ejemplo:

> ojos negros
> *Carlos tiene ojos negros.*

¿Cómo es él? ¿Y ella?

1. ojos azules
2. pelo corto
3. ojos cafés
4. anteojos
5. pelo rubio
6. frenos en los dientes
7. pelo negro
8. lentes de contacto
9. pelo rizado

Varilux de Essilor.
Para ver bien a cualquier distancia.

No sé quién dijo que la distancia más corta entre un beso y las estrellas es apenas una lente *Varilux*.

Absolutamente cierto. *Varilux* es la lente progresiva que permite ver correctamente a cualquier distancia.

Con *Varilux* unas únicas gafas sirven lo mismo para besar... que para ver el cielo.

De cerca. A media distancia. A lo lejos. *Varilux* de *Essilor*. Así de claro.

Pida a su Optico el Certificado de Origen.

essilor
el placer de ver bien

Lección 4 **281**

Actividades

Actividades A, B, and C Answers
Answers will vary.

Reteaching

Using the vocabulary items on page 280, describe an imaginary person to the class. Have each student draw the person you are describing on a piece of paper. Then have each student share his or her drawing with the class.

Muéstrenme la figura del color de los ojos de su madre.
(Repeat with other family members.)

TPR 2

Levanten las manos si tienen pelo rubio.
Toquen los pies si tienen pelo corto.
Pongan la cabeza en su escritorio si tienen pelo rizado.
Quítense los anteojos.

Cierren los ojos si tienen lentes de contacto.

TPR 3

Habla con una chica con pelo corto.
Saluda a un chico con barba o bigote.
Sonríe a una chica con pelo rubio.
Dale tu número de teléfono a un(a) chico(a) con ojos azules.
(Interchange commands and words.)

Learning From Photos

You may want to have students look at the photo on page 282 and have them describe hairstyles for Spanish male and female teens, based on what they see in the photo.

Unos viajeros jóvenes en la Estación de Atocha.

B **No somos gemelos.** Think of a friend and compare what the two of you look like, what characteristics you have in common, and what you like to do. Complete the following statements.

1. **Mi amigo(a) se llama _____.**
2. **Los (Las) dos somos _____.**
3. **A _____ le gusta _____, y a mí también (pero a mí _____).**

C **Mis parientes.** Choose two of your favorite relatives and describe each one as completely as you can, answering the following questions.

Por ejemplo:

> **¿Usan anteojos?**
> *Mi prima Kay usa anteojos pero mi tío Luke usa lentes de contacto.*

1. **¿De qué color tienen los ojos y el pelo?**
2. **¿Cuántos años tienen?**
3. **¿Qué les gusta? ¿Qué no les gusta?**
4. **¿Dónde viven?**
5. **¿Cómo son?**

282 CAPÍTULO 4

CULTURA VIVA 1

¡Vamos a tomar el tren!

La **RENFE (Red Nacional de los Ferrocarriles Españoles)** es el sistema nacional de trenes. Viajar en tren es muy popular y muy rápido en España. Hay varias clases de trenes: el tranvía es el más lento porque tiene muchas paradas en todos los pueblos pequeños. El rápido y el expreso son, claro, más rápidos. Pero el más rápido y el más cómodo de todos es el famoso Talgo. Durante los 260 "días azules", es posible comprar billetes más baratos y ahorrar dinero.

Actividades

A When are train tickets cheaper?

B Scan the following ad for information on a special student card **(la tarjeta joven)** for the railway system. Find out the following.

1. ¿Cuántos años debes tener para usar la tarjeta?
2. ¿Cuánto vale la tarjeta?
3. ¿Cuándo es posible viajar?
4. ¿Cuántos kilómetros necesitas viajar?
5. ¿Dónde compras la tarjeta?

¡¡Ésta es tu marcha!!
Tarjeta Joven de la Renfe.

Ésta es la marcha del tren. La Marcha de la Tarjeta Joven de la RENFE. Con ella, si tienes de 12 a 26 años, puedes viajar en tren a mitad de precio de la Tarifa General. Al precio que tú puedes.

Con la Tarjeta Joven no tienes excusas, cuesta sólo 2.500 ptas. y puedes recorrerte España de punta a punta siempre que salgas en días azules y a más de 100 Kms. de donde estés.

Además, por sacarte la Tarjeta, tienes un recorrido en litera gratis.

Y por si fuera poco, RENFE te dedica un super programa musical: todos los sábados, de 13.00 a 14.00 h., Emilio Aragón en directo en "Entrentenidísimo." (Cadena Ser O. M. y F. M.)

Cómprala ya.
Puedes hacerlo en Estaciones. Oficinas de Viaje RENFE y Agencias de Viaje autorizadas.

Bell Ringer Review

Directions to students: Write the name of a classmate who has each of the following characteristics:

1. **Tiene ojos azules y pelo rubio.**
2. **Tiene pelo negro y frenos en los dientes.**
3. **Tiene pelo negro y usa anteojos.**
4. **Tiene pelo corto, rizado y rubio.**

Presentation

Lead students through steps 1–4 on page 284. For step 1, you may wish to give additional examples of the personal **a,** such as: **Veo a Carmen. También veo su libro. Escucho discos. Escucho a Sofía.** For step 2, you may wish to add examples of **a** + **el** = **al.** For example, **Veo al maestro. Busco al amigo de Karen.**

Estructura 1

How to Talk about Specific People   The personal **a**

In the following pairs of sentences, in one sentence in each pair the direct object refers to a person; in the other, the direct object refers to a thing.

> **Veo a Julia en la clase de arte. En la clase vemos muchas fotos.**
>
> **No comprendo a la maestra de geometría. No comprendo el libro tampoco.**
>
> **En julio pensamos visitar Nueva York. Allí pensamos visitar a mis abuelos.**

1. Did you notice that if a word referring to a specific person or persons follows the verb, you use **a** before that word?

> **Los domingos visito _a_ mi amiga Inés. Inés y yo vamos al parque donde siempre vemos _a_ mis compañeros. También vemos _al_ hermano de Inés, que juega baloncesto con sus amigos. Generalmente invito _a_ Inés a tomar algo después en una cafetería.**

En el comedor del apartamento de la familia Mestre. ¿A quiénes ves?

2. Did you notice in the above paragraph that if the **a** comes before **el,** the two words combine to form **al?**

> **Inés piensa invitar al primo de Susan a la fiesta. También va a llamar al hermano de Eva.**

3. The personal **a** also appears in questions about specific people.

> **¿A quién llamas?**   **Llamo a Pilar.**
> **¿A quién invitas al baile?**   **Invito a José Luis.**

4. You do not use **a** before specific people after the verb **tener.**

> **Tengo dos hermanos.**

Actividades

A **Mi mundo.** Think of three people you visit frequently. Tell when you usually visit each of them.

Por ejemplo:

> mi amigo Sam
> *Visito a mi amigo Sam los sábados por la tarde.*

B **Mis amigos.** Tell about the people who are important to you by answering the following questions.

Por ejemplo:

> ¿A quién llamas cuando no entiendes la tarea?
> *Llamo al hermano de Pat.*

1. ¿A quién invitas al cine?
2. ¿A quién ves cuando vas a las fiestas?
3. ¿A quién ayudas (help) con la tarea?
4. ¿A quién visitas los fines de semana?
5. ¿A quién llamas cuando tienes un problema?

C **Un mensaje.** When Pilar and Kim return home one day, they find a phone message Pilar's mother left. Complete it by inserting a personal **a** in the blanks where necessary.

> Pilar:
> Debes llamar ___ Maura. Parece
> que ___ todos van a ver ___ José
> Antonio porque sale para Segovia
> el sábado. Maura quiere saber
> si debe invitar ___ Felipe y ___ su
> novia. Sabes ___ el número de
> teléfono de Maura, ¿no?

Lección 4 **285**

Actividades

Actividad A Answers
Answers will vary, however students should use the personal **a** in each response.

Actividad B Answers
Answers will vary but should include the following:

1. Invito a . . .
2. Escribo a . . .
3. Ayudo a . . .
4. Visito a . . .
5. Llamo a . . .

Actividad C Answers
The personal **a** should appear before the words **Maura, José Antonio, Felipe, su novia.**

Additional Practice
After completing Actividades A, B, and C, you may wish to reinforce the lesson by having Student A ask Student B the pair of questions in No. 1 below. Student B will respond. Then Student B will ask Student C the same question. Continue until all students in the class have had a chance to both ask and answer each pair of questions. Then repeat with question No. 2, etc.

1. ¿A quién buscas?
   Busco a _____.
   ¿Qué buscas?
   Busco _____.
2. ¿A quién ves en la cafetería?
   Veo a _____.
   ¿Qué ves?
   Veo _____.
3. ¿A quién escribes?
   Escribo a _____.
   ¿Qué escribes?
   Escribo _____.
4. ¿A quién escuchas?
   Escucho a _____.
   ¿Qué escuchas?
   Escucho _____.

285

Presentation

Read the Cultura viva on this page. You may wish to use a map of central Spain to show the location of each city described in the reading. If possible, bring to class additional photos of these cities. Then proceed to the Actividad.

Did You Know?

Toledo is located 41 miles southwest of Madrid. Because of its many historic structures, the Spanish government has declared the entire city a national monument. The architecture of Toledo shows a strong Moorish influence. The Moors captured Toledo in 712 A.D. and made the city its headquarters for that part of Spain.

Avila is located northwest of Madrid. The walls that surround Avila are the oldest and best preserved in Spain.

Segovia is also located northwest of Madrid. Its aqueduct is still in use. Segovia's second landmark is the **Alcázar** (castle).

Critical Thinking Activity

What does the reading tell you about Spain's history? In general, how would you compare Spain's history to U.S. history?

Actividad

Actividad Answers

Answers will vary but may include the following:

1. **Si estamos en Toledo debemos visitar la Catedral y la Iglesia de Santo Tomás.**
2. **Si estamos en Ávila debemos ver la Catedral y la Iglesia de Santa Teresa.**
3. **Si estamos en Segovia debemos ver el Acueducto Romano y el Alcázar.**

CULTURA VIVA 2

Toledo, Ávila y Segovia

Muchos turistas que visitan Madrid hacen excursiones a tres ciudades pequeñas que están a poca distancia de la capital: Toledo, Ávila y Segovia.

Toledo es una ciudad histórica. Como tiene influencia árabe, hebrea y católica, los turistas se maravillan ante la sinagoga, la catedral, las iglesias, los monasterios y calles y edificios medievales. También visitan la casa de El Greco, uno de los pintores más famosos de España.

Ávila es una ciudad medieval, completamente rodeada por una muralla construida como protección contra los moros. En Segovia, vemos el acueducto romano que pasa por el centro de la ciudad.

EXCURSIONES Y VISITAS

VIAJES ORBE, S.A.

MEDIO DÍA EN TOLEDO

En Toledo, ciudad-museo de gran belleza artística, visitamos la Catedral y su riquísimo Tesoro, y la Iglesia de Santo Tomás, donde está la obra más importante de El Greco: "El Entierro del Conde de Orgaz." Visitamos también la Sinagoga de Santa María la Blanca y el Monasterio de San Juan de los Reyes.

Salidas julio: 9, 10, 12, 13, 14, 21, 22, y 24.

Precio por persona: 2.200 ptas.

ÁVILA-SEGOVIA

En Ávila, visitamos la Catedral y la Iglesia de Santa Teresa. Más tarde salimos para Segovia, donde comemos cochinillo asado en un restaurante típico. En esta ciudad podemos contemplar el Acueducto Romano, de unos 2.000 años de antigüedad, y visitar el Alcázar.

Salidas julio: 11, 16, 19, 20 y 21.

Precio por persona: 4.700 ptas.

Actividad

Help Kim give advice on what to see in the following cities.

1. **Si estamos en Toledo, ¿qué debemos hacer?**
2. **¿Y si estamos en Ávila?**
3. **¿Y si estamos en Segovia?**

Estructura 2

How to Say What You Must Do   **Tener que** + *infinitive*

To say what you or others must do or have to do, use a form of the verb **tener,** followed by **que** and the activity.

> **Tengo que hacer la tarea.**
> **¿Tienes que llamar a tu hermano?**
> **José no tiene que trabajar hoy.**
> **Todos tenemos que ganar dinero.**
> **Raquel y su prima tienen que visitar a sus abuelos.**

Actividades

A **¡Vamos a España!** A group of students is going to Spain for a week. You are in charge of giving them final instructions. Which of the following must they do? Which do they not need to do?

Por ejemplo:

> recibir el pasaporte
> *Tienen que recibir el pasaporte.*
> llevar el libro de inglés
> *No tienen que llevar el libro de inglés.*

1. saber la dirección del hotel
2. llevar cheques de viajero
3. estudiar el mapa
4. llegar temprano al aeropuerto
5. comprar regalos para la maestra
6. hablar español
7. ser muy amables
8. ahorrar cinco mil dólares

Una vista de Toledo.

B **En tu casa.** List five things that your parents would say you have to do at home. Use **primero, luego, después, entonces.**

Por ejemplo:

> **Primero tienes que limpiar tu habitación.**

Cooperative Learning

Within teams, have students form pairs. Then have them write down activities they either have to do or don't have to do, using the following categories: **Tenemos que hacer. No tenemos que hacer.** Then have the entire team compare papers. The recorder will write down things everyone has in common.

Estructura 2

Structure Teaching Resources
1. Workbook, p. 129
2. Cassette 4.4
3. Student Tape Manual, p. 103
4. Estructura Masters 4.4
5. Lesson Quizzes, p. 87

Bell Ringer Review

Directions to students: List your classes in order, using words such as **primero, segundo, etc.**

Presentation

Lead students through the presentation on page 287. For emphasis, you may wish to write on the chalkboard things you have to do today. For example,
Tengo que leer.
Tengo que preparar lecciones.
Tengo que hablar con los estudiantes. Etc.
Then ask individual students:
¿Tienes que estudiar?
¿Tienes que hacer la tarea?
¿Tienes que practicar el piano? Etc.
For a review of the verb **tener,** you may want to use other forms in your questions.

Actividades

Actividad A Answers
1. **Tienen que saber la dirección del hotel.**
2. ... **llevar cheques de viajero.**
3. ... **estudiar el mapa.**
4. ... **llegar temprano al aeropuerto.**
5. **No... comprar regalos para la maestra.**
6. **Tienen que hablar español.**
7. ... **ser muy amables.**
8. **No... ahorrar cinco mil dólares.**

Actividad B Answers
Answers will vary.

Actividad C Answers
Answers will vary.

Classroom Management
You may wish to do Actividad C as a whole class activity initially. Take the role of Student A, calling on individual students to answer for Student B. You may want to do this as a paired activity the second time.

Actividades D and E Answers
Answers will vary.

Additional Practice
After doing Actividades A, B, C, D, and E, you may wish to reinforce the lesson by doing the following: In pairs have students invite each other to do certain things. The partner will refuse and say that he or she has to do something instead. For example:

ESTUDIANTE A	ESTUDIANTE B
¿Quieres ir al cine?	No, gracias, tengo que estudiar.

Reteaching
Have students list five things they have to do after school.

C **Estoy muy ocupado.** Bruno asks you to go to the following places, but you think he's boring. Tell him that you have to do something else.

Por ejemplo:

> ¿Quieres tomar algo en la cafetería?
> *¡Qué pena! Tengo que ver al maestro de inglés.*

1. ¿Quieres ir al centro comercial?
2. ¿Por qué no jugamos tenis?
3. ¿Quieres ir al cine el sábado?
4. ¿Por qué no vamos al partido esta noche?
5. Te gusta el fútbol, ¿verdad? ¿Quieres jugar?

D **Imposible.** Suggest to a classmate that the two of you do the following things. Your classmate will reject your suggestions and say something else you both have to do instead.

Por ejemplo:

> ir al cine

¿Qué tienen que hacer los muchachos?

ESTUDIANTE A	ESTUDIANTE B
¿Por qué no vamos al cine?	No. Tenemos que ir al centro.

1. ir al partido
2. tomar algo
3. bailar
4. hablar inglés
5. descansar
6. salir esta noche
7. limpiar tu habitación

E **Resoluciones.** Think of three things that you don't do enough of. Share these with a classmate. Then tell what you have to do to improve. Report back to the class.

Por ejemplo:

ESTUDIANTE A	ESTUDIANTE B
No trabajo bastante en mis clases. Tengo que trabajar más.	Nunca llevo a mi hermano menor al cine. Tengo que llevar a mi hermano al cine más.

(A la clase:) Jill dice que tiene que trabajar más. Yo también.

Finalmente

Finalmente

Situaciones

A conversar A classmate has witnessed a robbery. You will play the role of a police officer who asks about what the suspect looks like.

1. Find out if the person is a man or a woman.
2. Find out the person's approximate **(más o menos)** age.
3. Ask if the person is tall or short, thin or heavy.
4. Ask about the color, length, and type of hair. If it is a man, ask about facial hair and its color and length.
5. Find out if the person wears glasses.

A escribir Write a note to a classmate describing a well-known personality, such as an athlete, politican, musician, actor, or actress. Don't give the person's name; your classmate will guess whom you are describing.

1. Give the person's profession.
2. Describe what the person looks like.
3. Give one or two other details, such as the person's recent achievements or favorite activities.

Repaso de vocabulario

DESCRIPCIÓN PERSONAL	DESCRIPCIÓN DE PELO	EXPRESIÓN
los anteojos	corto	tener que
la barba	lacio	
el bigote	largo	
los dientes	pelirrojo(a)	
los frenos	rizado	
los lentes de contacto	rubio(a)	
el ojos		
el pelo		

For the Native Speaker

Native speakers will talk about places in their countries they like and tell why. They should make a list for their classmates.

Situaciones

Lesson 4 Evaluation
The A conversar and A escribir situations on this page are designed to give students the opportunity to use as many language functions and as much vocabulary from this lesson as possible. The A conversar and A escribir are also intended to show how well students are able to meet the lesson objectives.

Presentation
Prior to doing the A conversar and A escribir, you may wish to play the Situaciones listening activities on Cassette 4.4 as a means of helping students organize the material.

Lección 5

Objectives

By the end of this lesson, students will be able to:

1. say what they and others prefer to do
2. identify television programs and pastimes
3. talk about another or others
4. report on what someone says

Lesson 5 Resources

1. Workbook, pp. 130–135
2. Vocabulario Transparencies 4.5
3. Cassette 4.5
4. Student Tape Manual, pp. 105–108
5. Lesson Quizzes, pp. 88–91
6. Computer Software, Disk 2
7. Video Cassette
8. Estructura Masters 4.5
9. Diversiones Masters 4.5

Bell Ringer Review

Directions to students: Draw a picture of this Halloween monster. Follow the description given of its physical characteristics. The rest is up to you and your imagination!
El monstruo es muy alto y flaco. Tiene el pelo muy rizado y verde. Tiene frenos enormes en sus dientes. También usa anteojos negros porque tiene problemas con los ojos. ¡Es muy feo!

¡A comenzar!

Presentation

A. Lead students through each of the three functions given on page 290, progressing from the English to the Spanish for each function. Then have students find these words and phrases in the letter on page 291.

Lección 5

¡Qué divertido es Madrid!

¡A comenzar!

The following are some of the things you will be learning to do in this lesson.

When you want to . . .	You use . . .
1. say what someone prefers to do	• **Prefiere** + activity.
2. report what someone says	• **Dice que...**
3. talk about other things	• **otros(as)...**

Now find examples of the above words and phrases in the following letter.

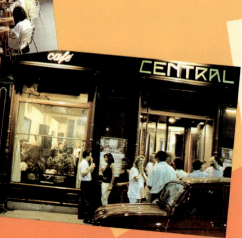

Madrid de Noche

DISCOTECAS Y SALAS DE FIESTA

BOITE DEL PINTOR. Goya, 59. Metro Goya. Tel. 465 06 17. Discoteca de 20 a 3 h. de la madrugada. Domingo cerrado.
CARIBIANA - Boite. Paseo de la Castellana, 23 (Nuevos Ministerios). Autobuses 27 y 14. Tels. 295 77 69 y 268 78 07.
CARNAVAL. Cartagena, 89. Metro Avenida América/ Tel. 266 71 67. Abierto todos los días de 19 a 22 h. Baile.
LA CARROZA. Flor Baja, 6 (entre Isabel La Católica y Leganitos). Tel. 372 53 77. Sesión continua de 18 a 4 madrugada Bailes con tres orquestas recordando los años 40 al 60.
EL CASINO. Boite-espectáculo. Carrera de la Coruña, km. 28,300. Torrelodones. Tel. 253 03 12. Abierto de 24 a 4 de la madrugada.

Getting Ready for Lesson 5

You may wish to use one or more of the following suggestions to prepare students for the lesson:

1. Bring a TV schedule to class and describe the types of programs that are on television today and tonight. Have students respond according to their likes and dislikes. Also have them agree or disagree with your opinion of various programs. For example: **Por la mañana hay muchos concursos. Por ejemplo, a las diez hay _____. (No) Me gustan los concursos porque _____. Prefiero _____. A las seis de la tarde siempre veo las noticias, etc.**

2. Tell students some common complaints about television viewing. Have them respond in agreement **(De acuerdo)**

Kim le escribe una carta a Josh, un compañero de clase en Los Ángeles.

Querido Josh:

Aquí estoy en Madrid con Pilar. Madrid es fantástico y Pilar es sensacional, tan guapa y simpática como siempre. Por la tarde, Pilar y yo salimos con su hermano mayor, José Luis, y sus amigos. Vamos al cine y comemos tapas, o vamos a las discotecas y después tomamos un café en una de las plaza. Hay muchas discotecas — son fantásticas y tienen toda la música de los Estados Unidos, Inglaterra, Alemania y, claro, de España también. Si no salimos, a veces veo telenovelas y otros programas interesantes. Pero a Pilar no le gustan las telenovelas. Prefiere hacer otras cosas. Por ejemplo, le encanta leer. También vive con la familia la abuela de Pilar. A la abuela no le gustan las discotecas — dice que son malas para las jóvenes. (Me gusta mucho la familia de Pilar, pero no comprendo a la abuela). Bueno, termino la carta ahora. Esta tarde empiezo un curso de arte en el Museo del Prado.

¡Hasta pronto!

Tu amiga,

Kim

Actividades preliminares

A Based on Kim's letter, tell whether the following statements are true **(Es verdad)** or false **(No es verdad)**.

1. Kim cree que Pilar es amable.
2. Kim y Pilar nunca salen por la tarde.
3. Parece que a Kim le gusta Madrid.
4. Pilar ve la tele muy poco.
5. A las chicas les gusta bailar.
6. A Kim no le gusta escribir a su maestra de español.

B Tell at what time each of the following begins and ends.

Por ejemplo:

tu primera clase
Empieza a las ocho y cuarto y termina a las nueve.

1. tu clase de español
2. tu programa favorito
3. el programa favorito de tu hermano (mamá, papá, etc.)

Lección 5   **291**

---

or disagreement **(No es verdad)**. For example:

a. Dicen que hay demasiada violencia en los programas.
b. Dicen que la violencia en la televisión causa crímenes.
c. Dicen que los jóvenes ven la tele 25 horas a la semana.
d. Dicen que la televisión es mala para los niños.
e. Dicen que los jóvenes no leen bastante porque ven demasiado la tele.
f. Dicen que los niños creen todo lo que ven en la televisión.

B. Introduce the Lesson 5 letter by reading it aloud or by playing the cassette version. Tell students they are going to hear Kim read a letter she wrote to a friend in Los Angeles. Have students listen to the tape to find out the following information:

1. **dos cosas que a Kim y Pilar les gusta hacer**
2. **una cosa que a la abuela de Pilar no le gusta**

C. Now ask students to open their books and look at the letter on page 291. Ask students to list the following:

1. **las cosas que a Kim le gusta hacer**
2. **las cosas que a Pilar le gusta hacer**

D. Have each student compare his or her preferences to those of Kim and Pilar. For example:
A Kim le gusta _____ pero a mí, no. Prefiero _____.
A Pilar le gusta _____ y a mí también.

E. Help students summarize what Kim says in her letter using the expression **dice que.** For example:
Kim dice que salen con José Luis y que comen . . .

Actividades preliminares

Actividad A Answers
1. Es verdad.
2. No es verdad.
3. Es verdad.
4. Es verdad.
5. Es verdad.
6. No es verdad.
7. Es verdad.

Actividad B Answers
Answers will vary.

Bell Ringer Review

Directions to students: List one important thing that each member of your family has to do very soon. Follow this model: **Mi hermana Susan tiene que practicar el piano para el concierto.**

Presentation

A. Have students open their books to the Vocabulario on pages 292 and 293. Model each new word or phrase, beginning with **En los ratos libres quiero aprender a...** Have students repeat after you in unison.

B. Find out what students like to do in their spare time. For example, **¿Cuántos saben jugar cartas? ¿ajedrez? ¿Cuántos quieren aprender?** Have students respond with their preferences. For example, **¿Prefieres leer or jugar cartas? ¿Con quién juegas cartas? ¿Quién gana? ¿Qué lees? ¿Prefieres jugar ajedrez o leer libros de ciencia ficción? ¿Con quién juegas ajedrez? ¿Quién gana? ¿Cómo se llama tu libro de ciencia ficción favorito?**

C. Have students tell what things they are learning to do now in school. For example, **Aprendo a hablar español.**

D. After modeling the words and phrases on page 293, ask students to list their two favorite TV

Vocabulario

En los ratos libres quiero aprender a...

jugar cartas

jugar ajedrez

A veces prefiero leer novelas...

románticas

policiales

de ciencia ficción

También me gusta leer revistas de...

historietas

moda

Y me gusta jugar juegos de mesa.

Me gusta ganar pero a veces pierdo.*

* perder (ie)

292 CAPÍTULO 4

Total Physical Response

Getting Ready
Bring to class magazine covers, novels, and TV listings of programs students will recognize. Each student should have at least one of the above.

New Words
coloquen
título

TPR 1

Pongan los programas deportivos en la pizarra.
Pongan las revistas de moda en la pared.
Coloquen las telenovelas en la pared a mi derecha.
Coloquen las novelas de ciencia ficción en la pared a mi izquierda.
Denme los programas educativos.
Denle a _____ los programas cómicos.

¿Qué clase de programa prefieres?
Prefiero ver...

las telenovelas

las noticias

los concursos

los programas deportivos

los programas educativos

los programas cómicos

las películas extranjeras

las películas de terror

las películas de aventuras

Actividades

A **Las películas.** List a recent movie for each of the following categories.

1. películas cómicas
2. películas de aventuras
3. películas románticas
4. películas de ciencia ficción
5. películas de terror
6. películas policiales

Actividades B and C Answers
Answers will vary.

Extension
After doing Actividad B, you may wish to extend it in the following ways:

1. If students disagree with the statement, have them say what should be done instead. For example:
   1. No estoy de acuerdo. Deben incluir más programas deportivos.
2. Tally on the chalkboard how many students agree and disagree with each statement. Then summarize the results. For example, **Parece que (no) deben incluir más programas cómicos. Etc.**

Actividad D Answers
1. Practico deportes (Juego cartas).
2. Juego cartas (ajedrez).
3. Veo programas deportivos (telenovelas).
4. Leo libros románticos (libros de terror).
5. Veo programas cómicos (programas policiales).
6. Leo novelas (biografías).
7. Me gusta leer…
8. Prefiero las películas de…
9. Cuando juego juegos de mesa…

Extension
When doing Actividad D, you may wish to extend it by keeping a tally on the chalkboard of students' preferences. Then have students summarize the results.

Reteaching
Ask individual students the following questions: **¿Qué te gusta hacer en los ratos libres?** or **¿Qué prefieres hacer en tus ratos libres?** or **¿Qué clase de programas prefieres?** Ask other students to summarize. For example: **A Raúl le gusta jugar ajedrez pero a veces prefiere leer revistas de deportes. Prefiere los programas deportivos.**

B **Opinión pública.** The following are the opinions some people have expressed about U.S. television programming. For the statements you agree with, say or write **De acuerdo.** If you disagree, say or write **No estoy de acuerdo.**

1. **Deben incluir más programas cómicos.**
2. **Existe un exceso de telenovelas.**
3. **Deben incluir más programas educativos.**
4. **Deben prohibir las películas de terror.**
5. **Un programa de noticias a las 7:00 de la mañana y otro a las 6:00 de la tarde es suficiente.**
6. **Deben incluir más programas deportivos, por ejemplo de fútbol y de otros deportes también.**
7. **Deben presentar más programas extranjeros.**
8. **Hay demasiados concursos.**

C **Quiero aprender.** List five things that you would like to learn how to do some day.

Por ejemplo:
> **Quiero aprender a esquiar.**

D **¿Cuál prefieres?** Interview a classmate using the following questions. Then report back to the class about his or her preferences.

Por ejemplo:

ESTUDIANTE A	ESTUDIANTE B
¿Lees libros o ves la tele?	**Leo libros.**
(A la clase:) Bob dice que prefiere leer libros.	

1. **¿Practicas deportes o juegas cartas?**
2. **¿Juegas cartas o juegas ajedrez?**
3. **¿Ves programas deportivos o telenovelas?**
4. **¿Lees libros románticos o libros de terror?**
5. **¿Ves programas cómicos o programas policiales?**
6. **¿Lees novelas o biografías?**
7. **¿Qué clase de revistas te gusta leer?**
8. **Cuando vas al cine, ¿qué clase de película prefieres?**
9. **Cuando juegas juegos de mesa, ¿a veces pierdes o siempre ganas? ¿Y cuando practicas deportes?**

294 CAPÍTULO 4

For the Native Speaker
A. Have native speakers make a list of five television programs shown in their country. They should then explain what each program is about.
B. Ask native speakers to describe five different television programs shown in the U.S.

Cooperative Learning
Ask reporters from each team to exchange places with reporters from other teams in the class. After asking questions 1–9 in Actividad D, each reporter will return to his or her own team and share his or her findings from the other team.

El cine y la tele en España

A los españoles (como a los norteamericanos) les gusta mucho ir al cine. Pero en España no es raro ir a ver una película después de cenar, como a las once de la noche.

En España la televisión es muy popular también. Muchos de los canales son controlados por el gobierno. Por eso, ves menos anuncios comerciales, y los programas no siempre empiezan y terminan a la hora o a la media hora como en los Estados Unidos.

Actividad

Find at least one program in the Madrid listing below that fits each of the following categories.

1. programas extranjeros
2. de niños
3. concursos
4. cómicos
5. de noticias
6. deportivos
7. de música
8. de aventuras

DOMINGO

09.15 `TVE-1` **CONCIERTO**

12.00 `TVE-2` **DOMINGO DEPORTE**
Espacio deportivo que presenta MARÍA ESCARIO, y que ofrece las siguientes transmisiones:
12.15: BALONCESTO. En directo, desde el Pabellón de Villalba, se ofrece la transmisión del encuentro correspondiente a la Liga ACB, que enfrenta a los equipos del ATLÉTICO DE MADRID VILLALBA y al JOVENTUT DE BADALONA. **15.00: GOLF.** En directo, desde el campo de Valderrama se ofrece la transmisión de la última jornada del TROFEO VOLVO MASTERS. **CICLISMO:** Resumen de la Escalada al Montjuich. **GIMNASIA.** En directo, desde el Pabellón de Bruselas, transmisión de la final de la Copa del Mundo de este deporte.

13.00 `CANAL +` **EL GRAN MUSICAL**

14.30 `ANTENA-3` **NOTICIAS**

16.30 `CANAL +` **PREVIO LIGA DE FÚTBOL**

17.20 `TELE-5` **LASSIE**

17.45 `TVE-1` **JUEGO DE NIÑOS**
XAVIER SARDÁ presenta este concurso en el que los participantes deben adivi...

19.00 `TVE-2` **PLAYA DE CHINA:**
"EL MUNDO" (II)
Capítulo 21 de esta serie estado-unidense que consta de 22 episodios. Colleen, tras el entierro de su padre, está muy confundida y se plantea el permanecer en Estados Unidos en lugar de regresar a Vietnam.

19.35 `TVE-5` **MISIÓN IMPOSIBLE:**
"LA PRUEBA" (Capítulo 16)

19.45 `TVE-2` **NOTICIAS**

20.00 `TVE-5` **EL NUEVO BENNY HILL**

20.05 `ANTENA-3` **LA RULETA DE LA FORTUNA**
Concurso presentado por IRMA SORIANO.

20.30 `ANTENA-3` **DIBUJOS ANIMADOS:**
"EL CAMPEÓN"

21.30 `TVE-2` **CHEERS:**
"LOS CHICOS DEL BAR"
Un antiguo compañero de equipo de Sam decide organizar en Cheers una rueda de prensa. En el transcurso de la misma va a presentar un libro autobiográfico en el que relata las juergas que él y Sam disfrutaron en su juventud.

Pronunciation

A. You may wish to play the recorded version of these pronunciation lines, located at the end of Cassette 4.5. You may also wish to write this verse on the chalkboard and have students copy it into their notebook:
Cuando vemos películas de amor no siempre creemos al actor.

Y cuando leemos libros de amor no siempre creemos al escritor.

B. Have students repeat words and phrases individually and in unison. You may wish to focus on the /r/ sound as in **amor; actor; escritor.**

Cultura viva 1

Presentation
Read the Cultura viva on this page. You may wish to have students guess the meaning of **canal(es)** and **gobierno.**

Did You Know?
TV is not as popular in Spain and other countries as it is in the U.S. In fact, many programs shown in Spain are imported from the U.S. American movies are popular in Spain and in many other countries.

Critical Thinking Activity
Based on the reading selection, make some comparisons between Spanish television and U.S. television.

Actividad

Actividad Answers
1. Playa de China, La ruleta de la fortuna, Cheers, El nuevo Benny Hill, Lassie, Misión imposible.
2. Juego de niños, Dibujos animados.
3. La ruleta de la fortuna.
4. El nuevo Benny Hill, Dibujos animados.
5. Noticias.
6. Domingo deporte, Previo liga de fútbol.
7. Concierto, El gran musical.
8. Misión imposible

Additional Practice
After completing the Actividad on page 295, you may wish to reinforce the lesson with the following: Compare the times people go to the movies in Spain with the times they go where you live. **Por ejemplo:**
En España van al cine _____.
Donde yo vivo, van al cine _____.

Estructura 1

Bell Ringer Review

Directions to students: Write these three categories across the top of your paper. Then list your preferred programs and movies in the appropriate column. Add other categories if you wish.

**programas cómicos
telenovelas
películas de terror
películas policiales
películas de aventuras**

Presentation

Lead students through steps 1–3 on page 296. To establish familiarity, you may wish to model each form of the verb **preferir,** having students repeat in unison. You may also wish to remind students that they have already learned the verbs **pensar** and **querer** and that these have the same stem changes as **preferir.**

Learning From Photos

You may want to have students look at the photos on page 296 and have them identify the various kinds of magazines they see.

Estructura 1

How to State Preferences   *The verb* **preferir**

1. When you want to state your preferences or those of others, use the appropriate form of the verb **preferir (ie),** followed by the activity you prefer to do.

SINGULAR	PLURAL
prefiero	**preferimos**
prefieres	**preferís***
prefiere	**prefieren**

*This form is rarely used in the Spanish-speaking world, except for Spain.

2. When you want to ask which one someone prefers, use **¿cuál?**
   **¿Cuál película prefieres ver?
   Prefiero ver la película romántica.**

3. When you want to offer someone choices, use the word **o.**
   ¿Prefieres nadar o descansar?

En un quiosco de Madrid.

296   CAPÍTULO 4

296

Actividades

A **En los ratos libres.** Choosing from the following list, decide which types of magazines you, your family, and your friends prefer.

revistas de casa y cocina	revistas cómicas
revistas de coches	revistas de moda
revistas de deportes	revistas de noticias
revistas policiales	revistas de política
revistas de historietas	revistas financieras

1. tú
2. tu hermano(a)
3. tu mamá o tu papá
4. tú y tus amigos
5. tus abuelos

B **¿Cuál prefieres?** Interview a classmate to find out which activity from the list below he or she prefers to do. Report back to the class.

Por ejemplo:

> ir al cine o jugar videojuegos

ESTUDIANTE A	ESTUDIANTE B
¿Prefieres ir al cine o jugar videojuegos?	Prefiero ir al cine (jugar videojuegos).

(A la clase:) Jill dice que prefiere...

1. salir con los amigos o descansar en casa
2. ver telenovelas o escuchar música
3. leer en la biblioteca o estudiar en casa
4. tomar un café o un refresco
5. comer tapas o papas fritas
6. practicar deportes o correr
7. comer en la cafetería de la escuela o comer afuera
8. limpiar tu habitación o estudiar
9. jugar cartas o escuchar música
10. jugar juegos de mesa o ajedrez
11. ver películas extranjeras o películas de ciencia ficción

Lección 5 **297**

C U L T U R A   V I V A   2

¡Me gusta esta ciudad!

Presentation

Read the Cultura viva on this page. You may wish to read Kim's diary entry to the class aloud, or you may want to ask students to take turns reading one sentence each. You may also wish to remind students that José Luis is Pilar's older brother.

Did You Know?

Spaniards tend to stay up later and go out late at night more than Americans. Spanish teenagers don't have to obey a curfew. That's why Kim and José Luis are in a café at 2 o'clock in the morning.

Critical Thinking Activity

What do you think American TV programs and movies shown in Spain tell Spaniards about life in the U.S.? Do they give a true picture of life in the U.S.?

Actividades

Actividad A Answers
Kim fue a una tienda, a la discoteca y a un café con José Luis. Kim piensa ir al Parque del Retiro y a una fiesta en casa de un amigo de Pilar.

Actividad B Answers
Kim went: **fui.**
Kim and José Luis went: **fuimos.**
Pilar went: **fue.**

Actividad C Answers
A Kim le gusta Madrid, le gusta bailar y le gustan Pilar y José Luis.

Actividad D Answers
Answers will vary.

Querido diario:

6 de agosto

Ayer por la tarde fui a una tienda a comprar un regalo para la señora Rivera. Anoche fuimos a la discoteca a bailar Pilar, José Luis y yo. ¡Qué bien baila ese chico! Después, Pilar fue a casa y José Luis y yo fuimos a tomar algo en el café ¡a las dos de la noche! Mañana él y yo vamos a hacer un picnic y pasar el día en el Parque del Retiro. Dice que es muy divertido pasear en bote en el lago. Luego, por la noche, vamos a ir a una fiesta en casa de un amigo de Pilar y José Luis. ¡Me gusta esta ciudad! (También me gusta José Luis).

Actividades

A Name the places Kim went in Madrid. Name the places she is going to go.

B What word does Kim use to say she went somewhere? To say that she and José Luis went somewhere? To say Pilar went somewhere?

C What can you tell about what Kim likes?

D Compare where you went yesterday **(ayer)** to where you're going to go tomorrow. Complete the following sentences.

Ayer fui a _____. Mañana voy a _____.

For the Native Speaker

Have native speakers write a 2–3 minute TV commercial and present it to the class. Students can use props or illustrations in presenting their commercial. You may wish to read over the script before asking the native speakers to present it to the class.

Estructura 2

How to Talk about Another or Others   Otro

1. If you want to express the idea of "another" or "others," use the word **otro.** This word will come before the person(s) or thing(s) you are referring to and end in **-o, -os, -a,** or **-as.**

    ¿Quieres otra cosa? Sí, necesito otro bolígrafo.
    Muchos estudiantes son aplicados, otros son perezosos.

2. If you want to express the idea of "the other one" or "the other ones," use the word **el, la, los,** or **las** before the appropriate form of **otro.**

    ¿Te gustan los anteojos negros? No, prefiero los otros.
    ¿Hablas del chico rubio? No, hablo del otro, del pelirrojo.

Actividades

A **¿Quieres otro?** Tell whether you are satisfied with the following things or whether you want others. Explain why.

Por ejemplo:

> tu cama
> *No me gusta mi cama. Es vieja y no es muy cómoda. Quiero otra. (Me gusta mi cama. Es nueva y grande. No necesito otra).*

1. tus discos
2. tu mochila
3. tu estéreo
4. tu habitación
5. tu gaveta
6. tu libro de matemáticas
7. tu perro o tu gato

El Escorial, al norte de Madrid.

Estructura 2

Structure Teaching Resources
1. Workbook, pp. 134–135
2. Cassette 4.5
3. Student Tape Manual, p. 106
4. Estructura Masters 4.5
5. Lesson Quizzes, pp. 90–91

Bell Ringer Review

Directions to students: Write these three categories across the top of your paper. Now list your preferences under each column.
novelas
revistas
juegos de mesa

Presentation

Lead students through steps 1–2 on page 299. You may wish to give additional examples by holding up two of the same object. For example, **Aquí tengo dos libros. Kelly, ¿quieres este libro o el otro? Aquí tengo dos revistas. Mark, ¿quieres esta revista o la otra?**

Actividades

Actividad A Answers
Answers will vary, however students should use a form of **otro** in each response.

B **¿De acuerdo o no?** Write down your preferences for each of the following topics. Then, with a partner, find out how many topics the two of you agree on. Report back to the class.

Por ejemplo:

> leer (una revista)

ESTUDIANTE A	ESTUDIANTE B
(1) ¿Quieres leer la revista *People*?	(2) **Sí, me gusta.** (No, prefiero leer otra).
(3) ¿Cuál prefieres?	(4) **Prefiero** *Sports Illustrated*.

(A la clase:) Yo prefiero la revista *People* pero Jaime dice que prefiere *Sports Illustrated*.

1. ver (una película)
2. ver (un programa de televisión)
3. practicar (un deporte)
4. ir a (un partido)

5. ser (una ocupación)
6. tener (un animal)
7. comer (una comida)
8. tomar (un refresco)

C **¿Cómo es diferente?** Describe the people and things below by telling how one of each group is different from the others.

Por ejemplo:

> Uno de los chicos no tiene anteojos, los otros tienen anteojos.

1.
2.
3.

Finalmente

....

Situaciones

A conversar Converse with a classmate about leisure activities.

1. Ask what kinds of leisure activities your partner likes to do.
2. Find one activity that you both have in common and invite your classmate to do something related to that activity.
3. Agree on a day, time, and place.

A escribir Your school has decided to begin a Spanish-language collection for the library. Complete the following note to your librarian, telling all the types of books, magazines, and videos that would appeal to a wide variety of students in your school.

Estimado(a) _____:

A muchos estudiantes les gusta(n) _____, _____ y _____. Entonces, usted debe comprar _____, _____ y _____.

Repaso de vocabulario

PREGUNTAS	ACTIVIDADES	DESCRIPCIONES	OTRAS PALABRAS Y EXPRESIONES
¿Cuál prefiere(s)?	**aprender a**	**cómico(a)**	
¿Qué clase de...?	**empezar (ie)**	**de aventuras**	**Dice que**
	ganar (to win)	**de ciencia ficción**	**otro(a)**
DIVERSIONES	**perder (ie)**	**de moda**	**preferir(ie)**
el ajedrez	**terminar**	**de terror**	**las noticias**
las cartas (cards)		**deportivo(a)**	**los ratos libres**
el concurso		**educativo(a)**	
la historieta		**extranjero(a)**	
el juego de mesa		**policial**	
la novela		**romántico(a)**	
el programa			
la telenovela			
el vídeo musical			

Lección 5 **301**

Finalmente

Situaciones

Lesson 5 Evaluation
The A conversar and A escribir situations on this page are designed to give students the opportunity to use as many language functions and as much vocabulary from the lesson as possible. The A conversar and A escribir are also intended to show how well students are able to meet the lesson objectives.

Presentation
Prior to doing the A conversar and A escribir on this page, you may wish to play the **Situaciones** listening activities on Cassette 4.5 as a means of helping students organize the material.

Lección 6

Objectives

By the end of this lesson, students will be able to:

1. talk about what they and others can or can't do
2. tell the day and month something occurs
3. request information
4. talk about an event to take place in the future

Lesson 6 Resources
1. Workbook, pp. 136–140
2. Vocabulario Transparencies 4.6
3. Cassette 4.6
4. Student Tape Manual, pp. 109–114
5. Lesson Quizzes, pp. 92–95
6. Test Booklet, pp. 65–70
7. Computer Software, Disk 2
8. Video Cassette
9. Estructura Masters 4.6
10. Diversiones Masters 4.6

Bell Ringer Review

Directions to students: Divide your paper into blocks representing the next seven days of the week. Label each day in Spanish. Now in each block write what you have to do on that day.

¡A comenzar!

Presentation

A. Lead students through each of the four functions on page 302, progressing from the English to the Spanish for each function. Then have students find these words and phrases in the letter on page 303.

Lección 6

Escribe la señora Rivera

....

¡A comenzar!

The following are some of the things you will be learning to do in this lesson.

When you want to . . .	You use . . .
1. tell a friend what he or she can do	• **Puedes** + activity.
2. say what someone else can or can't do	• **(No) Puede** + activity.
3. refer to an event to take place one day next week	• **el lunes (martes, etc.) que viene**
4. to say the day and the month something occurs	• **el** + date + **de** + month

Now find examples of the above words and phrases in the following letter.

Getting Ready for Lesson 6

You may wish to use one or more of the following suggestions to prepare students for the lesson:

1. Talk about your plans for next summer or next year. For example: **El verano que viene (el año que viene) voy a viajar a _____ (voy a trabajar en _____, voy a aprender a _____, voy a leer _____, etc.).**

2. Have students raise their hands in response to your questions about plans for next summer or next year. For example:

   a. **¿Cuántos van a trabajar?**
   b. **¿Cuántos van a hacer un viaje con los padres? Etc.**

Kim recibe una carta de la señora Rivera.

15 de agosto
Los Ángeles

Querida Kim:

¡Gracias por todas tus cartas y tarjetas postales! Y ¡qué bien escribes en español! Parece que te gustan mucho José Luis y su grupo y veo que puedes salir con ellos por la noche. ¡Qué experiencia para ti!

Creo que con el tiempo vas a comprender a la abuela. Es de otra generación y no puede comprender bien los intereses de los jóvenes como Pilar y tú, José Luis y los otros. Debes comprender también que, para los hispanos, la abuela es una parte muy importante de la familia. Por eso, creo que ella no va a regresar a su pueblo.

Bueno, tu mamá dice que vas a regresar a Los Ángeles el lunes que viene. ¡Quiero saber todas las noticias de tu viaje a Madrid!

Saludos afectuosos de

Sonia Rivera

P.D. Otra cosa: Si tienes tiempo antes de regresar, ¿me puedes comprar unas revistas y periódicos españoles?

Actividades preliminares

A Tell two things you plan to do on the following days next week.

Por ejemplo:

el viernes que viene
El viernes que viene pienso ir al cine.

1. el sábado que viene
2. el domingo que viene
3. el martes que viene

B Tell what time you return home in the following situations.

Por ejemplo:

después de las clases
Regreso a las tres y media.

1. después de un partido
2. después de una fiesta
3. después del cine

Lección 6   **303**

B. Introduce the letter in Lesson 6 by reading it aloud or by playing the cassette version. Tell students they will hear Sra. Rivera read a letter she wrote to Kim. Have students listen to determine the purpose of the letter.

1. Is it to tell Kim what she (Sra. Rivera) has been doing this summer?
2. Is it to explain something to Kim?
3. Is it to tell Kim about her plans for next year?

C. Now ask students to open their books and look at the letter as you lead them through what is said. For example:

1. What explanation does Kim's teacher give for the grandmother's attitude toward teenage lifestyles? Give the sentence.
2. Is this just a "generation gap" or does it also have to do with the country? Give the sentence that makes you think so.
3. Cite the phrases that begin with "I think that . . . ," "I see that . . . " and "It seems that. . ."

D. Have students tell which of the following is the main message of Sra. Rivera's letter:

1. **Es muy divertido salir por la noche.**
2. **A veces es difícil comprender los cambios.**
3. **La abuela es de un pueblo y no le gusta la ciudad.**
4. **A la abuela no le gustan las discotecas.**

E. Have students read the letter and select the two clauses or groups of words that they think are the most important in the letter.

Actividades preliminares

Actividades A and B Answers
Answers will vary.

Bell Ringer Review

Directions to students: Write a description of one of your favorite singers, actors, or actresses. Identify his or her profession and give a description in terms of physical appearance. Then see whether the class can guess whom you have described.

Presentation

A. Have students open their books to the Vocabulario on pages 304 and 305.
   Model each month of the year, beginning with **enero.** Have students repeat each month in unison.

B. Ask individual students what they like to do during different months of the year. For example, **Karen, ¿qué te gusta hacer en julio?** Encourage students to give a complete response. For example, **Me gusta nadar, montar a caballo, etc.**

C. Now have students look at the vocabulary presentation on page 305. Model the question **¿Qué vas a hacer...** Then model each new word or phrase.

D. You may wish to use Vocabulario Transparencies 4.6 when making the following statements, or you may choose to write the following on the chalkboard:

Vocabulario

¿Qué vas a hacer...?

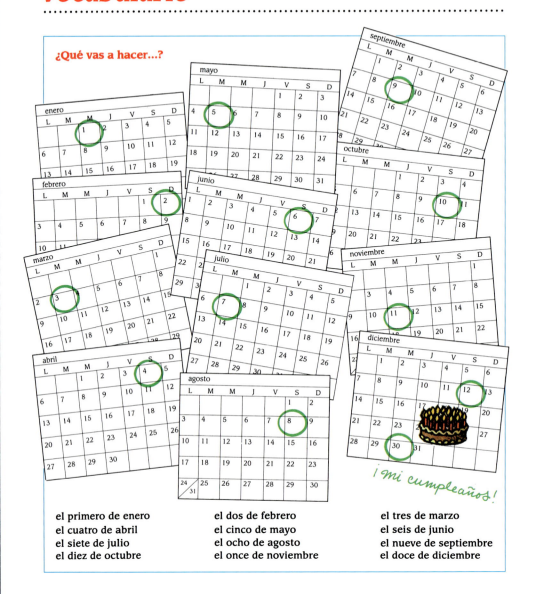

el primero de enero	el dos de febrero	el tres de marzo
el cuatro de abril	el cinco de mayo	el seis de junio
el siete de julio	el ocho de agosto	el nueve de septiembre
el diez de octubre	el once de noviembre	el doce de diciembre

Total Physical Response

Getting Ready
Draw a calendar for the month of February and make one copy for each student. Write in **miércoles, viernes,** and **domingo** only. Leave blocks open for students to write in numbers. At the end of each **TPR** activity, show students a transparency of your calendar so they can match it with their own.

New Words

dibujen	corazón
cuadro	círculo
rectángulo	

TPR 1

Escriban lunes en el primer cuadro.
Marquen sábado en el sexto cuadro.
Indiquen martes en el segundo cuadro.
Escriban jueves en el cuarto cuadro.

	L	M	M	enero	J	V	S	D
						1	2	3

el año/el mes que viene

diciembre	L	M	M	J	V	S	D
		1	2	3	4	5	6
	7	8	9	10	11	12	13
	14 hoy	15 mañana	16 pasado mañana	17	18	19	20
	21 el lunes que viene	22 el martes que viene	23	24	25	26	27
	28	29	30	31			

la semana que viene

(enero continued: 10, 17, 24, 31)

Actividades

A **El año que viene.** Imagine that New Year's Day is coming up. List five of your resolutions.

Por ejemplo:

> El año que viene voy a hacer la tarea todos los días.

B **Mis planes.** Interview a classmate about his or her plans for the following times.

Por ejemplo:

> esta tarde

ESTUDIANTE A

¿Qué vas a hacer esta tarde?

ESTUDIANTE B

Voy a trabajar.

1. pasado mañana
2. esta noche
3. la semana que viene
4. el miércoles que viene
5. el mes que viene
6. el año que viene

Escriban los números en la primera semana.
Marquen los números en la segunda semana.
Indiquen los números en la tercera semana.
Escriban los números en la cuarta semana.

TPR 2

Busquen el día _____ y escriban "partido de fútbol".
Encuentren el día _____ y marquen "examen de español".
Dibujen un corazón el día 14.
Marquen el día _____ con "vacaciones".
Dibujen un círculo el lunes, día _____.
Hagan un rectángulo el jueves, día _____.

Sidebar (teacher notes):

1. Pasado mañana hay una fiesta en la clase.
2. El año que viene no voy a dar más exámenes en la clase de español.
3. El mes que viene no hay clases.
4. La semana que viene tus padres van a vender su coche y no van a comprar otro.

Ask students to make their own statements using these time referents.

Note: In some parts of the Spanish-speaking world the *p* is dropped from **septiembre**.

When Students Ask

The following additional vocabulary may be provided to allow students to talk about expressions of time.

ahora mismo
en dos semanas, tres semanas, etc.
en tres días, cuatro días, etc.

Actividades

Actividades A and B Answers
Answers will vary.

Extension
You may wish to extend Actividad B by having each partner take notes on what the other student said. Then have each partner report back to the class.

Answers will vary but should include each month of the year.

Actividad D Answers
1. el 1 de enero
2. el 11 de noviembre
3. el 4 de julio
4. el 25 de diciembre
5. el 12 de octubre
6. Answers will vary.

Actividades E and F Answers
Answers will vary.

Additional Practice
After completing Actividades A, B, C, D, E, and F on pages 305 and 306, you may wish to reinforce the learning with the following activity:
Write a letter to the school board protesting the change of your vacation time from summer to November, December, and January. Tell why you and your classmates want the vacation time returned to the usual months.
Por ejemplo:
Estimados señores:
Quisiéramos tener las vacaciones los meses de _____ porque _____.
No queremos tener las vacaciones en _____ porque _____.

Reteaching

Using the Vocabulario on pages 304 and 305, have volunteers think of a particular month. Then they will ask the class, **¿Qué mes es?** They may also want to give a clue, for example, **Es un mes cuando vemos los partidos de fútbol. Etc.** Other students will guess the month. The student who guesses correctly starts the game once again.

C **Cada mes del año.** Tell what you do each month of the year.

Por ejemplo:

> enero
> *En enero juego baloncesto y esquío.*

D Give the dates of the following celebrations.

Por ejemplo:

> **el día de San Valentín**
> *el 14 de febrero*

1. el Año Nuevo
2. el Día de los Veteranos
3. el Día de la Independencia
4. la Navidad (Christmas)
5. el Día de la Raza
6. tu cumpleaños

E **¿Vacaciones de invierno?** Your school board plans to change your vacation time from summer to November, December, and January. Compare the winter vacation plan to your summer vacation plan in terms of your usual activities.

Por ejemplo:

> **En junio voy a la playa, pero en noviembre no quiero (no es posible, no me gusta, etc.) ir a la playa.**

F **El sábado que viene.** Ask two or three classmates what their plans are for the weekend. Then report back to the class, comparing your plans with those of your classmates.

Por ejemplo:

ESTUDIANTE A	ESTUDIANTE B
¿Qué vas a hacer el sábado (domingo) que viene?	Voy a ir a la biblioteca por la tarde.

(A la clase:) Yo voy a correr, pero Sue va a ir a la biblioteca y Tom va a ir al partido de baloncesto. Gina y Eva van a trabajar.

306 CAPÍTULO 4

Cooperative Learning

After listing five resolutions in Actividad A, page 305, have each team choose the most interesting ones. The team recorder will list these on the board. While this is being done, others on the team can have a three-way interview of Actividad B. They should alternate asking and answering questions. Once all team reporters have written their list on the chalkboard, Actividad A's results can be discussed as a whole class activity in order to find similarities and differences among class members.

Los jóvenes españoles

A los jóvenes españoles les gusta tomar clases particulares (lecciones privadas) para aprender, por ejemplo, a tocar un instrumento, a bailar, a practicar ciertos deportes o artes marciales o aprender idiomas, especialmente inglés.

Pero los jóvenes no pasan todo el tiempo en clases. Por la noche, desde las once hasta la una o las dos de la mañana, muchos bailan, comen y conversan en las discotecas.

Actividad

Spanish teenagers like to spend free time taking lessons on things of interest to them. List the classes below that (a) you would like to take, (b) you are already taking, and (c) you already know how to do.

Por ejemplo:

Quisiera estudiar (Ya estudio, Ya sé)...

IDIOMAS	INSTRUMENTOS	DEPORTES	OTRAS CLASES
francés	guitarra	tenis	artes marciales
español	piano	vóleibol	baile moderno
chino	batería (drums)	fútbol	ajedrez
japonés	saxofón	natación	
italiano	violín	esquí	
		gimnasia	

Cultura viva 1

Presentation
Read the Cultura viva on this page. Then, as a class activity, you may wish to list on the chalkboard the various activities Spanish teenagers do, according to the reading.

Did You Know?
High school students are allowed to go to **discotecas** in Spain, even though alcoholic beverages are served.
Wine is a normal part of meals in Spain.
Since most people in Spain live in cities rather than suburban or rural areas, people have access to an extensive public transportation system. It is therefore easier for young people to go out since they don't have to rely on adults to take them to their destination.

Critical Thinking Activity
What are some similarities and differences in leisure activities of teenagers in the U.S. and in Spain? Imagine you are a Spanish teenager. What might your day be like?

Actividad

Actividad Answers
Answers will vary.

Learning From Photos
You may want to have students look at the photos on page 307. Have them choose one of the photos and imagine what plans the Spanish teenagers are making for later in the day.

Pronunciation
A. You may wish to play the recorded version of these pronunciation lines, located at the end of Cassette 4.6. You may also wish to write this verse on the chalkboard and have students copy it into their notebook:
En los ratos libres
muchos estudian inglés;
algunos escriben a amigos
en francés
y otros aprenden a jugar
ajedrez.

B. Have students repeat words and phrases individually and in unison. You may wish to focus on the stressed final syllable in words such as **inglés, francés,** and **ajedrez.**

Bell Ringer Review

Directions to students: On your paper list all the things you have to do at home and at school to avoid getting into trouble with your parents and your teachers.

Presentation

Lead students through steps 1–11 on pages 308 and 309. Remind students that they have learned all of these question words in previous lessons and that this is a review. You may wish to encourage students to refer to this page from now on when they need help with asking questions in Spanish.

Estructura 1

How to Request Information   **Summary of Question Words**

You have learned to request information using question words.

1. You have learned to ask where people and things are located, using **dónde**.

   ¿Dónde está la calle Serrano? Está a la derecha.

2. You have asked where people go, using **adónde**.

   ¿Adónde vas mañana? No voy a ningún lugar.

3. You have asked where people are from, using **de dónde**.

   ¿De dónde son ustedes? Somos de Puerto Rico.

4. You have used **cómo** with forms of the verb **ser** to ask what someone or something is like.

   ¿Cómo es la muchacha de Colombia? Es muy lista.

5. You have used **cómo** with **estar** to ask how people feel.

   ¿Cómo está, señora Dávila? Estoy bien, gracias.

En una escuela de Madrid.

6. To ask when someone does something or when something takes place, you have used **a qué hora** and **cuándo**.

   ¿A qué hora es el baile? Es a las ocho.
   ¿Cuándo sales para España? El viernes a la una y media.

7. To ask for a reason, you have used **por qué**.

   ¿Por qué necesitas estudiar esta noche?
   Porque tengo dos exámenes mañana.

8. You have asked "what," using **qué**.

   Oye, ¿qué quieres hacer esta noche? Bueno, no sé.

9. You have used a form of **cuánto** to ask how much or how many.

   ¿Cuánto dinero necesitas? Necesito dos dólares.
   ¿Cuántas chicas juegan tenis en tu escuela? Veinte y dos.

Cooperative Learning

Have students ask each other questions using each one of the question words. Students should write down the answers to the questions. Allow 5–10 minutes for practice. Then call on students to volunteer their results.

10. You have used **quién** to ask who does something and **de quién** to ask to whom something belongs.

> **¿Quién sabe hacer la tarea de español?   Marta González.**
> **¿De quién es el libro?   Es de Jaime Suñer.**

11. To ask someone to choose between two things, you have used **cuál**.

> **¿Cuál prefieres ver, el programa deportivo o la telenovela?**
> **Me gusta más el programa deportivo.**

Actividades

A **La carta de presentación.** Your class has decided to exchange letters with students studying English in Spain. Write a letter introducing yourself, answering the following questions.

1. **¿Cómo te llamas?**
2. **¿De dónde eres? ¿Dónde vives?**
3. **¿Cuántos hermanos tienes? ¿Cuántos años tienen? ¿Cómo son?**
4. **¿Cómo eres?**
5. **¿Qué te gusta hacer en los ratos libres?**
6. **¿Te gusta practicar deportes? ¿Cuál prefieres?**
7. **¿Sales mucho con los amigos? ¿Cuándo? ¿Adónde van?**
8. **¿Quién es tu músico favorito?**

B **La invitación.** A classmate invites you to go someplace with a friend of his or hers this weekend. Since you don't know your classmate's friend, find out the following information.

Por ejemplo:

> **¿Quién es el (la) amigo(a)?**

ESTUDIANTE A	ESTUDIANTE B
¿Quién es tu amigo(a)?	**Es Dana.**

1. **¿Cómo es?**
2. **¿De dónde es?**
3. **¿Cuánto dinero van a necesitar?**
4. **¿Adónde van a ir?**
5. **¿Dónde van a comer?**
6. **¿A qué hora van a regresar a casa?**

Lección 6   **309**

Extension
A. You may wish to extend Actividad A by having students answer the following additional questions.

1. **¿Te gusta practicar deportes? ¿Cuál prefieres?**
2. **¿Sales mucho con los amigos? ¿Cuándo? ¿Adónde van?**
3. **¿Quién es tu músico favorito?**

B. After students finish Actividad B, you may want to have them share their plans with the class.

Additional Practice
After completing Actividades A and B, you may wish to reinforce the lesson by doing the following activity: Prepare five questions to ask a classmate to get to know him or her better. Use the following words or phrases:
¿adónde? ¿cuál? ¿dónde? ¿cómo? ¿cuándo? ¿qué? ¿cuánto? ¿por qué? ¿quién? ¿de dónde? ¿a qué hora?

Reteaching

Make answers in the form of statements. Have individual students form the corresponding question, using one of the question words on page 308. For example, **José va a España en Abril. Soy de Chicago. Francisca es muy aplicada. Etc.**

Presentation

Read the Cultura viva on this page. You may also want to have students look at the photos on this page and identify what they see that represents Hispanic culture.

Did You Know?

Los Angeles has the largest Mexican population outside of Mexico City. It was founded by a group of Mexican settlers in 1781. Today, Hispanics account for approximately twenty-eight percent of Los Angeles' total population. Although people of Mexican ancestry make up the largest Hispanic group, many other nationalities are also represented.

Critical Thinking Activity

Do you think the percentage of Hispanics living in major U.S. cities will increase or decrease in the next five years? Give some reasons for your answer.

Actividad

Actividad Answers
1. Son de Guatemala.
2. ... Honduras.
3. ... Nicaragua.
4. ... El Salvador.
5. ... México.

Learning from Realia

You may want to have students look at the realia pieces on page 310. Have students tell what day and at what time they could watch **Desde Hollywood**. Ask students what kind of program it is. Using the restaurant ads from the yellow pages, have students tell you what number(s) they would call to make reservations at various restaurants.

Los Ángeles: una ciudad bilingüe

Kim y la señora Rivera son de Los Ángeles, California. Los Ángeles es una gran ciudad con mucha gente hispana de origen mexicano, centroamericano y sudamericano. Si visitas Los Ángeles, vas a ver que el español está por todas partes. Puedes hablar español en las calles, los restaurantes y las tiendas. Puedes leer revistas y periódicos en español. Y puedes oír español en la radio y la televisión.

UNIVISION PRESENTA

DESDE HOLLYWOOD

Revista de Espectáculos

Noticias del mundo del cine y el espectáculo. Entrevistas a talento hispano, los nuevos artistas cross-over y estrellas internacionales.

Con Luca Bentivoglio

El popular animador, de importante trayectoria en la televisión hispana, es también creador de "Tu Música," el exitoso show video-musical de Univisión.

todos los martes a las 10 pm este

UNIVISION

VEALO EXCLUSIVAMENTE POR UNA AFILIADA DE UNIVISION. LO NUESTRO

Actividad

Name the countries from which the following groups of residents in Los Angeles come.

Por ejemplo:

> los costarricenses
> Son de Costa Rica.

1. los guatemaltecos
2. los hondureños
3. los nicaragüenses

4. los salvadoreños
5. los mexicanos

Guía de Restaurantes

Una guía práctica de restaurantes, según clase de com

Colombianos

LOS ARRIEROS RESTAURANT
2619 W Sunset Bl LA **583 0074**

Cubanos

EL CHORI RESTAURANT
5147 E Gage Av Bell **873 3011**

Guatemaltecos

EL NAYARIT RESTAURANT
18822 W Sunset Bl LA **584 0766**
GUATELINDA RESTAURANT
2220 W 7th LA **485 7420**
MI GUATEMALA RESTAURANT
Especialidad En Comida
Guatemalteca
695 S Hoover LA **487 4296**

Espar

MADRID RES
Comida
Especial
Y Tapas
Diario 1ª
Especia
Salón d
1712 W

Filip

Amihan Grill
3253 B
EVA'S LEC
Especi
Lecho
Difere
4252 W

For the Native Speaker

Have native speakers make a collage of a city of the future. They should also write a description of this future city. In their writing they should include future occupations, leisure time activities, what schools will be like, etc. Have them read their description to the class.

Estructura 2

How to Describe What People Can and Can't Do

The verb poder

To say what you or others can and can't do, use a form of the verb **poder (ue)**.

SINGULAR	PLURAL
puedo	**podemos**
puedes	**podéis***
puede	**pueden**

*This form is rarely used in the Spanish-speaking world, except for Spain.

> **No puedo salir esta noche. ¿Puedes ir al cine mañana?**
> **Pilar no puede ir con nosotros al campo.**
> **Podemos invitar a quince personas a la fiesta.**
> **¿Pueden ustedes traer discos a la fiesta?**

Actividades

A **Soy increíble.** Write down four things that you can do very well.

Por ejemplo:

> **Puedo nadar muy bien.**

B **Mi compañero y yo.** Now ask a classmate if he or she can do each of the things on your list from activity **A**. Take notes and report back to the class, comparing what you and your partner can do.

Por ejemplo:

ESTUDIANTE A
¿Puedes nadar muy bien?

ESTUDIANTE B
Sí, puedo. (No, no puedo).

(A la clase:) Puedo esquiar muy bien, pero Ana no puede. Ella puede montar a caballo, pero yo no puedo. Los (Las) dos podemos nadar muy bien.

Estructura 2

Structure Teaching Resources
1. Workbook, pp. 139–140
2. Cassette 4.6
3. Student Tape Manual, p. 112
4. Estructura Masters 4.6
5. Lesson Quizzes, p. 95

Bell Ringer Review

Directions to students: Write the name of the appropriate month beside each of the following events.

1. tu cumpleaños
2. el primer día de la escuela
3. las vacaciones de...
4. el cumpleaños de Jorge Washington
5. el cumpleaños de Martin Luther King

Presentation

A. Lead students through the presentation on page 311. To establish familiarity, you may wish to model each form of the verb **poder,** having students repeat in unison.

B. You may wish to make statements regarding things you are able to do. For example: **Puedo esquiar, puedo hablar español, puedo jugar ajedrez, etc.** Ask students to volunteer additional examples for you to write on the board. For example: **Puedo bailar. Puedo montar en bicicleta, etc.** Then have students ask each other what they are able do.

Actividades

Actividades A and B Answers
Answers will vary.

C **Prohibido.** Tell whether or not you are allowed to do the following things at home.

Por ejemplo:

> comer en la cama
> *En mi casa no puedo comer en la cama.*

1. salir muy tarde por la noche
2. ver la tele después de las diez de la noche
3. escuchar el estéreo durante la cena
4. tener un perro
5. decir (to say) malas palabras

D **¿Quién puede?** Working in groups of three, find out whether your classmates are allowed to do the things listed in activity **C**. Take notes and report back to the class.

Por ejemplo:

> ¿Quién puede comer en la cama?

> (A la clase:) Ana y Curt pueden comer en la cama, pero yo no puedo.

E **Cuando están aburridos.** List five suggestions about what your classmates can do when they are bored.

Por ejemplo:

> Cuando ustedes están aburridos, pueden jugar con el perro.

F **El último día de clases.** Ask your teacher to change five class or school rules for the last day of school. How many of your requests will your teacher grant?

Por ejemplo:

> ¿Podemos tener clase afuera?

¿Quién puede contestar la pregunta?

Finalmente

Finalmente

Situaciones

A conversar Converse with a classmate about the next school vacation.

1. Ask your partner where he or she plans to go. Give your reaction.
2. Find out what your partner will do there.
3. Ask if your partner will go with family or friends.
4. Find out when your partner will return.
5. Reverse roles.

A escribir

1. Write a note to several friends telling them about a party at a classmate's home.
2. Give a specific date and time when the party will be.
3. Tell the various activities that all of you can do at the party.
4. Ask who can contribute **(llevar)** various items (cassettes, food, etc.).
5. Say that you need to know if they can go to the party by next Monday.

Repaso de vocabulario

EXPRESIONES DE TIEMPO	abril	ACTIVIDAD
el año (que viene)	mayo	regresar
el mes (que viene)	junio	
pasado mañana	julio	OTRAS PALABRAS
la semana (que viene)	agosto	el cumpleaños
	septiembre	poder (ue)
LOS MESES	octubre	
enero	noviembre	
febrero	diciembre	
marzo		

Situaciones

Lesson 6 Evaluation
The A conversar and A escribir situations on this page are designed to give students the opportunity to use as many language functions and as much vocabulary from this lesson as possible. The A conversar and A escribir are also intended to show how well students are able to meet the lesson objectives.

Presentation
Prior to doing the A conversar and A escribir on this page, you may wish to play the Situaciones listening activities on Cassette 4.6 as a means of helping students organize the material.

A. Before reading the Lectura, you may wish to have students work in groups to discuss the following questions. These questions are intended to help students think about the theme of the reading.

1. What are some advantages and disavantages of having a pen pal?
2. If you could have a pen pal from any country in the world, what country would you choose and why?
3. What qualities would you look for in a pen pal?

B. Have one student from each group report back to the class.

C. Now have students read the Lectura silently to themselves, or work with a partner. Have them answer the Actividades questions on page 315.

Lectura

You'll be able to figure out many of the words from the context in which they appear or because they look like English words that have similar meanings. First, look over the reading below. Then complete the activities, which follow.

Correo
VÍA SATÉLITE

¿Quieres ponerte en contacto con amigos de todas partes? Envíanos tus datos utilizando este cupón.

Nombre: _____

Dirección: _____

Edad: _____
Pasatiempos: _____

El cupón dirígelo a:
Correo vía Satélite

Nombre: Silvia Ortiz
Dirección: Heredia, Urb. La Esperanza 15, COSTA RICA
Edad: 15 años
Pasatiempos: Coleccionar todo lo referente al joven cantante Chayanne, tomar fotografías, estudiar, ver televisión y tener amigos de diferentes nacionalidades.

Nombre: Alfonso Marín
Dirección: Calle 19 #4-56, Apto. 1117, Edificio Sabana, Bogotá, COLOMBIA
Edad: 16 años
Pasatiempos: Leer, practicar deportes, escuchar música variada, escribir poemas, salir con mis amigas y coleccionar monedas de diferentes países.

Nombre: María del Carmen Sánchez
Dirección: Rdo. Rosendo Llanes, Danlí, El Paraíso, HONDURAS
Edad: 18 años
Pasatiempos: Intercambiar correspondencia, estampillas, carteles, escuchar música romántica, leer artículos sobre la cultura de diferentes países y escribir versos.

Nombre: Eugenia Vila Ávila
Dirección: Libertad 1261, Huancayo, PERÚ
Edad: 16 años
Pasatiempos: Practicar deportes, bailar, ver los vídeos musicales de mis artistas favoritos, salir con mis amigos y mantener correspondencia con jóvenes de todo el mundo.

Nombre: Juan José Pereira
Dirección: 15668 San Miguel de Sarandón, Santiago de Compostela, La Coruña, ESPAÑA
Edad: 15 años
Pasatiempos: Escribir, practicar deportes, ir al cine y a la playa, escuchar música variada, leer artículos sobre mis artistas favoritos y viajar.

Nombre: Lilia Calas
Dirección: Calle 8° de Los Jardines #4, H. Caborca, Sonora, MÉXICO.
Edad: 14 años.
Pasatiempos: Intercambiar correspondencia con otros jóvenes, cantar, bailar, tocar piano y coleccionar todo lo referente al grupo musical Flans.

Nombre: Angélica Trujillo
Dirección: 2351 Penn Rd., El Monte, California, 91765, ESTADOS UNIDOS
Edad: 16 años
Pasatiempos: Bailar, ver televisión, leer revistas, escuchar música variada, estudiar con mis amigas, coleccionar versos, practicar deportes e ir a la playa.

Nombre: Gromyko Watts
Dirección: Santa Rosa, Weg 173, Curaçao, ANTILLAS HOLANDESAS
Edad: 17 años
Pasatiempos: Mantener correspondencia con chicos y chicas de todo el mundo, practicar deportes, ver televisión, coleccionar carteles de mis artistas favoritos.

Nombre: Griselda M. Álvarez
Dirección: Col. Serramonte 3, Senda 3, Casa # 51, EL SALVADOR
Edad: 19 años
Pasatiempos: Coleccionar calcomanía y posters, escuchar música e intercambiar correspondencia con chicos y chicas de diferentes países.

Nombre: Cinthya Miralda
Dirección: Boul. de las Rosas, 256, Loacalco, Estado de México C.P. 5570, MÉXICO.
Edad: 17 años
Pasatiempos: Dibujar, leer, escuchar música variada, planear actividades con mis amistades, practicar deportes e intercambiar correspondencia con chicas y chicos de diferentes países.

314

Getting Ready for Reading

You may want to discuss the following keys to successful reading with your students before having them read the Lectura on page 314:

1. Skim the following magazine columns. That is, read over the selection quickly to get the main idea.

2. Don't stop to figure out the meaning of unknown words.
3. Look for cognates. For example, **contacto, variada, planear, nacionalidades.**
4. Try to read in groups of words, instead of word-for-word.

Actividades

A The magazine column on page 314 publishes requests from young people looking for pen pals. Look at the coupon in the upper left corner. Which of the following questions do you need to answer when writing to this column?

1. ¿Cómo te llamas?
2. ¿Cuántos hermanos tienes?
3. ¿Dónde vives?
4. ¿Cuál es tu apellido?
5. ¿Adónde vas?
6. ¿Cuál es tu número de teléfono?
7. ¿Cómo eres?
8. ¿Cuántos años tienes?
9. ¿De dónde eres?
10. ¿Qué te gusta hacer?

B Determine which pastimes are the most popular for these young people by listing the activities mentioned and tallying the number of times each activity is mentioned.

Por ejemplo:

> **Escribir cartas: 2**

Determine the five most popular activities and tell whether you like to do each of them.

C Choose one of the people who interests you the most and write a letter to him or her by responding to the questions below. Use the following format for your letter.

1. ¿Cuántos años tienes?
2. ¿En qué grado estás?
3. ¿Cómo es tu familia?
4. ¿Cómo es tu ciudad?
5. ¿Qué te gusta hacer?
6. ¿Qué haces todos los días?
7. ¿Qué estudias?
8. ¿Qué haces los fines de semana?
9. ¿Cuál es tu pasatiempo favorito? ¿Por qué?
10. ¿Cómo eres?

> Estimada Raquel:
> ¿Como estás? Me llamo Julia.
> Tengo diez y seis años.
> Estoy en el décimo grado.
> Mi familia .....
>
> Saludos de
> Julia Allen

Actividades

Actividad A Answers
1. Sí.
2. No.
3. Sí.
4. Sí.
5. No.
6. No.
7. No.
8. Sí.
9. No.
10. Sí.

Actividades B and C Answers
Answers will vary.

Repaso Resources
1. Workbook, pp. 141–143
2. Cassette 4.6
3. Student Tape Manual, pp. 115–116
4. Cumulative Test for Chapters 3 and 4, pp. 71–80

Bell Ringer Review

Directions to students: Tell how old your best friend is and describe him or her in five sentences.

¿Recuerdas?

Presentation

To review Chapter 4, call on individual students to give an example for each communicative function listed for Lecciones 1–3 and Lecciones 4–6, page 316. The numbers in parentheses on page 316 refer to the actual page(s) in Chapter 4 where each function was presented and practiced. You may wish to have your students go back to these pages for additional review and practice before continuing on to the Actividades, pages 317–319.

Lecciones 1–3 Answers

The following words and phrases are examples for each of the 14 functions listed under Lecciones 1–3. These words and phrases should be included in the students' response to each function listed below.

1. Parece...
2. Los hermanos, la mamá, el papá, etc.
3. Su... , sus...
4. Le(s) gusta...
5. ¿Cuánto vale?
6. ¿Cuántos años tiene?
7. Creo que...
8. Estudia para...
9. Es ingeniero, empleado(a) de banco, etc.
10. ¿Cuánto(s)...? ¿Cuánta(s)...?
11. Cien, doscientos, trescientos, etc.

Capítulo 4 Repaso

¿Recuerdas?

Do you remember how to do the following things, which you learned in **Capítulo 4**?

LECCIONES 1–3

1. describe what someone or something seems to be like (p. 242)
2. identify family members (p. 244)
3. describe possession or ownership (p. 248)
4. talk about what others like to do (p. 251)
5. ask how much something costs (p. 254, 261)
6. ask about someone's age (p. 254)
7. express an opinion (p. 254)
8. tell what someone is studying to be (p. 254)
9. name common occupations (pp. 256–257)
10. ask how much or how many there is of something (p. 261)
11. use numbers from 100 to 500 (p. 264)
12. identify common pets and zoo animals (pp. 268–269)
13. talk about things that others like (p. 272)
14. use numbers from 600 to the thousands (p. 275)

LECCIONES 4–6

1. describe someone's physical characteristics (p. 280)
2. talk about specific people (p. 284)
3. tell what you and others must do (p. 287)
4. report what someone says (p. 290)
5. identify pastimes (pp. 292–293)
6. tell and ask about preferences (p. 296)
7. talk about another or others (p. 299)
8. tell what will take place at a given time in the future (pp. 304–305)
9. give dates (pp. 304–305)
10. request information (pp. 308–309)
11. say what people can and can't do (p. 311)

Actividades

A **Sueños.** Compare your home with one you want to have. Use two paragraphs, starting one with **En mi casa...** and the other with **Pero en la casa que quiero...**

B **Mi gente preferida.** Find out from a classmate the following: (a) who his or her two favorite people are, (b) what they do, (c) what relationship they have to him or her, (d) what they like and dislike the most, and (e) why your classmate likes them. Then report back to the class.

C **Mi horario.** Tell the class about your schedule. Include the following.

1. cinco cosas que haces todos los días
2. un lugar adonde fuiste (you went) la semana pasada (Fui a...)
3. dos cosas que vas a hacer la semana que viene

D **¿Cuál es mi trabajo?** Work in pairs or small groups and think of a profession. The other pairs or groups in the class will then ask yes/no questions to try to guess what the profession is.

Por ejemplo:

> bombero
> *¿Trabaja usted en casa?*
> *¿Tiene que trabajar por la noche?*
> *¿Trabaja con niños?*
> *¿Gana mucho dinero?*

E **¿Dónde está el señor X?** Draw the face of a fictitious person. On a separate sheet, describe the person, giving a name, occupation, and personality. Your teacher will distribute the drawings around the class. Read your description as a "missing person report." Which of your classmates has your "person"?

---

12. Le gusta(n)/Les gusta(n)...
13. Los elefantes, los monos, etc.
14. seiscientos(as), setecientos(as), etc.

Lecciones 4–6, Answers

The following words and phrases are examples for each of the 11 functions listed under Lecciones 4–6. These words and phrases should be included in the students' response to each function listed below.

1. Tiene barba, bigote, pelo rubio, etc.
2. Llamo a...
3. Tengo (Tienes, tiene, etc.) que...
4. Dice que...
5. Jugar cartas, jugar ajedrez, etc.
6. Preferir
7. Otro, otros, etc.
8. La semana que viene; el año que viene, etc.
9. El... de marzo de 199_____
10. ¿Dónde?, ¿adónde?, ¿de dónde?, ¿cómo?, ¿a qué?, ¿cuándo?, ¿por qué?, ¿cuánto?, ¿quién?, ¿cuál?
11. Poder (ue)

Actividades

Presentation

Each practice activity in this Chapter 4 review combines several of the language functions listed on page 316. Students are asked to use the language they have learned at a higher, more integrated level, compared to the individual practice activities in Lessons 1–6 of Chapter 4.

Actividad A Answers
Answers will vary.

Actividad B Answers
Answers will vary, however the questions asked will approximate the following:
a. ¿Quiénes son las dos personas que te gustan más?
b. ¿Qué hacen estas personas?
c. ¿Son tus parientes?
d. ¿Qué les gusta(n) ¿Qué no les gusta(n)
e. ¿Por qué te gustan...?

Actividades C, D, and E Answers
Answers will vary.

Actividad F Answers

1. ¿Por qué no vemos Club Disney?
2. ... Jazz entre amigos?
3. ... Rockopop?
4. ... Buenos días, buenos clips?
5. ... De película?
6. ... Queenie?

Actividad G Answers

Answers will vary.

Actividad H Answers

1. Don Gilberto
2. Tomás
3. Úrsula
4. Ildefonso
5. Érica
6. Roberto
7. Raquel
8. Esteban
9. Zacarías

Actividades I and J Answers

Answers will vary.

F **En la tele.** Using the Madrid TV listing at right, what would you suggest to a friend that the two of you watch at the following times of day?

Por ejemplo:

a las ocho de la noche
¿Por qué no vemos _____?

1. a las seis y media de la tarde
2. a la una de la mañana
3. a las tres de la tarde
4. a las siete y media de la mañana
5. a las siete de la tarde
6. a las diez y media de la noche

G **Recomendaciones.** Choose one of the programs listed in activity **F** for a member of your family and one of your friends. Tell what time it is on and why that person should watch it.

Por ejemplo:

Mi papá debe ver el noticiero a las nueve porque le gustan las noticias.

H **La familia de Ildefonso.** Pilar describes a family she knows in Los Angeles. Fill in the name of each family member to show their relationship.
In the chart below, + means they are married; / means children.

Mi hermano dice que el año que viene, va a los Estados Unidos. Tiene un amigo, Ildefonso, que vive en Los Ángeles. Creo que la casa está en las afueras de la ciudad, en un barrio donde hay mucha gente de habla española.

Los padres de Ildefonso son españoles y amigos de mis padres. Bueno, el papá, Tomás, es español. Creo que la mamá, Úrsula, es argentina. Ildefonso es muy amable y tiene un hermano

Buenos días, buenos clips
7:30 / Canal +

Vídeos musicales de todo tipo y condición para comenzar el día con buen pie.

Jazz entre amigos
1:00 / TVE-1

Celebración del sexto aniversario del programa con la actuación del quinteto de Tom Harrell y la entrega de los premios de *Jazz entre amigos*.

Rockopop
15:00 / TVE-1

Programa musical con entrevistas y actuaciones, presentado por Beatriz Pécker.

Club Disney
18:30 / TVE-1

Programa infantil nuevo en emisión que incluye dibujos animados, telefilmes, juegos y concursos.

De película
19:00 / TVE-2

Espacio cinematográfico con entrevistas y reportajes sobre el Festival Internacional de Cine de San Sebastián.

Queenie
22:30 / TVE-2

Serie que trata de la historia de una niña mestiza, de padre ingles y madre india, en la Calcuta de 1931. La mezcla de su origen le complicará tremendamente la vida.

mayor, Roberto. ¡Fíjate qué guapo! Tengo una foto aquí en el escritorio. ¿Ves?

Aquí está la familia entera: la esposa de Ildefonso, Érica y el hijo, Esteban. ¿Precioso, no? Erica es norteamericana pero habla español. Y el pequeñito es el primo de Esteban, Zacarías. Es una familia de varones. La mamá de Zacarías es Raquel. Sí, Roberto está casado. Qué pena, ¿no? Pues, mira la casa. ¡Qué elegante! Y debe ser muy grande, porque todos viven allí, también el abuelo, don Gilberto. Es un señor muy divertido. Juega con los nietos todo el día.

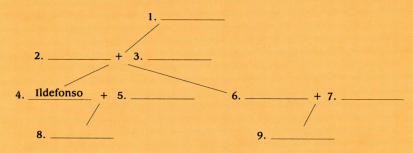

1. _____

2. _____ + 3. _____

4. _Ildefonso_ + 5. _____   6. _____ + 7. _____

8. _____   9. _____

I **Ya sé muchas palabras.** List as many words as you can think of to identify and describe people in terms of the following categories.

1. los parientes
2. las ocupaciones
3. la apariencia
4. la personalidad

J **Sabelotodo.** In groups of three or four, play the Spanish version of Trivial Pursuit **(Sabelotodo).** Think of three or four questions dealing with information or vocabulary that you have studied so far in Spanish class. Use the following categories of questions:

(C) Cultura (L) Lengua (G) Geografía (CSD) ¿Cómo se dice?

Have your teacher look over your questions and then see who can stump the rest of the class.

Chapter Overview

Cultural setting

The remaining two chapters in Level 1 take place in Miami and focus on the Cuban-American population. In Chapter 5, you will meet Carmen Marín and her parents who are originally from Cuba. The Marín family now lives in the Miami area, where Carmen was born. Carmen is bilingual and Spanish is the language of her household. However Carmen's constant mixing of Spanish and English is a source of aggravation to her father, who fears that the language of his family will ultimately be lost.

Rationale

A The use of circumlocution, that is, describing things you don't know the word for, as an oral communication strategy has tremendous utility when one's communicative motives outstrip linguistic capabilities. The activities presented are designed to help students decrease "exact word" dependence and to develop greater flexibility in speech by "talking around" the unknown vocabulary. Chapter 5 also presents techniques for self-correction (**digo,...**), stalling, and paraphrasing.

B Indirect object pronouns (**me, te, le**) are introduced through the function of asking and granting favors, first with **¿me** + conjugated form of **poder?** and later with conjugated forms of verbs such as **prestar, traer, ayudar, dar.** It is our experience that such a real life "hook" allows students to grasp more rapidly the concept of and need for indirect object pronouns in both oral and written communication.

Estructura

This chapter focuses on the following structure topics:
- asking and describing favors with the indirect pronouns **me** and **te;**
- requesting and giving descriptions of objects in terms of compostion, appearance, and purpose, and the use of circumlocution;
- giving nationalities and languages spoken;
- counting from the thousands to a million, giving dates (day, month, year), and describing time periods, using **desde** and **hace . . . que;**
- telling where people went, using **ir** in the preterit;
- describing what belongs to you and others (our);

CAPÍTULO 5

¡Me gusta vivir en Miami!

The presentation of the indirect object pronouns **les** and **nos** is delayed until Chapter 6 in order to allow students digestion and familiarity time and the opportunity to both grasp the concept and begin to develop some automaticity in limited aspects of its application.

C Chapter 5 begins the development of one function of the preterit, namely serialized reporting of past events, using the high frequency verbs **ir** and **ver.** It is our experience that this approach allows students to rather painlessly achieve a grasp of the forms of the preterit and begin to perceive, through contextualized practice, the function of the preterit tense.

The irregular verb **ir** is presented in all its forms for student production in **Dirección 2** of Lesson 3, building off the receptive **Cultura viva 2** activities of Chapter 4 as well as two additional ones in this chapter. This is followed by first and second person singular of **-er** and **-ir** (capitalizing on familiarity with the **-i** (albeit with no written stress) and **-iste** endings) and then by first and second person singular of **-ar** verbs.

We hope you enjoy your visit to the Miami area!

- telling with whom we do things, using **con;**
- enumerating past events, using **yo** and **tú** forms of the preterit tense;
- identifying what people say, hear and request or order, using present tense forms of the verbs **decir, oír** and **pedir;**
- saying what we do to or for another person, using **le.**

A complete listing of the language functions of this chapter appears in the **Repaso** section on page 400.

Lección 1

Objectives

By the end of this lesson, students will be able to:

1. request a favor of one or more people.
2. offer to do something for a friend.

Lesson 1 Resources
1. Workbook, pp. 144–149
2. Vocabulario Transparency 5.1
3. Cassette 5.1
4. Student Tape Manual, pp. 117–120
5. Lesson Quizzes, pp. 96–98
6. Computer Software, Disk 2
7. Video Cassette
8. Estructura Masters 5.1
9. Diversiones Masters 5.1

Bell Ringer Review

Display a picture of a celebrity familiar to students, a rock star, for example. Directions to students: Study the picture on the board carefully. Then write at least five questions about this person. Use the interrogative words we have studied to form your questions.

¡A comenzar!

Presentation

A. Lead students through each of the three functions given on page 322, progressing from the English to the Spanish for each function. Then have students find these words and phrases in the dialogue on page 323.

Lección 1

¡Gran oferta!

¡A comenzar!

The following are some of the things you will be learning to do in this lesson.

When you want to . . .

1. ask a favor of a friend
2. ask a favor of several people
3. offer to do something for a friend

You use . . .

- **¿Me puedes** + activity?
- **¿Me pueden** + activity?
- **Te puedo** + activity.

Now find examples of the above words and phrases in the following conversation and advertisement.

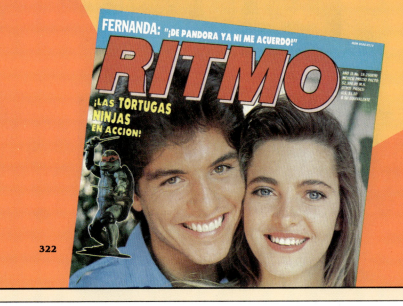

322

Getting Ready for Lesson 1

You may wish to use one or more of the following suggestions to prepare students for the lesson.

1. Tell students in Spanish that you're planning to take a trip to Miami soon and you're going to go to a travel agency. Tell the following things the travel agent can do for you. Have students raise their hands when you say something that is not true. For example:

Voy a la agencia de viajes. Allí el agente me puede ayudar mucho.
a. Me puede hacer las reservaciones.
b. Me puede dar información.
c. Me puede pagar la transportación.
d. Me puede dar dinero para el viaje.
e. Me puede llamar a los hoteles.
f. Me puede hacer las maletas.

Carmen Marín vive en Miami. Habla por teléfono con su amiga Elena.

CARMEN: ¿Recibes la revista *Ritmo*, ¿verdad?

ELENA: Sí, ¿por qué?

CARMEN: ¿Me puedes prestar el nuevo número? Tiene un anuncio muy interesante.

ELENA: Bueno, te puedo llevar la revista esta noche después de comer. Paso por tu casa a las siete.

CARMEN: Perfecto. Muchas gracias, ¿eh? Hasta luego.

Actividad preliminar

Ask a classmate for the following favors.

Por ejemplo:
cuidar al perro

ESTUDIANTE A
¿Me puedes cuidar al perro?

ESTUDIANTE B
Sí, cómo no. (No, no puedo).

1. llamar esta noche
2. comprar un refresco
3. limpiar la habitación esta tarde
4. visitar el sábado

Lección 1 **323**

g. Me puede mandar mapas de la ciudad.
h. Me puede comprar zapatos.
i. Me puede ahorrar dinero.

2. Tell students that in this lesson they are going to meet Carmen Marín and her family, who live in Miami. Tell them about Carmen.

Tiene quince años. Es muy lista y muy simpática. A Carmen le gusta mucho la música. Toca el piano y estudia la guitarra. Prefiere la música "rock" y le encanta ir a los conciertos y escuchar discos.

Bell Ringer Review

Directions to students: Pretend you live in Argentina, where the seasons are the opposite of ours. Copy the following activities and write beside each one the names of the months in which you would most likely do each one.

1. ir a la playa
2. esquiar
3. andar en monopatín
4. tener vacaciones
5. ir a la escuela

Presentation

Have students open their books to the Vocabulario on page 324.

1. Model the question **¿Me puedes hacer un favor?** Then model each phrase, beginning each one with **Me puedes...** Have students repeat each phrase in unison.
2. Ask for volunteers to do favors for you. For example:
   Maestro(a): ¿Quién me puede prestar un lápiz?
   Estudiante: Yo (puedo)
   Maestro(a): Gracias, muy amable.
   a. dar un sello
   b. prestar un sobre
   c. llevar la carta al correo
   d. enseñar a escribir mi nombre
   e. traer la tarjeta de crédito
   f. ayudar a preparar las tareas

Vocabulario

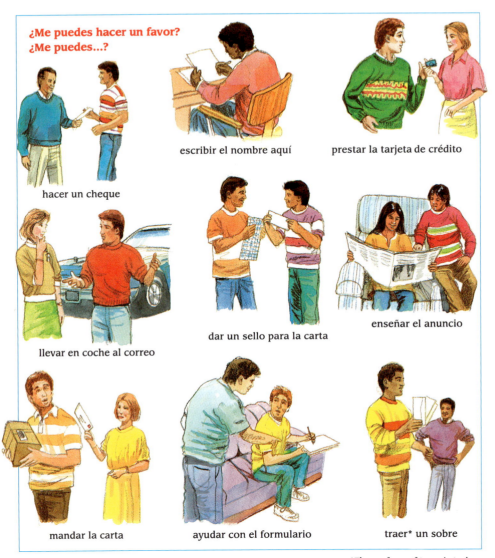

¿Me puedes hacer un favor?
¿Me puedes...?

hacer un cheque

escribir el nombre aquí

prestar la tarjeta de crédito

llevar en coche al correo

dar un sello para la carta

enseñar el anuncio

mandar la carta

ayudar con el formulario

traer* un sobre

*The **yo** form of **traer** is **traigo**.

Total Physical Response

Getting Ready

1. Make pictures of a check, credit card, and stamp on a sheet of paper.
2. Cut out an ad for cassettes and one for records from a magazine, and make copies of each. Draw five lines under each ad for students to fill out their order forms.
3. Number each of the above items 1 through 5.
4. Have students bring an envelope from home.

New words

llenen firmen
miren el costo

Muéstrenme con los dedos el número del formulario.

Actividades

A **¿Te gusta escribir cartas?** Complete the following sentences about writing and sending letters.

1. Me gusta escribir a _____.
2. Para escribir la carta, necesito _____.
3. En la dirección, escribo _____.
4. En la carta a un amigo, pregunto _____.
5. Para mandar la carta, necesito _____.
6. En el correo puedo comprar _____.

B **Por favor.** Ask a classmate if he or she can lend you the following things.

Por ejemplo:

un bolígrafo

ESTUDIANTE A

Por favor, ¿me puedes prestar un bolígrafo?

1. diez dólares
2. unos lápices
3. un sobre
4. tu calculadora
5. tu estéreo
6. la tarea
7. el libro de español
8. unos discos
9. dinero para comprar algo en la cafetería

ESTUDIANTE B

Sí, cómo no. (No, no puedo).

Hallmark llega al corazón

Hallmark

Lección 1 **325**

Indiquen con los dedos el número del cheque.
Muéstrenle el anuncio a un/a amigo(a). (Interchange commands and items.)
Miren el formulario de los discos.
Escriban su nombre en la primera línea.
Escriban dos títulos de discos en la segunda línea.
Indiquen el costo de cada disco en la tercera línea.

Marquen el total en la cuarta línea.
Escriban la fecha. Llenen el cheque con el total del primer disco. Firmen el cheque.
Marquen el número de la tarjeta en el formulario en la quinta línea.
Escriban su nombre y dirección en el sobre.
Dibujen un sello en el lugar apropiado.

Servicio "Express Mail".®

Obtenga seguridad de entrega "al-día-siguiente" más conveniente y más económica.

Por sólo $8.75.

C **Regalos y préstamos.** Tell five things you are willing to lend, and five things you are willing to give.

Por ejemplo:

> prestar / dar
> *Puedo prestar cinco dólares. Puedo dar mis discos viejos.*

D **¿Me puedes hacer un favor?** For each problem below, request some help and give a reason.

Por ejemplo:

> No tienes coche y quieres ir al baile.
> *Papá, ¿me puedes prestar el coche? Quiero ir al baile.*
> *(Tía, quiero ir al baile. ¿Me puedes llevar?)*

1. No tienes una camiseta buena para ir a la playa.
2. Necesitas mandar unas cartas y no tienes sellos.
3. Necesitas hacer la tarea pero no tienes el libro en casa.
4. Quieres comprar el nuevo disco de tu cantante favorito pero no tienes el dinero.
5. Estás en el centro comercial y necesitas llamar a tu casa pero no tienes dinero.
6. Tu amiga dice que hay un anuncio para un concierto de tu cantante favorito pero no sabes dónde está el periódico.
7. Tu amigo dice que tiene una amiga muy guapa. Quieres ver una foto.

326 CAPÍTULO 5

Aquí pueden hablar español

Hoy día hay más o menos setecientos cincuenta mil (750.000) cubanoamericanos en la ciudad de Miami. Este número representa casi el cincuenta por ciento de la población total de la ciudad. Muchos de ellos son doctores, abogados, profesores, directores de compañías y otros profesionales. Las contribuciones de todos los cubanos al comercio y a la economía de la ciudad son muy grandes.

El éxito de los cubanos y su decisión de mantener su idioma y cultura maternos son evidentes en la gran cantidad de periódicos, revistas, programas de radio y televisión en español.

Actividad

In the above reading, see if you can determine the following.

1. what percentage of Miami's current population is Cuban
2. what professions many Cubans practice
3. how Cubans have contributed to Miami's success as a city
4. how you could use your Spanish in Miami

Pronunciation

A. You may wish to play the recorded version of this pronunciation activity, located at the end of Cassette 5.1.
Hace mucho tiempo que vivimos en la Florida, pero nunca olvidamos nuestra isla querida.
B. Have students repeat words and phrases individually and in unison.

Focus on the following sound:
/v/ **vivimos; olvidamos**

For the Native Speaker

You may wish to have students write a 150–200 word composition about a trip they once took to a neighboring city, amusement park, or other place of interest.

Cultura viva 1

Presentation

In connection to Cultura viva 1, you may wish to discuss with the class some of the many ethnic groups that live in the U.S.

Did You Know?

After Fidel Castro became dictator of Cuba in 1959, thousands of Cubans left the country. They went to the United States, Mexico, and Spain. Half a million Cubans came to the United States. The majority of those who came settled in Miami because of that city's proximity to Cuba and its similar climate.

Cubans have given Miami a strong Latin flavor. They have attracted many banks and companies that handle Latin-American trade. Cuban Americans hold seats in the City Council, and the current mayor is Cuban-born.

Critical Thinking Activities

1. Do a research paper on the Cuban Revolution.
2. If you had to leave the United States and live in another country where you didn't speak the language, know the customs or the culture, how do you think you would adjust to your new life?
3. Think of reasons why people leave their country for another.

Actividad

Actividad Answers

1. Almost fifty percent.
2. Professions such as doctors, lawyers, and business people.
3. Cubans have contributed to the commercial and economic life of the city.
4. By reading newspapers and magazines, by listening to the radio, and by watching TV.

Structure Teaching Resources

1. Workbook, pp. 146–147
2. Cassette 5.1
3. Student Tape Manual, p. 118
4. Estructura Masters 5.1
5. Lesson Quizzes, p. 97

Bell Ringer Review

Directions to students: Copy the following words and phrases on your paper. Then draw a picture representing each one.

1. un sello
2. una tarjeta de crédito
3. una carta con un sobre
4. un cheque
5. un formulario

Structure Focus

The object pronoun **me** is presented in this lesson. Students will learn how to request favors. Students have been using **me** + **gusta(n)** since Chapter 1.

Presentation

1. Lead students through steps 1–3 on page 328.
2. You may want to introduce **me puedes(n)** asking students for favors. For example:
   ¿Me puedes prestar... ?
   ¿Me pueden ayudar con... ?

Actividades

Actividad A Answers

1. No, señor(a, -ita), ya escribimos bastante.
2. ... hablamos...
3. ... escuchamos...
4. ... leemos...
5. ... ayudamos...

Estructura 1

How to Request Favors   *Object pronoun* me

l. When you want to request help or a favor from a friend, use **¿Me puedes** + activity?

   ¿Me puedes prestar tu coche?

2. When you want to request help from someone you address formally, use **¿Me puede** + activity?

   Señorita, ¿me puede ayudar con la tarea?

3. When you want to request help from more than one person, use **¿Me pueden** + activity?

   Tíos, ¿me pueden llevar al cine?

Actividades

A **¡Qué exigente!** Your teacher makes some extra requests of the class. Tell your teacher that you and your classmates can't do what he or she asks because you already do each activity enough.

Por ejemplo:

   ¿Me pueden limpiar la clase?
   No, señor(a, -ita), ya limpiamos bastante.

1. ¿Me pueden escribir diez palabras más?
2. ¿Me pueden hablar más de la cultura hispana?
3. ¿Me pueden escuchar dos minutos más?
4. ¿Me pueden leer dos páginas más?
5. ¿Me pueden ayudar después de la clase?

Una clase de inglés en Buenos Aires, Argentina.

B **¿Qué puedes decir?** What do you say in the following situations to get what you want? Choose either the formal or friendly form of address, depending on the person to whom you are speaking.

Por ejemplo:

> Quieres ir al cine con Marta y no tienes dinero.
> Marta,...
> *Marta, ¿me puedes prestar diez dólares? (¿Me puedes hacer un favor?)*

1. Estás en el gimnasio y necesitas tu mochila que está en tu gaveta. Pablo,...
2. Estás en la oficina de la escuela y necesitas ayuda. Señorita,...
3. Estás en el correo y quieres mandar una carta. Señor,...
4. Estás en la clase de español y necesitas ayuda con la tarea. Susan,...
5. Tu cumpleaños es el sábado y quieres una grabadora nueva. Tía,...
6. El club de español va a hacer un viaje y necesitas un cheque. Mamá,...

C **Favores.** Write down the name of the person you would ask for each of the favors listed below. Then, ask the favor of each person you listed.

Por ejemplo:

> hablar en inglés
> *Señor(a, -ita), por favor, ¿me puede hablar en inglés?*

1. prestar cinco dólares
2. ayudar con la tarea
3. dar buenas notas
4. prestar el cuaderno
5. llevar en coche al centro comercial
6. comprar un regalo
7. hablar más despacio (slowly)
8. limpiar la habitación
9. prestar tus discos
10. escuchar
11. llamar esta noche
12. enseñar las fotos de tu fiesta

Lección 1 **329**

You may want to have students look at the photo on page 328. Have them formulate five questions they would like to ask the Argentine student about his English studies. Have them guess what five questions he would like to ask them about their study of Spanish.

Actividad B Answers
Answers will vary but may include the following.

1. Pablo, ¿me puedes traer mi mochila?
2. Señorita, ¿me puede ayudar?
3. Señor, ¿me puede dar un sello?
4. Susan, ¿me puedes ayudar con la tarea?
5. Tía, ¿me puedes comprar una grabadora nueva?
6. Mamá, ¿me puedes hacer un cheque?

Actividad C Answers
Answers will vary, but students must decide whether to use **puedes** or **puede,** according to whom they are addressing.

Reteaching

Directions to students: Your friend wants you to do some favors for him or her. What favors does he or she ask you? Write down four.

Presentation

Read the Cultura viva on this page. Point out Argentina on a map of South America.

Did You Know?

Mar del Plata, located about 400 kilometers south of Buenos Aires, is Argentina's largest summer resort.

Critical Thinking Activity

Have teams research Argentina. Divide the class into four large groups made up of all the 1's, 2's, 3's, and 4's from each group. Each group looks up something different. For example, mountain ranges; cities; industry; immigrants; economy; government; etc. They come back and compile information. Then they return to their regular teams and share their findings. Have each team share the information it has gathered with the class.

Actividades

Actividad A Answers
Disneyworld, Epcot Center.

Actividad B Answers
Sola: Epcot Center.
Acompañada: Disneyworld.

Actividad C Answers
El fin de semana pasado, la semana pasada./Both refer to the past.

Actividad D Answers
Answers will vary.

Una tarjeta postal a la Argentina

> 24 de febrero
>
> Querido primo:
> ¿Cómo estás? Aquí estamos de vacaciones ahora. Aquí tienes una postal de Disneyworld. Mi familia y yo fuimos allí el fin de semana pasado. ¡Es fantástico! Yo también fui al Epcot Center pero mis padres no fueron.
> Mis padres me dicen que ustedes fueron a Mar del Plata la semana pasada. Dicen que la playa es muy linda.
> Abrazos para tío y tía.
> muchos cariños de tu prima Carmen

> Sello
>
> Rafael Revueltas
> av. Libertad 642
> Buenos Aires
> A R G E N T I N A
>
> Correo aéreo

Actividades

A Name the places Carmen went.

B Tell where she went alone. Tell where she went with someone.

C Find the words that answer the question **¿cuándo?** Which of these refer to time in the past?

D Complete the sentences below to tell the following.

1. where you went last week: **Fui a _____.**
2. where you and family members or friends went:
   _____ y yo fuimos a _____.
3. where friends or family members went without you: **_____ fueron a _____. Yo no fui.**

Estructura 2

How to Offer Favors   ***Object pronoun* te**

You have used the word **me,** which means "to me" or "for me," when you want to request favors for yourself.

>**¿Me puedes ayudar con la tarea?**

When you want to offer a favor to a friend or family member or describe what you can do for him or her, use **te,** which means "to you" or "for you."

>**Te puedo prestar mi libro.**
>**No te puedo prestar mis discos.**
>**Miguel te puede ayudar con la tarea.**
>**Mis padres te pueden llevar al centro comercial.**
>**David y yo te podemos dar cinco dólares, si quieres.**

Actividades

A   **Buenos amigos.**   Tell a classmate three things that you can do for him or her. Then say three things you cannot do.

Por ejemplo:

>**Te puedo visitar si estás enfermo(a).**
>**No te puedo ayudar con la tarea de historia.**

B   **El estudiante nuevo.**   Tell five places in your area that you and your friends can show a new student. Say something interesting about each place. Use the suggestions below or think of your own.

Por ejemplo:

>**Te podemos enseñar el zoológico. Es muy grande y divertido. Tiene muchos animales.**

el centro	una tienda	un parque
un centro comercial	un lugar secreto	una playa
un estadio	una calle	un restaurante

Estructura 2

Structure Teaching Resources
1. Workbook, pp. 148–149
2. Cassette 5.1
3. Student Tape Manual, p. 119
4. Estructura Masters 5.1
5. Lesson Quizzes, p.98

Bell Ringer Review

Directions to students: You have just won a hundred thousand dollars in the lottery! What will you do with the money? List at least eight things.

Structure Focus

The object pronoun **te** is presented in this lesson. Students will learn how to offer favors. Students have been using **te** + **gusta(n)** since Chapter 1.

Presentation

1. Lead students through the explanation on page 331.
2. Have students ask you for favors. For example:

ESTUDIANTE	MAESTRO(A)
¿Me puede dar poca tarea?	No, pero te puedo dar pocos exámenes.

Cooperative Learning

Have students list two things they can't do (but want to learn [**enseñar**]): **No puedo esquiar. No puedo tocar la guitarra.** Then students ask other classmates to identify someone who can do each thing on their list: **¿Puedes... ?** Students report back to the class on who can teach them what they want to do. **No puedo esquiar, pero Julie me puede enseñar.**

Actividades

Actividades Answers
Actividades A, B, and C, pp. 331–332
Answers will vary but should follow the models.

Reteaching

Ask a classmate for three favors.

Learning from Photos

You may want to have students look at the photos in the realia piece on page 332. Have them imagine that they're going on the student trip to Mexico. Based on the photos, what are some of the things that they will be able to do and see while there?

C **Donaciones.** The Spanish Club is having a sale of used items to raise money for a trip to Mexico. You have been asked to collect items. Your partner will tell you five things he or she can give you. Write down your partner's responses and report back to the class.

Por ejemplo:

ESTUDIANTE A
¿Qué me puedes dar?

ESTUDIANTE B
Te puedo dar mis tarjetas de béisbol.

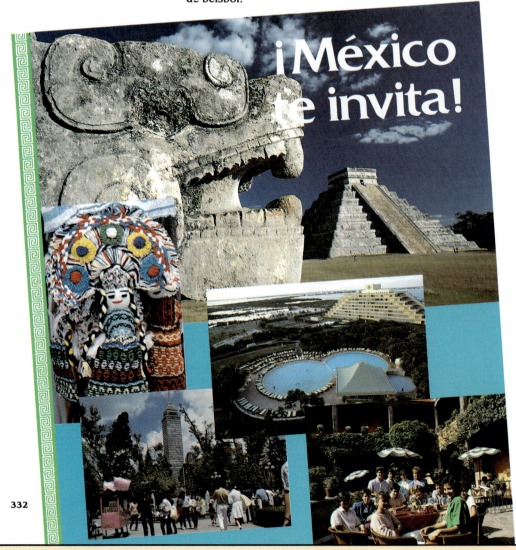

¡México te invita!

Finalmente

Finalmente

Situaciones

A conversar You need to borrow some money from a classmate to buy a birthday gift for a friend.

1. Ask if your partner can lend you some money.
2. Your partner asks you why you need the money.
3. Tell what you plan to buy and for (para) whom. Then tell how much it costs.
4. Your partner hesitates about lending the money.
5. Tell what favor you can do for your partner if he or she lends you the money.
6. Your partner agrees to give you the money but asks you for a favor in return.

A escribir You have seen an advertisement for some of your favorite audio cassettes for only four dollars each. Order several cassettes. Begin your letter with **"Estimados señores"** and include the following information.

1. Give the titles of the cassettes you want to buy.
2. Give the price of each title and the total amount of your purchase **(El precio total es...).**
3. Ask if you can pay by credit card or check.
4. Give your name, address, and telephone number.

Repaso de vocabulario

COSAS		hacer un favor	LUGAR
el anuncio	el sobre	llevar	el correo
el cheque	la tarjeta de crédito	mandar	
el favor		prestar	EXPRESIONES
el formulario	ACTIVIDADES	traer	hacer un cheque
el nombre	ayudar		por favor
	dar		
	enseñar		

Lección 1   **333**

Situaciones

Lesson 1 Evaluation
The **A conversar** and **A escribir** situations on this page are designed to give students the opportunity to use as many language functions and as much vocabulary from this lesson as possible. The **A conversar** and **A escribir** are also intended to show how well students are able to meet the lesson objectives.

Presentation

Prior to doing the **A conversar** and **A escribir** on this page, you may wish to play the **Situaciones** listening activities on Cassette 5.1 as a means of helping students organize the material.

Repaso de vocabulario

The words and phrases in the Repaso de vocabulario have been taught for productive use in this lesson. They are summarized here as a resource for both students and teacher. The Repaso de vocabulario also serves as a convenient resource for the A conversar and A escribir activities on this page. It also gives the teacher a source for writing either additional practice or evaluation activities such as quizzes and tests in addition to those provided by the publisher.

For the Native Speaker

In pairs have students pick out sale ads from a newspaper or a magazine. Have them order merchandise from the ads. They should write to those stores with the full address on the letter and envelope.

333

Lección 2

Objectives

By the end of this lesson, students will be able to:

1. give the meaning of a word in Spanish.
2. tell what things are made of.
3. describe something they don't know that word for.
4. request, offer, and describe favors.

Lesson 2 Resources
1. Workbook, pp. 150–154
2. Vocabulario Transparencies 5.2
3. Cassette 5.2
4. Student Tape Manual, pp. 121–125
5. Lesson Quizzes, pp. 99–101
6. Computer Software, Disk 2
7. Video Cassette
8. Estructura Masters 5.2
9. Diversiones Masters 5.2

Bell Ringer Review

Directions to students: Several friends ask you favors this week. How do you respond? Make two columns: **Te puedo ayudar a...** and **No te puedo ayudar a...** List each of the following favors in the appropriate column. Remember to add **"Lo siento"** if you can't help.

1. lavar el coche papá
2. limpiar la casa
3. comprar un regalo
4. llevar al centro comercial
5. ayudar con la tarea de historia

¡A comenzar!

Presentation

A. Lead students through each of the three functions given on

---

Lección 2

¿Cómo se dice "T-shirt"?

¡A comenzar!

The following are some of the things you will be learning to do in this lesson.

When you want to . . .	You use . . .
1. ask a favor of someone	• ¿Me + activity?
2. give the meaning of a word in Spanish	• Se dice...
3. tell what things are made of	• Son de + material.

Now find examples of the above words and phrases in the following conversation.

Getting Ready for Lesson 2

You may wish to use one or more of the following suggestions to prepare students for the lesson.

1. Describe to the class what you did yesterday, last week, etc., pretending to forget certain words. The sounds of the preterit tense are important here since students will be learning some forms of this tense in Lessons 3, 5, and 6 of this chapter. For example:

   Ayer fui al correo y pedí esas cosas que ponemos en el sobre para mandar la carta (use gestures). **¿Cómo se dice?** (elicit student response). **Sí, eso es— sellos. Luego fui a una tienda a comprar esa cosa que usamos para escribir. ¿Cómo se dice?** (Elicit student response.) **Sí, un bolígrafo.**

Carmen habla con su papá.

CARMEN: Oye, papá, ¿me das un cheque, por favor?

PAPÁ: ¿Para qué? A ver.

CARMEN: Mira, quiero comprar dos "T-shirts".

PAPÁ: *Camisetas*, Carmen. Y no comprendo por qué necesitas dos. Son muy caras.

CARMEN: Pero, papá, son del último "tour". Y además, son de puro "cotton".

PAPÁ: *Algodón*, Carmen. ¡Por Dios! Se dice "algodón".

Actividades preliminares

A Think of five of the most difficult words you know in Spanish. Write them down in English. Quiz a classmate.

Por ejemplo:

ESTUDIANTE A	ESTUDIANTE B
¿Cómo se dice "chemistry" en español?	Se dice "química". (No sé cómo se dice).

B Ask a classmate for the following items.

Por ejemplo:

un dólar

ESTUDIANTE A	ESTUDIANTE B
¿Me prestas un dólar, por favor?	Sí, cómo no. (No tengo, No puedo, etc.).

1. papel   2. un bolígrafo   3. la calculadora   4. la tarea

Lección 2   **335**

---

page 334, progressing from the English to the Spanish. Then have students find these words and phrases in the dialogue on page 335.

B. Introduce the Lesson 2 dialogue by reading it aloud or by playing the cassette version.

C. Now ask students to open their books and look at the dialogue as you lead them through what is said. For example:

1. ¿Qué dice Carmen para pedir el cheque?
2. Cuando Carmen pide el cheque, ¿qué dice su papá?
3. ¿Por qué quiere el cheque Carmen?
4. Cuando Carmen dice "T-shirts", ¿qué dice su papá?
5. ¿Por qué no quiere comprar las camisetas el papá?
6. Según Carmen, ¿por qué son caras?
7. Cuando Carmen dice que son de puro "cotton", ¿qué dice su papá?

D. Have students listen to the tape of the Lesson 2 dialogue again and raise their hands when they hear Carmen's father getting upset. Describe Carmen's father's mood, choosing from the following.

1. ¿Está enojado?
2. ¿Está nervioso?
3. ¿Está emocionado?
4. ¿Está contento?

E. Have students look at the dialogue and determine why Carmen's father is upset. **¿Por qué está enojado el papá de Carmen?**

1. ¿porque a él no le gustan los conjuntos de rock?
2. ¿porque no le gustan las camisetas?
3. ¿porque las camisetas son muy caras?
4. ¿porque Carmen dice palabras en inglés cuando habla español?

Actividades preliminares

Actividad A and B Answers
Answers will vary.

Vocabulario

Bell Ringer Review

Directions to students: Your best friend is in the hospital and is bored. What could you buy or lend him or her to make the time pass more quickly? Make two lists under the headings **Te puedo prestar...** and **Te puedo comprar...**

Presentation

A. Have students open their books to page 336.
1. Model each of the four words at the top of page 336. Begin each phrase with **Es...** Have students repeat each phrase in unison.
2. Using vocabulary transparencies, point to the word and ask individual students **¿Es una llave?** Encourage students to give a complete answer. For example: **Sí, es una llave.**

B. Have students look at the following groupings of vocabulary on pages 336–337.
1. Model the questions **¿Qué es? ¿Para qué sirve? ¿De qué es? ¿Cómo es?**
2. Pointing to objects in the classroom, ask students the questions presented in the vocabulary. For example: **Maestro(a):** (pointing to a pencil) **¿Qué es? Estudiante: Es un lápiz**

¿Qué es? Es...

una llave

un bolsillo

una billetera

un reloj

¿Para qué sirve? Sirve para...

guardar libros y otras cosas

abrir la puerta

llevar cosas

saber la hora

336 CAPÍTULO 5

Total Physical Response

Getting Ready

For **TPR 1**, use transparencies and color transparency pens. For **TPR 2**, obtain real items or pictures of items to be used in the activity. Bring multiples of the same item in various materials and display them in front of the room.

New Words

echa   devuelve   ponte

TPR 1

(Whole class or pairs)
Toquen la mochila.
Apunten al armario.
Indiquen la llave.
Hagan un círculo negro en el bolsillo.
Dibujen un cuadro azul en la billetera.

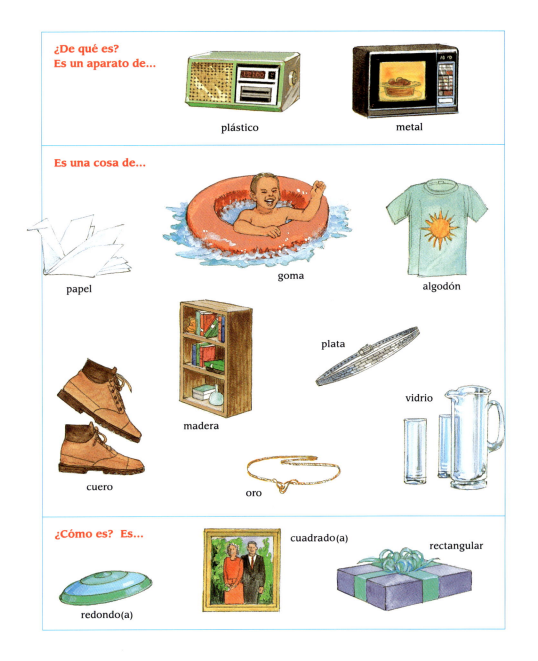

¿De qué es?
Es un aparato de...

plástico

metal

Es una cosa de...

papel

goma

algodón

madera

plata

cuero

oro

vidrio

¿Cómo es? Es...

cuadrado(a)

rectangular

redondo(a)

Maestro(a): ¿Para qué sirve?
Estudiante: Sirve para escribir.
Maestro(a): ¿De qué es?
Estudiante: Es de madera.
Continue with different objects.

3. You may wish to follow up with having students find the following things in the classroom.
   a. cosas recondas
   b. cosas cuadradas
   c. cosas rectangulares

When Students Ask

You may wish to give students the following additional vocabulary to allow them to describe objects.

triangular	ovalado(a)
la tela	la seda
la lana	el poliéster

Regionalisms

You may wish to tell students that in some parts of the Spanish-speaking world the following word are alternatives to those presented in the Vocabulario.
la billetera (la cartera)
el bolsillo (la bolsa) (Perú)

Toquen el objeto de plata.
Indiquen el objeto de oro.
Apunten al objeto de papel.
Hagan dos rectángulos verdes en el objeto de madera.
(Interchange commands and items.)

TPR 2

(Individual students)
Toca el reloj de oro.

Toma agua del vaso de plástico.
Ponte la camiseta de algodón.
Echa jugo en la jarra de vidrio.
Lleva el lápiz de madera a _____.
Lleva el lápiz de metal a _____.
Guarda los zapatos de cuero en mi escritorio.
Guarda el reloj de plata en el bolsillo.
Llévale la billetera a _____.
(Interchange commands and items.)

Actividades

Actividad A and B Answers
Answers will vary.

Actividad C Answers
Answers will vary but should approximate the following.

1. Una llave es de metal. Es pequeña y delgada. Sirve para abrir la puerta.
2. Una tarjeta de crédito es de plástico. Es rectangular y delgada. Sirve para comprar cosas.
3. Un calendario es de papel. Es rectangular y tiene números y los nombres de los meses y de los días de la semana. Sirve para enseñar los días.

Actividad D Answers
Answers will vary.

Reteaching

Ask students to bring or show you objects in the classroom without mentioning the name of the object. For example:
Linda, ¿me traes (enseñas) el aparato para escuchar casetes?

1. la cosa para escribir en la pizarra
2. la cosa para limpiar la pizarra
3. la cosa para escribir en el papel
4. la cosa que abrimos cuando queremos aire fresco
5. la cosa que usas para llevar tus libros

Actividades

A ¿De qué es? Tell what five things in your classroom are made of.

Por ejemplo:

> la silla
> *La silla es de metal (madera).*

B Para mí es de oro. Name five of your most prized possessions and tell what they are made of.

Por ejemplo:

> tu radio
> *Mi radio es de plástico. (Tengo un radio de plástico).*

C Descripción. Tell what the following items are made of, what they look like, and what they are for.

Por ejemplo:

> un lápiz
> *Un lápiz es de madera y de goma. Es delgado y largo. Sirve para escribir.*

1. una llave
2. una tarjeta de crédito
3. un calendario
4. un reloj
5. una billetera
6. una mochila
7. unas monedas
8. un bolsillo
9. un televisor
10. un teléfono
11. una cámara
12. una maleta

D Adivina, buen adivinador. Prepare descriptions of three objects and see if a classmate can guess what you are talking about. In your description, answer the following questions.

¿Para qué sirve?   ¿De qué es?   ¿Cómo es?

Por ejemplo:

ESTUDIANTE A
Es un aparato para trabajar con números. Es de plástico. Es rectangular.

ESTUDIANTE B
Es una calculadora, ¿verdad?

For the Native Speaker

Directions to students: Write a newspaper ad for two objects you wish to sell. Describe the objects by giving color, size, use, appearance, and condition. Include your address or telephone number. Read the ad to the class without mentioning the name of the objects. The class guesses what objects you are selling.

CULTURA VIVA 1

La música latina

El ritmo latino, que es la base de la "salsa" y la música "disco" en los Estados Unidos, tiene su origen en Cuba y el Caribe. La música del Caribe es una combinación de ritmos africanos e hispanos. Muchos bailes como la rumba, la conga y el chachachá tienen su origen en el Caribe.

Los instrumentos de percusión son muy importantes para estos ritmos. Aquí hay algunos de los instrumentos usados en Cuba y el Caribe.

Pégate... **Suave** 12-60 AM
Tenemos lo que te gusta.

Claves
Conga
Bongó
Maracas
Cencerro
Cuatro
Güiro

Actividad

Éstas son las diez canciones más populares durante una semana en Miami.

1. ¿Qué estación de radio debes escuchar si te gustan estas canciones?
2. ¿Qué canción es la más popular?
3. ¿Qué canciones son menos (less) populares?
4. ¿Quiénes son los cantantes más populares?

SUPER Q 108 SUPER HITS

SUPER HIT	ARTISTA(S)
1. UN BUEN PERDEDOR	Franco de Vita
2. DÉJALO QUE REGRESE	Hansel y Raúl
3. TÚ Y YO	Julio Iglesias
4. ME VAS A ECHAR DE MENOS	José José
5. CREO EN EL AMOR	José Luis Rodríguez
6. EN CARNE VIVA	Charanga '76
7. SERÉ	Salsa Latina
8. AMAR A MUERTE	Luis Ángel
9. POR SI ACASO	Braulio
10. TE QUIERO TE QUIERO	Orq. Éxito

Cultura viva 1

Presentation

Read the Cultura viva 1 on this page. You may wish to bring in tapes or records of Latin music to play for the class. Point out the instruments mentioned so students can appreciate the strong percussion base of this music. If you have a way of obtaining some of the instruments, bring them to class so that students can feel them and try to play them.

Did You Know?

Cuban composers have combined African and European musical traditions to create the Cuban sound. The combination of the guitar and the African drum gives Cuban music its characteristic beat.

Critical Thinking Activity

Working in groups, find out more information about dances such as **la rumba, la conga,** and **el chachachá.** Learn the basic steps and present them to the class.

Actividad

Actividad Answers

1. **Super Q (108).**
2. **"Un buen perdedor".**
3. **"Por si acaso"; "Te quiero, te quiero".**
4. **Franco de Vita; Hansel y Raúl.**

Pronunciation

A. You may wish to play the recorded version of this pronunciation activity, located at the end of Cassette 5.2 You may also wish to write this poem on the board and have students copy it into their notebook.

Sóngoro cosongo,
songo be;
Sóngoro cosongo,
de mamey;
Sóngoro, la negra
baila bien;
sóngoro de una,
sóngoro de tré.

(Nicolás Guillén, poeta cubano, 1902-1989)

B. Have students repeat the words and phrases individually and in unison. Ask students to focus on the rhythm.

Bell Ringer Review

Bring a recording of "salsa" music to class. Directions to students: Turn to page 339. Listen to the music carefully and write on your paper any of the instruments shown on this page that you hear.

Structure Focus

In this lesson students will learn to circumlocute.

Presentation

Lead students through steps 1–5 on page 340.
Show the class pictures of objects they know. Ask questions. **A ver... ¿cómo se dice _____? ¿Para que sirve?**

Actividades

Actividad A Answers

1. c
2. a
3. e
4. f
5. b
6. d

Estructura 1

How to Describe Something You Don't Know the Word For

If you forget a word or don't know the word for something, you can still communicate by using the following strategies.

1. Use stalling devices to gain time to think.
   A ver... Bueno... Pues...

2. Use general terms when you can't remember a word. For example, **la cosa** (thing) or **el aparato** (mechanical thing).
   ¿Dónde está la cosa redonda?
   ¿Me das el aparato para el pelo?

3. Ask how to say something.
   ¿Cómo se dice "key"? **Se dice "llave".**

4. Describe what something is used for.
   ¿Para qué sirve? Sirve para escribir.

5. Ask what a word means.
   ¿Qué quiere decir "mochila"?

Actividades

[A] **Descripciones.** Match the following objects with their descriptions on page 341.

A.

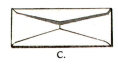
C.

B.

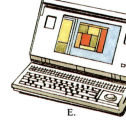
D.

E.

F.

1. Es la cosa en que mandas una carta. Aquí escribes el nombre y la dirección. Tiene un sello.
2. Es el aparato de plástico con los números de cero a nueve. Ayuda mucho en las clases de matemáticas y ciencias.
3. Es el aparato que sirve para escribir algo oficial o formal. Las secretarias usan este aparato.
4. Es la cosa para llevar dinero, las tarjetas de crédito y otras tarjetas importantes.
5. Es la cosa que sirve para abrir puertas, maletas y otras cosas.
6. Es el aparato que sirve para saber qué hora es. Puede ser grande o pequeño.

B **Así se dice.** Describe each of the objects below to a class-mate. Your classmate will tell you what you've described. Provide the following types of information:

color   size   shape   use   material   appearance   condition

Por ejemplo:

ESTUDIANTE A
Es una cosa rectangular para llevar libros. Es azul y bastante vieja.

ESTUDIANTE B
Es la mochila.

1.

2.

3.

4.

5.

Lección 2 **341**

Cultura viva 2

Presentation

Read the Cultura viva 2 on this page. You may wish to discuss with your students the importance of being bilingual.

Did You Know?

Because there are many Hispanic communities in the United States, the opportunity to use Spanish in the workplace is increasing. For example, bilingual teachers are in great demand in states that have a large Spanish-speaking populations. In some districts, bilingual teachers can command a higher salary than their monolingual counterparts.

Critical Thinking Activities

1. Invite a member of your community who uses Spanish in his or her work to speak to the class. Have students prepare questions to ask the visitor.
2. In groups, have students think of as many reasons as possible why Spanish would be useful in the following occupations: real estate agent, hotel manager, secretary, social worker, and doctor.

Actividad

Actividad Answers
Answers will vary.

Learning from Realia

You may want to have students look at the realia on page 342. Ask students what number the following people would call to learn more about one of the positions offered.

1. un/a doctor/a
2. una persona que quiere trabajar con abogados
3. una persona que sabe reparar coches
4. un/a secretario(a) o recepcionista

342

El español en el trabajo

El papá de Carmen es abogado y trabaja en una compañía internacional en Miami. Todos los días habla inglés y español con sus clientes.

Si sabes más de un idioma, hay muchos trabajos que puedes hacer. Hay muchas instituciones y compañías en los Estados Unidos que necesitan empleados que hablen inglés y español. Por ejemplo, los bancos, hospitales y clínicas; las agencias de servicios sociales y las escuelas; toda clase de compañías internacionales; los canales de televisión, los periódicos, las estaciones de radio, compañías de aviación y muchísimas otras. Si sabes dos idiomas, no sólo tienes más oportunidades de trabajo, sino que tu trabajo puede ser más interesante.

Actividad

Based on the above reading, list five occupations in which you think you could use Spanish.

Por ejemplo:

Empleados de bancos, compañías como...

EMPLEOS

Solicito médico bilingüe para curso de enfermería con E. K. G. 822-5951

Necesito hombre o mujer con experiencia para tienda de ropa. Servir al público bilingüe. Salario y comisión. 558-3978.

Se solicita ayudante legal, preferible hablar inglés. Llamar lunes a viernes de 10 a 6 pm. 823-9831

Mecánico para trabajar en gasolinera. Debe ser bilingüe. Inf. 853-9800.

¿Necesita trabajo? Llame Avance Personal para empleos de oficina. Poco inglés necesario. Llamar 245-8761.

Barnett Bank

En La Florida, Barnett es el Banco.

Estructura 2

How to Request, Offer, and Describe Favors

Me *and* te *with conjugated verbs*

You have learned to request favors and tell favors you do for others, using **me** or **te** and a form of the verb **poder.**

> **¿Me puedes traer mi camiseta verde?**
> **Te puedo dar mi bolígrafo, si quieres.**

1. You can use **me** and a form of other verbs to request a favor.

   > **¿Me traes mi camiseta verde?**
   > **¿Me das el bolígrafo?**
   > **Señorita, ¿me hace un favor?**

2. You also use **me** to describe what people do or don't do for you or to you.

   > **Mi maestra me da buenas notas.**
   > **Mi hermana siempre me ayuda con la tarea.**
   > **Mis amigos no me prestan dinero.**

3. To offer a favor to a friend or family member, or to describe what you do for that person, use **te.**

   > **Te invito a mi fiesta.**
   > **Te voy a comprar unos discos para tu cumpleaños.**

4. The following are some things friends or family might offer to do for each other.

-ar verbs		-er and -ir verbs
mandar	hablar	hacer
escuchar	llamar	leer
enseñar	dar	escribir
ayudar		abrir
prestar		traer
llevar		
guardar		
comprar		

Una familia cubanoamericana en Miami.

Estructura 2

Structure Teaching Resources

1. Workbook, pp. 153–154
2. Cassette 5.2
3. Student Tape Manual, p. 123
4. Estructura Masters 5.2
5. Lesson Quizzes, p. 101

Bell Ringer Review

Directions to students: Look around the classroom and write down the names in Spanish of as many objects as you can. Then write what each item is made of.

Structure Focus

Me and **te** with conjugated verbs are presented in this lesson. Students will learn how to request, offer, and describe favors. The object pronouns **le, les,** and **nos** will be presented in Lesson 6 of this chapter; Chapter 6, Lesson 1; and Chapter 6, Lesson 2, respectively.

Presentation

1. Lead students through steps 1–4 on page 343.
2. Ask students to lend you three different things. Tell them why you need them. For example: **¿Me das un lápiz? Tengo que escribir algó. ¿Me prestas papel? Tengo que preparar un examen. ¿Me traes el libro? Tengo que enseñar la lección.**

343

Actividades

Actividades

Actividad A Answers

Answers will vary but should include the following.

1. ... me hace favores.
2. ... me ayudan.
3. ... me llaman.
4. ... me escuchan.
5. ... me escriben.
6. ... me dan regalos.

Actividad B Answers

Answers will vary.

Actividad C Answers

1. ¿Por qué no me traes regalos de tus viajes?
2. ¿... no me das dinero cuando lavo el coche?
3. ¿... no me hablan cuando me ven?
4. ¿... no me da buenas notas cuando trabajo mucho?
5. ¿... no me das regalos para mi cumpleaños?

Additional Practice

After completing Actividades A, B, and C, you may wish to reinforce the lesson by doing the following activity. Directions to students: Write down three things you have that you are willing to exchange with a classmate. In another column, write down three things you want from a classmate.
Por ejemplo:
Tengo....
una colección de revistas de tenis
un bolígrafo negro
una raqueta de tenis
Quiero...
tu colección de discos de los Rolling Stones
tu camiseta verde
tu calculadora

Now offer your classmate a trade.

Reteaching

Have students tell you one thing their friends do for them and one their friends don't do for them. **Por ejemplo:**
Mis amigos me llevan a fiestas pero no me ayudan con mi tarea.

344

A **¿Quién te hace favores?** Tell who does things for you by responding to the following questions.

Por ejemplo:

> ¿Quién te da dinero en tu familia?
> *Mi mamá me da dinero.*

1. ¿Quién te hace favores?
2. ¿Quién te ayuda cuando no entiendes algo?
3. ¿Quiénes te llaman por teléfono?
4. ¿Quiénes te escuchan cuando tienes problemas?
5. ¿Quiénes te escriben cartas o tarjetas postales?
6. ¿Quiénes te dan regalos?

B **Consecuencias.** Tell what will happen if the following favors are not granted.

Por ejemplo:

> Si no me prestas tus discos...
> *Si no me prestas tus discos, mi fiesta va a ser un poco aburrida.*

1. Si no me ayudas con la tarea...
2. Si no me traes tus discos nuevos...
3. Si mis padres no me permiten salir esta noche...
4. Si mi maestro no me da exámenes fáciles...
5. Si mis compañeros no me prestan sus vídeos nuevos...
6. Si no me guardas una silla en la cafetería...

C **¿Qué pasa?** Ask the following people why they don't do what you expect them to.

Por ejemplo:

> Tu amiga nunca te manda cartas cuando viaja.
> *¿Por qué no me mandas cartas cuando viajas?*

1. Tu amigo nunca te trae regalos de sus viajes.
2. Tu papá nunca te da dinero cuando lavas el coche.
3. Tus amigos nunca te hablan cuando te ven.
4. Tu maestra nunca te da buenas notas cuando trabajas mucho.
5. Tu primo nunca te da regalos para tu cumpleaños.

Finalmente

Finalmente

Situaciones

Lesson 2 Evaluation
The **A conversar** and **A escribir** situations on this page are designed to give students the opportunity to use as many language functions and as much vocabulary from this lesson as possible. The **A conversar** and **A escribir** are also intended to show how well students are able to meet the lesson objectives.

Presentation

Prior to doing the **A conversar** and **A escribir** on this page, you may wish to play the **Situaciones** listening activities on Cassette 5.2 as a means of helping students organize the material.

Repaso de vocabulario

The words and phrases in the Repaso de vocabulario have been taught for productive use in this lesson. They are summarized here as a resource for both students and teacher. The Repaso de vocabulario also serves as a convenient resource for the A conversar and A escribir activities on this page. It also gives the teacher a source for writing either additional practice or evaluation activities such as quizzes and tests in addition to those provided by the publisher.

Situaciones

A conversar You have lost your backpack at school. Your partner is working in the office where the lost-and-found box is.

1. Greet your partner.
2. Tell your partner you don't know where your book bag is and ask for help.
3. Your partner asks what the bag is like. Describe it, telling the color, size, shape, and material.
4. Your partner asks what's in the bag. Describe the contents.
5. Your partner asks if you can come back in 15 minutes. Tell your partner why you need the book bag now.

A escribir A close friend suddenly decides you're not a good friend. Write your friend a note, listing all the favors you do for him or her. Then invite him or her to do something with you this weekend.

Repaso de vocabulario

PREGUNTAS
¿Cómo se dice?
¿De qué es?
¿Para qué sirve?

COSAS
el aparato
la billetera
el bolsillo
la cosa
la llave
el reloj

ACTIVIDADES
abrir
guardar
llevar (to carry)

MATERIALES
el algodón
el cuero
la goma
la madera
el metal
el oro
el papel

el plástico
la plata
el vidrio

FORMAS
cuadrado(a)
rectangular
redondo(a)

EXPRESIONES
se dice
sirve para

Lección 3

Objectives

By the end of this lesson, students will be able to:

1. say what nationality they and others are
2. say that something has been going on since a certain date
3. tell the year in which an event occurred
4. give the year they were born
5. tell where they went at one point in the past and ask where others went

Lesson 3 Resources

1. Workbook, pp. 155–159
2. Vocabulario Transparencies 5.3
3. Cassette 5.3
4. Student Tape Manual, pp. 126–130
5. Lesson Quizzes, pp. 102–105
6. Test Booklet, pp. 81–87
7. Computer Software, Disk 2
8. Video Cassette
9. Estructura Masters 5.3
10. Diversiones Masters 5.3

Bell Ringer Review

Directions to students: Where would you be most likely to find the following items—in a pocket or a wallet? Make two columns on your paper labeled **bolsillo** and **billetera**. Then write each of the following items in the appropriate column.

1. monedas
2. llaves
3. tarjetas de crédito
4. cheques
5. fotos
6. bolígrafos
7. calculadoras
8. documentos importantes

Lección 3

Tienes que practicar el español

¡A comenzar!

The following are some of the things you will be learning to do in this lesson.

When you want to . . .	You use . . .
1. say what nationality you and others are	• **Somos** + nationality.
2. say that something has been going on since a certain date	• Activity + **desde** + date.
3. give a year in the twentieth century	• **Mil novecientos...**
4. ask a friend or relative if he or she went somewhere	• **¿Fuiste a** + place?
5. say that you went someplace yesterday	• **Fui ayer.**

Now find examples of the above words and phrases in the following conversation.

DIARIO LAS AME

Fundado el 4 de Julio de 1953

Por la Libertad, la Cultura y la Solidaridad Hemisférica.

AÑO XXXVIII   NUMERO 89   MIAMI, FLA., MIERCOLES 17 DE OCTUBRE   EDIC

Getting Ready for Lesson 3

You may wish to use the following suggestions to prepare students for the lesson.

1. Give students a list of events in your life, using as many cognates and familiar words as possible. Do not list events in chronological order. For example:

a. viaje a Puerto Rico
b. graduación de la universidad
c. viaje a México
d. nacimiento de mi hijo(a) _____
e. matrimonio con _____

Give an account of these events arranged by topics rather than chronologically. Give years in terms of the decade (for example, **en el año ochenta y cinco**). As you speak, have students record the year

Carmen habla con su padre.

PAPÁ: ¿Ya fuiste al correo a mandar el cheque?

CARMEN: Sí, papá. Fui ayer. Gracias por el cheque. Te van a gustar las "T-shirts".

PAPÁ: Carmen, tienes que practicar el español.

CARMEN: Pero, papá, estamos aquí en Miami desde mil novecientos sesenta y tres. ¿Por qué no puedo hablar inglés en casa?

PAPÁ: Bueno, porque somos cubanos y tienes que hablar bien el español.

EXPRESS MAIL

Cuando decimos "al-día-siguiente"... ¡es al-día-siguiente!

Actividad preliminar

Ask a classmate if he or she went to the following places yesterday.

Por ejemplo:

al cine

ESTUDIANTE A	ESTUDIANTE B
¿Fuiste al cine?	Sí, fui con Miriam. (No, no fui).

1. al partido de _____
2. a la cafetería
3. al centro comercial
4. al trabajo
5. a la casa de _____

Miembro de la Sociedad Interamericana de Prensa

25 CENTAVOS EN MIAMI

Lección 3 **347**

Vocabulario

Vocabulario

Bell Ringer Review

Directions to students: Draw ten circles on a sheet of paper. In the center of each one write one of the following materials: **vidrio, oro, plata, madera, cuero, algodón, goma, papel, plástico, metal.** Draw lines out from each circle and write as many things as you can think of that are made of that material.

Presentation

A. Have students open their books to page 348. Model each new word on page 348. Begin each phrase with **Soy...** Have students repeat each phrase in unison.

B. Now have students look at the vocabulary presentation on page 349.

1. Model the phrases **¿Qué idioma estudias? Estudio...** Have students repeat each phrase in unison.
2. Ask which language is spoken by each of the nationalities. For example: **Los cubanos hablan español.**
3. Using the names of well-known people from foreign countries, ask individual students questions. For example: **¿Qué es Julio Iglesias?** Encourage students to give complete responses. For example: **Es español.**

Soy...

CANADIENSE

(NORTEAMERICANO)

ESTADOUNIDENSE

JAPONÉS(ESA)

RUSO(A)

INGLÉS(ESA)

ALEMÁN(ANA)

ITALIANO(A)

FRANCÉS(ESA)

ESPAÑOL(A)

CHINO(A)

CUBANO(A)

DOMINICANO(A)

PUERTORRIQUEÑO(A)

MEXICANO(A)

HONDUREÑO(A)

NICARAGÜENSE

COLOMBIANO(A)

GUATEMALTECO(A)

VENEZOLANO(A)

SALVADOREÑO(A)

COSTARRICENSE

PANAMEÑO(A)

ECUATORIANO(A)

PERUANO(A)

BOLIVIANO(A)

PARAGUAYO(A)

CHILENO(A)

URUGUAYO(A)

ARGENTINO(A)

348 CAPÍTULO 5

Total Physical Response

Getting Ready

Make up poster strips with the names of each nationality presented in feminine and masculine form. Distribute two per student, having students use only one strip at a time. Show Vocabulary Transparency 5.3 during the activity for reference.

New Words

pasen   al fondo de

Pre-activity

Review the world map pointing out the locations of the different countries, nationalities, and the names of the continents.

¿Qué idioma estudias? Estudio...

español

inglés

francés

alemán

japonés

italiano

chino

ruso

Actividades

A **¿De dónde son?** What countries are the following people from?

Por ejemplo:

los cubanos
Los cubanos son de Cuba.

1. los hondureños
2. los colombianos
3. los guatemaltecos
4. los venezolanos
5. los ecuatorianos
6. los bolivianos
7. los dominicanos
8. los peruanos
9. los norteamericanos
10. los uruguayos
11. los costarricenses

B **Una ciudad internacional.** Tell what kinds of food you can eat in Miami based on the following restaurant ads. Then tell what kinds of restaurants there are in your area.

Por ejemplo:

En Miami hay restaurantes _____.
En mi ciudad hay restaurantes _____.

Casona de Carlitos

El restaurante argentino de la esquina de la alegría con motivo de cumplir un año de su apertura, se hace un deber en agradecer a toda su estimada clientela el apoyo brindado, esperando continuar contando con su presencia en su casa, con la seguridad de una continua superación para una excelente atención.

LES RECORDAMOS NUESTRA ÚNICA DIRECCIÓN:
COLLINS AVE. Y 23 ST. MIAMI BEACH
TELÉFONO: 354-7013

TABLAO-FLAMENCO
del Restaurante
MADRID

RESERVACIONES: 558-4224

477 S. W. 8TH ST. Miami, Fl.

SHIBUI
A JAPANESE RESTAURANT
En la Ave. 102 del S.W. unos pasos al norte de Sunset (S.W. 72 St.)
abierto diariamente para la cena solamente de 6 P.M. a 12 A.M.
277-7785
Se aceptan reservaciones.

El Inka Restaurant
Presenta Directamente de LIMA a:
ARMANDO DE DIOS y su PIANO
Todos los sábados a partir de las 10 p.m.
LA GRAN PEÑA CRIOLLA DE PAPÁ JUAN
(Guitarras y Cajón)
Participe Ud. cantando o tocando algún instrumento
Saboree la mejor comida peruana e internacional
Sirviéndoles en Miami por 7 AÑOS.
Menú Especial   De lunes a jueves   Se atienden Buffets
Reserv. 885-0432 1756 S. W. 8 St.

CANTON DRAGON
CANTONESE & SZECHUAN CUISINE
CHOP SUEY - SEAFOOD
14051 S.W. 40 ST. (Bird Road) Miami
TARJETAS DE CRÉDITO
ABIERTO LOS 7 DÍAS
11:30 a 10:30
ÓRDENES PARA LLEVAR
522-5577 • 533-9144

CALLE OCHO
DIVIÉRTASE ESCUCHANDO MELODÍAS, TANGOS Y MÚSICA COLOMBIANA
3610 S. W. 8 ST. TEL. 445-8965

LA CARRETA
UN RESTAURANTE
UN RESTAURANTE CAMPESTRE EN ESTILO Y SABOR AL SERVICIO DE USTED CON GRAN ESPECIALIDAD EN COMIDAS TIPICAS CUBANAS
PARA COMPLACER A NUESTROS CLIENTES
17704 S.W. 87 ST. 659-4646

C **¿Qué idioma habla?** Tell the language that each of the following people speaks.

Por ejemplo:

una mexicana
Una mexicana habla español.

1. una chilena
2. una japonesa
3. un italiano
4. un canadiense
5. una puertorriqueña
6. un francés
7. un norteamericano
8. un guatemalteco
9. una alemana
10. una española

C U L T U R A   V I V A   1

La televisión en español

En Miami así como en Nueva York, Los Ángeles, Chicago y en casi todas las otras grandes ciudades de los Estados Unidos, puedes ver televisión en español. Hay casi 500 canales que transmiten programas en español en nuestro país.

Actividad

Using the advertisements below, tell each of the following persons the name and time of a show he or she should watch.

Por ejemplo:

Gabriela: Me gustan los concursos.
Debes ver "Super Sábados" a las cuatro de la tarde.

1. Sarita: Me gustan los programas de mujeres.
2. Paco: Yo prefiero ver programas cómicos.

¡PARTICIPE Y GANE DESDE SU CASA!

SUPER SABADOS

DESDE EL
1ʳᵒ DE AGOSTO
4PM A 9PM

CANAL 51
WSCV-TV
TELEMUNDO

UNIVISION PRESENTA

SABADO GIGANTE

Concursos y Variedades

Tres horas y media de concursos, juegos, música, comedia, conversación y mucho más.

Con "Don Francisco"

Todos los sábados a las 7 pm

UNIVISION PRESEN

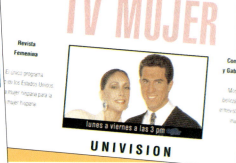

TV MUJER

Revista Femenina

El único programa en los Estados Unidos... la mujer hispana para la mujer hispana.

Con... y Gab...

lunes a viernes a las 3 pm

U N I V I S I O N

Lección 3 **351**

351

Bell Ringer Review

Directions to students: Draw an outline map of the South American continent. Label the countries and their capitals. Write the nationality of the people who live in each country on the map.

Structure Focus

In this lesson students will learn how to give dates in terms of years, tell when they were born, say how long they have been doing certain activities, and use numbers to the millions.

Presentation

1. Lead students through steps 1–4 on page 352.
2. Ask students what year they were born. Write a few of the years on the board. Then ask students to read the years in Spanish.

Actividades

Actividad A Answers

1. g	3. c	5. f	7. a
2. e	4. b	6. d	

Actividades B and C Answers
Answers will vary.

Additional Practice
After completing Actividades A, B, and C, you may wish to reinforce

Estructura 1

How to Give Dates and Count to a Million

You have learned to use numbers in the thousands.

> **La computadora vale mil trescientos quince dólares.**
> **El coche vale diez mil dólares.**

1. To tell the year of an event, use the numbers you have already learned. For example, the year 1992 would be the same as the number 1,992: **Mil novecientos noventa y dos.**

   Notice how to give various years in the twentieth century.

1963	mil novecientos sesenta y tres
1975	mil novecientos setenta y cinco
1980	mil novecientos ochenta

2. To give the year you were born, use **Nací en...**

   > **Nací en 1972.**
   > **Nací en 1981.**

3. To give the date on which you first started doing something, you use *activity* + **desde** + *date.*

   > **Vivo en Orlando desde 1980.**
   > **Estudio español desde 1990.**

4. A million is **un millón.** To state that there are a million of something, say **Hay un millón de...** To form the plural, add **-es** to **millón** and drop the accent mark.

   > **Hay un millón de dólares en el banco.**
   > **Cuatro millones de personas viven en Madrid.**

LATINOS EN HOLLYWOOD
AHORA Y ANTES

★ ★ ★ ★ ★ ★ ★ ★ ★

1980-1989

Julie Carmen
Milagro Beanfield War;
Fright Night II

Elpidia Carrillo
The Border; Beyond the Limit

Rosanna De Soto
Ballad of Gregorio Cortez;
La Bamba

Emilio Estévez
The Outsiders;
The Breakfast Club

Jenny Gago
Under Fire; Old Gringo

Andy García
The Untouchables; Black Rain;
Internal Affair

Raúl Juliá
The Morning After; Tango Bar;
Romero

Lorenzo Lamas
Grease

Esai Morales
Bad Boys; La Bamba

Edward James Olmos
Ballad of Gregorio Cortez;
Stand and Deliver

Elizabeth Peña
Down and Out in Beverly Hills
La Bamba

Paul Rodríguez
D C Cab; Born in East L A

Charlie Sheen
Platoon; Wall Street

Jimmy Smits
The Believers; Old Gringo

Talisa Soto
Licence to Kill

Eddie Vélez
Repo Man; Romero

Actividades

A **Estudiante de historia.** Tell the year in which each of the following events took place, choosing from the list on the right.

Por ejemplo:

> independencia de los Estados Unidos
> *1776 (mil setecientos setenta y seis)*

1. Los primeros hombres llegan a la luna (moon).
2. asesinato del presidente Kennedy
3. asesinato del presidente Lincoln
4. Constitución de los Estados Unidos
5. asesinato de Martin Luther King, Jr.
6. Alexander Graham Bell inventa el teléfono.
7. Cristóbal Colón llega a América.

a. 1492
b. 1787
c. 1865
d. 1876
e. 1963
f. 1968
g. 1969

B **¿Desde cuándo?** Tell how long you have been doing the following things.

Por ejemplo:

> ¿Desde cuándo vives aquí?
> *Vivo aquí desde 1978.*

1. ¿Desde cuándo practicas tu deporte favorito?
2. ¿Desde cuándo estudias español?
3. ¿Desde cuándo sabes leer?
4. ¿Desde cuándo eres miembro de un club?
5. ¿Desde cuándo eres amigo(a) de *(nombre de la persona)*?

C **Autos usados.** A favorite relative is thinking of buying you a used car. Look at the ads to the right. Decide on a model you like, tell how much it costs, then tell the telephone number your relative needs to call for further information.

Por ejemplo:

> Me gusta el Nova. Vale mil cincuenta dólares. Debes llamar al ocho, cincuenta y ocho, sesenta y ocho, treinta.

9901 - VENTA AUTOS

Nova '87, 6 cil. Buen estado $1,050. Llamar al 858- 6830

Toyota Corolla,'86, 1.8,4 ptas, 5 vel. A-C, PB, exc. conds. $1,795. Telf 635-2267

Mustang II '84, motor 302 stereo aire $800 o mejor oferta 823-9660

VW Rabbit '86, a/c, radio casete, azul $19,999. 262-5289

Chevette '88,hatchback, 4 ptas. A/C, PS-PB, AM-FM, stereo, $1950. (559-2909)

HONDA '86, AUTO CHIQUITO, 2 PTAS. $1,250. TELF: 556-0084

'85 Subaru DL, 5 veloc. pocas millas, A/C, $1,750. Inf 844-5752

Camaro '83, A/C, 45,000 millas, extras, como nuevo, $1,950. Telf. 860-1721

---

the lesson by doing the following activities.

1. Give the dates for the following events in your life.
   Por ejemplo:
   un viaje especial: *1982*
   a. cuando naciste
   b. tu primer año de la escuela
   c. el año más importante de tu vida
   d. el año que aprendes a manejar un coche
   e. el año de tu graduación
2. Tell five things you're going to do in the future and give the year you're probably going to do each. Use the suggestions below, then think of one of your own.
   Por ejemplo:
   viajar a España
   Voy a viajar a España en 1995.
   a. graduarme
   b. aprender a manejar
   c. ganar un millón de dólares
   d. ser famoso(a)
   e. recibir tu primera tarjeta de crédito
   f. viajar a un país latinoamericano
   g. empezar a trabajar

Reteaching

Ask students to give you two important dates (including years) in their lives. Write them on the board. Call on individual students to read the dates on the board.

Learning from Realia

A. See if students can determine the meaning of the following words, phrases, and abbreviations in the realia on page 353.

1. **buen estado** (good condition)
2. **5 vel. (veloc).** (5 speeds)
3. **exc. conds.** (excellent condition; **excelentes condiciones**)
4. **aire** (air conditioning)
5. **mejor oferta** (best offer)
6. **bajas millas** (low mileage)
7. **millas** (miles)

B. Have students give in Spanish the phone numbers, prices, and years of the models listed.

Cultura viva 2

Presentation

Read the Cultura viva on this page. You may wish to discuss letter writing with students.

Did You Know?

In writing letters, Hispanics tend to be more effusive and cordial than Americans are. When writing to friends or relatives, it is common to open with **Querido(a)...** or **Queridísmo(a)...** and to close with a phrase such as **Un fuerte abrazo de tu hijo (prima, tío, hermana que te quiere mucho...).**

Critical Thinking Activity

Write a letter inviting someone you like very much to spend two weeks with you and your family. Use the letter in Cultura viva 2 as a model.

Actividades

Actividad A Answers

1. hermanos
2. Cuba; Miami
3. está demasiado ocupado; descansar

Actividad B Answers

¿No fuiste al doctor? ¿Fuiste a...?

Learning from Photos

You may want to have students look at the photos on page 354. Have them describe each person physically. Then have them describe what the person appears to be like (**El tío Lucas parece...**).

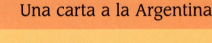

Una carta a la Argentina

La mamá de Carmen le escribe a su hermano Lucas, el papá de Rafael.

Miami, 25 de marzo

Querido hermano Lucas:

Te escribo para saber cómo estás; ¿todavía estás enfermo? Estoy un poco preocupada por ti. ¿No fuiste al doctor? Sé que él te va a decir que trabajas demasiado y que necesitas descansar. ¿Por qué no descansas aquí en Miami? Y ¿por qué no vienes con Rafael? Aquí puede practicar el inglés y conocer a los amigos de Carmen.

Bueno, hermanito, te mando un gran abrazo y una sincera invitación a nuestra casa. Todos esperamos tu visita. Hasta entonces te manda un fuerte abrazo

tu hermana que te quiere,

Alicia

Actividades

A Tell about the person writing the letter and the person who will receive it by choosing the appropriate words in parentheses.

1. Alicia y Lucas son (**hermanos / primos**).
2. Alicia es de (**la Argentina / Cuba**) pero vive en (**Miami / Buenos Aires**).
3. Alicia cree que Lucas (**está demasiado ocupado / es muy listo**) y que debe (**trabajar más / descansar**).

B Give the sentence that Alicia uses to ask if Lucas went somewhere. Ask a classmate if he or she went somewhere (movies, game, mall, etc.) last Saturday.

Estructura 2

How to Say Where People Went
The preterit of ir

1. To say where people went, use forms of the verb **ir** in the past (preterit) tense. Here are the forms of the verb you will need to talk about different people.

SINGULAR	PLURAL
fui	**fuimos**
fuiste	**fuisteis***
fue	**fueron**

*This form is rarely used in the Spanish-speaking world, except for Spain.

2. To ask where someone went, use **¿adónde?**

   ¿Adónde fueron ustedes anoche?   Fuimos al centro.

3. To say you went somewhere to do something, use **ir** + **a** + place + **a** + infinitive.

   ¿Fuiste a casa a descansar? No, fui a la piscina a nadar.

4. The following are words and phrases you can use to talk about various times in the past.

ayer	la semana pasada	el lunes (martes,
anoche	el año pasado	etc.) pasado

Actividades

A **Lugares.** Tell three places you went last week and three places you have to go next week.

Por ejemplo:

> La semana pasada fui a _____.
> La semana que viene tengo que ir a _____.

Structure Teaching Resources
1. Workbook, pp. 158–159
2. Cassette 5.3
3. Student Tape Manual, p. 128
4. Estructura Masters 5.3
5. Lesson Quizzes, pp. 104–105

Bell Ringer Review
Directions to students: Write out the dates of birth of at least three family members.
Por ejemplo:
mi prima Sue: 1975
Do you know in what year a grandparent (aunt, uncle, cousin, etc.) was born?

Structure Focus
The preterit of **ir** is presented. Students will learn how to say where they and others went at one point in the past.

Presentation

1. Lead students through steps 1–4 on page 355.
2. You may wish to introduce the preterit of **ir** using TPR techniques. For example: **Ve a la ventana.** Then ask a series of questions in the preterite: **¿Adónde fuiste? ¿Quién fue a la ventana?**, etc.

Actividades

Actividades A, B, C, and E Answers
Answers will vary.

B **¿Adónde fue el maestro?**   With a classmate, make a list of five places you think your teacher went after school yesterday. Read your list to your teacher, who will say whether you're right or wrong.

Por ejemplo:

> **¿Fue usted anoche a una fiesta a bailar?**

C **Mi compañero y yo.**   Have a classmate tell you three places he or she went yesterday. Then report back to the class, comparing where you went to where your classmate went.

Por ejemplo:

ESTUDIANTE A	ESTUDIANTE B
(1) **¿Adónde fuiste ayer?**	(2) **Fui a un partido.**
(3) **¿Y luego?**	(4) **Fui al centro comercial.**

(A la clase:) Pam fue ayer a un partido y luego al centro comercial. Yo fui a casa y después a la piscina. Anoche los (las) dos fuimos al cine.

D **El diario de Carmen.**   To the right are some of the headings of Carmen's diary last year. Tell the places she went, the things she did, and when she did them.

Por ejemplo:

> *El 22 de enero fue al Carnaval con Jorge a las siete.*

E **Mi conjunto.**   You are part of a rock group touring Latin America and the U.S. Give your group a name. Tell a classmate six places where you and your group went. Your classmate will report back to the class.

Por ejemplo:

> **Somos "Las Serpientes" y somos muy populares. El mes pasado fuimos a Buenos Aires, Santiago...**

> **(A la clase:) El mes pasado "Las Serpientes" fueron a Buenos Aires, Santiago...**

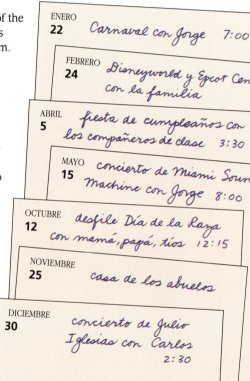

ENERO 22 Carnaval con Jorge 7:00

FEBRERO 24 Disneyworld y Epcot Center con la familia

ABRIL 5 fiesta de cumpleaños con los compañeros de clase 3:30

MAYO 15 concierto de Miami Sound Machine con Jorge 8:00

OCTUBRE 12 desfile Día de la Raza con mamá, papá, tíos 12:15

NOVIEMBRE 25 casa de los abuelos

DICIEMBRE 30 concierto de Julio Iglesias con Carlos 2:30

356   CAPÍTULO 5

Finalmente

Finalmente

Situaciones

Lesson 3 Evaluation
The **A conversar** and **A escribir** situations on this page are designed to give students the opportunity to use as many language functions and as much vocabulary from this lesson as possible. The **A conversar** and **A escribir** are also intended to show how well students are able to meet the lesson objectives.

Presentation

Prior to doing the **A conversar** and **A escribir** on this page, you may wish to play the **Situaciones** listening activities on Cassette 5.3 as a means of helping students organize the material.

Situaciones

A conversar Converse with a classmate about a memorable trip you once took. Reverse roles.

1. Tell where you went, with whom, and give the month and year of the trip. Ask if your partner knows where the place is.
2. Tell your partner why he or she should go there.

A escribir Write a letter of application to a pen pal club; include the following information.

1. Tell what nationality the pen pal should be.
2. Tell where you live. Give your date of birth.
3. Describe your appearance and your personality.
4. Tell about the activities you like to do in your free time.

Repaso de vocabulario

TIEMPOS EN EL PASADO

anoche
el año pasado
ayer
el lunes (martes, etc.)
    pasado
el mes pasado
la semana pasada

NACIONALIDADES

alemán, alemana
argentino(a)
boliviano(a)
canadiense
colombiano(a)
costarricense
cubano(a)
chileno(a)
chino(a)
dominicano(a)
ecuatoriano(a)
español, española
estadounidense
    (norteamericano[a])
francés, francesa
guatemalteco(a)
hondureño(a)
inglés, inglesa
italiano(a)
japonés, japonesa

mexicano(a)
nicaragüense
panameño(a)
paraguayo(a)
peruano(a)
puertorriqueño(a)
ruso(a)
salvadoreño(a)
uruguayo(a)
venezolano(a)

IDIOMAS

el alemán
el chino
el italiano

el japonés
el ruso

OTRAS PALABRAS

desde
un millón de
nací

Lección 3   **357**

For the Native Speaker

Have native speakers make a list of twenty-five words in ''Spanglish''. Have them find out the correct Spanish for each term.

Lección 4

Objectives

By the end of this lesson, students will be able to:

1. say with whom they do things
2. say what belongs to them and others

Lesson 4 Resources
1. Workbook, pp. 160–164
2. Vocabulario Transparencies 5.4
3. Cassette 5.4
4. Student Tape Manual pp. 131–134
5. Lesson Quizzes pp. 106–109
6. Computer Software, Disk 2
7. Video Cassette
8. Estructura masters, 5.4
9. Diversiones Masters 5.4

Bell Ringer Review

Directions to students: Copy the following countries on your paper. Beside each country write the language(s) spoken there.

Japón	China
Alemania	Italia
Inglaterra	Canadá
Rusia	Francia
los Estados	Perú
Unidos	España

¡A comenzar!

Presentation

A. Lead students through each of the three functions given on page 358, progressing from the English to the Spanish for each function. Then have students find these words and phrases in the dialoguc on pagc 359.

358

Lección 4

Nuestro idioma

¡A comenzar!

The following are some of the things you will be learning to do in this lesson.

When you want to . . .	You use . . .
1. say "with me"	• **conmigo**
2. say "with you" to a friend or family member	• **contigo**
3. talk about what belongs to you and someone else ("our")	• **nuestro(a)**

Now find examples of the above words and phrases in the following conversation.

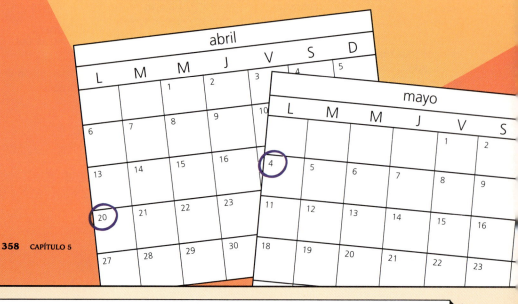

358 CAPÍTULO 5

Getting Ready for Lesson 4

You may wish to use of the following suggestions to prepare students for the lesson.

1. Talk about what you and your family do at the beach during your vacation. Use gestures or bring in photos or pictures from magazines to help illustrate your narration.
   Durante las vacaciones me gusta ir a la playa con mi familia pero no me gusta bucear. Prefiero practicar el esquí acuático con mi primo. A él no le gusta ir de pesca conmigo porque dice que es aburrido. También paseo en velero y tomo el sol. Nuestras vacaciones son muy divertidas.

2. Ask students where they can go to do the activities you mentioned above.

Carmen habla con su mamá.

CARMEN: Mamá, ¿me puedes explicar por qué papá está enojado conmigo?

MAMÁ: No está enojado contigo, Carmen. Es otra cosa. En nuestra casa todos tenemos que hablar español.

CARMEN: Claro, entiendo, pero...

MAMÁ: Y tienes que practicar porque tu tío y tu primo llegan de la Argentina el 20 de abril. Con ellos en casa, debes hablar nuestro idioma.

CARMEN: ¿Tío Lucas y mi primo Rafael? ¡Qué bueno! ¿Cuánto tiempo van a pasar con nosotros?

MAMÁ: Hasta el 4 de mayo —dos semanas. ¿No viste su carta?

Actividades preliminares

A Complete the following conversation between Carmen and her friend Carlos, using **conmigo** and **contigo**.

CARLOS: ¿Quieres ir al concierto el sábado?

CARMEN: Lo siento, no puedo ir _____ el sábado porque tengo que trabajar.

CARLOS: ¿Quieres ir al parque _____ el domingo a ver el partido?

CARMEN: Gracias por la invitación, pero tengo que estudiar para el examen de computadoras. No puedo ir _____ el domingo, tampoco.

CARLOS: Carmen, ¿no quieres salir _____?

CARMEN: Ay, Carlos. Claro que quiero salir _____. ¿Por qué no vamos al cine el viernes?

B Complete this sentence to tell what people in your house have to do: **En nuestra casa todos tenemos que _____.**

Lección 4 **359**

B. Introduce the Lesson 4 dialogue by reading it aloud or by playing the cassette version. Have students listen to the tape of the Lección 4 dialogue to find out the following.
   1. What advice does Carmen's mother giver her?
   2. What event is going to take place?

C. Now ask students to open their books and look at the dialogue as you lead them through what is said. For example:
   1. Carmen quiere saber algo. ¿Qué dice?
   2. La mamá de Carmen explica que Carmen está equivocada. ¿Qué dice?
   3. En la casa de los Marín todos tienen que hacer algo. ¿Qué tienen que hacer?
   4. ¿Por qué tiene que practicar español Carmen?
   5. Su mamá dice: "En casa todos tenemos que hablar nuestro idioma". ¿Qué idioma?
   6. ¿Cómo se llama el tío? ¿Y el primo?
   7. ¿Dónde viven? ¿Cuándo llegan? ¿Cuándo regresan a Argentina? ¿Cuánto tiempo van a pasar en Miami?
   8. La mamá de Carmen le pregunta: "¿No viste sus cartas?" (Ask a student:) ¿Viste tú sus cartas, Tom?

Actividades preliminares

Actividad A Answers
1. contigo
2. conmigo
3. contigo
4. conmigo
5. contigo

Actividad B Answers
Answers will vary.

359

Bell Ringer Review

Directions to students: Draw a large circle, rectangle, and square on your paper. Inside each shape write in Spanish the names of as many things as you can think of that have that shape.

Presentation

Have students open their books to page 360.

1. Model each new word and phrase on pages 360 and 361.
2. Ask individual students whether or not they like or know how to do the activities listed. For example: **¿Te gusta (Sabes) bucear?** Encourage students to give a complete response. For example: **Me gusta bucear.**

When Students Ask

The following additional vocabulary may be provided to allow students to talk about other beach-related activities.
la vela
la regata
la arena
el bote de motor
la barca
la loción
la tabla de velero
el castillo de arena

Vocabulario

Te invito a mi casa.

¿Vas a pasar dos semanas con nosotros? ¡Qué bueno!

Voy a planear una semana estupenda.

Vamos a ir a la playa y tomar el sol.

También podemos saltar las olas.

Total Physical Response

Getting Ready

For TPR 1 use pictures of the various locations and activities listed in the **Vocabulario** or sketch each one on a separate sheet of paper. Display them around the room.

For TPR 2 make a grid, dividing a sheet of paper into four columns and three rows (twelve squares) and labeling them **fila** and **columna.** Make copies and give one to every student.

Display the grids around the room. Working in teams, students will write down the activities they would like to to when they go to the beach.

TPR 1

Ve a la playa.
Saca fotos del concierto.

Te puedo enseñar a...

practicar el esquí
acuático

bucear

También podemos ir de
pesca en el mar.

pasear en velero

No necesitas gastar mucho dinero.

Podemos asistir a conciertos
y a fiestas por la noche.

Bucea.
Ve a practicar el esquí acuático.
Muéstrenme ''ir de pesca''.
(Continue until all words have been
shown.)

TPR 2
Students place pictures in the correct positions.)
Pongan ''bucear'' en la primera fila,
tercera columna.

Pongan ''saltar las olas'' en la segunda
fila, cuarta columna.
Pongan ''practicar el esquí acuático''
en la segunda fila, primera columna.
(Continue placing all pictures into different squares. Do an oral check.)

Actividades

A **Sé hacer muchas cosas.** Tell whether you know how to do the following activities. If you don't know how to do something, say whether you want to learn how.

Por ejemplo:

> jugar ajedrez

ESTUDIANTE A	ESTUDIANTE B
(1) **¿Sabes jugar ajedrez?**	(2) **No, no sé. ¿Y tú?**
(3) **Sí. Si quieres, te puedo enseñar.**	(4) **Gracias, quiero aprender. (No, gracias, no me gusta).**

1. ir de pesca	4. bucear
2. practicar el esquí acuático	5. saltar las olas
3. pasear en velero	6. cuidar niños pequeños

Actividades A and B Answers
Answers will vary but should follow the model.

Actividad C Answers
Answers will vary but should include the following.

1. Vamos a planear...
2. Va a ser el... a la(s)... Va a ser en...
3. Vamos a pasar...
4. Necesitamos llevar...
5. Podemos...

B **¿Qué te gusta hacer?** Converse with a classmate about whether you like or dislike doing the following activities. If you dislike an activity, tell what you prefer to do. Reverse roles.

Por ejemplo:

> cantar

ESTUDIANTE A	ESTUDIANTE B
¿Te gusta cantar?	Sí, me gusta mucho. (No, no me gusta. Prefiero bailar).

1. ir al mar	4. pasar unos días con tus parientes
2. asistir a conciertos	5. gastar dinero
3. tomar el sol	6. planear fiestas

Additional Practice
After completing Actividades A, B, and C, you may wish to reinforce the learning with the following. Invite a classmate to do one of the activities in the **Vocabulario.** Your classmate will either accept or reject your invitation and give an explanation.
Por ejemplo:

ESTUDIANTE A	ESTUDIANTE B
(1) ¿Te gusta ir a la playa?	(2) Sí, por qué?
(3) ¿Quieres ir el sábado?	(4) ¡Estupendo! (El sábado no puedo. Tengo que cuidar a mi hermano menor).

C **Un plan estupendo.** You and a classmate are in charge of planning one of the following activities at school: **una fiesta / una excursión / un baile / un viaje / un partido.** Write the details of the event by answering the questions below. Report to the class.

1. ¿Qué clase de actividad van a planear?
2. ¿Cuándo va a ser? ¿Dónde?
3. ¿Cuánto tiempo van a pasar allí tus compañeros?
4. ¿Qué necesitan llevar?
5. ¿Qué pueden hacer?

Reteaching

Have students open their books to page 360. Write two columns on the board: **Adentro podemos...** and **Afuera podemos...** Have students write each of the activities pictured under the appropriate column.

362 CAPÍTULO 5

For the Native Speaker

Imagine that you have been shipwrecked on a desert island. Answer the following questions in Spanish.

1. Who is shipwrecked with you?
2. How long will both of you be there?
3. Who will rescue you?
4. What will you do on the island (for example: fish, sunbathe, swim)?

CULTURA VIVA 1

Cuba linda

Cuba es la más grande de las islas del Caribe. Es una isla tropical de gran belleza natural. Hay muchas playas bonitas como Varadero en la costa norte. También tiene valles y bahías preciosos y puertos excelentes.

La Habana, la capital, es la ciudad más grande del país. También es un puerto muy importante.

España gobernó a Cuba de 1492 a 1898. Los españoles llamaron a Cuba la "llave del Golfo". Durante la época colonial de Cuba salían barcos llenos de oro, plata, café, azúcar, especias y otros productos importantes de las Américas.

Actividades

A Which of the following could be said about where you live?

1. Tiene un clima tropical.
2. Hay playas bonitas.
3. Es una isla.
4. Tiene montañas y valles.
5. Hay puertos importantes.

B Which of the following words are *not* related to the ocean?

el puerto	la isla
el barco	la bahía
el azúcar	el golfo
la costa	el valle

C What does the phrase **"la llave del Golfo"** refer to?

a. Cuba's key location in the Caribbean
b. the wealth of the island
c. a beautiful bay

EL GOLFO DE MÉXICO
CUBA
CENTROAMÉRICA
N

Presentation

Read the Cultura viva on this page. You may wish to have students locate Cuba on a map of the Western Hemisphere to illustrate its strategic location in the Caribbean.

Did You Know?

Often called the "Pearl of the Antilles," Cuba is located about 90 miles from the southern tip of Florida. Havana is the largest city and its commercial and industrial center. It is also the largest and one of the oldest cities in the the West Indies. About twenty percent of the Cuban population lives in Havana.

Critical Thinking Activity
Why is Cuba is called the "Pearl of the Antilles"?

Actividades

Actividad A Answers
Answers will vary.

Actividad B Answers
el azúcar, la isla, el valle

Actividad C Answer
a

Learning from Photos and Maps

You may want to have students look at the photo and map on page 363. Have them tell what kinds of activities Cubans who go to **la playa de Varadero** can do. Have students look at the map and locate Florida. Also have them identify the other islands to the south, east, and northeast of Cuba (Jamaica; Haiti and the Dominican Republic; the Bahamas).

Pronunciation

A. You may wish to play the recorded version of this pronunciation activity, located at the end of Cassette 5.4. You may also wish to write this verse on the board and have students copy it into their notebook.
Yo soy un hombre sincero
de donde crece la palma,
y antes de morirme quiero

echar mis versos del alma.
("Versos sencillos" by José Martí, poeta cubano, 1853-1895)

B. Have students repeat words and phrases individually and in unison. You may also want to play the song "Guantanamera" by the Sandpipers, which features this verse.

Bell Ringer Review

Directions to students: Make four columns on your paper: **mar, lago, río,** and **piscina.** Then list each of the following activities under the appropriate column, according to where you would be likely to do each activity. Some activities might appear in more than one column.

bucear
ir de pesca
pasear en velero
nadar
saltar las olas
tomar el sol
practicar el esquí acuático

Structure Focus

In this lesson **nuestro(s)/ nuestra(s)** will be presented. Students will learn how to say what they and others possess in common.

Learning from Realia

You may want to have students look at the realia on page 364. Have students guess at the meaning of "**cariño.**" You may also have them write a brief message for the inside of the card.

Presentation

A. Lead students through the explanation on page 364.

B. Ask students for various items belonging to them. Add some that belong to you. Display items around the room. Ask questions such as: **¿Dónde están nuestros lápices? ¿Cómo es nuestro libro?**

364

Estructura 1

How to Say What People Possess Nuestro(s) / Nuestra(s)

You have learned to say what is yours, his, hers, and theirs, using **mi, tu,** and **su** to describe one possession and **mis, tus,** and **sus** to describe several.

> **Mi papá está enfermo.**
> **¿Cómo están tus padres?**
> **Señora, ¿cómo está su hija?**

You have also indicated what belongs to someone else by using **de** + person.

> **Es la camiseta de Fernando.**
> **Me gustan las clases del señor García.**

When you want to talk about what you and someone else have, use **nuestro, nuestra, nuestros,** or **nuestras,** depending on what or whom you are describing.

> **En nuestra casa debemos hablar español.**
> **Nuestros padres son cubanos.**
> **Nuestro maestro de inglés es del Canadá.**

The following chart summarizes how to say what people possess.

SINGULAR	PLURAL
mi casa	mis padres
tu casa	tus cosas
su maestro	sus clases
nuestro tío	nuestros discos
nuestra tía	nuestras clases

En Tu Cumpleaños, Mamá
CON NUESTRO CARIÑO

Actividades

A **Somos amigos.** Think of a friend whose likes are similar to yours. Write down your and your friend's favorite people and things, using the categories below.

Por ejemplo:

> un deporte
> *Nuestro deporte favorito es el béisbol.*

1. un programa de televisión
2. un equipo
3. una comida
4. una clase
5. una película
6. un disco
7. un conjunto musical
8. un/a cantante
9. un actor
10. una actriz

B **Un extranjero.** A visitor from Argentina comes to your class and asks all about your town, school, and Spanish class. Respond to the questions, either as a class or in groups.

Una fiesta de cumpleaños en Buenos Aires. ¿Cuántos años tiene el niño?

Por ejemplo:

> En su clase de español, ¿qué hacen?
> *En nuestra clase leemos, hablamos y estudiamos.*

1. En su ciudad, ¿qué hay?
2. En sus fiestas, ¿qué hacen?
3. En sus clubes, ¿qué hacen?
4. En su estado, ¿cuáles son las ciudades más grandes? ¿las ciudades más divertidas?
5. En su escuela, ¿cuántos estudiantes hay?

Actividades

Actividad A Answers
Answers will vary but should include the following.

1. Nuestro programa favorito...
2. Nuestro equipo favorito...
3. Nuestra comida favorita...
4. Nuestra clase favorita...
5. Nuestra película favorita...
6. Nuestro disco favorito...
7. Nuestro conjunto favorito...
8. Nuestro(a) cantante favorito(a)...
9. Nuestro actor favorito...
10. Nuestra actriz favorita...

Actividad B Answers
Answers will vary but should include the following.

1. En nuestra ciudad...
2. En nuestras fiestas...
3. En nuestros clubes...
4. En nuestro estado...
5. En nuestra escuela...

Learning from Photos

You may want to have students look at the photo on page 365. Have them tell who they think each of the people in the photo is in terms of family relations.

Reteaching

Have students imagine that a friend from out of town is visiting them. Have them tell him or her what things are found in their school and what there school is like. For example: **En nuestra escuela hay una biblioteca grande y moderna.**

Presentation

Read the Cultura viva on this page. Have students locate Argentina on a map.

Did You Know?

The **gaucho** was usually of mixed Spanish and Indian blood. He was an excellent horseman and spent most of his time on horseback. His costume consisted of baggy pants, silver belt, and a bright scarf. In the early days he made his living by selling the hides of wild horses. His weapon was the **bola,** a type of sling consisting of heavy balls tied to the ends of a cord. It was thrown to entangle and capture cattle or game. During the 1800s, the **gaucho** became a symbol of the Argentine nation and its values.

The **gaucho's** way of life ended with the invention of refrigerated ships, which facilitated the rapid development of the international meat industry. Today, day laborers have largely replaced the **gauchos** in Argentina.

Critical Thinking Activity

What are the differences and similarities between the American cowboy and the **gaucho**?

Actividades

Actividad A and B Answers
Answers will vary.

Actividad C Answers
Answers will vary but may include the following.

1. **En Argentina hay muchos inmigrantes. En los Estados Unidos también hay muchos inmigrantes.**
2. **Como en Argentina, gran parte del territorio norteamericano es una extensa "pampa".**

366

La Argentina

Los parientes de Carmen viven en la Argentina, en Sudamérica. La Argentina es el país más grande del mundo hispano. Tiene una población de unos 31 millones de habitantes y 14 o 15 millones de ellos viven en el área metropolitana de Buenos Aires, la capital del país.

Como los Estados Unidos, la Argentina es un país de inmigrantes. Los inmigrantes forman el 95 por ciento de la población nacional. Son principalmente de Europa: Italia, Alemania, Rusia, Polonia, Hungría, Inglaterra, Irlanda e Escocia.

Gran parte del territorio argentino es una extensa pampa, donde hay grandes haciendas, en que trabajan los gauchos —los vaqueros o "cowboys" **argentinos.**

Actividades

A Describe the region where you live: **una ciudad grande / la capital del estado (del país) / el campo / las afueras** (suburbs) **de una ciudad.**

B Which is the principal group of immigrants in your area?

Por ejemplo:

> Hay muchos _____ donde yo vivo.

C Tell one thing that Argentina has in common with the U.S.

Por ejemplo:

> En la Argentina _____. También en los Estados Unidos _____.

En Buenos Aires.

En la pampa.

Estructura 2

How to Say with Whom You Do Things

The preposition **con**

1. To say with whom you do something, use the word **con** and the name of the person or the appropriate pronoun (him, her, you, them, us).

SINGULAR	PLURAL
conmigo	**con nosotros(as)**
contigo	**con vosotros(as)** *
con Juan (con él)	**con mis amigos (con ellos)**
con María (con ella)	**con mis hermanas (con ellas)**
con usted	**con ustedes**

*This form is rarely used in the Spanish-speaking world, except for Spain.

2. Notice that to say "with me" and "with you" (a friend), you use **conmigo** and **contigo**.

> **¿Quieres ir al cine conmigo?**   Sí, gracias.
> **¿José va contigo al partido?**   No, no puede.

3. To ask "with whom?", say **¿con quién?**

> **¿Con quién fuiste al cine anoche?**   Fui con Marilú.

Actividades

A **¿Con los amigos o con la familia?**
Name six places you like to go or things you like to do with others.

Por ejemplo:

> **hablar por teléfono**
> *Me gusta hablar por teléfono con mi amiga Eva.*

Una familia urgentina que vive en el campo.

Cooperative Learning

After students have completed **Actividad A** on page 367, have teams categorize all their answers into two columns: **lugares** and **cosas**. They roundtable the paper until all members have written their comments under each category. Then they add a third category: **con quién**. The paper is roundtabled again, with everyone adding the name of the person.

Estructura 2

Structure Teaching Resources
1. Workbook, pp. 163–164
2. Cassette 5.4
3. Student Tape Manual, p. 132
4. Estructura Masters 5.4
5. Lesson Quizzes, p. 109

Bell Ringer Review

Directions to students: Use a possessive adjective to show who owns each of the following items in your home. Since **su** can have several meanings (''his, her, your, their''), give an explanation, as in the model. **Mi, tu,** and **nuestro** do not need to be explained because they can only mean one thing.
Por ejemplo: su sofá (el sofá de mi mamá)

1. _____ casa
2. _____ perro
3. _____ gato
4. _____ estéreo
5. _____ cámara
6. _____ coche
7. _____ patio
8. _____ videojuegos

Structure Focus
The words **conmigo** and **contigo** are presented in this lesson. The preposition **con**, introduced in Chapter 1, and subject pronouns, introduced in Chapter 3, are reinforced here.

Presentation

A. Lead students through steps 1–3 on page 367.

B. Ask students to do certain things with you. **¿Quieres ir conmigo al gimnasio? ¿Quieres conmigo a la cafetería?**

Actividades

Actividad A Answers
Answers will vary.

B ¿Con quién? Tell things you do with the following people and pets.

Por ejemplo:

> tu hermano
> *Juego tenis con él los domingos.*

1. tu amiga   4. tus padres
2. tu amigo   5. tus primos
3. tu mamá   6. tu perro (gato, caballo, etc.)

C ¿Qué dices? What would you say in response to each of the following situations?

Por ejemplo:

> Tu amigo te dice que no puede ir contigo a la fiesta.
> (A tu amigo:) *¿Por qué no puedes ir conmigo a la fiesta?*

1. Tus padres están enojados contigo y no sabes por qué.
2. Tu mamá dice que tienes que ir al banco con ella pero no quieres.
3. Tu hermana mayor dice que no puedes ir al centro con ella.
4. No sabes por qué tus padres te dicen que no debes salir con Bruno.
5. Tus primos van a ver una película estupenda y quieres ir con ellos.
6. Quieres invitar a Julia a ir contigo al concierto.

Unos estudiantes argentinos.

D ¿Quieren ir conmigo? Work in groups of three or four. One person in the group will invite the others to do something after school or on the weekend. Another person will report back to the class.

Por ejemplo:

ESTUDIANTE A
¿Quieren ir al cine conmigo?

ESTUDIANTE B
Sí, cómo no.

ESTUDIANTE C
No puedo ir contigo. Tengo que trabajar.

(A la clase:) Todd y Alicia van a ir al cine pero Julie dice que no puede ir con ellos porque tiene que trabajar.

Finalmente

Finalmente

Situaciones

Situaciones

A conversar

1. Your partner will invite you to go someplace with him or her.
2. If you've already gone there, tell when. If you haven't gone, ask what the place is like. Also find out what the two of you can do there.
3. Decide on a day and time for your visit.

A escribir Write a letter to a friend inviting him or her to go with you to the beach this summer **(este verano)**.

1. Tell where you plan to go.
2. Tell when you will leave, how much time you will spend there, and when you will return.
3. Tell all the activities that the two of you can do at the beach.
4. Ask if your friend already knows how to do several water activities.
5. Tell what activities you can teach him or her to do, or that you both can learn to do.

Repaso de vocabulario

PREGUNTA
¿cuánto tiempo?

POSESIÓN
nuestro(a)

ACTIVIDADES
asistir a
bucear
enseñar a (to teach how to)
gastar (dinero)
invitar (a)
ir de pesca
pasar (tiempo)
pasear en velero
planear

practicar el esquí acuático
saltar las olas
tomar el sol

OTRAS PALABRAS Y EXPRESIONES

conmigo
contigo
estupendo(a)
el mar

Lección 4   **369**

Situaciones

Lesson 4 Evaluation
The **A conversar** and **A escribir** situations on this page are designed to give students the opportunity to use as many language functions and as much vocabulary in this lesson as possible. the **A conversar** and **A escribir** are also intended to show how well students are able to meet the lesson objectives.

Presentation

Prior to doing the **A conversar** and **A escribir** on this page, you may wish to play the **Situaciones** listening activities on Cassette 5.4 as a means of helping students organize the material.

For the Native Speaker

Have students make up invitations to a party they will give this weekend. They must come up with a theme and answer when, why, what, where, etc. You may wish to display invitations on a bulletin board.

Lección 5

Objectives

By the end of this lesson, students will be able to:

1. say how long they and others have been doing something
2. correct themselves as they speak, using "**digo,...**"
3. say what they did at one point in the past
4. tell or ask a friend or relative what he or she did
5. report what someone says or hears
6. say what they and others request

Lesson 5 Resources

1. Workbook, pp. 165–169
2. Vocabulario Transparencies 5.5
3. Cassette 5.5
4. Student Tape Manual, pp. 135–139
5. Lesson Quizzes, pp. 110–113
6. Computer Software, Disk 2
7. Video Cassette
8. Estructura Masters 5.5
9. Diversiones Masters 5.5

Bell Ringer Review

Directions to students: Tell whether each of the following items refers to Cuba or to Argentina. Make two columns and list each item under the appropriate column.

1. **Es la llave del Golfo.**
2. **La Habana es su capital.**
3. **Buenos Aires es su capital.**
4. **Exporta azúcar.**
5. **Exporta carne.**
6. **Hay pampas.**
7. **Es una isla tropical.**
8. **Viven allí muchos inmigrantes de Europa**.

Lección 5

Somos todos americanos

¡A comenzar!

The following are some of the things you will be learning to do in this lesson.

When you want to . . .	You use . . .
1. say how long someone has been doing something	• **Hace** + time + **que** + activity.
2. correct yourself as you speak	• **Digo...**
3. say what you did	• **-i** on the end of **-er** and **-ir** verbs
4. tell a friend or relative what he or she did	• **-iste** on the end of **-er** and **-ir** verbs

Now find examples of the above words and phrases in the following conversation.

Los cubanos llegan de Cuba a Miami en 1963.

370 CAPÍTULO 5

Cooperative Learning

Carmen's intermingling of English and Spanish words is called "codeswitching." After completing Actividad preliminar B, have teams come up with other examples of codeswitching. Have teams cut up strips of paper. On one strip they write a Spanish word and on another its English equivalent. Then distribute the various strips around the room and have students match up the English and Spanish words. For example:

ESTUDIANTE A	ESTUDIANTE B
"Milk."	Digo, leche.

Carmen habla con su mamá.

CARMEN: **Mamá, no me molesta practicar el español, ¿entiendes? Pero hace casi treinta años que ustedes están aquí. Tú saliste de Cuba en el sesenta y tres, y papá en el sesenta y cuatro.**

MAMÁ: **Sí, hija. Salí de Cuba en el sesenta y tres, pero nací en la isla y allí viví diez y seis años.**

CARMEN: **Pero yo nací aquí en la Florida y aquí aprendí a hablar inglés. Somos todos "Americans", digo, americanos. ¿Por qué es tan importante el español?**

Actividades preliminares

A Complete the sentences below to tell how many days, months, or years you have been doing the following.

1. Hace _____ que vivo aquí.
2. Hace _____ que estudio español.
3. Hace _____ que me gusta la música de _____.

B Carmen continually mixes English with her Spanish. Help her correct herself in the following sentences.

Por ejemplo:

> Somos todos "Americans".
> *Somos todos "Americans", **digo, americanos.***

1. **Mira, papá, quiero comprar estas dos "T-shirts".**
2. **Son de puro "cotton".**
3. **Estamos aquí desde "nineteen sixty-three".**
4. **Me gusta mucho la clase de "computers".**
5. **¿Me prestas la "magazine" nueva?**

Lección 5 **371**

Bell Ringer Review

Directions to students: With whom did you go to the following places last year? Choose five and write a complete sentence about each one. Begin with **Fui**. Add a date if you wish.

Por ejemplo: el mar
Fui al mar con mi papá.
Fuimos en agosto.
un concierto
la piscina
un partido de baloncesto
la playa
un partido de fútbol americano
la biblioteca
el parque
la fiesta de tus amigos

Presentation

A. Have students open their books to page 372.
  1. Model each new phrase on pages 372 and 373. Have students repeat each phrase in unison.
  2. Ask individual students the following questions, allowing them to answer with just the time period (**dos meses, tres años, media hora, etc.**).
     ¿Cuánto tiempo hace que...
     a. haces cola?
     b. juegas en el equipo de baloncesto (vóleibol, tenis, etc.)?

Vocabulario

¿Cuánto tiempo hace que...?

Hace tres días que estoy enferma.

Hace catorce años que estamos aquí.

(de 1977 a 1991)

(lunes, martes, miércoles)

Hace mucho tiempo que conozco* a Paco.

Hace poco tiempo que la señorita Chávez conoce a sus vecinos.

Hace seis meses que estudio español.

(del 2 de abril a el 15 de abril)

Hace dos meses que pertenezco* al club de español. Las reuniones son muy divertidas.

(de septiembre a marzo)

Hace un mes que Anita pertenece al club de ajedrez.

(de septiembre a octubre)

(de noviembre a enero)

*Conocer and pertenecer are regular -er verbs, with the exception of the yo form: conozco and pertenezco.

Total Physical Response

Getting Ready
Make copies of the vocabulary transparencies and give one to each student.

New Words
el corazón   la estrella
el globo   la cara
feliz   serio(a)

TPR 1

Hagan un círculo en la reunión del club de español.
Hagan un rectángulo en la chica que espera.
Dibujen un corazón en la muchacha con la gripe.
Dibujen una estrella en el chico que compra entradas.

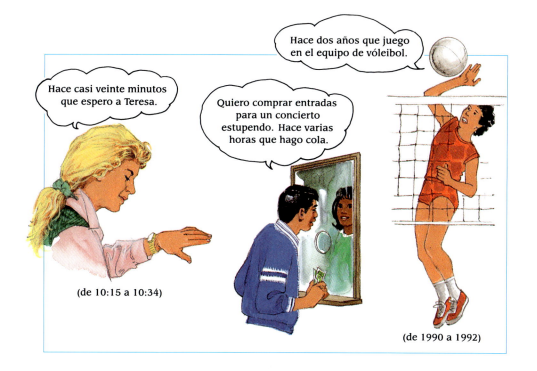

Hace casi veinte minutos que espero a Teresa.

(de 10:15 a 10:34)

Quiero comprar entradas para un concierto estupendo. Hace varias horas que hago cola.

Hace dos años que juego en el equipo de vóleibol.

(de 1990 a 1992)

Actividades

A **Una escuela internacional.** Many of Carmen's classmates and teachers are from Cuba as well as other countries. Below are their names, their countries of origin, and the years they left their countries. Tell each person's nationality and how long he or she has been in Miami.

Por ejemplo:

> Rodrigo: Guatemala, 1988
> *Rodrigo es guatemalteco. Hace _____ años que está en Miami.*

1. Manuel: la Argentina, 1980
2. Graciela: Nicaragua, 1982
3. Margarita: Costa Rica, 1990
4. la Srta. Camacho: Cuba, 1963
5. el Sr. Jiménez: la República Dominicana, 1975
6. la Sra. Costas: el Ecuador, 1969

Lección 5 **373**

c. tocas *(instrumento)*?
d. sabes *(hacer algo)*?
e. conoces a _____?
f. perteneces al club de _____?

3. Ask pairs of students how long they have been friends. **¿Cuánto tiempo hace que son amigos(as)?**

Actividades

Actividad A Answers
The years of residence will vary.

1. **Manuel es argentino. Hace... años que está en Miami.**
2. **Graciela es nicaragüense...**
3. **Margarita es costarricense...**
4. **La Srta. Camacho es cubana...**
5. **El Sr. Jiménez es dominicano...**
6. **La Sra. Costas es ecuatoriana...**

Coloquen un cuadro en los nuevos vecinos.
Dibujen una cara feliz en la chica que está en el equipo de vóleibol.
Dibujen una cara seria en la chica que espera.
Dibujen una cara muy feliz en el chico que hace cola para las entradas.
(Interchange commands with other vocabulary. Use a transparency to check results.)

TPR 2

Escriban "¡Qué lástima!" en el globo de la chica enferma.
Escriban "¡Estupendo!" en el globo del chico que compra entradas.
Escriban "¡Caramba!" en la foto del club de ajedrez.
Escriban "Mucho gusto" en el globo de los nuevos vecinos.
(Check answers with a transparency.)

B **¿Cuánto tiempo hace que los conoces?** Say how long you have known the following people.

Por ejemplo:

> tu amigo _____.
> *Hace varios meses que conozco a mi amigo Paco.*

1. tu amiga _____
2. tu amigo _____
3. tu maestro(a) de español
4. tu maestro(a) de educación física
5. un vecino
6. una vecina

C **¡Paciencia!** How long do you have to wait for the following people or things? Also tell whether or not you have to wait in line.

Por ejemplo:

> el autobús
> *A veces espero diez minutos. (No) Tengo que hacer cola.*

1. en la oficina del dentista
2. para comprar entradas en el cine
3. la nota después de un examen
4. en la cafetería a la hora de comer
5. a tu amigo(a) en el centro comercial
6. para comer en un restaurante
7. en el supermercado
8. en la tienda de vídeos

D **Somos miembros.** Ask a classmate if he or she belongs to the school clubs and teams below. Also find out how long he or she has been a member. Reverse roles.

Por ejemplo:

> el club de vídeo

ESTUDIANTE A	ESTUDIANTE B
(1) ¿Perteneces al club de vídeo?	(2) Sí.
(3) ¿Cuánto tiempo hace que perteneces al club?	(4) A ver... hace casi tres meses que pertenezco al club.

el club...
  de ajedrez
  de español
  de esquí
  internacional
  de agricultores
  de periodismo

el equipo de...
  baloncesto
  béisbol
  tenis
  fútbol
  fútbol americano
  vóleibol

For the Native Speaker
Write a 150-word composition telling how long your family has lived in the U.S. and what you like and dislike about living here.

Los cubanoamericanos

Aunque hoy día muchos cubanos son ciudadanos de los Estados Unidos, todavía son parte de dos culturas. Para los cubanoamericanos es muy importante mantener su idioma y cultura originales. También quieren mantener contacto con los amigos y familiares de su tierra. Muchos cubanoamericanos mandan dinero, ropa y medicinas a sus parientes y amigos que viven en la isla.

Carmen es parte de una nueva generación de cubanoamericanos que vive en dos culturas: la cubana (el idioma, la música, las costumbres, la comida, la familia) y la norteamericana (la escuela, las actitudes de sus compañeros de clase, las películas, la televisión).

Actividades

A In the first paragraph, to what place do the following phrases refer?

su tierra / la isla / la cultura original

B Cuban Americans live in two cultures. In the second paragraph, find as many things as you can that make up a "culture."

Open Abierto

ABIERTO DE
8:00 A.M. A 7:00 P.M.
LUNES A SABADO
COBRO DE:
LUZ, GAS Y TELEFONO
MONEY ORDERS

SE HABLA ESPAÑOL

Lección 5 **375**

Cultura viva 1

Presentation

Read the Cultura viva on this page. You may wish to discuss with your students the contributions of Cuban Americans to American society.

Did You Know?

Many other ethnic groups in the U. S. have maintained strong ties to their native culture and language. You may wish to have students identify those groups in your area.

Critical Thinking Activity

In groups, have students discuss the following questions.

1. If you had to leave your country, what would you miss the most?
2. What would be the most dificult thing to adjust to in your new country?
3. What do you think would be the most difficult thing about living in two cultures?

Actividades

Actividad A Answers
Cuba.

Actividad B Answers
El idioma, la música, las costumbres, la comida, la familia, la escuela, las actitudes de la gente, las películas, la televisión.

Pronunciation

A. You may wish to play the recorded version of this pronunciation activity, located at the end of Cassette 5.5. You may also wish to write these lines on the chalkboard and have students copy them into their notebook.
**Hace quince años
nací en la Florida:
chispa de cubana,**
lengua americana.

B. Have students repeat words and phrases individually and in unison. You may wish to focus on the elision of vowel sounds across word boundaries. For example:
"quinceaños"
"nacíen"
"lenguaamericana"

375

Bell Ringer Review

Directions to students: On your paper, draw a picture representing each of these new vocabulary words.

1. la entrada
2. la reunión
3. hacer cola
4. el ajedrez
5. el equipo

Structure Focus

In this lesson the **yo** and **tú** forms of the preterit of -**er** and -**ir** verbs are presented. The **yo** and **tú** forms of -**ar** verbs will be presented in Lesson 6.

Note: The following are infinitives students have used but whose preterit forms will not be introduced in Level 1.

decir   traer
querer   tener
poder

Presentation

1. Before presenting the **yo** and **tú** -**er** and -**ir** forms of the preterit, remind students of the difference between the present and the past. For example: **Hoy voy a la biblioteca. Ayer fui al gimnasio. Hoy tú vas al cine. Ayer tú fuiste al estadio,** etc.

2. Now lead students through steps 1–5 on page 376.

3. After presenting the preterit you may wish to have students practice the stressed -**í** as a quick drill. Give them an infinitive and have them give you the first person form, clapping hands or tap-

376

Estructura 1

How to Say What You Did, What I Did

Yo *and* tú *forms of the preterit of* -er *and* -ir *verbs*

You have already learned to say where you went in the past. You have also learned to ask where a friend or family member went.

> **Anoche fui a casa de mi amiga Carmen.**
> **¿Fuiste a la fiesta de Juan Carlos el sábado pasado?**

1. To tell other things you did in the past using -**er** or -**ir** verbs, replace the -**er** or -**ir** with the ending of the past (preterit) tense: -**í.** You must write an accent mark over the letter **i** to indicate that it is stressed when you pronounce the word.

escribir	Ayer escribí una carta a mi prima.
salir	El domingo pasado salí con mis amigos.
comer	No comí en la cafetería ayer.

2. When you talk about people or things you saw (**ver**), there is no written accent over the **i.**

   > **Anoche vi una película fantástica. Y en el cine vi a mi primo Carlos.**

3. To tell or ask a friend or relative what he or she did in the past using -**er** or -**ir** verbs, replace the -**er** or -**ir** with -**iste.**

escribir	¿Ya escribiste a tu abuela?
aprender	¿Aprendiste el vocabulario nuevo?
ver	¿Viste a Irene en la clase de inglés?

4. To ask a friend what he or she did, say **¿Qué hiciste?**

   > **¿Qué hiciste cuando fuiste a California?**

5. To say that you didn't do anything, say **No hice nada.**

   > **Anoche no salí. No hice nada.**

These two forms (**hice, hiciste**) are the past tense (preterit) forms of the verb **hacer.**

Una clase de química en Buenos Aires.

Cooperative Learning

Play the game of "Teléfono." The person sitting in the first seat of each row creates a "rumor" and passes it down the row. The last person writes it on the board. The person who started the "rumor" is asked to say **verdad** or **falso** to the "rumor". Remind students not to say anything that might be embarrassing or offensive.

Actividades

A **¿Qué viste?** Tell three things or people you saw on your way to school this morning.

Por ejemplo:

> Vi a mi amiga Raquel.
> Vi un gato negro en la calle Oak.

B **Te vi ayer.** Tell three classmates that you saw each of them with someone yesterday and say where (even if it's not true). Each classmate will say whether it is possible or not.

Por ejemplo:

ESTUDIANTE A	ESTUDIANTE B
Sam, te vi ayer con Carmen en la reunión del club de español.	No me viste allí con ella. (Sí, es posible).

C **¿Qué viste?** Ask two classmates how many hours they watch television during the week. Then ask what programs they saw last week.

Por ejemplo:

ESTUDIANTE A	ESTUDIANTE B
(1) ¿Cuántas horas a la semana ves la tele?	(2) Veo la tele seis horas a la semana.
(3) ¿Qué programas viste la semana pasada?	(4) Vi _____.

D **¿Qué hiciste ayer?** Answer the following questions about what you did yesterday.

1. ¿Saliste anoche? ¿Con quién?
2. ¿Leíste un libro ayer? ¿Cuál?
3. ¿Viste a todos tus amigos ayer? ¿A quiénes? ¿Dónde?
4. ¿Comiste algo delicioso? ¿Qué comiste? ¿Dónde?
5. ¿Recibiste una carta? ¿De quién?
6. ¿Fuiste a una reunión? ¿Dónde? ¿Con quién?

El correo argentino.

ping their pencils on their desks at the sound of the stressed syllable. For example:

Maestro(a): salir
Estudiante: sa-*lí* (clap)

Actividades

Actividades A, B, and C Answers
Answers will vary but should follow the model.

Actividad D Answers
Answers will vary but should include the following

1. (No) Salí...
2. (No) Leí...
3. (No) Vi...
4. (No) Comí...
5. (No) Recibí...
6. (No) Fui...

Actividad E Answers
Answers will vary but should include the following.

1. ¿A qué hora saliste...?
2. ¿... hiciste...?
3. ¿... viste...?
4. ¿... fuiste...?
5. ¿... comiste...?

Actividad F Answers
Answers will vary.

Reteaching

Choose several **-er** and **-ir** infinitives and write them on the board. Ask individual students to tell you whether or not they did each of the activities yesterday. Then have them ask a classmate if he or she did any of the activities.

E **¿A qué hora?** Ask a classmate what time he or she did the following things yesterday. Then ask if he or she always does each thing at that time.

Por ejemplo:

> hacer la cama

ESTUDIANTE A	ESTUDIANTE B
(1) ¿A qué hora hiciste la cama ayer?	(2) A las siete.
(3) ¿Siempre haces la cama a las siete?	(4) Sí, siempre. (No, no siempre).

1. salir para la escuela
2. hacer la tarea de español
3. ver a tus amigos
4. ir a la clase de inglés
5. comer en la escuela

F **Chismes.** Make up a rumor about what three of your classmates have done. They will say whether the rumor is true (**"Es verdad"**) or false (**"No es verdad"**) and give an explanation. Use the verbs suggested below.

leíste	saliste	perdiste	hiciste	recibiste
comiste	viste	fuiste	aprendiste	escribiste

Por ejemplo:

> recibiste / escribiste

ESTUDIANTE A	ESTUDIANTE B
(1) Sandra, dicen que recibiste una "A" en el examen de álgebra.	(2) Es verdad. Siempre saco buenas notas en álgebra.
(3) Paul, dicen que escribiste en tu pupitre (desk).	(4) ¡No es verdad! Nunca escribo en mi pupitre.

Una compañera de clase.

Una carta de la Argentina

Buenos Aires
6 de abril

Queridísima Alicia:

Muchas gracias por la invitación a Miami. Te llamé anoche para hablar del viaje, pero nadie contestó. Rafael va a ir conmigo a Miami. Está muy entusiasmado con la idea de visitar los Estados Unidos. Vamos a llegar el día 20 de abril a las 7:55 de la mañana, vuelo de Aerolíneas Argentinas número 445. Recibí el cheque que me mandaste. Gracias, hermanita.

Si no me llamas este domingo, te llamo el lunes por la noche.

¡Hasta pronto!

Un fuerte abrazo de tu hermano que te quiere,

Lucas

Actividad

From Lucas's list of things to do, tell which he did by answering **sí** or **no**.

1. escribir a Alicia
2. llamar a Alicia
3. hacer las reservaciones en Aerolíneas Argentinas
4. hacer las compras para Alicia
5. recibir el cheque de Alicia
6. hacer las maletas
7. mandar a Alicia la información sobre el vuelo

Presentation
Read the Cultura viva on this page.

Did You Know?
Lucas and Rafael plan to fly Aerolíneas Argentinas to Miami. Most airline companies in Latin America are government-owned. For example: LAN Chile (Líneas Aéreas Nacionales de Chile), Aeronaves del Perú, Air Panamá Internacional, Aerolíneas de Guatemala, Aviateca, Aeroméxico, Viasa (Venezolana Internacional de Aviación).

Critical Thinking Activity
In groups, have students plan a trip to a Latin American city. Have them do research to answer the following questions. What airline would they take? Can they take a direct flight? If not, where do they have to stop?

Actividad Answers
1. Sí.
2. Sí.
3. Sí.
4. Sí.
5. Sí.
6. No.
7. Sí.

Learning from Photos
You may want to have students look at the photo on page 379. Have students guess what sorts of things Rafael likes to do in his free time. Also have students think of five things that Rafael has to do to prepare for his upcoming trip to Miami.

Bell Ringer Review

Directions to students: Tell how long you've been doing each of the following.

1. estudiar español
2. jugar _____.
3. conocer a tu amigo(a) _____
4. escuchar la música de _____
5. vivir en tu casa (apartamento)

Structure Focus

The present tense of the verbs **decir, oír,** and **pedir** are presented in this lesson. Students will learn how to report what others say, hear, and request.

Presentation

A. Lead students through steps 1–3 on page 380.

B. To introduce **oír**, ask individual students simple questions. When they respond, pretend you didn't hear, gesturing and saying **¿Cómo? No te oigo.** List on the board different noises you hear in the class. For example:
Oigo a Jane abrir un libro.
Oigo a Ralph hablar con su compañero, etc.
Summarize by saying, **Oímos muchas cosas.** Then lead them through step 4.

Estructura 2

How to Report What Someone Says or Hears	The verbs decir and oír
How to Request Things	The verb pedir

You have already seen some forms of the verb **decir**, which means "to say" or "to tell." For example, when you use the wrong word and want to correct yourself, you have said **digo**.

> **Todos somos** "Americans", **digo, americanos.**

To report or summarize what someone said, you have used **Dice(n) que...**

> **Miguel dice que Juanita está enferma hoy.**
> **Mis padres dicen que no puedo salir esta noche.**

1. The following are all the forms of **decir** in the present tense.

SINGULAR	PLURAL
digo	decimos
dices	decís*
dice	dicen

¿Qué dices? No te oigo.

2. Use a form of **decir** when you want to quote directly what someone says to you.

> **Siempre me dice: "Eres muy guapa".**

3. Use a form of **decir** to summarize what someone says to you.

> **Siempre me dice que soy muy guapa.**

4. You use the verb **oír** to tell what you and others hear. The following are all the forms of **oír** in the present tense.

SINGULAR	PLURAL
oigo	oímos
oyes	oís*
oye	oyen

5. The verb **pedir** ("to request, to ask for, or order something") changes from **e** to **i** in the same way **decir** does.

SINGULAR	PLURAL
pido	pedimos
pides	pedís*
pide	piden

Cuando vas a la cafetería, ¿qué bebida **pides**?
Para su cumpleaños mi hermana siempre **pide** ropa.

*This form is rarely used in the Spanish-speaking world, except for Spain.

Actividades

A **¿Qué me dices?** Ask a classmate what he or she says in the following situations.

Por ejemplo:

cuando salgo de clase

ESTUDIANTE A
¿Qué me dices cuando salgo de clase?

ESTUDIANTE B
Te digo ¡Adiós!

1. cuando te doy un regalo
2. cuando te digo gracias
3. cuando te llevo tu mochila
4. cuando no puedes salir conmigo
5. cuando te pido dinero
6. cuando te digo algo increíble

B **¿Qué dicen?** What do you and your friends say about the following?

Por ejemplo:

Los maestros dicen que ustedes van a tener clases los sábados.
Nosotros decimos que no queremos ir a la escuela los fines de semana.

1. Su maestro dice que ustedes deben tener muchos exámenes.
2. Dicen que la comida de la cafetería es excelente.
3. Los padres dicen que deben regresar a casa antes de las once de la noche.
4. Los dentistas dicen que los jóvenes no deben comer postres.

Lección 5 **381**

C. To introduce **pedir,** tell students something like the following: **Cuando voy a un restaurante, pido carne y legumbres. Mi esposo(a) pide pollo y una ensalada. Mis hijos piden hamburguesas y papas fritas. Todos pedimos helado. Y tú, ¿qué pides?**
Then lead them through step 5.

Actividades

Actividades A and B Answers
Answers will vary.

C **¿Qué oyen?** Tell what or whom the people below might be hearing, according to where they are.

Por ejemplo:

> Miguel está en una fiesta.
> *Oye música (un vídeo musical, una guitarra, a sus amigos).*

1. Los turistas están en el parque zoológico.
2. Estás en tu habitación.
3. Tú y los compañeros están en tu casa. Escuchan la radio.
4. Estoy en la oficina del veterinario.
5. Maricarmen está en la casa de sus tíos en el campo.
6. Jorge y Elena están en la clase de español.

D **Todos me piden favores.** Tell one possession the following people frequently request from you.

Por ejemplo:

> tu mamá
> *Mi mamá me pide la bicicleta.*

1. tu compañero(a) de clase
2. tu papá
3. tus hermanos
4. tus maestros
5. tu abuelo(a)
6. tu amigo(a)

E **Los platos favoritos.** Working with a classmate, find out what each of you usually orders to eat in the following places or circumstances. Then report back to the class.

Por ejemplo:

> en la cafetería de la escuela

ESTUDIANTE A	ESTUDIANTE B
(1) ¿Qué pides en la cafetería de la escuela?	(2) Pido hamburguesas. ¿Y tú?
(3) Yo también.	

(A la clase): Miguel y yo pedimos hamburguesas en la cafetería.

1. en un restaurante muy elegante
2. en un partido de béisbol
3. en un restaurante mexicano
4. en McDonald's
5. el día de tu cumpleaños

Finalmente

Finalmente

Situaciones

Situaciones

A conversar Converse with a classmate about birthday gifts.

1. Find out what gifts your partner asked for on a recent birthday.
2. Find out what gifts he or she actually received.
3. Ask which gift your partner likes best. Ask him or her to describe it.
4. Find out what your partner plans to ask for next year.
5. Reverse roles.

A escribir Write a note to a friend describing a memorable weekend. Include details about places you went, with whom, what you did and saw, what new friends you met **(Conocí a...),** what new things you may have learned how to do, and special foods you ate.

Repaso de vocabulario

PREGUNTA
¿Cuánto tiempo hace que...?

ACTIVIDADES
conocer (-zco)
decir
esperar
hacer cola
oír
pedir
pertenecer (-zco)

PERSONA
el/la vecino(a)

COSAS
el club
la entrada
el equipo
la hora (hour)
el minuto
la reunión
el tiempo

OTRAS PALABRAS
casi
varios(as)

EXPRESIÓN
Hace... que...

CRAZY LOBSTER

LANGOSTA · LOCA

MIAMI · FLORIDA

SERVICIO A DOMICILIO
Con un día de anticipación
Teléfono: 266-3033

Lección 5 **383**

For the Native Speaker

1. Explain in a composition your feelings about living in two cultures. Be sure to mention the advantages, disadvantages, as well as your likes and dislikes.
2. Write a 150-word composition describing the advantages of being bilingual.

Situaciones

Lesson 5 Evaluation
The **A conversar** and **A escribir** situations on this page are designed to give students the opportunity to use as many language functions and as much vocabulary from this lesson as possible. The **A conversar** and **A escribir** are also intended to show how well students are able to meet the lesson objectives.

Presentation
Prior to doing the **A conversar** and **A escribir** on this page, you may wish to play the **Situaciones** listening activities on Cassette 5.5 as a means of helping students organize the material.

Learning from Realia
You may want to have students look at the realia on page 383. Have them guess what "servicio a domicilio" and "con un día de anticipación" mean.

Lección 6

Objectives

By the end of this lesson, students will be able to:

1. say what they do for another person
2. say what they did at one point in the past
3. tell a friend or family member what he or she did at one point in the past
4. name common household chores
5. give a result of an action, using **por eso**

Lesson 6 Resources
1. Workbook, pp. 170–175
2. Vocabulario Transparencies 5.6
3. Cassette 5.6
4. Student Tape Manual, pp. 140–144
5. Lesson Quizzes, pp. 114–116
6. Test Booklet, pp. 89–97
7. Video Cassette
8. Computer Software, Disk 2
9. Estructura Masters 5.6
10. Diversiones Masters 5.6

Bell Ringer Review

Directions to students: Which of the following statements are true about your life? Which are false? Turn your notebook paper sideways and make two columns at the top (**Verdad** and **Mentira**). List each of the following statements under the appropriate column.

1. **Nunca pido hamburguesas en los restaurantes.**
2. **Nunca oigo música en la sala de mi casa.**
3. **Siempre digo la verdad.**
4. **Cuando no comprendo algo,**

Lección 6

El idioma es muy importante

¡A comenzar!

The following are some of the things you will be learning to do in this lesson.

When you want to . . .	You use . . .
1. say what you do for another person	• **Le** + activity + **a** + person.
2. say what you did at one point in the past	• **-é** at the end of **-ar** verbs
3. tell a friend or family member what he or she did at one point in the past	• **-aste** at the end of **-ar** verbs
4. tell a friend or family member what he or she gave	• **diste** + object
5. give a result of an action ("therefore," "that's why")	• **por eso**

Now find examples of the above words and phrases in the following conversation.

Getting Ready for Lesson 6

You may wish to use the following suggestion to prepare students for the lesson.

1. Give students a list of things you did and intended to do yesterday, using regular **-ar** verbs. For example:
   1. **llamar a mamá**
   2. **firmar el formulario**
   3. **cortar el césped**
   4. **mandar cartas**
   5. **planchar la ropa**
   6. **lavar el coche**
   7. **limpiar la casa**
   8. **preparar una comida especial**
2. Tell students about your day yesterday. Say that you just didn't get around to doing some things. Have students cross off of their lists the things you were able to accomplish.

Sigue la conversación entre Carmen y su mamá.

CARMEN: **Mamá, no me escuchaste.**

MAMÁ: **Claro que te escuché, hijita.**

CARMEN: **Pues, entonces...**

MAMÁ: **Mira, Carmencita, tú puedes hablar inglés todo el día en la escuela, con tus amigos, por todas partes. Pero también somos cubanos y el idioma es muy importante para nosotros.**

CARMEN: **Pero, mamá...**

MAMÁ: **Escúchame, Carmen. Cuando le hablaste ayer a tu papá en inglés, cuando olvidaste las palabras en español, le diste la impresión de que no respetas ni el idioma ni nuestra cultura. Por eso le debes hablar en español.**

Actividades preliminares

A Complete the following sentences to say what you do for the people indicated.

1. **A mi maestro le doy _____ todos los días.**
2. **A mi hermano le doy _____ para su cumpleaños.**
3. **A mi hermano nunca le presto mi(s) _____.**
4. **A mi amigo le compro _____ porque le gusta(n) mucho.**

B Give a result of the following actions, using **por eso**.

Por ejemplo:

> **Enrique nunca estudia.**
> *Por eso saca malas notas (no sabe contestar en clase, etc.).*

1. **Mi papá no me puede llevar a la escuela hoy.**
2. **A Raúl no le gusta practicar la guitarra.**
3. **Hace tres días que Susana llega tarde a la clase de español.**

---

le pido ayuda al (a la) maestro(a).

¡A comenzar!

Presentation

A. Lead students through each of the five functions given on page 384, progressing from the English to the Spanish for each function. Then have students find these words and phrases in the dialogue.

B. Introduce the Lesson 6 dialogue by reading it aloud or by playing the cassette version.
Tell students that they will hear a conversation between Carmen and her mother about something Carmen has done that hurt her father's feelings. Have students listen to the tape of the **Lección 6** dialogue to find out how Carmen's father interprets her constant use of English in the home. This may require two listenings.

C. Ask students to open their books and look at the dialogue as you guide them with the following questions.
   1. **Carmen cree que su mamá no escucha. ¿Qué dice?**
   2. **Su mamá le contesta. ¿Qué dice?**
   3. **Según la mamá, ¿cuándo puede hablar inglés Carmen?**
   4. **Según la mamá, ¿qué le molesta al papá? ¿Cómo lo explica la mamá?**
   5. **¿Qué favor le pide la mamá a Carmen?**

Actividades preliminares

Actividad A Answers
Answers will vary.

Actividad B Answers
Answers will vary but may include the following.

1. **Por eso tengo que ir en bicicleta (llegar tarde).**
2. **Por eso no puede tocar bien.**
3. **Por eso el maestro está enojado.**

---

3. Follow up by asking about each thing on your list. For each thing that you failed to do, students should respond with **No. ¿Por qué no _____ hoy?** For example:
MAESTRO(A): ¿Llamé a mi mamá ayer?
ESTUDIANTE: No. ¿Por qué no llama hoy?

Vocabulario

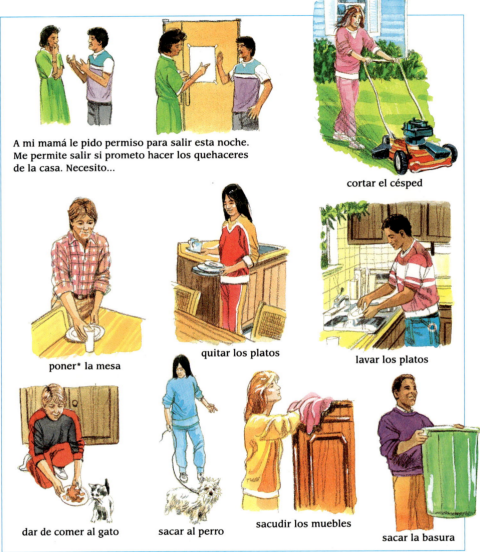

A mi mamá le pido permiso para salir esta noche. Me permite salir si prometo hacer los quehaceres de la casa. Necesito...

cortar el césped

poner* la mesa

quitar los platos

lavar los platos

dar de comer al gato

sacar al perro

sacudir los muebles

sacar la basura

*The **yo** form of **poner** is **pongo**.

386 CAPÍTULO 5

Vocabulary Teaching Resources
1. Vocabulario Transparencies 5.6
2. Workbook, pp. 170–171
3. Cassette 5.6
4. Student Tape Manual, p. 141
5. Lesson Quizzes, p. 114

Presentation

A. Have students open their books to page 386.
  1. Model each new word on page 386. Begin each phrase with **Tengo que**... Have students repeat each phrase in unison.
  2. Ask individual students whether or not they have to do the chores on pages 386 and 387. For example, **¿Tienes que poner la mesa?** Encourage students to give a complete response. For example, **Sí, tengo que poner la mesa.**

B. Ask students questions about chores they do at home. For example:
  1. **¿Cuándo cortas el césped? ¿En qué meses no lo tienes que cortar?**
  2. **¿Quién plancha en tu casa?**
  3. **¿En qué habitaciones pasas la aspiradora?**
  4. **En tu casa, ¿quién da de comer al gato?**
  5. **¿Para qué pides permiso?**
  6. **¿Quién saca la basura?**

Note: Students will not be able to use the preterit of **poner**. The preterit of **poner** will be introduced in Level 2.

386

Total Physical Response

Getting Ready
Bring to class real items or pictures of items for the underlined vocabulary in the activity. Arrange items or pictures on a table. Students will be using a combination of real items, pictures, and pantomime to perform the TPR.

TPR 1
(Call on pairs of students.)
Quiten los platos de la mesa.
Pónganlos en la silla cerca de la puerta.
Saquen la basura.
Pongan la basura en el pasillo.
Sacudan los pupitres y mi escritorio.
Vayan a la silla donde están los platos.
Laven los platos. Pónganlos en la mesa.
Corten el césped.

cuidar a mi hermano menor

pasar la aspiradora

barrer el piso

planchar la ropa

A mi papá le explico mis problemas.

Me da buenos consejos.

Le presento a mis amigos.

A mi amigo le vendo mi estéreo.

Me paga veinte dólares.

Lección 6 **387**

Actividades

A **Le hago favores.** Tell whether or not you do the following favors for your best friend.

Por ejemplo:

> prestar dinero
> *Le presto dinero (No le presto dinero).*

1. mandar tarjetas postales cuando vas de vacaciones
2. dar regalos caros para su cumpleaños
3. explicar tus problemas
4. prometer decir la verdad (truth)
5. permitir usar tus cosas
6. presentar a tu familia
7. dar buenos consejos

B **¿Tienes que pedir permiso?** Tell whether or not you must ask permission at home to do the following things.

Por ejemplo:

> salir con tus amigos
> *(No) Tengo que pedir permiso para salir con mis amigos.*

1. escuchar música
2. invitar a un(a) amigo(a) a casa
3. ver la tele
4. ir al cine por la tarde
5. salir por la noche
6. dormir en casa de un(a) amigo(a)
7. comer en casa de un(a) amigo(a)
8. dar una fiesta
9. ir a una fiesta
10. hablar por teléfono
11. regresar a casa después de las diez de la noche
12. vender tu radio o tu grabadora

En la cocina después de comer. ¿Qué hace el muchacho?

C **¿Estrictos o no?** Tell how often your mother or father allows you to do each of the things in activity **B**.

Por ejemplo:

> salir con tus amigos
> *Mi mamá siempre me permite salir con mis amigos.*

D **Los quehaceres de la casa.** Find out from a classmate if he or she does the following household chores. Reverse roles and report back to the class.

Por ejemplo:

limpiar la habitación

ESTUDIANTE A	ESTUDIANTE B
En tu casa, ¿tienes que limpiar la habitación?	Sí, todos los sábados. (No, es el quehacer de mi hermana mayor).

(A la clase): Elena tiene que limpiar la habitación todos los sábados. (En la casa de Elena su hermana mayor limpia la habitación).

En un parque de Miami.

1. dar de comer al perro (gato, conejo, etc.)
2. sacar la basura
3. cocinar
4. poner la mesa
5. quitar los platos
6. lavar los platos
7. sacar al perro
8. cuidar a los hermanos menores
9. pasar la aspiradora
10. sacudir los muebles
11. cortar el césped
12. lavar el coche
13. hacer la cama
14. planchar la ropa
15. barrer el piso

E **Buenos negocios.** Make a list of some of your possessions that you are willing to sell. Share the list with a classmate. Your classmate tells you what items he or she would like to buy. Come to an agreement on the price of each item. Choose from the items below or think of your own.

bicicleta	casetes	grabadora	muebles
cámara	colecciones	historietas	revistas
camisetas	discos	juegos de mesa	vídeos musicales
carteles	estéreo	libros	videojuegos

Por ejemplo:

ESTUDIANTE A	ESTUDIANTE B
(1) ¿Me vendes tu cámara de marca Kodak?	(2) Depende. ¿Cuánto me pagas?
(3) Bueno, te doy veinte dólares.	(4) Es muy poco. La cámara es casi nueva.
(5) No puedo pagar más.	(6) Bueno, está bien.

Lección 6 **389**

Presentation
Read the Cultura viva on this page.

Critical Thinking Activities
In groups, have students write a list of diminutives in English. For example: John (Johnny), Thomas (Tom, Tommy), dog (doggy), etc. How are these words formed? How are they different from diminutives in Spanish?

Actividad Answers
1. mi hermanito
2. mi primita
3. mi perrito
4. mi gatito
5. mi conejito

Learning from Photos
You may want to have students look at the photos on page 390. Have them guess what the relationship between the girl and the woman might be. Also have students tell what the girl is doing.

Los diminutivos

Cuando Carmen habla con su mamá, su mamá le dice "hijita" y "Carmencita". Cuando el tío Lucas le escribe a la mamá de Carmen, le dice "hermanita". Cuando la mamá le contesta sus cartas, le dice "hermanito".

Los hispanos usan *-ito* e *-ita* al final de los nombres de las personas para indicar que sienten cariño por esas personas.

Actividad

How would you refer to the following to show affection?

Por ejemplo:
tu abuela
mi abuelita

1. tu hermano
2. tu prima
3. tu perro
4. tu gato
5. tu conejo

Pronunciation

A. You may wish to play the recorded version of this pronunciation activity, located on Cassette 5.6. You may also wish to write these lines on the chalkboard and have students copy them into their notebook.
Mamacita, cómprame un regalito.
Papacito, ayúdame un poquito.
Hermanita, hazme un favorcito.
Abuelito, préstame un dinerito.

B. Have students repeat words and phrases individually and in unison. You may wish to focus on the /t/ sound: **mamacita, papacito, poquito, hermanita,** etc.

Estructura 1

How to Say What You Do to or for Another Person

Indirect object pronoun le

You have used **me** to request a favor for yourself or to describe favors done for you.

> **¿Me puedes prestar un sello?**

You have used **te** to offer a favor to a friend or a family member or to describe what you do for him or her.

> **Te puedo dar cinco dólares.**

1. To say that someone is doing something to or for another person, use **le** + activity.

   > **Pobre Miguel está enfermo. Sus amigos le hacen muchos favores.**

2. Also use **le** to say what you do to or for someone you address formally **(usted).**

   > **Señorita, le doy mi tarea esta tarde.**

3. The words **me, te,** and **le** go before the verb form that indicates who is doing the action. Word groups such as **voy a decir, puedo dar,** and **quieres prestar** cannot be broken up. The words **me, te** and **le** go before them.

   > **Te puedo dar mi tarea de inglés.**
   > **¿Me quieres prestar tu bolígrafo?**

4. If you use the word **no,** it goes before the **me, te,** or **le.**

   > **No le voy a decir mis secretos.**

5. Since **le** can refer to him, her, or you **(usted),** you will sometimes need to clarify who the **le** is. You do this by adding **a** + the name of the person.

   > **Todos los meses Ron le manda cartas** *a Raquel,* **pero Raquel no le escribe** *a Ron* **porque ella no sabe inglés.**
   > **Señora, le voy a prestar cinco dólares** *a usted,* **pero no le puedo prestar nada** *a Miguel.*

Lección 6 **391**

Structure Teaching Resources
1. Workbook, pp. 172–173
2. Cassette 5.6
3. Student Tape Manual, p. 141
4. Estructura Masters 5.6
5. Lesson Quizzes, p. 115

Bell Ringer Review

Directions to students: Tell whether you heard or saw the following things or events. Make two columns: **Oí** and **Vi.** List each item under the appropriate column. Could some fit in both categories?

la tele
el partido de tenis
el postre
los exámenes
el casete
la música rock
el centro comercial
la fiesta
la cola
el león
el videojuego
los platos

Structure Focus

In this lesson the indirect object pronoun **le** will be presented. Students will learn how to say what they do to or for another person. Students have already used **le + gusta(n)** to talk about the likes and dislikes of someone else. Students learned to use the indirect object pronouns **me** and **te** in Lesson 1 of this chapter. They will learn **les** and **nos** in Chapter 6, Lessons 1 and 2, respectively.

Presentation

1. Act out situations such as **Le doy consejos a Manuel. Le pago cinco dólares a Irma. Le prometí a Tom no dar mucha tarea esta noche.**
2. Lead students through steps 1–5 on page 391.

391

Actividades

Actividad A Answers

Answers will vary.

Actividad B Answers

1. sé
2. contigo
3. te
4. me
5. estoy
6. me
7. dices
8. tu
9. me
10. permites
11. te
12. traigo

Actividad C Answers

1. ¿Por qué no le escribes una carta?
2. ¿... le haces un favor?
3. ¿... le das un regalo?
4. ¿... le dices "perdón"?
5. Answers will vary.

Actividades

A **¿A quién?** Name one person to whom or for whom you do each of the following things.

1. Le digo mis secretos a _____.
2. Le presto dinero a _____.
3. Le mando cartas a _____.
4. Le doy regalos especiales a _____.
5. Le hago muchos favores a _____.

B **Pobre Alfredo.** Read the story below; then complete the paragraph following it as if you were Alfredo's father.

Nadie sabe qué pasa con Alfredo. Cuando su papá le habla, Alfredo no le contesta. Está muy triste estos días y el papá está preocupado. No le dice nada a su papá. Prefiere estar en su habitación y tampoco le permite entrar cuando él le trae su comida.

(El papá de Alfredo le dice): Alfredo, yo no _____ qué pasa _____. Cuando _____ hablo, no _____ contestas. Veo que estás muy triste estos días. Francamente, _____ preocupado. No _____ _____ nada. Prefieres estar en _____ habitación y tampoco _____ _____ entrar cuando _____ _____ tu comida.

C **Están peleados.** Carmen had a fight with her friend Jorge. Use the ideas below to suggest things she can do for him to make up; then think of one idea of your own.

Por ejemplo:

 hablar
 ¿Por qué no le hablas?

1. escribir una carta
2. hacer un favor
3. dar un regalo
4. pedir perdón

La mamá le prepara el desayuno a su hija.

D **Hoy y mañana.** Name two things you do for someone else during the course of the day. Then name two things you are going to do for someone tomorrow.

Por ejemplo:

> Todos los días le hablo a mi amiga
> Eva por teléfono...
> Mañana le voy a comprar un regalo
> a mi hermano...

Unos amigos en Miami.

E **Le quiero presentar a mis amigos.** Tomorrow a local Hispanic businesswoman will come to your Spanish class. Practice introducing four of your classmates to her. Also say something about each one.

Por ejemplo:

> Señora, le quiero presentar a Tony. Tony pertenece al
> equipo de baloncesto. Juega muy bien.

F **¿Qué le dices?** In the situations below, what would you say to or ask each person?

Por ejemplo:

> a tu prima cuando te visita
> *Le pregunto si quiere escuchar mi nuevo disco.*

1. a tu mamá o a tu papá cuando te pide sacar la basura
2. a tu amigo cuando no puedes ir a una fiesta porque tienes que cuidar a tu hermano menor
3. a tu maestro cuando no haces la tarea
4. a tu amigo cuando te pide consejos
5. a tu mamá o a tu papá cuando te pide poner la mesa
6. a tu abuela cuando le dices que necesitas cinco dólares
7. a tu compañero de clase cuando le dices que sacaste una "A" en el examen

Lección 6 **393**

Cultura viva 2

El lenguaje: algo muy frágil

Para los inmigrantes hay, en realidad, dos problemas enormes. El primero es adaptarse rápidamente y aprender el idioma del nuevo país. El segundo es mantener el idioma materno —el idioma de los padres, los abuelos y los bisabuelos.

Parece increíble, pero puedes perder tu idioma. Tu idioma es muy frágil y si no lo usas, lo puedes olvidar. Los extranjeros que vienen a los Estados Unidos dicen que después de sólo dos años de no usar su idioma, empiezan a tener problemas con el vocabulario.

Actividades

A The following are some words used to describe what can happen to our language. Decide which of these words relate to remembering the language **(recordar)** and which relate to not remembering **(no recordar)**. List them in the appropriate category.

1. abandonar
2. mantener
3. perder
4. olvidar
5. usar
6. practicar

B What two pieces of advice can you give a classmate about what he or she should do over summer vacation so as not to forget the Spanish he or she has learned this year?

Por ejemplo:

Debes hablar español con los amigos por teléfono.

Estructura 2

How to Say What You Did and Ask What a Friend Did

Yo and tú forms of the preterit of -ar verbs

You have learned to say what you did and to ask a friend what he or she did in the past using -er and -ir verbs.

¿Qué hiciste anoche?   Fui al cine.
¿Viste a Julia allí?   Claro, ¡salí con ella!

1. To talk about what you did in the past using -ar verbs, use -é to replace the -ar.

   Estudié mucho anoche. Terminé mi composición a las diez y media.

2. To ask what a friend did in the past using -ar verbs, use -aste to replace the -ar.

   ¿Le hablaste a tu papá anoche? ¿Le enseñaste tus notas?

3. The verb **dar** is irregular in the preterit tense. Although it is an -ar verb, it uses endings of -er and -ir verbs: **di, diste.**

   ¿Qué le diste a Sara?   **Le di una camiseta.**

Actividades

A **Favores que le hice yo.** Tell for whom you did each of the following favors recently. If you didn't do one of the favors, use the sentence *No le (activity) a nadie.*

Por ejemplo:

mandar una carta
Le mandé una carta a mi abuelo (No le mandé una carta a nadie).

1. enseñar unas fotos
2. comprar un regalo
3. ayudar
4. presentar a tus amigos(as)
5. prestar discos
6. dar dinero

Cooperative Learning

After completing **Actividad C,** p. 396 each team will come up with their own list of seven questions and then exchange papers with another team. The other team will answer the questions.

Estructura 2

Structure Teaching Resources
1. Workbook, pp. 174–175
2. Cassette 5.6
3. Student Tape Manual, p. 142
4. Estructura Masters 5.6
5. Lesson Quizzes, p. 116

Bell Ringer Review

Directions to students: Draw a picture representing the following household chores. Be prepared to tell the class who does these chores in your home.

1. planchar la ropa
2. barrer el piso
3. sacar al perro
4. lavar los platos
5. pasar la aspiradora

Structure Focus
The **yo** and **tú** forms of the preterit of -ar verbs will be presented. Students will learn how to say what they did and ask a friend what he or she did.

Presentation

1. Review the **yo** and **tú** forms of the preterite of -er and -ir verbs. Tell students what you did yesterday: **Ayer fui a un restaurante y comí pescado. Después leí un libro y escribí una carta.**
2. Lead students through steps 1–3 on page 395.

Actividades

Actividad A Answers
Answers will vary but should include the following.

1. Le enseñé unas fotos a... (No le enseñé fotos a nadie).
2. Le compré un regalo a...
3. Le ayudé a...
4. Le presenté a mis amigos a...
5. Le presté discos a...
6. Le di dinero a...

B **Para mí, es muy fácil.** Ask a classmate if he or she did the activities below yesterday. Your classmate will answer and tell his or her opinion of that activity, choosing from the following words.

interesante   fácil   difícil   aburrido   divertido

Por ejemplo:

gastar mucho dinero

ESTUDIANTE A	ESTUDIANTE B
¿Gastaste mucho dinero ayer?	Sí, para mí es fácil gastar dinero.

1. escuchar música
2. cuidar niños
3. practicar deportes
4. ayudar a mis padres
5. limpiar la habitación
6. estudiar mucho
7. llamar a mis amigos

C **Este año y el año pasado.** Compare this school year to last year, considering the following questions.

Por ejemplo:

¿Vas a muchos partidos?
Este año voy a muchos partidos pero el año pasado fui a dos partidos.

1. ¿Qué estudias?
2. ¿Vas a muchas reuniones?
3. ¿Lees muchos libros?
4. ¿Haces muchas tareas?
5. ¿Sales con muchos amigos?

Unos compañeros de clase.

D **Lugares.** What would you say you did in the following places?

Por ejemplo:

en la tienda
Vi camisetas bonitas pero no compré nada.

1. en la biblioteca
2. en la escuela
3. en el parque
4. en casa
5. en la playa
6. en el trabajo
7. en casa de los abuelos
8. en la fiesta
9. en las vacaciones

Finalmente

Finalmente

Situaciones

Situaciones

A conversar Converse with a classmate about your activities last weekend.

1. Ask your partner what he or she did at various times during the weekend. Find out where your partner went, what he or she did, and with whom. Give your reactions.
2. Reverse roles.

A escribir There's a special meeting you want to attend next week in school, but it's at the same time as Spanish class. You must get your teacher's permission to attend the meeting. Write your teacher a note of explanation.

1. Ask for permission to go to the meeting.
2. Give the date you will not be in class.
3. Promise to do the homework for that day.
4. Tell what favor you will do for your teacher if he or she allows you to go to the meeting.

Repaso de vocabulario

ACTIVIDADES
barrer
cortar el césped
dar consejos a
dar de comer (al gato, al perro, etc.)
explicar
hacer los quehaceres
pagar
pasar la aspiradora
pedir permiso (para)

permitir
planchar
poner la mesa
presentar
prometer
quitar los platos
sacar la basura
vender

OTRA PALABRA
el problema

Situaciones

Lesson 6 Evaluation
The **A conversar** and **A escribir** situations on this page are designed to give students the opportunity to use as many language functions and as much vocabulary from this lesson as possible. The **A conversar** and **A escribir** are also intended to show how well students are able to meet the lesson objectives.

Presentation

Prior to doing the **A conversar** and **A escribir** on this page, you may wish to play the **Situaciones** listening activities on Cassette 5.6 as a means of helping students organize the material.

For the Native Speaker

Have students write a 150–word composition about what they did during their last vacation.

Lectura

You may want to stress the following points to your students.

1. A good technique that helps you to understand a reading selection is to try to predict what the selection is about before you read it. You can do that by reading the title and subtitles and looking at the pictures and drawings, as well as by using what you know about the topic before you read about it.

2. Look for cognates to help you predict what the reading is about. For example: **ritmos, clásica, trópico, tradicional.**

   Before reading the **Lectura,** you may wish to have students discuss in groups the following questions related to the **Lectura** topic.

   a. What are some of the dances that come from Cuba?

   b. Why would people in other countries be interested in Cuban dances?

Discussing the above questions will help students think about the theme of the **Lectura.**

Lectura

You will be able to figure out many of the words in the following reading from the context in which they appear or because they look like English words that have similar meanings. First, look over the article below and complete activities **A** and **B.** Then, after reading the article more carefully, complete activities **C** and **D.**

DANZA

Los ritmos de la danza afrocubana clásica invaden la Plaza España de Madrid

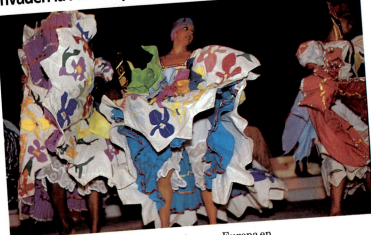

La llegada de nuevos inmigrantes cubanos a Europa en estos últimos años ha despertado el interés por los ritmos afrocubanos, especialmente en España, donde el número de exiliados es mayor. En numerosas escuelas de ballet y danza madrileñas se puede escuchar, junto al tradicional sonido de palmas y castañuelas, los ritmos sensuales del trópico expresados con exquisito lirismo por bailarines clásicos, verdaderos maestros en su género, como María Elena García, que baila en todas partes, "¡hasta en la mismísima Plaza España, y Olé!".

Actividades

A List the words you know or think you recognize in the above reading.

Por ejemplo:

> nuevos, inmigrantes, cubanos...

B The following look like Spanish words you've learned. Can you identify the root word?

Por ejemplo:

> llegada
> *(looks like)* **llegar**

1. madrileñas
2. numerosas
3. expresados
4. verdaderos

C Which of the following could be an appropriate title for this article?

1. Cubanos de vacaciones en Madrid
2. La música del trópico llega a España
3. La Plaza España —sitio de muchos conciertos

D Answer the following questions about the above article.

1. Según la primera frase de este artículo, ¿qué país europeo tiene más cubanos exiliados?
2. ¿Cómo describe el artículo la música tradicional de España? ¿Cómo describe la música de Cuba?
3. Según el artículo, ¿por qué es tan popular en España la danza afrocubana?

El Ballet Folklórico de Cuba.

400

Capítulo de Repaso

Tell three places you went last week and with whom.

Repaso Resources
1. Workbook, pp. 176–177
2. Cassette 5.6
3. Student Tape Manual, pp. 145–146
4. Video Cassette

¿Recuerdas?

Presentation

To review Chapter 5, call on individual students to give an example for each communicative function listed for Lecciones 1–3; and Lecciones 4–6, p. 400. The numbers in parentheses on page 400 refer to the actual page(s) in Chapter 5 where each function was presented and practiced. You may wish to have your students go back to these pages for additional review and practice before going on to the Actividades, pages 401-403

Lecciones 1–3 Answers

The following words and phrases are examples for each of the eleven functions lister under Lecciones 1–3. These words and phrases should be included in the students response to each function listed.

1. ¿Me puedes... ?
2. Te puedo...
3. la cosa, el aparato...
4. Se dice...
5. Mi(s) amigo(s) me...
6. alemán(ana), boliviano(a), cubano(a), español(ola), etc.
7. Mi novecientos noventa y dos, etc.
8. Vivo aquí desde 1991, etc.
9. Dos mil, cuatro mil quinientos, un millón etc.
10. fui, fuiste, fue, fuimos, fueron
11. ayer, la semana pasada, anoche, etc.

Capítulo 5 Repaso

¿Recuerdas?

Do you remember how to do the following things, which you learned in **Capítulo 5**?

LECCIONES 1–3

1. ask favors of others (p. 328)
2. offer favors to a friend or family member (p. 331)
3. describe things you don't know the name for in terms of size, shape, material, and use (p. 340)
4. give the meaning of a word in Spanish (p. 340)
5. ask or say what others do to or for you (p. 343)
6. give nationalities and tell what languages people speak (pp. 348–349)
7. give the year an event occurred (p. 352)
8. say that something has been going on since a certain date (p. 352)
9. give numbers to the millions (p. 352)
10. say where you and others went (p. 355)
11. tell when you and others went places (p. 355)

LECCIONES 4–6

1. say what belongs to you and others (p. 364)
2. talk about activities you do with others (p. 367)
3. say or ask how long someone has been doing something (pp. 372–373)
4. tell what you did at one point in the past (pp. 376, 395)
5. ask or tell a friend what he or she did in the past (pp. 376, 395)
6. report what you and others say (p. 380)
7. tell what you and others request or ask for (p. 380)
8. say what you do for others (p. 391)

Actividades

A **Regalos de cumpleaños.**

1. List the things your relatives or friends typically give you for your birthday.

Por ejemplo:

> Mis abuelos me dan ropa.

2. List three items you are going to ask your parents for on your next birthday.

Por ejemplo:

> Les voy a pedir un estéreo...

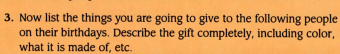

Un padre con su hija.

3. Now list the things you are going to give to the following people on their birthdays. Describe the gift completely, including color, what it is made of, etc.

a. a tu amigo(a)

b. a tu maestro(a)

c. a tu abuelo, tía, hermano, madre, etc.

B **Persuasión.** You want permission from your mother or father to do something. Offer to do something for him or her in exchange.

Por ejemplo:

> Mamá, si me haces un cheque para comprar _____, yo te lavo la ropa.

C **Amigos otra vez.** List three or four things that you would do to make up with a friend after an argument.

Por ejemplo:

> Le puedo decir que _____. También le puedo mandar _____ o le puedo ayudar con _____.

Lecciones 4–6 Answers

The following words and phrases are examples for each of the eight functions listed under Lecciones 4–6. These words an phrases should be included in the students' response to each function listed.

1. nuestro(a)/nuestros(as)
2. contigo, con él, ellos, ella(s), usted(es)
3. Hace que
4. Escribí, comí, escuché, etc.
5. escribiste, comiste, escuchaste, etc.
6. digo, dices, dice, decimos, dicen; oigo, oyes, oye, oímos, oyen
7. pido, pides, pide, pedimos, piden
8. Le...

Actividades

Presentation

Each practice activity in this Repaso of Chapter 5 reviews several of the language functions listed on page 400. Students are asked to use the language they have learned at a higher, more integrated level, compared to the individual practice activities in Lessons 1–6 of Chapter 5.

Actividades A, B, and C Answers
Answers will vary.

Actividad D Answers

1. *El Universal es un periódico venezolano.*
2. *El Miami Herald*... estadounidense (norteamericano)
3. *El Espectador*... colombiano.
4. *El Día*... uruguayo.
5. *El Heraldo de México*... mexicano.
6. *El País*... español.
7. *El Diario/La Prensa*... estadounidense (norteamericano).

Actividad E Answers

1. Answers will vary.
2. ¿Cómo te llamas? / ¿Cuándo empezaste a estudiar aquí? (¿Cuándo llegaste?) / ¿Cuándo naciste? / ¿Cuántos años tienes? / ¿Cómo se llama tu papá? ¿tu mamá? / ¿Con quién vives? / ¿Cuál es tu dirección? ¿tu número de teléfono? / ¿Dónde viviste antes? / ¿En qué escuela estudiaste? / Answers will vary
3. Les quiero presentar a...

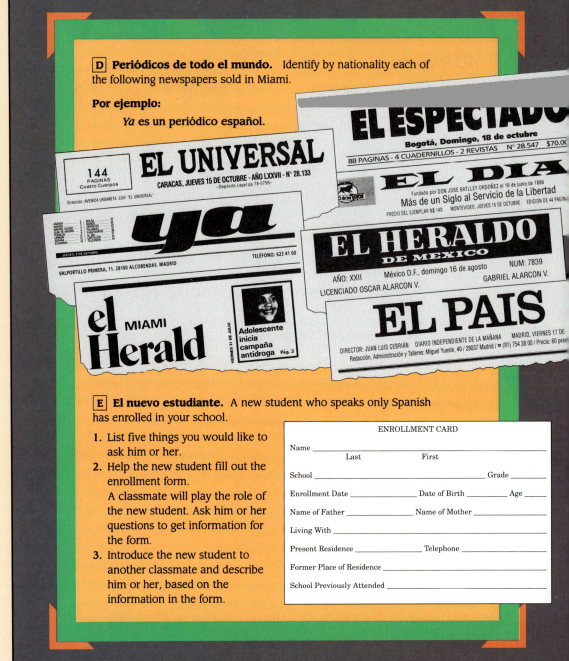

D **Periódicos de todo el mundo.** Identify by nationality each of the following newspapers sold in Miami.

Por ejemplo:

Ya es un periódico español.

E **El nuevo estudiante.** A new student who speaks only Spanish has enrolled in your school.

1. List five things you would like to ask him or her.
2. Help the new student fill out the enrollment form.
   A classmate will play the role of the new student. Ask him or her questions to get information for the form.
3. Introduce the new student to another classmate and describe him or her, based on the information in the form.

ENROLLMENT CARD

Name _____
    Last   First

School _____ Grade _____

Enrollment Date _____ Date of Birth _____ Age ____

Name of Father _____ Name of Mother _____

Living With _____

Present Residence _____ Telephone _____

Former Place of Residence _____

School Previously Attended _____

F **Diccionario moderno.** Make a list of four or five special
words you use with friends that might not be understood by persons
from a different generation or region. Give a definition in Spanish
for each word or expression. Share the list of definitions with the
class and see if they agree.

Por ejemplo:

"dude"
Es un muchacho.

G **Bienvenido.** List five or six things you could do to welcome a
new student.

Por ejemplo:

Le puedo enseñar dónde está la cafetería.

H **Un viaje.** You have just come back from an exciting trip and
try to persuade a classmate to take a trip to the same place, telling
all the places one can visit, the things one must see, and what one
should do there. Your classmate will ask you what you did there,
where you went, and what you saw.

Por ejemplo:

ESTUDIANTE A	ESTUDIANTE B
Fui a _____. Es fantástico.	Ah, ¿sí? ¿Cuándo fuiste?

I **El sospechoso.** Alicia wasn't home last night when Bruno
called. He asks her where she went, with whom, and then makes
accusations, which she denies. Play the roles of Bruno and Alicia
with a partner. End up as friends again—somehow.

Por ejemplo:

ESTUDIANTE A	ESTUDIANTE B
¿Adónde fuiste anoche?	...
¿Con quién?	...
¿Qué hiciste?	...
¡Qué va! Yo sé que...	...

Chapter Overview

Cultural setting

This chapter continues with Carmen Marín and her family in Miami. We also meet Carmen's uncle Lucas and her cousin Rafael, from Buenos Aires, Argentina, who come to spend several weeks with the Marín family. The major cultural issues deal with

- the confusion that can arise over the disparity between the metric system and the system used in the U.S. for measuring height, weight, distances, and clothing;
- the difference in seasons between the Northern and Southern hemispheres.

Rationale

A The presentation of the preterit is completed in this chapter: first person plural endings are introduced in Lesson 1, third person singular endings in Lesson 3, and third person plural endings in Lesson 4. A summary and practice of all preterit forms is given in Lesson 6.

B Presentation of indirect object pronouns is also completed here. The functions of **me, te,** and **le** should be solidly rooted by now. Students should not have trouble grasping the functions of the plural forms **les** and **nos.**

C The third person direct object pronouns **lo, la, los,** and **las** are presented in Lesson 4. No attempt is made to contrast the use of indirect and direct object pronouns. This distinction will be made and practiced in Level 2.

D Finally, to enable students to compare and contrast persons and things, the functions of **tanto como, tanto(a)... como, más (menos)... que** are introduced.

We hope you enjoy the remainder of your stay in Miami!

Estructura

This chapter focuses on the following:

- identification of articles of clothing and accessories
- use of **les** to tell what you do for others
- use of **nos** to tell what people do for you and others
- identification of means of transportation
- giving and getting directions
- telling what you and others did in the past
- referring to people and things already mentioned
- describing the weather
- describing and asking how you and others feel

De visita en Miami

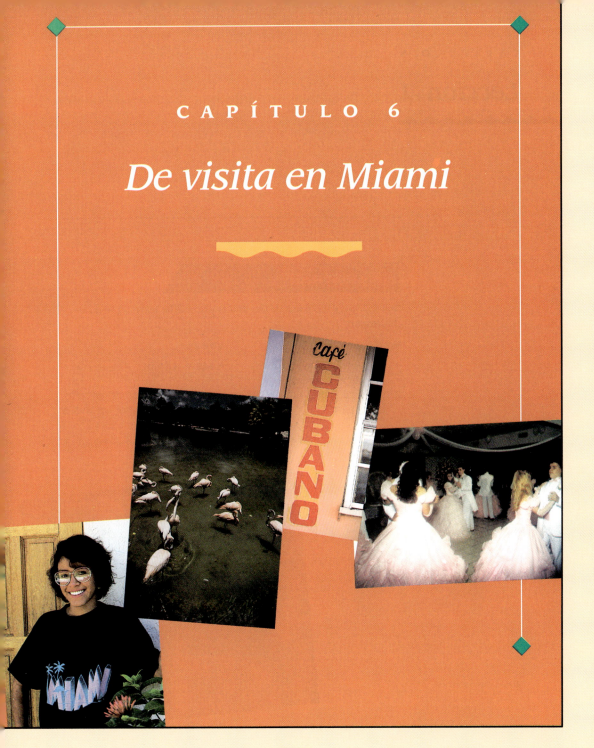

- comparing and contrasting people and things
- giving weights, measurements, and distances
- distinguishing one thing from another

A complete listing of the language functions of this chapter appears in the Repaso section on page 486.

Lección 1

Objectives

By the end of this lesson, students will be able to:

1. talk about doing something for others
2. tell what they and others did in the past
3. name articles of clothing

Lesson 1 Resources

1. Workbook, pp. 178–182
2. Vocabulario Transparencies 6.1
3. Cassette 6.1
4. Student Tape Manual, pp. 147–151
5. Lesson Quizzes, pp. 117–120
6. Computer Software, Disk 2
7. Video Cassette
8. Estructura Masters 6.1
9. Diversiones Masters 6.1

Bell Ringer Review

Directions to students: Write as many expressions as you can using each of these verbs: **dar, pedir, hacer, pasar, sacar.**

¡A comenzar!

Presentation

A. Lead students through each of the two functions given on page 406, progressing from the English to the Spanish for each function. Then have students find these words and phrases in the advertisement on page 407.

B. Introduce the Lesson 1 advertisement by reading it aloud or by playing the cassette version. Have students listen to determine the following:

Lección 1

¡Liquidación de temporada!

¡A comenzar!

The following are some of the things you will be learning to do in this lesson.

When you want to . . .

1. talk about doing something for others **(ustedes)**
2. tell what you and others did in the past

You use . . .

- **Les** + activity.
- **-amos** on the end of **-ar** verbs
- **-imos** on the end of **-er** and **-ir** verbs

Now find examples of the above words and phrases in the following advertisement.

Getting Ready for Lesson 1

You may wish to use one or more of the following suggestions to prepare students for the lesson:

1. Ask for three or four volunteers to take part in a fashion show. As students walk across the front of the classroom, describe what they are wearing (**llevar**), including colors and other adjectives, for example: **elegante, sensacional, fenomenal,** etc.

2. Borrow the lost-and-found box from the school office. Screen out any objectionable items. Then go through the contents with the class, naming and describing articles of clothing and having students speculate on **¿De quién es?**

Carmen lee con mucho interés un anuncio en el periódico.

¡Liquidación de temporada en Levy!

¡Grandes rebajas!

¡Ya rebajamos ropa de primavera un 50 por ciento o más! Todo para ustedes, nuestros clientes. Camisas, pantalones, chaquetas. Ropa elegante para toda la familia. Sensacional liquidación total. Descuentos increíbles.

➤ Camisas y blusas   Antes: $23.99   Ahora: sólo $11.99

➤ Pantalones de moda   Antes: $36.50   Ahora: sólo $17.50

➤ Jeans para damas o caballeros   Antes: $37.25   Ahora: sólo $18.99

Y para su comodidad, abrimos una nueva sucursal en el centro comercial Bayside. Abierto los domingos y días de fiesta de las 12 a las 5:30. Todas las tiendas abren de las 9 de la mañana a las 9 de la noche. Cerrado los domingos.

Almacenes LEVY, donde lo bueno cuesta barato.   *¡Siempre les ofrecemos lo mejor!*

Actividades preliminares

A Find out the following about what your classmates are wearing (llevar) today.

1. **¿Cuántos llevan chaqueta hoy?**
2. **¿Cuántos llevan camisa? ¿Y un suéter?**
3. **¿Cuántos llevan "jeans"?**

B Complete the following about shopping in your area.

1. **Las mejores liquidaciones en las tiendas de mi ciudad son en los meses de _____.**
2. **Me gusta comprar ropa cuando hay descuentos de un _____ por ciento.**

C Offer something to your classmates.

Por ejemplo:

> **Les doy (presto, compro, vendo) mi _____.**

Lección 1   **407**

---

1. What is being advertised?
2. Is this a grand opening, a sale, or a celebration?

C. Now ask students to open their books and look at the advertisement. Ask them to do the following:

1. Find all the words they think might relate to a sale or low prices. Possible answers are: **liquidación, rebajas, 50 por ciento, descuentos, antes… ahora, barato.**
2. Find words they recognize as articles of clothing.
3. Name articles that are for women, for men, and for both.
4. Find words related to seasonal clothing.

D. Have students look at the advertisement and give appropriate prices for the following:

1. **El mes pasado fui a Levy y compré una blusa. ¿Cuánto pagué?**
2. **Mañana le voy a comprar una camisa a mi esposo (una blusa a mi esposa). ¿Cuánto voy a pagar?**
3. **La semana pasada fui a Levy y compré pantalones. ¿Cuánto pagué? ¿Cuánto voy a pagar hoy?**
4. **Mañana voy a Levy a comprar jeans. ¿Cuánto voy a pagar? ¿Cuánto pagué hace tres meses?**

E. Have students look at the store schedule and answer the following questions:

1. **¿Cuándo está abierto el almacén?**
2. **Si quiero ir de compras el domingo, ¿adónde debo ir?**
3. **¿Hay almacenes en nuestra ciudad? ¿Cómo se llaman algunos?**
4. **¿Hasta qué hora están abiertos?**
3. **¿Están abiertos los domingos?**

Actividades preliminares

Actividades A, B, and C Answers
Answers will vary.

Vocabulario

Vocabulary Teaching Resources
1. Vocabulario Transparencies 6.1
2. Workbook, pp. 178–179
3. Cassette 6.1
4. Student Tape Manual, p. 148
5. Lesson Quizzes, pp. 117–118

Bell Ringer Review

Directions to students: Draw the appropriate number of circles on your paper to represent the members of your immediate family. Draw lines out from each circle and list the chores that each member is responsible for doing. Don't forget shopping, cooking, etc. Are the chores divided evenly or not?

Presentation

A. Have students open their books to the Vocabulario on pages 408 and 409. Lead students through the Vocabulario, beginning with the phrase **Quisiera comprar...** Have students repeat each phrase in unison.

B. You may wish to ask individual students whether they want to buy the articles of clothing or jewelry on pages 408 and 409. For example, **Daniela, ¿quieres comprar un vestido?**

C. You may wish to stand in the back of the classroom and describe students individually in terms of what they're wearing. The person being described will raise his or her hand. If students are unable to identify themselves based on the clothing description, provide more details such as hair color, etc.

Quisiera comprar...

unos pantalones

una corbata

un traje de caballero

una chaqueta

una camisa

un cinturón de cuero

unos calcetines

Ayer compré...

una blusa de algodón

un traje de baño

unas pantimedias

un vestido

unas sandalias

un traje de dama

unos shorts

una bolsa grande

unos anteojos de sol

una falda

unos tenis

408 CAPÍTULO 6

Total Physical Response

Getting Ready
Collect two sets of the articles of clothing taught in the Vocabulario. Bring in a large stuffed animal, or a dummy to dress.

New Words

denle	denles
ponte	pónganse
póngale	póngales

TPR 1

(Call on pairs of students.)
Denle las camisas a _____.
Denles las faldas a dos chicas rubias.
Denle los guantes a un chico alto.
Pónganse los anteojos de sol.
Póngale el abrigo a _____.
Póngale el vestido de baño y las medias al mono.
Pónganse las corbatas.

Hoy debes llevar...

un abrigo

una bufanda

un suéter

un gorro

un impermeable

unas botas

unos guantes

un paraguas

Me gustan las joyas. Quiero...

un collar de oro

un anillo pequeño

una pulsera de plata

unos aretes de plástico

Actividades

A **En la tienda.** Organize the words and phrases in the **Vocabulario** according to the following categories.

Por ejemplo:

> ropa para hombres
> *pantalones, camisas, corbatas...*

1. ropa para mujeres
2. ropa para jóvenes
3. artículos para mujeres
4. artículos para hombres
5. joyas

Lección 1 **409**

Quítenle el vestido de baño al mono y pónganle la bufanda.
Busquen al chico con los guantes y llévenle el suéter.
Busquen a los chicos con las chaquetas y denles los gorros.
(Continue interchanging commands and clothing items.)

TPR 2

(Individual students.)
Dale la bolsa grande a _____.
Dale el cinturón de cuero a un chico.
Ponte una sandalia.
Ponle los pantalones al mono.
Ponles las corbatas a _____ y a _____.
Ponte el impermeable.
(Continue interchanging commands and clothing.)

When Students Ask

You may wish to give students the following additional vocabulary to allow them to talk about clothes.
el piyama   la bata
el chaleco   la ropa interior

Regionalisms

You may wish to tell students that in some parts of the Spanish-speaking world the following words or phrases are alternatives to those presented in the Vocabulario.
el abrigo (el gabán) (Argentina), **(el tapado)** (Uruguay), **(el sobretodo)** (Spain);
la bufanda (el echape) (Argentina), **(el tapabocas)**
los calcetines (las medias);
la chaqueta (la chamarra) (Mexico), **(la americana)** (Spain);
la falda (la pollera) (Argentina), **(la saya)** (Caribbean);
el impermeable (la gabardina);
el suéter (el jersey) (Spain), **(la chompa)** (Perú);
el traje de baño (la trusa) (Cuba), **(el bañador)** (Spain), **(la malla)** (Argentina), **(la ropa de baño)** (Perú);
los aretes (los aritos) (Perú, Argentina), **(los zarcillos)** (Venezuela), **(los pendientes, las pantallas)** (Caribbean);
la pulsera (el brazalete);
el cinturón (el cinto, la correa) (Caribbean)

Actividades

Actividad A Answers
Answers may vary but should include the following:

1. **Vestidos, blusas, faldas, medias**
2. **Pantalones, camisetas, chaquetas**
3. **Bolsas, anteojos de sol, paraguas**
4. **Cinturones, anteojos de sol**
5. **Pulseras, anillos, collares, aretes**

B **¿De qué es?** List articles of clothing and accessories according to what they are made of.

Por ejemplo:

> artículos de plata
> *un collar, unos aretes, un anillo...*

1. artículos de algodón
2. artículos de cuero
3. artículos de goma
4. artículos de plástico
5. artículos de oro
6. artículos de lana (wool)

C **¿Qué ropa usan?** Tell what you and your classmates wear during the following months.

1. En enero llevamos _____.
2. En abril llevamos _____.
3. En julio llevamos _____.
4. En octubre llevamos _____.

D **¿Elegante o informal?** Converse with a classmate about what you wear when you go to the following places.

Por ejemplo:

> el centro comercial

ESTUDIANTE A

(1) ¿Qué ropa llevas cuando vas al centro comercial?

(3) Yo prefiero llevar pantalones, una camisa y un suéter.

ESTUDIANTE B

(2) A veces llevo "jeans" y una camiseta. ¿Y tú?

1. un partido de fútbol americano
2. una fiesta
3. un restaurante
4. la escuela

E **Las compras.** Tell where you went shopping last and what clothes or other items you bought.

Por ejemplo:

> El sábado pasado fui al centro comercial y compré un cinturón. (Anoche fui al centro, pero no compré ropa. Compré un casete).

410   CAPÍTULO 6

For the Native Speaker

Describe in detail the clothing you would use to participate in three of your favorite activities.

Cooperative Learning

Have each team make a collage of clothing. It should include items that students can describe in terms of article of clothing, material, and price. Then have the members of each team describe their collage to the class.

Los anuncios

En Miami, como en otras grandes ciudades bilingües, puedes ver anuncios en inglés y español.

La Misma de la Habana
ÓPTICA BRAVO

* Lentes de Contacto
* Armaduras de Marcas
* Envío de Espejuelos a Cuba

(305) 626-2717
603 S.W. 57 Ave. Miami, Fl.

PET'S PARADISE
nos especializamos en pájaros exóticos y todo tipo de cotorras
4085 E. 8 Ave. Hlh. Fl. 863-1966

EDICIÓN EN ESPAÑOL
LEVI'S
$15⁹⁹
Alteraciones gratis mientras Usted espera
Camisas y Blusas Compre una y reciba una por
1¢
DENIM WORLD
Abierto de 9 de la mañana a 9 de la noche excepto los domingos: de 11 a 7. Tel. (305) 393-3918.

con crédito, sin crédito o con mal crédito,
...Tito nunca dice «no»!
Tito Soto, gerente de **Potamkin**
OFERTAS de la SEMANA**

CHEVY CAVALIER '86 aire, aut	PLYMOUTH COLT '86 aire, a
$6999	$6999
CHEVY CAVALIER '84 aire, aut	Plymouth Chrysler Le Baron '82
$3999	$3999

FINANCIAMOS AUN CON CRÉDITO INSUFICIENTE O SIN CRÉDITO
$2,000 por su carro en "trade in", ...aunque lo traiga a remolque!
Pregunte por «Tito», ...pregunte por Tito Soto!
16600 NW 57 AVE.
(salida Palmetto y 57 Ave.)
585-1400

Riviera Supermarket
CON LA MEJOR CARNE DE MIAMI Y EN EL DEPARTAMENTO DE ARTÍCULOS PARA REGALOS LE BRINDAMOS EL 20% DE DESCUENTO. AMPLIO PARQUEO
1710 N.W. 17 AVE. ☎ 225-0056

Actividades

A What number would you call in the above ads to check prices on the following items?

1. comida
2. un coche
3. anteojos nuevos
4. ropa para jóvenes
5. un conejo o un gato

B List as many things as you can think of that would be sold in each of the stores above.

Por ejemplo:

En _____ venden _____.

Cultura viva 1

Presentation
Read the Cultura viva on this page. Lead students through each of the advertisements, asking them what is being advertised, and whether they can guess the meaning of any new words. You may wish to have a class discussion about advertising.

Did You Know?
Major American companies have done a great deal of market research about the Hispanic population in the U.S. because the buying power of Hispanics in this country is in the millions of dollars. Many major U.S. companies advertise in Spanish. Hispanics tend to be loyal to brands. Also, a greater percentage of advertisements in Spanish are designed to appeal to the family.

Critical Thinking Activities
1. Have students think of several reasons why many American companies advertise in Spanish for the Hispanic population in the U.S.
2. If Spanish-language newspapers are available in your area, you may want to ask each student to cut out ads, paste them on a poster board, and explain the ads to the class.

Actividades

Actividad A Answers
1. 225–0056
2. 585–1400
3. 626–2717
4. 393–3918
5. 863–1966

Actividad B Answers
Answers will vary.

Pronunciation

A. You may wish to play the recorded version of this pronunciation activity, located at the end of Cassette 6.1. You may also wish to write these lines on the chalkboard and have students copy them into their notebook:
Venga a Almacenes Levy donde lo bueno cuesta barato.

Levy, la tienda de la oferta barata. Todo por poco plata.

B. Have students repeat words and phrases individually and in unison. You may wish to focus on the /v/ sound: **venga, bueno, barato,** Levy.

Bell Ringer Review

Directions to students: On a Saturday afternoon, you come home to find your older brother dressed for the beach, your mother dressed for the theater, and your younger sister dressed for the tennis championship. Draw a sketch of each person and label their clothing.

Structure Focus

The indirect object pronoun **les** is presented in this lesson. Students have used the indirect object pronoun **les** with the verb **gustar** in Chapter 4, Lessons 1 and 3. The indirect object pronoun **le** was presented in Chapter 5, Lesson 6.

Presentation

A. Lead students through steps 1–2 on page 412.
B. You may wish to review the uses of the indirect object pronoun **le** in Chapter 5, Lesson 6.

Actividades

Actividad A Answers
Answers will vary but should include the following:

1. A mis padres les...
2. A mi maestro le...
3. A mi mejor amigo le...
4. A todos mis amigos les...
5. A mis parientes les...

Estructura 1

How to Say What You Do for Others   *Indirect object pronoun* **les**

You have used **le** to tell what you do to or for someone else.

> **A Miguel le voy a dar una billetera para su cumpleaños.**
> **A Susana le voy a dar unos aretes.**

1. To say what you do to or for more than one person, use **les**.

> **¿Conoces a mis amigos Paco y Raúl? Siempre les tengo que explicar las tareas. Les digo que deben estudiar más.**

2. Notice that **les** can refer to "you" (plural) or "them." If it is not clear to whom you are referring, add **a** + the name of the group. For example, **a ustedes, a ellos, a ellas, a mis padres, a mis amigos, a Roberto y a Julia.**

> **A ustedes les voy a decir la verdad. Si visitan mi pueblo, no les puedo enseñar nada. A mis padres siempre les digo que es un pueblo aburrido.**

Actividades

A **¿Siempre o no siempre?** Tell how often you do favors for the following people.

Por ejemplo:

> a tus hermanos
> *A mis hermanos siempre les hago favores.*

1. a tus padres
2. a tu maestro de inglés
3. a tu mejor amigo
4. a todos tus amigos
5. a tus parientes

B **Un millón de dólares.** You have just won a million dollars! Tell what you will buy or do for the following people.

Por ejemplo:

> tus amigos
> *A mis amigos Mark y Paula les voy a comprar un Porsche.*

1. a tus padres
2. a tus hermanos
3. a tus amigos
4. a tus maestros
5. a tus abuelos
6. a tus primos

C **¿Qué les diste?** You still had money left over, so you gave all your old possessions away to friends and family and bought everything new. Tell to whom you gave five of your possessions.

Por ejemplo:

> A mis primos les di mi estéreo.
> A Laura y a Ken les di mis discos.

D **¿Eres generoso?** Tell what you can do for the following people.

Por ejemplo:

> dos compañeros de clase
> *Les voy a (puedo, quiero, etc.) ayudar con la tarea.*

1. dos amigos
2. dos maestros
3. tus padres
4. tus hermanos
5. tus abuelos

Actividad B Answers
Answers will vary.

Class Management
You may wish to do Actividad B in small groups initially. Then have the members of each group report to the whole class. This approach will generate more ideas in preparation for doing Actividades C and D on this page.

Actividades C and D Answers
Answers will vary.

Reteaching
Make a list of the people for whom you do favors. Write down the favors you do for them.

Learning from Photos
You may want to have students look at the photo on page 413. The boy on the left is helping his classmate with the lesson. Ask students what favor the boy on the right will do in return.

Cultura viva 2

Presentation

Read the Cultura viva on this page. First, you may wish to read Rafael's letter to the class. Then read the letter a second time, calling on individual students to read one line each.

Did You Know?

Baseball has always been a favorite pastime of Cubans. It is also Cuba's national sport. Before Fidel Castro became dictator of Cuba, the country had a team, the Cuban Sugar Kings, which played in the minor leagues in the U.S. In recent years the Dominican Republic is the nation that has contributed the greatest number of players to American baseball teams, including Pedro Guerrero, and Ramoncito Martínez. Baseball is not played in Argentina; soccer is Argentina's national sport.

Critical Thinking Activity

Read Rafael's letter to his mother once more, paying particular attention to the opening and closing portions. How is his letter different from one you might write to your mother?

Actividad Answers

1. **Sí.**
2. **No.**
3. **No.**
4. **Sí.**
5. **Sí.**
6. **Sí.**

Learning from Photos

You may want to have students look at the photos on page 414. Have them guess what Carmen might be saying to her cousin Rafael in the top photo. In the bottom photo, what might Rafael and his companion be talking about? Have students describe the clothing each person is wearing in both photos.

¡Tío Lucas y Rafael ya están en Miami!

Desde Miami, Rafael le escribe una carta a su mamá, que está en Buenos Aires.

Miami, 27 de abril

Querida mamita:

Papá y yo llegamos bien el jueves pasado y pasamos la primera semana aquí bastante ocupados. Estamos bien. Y tú, ¿cómo estás? ¿Muy solita? Ayer Carmen y yo tomamos el tren (el "Metrorail") y visitamos varias partes de la cuidad, incluso la "Pequeña Habana". ¡Hasta jugué béisbol con unos chicos en el parque! Y saqué un montón de fotos. Anoche fui con Carmen a una fiesta en casa de una de sus compañeras. Practiqué el inglés con todos sus amigos. Dicen que hablo bastante bien. ¿Qué te parece?

Bueno, mamá, el domingo te escribo. Los tíos te mandan un abrazo y yo, un beso grande.

Tu hijo que te quiere mucho, *Rafael*

Actividad

The following are some of the things Rafael wanted to do during his stay in Florida. Tell which of the following happened, according to his letter to his mother, by responding **sí** or **no**.

1. **llegar sin problemas**
2. **ir a la playa**
3. **visitar Tampa**
4. **sacar muchas fotos**
5. **practicar el inglés**
6. **conocer a jóvenes**

Estructura 2

How to Say What You and Others Did in the Past   **Preterit nosotros *forms***

You have learned to say what you did in the past (preterit) by using the following verb endings.

- for **-ar** verbs: **-é**
- for **-er** and **-ir** verbs: **-í**

Llamé a Carmen anoche a las seis. A las siete salí con ella.

You have learned to tell or ask a friend or family member what he or she did using the following verb endings.

- for **-ar** verbs: **-aste**
- for **-er** and **-ir** verbs: **-iste**

¿Cuándo llegaste a Miami? ¿Ya viste muchas cosas?

1. To say what you and another person ("we") did in the past, use the following verb endings.

   - for **-ar** verbs: **-amos**
   - for **-er** and **-ir** verbs: **-imos**

   En el picnic jugamos béisbol y después comimos.

Notice that for **-ar** and **-ir** verbs, these are the same endings you use to form the present tense.

2. The following verbs are exceptions to the above rules.

ir	fuimos	**El sábado pasado fuimos al cine.**
dar	dimos	**Ayer por la tarde dimos un paseo por la playa.**
hacer	hicimos	**Anoche no hicimos nada.**

For the Native Speaker

Imagine that you have a part-time job in a record/tape store. In writing, describe a recent day at work. What kind of customers did you have? What type of records/tapes did you sell? What else did you have to do?

this lesson they will be using the **nosotros** form.

B. You may wish to practice **yo** and **tú** forms of the preterit by reviewing some of the activities in Chapter 5, Lessons 5 and 6 .
Note. Oímos and **leímos** take an accent on the **i**.

Actividades

Actividad A Answers

Answers will vary but should include:

1. **(No) Visitamos...**
2. **(No) Hablamos...**
3. **(No) Jugamos...**
4. **(No) Salimos...**
5. **(No) Comimos...**
6. **(No) Dimos...**
7. **(No) Hicimos...**
8. **(No) Recibimos...**

Actividades B and C Answers

Answers will vary.

Reteaching

Ask students how they would say they and their friends did each of the following activities yesterday: **ir a la escuela; comprar ropa; jugar tenis; comer hamburguesas; hacer la tarea; recibir regalos; salir temprano; dormir mucho; escribir cartas.**

Actividades

A **¿Y ustedes?** Tell whether or not you and your family or friends did the following activities in the past few months.

Por ejemplo:

> ir al zoológico
> *(No) Fuimos al zoológico.*

1. visitar Miami
2. hablar español
3. jugar béisbol
4. salir a la playa
5. comer comida cubana
6. dar un paseo por la ciudad
7. hacer un picnic
8. recibir invitaciones a una fiesta

B **Mi compañero y yo.** Ask a classmate the following questions about things the two of you did. Report to the class those things the two of you have in common.

Por ejemplo:

> ¿Saliste anoche?

ESTUDIANTE A	ESTUDIANTE B
(1) ¿Saliste anoche?	(2) **Sí, salí con mis amigos.**
(3) **Yo también.**	

(A la clase:) **Victoria y yo salimos anoche.**

1. ¿En qué año naciste?
2. ¿Practicaste un deporte ayer?
3. ¿Qué programas viste anoche?
4. ¿Adónde fuiste ayer después de las clases?
5. ¿Qué estudiaste anoche? ¿Dónde estudiaste?
6. ¿Qué hiciste el fin de semana pasado?
7. ¿A qué hora llegaste a la escuela esta mañana? (Llegué...)

C **¡Muchas gracias, maestros!** Your teachers have agreed to give less homework. You and your classmates have thanked them by giving each a present. Tell what gifts you have given to four of your teachers and tell why you selected each gift.

Por ejemplo:

> A la maestra de español le dimos un diccionario grande porque le gustan las palabras raras.

Finalmente

Situaciones

A conversar You've saved enough money to buy some new clothes. Your partner will play the role of the department store salesperson.

1. Ask the salesperson to show you certain articles of clothing.
2. Ask about prices and alternate colors.
3. Inquire about matching accessories.
4. Make your selections. The salesperson will tell you the total cost.

A escribir Think of an exciting place you went to once with family or friends. Write a letter to a classmate telling about your trip.

1. Describe the activities that you and others did during the day.
2. Tell what you did in the evening. Tell with whom you did each activity.
3. Describe any souvenirs or other items you bought for yourself or others.

SOLAMENTE EL MIÉRCOLES EN JBYRONS

REBAJA DE UN DÍA
OCTUBRE 17

OBTENGA UN DESCUENTO DEL

10%
ADICIONAL*

*DESPUÉS DE TOTALIZADAS SUS COMPRAS

¡EN TODA LA TIENDA¡
¡HASTA EN LOS ARTÍCULOS YA REBAJADOS!

JBYRONS

Repaso de vocabulario

ROPA
el abrigo
la blusa
las botas
la bufanda
los calcetines
la camisa
la corbata
la chaqueta
la falda
el gorro
los guantes

el impermeable
los pantalones
las pantimedias
las sandalias
los "shorts"
el suéter
los tenis
el traje de baño
el traje de caballero
el traje de dama
el vestido

JOYAS
el anillo
el arete
el collar
la pulsera

ARTÍCULOS
los anteojos
   de sol
la bolsa
el cinturón
el paraguas

ACTIVIDAD
llevar (to wear)

Lección 1 **417**

Situaciones

Lesson 1 Evaluation
The A conversar and A escribir situations on this page are designed to give students the opportunity to use as many language functions and as much vocabulary from this lesson as possible. The A conversar and A escribir are also intended to show how well students are able to meet the lesson objectives.

Presentation
Prior to doing the A conversar and A escribir on this page, you may wish to play the Situaciones listening activities on Cassette 6.1 as a means of helping students organize the material.

Learning from Realia
You may want to have students look at the realia on page 417. If they were to buy the following items during this sale, how much would they pay for each with the 10% discount?

1. zapatos: $40
2. chaqueta: $50
3. abrigo: $77

Lección 2

Objectives

By the end of this lesson, students will be able to:

1. say what people do for them and others
2. say that they did certain activities in the past
3. describe clothing and accessories

Lesson 2 Resources
1. Workbook, pp. 183–188
2. Vocabulario Transparencies 6.2
3. Cassette 6.2
4. Student Tape Manual, pp. 153–158
5. Lesson Quizzes, p. 121–124
6. Computer Software, Disk 2
7. Video Cassette
8. Estructura Masters 6.2
9. Diversiones Masters 6.2

Bell Ringer Review

Directions to students: Write down what you would suggest your father, mother, and 6-year-old brother wear on the following occasions:
papá — para el trabajo
mamá — para el trabajo
hermanito — para la playa

¡A comenzar!

Presentation

A. Lead students through each of the two functions given on page 418, progressing from the English to the Spanish for each function. Then have students find these words and phrases in the dialogue on page 419.

Lección 2

¿Vamos al centro comercial?

¡A comenzar!

The following are some of the things you will be learning to do in this lesson.

When you want to . . .	You use . . .
1. say what people do for you and others	• **Nos** + activity.
2. say that you did certain activities in the past	• **-cé** or **-qué** on certain **-ar** verbs

Now find examples of the above words and phrases in the following conversation.

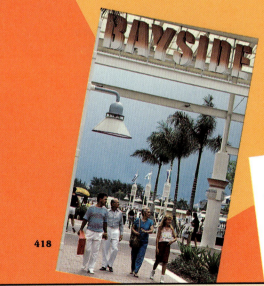

BAYSIDE

¡Liquidación de temporada!

418

Getting Ready for Lesson 2

You may wish to use one or more of the following suggestions to prepare students for the lesson:

1. Cut out illustrations from magazines to present various types of clothing. Describe the illustrations. For example: **Este hombre lleva una camisa de manga larga y pantalones de rayas. Esta mujer lleva un traje elegante de seda... un vestido de flores de manga corta... un traje de invierno... una camiseta y pantalones deportivos, etc.**

2. Describe the clothing worn by students in the class. After your descriptions, ask questions about what the students are wearing. For example: **¿Lleva Eric una camiseta de rayas? ¿Lleva Janet una blusa de manga larga? ¿Lleva Tom**

Carmen está en casa con su primo Rafael y su tío Lucas.

RAFAEL: Carmen, ya empecé a estudiar las palabras que me enseñaste en inglés. Y ayer practiqué mucho pero no entiendo qué dice aquí en el periódico.

CARMEN: A ver... Dice que hay una liquidación de temporada.

RAFAEL: Bueno, quisiera comprar unos regalos antes de regresar a Buenos Aires.

TÍO LUCAS: Oye, Carmencita, ¿por qué no llevas a tu primo al centro comercial? Le puedes enseñar las tiendas y también le puedes presentar a tus amigos.

RAFAEL: ¿Vamos a la calle Ocho?

CARMEN: No, Rafael. Voy a ver si mamá nos da permiso para ir al centro comercial Bayside.

RAFAEL: ¡Qué bueno! Oye, papá, ¿nos puedes prestar dinero?

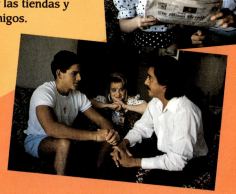

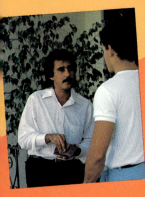

Actividades preliminares

A Tell where the following are located.

Por ejemplo:

> Argentina
> *Está en la América del Sur.*

1. Florida
2. Buenos Aires
3. la calle Ocho
4. Miami

B Complete the following sentences about what you did recently.

1. Compré _____. Pagué _____.
2. Saqué una buena nota en la clase de _____.
3. Llegué tarde a la clase de _____.
4. Jugué _____ con mis amigos.
5. Practiqué _____.

B. Introduce the Lesson 2 dialogue by reading it aloud or by playing the cassette version. Tell students they are going to hear a conversation between Carmen, her Uncle Lucas, and her cousin Rafael. Have them listen to find out:

1. ¿Qué quiere hacer Rafael?
2. ¿Adónde quieren ir Carmen y Rafael?

C. Now ask students to open their books and look at the dialogue as you lead them through what is said. For example:

1. ¿Qué no entiende Rafael? ¿Qué dice el periódico?
2. ¿Qué quiere hacer Rafael?
3. Lucas le recomienda algo a Carmen. ¿Qué dice?
4. Rafael quiere saber si van a cierto lugar. ¿Dónde? ¿Adónde van a ir?
5. ¿Qué le pregunta Rafael a su papá?

D. After reading the dialogue with your students, you may wish to follow up with these questions:

1. Cuándo vas al centro comercial, ¿te prestan dinero tus padres?
2. Si quieres comprar pantalones deportivos, ¿adónde vas (¿a qué tienda vas?)?
3. Si quieres comprar un vestido elegante, ¿adónde vas?
4. Si quieres comprar camisetas de moda, ¿adónde vas?, etc.

Actividades preliminares

Actividad A Answers
1. Está en los Estados Unidos (la América del Norte).
2. Está en Argentina.
3. Está en Miami.
4. Está en Florida.

Actividad B Answers
Answers will vary.

---

pantalones de lunares?, etc. Students may respond with **Sí** or **No**.

3. Using the magazine pictures and any other available illustrations, ask individual students either/or questions about their clothing preferences. For example:

John, ¿qué te gustan más, los pantalones de cuadros o de un sólo color?

Angela, ¿qué te gusta más, un vestido de lunares o un vestido de flores?

Michael, ¿qué te gusta más, una camisa de manga corta o de manga larga?

Amy, ¿qué te gusta más, una falda de rayas o de un sólo color?, etc.

419

Vocabulario

Bell Ringer Review

Directions to students: Sometimes when we hear a word we immediately think of an image we associate with it. Copy down these words and beside each write the first word or expression you associate with it. Be spontaneous!

los aretes de oro
un anillo
un paraguas
un gorro
botas
guantes
el béisbol
diciembre

Presentation

A. Have students open their books to the Vocabulario on pages 420 and 421. Model the question at the top of page 420, **¿Qué clase de ropa buscas?** Then introduce each phrase in the Vocabulario, beginning each time with **Busco...** Have students repeat after you each time. Then introduce each word or phrase on page 421, beginning with the questions **¿Qué diseño te gusta?** and **¿Qué tela prefieres?**

B. You may wish to ask students personalized questions such as, **¿Te gusta la blusa de seda? ¿Les gustan los pantalones de lana? ¿Necesitas un vestido de un solo color? ¿Cuándo llevas un abrigo de lana?**, etc.

Vocabulario

¿Qué clase de ropa buscas? Busco...

una blusa...
sin mangas
de manga larga
de manga corta
unos pantalones de moda
un vestido elegante
una camisa deportiva

ropa para damas
ropa para caballeros

un traje de...
primavera
verano
otoño
invierno

Total Physical Response

Getting Ready
Bring to class the articles of clothing mentioned in the TPR activities below. Display the clothing on hangers and add prices to each item. Have fake paper money in $5 and $10 bills.

New Words
pruébate   pruébense
escoge   escojan
págale   páguenle

TPR 1
Toquen la blusa con lunares.
Apunten al vestido elegante.
Escojan tres artículos de ropa para mujeres.
Escojan tres artículos de ropa para hombres.

420

¿Qué diseño te gusta? Quiero una camisa...

de cuadros

de lunares

de rayas

de un solo color

de flores

¿Qué tela prefieres? Prefiero ropa de...

seda

lana

Actividades

A **Ropa adecuada.** Make four columns, one for each season of the year. Under each season, list two articles of clothing you would typically wear.

Por ejemplo:

> verano
> *ropa de algodón, sandalias...*

B **Inventario.** List three articles of clothing that you wear in summer and three you wear in winter. Describe each article in detail.

Por ejemplo:

> **En verano llevo pantalones grises. Son de algodón. Son viejos. En invierno llevo botas negras de cuero. Me gustan mucho.**

Lección 2 **421**

C. Have students compliment each other on one article of clothing they are wearing. For example: **¡Qué vestido más lindo! Me gusta mucho tu camisa de lunares, etc.**

When Students Ask

You may wish to give students the following additional vocabulary to allow them to talk about clothing.

el encaje
el lino
la piel
el nilón
el probador
las rebajas
la talla
el estampado
me/te queda(n)
pasado(a) de moda
bordado(a)
la camisa de vestir
apretado(a)
ancho(a)
no me queda
no hace juego con

Actividades

Actividades A Answers
Answers may vary but might include the following:
verano: una camisa de manga corta, unos shorts
otoño: una camisa de manga larga, un suéter
invierno: ropa de lana; un abrigo
primavera: ropa de algodón, una chaqueta

Actividad B Answers
Answers will vary.

Pruébense las blusas de flores.
Pruébense las blusas de algodón.
Páguenle a la maestra (al maestro) $20 por la camisa deportiva.
Páguenle a la maestra (al maestro) $100 por el vestido elegante.
(Continue interchanging commands and clothing.)

TPR 2

(Call on pairs of students to respond. Alternate your commands between them.)
1. Dale el vestido elegante a _____.
2. Pruébate el vestido elegante.
1. Dile que es bonito.
2. Pregúntale el precio y págale.
(Interchange clothing, prices, and descriptions.)

422

Actividades C and D Answers
Answers will vary.

Class Management
You may wish to model Actividad C with several of your better students initially. The teacher may play the role of Student A. After modeling in this way, have students do Actividad C in pairs according to the directions.

Actividad E Answers
Sonia: Lleva una falda amarilla de lunares.
Yolanda: Lleva una blusa de seda, una falda blanca, sandalias, joyas de plástico de muchos colores.
Paco: Lleva una camisa de cuadros anaranjados, negros y blancos, "jeans", zapatos de cuero, anteojos de sol.
Cristina: Lleva un traje de baño de rayas azules y rojas, anteojos de sol, sandalias.
Héctor: Lleva un traje de baño de flores, una camiseta amarilla.
David: Lleva una camisa de flores verdes, amarillas y rojas, "shorts" blancos, calcetines blancos, tenis.

Additional Practice
After completing Actividades A, B, C, D, and E, you may wish to reinforce the learning with the following activity:
Create and describe a situation in which someone was inappropriately dressed for an event. **Por ejemplo:**

ESTUDIANTE A	ESTUDIANTE B
Mi amiga fue a la iglesia. Llevó un traje de baño.	¡Qué horror!

Reteaching

Tell students where you went yesterday, last weekend, etc. Describe what you wore. Have students write down the clothing you describe.

C **Lo que buscas.** Write down five items of clothing you need to buy for winter or summer. Describe each item.

Por ejemplo:

> Para el verano necesito una camiseta de rayas. Prefiero una blanca y azul.

D **¿Me compras algo, por favor?** A classmate will play the role of a parent. Ask him or her for each of the items you listed in activity C. He or she says no to each request, but gives a good reason. Student A then reports back to the class.

Por ejemplo:

ESTUDIANTE A
Mamá (Papá), ¿me compras una camiseta de rayas?

ESTUDIANTE B
No, ya tienes muchas camisetas.

(A la clase:) Mi mamá (papá) no me quiere comprar una camiseta porque dice que ya tengo muchas camisetas.

E **En la fiesta.** Describe to a classmate with as much detail as possible what each person is wearing in the picture below. Your classmate will identify whom you are describing.

Por ejemplo:

ESTUDIANTE A
Una muchacha lleva una falda amarilla de lunares.

ESTUDIANTE B
Hablas de Sonia, ¿no?

422 CAPÍTULO 6

La Pequeña Habana

La Pequeña Habana es un barrio de Miami. En este barrio puedes ver muchos cafés, bodegas, tiendas y puntos de reunión donde la cultura cubana está en todas partes. Allí puedes comprar cosas que no hay en muchas otras ciudades de los Estados Unidos, como, por ejemplo, frutas y verduras tropicales, guayaberas, piñatas, churros y helados de frutas tropicales.

Las fiestas más importantes del año son el Desfile del Día de la Herencia Hispánica y el "Carnaval Miami". Dicen que el carnaval atrae más gente que todas las otras festividades hispanas de los Estados Unidos.

CHURROS 10 POR $1⁰⁰

Actividad

Tell what a visitor to **La Pequeña Habana** could do, based on the photos.

Por ejemplo:

    Puede comer comida nicaragüense.

GUAYACAN RESTAURANT
The Best Nicaraguan Food

PLATOS TÍPICOS DE EL SALVADOR
PUPUSAS de chicharrón, frijoles y queso   TAMALES
YUCA FRITA con chicharrón y col curtida   DESAYUNOS
CHURROS y CHOCOLATE A LA ESPAÑOLA
CAFÉ CUBANO
FARMACIA CEN

Lección 2 **423**

Estructura 1

Bell Ringer Review

Directions to students: In Spanish, write the name of each season on your paper. Then beside each season, write the three months that belong to it.

Structure Focus

In this lesson the object pronoun **nos** is presented. The indirect object pronoun **le** was presented in Chapter 5, Lesson 6. The indirect object pronoun **les** was presented in Chapter 6, Lesson 1.

Presentation

A. Lead students through steps 1–2 on page 424. In step 1, you may wish to have students read the illustrated dialogue. As review, you may also ask various students to read the dialogue, pretending that Diana is not there.

B. You may wish to review earlier exercises that practice the use of **gustar,** this time substituting **nos** as the indirect object pronoun. See Chapter 1, Lessons 4 and 6; Chapter 4, Lessons 1 and 3.

Estructura 1

How to Say What People Do for You and Others   **Object pronoun nos**

How to Talk about What You and Others Like and Dislike

You have used **me, te, le,** and **les** to talk about what people do to or for you and others.

> **Si me ayudas con la tarea, te regalo mi nuevo casete.**
>
> **Todos me piden favores. Ayer le presté mi libro de inglés a Jaime. También les presté cinco dólares a Raquel y a Yolanda.**

1. To say that someone does something for you and others ("for us"), use **nos** + activity.

Papá, Diana y yo queremos saber si nos puedes prestar el coche.

No les puedo prestar el coche porque tengo que ir al centro.

Entonces, ¿nos das el dinero para tomar un taxi?

2. To say what you and others like or dislike, use **(no) nos + gusta(n).**

> **Nos gusta la clase de arte porque nos gusta dibujar.**
> **No nos gustan mucho los partidos de tenis.**

Actividades

A **El maestro ideal.** Tell whether or not the ideal teacher does the following for you and your classmates.

Por ejemplo:

hacer exámenes fáciles
Sí, nos hace exámenes fáciles.

1. escuchar
2. dar dos horas de tarea
3. explicar bien las lecciones
4. criticar mucho
5. enseñar cosas interesantes
6. hacer exámenes todos los días
7. dar buenos consejos

B **Maestro, ¡por favor!** Work with a classmate to make five unusual requests of your teacher. Then report your requests to the class.

Por ejemplo:

Señorita, ¿nos puede dar tareas muy fáciles? (Señor, ¿nos permite comer en clase?)

C **Durante todo el año.** Tell two things that you and your family or friends like about each of the four seasons.

Por ejemplo:

en verano
En verano nos gusta ir a la playa.
También nos gustan los partidos de béisbol.

1. en verano
2. en otoño
3. en invierno
4. en primavera

CULTURA VIVA 2

La comida cubana

En la Florida y en otras partes de los Estados Unidos, puedes comer comida cubana. Algunos de los ingredientes básicos son: el arroz, frijoles de distintos colores, varias verduras y frutas tropicales (como los plátanos y las guanábanas), papas, pescado, carne de puerco y pollo. La comida cubana no es tan picante como la mexicana. Para terminar, el café cubano es muy rico y los helados de frutas tropicales son deliciosos.

arroz blanco con frijoles negros

plátanos fritos

naranjas, guavas, chirimoyas y mangos

Actividad

This is a portion of the bilingual menu from a restaurant on **la calle Ocho**. The chef mixed up the English translations. Can you match the items on the menu with their correct English translations?

Especialidades	Today's Specials
ARROZ FRITO Plátanos Maduros	Beef vegetable stew, with yellow rice and fried bananas
CHICHARRONES DE POLLO Con Arroz Blanco	Cheese melt steak, with mashed potatoes
BISTEC AL QUESO Con Puré de Papas	Breaded steak, with french fries
ARROZ CON POLLO Con Plátanos Maduros	Fried rice, with fried bananas
BISTEC EMPANIZADO Con Papas Fritas	Fried chicken chunks, with white rice
CARNE DE RES CON VEGETALES Con Arroz Amarillo y Plátanos Maduros	Chicken and rice, with fried plantains

Estructura 2

How to Write about the Past

Irregular yo forms of certain -ar verbs in the preterit

You have learned to say what you did in the past using **-ar** verbs.

> **Anoche llamé a mi amigo Tomás.**
> **Después hablé con mi amiga Inés.**

1. In Rafael's letter to his mother on p. 414, he used the past tense forms **jugué, saqué,** and **practiqué.**

> **Jugué béisbol. Saqué muchas fotos. Practiqué el inglés.**

If you pronounce these words aloud, you can hear the sound of the past tense. When you write certain verbs using the **"yo"** form in the past tense, you must change the spelling.

2. The following verbs ending in **-car, -gar,** and **-zar** will make these changes.

-qué	tocar	**Anoche toqué la guitarra.**
	sacar	**Saqué una "A" en el examen.**
	practicar	**Practiqué el español con Eva.**
	explicar	**Le expliqué la tarea a José.**
	buscar	**En el centro le busqué un regalo a mi primo.**
-gué	llegar	**El lunes llegué tarde a la escuela.**
	jugar	**Jugué béisbol con los amigos.**
	pagar	**Compré un traje de baño. No pagué mucho.**
-cé	empezar	**Anoche empecé la composición. Voy a terminar hoy.**

These changes affect the way you spell the words, not how you pronounce them.

Structure Teaching Resources
1. Workbook, pp. 187–188
2. Cassette 6.2
3. Student Tape Manual, p. 156
4. Estructura Masters 6.2
5. Lesson Quizzes, p. 124

Bell Ringer Review

Directions to students: Make four columns across the top of your paper, one for each season. Then list under each column the appropriate articles of clothing you would wear in that season. (It might be possible to include some articles under more than one season.)
sandalias, trajes de caballero, botas, camisas de manga larga, camisas de manga corta, chaquetas de cuero, zapatos de tenis, impermeables, blusas de seda, sombreros, bufandas, suéteres, abrigos, gorros, vestidos de lana, los shorts, trajes de baño, calcetines, pantalones de algodón, pantalones de lana

Struture Focus

In this lesson, the presentation of the preterit is limited to irregular **yo** forms of certain **-ar** verbs. The **yo** and **tú** forms of the preterit were presented in Chapter 5, Lessons 5 and 6. The **nosotros** preterit forms were presented in Chapter 6, Lesson 1. The third person singular and plural preterit forms will be presented in Chapter 6, Lessons 3 and 4. A summary of preterit forms is presented in Chapter 6, Lesson 6.

Presentation

Lead students thorough steps 1–2 on page 427. In step 2, you may wish to write some or all of the examples on the chalkboard for emphasis, underlining the spelling changes. Model these examples and have students repeat after you.

Actividades

Actividad A Answers
1. empecé
2. Llegué
3. expliqué
4. pagué
5. busqué
6. empecé
7. Saqué

Actividad B Answers
Answers will vary but should include
the following:

1. Este año saco... pero el año
   pasado saqué...
2. ... estudio... estudié...
3. ... leo... leí...
4. ... hago... hice...
5. ... practico... practiqué...

Reteaching

How would you say you did the following things yesterday?
**buscar tu número de teléfono,
practicar la guitarra, empezer la
tarea, le explicar el problema de
química a Jorge, llegar temprano,
pagar cinco dólares, sacar muchas
fotos.**

Actividades

A **Notas.** Carmen wrote the following notes to her friend Jorge on
the days she was taking her computer class. Complete them, using
the **yo** form of the preterit of the following verbs.

buscar	**explicar**	**pagar**	**sacar**
empezar	**llegar**	**practicar**	

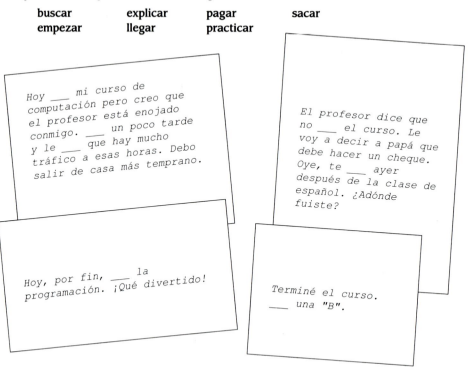

Hoy ___ mi curso de
computación pero creo que
el profesor está enojado
conmigo. ___ un poco tarde
y le ___ que hay mucho
tráfico a esas horas. Debo
salir de casa más temprano.

El profesor dice que
no ___ el curso. Le
voy a decir a papá que
debe hacer un cheque.
Oye, te ___ ayer
después de la clase de
español. ¿Adónde
fuiste?

Hoy, por fin, ___ la
programación. ¡Qué divertido!

Terminé el curso.
___ una "B".

B **Este año y el año pasado.** Compare this school year to last
year in terms of the following topics.

Por ejemplo:

> **los deportes que practicas**
> *Este año juego tenis pero el año pasado jugué baloncesto.*

1. **las notas que sacas**
2. **las materias** (subjects)
   que estudias
3. **los libros que lees**

4. **las tareas que haces**
5. **los deportes que practicas**

Cooperative Learning

Divide teams into pairs. Give each pair the
infinitive of the verbs presented in Actividad B, page 428. Have students write the
past tense of the verbs. Then as a team,
they should complete the sentences in
Actividad B.

Finalmente

Finalmente

Situaciones

A conversar A classmate will play the role of a new Spanish-speaking exchange student whose first day of school is tomorrow. You call him or her and make plans to meet tomorrow before classes start.

1. Say hello, introduce yourself, and ask where he or she is from.
2. Find out when he or she arrived in the U.S.
3. Say that you'd like to show him or her around school tomorrow and introduce him or her to your friends. Your partner accepts the invitation and thanks you.
4. Tell your partner what time you will arrive at school and where you will be.
5. Describe yourself so your partner will know who you are. Tell what you look like and what you will be wearing. Your partner does the same. Say good-bye.

A escribir Identify who, in your opinion, is the best-dressed and worst-dressed celebrity today. Write a review, describing each person's clothing and appearance in general, making reference to photos in magazines, an album cover, a poster, or a live concert or TV appearance. To make your review seem more lively, write in the present tense.

Repaso de vocabulario

CLASES DE ROPA	para damas	DISEÑOS	ESTACIONES
de manga corta	sin mangas	de cuadros	la primavera
de manga larga		de flores	el verano
de moda	**TELAS**	de lunares (m.)	el otoño
deportivo(a)	la lana	de rayas	el invierno
para caballeros	la seda	de un solo color	

Lección 2 **429**

Situaciones

Lesson 2 Evaluation
The A conversar and A escribir situations on this page are designed to give students the opportunity to use as many language functions and as much vocabulary from the lesson as possible. The A conversar and A escribir are also intended to show how well students are able to meet the lesson objectives.

Presentation
Prior to doing the A conversar and A escribir on this page, you may wish to play the Situaciones listening activities on Cassette 6.2 as a means of helping students organize the material.

Lección 3

Objectives

By the end of this lesson, students will be able to:

1. give directions
2. identify modes of transportation
3. say what someone did at one point in the past
4. say that someone is coming

Lesson 3 Resources

1. Workbook, pp. 189–194
2. Vocabulario Transparencies 6.3
3. Cassette 6.3
4. Student Tape Manual, pp. 159–164
5. Lesson Quizzes, pp. 125–128
6. Test Booklet, pp. 99–105
7. Computer Software, Disk 2
8. Video Cassette
9. Estructura Masters 6.3
10. Diversiones Masters 6.3

Bell Ringer Review

Directions to students: Write the names of the four seasons across the top of your paper and list each of the following activities in the appropriate column.

esquiar
bucear
saltar las olas
patinar sobre hielo
montar en bicicleta
nadar en la piscina
pasear en velero
jugar béisbol
jugar tenis
jugar fútbol americano
ir de pesca
practicar el esquí acuático

Lección 3

Aquí se dice "guagua"

¡A comenzar!

The following are some of the things you will be learning to do in this lesson.

When you want to . . .	You use . . .
1. say something is far / near	• **Está lejos / Está cerca.**
2. say what someone did in the past	• **-ó** at the end of **-ar** verbs
3. say that something or someone is approaching	• **Ya viene.**

Now find examples of the above words and phrases in the following conversation.

Getting Ready for Lesson 3

You may wish to use one or more of the following suggestions to prepare students for the lesson:

1. Sketch a map of your own town or area on a transparency and fill in places such as the library, a museum, the post office, hospital, hotel, school, church, synagogue, park, streets, and depart-ment stores as well as some students' houses. Use this map to describe the locations of various places and houses in relation to each other. For example: **El hospital está lejos de nuestra escuela pero el museo está cerca. La casa de Julia está en la esquina de las calles Vine y Elm. Al lado de su casa está la biblioteca. A dos cuadras de la casa de Don hay un restaurante, etc.**

Carmen y Rafael salen de compras.

RAFAEL: ¿Está muy lejos el centro comercial?

CARMEN: No, está bastante cerca.

RAFAEL: ¿A cuántos kilómetros?

CARMEN: Pues, en kilómetros, no sé. Pero no hay problema. Tomamos la guagua.

RAFAEL: ¿Tomamos *qué*?

CARMEN: Digo, el autobús. Aquí se dice "guagua". Oye, ¿cuánto dinero te prestó tu papá?

RAFAEL: Me prestó veinte dólares. Vamos, ya viene el autobús.

Actividades preliminares

A Tell whether the following are close to or far from school.

Por ejemplo:

> un restaurante
> *Un restaurante está cerca (lejos).*

1. un centro comercial
2. una tienda de computadoras
3. tu casa
4. el trabajo de tu papá (mamá)
5. un cine

B Tell what three people lent you recently.

Por ejemplo:

> Mi papá me prestó su coche.

¡A comenzar!

Presentation

A. Lead students through each of the three functions given on page 430, progressing from the English to the Spanish for each function. Then have students find these words and phrases in the dialogue on page 431.

B. Introduce the Lesson 3 dialogue by reading it aloud or by playing the cassette version. Have students listen to determine the following:

1. ¿Adónde van Carmen y Rafael?
2. ¿Qué hacen?

C. Now ask students to open their books and look at the dialogue as you lead them through what is said with the following questions:

1. Cuando Rafael pregunta: "¿Está muy lejos el centro comercial?", ¿qué le contesta Carmen?
2. ¿Sabe Carmen a cuántos kilómetros está?
3. Carmen dice: "Tomamos la guagua". ¿Qué quiere decir "guagua"?
4. Cuando Carmen pregunta "¿cuánto dinero te prestó tu papá?", ¿qué le contesta Rafael?

Actividades preliminares

Actividades A and B Answers
Answers will vary.

---

2. Describe to students a big party or family reunion you're going to have. Tell them you have to make hotel arrangements for those coming from out of town. Give students a list of guests you've invited. As you talk, have them place a check beside the names of those who are coming from out of town. Describe each guest in terms of the following:

- name
- relationship
- if he or she lives far or near
- how he or she will arrive (**Viene en coche, tren, etc.**). If the person lives close to your home, give location in terms of blocks (**Vive a tres cuadras de mi casa**).

Bell Ringer Review

Directions to students: What a weird circus! Draw the following animals according to their descriptions.

1. **El elefante lleva un traje de caballero, una camisa de lunares, una corbata de flores, un sombrero y unos zapatos de tenis.**
2. **El gorila lleva un vestido de cuadros, sandalias y una bufanda.**
3. **El león lleva una camisa de rayas, unos shorts, sandalias y un gorro de béisbol.**

Presentation

A. Have students open their books to the Vocabulario on pages 432 and 433. Model each new phrase. Have students repeat each phrase in unison.

B. You may want to use Vocabulario Transparencies 6.3 or the one you made of your area in "Getting Ready for Lesson 3" to direct students to various locations. They will tell you where they end up. For example: **Están en la esquina de _____ y _____. Siguen derecho dos cuadras. ¿Dónde están?**

C. Have students name places according to your questions. For example: **¿Qué hay al lado de _____/enfrente de _____/a la izquierda de _____/a tres cuadras de _____?**, etc.

Vocabulario

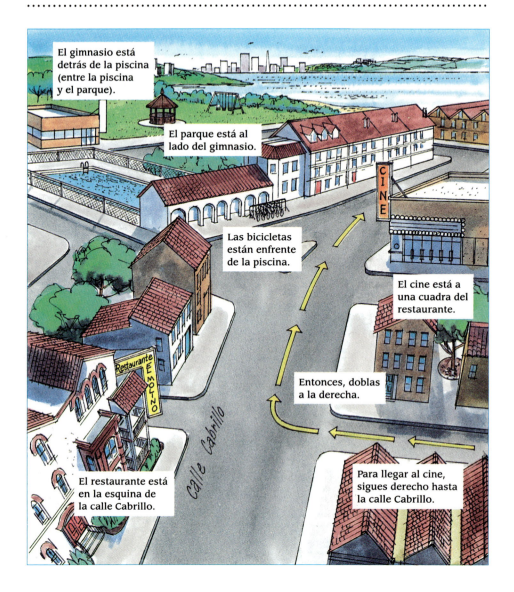

El gimnasio está detrás de la piscina (entre la piscina y el parque).

El parque está al lado del gimnasio.

Las bicicletas están enfrente de la piscina.

El cine está a una cuadra del restaurante.

Entonces, doblas a la derecha.

El restaurante está en la esquina de la calle Cabrillo.

Para llegar al cine, sigues derecho hasta la calle Cabrillo.

432   CAPÍTULO 6

Total Physical Response

Getting Ready
Use Vocabulario Transparencies 6.3, filling in appropriate places for the TPR commands. Or sketch a map of your own town or area on a transparency and fill in with the appropriate places for the TPR commands. Then make photocopies of the modes of transportation on page 433 and cut up into individual pieces.

New Words
estaciona   mueve   cielo

TPR 1
(Call individual students to the overhead projector.)
Pon el autobús enfrente del cine.
Pon el tren entre la piscina y el parque.
Estaciona la camioneta a la derecha del gimnasio.

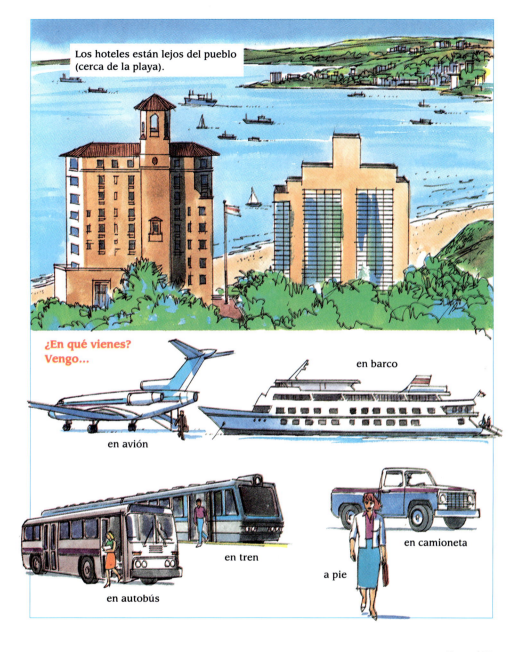

Los hoteles están lejos del pueblo (cerca de la playa).

¿En qué vienes?
Vengo...

en barco

en avión

en tren

en autobús

a pie

en camioneta

Lección 3 **433**

D. Have students tell places they went recently and how they got there. For example: **El sábado pasado fui a _____ en _____.** Have them talk about other people as well. For example: **Mis padres fueron a _____ en _____. (Mi amiga y yo fuimos... /José fue..., etc.)**

Regionalisms

You may wish to tell students that in some parts of the Spanish-speaking world the following words or phrases are alternatives to those presented in the Vocabulario.
el autobús (el camión) (México), **(la guagua)** (Cuba), **(el colectivo)** (Argentina), **(el ómnibus)** (Uruguay, Perú), **(el micro)** (Chile), **(la camioneta)** (Guatemala); **el barco (el navío); la camioneta (la furgoneta)**

Estaciona el tren a la izquerda del gimnasio.
Estaciona la camioneta al lado del restaurante.
Pon el avión en el cielo sobre la piscina.
Pon el barco en el océano.
Ve a pie al parque.
Ve en autobús al restaurante.
Mueve la camioneta a la esquina de la calle Cabrillo.
Mueve el tren al lado del restaurante.
Mueve el autobús al lado del cine.
Ve en camioneta al parque.
Ve a pie a la piscina.
Ve en tren al hotel.
Ve en avión a la piscina.
Regresa al hotel a pie.
Regresa al restaurante a pie.
(Interchange commands, locations, and modes of transportation.)

433

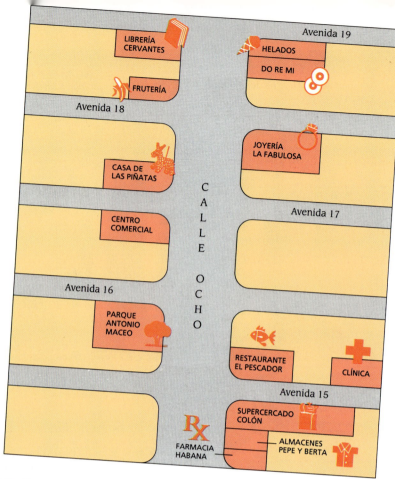

Actividades

Actividad A Answers

Answers will vary but may include the following:

1. Está en la esquina de la calle ocho y la avenida diez y seis.
2. ... y la avenida diez y siete.
3. ... y la avenida quince.
4. ... y la avenida diez y nueve.
5. ... y la avenida diez y nueve, cerca de la heladería.
6. y la avenida diez y ocho.

Actividades

A **El plano de la ciudad.** Using the map of **La Pequeña Habana,** describe where each of the following is.

Por ejemplo:

> el supermercado Colón
> *Está en la esquina de la calle Ocho y la avenida Quince.*
> *(Está al lado de Almacenes Pepe y Berta, etc.).*

1. el parque Antonio Maceo
2. el centro comercial
3. el restaurante El Pescador
4. la heladería
5. la librería Cervantes
6. la frutería

434 CAPÍTULO 6

B **En mi ciudad.** Where would you tell a new student to go in your town or city to do the following things?

Por ejemplo:

> **para comprar una tarjeta de cumpleaños**
> *Debes ir a la tienda "Marie's". Cuando sales de la escuela, doblas a la izquierda. Sigues tres cuadras y doblas a la derecha. La tienda está al lado del cine.*

1. **para comprar revistas**
2. **para comprar un videojuego**
3. **para comer hamburguesas**
4. **para ver una película nueva**
5. **para nadar**
6. **para sacar una novela de la biblioteca**

C **¿En qué vienes?** Ask three classmates how they get to school.

Por ejemplo:

ESTUDIANTE A	**ESTUDIANTE B**
John, ¿en qué vienes a la escuela?	A veces vengo a pie pero casi siempre vengo en autobús.

D **¿Adónde vamos?** In pairs or small groups, think of a place in your area where you want another group to go, but don't tell them their destination. Give them detailed directions. Have them tell you where they are.

Por ejemplo:

GRUPO A

(1) **Uds. salen de la escuela, doblan a la izquierda y siguen diez cuadras. Van al edificio al lado de la tienda de discos.**

(3) **¡Sí!** (¿"Wendy's"? **No, "Wendy's" está muy lejos. Están en el cine).**

GRUPO B

(2) **Estamos en "Wendy's", ¿verdad?**

Lección 3 **435**

Presentation

Read the Cultura viva on this page. You may wish to use a map to point out the different geographical references in the reading. You may also want to use a map to point out where different words are used to express the same object in the English-speaking world, most notably the U.S., Great Britain, and Australia.

Did You Know?

Just as some terms in the Spanish language vary considerably from one country or region to another, the same happens in the English language.
Have students notice the difference between the British and U.S. expressions, just in talking about cars.

British	U.S.
bonnet	hood
lorry	truck
boot	trunk
estate car	station wagon
wing	fender

Even within the U.S. people speak differently. For example, any one of the following expressions may be used to refer to a carbonated drink: "pop," "soda pop," "soda," "soft drink," "tonic."

Critical Thinking Activity

Can you give some examples of different words that are used to say the same thing in English? Where might you look for examples?

Actividad Answers

1. coche
2. habitación
3. anteojos
4. piscina
5. cinturón

CULTURA VIVA 1

Los dialectos de un idioma

En su conversación con Rafael, Carmen usó la palabra "guagua" en vez de "autobús". La gente de diferentes regiones muchas veces dice cosas de una manera diferente aunque habla el mismo idioma. El español que se habla en México es un poco diferente del que se habla en el Caribe, en España, en los países de la región andina, y en Chile o la Argentina.

Por ejemplo, aquí tienes tres palabras diferentes para una misma cosa.

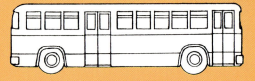

Así se dice generalmente:	un autobús.
Pero se dice así en el Caribe:	una guagua.
Y se dice así en México:	un camión.

Actividad

Each of the following groups of words contains different ways of saying the same thing. Choose the general term for each, which you have learned in this book.

1. carro	coche	auto	máquina
2. habitación	cuarto	dormitorio	recámara
3. gafas	anteojos	lentes	espejuelos
4. alberca	piscina	pileta	
5. cinturón	cinto	correa	

Pronunciation

A. You may wish to play the recorded version of this pronunciation activity, located at the end of Cassette 6.3. You may also wish to write these lines on the chalkboard and have students copy them into their notebooks:

Para ti es durazno
para mí es melocotón.
Yo tomo la guagua
y tú, el camión.
Un idioma, una herencia.
Digo yo: ¡Viva la diferencia!

B. Have students repeat words and phrases individually and in unison. You may wish to focus on the /t/ sound as in ti; melocotón; tomo; tú.

Estructura 1

How to Say That Someone Is Coming

The verb venir

1. To ask what mode of transportation a friend uses to arrive somewhere, ask **¿En qué vienes?**

    ¿En qué vienes a la escuela?   **A veces vengo en coche.**

2. Here are all the present tense forms of the verb **venir**.

SINGULAR	PLURAL
vengo	**venimos**
vienes	**venís***
viene	**vienen**

*This form is rarely used in the Spanish-speaking world, except for Spain.

¿Vienes a mi fiesta?
Sí, vengo con mi primo José. Venimos con los discos y los tacos. Creo que Miguel no viene; está enfermo.

Actividades

A **¿En qué vienen?** Tell how the following people or things get to the places below.

Por ejemplo:

> tu amigo(a) / a tu casa
> *Viene a pie (en bicicleta, en coche).*

1. tu abuelo(a) / a tu casa
2. tu mamá (papá) / del trabajo a tu casa
3. tu hermano(a) / de la escuela a tu casa
4. tu tío(a) / a tu casa
5. un coche importado / del Japón a los Estados Unidos
6. un hombre (una mujer) de negocios / de Nueva York a Los Ángeles
7. una carta / de la Argentina a los Estados Unidos

Lección 3   **437**

Estructura 1

Structure Teaching Resources
1. Workbook, p. 191
2. Cassette 6.3
3. Student Tape Manual, p. 160
4. Estructura Masters 6.3
5. Lesson Quizzes, p. 127

Bell Ringer Review

Directions to students: Imagine you will be taking several trips (both near and far) in the future. Write down what method of transportation you will use to get to the places listed.
Por ejemplo: a Francia
Voy a ir a Francia en avión.

1. a Canadá
2. a Puerto Rico
3. al banco
4. a tu restaurante favorito
5. a la casa de tus abuelos
6. a Nueva York
7. al cine

Presentation

Lead students through steps 1–2 on page 437. You may want to ask students the following questions using **venir**. For example: **¿Cómo vienes a la escuela? ¿Cómo vienen a... y... ? ¿Quién viene en moto? ¿Cuántos vienen en autobús?**, etc.

Actividades

Actividad A Answers
Answers 1–4 will vary.

5. Viene en barco.
6. Viene en avión.
7. Viene en avión.

B **Estás invitado.** You have been invited to a party at 8:00 at a friend's house. Your friend calls you to make sure you're coming. Answer his or her questions.

Por ejemplo:

> ¿De dónde vienes?
> *Vengo de mi casa (del partido, del centro, etc.).*

1. ¿En qué vienes?
2. ¿Con quién vienes?
3. ¿Con qué ropa vienes?
4. ¿A qué hora vienes?

C **¿De dónde vienen?** The U.S. has become home to many people from other countries. Tell where the following groups come from and how they arrive.

Por ejemplo:

> los cubanos
> *Los cubanos vienen de Cuba en avión o en barco.*

1. los canadienses
2. los portugueses
3. los japoneses
4. los dominicanos
5. los mexicanos
6. los argentinos
7. los ecuatorianos

D **Los meses del año.** Tell how you and your classmates are dressed when you come to school in the following months.

Por ejemplo:

> en abril
> *En abril venimos con pantalones de algodón, camisas o blusas...*

1. en septiembre
2. en enero
3. en mayo
4. en noviembre

438   CAPÍTULO 6

438

Una carta a los abuelos

Carmen les escribe una carta a sus abuelitos, que viven en Nueva York.

Miami, 27 de abril

Queridos abuelitos:

Gracias por su carta tan bonita. Mi tío Lucas llegó con mi primo Rafael de la Argentina la semana pasada. Fuimos anoche a un restaurante en La Pequeña Habana donde comimos comida típica cubana. Rafael comió arroz con pollo y de postre comió helado de mamey. Un día, mi tío Lucas nos preparó un plato al estilo argentino. ¡Qué rico!

El sábado pasado mi compañera Julia dio una fiesta y nos invitó a Rafael y a mí. Rafael tocó la guitarra, bailó mucho y habló inglés toda la noche.

Bueno, abuelitos, termino mi carta ahora. Les prometo escribir otra la semana que viene.

Un abrazo de su nieta que los quiere mucho,

Carmen

Actividad

Which of the following statements about what Rafael or tío Lucas did in Florida are correct, based on Carmen's letter? If the statement is correct, write **Sí, es cierto.** If the statement is incorrect, correct it as in the example.

Por ejemplo:

> Rafael tocó el saxofón en la fiesta.
> *No. Tocó la guitarra.*

1. Rafael llegó a la Florida con su papá.
2. Rafael habló español en la fiesta.
3. Rafael comió pescado en el restaurante cubano.
4. El tío Lucas preparó comida mexicana una noche.

Cultura viva 2

Presentation

Read the Cultura viva on this page. You may wish to read it aloud to the class, or have individual students take turns reading one or two sentences.

Did You Know?

Some popular Argentine dishes are **asado con cuero,** beef roasted in its hide over an open fire; **pucheros,** stews of chicken or other meat with vegetables; **empanadas,** pastries stuffed with meat or seafood; and **matahambre,** stuffed roast. The Argentine diet includes a considerable amount of meat, since a large area of the pampa, which covers about one fifth of Argentina, is a grazing area for cattle.

Like the U.S., Argentina is a country of immigrants: the Italians introduced spaghetti and other pastas into the Argentine diet, and the English introduced tea time — a custom many Argentines still observe.

Critical Thinking Activity

Compare the letter Carmen wrote to her grandparents to a letter you might write to your grandparents. How would your letter be different? How might it be similar?

Actividad Answers

1. **Sí.**
2. **No. Habló inglés.**
3. **No. Comió arroz con pollo.**
4. **No. Preparó un plato al estilo argentino.**

For the Native Speaker

Have students interview an immigrant who is now living in your area. They should ask him or her about final preparations for the trip to the U.S., buying tickets, the trip itself, first impressions, etc. Have students read their interviews to the class.

439

Bell Ringer Review

Directions to students: Draw a map of your school. Write out directions to go to three of your classes. Then exchange papers with a classmate and see whether or not you can follow each other's directions.

Structure Focus

In this lesson, the presentation of the preterit is limited to the third person singular. The third person plural preterit forms will be presented in Chapter 6, Lesson 4. A summary of preterit forms is presented in Chapter 6, Lesson 6.

Presentation

A. Lead students through steps 1–2 on page 440. You may wish to review forms of the preterit students have studied earlier by going over selected exercises in the lessons cited in the Structure Focus above.

B. You may wish to narrate the following, emphasizing the preterit forms of the verbs: **Ayer Carmen fue al centro. Antes de ir le pidió dinero a su papá para comprar discos. Su papá le dio veinte dólares. En el centro Carmen vio a su amiga Julia. Julia invitó a Carmen a una fiesta en su casa el sábado. Car-**

Estructura 2

*How To Say What Someone
Did in the Past*

*Third person singular
forms of the preterit*

You have already practiced asking or telling a friend what he or she did in the past.

¿Qué hiciste ayer? ¿Jugaste béisbol o fuiste al cine?

You have also learned to say what you did in the past.

**El invierno pasado aprendí a esquiar. Esquié con mis
amigos.**

In addition, you have learned to say what you and someone else ("we") did in the past.

Carmen y yo fuimos a la fiesta de Ana. Comimos mucho.

1. To describe the past actions of another person or thing (he, she, it) or to talk to a person formally **(usted)**, use these endings for the preterit tense.
   - for **-ar** verbs: **-ó**
   - for **-er** and **-ir** verbs: **-ió**

The written accent over the **-ó** tells you to stress that vowel sound. It is very important to write the accent and pronounce the vowel.

> **Carmen no compró nada en el centro comercial. Su primo
> compró un suéter y algunos discos. Después, en una
> cafetería, Carmen comió helado y su primo comió pizza.**
>
> **Señor Marín, ¿vivió usted muchos años en Cuba?**
> **Y usted, señora, ¿cuándo llegó a los Estados Unidos?**

2. The following verbs are formed differently.

ir	fue	El tío Lucas no fue al centro comercial con Rafael.
dar	dio	Pero le dio dinero.
ver	vio	El tío Lucas vio un programa en la tele.
hacer	hizo	También le hizo un favor a su hermana.
leer	leyó	Carmen le leyó el anuncio a Rafael.
oír	oyó	Creo que tu papá no te oyó.
pedir	pidió	Y pidió permiso para dar una fiesta.

Actividades

A **Favores.** Name someone who did each of the following favors for you recently. If no one did the favor, use the word **nadie**.

Por ejemplo:

> ayudar
> *La maestra de inglés me ayudó con mi composición. (Nadie me ayudó).*

1. prestar dinero
2. mandar una carta
3. llamar por teléfono
4. dar buenos consejos
5. comprar algo bonito
6. enseñar a hacer algo nuevo

B **Muchos planes.** Using the verb phrases below, write a short paragraph telling what Carmen's mother did at the following times: (a) prior to Lucas and Rafael's visit, (b) the day they arrived, and (c) during their visit.

Por ejemplo:

> antes / invitar a Lucas y a Rafael
> *Antes invitó a Lucas y a Rafael...*

ANTES

llamar a la Argentina
escribir una carta
dar instrucciones
buscar otra cama para la habitación
hacer la cama

EL DÍA DE SU LLEGADA

oír las noticias en la radio
ver a su hermano
llevar a sus parientes a casa

DURANTE LA VISITA

preparar una comida cubana
llevar a sus parientes a Orlando

Medios
EN ESPAÑOL

Medios de Comunicación en Español que Prestan Servicio Diariamente a la Comunidad Hispana...

RADIO

WCMQ	1220 AM	92.1 FM
1411 Coral Way		854-1830
WOCN	1450 AM	
1779 W. Flagler		649-1450
WRHC	1550 AM	
2260 S.W. 8th Street		541-3300
WQBA	1140 AM	
2828 Coral Way		447-1144
WSUA	1160 AM	

men regresó a casa temprano. Cuando llegó a casa Carmen le hizo un favor a su primo y leyó el periódico. También le pidió permiso a su papá para ir a la fiesta de Julia. Carmen no oyó cuando su papá le dijo, "Cómo no, puedes ir". Now ask students questions about the narrative. For example: **¿Adónde fue Carmen? ¿Cuánto dinero le dio su papá?**, etc.

Actividades

Actividad A Answers
Answers will vary, however they should include the following:

1. ... me prestó...
2. ... me mandó...
3. ... me llamó...
4. ... me dio...
5. ... me compró...
6. ... me enseñó...

Actividad B Answers
Answers will vary but should include the following:
Antes: llamó, escribió, dio, buscó, hizo.
El día de su llegada: oyó, vio, llevó.
Durante la visita: preparó, llevó.

Learning from Photos and Realia

You may want to have students look at the photo on page 440. Ask: **¿Qué pidió la señorita, un café, leche o un refresco?** You may also want to direct students' attention to the realia on page 441. Have them find out if there are any Spanish-language radio stations in your area. What are the call letters? What kinds of programs can they hear?

C **¿Qué hizo tu compañero?** Find out from a classmate three things that he or she did last week. Report back to the class.

Por ejemplo:

ESTUDIANTE A
¿Qué hiciste la semana pasada, Debra?

ESTUDIANTE B
Gané el partido de tenis. Salí con mis amigas el sábado por la noche...

(A la clase:) **Debra ganó el partido de tenis, salió con sus amigas el sábado por la noche...**

D **Gustos.** Do you always eat the same things as your friends? Tell when you ate with your friends last and what each of you ate.

Por ejemplo:

Joe y yo fuimos a comer en la cafetería ayer. Yo pedí una hamburguesa, Joe pidió un sandwich de queso. Los dos pedimos ensaladas.

E **Regalos.** Tell what gifts you have exchanged with five friends or family members during the last year.

Por ejemplo:

Para mi cumpleaños mi papá me dio entradas a un partido de béisbol. Yo le di una corbata.

F **Lecturas.** Carmen is reading more in Spanish to improve her vocabulary. Tell whether she probably read the following items in (a) **el periódico,** (b) **una revista,** or (c) **una carta.**

Por ejemplo:

las noticias
Leyó las noticias en el periódico.

1. un anuncio de una liquidación de faldas
2. una receta para arroz con pollo
3. instrucciones para hacer una falda
4. los planes de los abuelos para viajar a México
5. su horóscopo

Fútbol:

Brasil se enfrenta a Chile en Santiago

SANTIAGO, (AFP) - Las Selecci de Brasil y Chile protagonizarán un " cil" partido el próximo miércoles, e Estadio Nacional, pronosticó el téc brasileño Pablo Roberto Falcao al arrib Santiago junto al nuevo plantel brasileñ

"Si bien es cierto que es un amisto Chile cuenta con la base de Colo Col Universidad Católica, los líderes de Primera División. Será un juego muy d cil", expresó Falcao al referirse al prime de los dos encuentros de la Copa Exped Texeira, programado para las 20H locales (23H00 Gmt).

Ese partido -dijo Falcao- "me servi para observar lo que podemos ir elaboran para nuestro futuro futbolístico" y seña que, lamentablemente, sus jugadores só podrán realizar dos prácticas muy suaves Santiago.

Falcao, quien dirigió al equipo de Brasi que sufrió un revés por 3/0 ante España observó atentamente a sus futbolistas en e entrenamiento que hicieron en el césped del estadio San Carlos de Apoquind

Finalmente

Situaciones

A conversar Imagine you are a new student at your school. Converse with a classmate to find out the following information.

1. Ask how to get to your next class.
2. Find out where the gym is.
3. Ask about two other places that you have to go within the school.
4. Ask about a good place to get something to eat after school. Find out what mode of transportation you need to take and ask directions.

A escribir Write a brief composition about someone you admire a great deal, such as someone in your family, community, a celebrity, or a historical figure. Tell when and where the person was born and list several of his or her accomplishments.

Repaso de vocabulario

INSTRUCCIONES
al lado de
cerca de
detrás de
enfrente de
entre
lejos de

ACTIVIDADES
doblar
venir

TRANSPORTE
a pie
el autobús
el avión
el barco
la camioneta
el tren

OTRAS PALABRAS
la cuadra
la esquina
hasta (as far as, up to)
el lado

EXPRESIÓN
Está a + distance + **de** + place.
Sigue(s) derecho.

Lección 3 **443**

Finalmente

Situaciones

Lesson 3 Evaluation
The A conversar and A escribir situations on this page are designed to give students the opportunity to use as many language functions and as much vocabulary from the lesson as possible. The A conversar and A escribir are also intended to show how well students are able to meet the lesson objectives.

Presentation
Prior to doing the A conversar and A escribir on this page, you may wish to play the Situaciones listening activities on Cassette 6.3 as a means of helping students organize the material.

Learning from Photos
You may wish to have students look at the photo on page 443. Have students imagine the conversation the two young women are having.

Lección 4

Objectives

By the end of this lesson, students will be able to:

1. describe weather conditions
2. refer back to someone or something already mentioned
3. say what others did in the past

Lesson 4 Resources

1. Workbook, pp. 195–199
2. Vocabulario Transparencies 6.4
3. Cassette 6.4
4. Student Tape Manual, pp. 165–169
5. Lesson Quizzes, pp. 129–131
6. Computer Software, Disk 2
7. Video Cassette
8. Estructura Masters 6.4
9. Diversiones Masters 6.4

Bell Ringer Review

Directions to students: Villabonita is a small but pretty town. See whether you can draw a plan of the town from the instructions given.

En el centro hay un parque en la Plaza Mayor. Al lado del parque hay varias tiendas—de ropa, de discos, etc. Enfrente de las tiendas hay un cine y un banco. Entre el cine y el banco hay un pequeño mercado. Al lado del cine hay un hotel de diez pisos. Cerca del hotel grande hay un restaurante donde sirven comida italiana. Detrás del banco hay una discoteca muy popular. Lejos del centro comercial hay una piscina.

¡A comenzar!

Presentation

A. Lead students through each of the three functions given on page

Lección 4

Un regalo especial

¡A comenzar!

The following are some of the things you will be learning to do in this lesson.

When you want to . . .	You use . . .
1. say that it's hot or cool out	• **Hace calor / Hace fresco.**
2. refer back to someone or something already mentioned	• **la** (feminine words) • **lo** (masculine words)
3. say what others did in the past	• **-aron** at the end of **-ar** verbs • **-ieron** at the end of regular **-er** or **-ir** verbs

Now find examples of the above words and phrases in the following conversation.

Temperaturas para hoy 28 de abril

Ciudad	C°	F°
Buenos Aires	10	50
Caracas	25	77
La Habana	30	86
Lima	15	59
Ciudad de México	22	72
Miami	29	84
San Juan	27	81
Santiago	5	41

Getting Ready for Lesson 4

You may wish to use one or more of the following suggestions to prepare students for the lesson:

1. Use the weather map on page 448, or your daily newspaper's weather report (international listing, if possible). Distribute to students a list of cities such as those below and sketch or write beside each city the following articles of cloth-

ing: **abrigo, chaqueta, traje de baño.** Use gestures as you describe the weather in these cities. For example: **Hoy en nuestra ciudad hace fresco pero el periódico dice que en Tucson hace calor, con la temperatura máxima cerca de 95 grados. ¡Qué calor!**

As you describe the weather for these cities, have students circle the article of

Carmen y Rafael conversan en el autobús.

CARMEN: ¿Qué regalos necesitas comprar, Rafael?

RAFAEL: Bueno, primero le quiero comprar algo muy bonito a mi mamá.

CARMEN: No la conozco. Mis padres la conocieron cuando visitaron la Argentina el año pasado. Bueno, ¿qué le piensas comprar a tu mamá?

RAFAEL: Pues, sé que le gusta la ropa. Le puedo comprar un suéter de lana.

CARMEN: Pero, ¿de lana, en abril? ¡Hace mucho calor!

RAFAEL: Pero, Carmen, cuando aquí es primavera, en la Argentina es otoño y hace fresco.

CARMEN: Ah, sí, claro. Pues, vi un bonito suéter de lana en el centro comercial la semana pasada. ¿Por qué no lo compramos?

Actividades preliminares

A Complete the following sentences about the weather in your area.

1. Hace calor en los meses de _____.
2. Hace fresco en los meses de _____.
3. Cuando hace calor me gusta _____.
4. Cuando hace fresco me gusta _____.

B Complete the following sentences about what some of your friends did recently.

1. Fueron a _____.
2. Vieron _____.
3. Comieron _____.
4. Compraron _____.
5. Jugaron _____.

Lección 4   445

444, progressing from the English to the Spanish for each function. Then have students find these words and phrases in the dialogue on page 445.

B. Introduce the Lesson 4 dialogue by reading it aloud or by playing the cassette version. Have students listen to determine what the difference is between the weather in Miami and in Buenos Aires.

C. Now ask students to open their books and look at the dialogue as you lead them through the following questions:

1. ¿A quién quiere comprar un regalo Rafael?
2. ¿Conoce Carmen a la mamá de Rafael? ¿La conocen sus padres? ¿Cuándo la conocieron?
3. ¿Qué le piensa comprar?
4. ¿Qué tiempo hace en Miami en abril? ¿Qué tiempo hace en Buenos Aires?
5. ¿Dónde vio Carmen un bonito suéter de lana? ¿Cuándo?

Actividades preliminares

Actividad A Answers
Answers may vary but might include the following:

1. Hace calor en los meses de junio, julio y agosto.
2. Hace fresco en los meses de abril, mayo, septiembre, octubre.
3. and 4. Answers will vary.

Actividad B Answers
Answers will vary.

Additional Practice
Tell how often you see the following people.
Por ejemplo: tu hermana
La veo todos los días.

1. tu abuela
2. el director de la escuela
3. tu amigo _____
4. tu amiga _____
5. el dentista

---

clothing they would wear there. Be sure to use the temperature as this will key the meanings of **calor, fresco, frío,** etc. Use only extremes for comparison.

2. Ask individual students in the class if they know other students: **Jack, ¿conoces a Lisa?** After the student responds affirmatively, say: **Sí, la conoces.** Repeat this several times with different students, male and female. Then use **¿Ves a _____ mucho?** and repeat.

Vocabulary Teaching Resources
1. Vocabulario Transparencies 6.4
2. Workbook, p. 195
3. Cassette 6.4
4. Student Tape Manual, p. 166
5. Lesson Quizzes, p. 129

Bell Ringer Review

Directions to students: Reread the letter that Carmen wrote to her grandparents (page 439). Close your book. Then complete the following sentences from the letter by filling in the blanks. See how much you can remember.

1. Mi tío Lucas llegó con mi primo _____ de la _____ la semana pasada.
2. Fuimos anoche a un restaurante en La Pequeña _____ donde comimos comida típica _____.
3. Rafael comió arroz con _____ y de postre comió helado de _____.
4. Mi compañera Julia dio una _____ y nos invitó a Rafael y a _____.
5. Rafael _____ la guitarra, bailó mucho y habló _____ toda la noche.

Presentation

A. Have students open their books to the Vocabulario on pages 446 and 447. Model each new word on page 446, beginning with the question, **¿Qué tiempo hace?** Have students repeat each phrase or word in unison.

B. You may wish to ask students where they go and what they do in the following situations:

   1. **cuando hace sol**
   2. **cuando hace frío**
   3. **cuando llueve**

Vocabulario

¿Qué tiempo hace?

Hace buen tiempo.

Hace sol.

Hace calor.

Hace un tiempo regular.

Hace fresco.

Hace frío.

Nieva.

Está nublado.

Hace mal tiempo.

Llueve.

Hace viento.

446 CAPÍTULO 6

Total Physical Response

Getting Ready
For TPR 1 use Vocabulario Transparencies 6.4. Call students to the projector. For TPR 3, make photocopies of pages 446 and 447 on standard size paper. Make one copy per student.

TPR 1
(Pairs of students.)
Apunten al cuadro donde hace calor.
Apunten al cuadro donde llueve.
Toquen cl cuadro donde hay montañas.
Toquen el cuadro donde está el desierto.
Cubran el bosque con el papel.
Señalen al cuadro donde nieva.
Señalen al cuadro donde hace viento.
(Interchange commands and vocabulary.)

¿Por qué no vamos...?

al desierto

al lago

al bosque

al río

a las montañas

Podemos...

dar una caminata

dormir al aire libre

Actividades

A **De viaje.** Name three places in the U.S, or elsewhere, that you would like to visit because of the weather. Then name three places you would not like to visit.

Por ejemplo:

> Quisiera visitar _____ porque siempre _____. No quisiera visitar _____ porque _____.

Now tell one or two things that you could do in each of the places you listed.

Por ejemplo:

> En _____ puedo _____.

---

4. cuando nieva

C. Model the words and phrases on page 447, beginning with the question, **¿Por qué no vamos... ?** Then ask individual students whether or not they like to go to the places mentioned to do the activities shown in the Vocabulario. For example: **¿Te gusta ir al bosque cuando hace buen tiempo? ¿Te gusta dormir al aire libre cuando hace viento?** Encourage students to give a complete response. For example: **Me gusta ir al bosque cuando hace buen tiempo. No, me gusta dormir al aire libre.**

D. Ask individual students, **¿Qué te gusta hacer?** Encourage students to give a complete response. For example: **Me gusta dar una caminata.**

When Students Ask

You may wish to give students the following additional vocabulary to allow them to talk about weather conditions and outdoor activities.
hay neblina
acampar
explorar
escalar montañas
bajar el río en balsa
practicar tabla hawaiana

Actividades

Actividad A Answers
Answers will vary.

Actividad B Answers

1. En Lima hace fresco y está soleado.
2. En México hace fresco y está nublado.
3. En San Juan hace calor y llueve.
4. En Bogotá hace fresco y llueve.
5. En Santiago hace calor y está soleado.
6. En Caracas hace calor y está nublado.

Comparisons and contrasts will vary.

Extension

After doing Actividad B, you may wish to extend the learning by asking students to describe the weather in the remaining cities listed in the weather chart, i.e., **Nueva York, Los Ángeles, Montreal.**

Actividades C and D Answers

Answers will vary.

B **¿Qué tiempo hace?** Describe the weather in each of the following Latin American cities, based on the weather map. Then select two cities to compare or contrast. Compare weather conditions using **y**; contrast conditions using **pero.**

Por ejemplo:

> Buenos Aires
> *En Buenos Aires hace calor y está nublado.*
> Buenos Aires / La Habana
> *En Buenos Aires hace calor y está nublado*
> *pero en La Habana hace fresco.*

1. Lima
2. México
3. San Juan
4. Bogotá
5. Santiago
6. Caracas

C **Cosas de cada estación.** Working in small groups, each student tells what he or she does during each season. One student records all the activities mentioned. Another student uses this list to report back to the class on the group's activities.

Por ejemplo:

> en verano

ESTUDIANTE A
En verano nado y juego béisbol.

ESTUDIANTE B
(Escribe:) nadar, jugar béisbol

ESTUDIANTE C
En verano nadamos y jugamos béisbol.

D **Diversiones.** Write down at least three activities to do in each of the places listed on p. 449.

Por ejemplo:

> la playa
> *En la playa puedes practicar el esquí acuático, bucear, tomar el sol...*

448   CAPÍTULO 6

TEMPERATURAS EN OTRAS CIUDADES

CIUDAD	MIN	MAX	CONDICIONES
Nueva York	10	18	soleado
Los Angeles	51	74	soleado
Bogotá	45	64	lluvia
Buenos Aires	67	89	nublado
Caracas	57	81	nublado
La Habana	57	66	nublado
Lima	63	77	soleado
México	36	75	nublado
Montreal	-12	13	nieve
Nassau	53	66	nublado
San Juan	71	90	lluvia
Santiago	57	88	soleado

Cooperative Learning

Assign each team one of the places mentioned in Actividad D. Each team will decide on three or four activities that can be done in the place assigned to them. They must be activities that can be acted out in front of the class. When each team presents its activities in front of the class, team members should take turns miming their activities.

For the Native Speaker

Have native speakers write a short weather report. Then have each student present his or her weather report to the class. Students will indicate comprehension by telling what kind of clothing they will wear for the day.

1. el lago
2. el desierto
3. las montañas
4. el bosque
5. el río
6. el campo
7. la ciudad

E **Todo depende del tiempo.** Answer the following questions for each of these weather reports for Miami.

- ¿Qué ropa vas a llevar?
- ¿Qué piensas hacer?

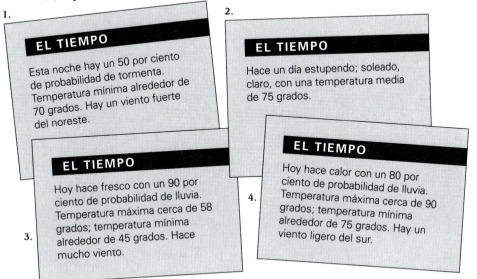

1.

EL TIEMPO

Esta noche hay un 50 por ciento de probabilidad de tormenta. Temperatura mínima alrededor de 70 grados. Hay un viento fuerte del noreste.

2.

EL TIEMPO

Hace un día estupendo; soleado, claro, con una temperatura media de 75 grados.

3.

EL TIEMPO

Hoy hace fresco con un 90 por ciento de probabilidad de lluvia. Temperatura máxima cerca de 58 grados; temperatura mínima alrededor de 45 grados. Hace mucho viento.

4.

EL TIEMPO

Hoy hace calor con un 80 por ciento de probabilidad de lluvia. Temperatura máxima cerca de 90 grados; temperatura mínima alrededor de 75 grados. Hay un viento ligero del sur.

F **De vacaciones.** The suitcase below was left behind by a forgetful traveler. Answer the following questions about this person by looking at the luggage.

1. ¿Cómo viaja?
2. ¿De dónde es?
3. ¿Qué le gusta hacer?
4. ¿Adónde va?
5. ¿Qué lleva?
6. ¿Va muy lejos de donde vive?
7. ¿Qué tiempo hace allí?

Lección 4 **449**

Presentation

Read the Cultura viva on this page. You may wish to use the map to illustrate the Northern and Southern hemispheres described in the reading.

Did You Know?

The closer one gets to the equator, the less extreme the seasonal changes are. Altitude and ocean currents also play a role. For example, in Ecuador one can follow the equator through three climate zones: coastal, mountain, and tropical jungle.

In the southern hemisphere the school year begins in March and ends in December.

Critical Thinking Activity

Ask students the following questions:

1. If you lived in Argentina, during which months would you be most likely to do each of the following activities?
   a. ir a la playa
   b. esquiar
   c. acampar
2. During which months would you have your summer vacation?
3. In what season would you celebrate Christmas (Chanukah)?

Actividad Answers

Answers will vary.

Extension

After doing the Actividad, you may wish to extend the learning by reviewing months and seasons.

Learning from Maps

You may want to have students look at the map on page 450 and locate the equator. Have them name the South American countries that are fully or partially below the equator.

Las estaciones del año

Las estaciones del año, el frío y el calor, dependen del hemisferio. Los Estados Unidos están en el hemisferio boreal (norte), pero la Argentina está en el hemisferio austral (sur). Cuando aquí estamos en invierno, en la Argentina están en verano.

LA ESTACIÓN	EN LOS ESTADOS UNIDOS	EN LA ARGENTINA
el verano	junio, julio, agosto	diciembre, enero, febrero
el otoño	septiembre, octubre, noviembre	marzo, abril, mayo
el invierno	diciembre, enero, febrero	junio, julio, agosto
la primavera	marzo, abril, mayo	septiembre, octubre, noviembre

Actividad

List the things students are probably doing right now in the Southern Hemisphere. What clothes are they probably wearing?

Pronunciation

A. You may wish to play the recorded version of this pronunciation activity, located at the end of Cassette 6.4. You may also wish to write these lines on the chalkboard and have students copy them into their notebook:

En enero hace frío,
en febrero también;
en marzo hace viento,
en abril está bien.

B. Have students repeat words and phrases individually and in unison. You may wish to focus on the /b,v/ sound as in febrero, también, viento, abril.

Estructura 1

How to Talk about What Others Did

Third person plural forms of the preterit

You have learned to tell what someone did in the past using **-ar**, **-er**, and **-ir** verbs. You used the same form to tell or ask what someone whom you address formally **(usted)** did in the past.

- Regular **-ar** verbs: **-ó**

Andrés terminó su tarea de álgebra y luego empezó su composición.

- Regular **-er** and **-ir** verbs: **-ió**

Escribió dos páginas y luego aprendió el vocabulario nuevo para la clase de español.

1. To tell what more than one person **(ellos, ellas)** did in the past or to talk to more than one person **(ustedes)** about their past actions, use the following forms of the preterit tense.

- **-ar** verbs: **-aron**
- **-er** and **-ir** verbs: **-ieron**

Carmen y Rafael tomaron el autobús para ir al centro comercial. Allí vieron muchas cosas bonitas y buscaron suéteres. Después comieron algo en la cafetería. Cuando regresaron a casa, los padres de Carmen les preguntaron: —¿Compraron algo bonito?

2. As you have seen, the following verbs are formed differently.

ir	Mis tíos *fueron* a Puerto Rico el mes pasado.
dar	Allí *dieron* muchos paseos por la playa.
hacer	*Hicieron* muchas cosas en San Juan.
leer	*Leyeron* libros sobre Puerto Rico antes de
oír	viajar. *Oyeron* música puertorriqueña.
ver	*Vieron* playas bonitas.
pedir	En los restaurantes siempre *pidieron* comida puertorriqueña.

Structure Teaching Resources
1. Workboook, pp. 196–197
2. Cassette 6.4
3. Student Tape Manual, p. 166
4. Estructura Masters 6.4
5. Lesson Quizzes, p. 130

Bell Ringer Review

Directions to students: Where would you most likely find the following people or things? Make headings for four columns on your paper: **bosque, desierto, lago, montaña.** Arrange the following people or things under the appropriate headings.
**agua
serpientes
veleros
esquís acuáticos
peces
caballos
animales
conejos
barcos
trenes**
Can you think of any other to add to the list?

Structure Focus
In this lesson, the presentation of the preterit is limited to the third person plural forms. The **yo** and **tú** forms of the preterit were presented in Chapter 5, Lessons 5 and 6. The **nosotros** forms were presented in Chapter 6, Lesson 1. The third person singular forms were presented in Chapter 6, Lesson 3. A summary of preterit forms is presented in Chapter 6, Lesson 6.

Presentation

Lead students through steps 1–2 on page 451. You may wish to review forms of the preterit students have studied earlier by going over selected exercises in the lessons cited in the Structure Focus above.

You may also wish to refer students to the preterit verb charts at the back of their textbook, or write several verb paradigms on the chalkboard, pointing out the preterit forms students have already learned, and those they will learn in this lesson.

Actividades

Actividad A Answers
1. Practicaron el inglés.
2. Compraron regalos.
3. Mandaron tarjetas postales.
4. Comieron comida...
5. Dieron paseos...
6. Hicieron amigos nuevos.
7. Vieron programas...
8. Fueron al cine.
9. Leyeron el periódico.
10. Oyeron música cubana.

Actividad B Answers
Answers will vary.

Actividad C Answers
Answers will vary, however students should use the third person preterit in each question.

Additional Practice
After completing Actividades A, B, and C, you may wish to reinforce the learning with the following activity: The school newspaper is asking you to interview two exchange students from Honduras. Make a list of five questions you will ask them about their first week in the U.S. Two classmates will play the roles of the exchange students. **Por ejemplo: ¿Cuándo llegaron? ¿Cuándo aprendieron a hablar inglés?**

Reteaching

How would you say your friends did the following things last week: **trabajar en casa, comer en la cafetería, ver la tele, hacer ejercicio, leer el periódico, ir a la playa, dar un paseo, pedir dinero a su papá**

Actividades

A **En los Estados Unidos.** Below is a list of some of the things that Tío Lucas and Rafael did during their visit to the U.S. Say what they did.

Por ejemplo:

> visitar el Epcot Center / vivir en casa de Carmen
> *Visitaron el Epcot Center. Vivieron en casa de Carmen.*

1. practicar el inglés
2. comprar regalos
3. mandar tarjetas postales
4. comer comida americana y cubana
5. dar paseos por la ciudad
6. hacer amigos nuevos
7. ver programas interesantes
8. ir al cine
9. leer el periódico
10. oír música cubana

B **¿Qué hicieron?** Tell a classmate five things that you and your friends did between your last Spanish class and this one. Your classmate will make a note of them and report to the class.

Por ejemplo:

> Jugamos "frisbee" y comimos hamburguesas.
>
> (A la clase:) David y sus amigos jugaron "frisbee" y comieron hamburguesas.

C **Mis compañeros.** Interview two of your classmates about recent activities, using the topics below. Use the following question words in your interview: **qué, cuándo, a qué hora, dónde, adónde, por qué, cómo, quién.** Take notes and report back to the class the things your classmates have in common.

Por ejemplo:

> programas de televisión
> *¿Qué programas vieron ustedes? (Juan, ¿a qué hora viste...?)*
>
> (A la clase:) Los dos vieron un partido de béisbol...

1. viajes
2. notas
3. comida
4. películas
5. fiestas
6. música
7. deportes
8. compras
9. quehaceres
10. ropa

La temperatura

Sólo en los Estados Unidos se usa el sistema Fahrenheit para medir la temperatura. En el resto del mundo se usa la escala de Celsius, o los "grados centígrados", para medir el frío y el calor. Para estimar la temperatura, usa estas fórmulas:

grados Fahrenheit − 32 × 0,55 = grados centígrados
grados centígrados × 1,8 + 32 = grados Fahrenheit

| 35° C | 18° C | 0° C | -12° C |

Actividades

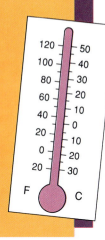

A In the above reading, can you find the word that means "to measure"?

B What temperature, in Fahrenheit, is it in the following cities?

1. **Buenos Aires**   15°C
2. **Ciudad de México**   30°C
3. **París**   17°C
4. **Madrid**   19°C
5. **Moscú**   10°C

C Tell what the weather is like in the cities in activity **B**. Imagine yourself in each of these cities. What are you wearing?

Cooperative Learning

Have each team do Actividad B on page 453. After each team completes the activity, the reporter will give the answers, using a map to point out where the cities mentioned in Actividad B are located.

For the Native Speaker

Have native speakers bring in world weather reports from a newspaper from the school library or some other source. Ask students to choose four different countries from the weather report, and write short paragraphs describing the weather in each of those countries and comparing it to what the weather is like in other countries. Have students present their weather reports to the class in a television news format.

Cultura viva 2

Presentation

Read the Cultura viva on this page. You may wish to write the formula for converting from Fahrenheit to Centigrade on the chalkboard. You may also wish to invite the science teacher, or a student who is taking advanced chemistry or physics, to talk to the class about the Celsius scale.

Did You Know?

The Celsius scale has 100 degress between the freezing and boiling temperatures of water. Water freezes at 0°C and boils at 100°C. In a Fahrenheit temperature scale the freezing point of water is at 32 degrees and the boiling point is at 212 degrees. In a Celsius scale normal body temperature of human beings is 37°C. In a Fahrenheit scale it is 98.6 degrees.

Critical Thinking Activity

Make copies of the weather report for several cities in the U.S. or Latin America, including the temperature for a particular day. Give one copy to each student. Have students convert the temperatures to Celsius. Then have them write a weather report for one city on the weather map.

Actividades

Actividad A Answers
Medir

Actividad B Answers
1. 59
2. 86
3. 63 (62.6)
4. 66 (66.2)
5. 50

Actividad C Answers
Answers will vary.

Bell Ringer Review

Directions to students: Copy each of the following weather expressions and draw beside each one an appropriate outfit to wear. Label your outfit in Spanish.
Llueve.
Hace frío y nieva.
Hace mucho calor en la playa.
Hace fresco con viento.

Presentation

Lead students through steps 1–4 on pages 454 and 455. You may wish to give students additional examples of the use of direct object pronouns, both in English and in Spanish, writing these additional examples on the chalkboard.

Reteaching

Place several classroom objects in a paper bag (pen, pencil, paper, book, etc.) . Pass the bag around the classroom. Have each student take one item out of the bag. Then ask the class, **¿Quién tiene mi lápiz?** The students who has the pencil answers, **Yo lo tengo.** Etc.

Estructura 2

....

How to Talk about Things or People Already Mentioned   *Direct object pronouns*

1. If you have already mentioned a person or thing, there is really no need to keep repeating the name of the person or thing.

   > Jan received a wallet for her birthday. The wallet is black leather. Her sister gave her the wallet. Yesterday she couldn't find the wallet. She thinks she lost the wallet at the movies.

   In English, we substitute words such as "it, her, him," and "them" (called pronouns) so we don't have to keep repeating the same word. In the above sentences, we can say "it" once we know we're talking about a wallet.

2. In Spanish, the words you use for these pronouns depend on whether the person or thing you are referring to is singular or plural, masculine or feminine.

MASCULINE		FEMININE	
SINGULAR	PLURAL	SINGULAR	PLURAL
lo	**los**	**la**	**las**

3. Notice where these words are placed.

   ENRIQUE: **Si buscas la revista de historia, la puedes encontrar en la biblioteca. Pero, ¿por qué la quieres?**
   JOSÉ: **No la quiero. La necesita mi papá. A él le gustan las revistas de historia. Siempre las lee.**

   ANA: **¿Viste a Rafael? Lo necesito ver, es muy importante.**
   CARMEN: **Pues, está en el gimnasio con sus amigos. Los vi durante el almuerzo.**

   As you can see, **la /las** and **lo /los** in the above examples are placed immediately before the verb that tells who is doing the action. If the sentence has **"no"** in it, the **"no"** is placed before **la /las** or **lo /los.**

454   CAPÍTULO 6

Cooperative Learning

Ask each team to select one or two individuals to describe. The individuals may be other classmates, or someone else known to thc class. After rehearsal, the team reporter will describe one of these individuals to the class. The class must then guess who this person is.

4. If you want to refer back to two or more persons or things, and some are masculine and some are feminine, use the masculine form **los**.

> ¿Conoces a Carmen y a Rafael?
> Claro, los conozco muy bien.

Actividades

A **Buenos recuerdos.**
To the right is part of a letter Rafael wrote to his grandmother after his trip to Miami. Make it sound better by replacing unnecessary words with pronouns.

B **Mañana, mañana.** Ask a classmate if he or she did the following things today.

Por ejemplo:

> limpiar tu habitación

ESTUDIANTE A

¿Limpiaste tu habitación hoy?

ESTUDIANTE B

Sí, la limpié esta mañana. (No, pero la voy a limpiar mañana, No la necesito limpiar, etc.).

1. escribir la composición
2. hacer la tarea de español
3. llamar a tus abuelos
4. hacer ejercicio
5. planchar los pantalones
6. leer la novela para la clase de inglés
7. sacar la basura
8. cortar el césped

Cuando fui a Miami, saqué muchas fotos de la gente que conocí y de los lugares que visité. Saqué fotos en todas partes: por la calle y en el coche. Ahora papá tiene las fotos porque quiere arreglar las fotos en un álbum. Si vienes a nuestra casa, puedes ver las fotos.

Lección 4 **455**

Actividades

Actividad A Answers
... lugares que visité. Las saqué en todas partes:... Ahora papá las tiene porque las quiere arreglar... nuestra casa, las puedes ver...

Actividad B Answers
Answers will vary but should include the following:

1. ¿Escribiste la composición hoy? / Sí, (No, no) la escribí...
2. ¿Hiciste la tarea de español hoy? / Sí, (No, no) la hice...
3. ¿Llamaste a tus abuelos hoy? / Sí, (No, no) los llamé...
4. ¿Hiciste ejercicio hoy? / Sí, (No, no) lo hice...
5. ¿Planchaste los pantalones hoy? / Sí, (No, no) los planché...
6. ¿Leíste la novela para la clase de inglés hoy? / Sí, (No, no) la leí...
7. ¿Sacaste la basura hoy? / Sí, (No, no) la saqué...
8. ¿Cortaste el césped hoy? / Sí, (No, no) lo corté...

Learning from Photos

You may want to have students look at the photo on page 455. Have them imagine that the boy asked the girl the following questions. How would the girl respond to each?
¿Hiciste la tarea? ¿Entendiste la lección? ¿Terminaste la composición? ¿Estudiaste las palabras?
What questions might the girl have asked him?

455

Actividad C Answers
Answers will vary but should include **lo** or **la.**

Actividad D Answers
Answers will vary.

Class Management
You may wish to give one or two additional examples of Actividad D while students think of how to describe one of their classmates. As an option, you may ask students to write their description as a homework assignment first, then read their description to the class.

Actividad E Answers
Answers will vary but should include the following.

1. ... las llevo...
2. ... las llevo...
3. ... las...
4. ... las...
5. ... los...
6. ... los...
7. ... los...
8. ... las...
9. ... los...
10. ... los...

Actividad F Answers
Answers will vary, however students should use the exclamatory **¡Qué... más...** and a direct object pronoun in each verbal exchange.

C Mis amigos. List four of your favorite people. Tell how long you have known each one, without using the people's names.

Por ejemplo:

> mi amiga Kate
> *Hace cuatro años que la conozco.*

D ¿Los conoces? Describe a classmate with as much detail as possible, without revealing his or her name. Describe the classmate's personality, appearance, likes, and dislikes. Your other classmates will guess whom you are describing.

Por ejemplo:

ESTUDIANTE A	ESTUDIANTE B
Hablo de un chico de la clase. Es muy simpático. No es muy alto. Tiene pelo negro. ¿Quién lo conoce?	Yo lo conozco. Es Jon, ¿no?

E Ropa. Tell whether you wear the following kinds of clothing or accessories. If you do, tell where or when. If not, tell why not.

Por ejemplo:

> zapatos blancos
> *Sí, los llevo. Los llevo cuando juego tenis.*
> *(No, nunca los llevo. No me gustan. Son feos).*

1. camisetas
2. sandalias
3. botas de cuero
4. corbatas
5. cinturones de plástico
6. gorros
7. trajes
8. camisas de manga larga
9. pantalones de rayas
10. calcetines blancos

F ¡De moda! Compliment three classmates on something they are wearing. Ask them where they bought each item.

Por ejemplo:

ESTUDIANTE A	ESTUDIANTE B
¡Qué camiseta más bonita! ¿Dónde la compraste?	La compré en la tienda "Val's".

Finalmente

Finalmente

Situaciones

A conversar Invite a classmate to do something with you this weekend.

1. Find out what your partner wants to do if the weather is good. Make alternate plans if the weather is bad.
2. Decide how much money you will need.
3. Talk about what you will probably wear in each case.
4. Decide on how you will get there.

A escribir A group of your friends went out last night, but you couldn't go with them. You tried to call them to find out what happened but you couldn't reach them. Write them a note to find out details such as where they went, what they wore, what they did, whom they saw, where they ate, and what time they returned home.

Repaso de vocabulario

PREGUNTA
¿Qué tiempo hace?

LUGARES
el bosque
el desierto
el lago
la montaña
el río

ACTIVIDADES
dormir al aire libre
dar una caminata

EXPRESIONES
Está nublado.
Hace...
    buen tiempo.
    calor.
    fresco.
    frío.
    mal tiempo.
    sol.
    un tiempo regular.
    viento.
Llueve.
Nieva.

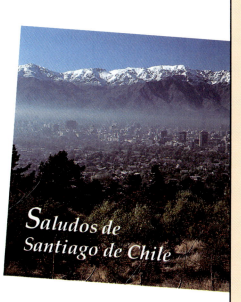

Saludos de Santiago de Chile

Lección 4   **457**

Lección 5

Objectives

By the end of this lesson, students will be able to:

1. describe physical sensations
2. compare people and things

Lesson 5 Resources

1. Workbook, pp. 200–204
2. Vocabulario Transparency 6.5
3. Cassette 6.5
4. Student Tape Manual, pp. 170–173
5. Lesson Quizzes, pp. 132–134
6. Computer Software, Disk 2
7. Video Cassette
8. Estructura Masters 6.5
9. Diversiones Masters 6.5

Bell Ringer Review

Directions to students: Carmen and Rafael are discussing what they do at different times of the year. Since Rafael lives in the southern hemisphere, everything is reversed. Follow the model as Rafael contrasts his activities with Carmen's.
Por ejemplo: Carmen: **En junio voy a la playa.**
You write for Rafael: **En junio esquío en las montañas.**

1. **En julio nado en la piscina.**
2. **En septiembre juego fútbol.**
3. **En enero y en febrero patino sobre hielo.**
4. **En mayo juego tenis.**
5. **En octubre hago caminatas.**

Lección 5

En el centro comercial

¡A comenzar!

The following are some of the things you will be learning to do in this lesson.

When you want to . . .

1. say someone is like someone else.
2. compare two people
3. say you're hungry

You use . . .

- **Es como** + person.
- **Es más** + description + **que** + person.
- **Tengo hambre.**

Now find examples of the above words and phrases in the following conversation.

458   CAPÍTULO 6

Getting Ready for Lesson 5

You may wish to use one or more of the following suggestions to prepare students for the lesson:

1. Use the weather reports from the previous lesson and make comparisons between cities. Give students the list of cities. Have them write today's temperature for your area at the top of the sheet. For each city you mention, have them write (+) if the temperature is higher there than in your city, (-) if it's lower, and (=) if it's the same. For example:
En St. Louis hace tanto calor como aquí en nuestra ciudad. Las dos ciudades tienen una temperatura de 76 grados. Pero en Dallas hace más calor. Allí la temperatura es 84 grados. Y en Boston hace menos calor con

En el centro comercial, Carmen y Rafael hablan del regalo.

CARMEN: **¿Sabes la talla de tu mamá? ¿Y los colores que le gustan?**

RAFAEL: **Bueno, a decir la verdad, no.**

CARMEN: **¿Sabes, por ejemplo, si le gusta el verde?**

RAFAEL: **Bueno, no. En realidad, prefiere el rojo.**

CARMEN: **Ah, es como yo. ¿Es alta?**

RAFAEL: **Pues, es más baja que tú.**

CARMEN: **Ajá, más baja. ¿Y más delgada?**

RAFAEL: **No, mamá es más gorda que tú. Pero es rubia como tú. Oye, compramos el suéter después. Tengo hambre. ¿No quieres comer algo?**

CARMEN: **Ay, Rafael, ¡eres imposible!**

Actividad preliminar

Compare the following pairs of items using the words in parentheses.

Por ejemplo:

los idiomas / las matemáticas (fácil)
Los idiomas son más fáciles que las matemáticas.
(Las matemáticas son más fáciles que los idiomas).

1. el fútbol / el béisbol (interesante)
2. los zapatos deportivos / las camisetas (popular)
3. la ropa deportiva / la ropa elegante (bonito)
4. la comida italiana / la comida mexicana (delicioso)

Lección 5 **459**

B. Introduce the Lesson 5 dialogue by reading it aloud or by playing the cassette version. Have students listen to determine what comparison is being made.

C. Now ask students to open their books and look at the dialogue as you lead them through what is said. For example:

1. ¿Cuál es la talla de la mamá de Rafael?
2. ¿Qué color le gusta?
3. ¿Es gorda o delgada?
4. ¿Quiere Rafael comprar el suéter ahora? ¿Por qué? ¿Qué dice?

D. Have students look at the dialogue again and compare Carmen and Rafael's mother, answering the following questions.

1. ¿Quién prefiere el rojo?
2. ¿Quién es más baja?
3. ¿Quién es más delgada?

Actividad preliminar

Actividad preliminar Answers
Note. The reverse of the following statements would also be correct:

1. El fútbol es más interesante que el béisbol.
2. Los zapatos deportivos son más populares que las camisetas.
3. La ropa deportiva es más bonita que la ropa elegante.
4. La comida italiana es más deliciosa que la comida mexicana.

¡A comenzar!

Presentation

A. Lead students through each of the three functions given on page 458, progressing from the English to the Spanish for each function. Then have students find these words and phrases in the dialogue on page 459.

---

una temperatura de 69 grados. En Chicago hace frío pero hace más frío en Minneapolis, etc.

2. Follow up with the following types of questions:
   a. ¿Dónde hace tanto calor como aquí?
   b. ¿Dónde hace más calor?
   c. ¿Dónde hace más frío que aquí?

3. Tell about a trip you took once. Tell where you went, what you did, and compare that place to your own city. For example: **Allí hay más discotecas que aquí. Pero no hay tantos museos buenos como aquí.** Have students take notes and then work with their partners for five minutes to come up with several statements about your likes and dislikes.

Bell Ringer Review

Directions to students: Draw a picture representing these weather conditions.

1. Está nublado.
2. Hace sol.
3. Llueve hoy.
4. Hace mucho frío.
5. Nieva mucho.
6. Hace calor.
7. Hace fresco.
8. Hace mucho viento.

Presentation

A. Have students open their books to the Vocabulario on page 460. Model each new phrase. Have students repeat each phrase in unison.

B. Ask individual students how they feel. For example: **¿Tienes frío? ¿Tienes sed?** Ask students to look at the Vocabulario on page 460 before they answer.

Vocabulario

Tengo mucha sed.
¿Quieres tomar algo?

Tengo mucha hambre.
¿Quieres comer algo?

Tengo mucho frío.
¿Me puedes traer mi suéter?

Tengo mucho sueño, mamá.
Voy a dormir.

Tengo mucha prisa.
No quiero llegar tarde.

Tengo mucho miedo.
Quiero regresar a casa.

Tengo mucho calor. ¿Por qué no vamos a la piscina?

460 CAPÍTULO 6

Total Physical Response

Getting Ready
Use Vocabulario Transparency 6.5 and felt pens.
Apunta a la persona que tiene frío.
Apunta al chico que tiene hambre.
Señala al chico que tiene calor.
Señala a la chica que tiene miedo.
Haz un círculo en el chico que tiene prisa.

Haz un rectángulo en la chica que tiene sed.
Haz un triángulo en el chico que tiene sueño.
Levanten la mano derecha si tienen frío en el invierno.
Levanten la mano izquierda si tienen calor en el verano.
Pongan la cabeza en el pupitre si tienen sueño a las doce de la noche.

Actividades

A ¿Cómo estás? Tell how you feel in the following situations.

Por ejemplo:

> Es un día de agosto a las tres de la tarde.
> *Tengo (mucho) calor.*

1. Hace doce horas que no comes.
2. Corriste cuarenta y cinco minutos y hace dos horas que no tomas agua.
3. Estudiaste hasta las dos de la noche y saliste para la escuela a las siete de la mañana.
4. La temperatura está a cinco grados bajo cero y hace mucho viento.
5. La temperatura está a cuarenta grados.
6. Das un paseo por el campo y ves una serpiente muy grande.
7. Estás en casa a las ocho de la mañana y tu primera clase es a las ocho y veinte.

B ¿Cuándo? Complete the sentences below to tell when you feel the following.

1. Tengo hambre cuando...
2. Tengo sed cuando...
3. Tengo prisa cuando...
4. Tengo miedo cuando...
5. Tengo frío cuando...
6. Tengo calor cuando...
7. Tengo sueño cuando...

En una cafetería cubana de la Calle Ocho.

Lección 5   **461**

461

Presentation

Read the Cultura viva on this page. After reading this selection once, you may wish to have students guess the meaning of the words **talla** and **tabla**. Then have students read the selection again before having them look up the sizes they would use if they were in Spain.

Critical Thinking Activity

Using the chart on page 462, ask students to write down their European size for each of the appropriate categories shown.

Actividad Answers

Answers will vary.

Learning From Realia

You may want to ask students to look again at the chart on page 462.

1. What is the European equivalent of American half sizes?
2. How many articles of clothing are missing from this chart? Give the names in Spanish.

462

Las tallas

Las tallas de la ropa varían de un país a otro. La tabla que sigue tiene las equivalencias entre el sistema de tallas europeo y el americano. Para comprar ropa, dices "Mi talla es…"

TALLAS EN ESTADOS UNIDOS Y EN EUROPA							
BLUSAS Y SUÉTERES							
Estados Unidos	32	34	36	38	40	42	44
Inglaterra	34	36	38	40	42	44	46
Europa	40	42	44	46	48	50	52
VESTIDOS Y TRAJES DE SEÑORA							
Estados Unidos		10	12	14	16	18	20
Inglaterra		32	33	35	36	38	39
Europa		38	40	42	44	46	48
TRAJES Y ABRIGOS DE CABALLERO							
Estados Unidos		36	38	40	42	44	46
Europa e Inglaterra		46	48	50	52	54	56
CAMISAS							
Estados Unidos	14	14½	15	15½	15¾	16	16½	17
Europa	36	37	38	39	40	41	42	43
CALCETINES							
Estados Unidos		9½	10	10½	11	11½	
Europa		38-39	39-40	40-41	41-42	42-43	
ZAPATOS DE SEÑORA							
Estados Unidos	4	5	6	7	8	9	10	11
Inglaterra	2	3	4	5	6	7	8	9
Francia	36	37	38	39	40	41	42	43
Italia y España	32	34	36	38	40	42	44	46
MEDIAS							
Estados Unidos e Inglaterra		8	8½	9	9½	10	10½
Europa		0	1	2	3	4	5

Actividad

Give the size you will buy for yourself for the following items in the countries named.

Por ejemplo:

> Estás en Francia y buscas un suéter.
> *Voy a comprar zapatos de la talla cuarenta y cuatro.*

1. Estás en España y quieres un traje.
2. Estás en Inglaterra y quieres una camisa / una blusa.
3. Estás en Italia y buscas un suéter.
4. Estás en Alemania y necesitas calcetines.

Estructura 1

How to Make Comparisons   **Más / menos... que...**
of Numbers and Amounts   **Tanto... como....**

1. To say that there is or are more of one than of another, use
   más... que...

   > **Hay más muchachos que muchachas aquí.**
   > **Mi padre gana más dinero que mi tío.**

2. To say that there is or are less or fewer of one than the other, use
   menos... que...

   > **Hay menos amarillo que rojo en la camisa.**
   > **Mi prima tiene menos vestidos que mi hermana.**

3. To say that there is as much or as many of one as the other, use
   tanto(a, os, as)... como...

   > **Necesito ahorrar tanto dinero como tú.**
   > **Miguel tiene tanta hambre como yo.**
   > **Mi hermano tiene tantos carteles como mi primo.**
   > **Tengo tantas clases como mis amigos.**

4. To say that there isn't as much of one as the other, use **"no"**
   before the above examples.

   > **No tengo tanto dinero como tú.**
   > **No tengo tantas clases como mis amigos.**

5. To say that someone does something as much
   as someone else, use **tanto como.**

   > **En la clase de historia, yo estudio tanto**
   > **como tú. Silvia puede ahorrar tanto**
   > **como María.**

   Notice that when **tanto como** is used this way,
   the ending **(-o)** of **tanto** never changes.

Estructura 1

Structure Teaching Resources
1. Workbook, pp. 201–202
2. Cassette 6.5
3. Student Tape Manual, p. 171
4. Estructura Masters 6.5
5. Lesson Quizzes, p. 133

Bell Ringer Review

Directions to students: What would be the solutions to the following problems? Copy each word and then draw a picture depicting a cure.

1. **Tengo mucha sed.**
2. **Tenemos calor.**
3. **Tienen hambre.**
4. **Tengo miedo.**
5. **Tenemos frío.**
6. **Tienes mucha prisa.**
7. **Tengo sueño.**

Structure Focus

The presentation in this lesson is limited to comparisons of numbers and amounts: **más/menos... que...** and **tanto... como...** Comparisons based on characteristics will be presented in Estructura 2 of this lesson.

Presentation

Lead students through steps 1–5 on page 463. You may wish to give additional examples, such as: **Hay más estudiantes en esta clase que en la clase a las diez; Hay menos páginas en este libro que en el libro de historia; etc.**

Actividades

Actividades

A **En la clase.** Tell what your Spanish classmates are like by comparing the categories below.

Por ejemplo:

> muchachos o muchachas
> *Hay más muchachas que muchachos en la clase.*
> deportistas o artistas
> *Hay más deportistas que artistas.*

1. cantantes o deportistas
2. rubios o pelirrojos
3. personas con anteojos o sin anteojos
4. personas con frenos o sin frenos en los dientes
5. estudiantes aplicados o estudiantes perezosos
6. muchachas de pelo largo o de pelo corto
7. estudiantes con "jeans" o con pantalones
8. muchachas con pantalones o con faldas

B **A decir la verdad.** Tell whether the following statements about you and your best friend are true or not.

Por ejemplo:

> Estudias tanto como él / ella.
> *Sí, estudio tanto como él. (No, estudio menos que él).*

1. En la clase de español sabes menos que él / ella.
2. Escuchas los problemas de los amigos tanto como él / ella.
3. Trabajas tanto como él / ella.
4. Sabes tanto como él / ella.
5. El mes pasado saliste por la noche más que él / ella.
6. Ayer estudiaste tanto como él / ella.
7. Anoche hablaste por teléfono menos que él / ella.
8. En la cafetería comiste menos que él / ella.

Cooperative Learning

You may wish to do Actividad A as a cooperative learning activity. Do an oral round robin, with all the team members taking turns and contributing answers:

For the Native Speaker

Write a 150-word comparison of two of your classes. Mention the quantity of work required, the teacher, activities that you like or dislike, etc.

C **No soy como él.** Compare yourself to a friend or family member in terms of the following topics.

Por ejemplo:

> tener tarea
> *Yo tengo más (menos) tarea que mi amiga Mónica. (Yo tengo tanta tarea como mi amiga Mónica).*

1. ir a bailes
2. practicar deportes
3. leer libros
4. ver películas
5. ahorrar dinero
6. tener problemas
7. hacer ejercicio

D **Mi compañero y yo.** Compare yourself to a classmate, answering the following questions.

Por ejemplo:

> ¿Tienes tantas clases como él / ella?
> *No tengo tantas clases como ella. Ella tiene más clases que yo.*

1. ¿Tienes tantos discos como él / ella?
2. ¿Ahorras tanto dinero?
3. ¿Ganas tantos partidos?
4. ¿Vas a tantos restaurantes?
5. ¿Ves tantas películas?
6. ¿Haces tanto ejercicio?

Presentation

Read the Cultura viva on this page. You may wish to discuss with your students which birthdays are special in the U.S.

Did You Know?

Most **quinceañera** celebrations include a church service, the purpose of which is to give thanks for having reached this important age. During the celebration, **la quinceañera** wears a formal dress, like a prom dress. Her father accompanies her to the altar where she remains for the entire ceremony. She may give a speech. Her court of honor, fourteen girls with their partners, go to the church with her. Following the religious ceremony, there may be a party, including a formal dance.
Quinceañera celebrations are common in Mexico, the Caribbean, and certain Central American nations.

Critical Thinking Activity

Is there any other celebration that is similar to the **quinceañera** in the U.S.? What do you think is the importance and meaning of a **quinceañera** for the girl's family?

Actividades

Actividad A Answers
Special U.S. birthdays: 16, 18, 21. Special birthday for Hispanic girls: 15; it is called the quinceañera.

Actividad B Answers
1. culta, encantadora
2. un matrimonio muy apreciado
3. grata
4. conocido

Actividad C Answers
Answers will vary.

466

La quinceañera

En algunos países hispanos, el cumpleaños de los quince años es muy importante para las muchachas. Los padres dan una gran fiesta con baile para presentar a la muchacha en sociedad.

Hoy cumple sus ansiados quince la culta y encantadora señorita Carmen Marín Revueltas, hija de un matrimonio muy apreciado, el abogado Luís Marín Armas y la señora Alicia Revueltas de Marín Armas. Con motivo de esta grata ocasión, la quinceañera celebrará un baile en un conocido club de esta ciudad. ¡Muchas felicidades!

Para una Amiga Especial

*Porque eres una amiga
En quien me gusta pensar.
Cuando viene tu cumpleaños
No te puedo olvidar.*

Feliz Cumpleaños

Éste es el anuncio que apareció en un periódico de Miami cuando Carmen cumplió sus quince años.

Y aquí está la tarjeta que Jorge, un compañero de clase de Carmen, le mandó para su cumpleaños.

Actividades

A Which birthdays are special in the U.S.? In the above reading, find out which birthday is special for many Hispanic girls. What is this celebration called?

B In the newspaper article what words are used to describe:
1. Carmen   2. los Marín   3. la ocasión   4. el club

C Tell the things you did or plan to do for your fifteenth birthday. Tell the things you received or asked for (or are going to ask for).

For the Native Speaker

Imagine that you are a newspaper reporter. Write an article about a **quinceañera** that you recently attended. Include information about the food, music, gifts, guests, other entertainment, etc.

Estructura 2

*How to Make Comparisons
Based on Characteristics*

**Tan... como...
Más/menos... que...**

1. You may want to compare people and things on the basis of their qualities or characteristics; for example, smaller, taller, prettier, cheaper. To say that someone or something is the same as another person or thing, use **tan... como.**

   > **Soy tan alto como tú.**
   > **Eva es tan guapa como Inés.**

2. If the persons or things are not the same, use **"no"** with the above examples.

   > **No soy tan alta como Mariví.**
   > **Jorge no es tan guapo como su hermano.**

3. To say that someone or something is more than another person or thing, use **más... que.**

   > **Soy más aplicado que mi hermana.**
   > **Teresa es más simpática que su prima.**

4. To say that someone or something is less than another, use **menos... que.**

   > **Soy menos puntual que tú.**

5. To compare people's ages, use **menor que** (younger than) and **mayor que** (older than).

   > **Mi hermana es menor que yo.**
   > **Mi amigo es mayor que yo.**

6. To say that something is better than something else, use **mejor que.** To say it is worse than something else, use **peor que.**

   > **El libro es mejor que la película.**
   > **La cantante es peor que la bailarina.**

¿OTRO RESTAURANTE TAN BUENO COMO BIG SPLASH? TIENE QUE SER UNA COPIA

Lección 5 **467**

For the Native Speaker

Who is your favorite athlete? Why? Compare your favorite with another famous athlete. Mention their training, past record, playing style, potential, etc.

Estructura 2

Structure Teaching Resources
1. Workbook, pp. 203–204
2. Cassette 6.5
3. Student Tape Manual, p. 172
4. Estructura Masters 6.5
5. Lesson Quizzes, p. 134

Bell Ringer Review

Directions to students: Think of four adjectives that could be used to describe you and a friend. Now write sentences comparing the two of you using the adjectives with phrases such as **tanto... como, más/menos... que.**

Presentation

Lead students through steps 1–6 on page 467. You may wish to write the comparisons **Tan... como...** and **Más/menos... que...** on the chalkboard, giving additional examples of each. You may also want to ask students to volunteer additional examples for you to write on the chalkboard.

Actividad A Answers

Answers will vary.

Actividad B Answers

Answers will vary but may include the following:

1. No es tan independiente como yo. Es más tímida que yo.
2. No es tan responsable como yo. Soy más responsable que ella.
3. No es tan antipática como yo. Es más simpática que yo.
4. No es tan alta como yo. Es más baja que yo.

Actividad C Answers

Answers will vary.

Reteaching

Ask individual students to compare the following. Tell which is better and why.

1. la clase de álgebra o la clase de inglés
2. el fútbol americano o el baloncesto
3. la música clásica o la música rock
4. las motos o los coches
5. un perro o un gato

Actividades

A **Comparaciones.** Think of two items for each of the categories below and compare them in terms of better or worse.

Por ejemplo:

> días de la semana
> *Los sábados son mejores que los lunes. (Los martes son peores que los viernes, etc.).*

1. películas
2. equipos de béisbol
3. equipos de baloncesto
4. coches

B **Elena y yo.** Carmen Marín is comparing herself to her friend Elena. For each statement she makes, give two other ways she could have said it.

Por ejemplo:

> Elena es menos gorda que yo.
> *No es tan gorda como yo. Es más delgada que yo.*

1. Es menos independiente que yo.
2. Es menos responsable que yo.
3. Es menos antipática que yo.
4. Es menos alta que yo.

C **Este año y el año pasado.** Compared to last year, give your opinion of what the following people and things are like this year (**este año**). Tell why.

Por ejemplo:

> la escuela
> *La escuela es más interesante este año porque...*

1. tus amigos
2. los equipos de la escuela
3. la música más popular
4. la ropa de moda
5. los programas de la tele
6. la comida de la cafetería
7. las tareas

Finalmente

....

Situaciones

A conversar Converse with a classmate about one of your favorite celebrities.

1. Decide on a category (such as athlete, musician, or movie star) that you both want to talk about.
2. Compare your favorite with your classmate's favorite in terms of appearance, abilities, and achievements.

A escribir Rate your school, comparing it to a rival school. Write about why your school is better than the rival school. Compare sports teams, equipment, facilities, the students, faculties, libraries, school colors, mascots, and so on.

Repaso de vocabulario

COMPARACIONES	EXPRESIONES
como	tener
más (... que)	calor (m.)
mejor (que)	frío
menos (... que)	hambre (f.)
peor (que)	miedo
tan... como	prisa
tanto(a, os, as)... como	sed (f.)
tanto como	sueño

Lección 5 **469**

Finalmente

Situaciones

Lesson 5 Evaluation
The A conversar and A escribir situations on this page are designed to give students the opportunity to use as many language functions and as much vocabulary from this lesson as possible. The A conversar and A escribir are also intended to show how well students are able to meet the lesson objectives.

Presentation
Prior to doing the A conversar and A escribir on this page, you may wish to play the Situaciones listening activities on Cassette 6.5 as a means of helping students organize the material.

Learning from Photos
You may want to have students look at the photo on page 469 and tell how they think the two young people are feeling.

Lección 6

Objectives

By the end of this lesson, students will be able to:

1. ask or tell how much someone or something weighs
2. ask or tell how tall someone is
3. distinguish "this one" from "that one"
4. talk about past events

Lesson 6 Resources

1. Workbook, pp. 205–210
2. Vocabulario Transparencies 6.6
3. Cassette 6.6
4. Student Tape Manual, pp. 174–178
5. Lesson Quizzes, pp. 135–137
6. Computer Software, Disk 2
7. Video Cassette
8. Estructura Masters 6.6
9. Diversiones Masters 6.6
10. Test Booklet, pp. 107–115
11. Cumulative Test of Chapters 5 and 6, pp. 117–125

Bell Ringer Review

Display pictures of two well-known personalities. Directions to students: Look at the pictures on the board. Think about the characteristics and interests of each person. Then write five sentences comparing the two people.

Lección 6

¿Qué talla, por favor?

¡A comenzar!

The following are some of the things you will be learning to do in this lesson.

When you want to . . .	You use . . .
1. distinguish "this..." from "that..."	• Este(a)... ese(a)...
2. ask how much someone weighs	• ¿Cuánto pesa?
3. ask how tall someone is	• ¿Cuánto mide?

Now find examples of the above words and phrases in the following conversation.

Getting Ready for Lesson 4

You may wish to use one or more of the following suggestions to prepare students for the lesson:

1. Select judiciously two or three students to come to the front of the classroom and help you estimate their heights (using the U.S. system of measurement: **pies** and **pulgadas**). For example: **Jim, ¿cuánto mides? Yo mido _____** y veo que tú eres más alto que yo. **¿Mides cinco pies y cuántas pulgadas? ¿cuatro? ¿cinco?** Estimate the heights of a few other individuals; then have students do the same for three or four volunteers. See who can give the closest estimate.

2. Have two volunteers come to the front of the classroom. Have them stand several feet apart. Stand next to one stu-

Carmen y Rafael hablan con la empleada de una tienda.

EMPLEADA: **Buenas tardes. ¿Qué buscan?**

CARMEN: **Buenas tardes, señorita. Quisiéramos ver ese suéter rojo, por favor.**

EMPLEADA: **Sí, cómo no, señorita. Este suéter es muy popular este año. ¿Qué talla?**

CARMEN: **Diez.**

RAFAEL: **No, Carmen, tiene que ser cuarenta y cuatro o cuarenta y seis.**

CARMEN: **No, Rafael. Si tu mamá es como yo, esa talla es muy grande. A ver... ¿cuánto pesa?**

RAFAEL: **No sé... sesenta, más o menos.**

CARMEN: **¿Sesenta? ¡No lo puedo creer! ¿Cuánto mide?**

RAFAEL: **Uno sesenta.**

CARMEN: **¿C-ó-m-o?**

Actividad preliminar

Say one thing about each of the following times or places.

Por ejemplo:
> esta tarde
> *Esta tarde voy a salir con mis amigos.*

1. este año
2. esta escuela
3. esta ciudad (este pueblo)
4. este mes
5. esta estación
6. este fin de semana

Lección 6 **471**

¡A comenzar!

Presentation

A. Lead students through each of the three functions given on page 470, progressing from the English to the Spanish for each function. Then have students find these words and phrases in the dialogue on page 471.

B. Introduce the Lesson 6 dialogue by reading it aloud or by playing the cassette version. Ask students to listen to answer the following:

 1. Where are Carmen and Rafael?
 2. To whom are Carmen and Rafael speaking?
 3. Why does Carmen get confused?

C. Now ask students to open their books and look at the dialogue as you lead them through what is said. For example:

 1. ¿Qué dice la empleada cuando entran Carmen y su primo?
 2. ¿Qué quieren ver?
 3. ¿Qué dice la empleada?
 4. ¿Qué talla pide Carmen?
 5. ¿Está de acuerdo Rafael?
 6. ¿Qué talla quiere él?
 7. Carmen cree que esta talla es demasiado grande. ¿Qué dice?
 8. ¿Qué quiere saber Carmen?
 9. ¿Cuánto pesa la mamá de Rafael, más o menos?
 10. Carmen no lo puede creer. ¿Qué dice?
 11. ¿Cuánto mide la mamá de Rafael? ¿Es posible eso?

Actividad preliminar

Actividad preliminar Answers
Answers will vary.

---

dent as you describe the students' heights in relation to each other, using **este(a)** and **ese(a)**. Use gestures as needed. For example:
Este estudiante es más alto que esa estudiante. Esa estudiante es más baja que este estudiante, etc.
Use pictures from magazines to illustrate people of different sizes and weights. Describe the pictures using

este(a) and **ese(a)**. For example:
Este hombre es más delgado que ese muchacho. Esa muchacha es más gorda que esa mujer, etc.

Vocabulario

Bell Ringer Review

Directions to students: Help Luisa straighten out her sentences by copying them on your paper and correcting the underlined words.

1. En el verano siempre tengo <u>frío</u> después de jugar tenis. Por eso tomo mucha agua.
2. Mi familia y yo tenemos <u>sueño</u> para llegar al cine a tiempo.
3. Cuando no como, tengo <u>calor</u>.
4. Tengo <u>sed</u> después de ver la tele hasta la medianoche.
5. Me gustan las películas de terror pero siempre tengo <u>prisa</u> cuando las veo.
6. Cuando hacen 35 centígrados, tengo mucha <u>hambre</u>.
7. Tengo <u>miedo</u> cuando nieva y hace mucho viento.

Presentation

A. Have students open their books to the Vocabulario on pages 472 and 473.
   1. Model each new phrase on page 472. Have students repeat each phrase in unison.
   2. Be sensitive in choosing certain students to ask how much they weigh and how tall they are. For example: **¿Cuánto pesas tú? ¿Cuánto mides tú?** Encourage students to give a complete response. For example: **Yo peso... , Yo mido...**

Total Physical Response

Getting Ready
Use the following items for TPR 1 and display them in front of the class.
un libro
una regla
un lápiz
un borrador
un bolígrafo
un saco de 5 libras de azúcar
un paquetito de espaguetis
una lata grande de frutas
unos platos de cartón
unos cubiertos de metal y de plástico
For TPR 2, borrow a scale and measuring tape.

New Words
coge   cojan

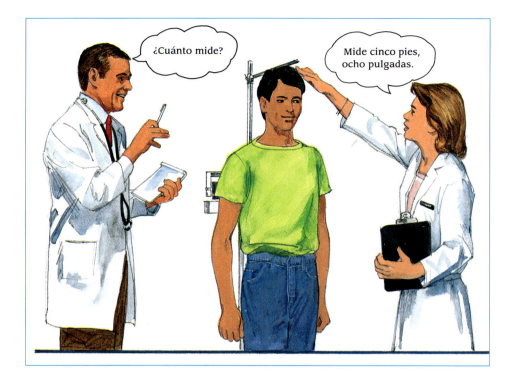

¿Cuánto mide?

Mide cinco pies, ocho pulgadas.

Actividades

A **¿Está muy lejos?** Take turns with a classmate estimating the distance from your school to each of the following places in miles or city blocks. Then give directions on how to get to each place.

Por ejemplo:

> **la biblioteca**
> *La biblioteca no está muy lejos. Está a dos millas de aquí, más o menos. Sales de la escuela, doblas a la derecha, sigues doce cuadras, entonces doblas a la izquierda y está en la esquina.*

1. la casa de tu amigo
2. un restaurante popular
3. el centro comercial
4. tu casa
5. un banco
6. el hospital

Lección 6 **473**

B. Now have students look at the Vocabulario on pages 472 and 473.
  1. Model the questions, **¿Está muy lejos? ¿Cuánto pesa? ¿Cuánto mide?** Then model each answer. Have students repeat each phrase in unison.
  2. Ask individual students how much they would like to weigh and how tall they would like to be. For example: **¿Cuánto quisieras pesar/ medir?**

When Students Ask

You may wish to give students the following additional vocabulary to allow them to talk about weights and measurements.
el galón
la yarda
la pinta
el cuarto
la tonelada

Actividades

Actividad A Answers
Answers will vary.

TPR 1

Toquen un artículo muy liviano.
Toquen un artículo muy pesado.
Levanten una comida que se vende por libras.
Levanten una comida que se vende por onzas.
Cojan el cubierto que pesa menos.
Cojan el cubierto que pesa más.

TPR 2

Coge el tenedor de plástico y mídelo.
Pesa el paquetito de espaguetis. Dile a la clase si pesa lo que dice el paquetito.
Pesa la lata de frutas. Dile a la clase si pesa lo que dice la lata.
Pesa el lápiz y diez platos de carton. Pregúntale a la clase cuál pesa más.
Pesa el libro y la lata de frutas. Pregúntale a la clase cuál pesa menos.

B **Vamos a viajar.** Tell whether the following places are near or far from where you live. Also tell how you would get to each place. Estimate how long a trip each would be.

Por ejemplo:

> la playa
> *La playa está muy lejos de aquí. Si quiero ir, tengo que viajar en coche (avión, etc.). Voy a tardar más o menos cinco horas.*

1. el desierto
2. un lago grande
3. un río
4. las montañas
5. el bosque
6. un parque

C **La tarea de matemáticas.** Carmen is babysitting for Miguelito and helping him with his math homework. He has to give the perimeters of the following shapes. What are the correct answers?

Por ejemplo:

> el rectángulo
> *El rectángulo mide 26 pulgadas.*

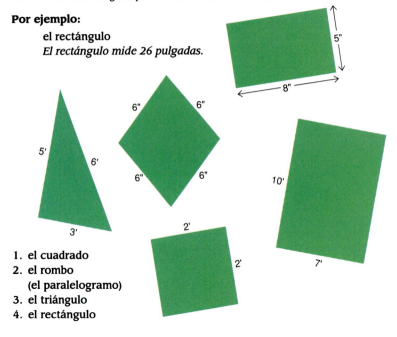

1. el cuadrado
2. el rombo
   (el paralelogramo)
3. el triángulo
4. el rectángulo

D **Comparaciones.** Compare the following pairs of persons or things and answer the questions.

Por ejemplo:

¿Quién es más alta?
Andrea, 5 pies / Julia, 4 pies, 8 pulgadas
Andrea es más alta.

1. ¿Quién pesa más?
   Julio Panza, 160 libras / David Winer, 126 libras

2. ¿Quién es más alta?
   Angélica Morán, 6 pies / Ann Darcey, 5 pies, 8 pulgadas

3. ¿Dónde hace más frío?
   Buenos Aires, 38 grados / Filadelfia, 53 grados

4. ¿Cuál café es más barato?
   Café Bustelo, 8 onzas, $3.29 / Nescafé, 12 onzas, $3.29

5. ¿Cuál es más pesado?
   azúcar, 5 libras / papas, 10 libras

6. ¿Cuál es más liviana?
   una tarjeta postal / una carta

**Publix.
El lugar para lo
bueno de comer.**

475

For the Native Speaker

Make a map of the United States that includes the following cities: Los Angeles, San Francisco, New York, Chicago, Philadelphia, Washington D. C., Seattle, Boston, Miami, Dallas, Bismark, New Orleans, Springfield. Using kilometers, indicate the distance between New York and all the other cities.
Make a chart that shows your findings.

Presentation

Read the Cultura viva on this page.

Critical Thinking Activity

1. Have students estimate the length of the following in centimeters:
   - your thumb
   - a new pencil
   - your elbow to your fingertips
   - the distance between the pupils of a classmate's eyes

   Then give students rulers marked off in centimeters and have them measure the above items. How well did they estimate?
2. What are the advantages and disadvantages of using the metric system and the English system?

Actividad Answers

1. kilómetros	3. gramos
2. centímetros	4. litros

Additional Practice

After completing the Actividad on this page, you may want to do the following activity:

How would the following things be measured: **gramos, litros, metros, kilómetros, kilos, centímetros?**

1. chocolates
2. refrescos o agua
3. tela para un traje
4. la distancia entre dos ciudades
5. azúcar
6. frijoles

Answers

1. gramos	4. kilómetros
2. litros	5. kilos
3. metros	6. kilos

CULTURA VIVA 1

El sistema métrico

Como ya sabes, en otros países usan el sistema métrico. Por ejemplo, usan grados centígrados para la temperatura, kilos y gramos para el peso, litros para los líquidos, y kilómetros y metros para la altura y la distancia.

Aquí tienes algunas maneras de estimar medidas con el sistema métrico.

un kilo (k.)	**Medio kilo (1/2 kilo)** is just over a pound.
un litro (l.)	Just over a quart.
un kilómetro (km.)	Slightly more than 1/2 mile.
un metro (m.)	Slightly longer than a yard.
un centímetro (cm.)	**Diez cm.** is about four inches.
un gramo (gr.)	A small piece of chalk weighs about a gram.

Actividad

What metric units of measurement would you use to respond to the following questions?

Por ejemplo:

> ¿Cuánto pesa Miguel?
> *kilos*

1. ¿Está muy lejos su casa?
2. ¿Cuánto mide Paco?
3. ¿Cuánto pesa la carta?
4. ¿Cuánta leche debo comprar?

476

Estructura 1

....

How to Distinguish One
Thing from Another　　　Este / ese

1. When you want to describe or point out someone or something that is nearby or close in time ("this class, these books"), use the following descriptive words.

MASCULINE		FEMININE	
SINGULAR	PLURAL	SINGULAR	PLURAL
este	**estos**	**esta**	**estas**

En esta tienda hay ropa bonita. Por ejemplo, me gustan estos pantalones y este suéter. ¿No te gustan estas camisas? Dicen que esta semana hay descuentos increíbles.

2. When you want to describe or point out something that is farther away from you or more remote in time ("that place, those years"), use the following descriptive words.

MASCULINE		FEMININE	
SINGULAR	PLURAL	SINGULAR	PLURAL
ese	**esos**	**esa**	**esas**

Pablo llegó en 1989. En ese año, jugó en el equipo de fútbol. ¡Siempre recuerda esos partidos, y esas fiestas, y esa muchacha rubia!

Notice that these words come before the word they describe.

Nuestra gente no necesita usar este libro.

Para pedir el servicio de gas natural u obtener información sobre su cuenta, medidor de gas o demás asuntos de la compañía de gas, llame a Ms. Colquitt el 522-1150, extensión 2110. Ella le asistirá con agrado. En su propio idioma.

Atlanta Gas Light Company
Georgia Natural Gas Company - Savannah Gas Company

477

Bell Ringer Review

Prepare Dictados A y B on half sheets of paper. Directions to students: Partner A: dictate your three sentences to Partner B. Then let him or her check the written work against your paper. Reverse roles: Partner B will dictate to Partner A, then check your work.

Dictado A.
1. **Ese jugador de fútbol americano pesa cien kilos.**
2. **El bebé mide diez y nueve pulgadas.**
3. **Este triángulo mide treinta y ocho centímetros.**

Dictado B.
1. **Dimos un paseo de cuatro millas.**
2. **Este suéter rojo es de talla cuarenta y cuatro.**
3. **¿Es liviana o pesada esta mochila?**

Structure Focus
In this lesson the demonstrative adjectives **este** and **ese** will be presented. Students will learn how to distinguish one thing from another.

Presentation

A. Lead students through steps 1–2 on page 477.

B. Point to objects in the classroom. For example: **Quiero ese bolígrafo, por favor.** Student answers: **¿Este bolígrafo?** Exaggerate gestures to emphasize distances.

Actividades

A **Ese año.** Think of a school vacation you had one year. Make five statements, comparing where you went and what you did that year with what you're going to do this year.

Por ejemplo:

> Recuerdo las vacaciones de verano de 1990. Ese año fui a _____. Pero este año voy a _____.

B **De mal humor.** One day Bruno was in a bad mood all day long. He hated everything he saw. How would he complain about the following?

Por ejemplo:

> en el desayuno: el jugo / el café / los huevos
> *No me gusta este jugo, ni este café, ni estos huevos.*

1. en casa: el televisor / el espejo / la habitación
2. en la escuela: las clases / los libros / los exámenes
3. en la cafetería: las papas fritas / el pescado / el refresco
4. en la ciudad: las tiendas / los empleados / los autobuses

C **En la tienda.** Ask the salesclerk in a store to show you each of the items in the display case where he or she is standing. The salesclerk wants to confirm which item you want to see. Play the roles with a classmate.

Por ejemplo:

ESTUDIANTE A
(1) **Señor (Señorita), quisiera ver ese anillo, por favor.**
(3) **Sí, gracias. Es muy bonito.**

ESTUDIANTE B
(2) **¿Este anillo?**

José Martí

 José Martí (1853-1895) es uno de los poetas más famosos de Cuba. Es también el héroe más importante para los cubanos porque trabajó mucho por la independencia cubana de España.

Aquí tienes un ejemplo de su poesía.

> Si dicen que del joyero
> tome la joya mejor,
> tomo a un amigo sincero
> y pongo a un lado el amor.
>
> Todo es hermoso y constante,
> todo es música y razón.
> Y todo, como un diamante,
> antes que luz es carbón.

("Versos sencillos")

Actividades

A ¿Quiénes son algunos de nuestros héroes en los Estados Unidos?

B Para ti, ¿son héroes...?

1. ¿los científicos?
2. ¿los escritores?
3. ¿los músicos?
4. ¿los políticos?
5. ¿los cantantes?
6. ¿los maestros?
7. ¿los deportistas?

Lección 6 **479**

Cultura viva 1

Presentation
Read the Cultura viva on this page. You may wish to have a discussion about heroes.

Did You Know?
José Martí was born in Havana, Cuba, on January 28, 1853. He devoted his life to the cause of Cuba's independence from Spain. He became interested in writing while in secondary school. Among his most important works are the *Versos Sencillos, Ismaelillo* (which he dedicated to his son), and *La Edad de Oro,* a magazine for children. He also wrote essays and newspaper articles. Martí died in a battle in Cuba on May 19, 1895.

Critical Thinking Activity
1. How are José Martí and George Washington similar and different?
2. Why are heroes important?

Actividades

Actividades A and B Answers
Answers will vary.

Bell Ringer Review

Directions to students: Draw three circles on your paper. In each circle draw one of the following: a sumo wrestler, a parakeet, and a giant sequoia tree. Now write descriptive phrases about each one, focusing on height, weight, and other physical characteristics. Be prepared to compare your pictures orally.

Structure Focus
This section summarizes all forms of the preterit taught in the text.

Presentation
A. Lead students through steps 1–3 on pages 480 and 481.
B. Ask students questions using the preterit.

Reteaching
Have students brainstorm endings for this sentence.
El verano pasado yo...

Estructura 2

How to Talk about the Past   ***Summary of the preterit***

1. To talk about people's actions in the past, you have learned to put the following endings on verbs.

-ar verbs	
-é	-amos
-aste	-asteis*
-ó	-aron

-er and -ir verbs	
-í	-imos
-iste	-isteis*
-ió	-ieron

2. You have also learned to spell the **yo** form of certain -ar verbs.

llegar	llegué	buscar	busqué
jugar	jugué	practicar	practiqué
pagar	pagué	explicar	expliqué
sacar	saqué	empezar	empecé
tocar	toqué		

3. You have learned the special forms of **ir, ver, dar, hacer, pedir, leer,** and **oír** in the past.

ir	
fui	fuimos
fuiste	fuisteis*
fue	fueron

ver	
vi	vimos
viste	visteis*
vio	vieron

dar	
di	dimos
diste	disteis*
dio	dieron

hacer	
hice	hicimos
hiciste	hicisteis*
hizo	hicieron

pedir	
pedí	pedimos
pediste	pedisteis*
pidió	pidieron

Cooperative Learning

In pairs have students write a letter in which they describe what they did on their last vacation. Students exchange letters and answer them.

leer	
leí	leímos
leíste	leísteis*
leyó	leyeron

oír	
oí	oímos
oíste	oísteis*
oyó	oyeron

* This form is rarely used in the Spanish-speaking world, except for Spain.

Actividades

A **¡Qué desastre!** Señor Ramírez's students had spring fever and didn't do the things they were supposed to. Say that no one **(nadie)** did the following things.

Por ejemplo:

> No escucharon al maestro.
> *Nadie lo escuchó.*

1. No hicieron las tareas.
2. No estudiaron la lección.
3. No leyeron el capítulo.
4. No comieron la comida en la cafetería.
5. No vieron la película en la clase de historia.
6. No oyeron las instrucciones.

B **¿Qué hiciste?** Using the cues below, interview a classmate about things he or she did recently. Then ask one additional question of your own for each. Take notes and report back to the class.

Por ejemplo:

> ir al cine

ESTUDIANTE A	ESTUDIANTE B
(1) ¿Fuiste al cine la semana pasada?	(2) Sí.
(3) ¿Qué viste? (¿Con quién fuiste? ¿Qué hiciste después?)	

(A la clase:) Elisa fue al cine. Vio... (Fue con..., Después...).

1. salir con los amigos
2. leer algo interesante
3. practicar deportes
4. comprar algo
5. comer en un restaurante
6. ver un programa bueno
7. ir a un partido
8. escuchar música
9. sacar una buena nota
10. viajar

C **La semana pasada.** List five things you did last week under a column labeled **"Yo."** Then ask two classmates what they did last week. List their activities under columns labeled by each student's name.

Por ejemplo:

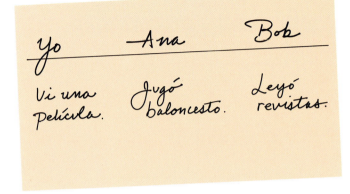

Yo   Ana   Bob

Vi una película.   Jugó baloncesto.   Leyó revistas.

D **¿Qué hicieron ustedes?** Using the list you made in activity **C,** tell the following.

1. Is there something similar that all of you did? Report on this, using the **nosotros** form of the verbs.
2. Is there something that your two classmates did that you didn't? Report on this using the **ellos** or **ellas** form of the verbs.
3. Then report on the other things that you did **(yo)** and the other things that each of your two classmates did **(él** or **ella).**

Finalmente

Situaciones

A conversar You are a customer in a clothing store. A classmate will play the role of a salesclerk.

1. Greet the salesclerk and tell him or her what you would like to see.
2. The salesclerk asks your preference of: (a) color, (b) fabric (cotton, wool, silk, etc.), and (c) style (sporty, dress, short sleeves, etc.). Respond with as much detail as possible.
3. The salesclerk tries to persuade you to buy the item, saying two nice things about it.
4. Ask the price. Then decide whether to buy it.

A escribir Yesterday your Spanish class had an end-of-year outing at a local park. Write a note to a friend who couldn't attend, telling about all the activities you, your classmates, and your teacher did or didn't do. Include details related to food, games, sports, music, and dancing.

Repaso de vocabulario

PREGUNTAS
¿Cuánto mide(s)?
¿Cuánto pesa(s)?

MEDIDAS
la libra
la milla
la onza
el pie
la pulgada

DESCRIPCIONES
liviano(a)
pesado(a)

OTRAS PALABRAS
ese, esa, esos, esas
este, esta, estos, estas

EXPRESIONES
más o menos
tardar + *tiempo* + en llegar

Lectura **483**

Finalmente

Situaciones

Lesson 6 Evaluation
The A conversar and A escribir situations on this page are designed to give students the opportunity to use as many language functions and as much vocabulary from this lesson as possible. The A conversar and A escribir are also intended to show how well students are able to meet the lesson objectives.

Presentation
Prior to doing the A conversar and A escribir on this page, you may wish to play the Situaciones listening activities on Cassette 6.6 as a means of helping students organize the material.

For the Native Speaker
Write a short composition about an imaginary shopping trip to your favorite mall. Include the stores you visited, a description and cost of the items you bought, how you got to the mall, and what you liked best and least about your shopping trip.

Lectura

Getting Students Ready for Reading

A. You may want to stress the following points to your students:

1. Read for general meaning without stopping to look up the words you don't understand.
2. Look for cognates. For example: **emoción, fantástico, casino**
3. Read a second time looking for specific detail.
4. Underline the words you didn't understand and try to guess their meaning by their context.
5. If you still don't know the meaning of the words, look them up in the dictionary.

B. Before reading the Lectura, you may wish to have students discuss in groups the following questions:

1. What are the advantages of traveling in a cruise ship?
2. If you were planning a cruise, where would you go and why?

Lectura

You will be able to figure out many of the words in the following reading from the context in which they appear or because they look like English words that have similar meanings.

The following is an ad for a trip Carmen's family took. Look at the pictures—what kind of trip is it? What might the word **"crucero"** mean?

Permita que el SeaEscape le lleve en un crucero por un día.

Toda la emoción de un crucero por más días en un día fantástico.

Disfrute de 3 deliciosas comidas (incluidas en el precio). Baile al compás de música en vivo. Tome baños de sol junto a la piscina. Diviértase con la revista musical estilo cabaret del SeaEscape. Y todos los lunes es la noche de Grandes Conjuntos Musicales.

Navegue desde Miami hasta Freeport-Lucaya y regrese por sólo $99. Desde Tampa navegue por el Golfo de México por sólo $79. O, desde Puerto Cañaveral, navegue por el Atlántico por sólo $79.

Tarifas especiales para personas mayores, adolescentes y niños. En el precio se incluye transportación por autobús de ida y regreso desde algunos hoteles hasta el muelle.

Para reservaciones e información, vea a su agente de viajes o al conserje de su hotel, o llame a las oficinas del SeaEscape cualquier día de la semana hasta las 11:00 p.m. desde cualquier lugar en los Estados Unidos al 1-800-555-0900 o desde la Florida al 555-6753.

SeaEscape

Actividades

A What kinds of information would you expect to find in an ad like this?

B Skim the ad to find out what types of information are included. Is there anything you did not list in question **A?**

C Scan the ad for the information needed in the following activities.

1. List the words that indicate the activities you could participate in.
2. List the words that indicate the duration of the trip.
3. What are the prices for the following?
   a. round-trip from Miami to Freeport
   b. Gulf of Mexico cruise
   c. Atlantic cruise
4. Which of the following people would be eligible for special rates?
   a. **Carmen**   d. **tú**
   b. **el tío Lucas**   e. **tus compañeros de clase**
   c. **la abuela de Carmen**   f. **tus padres o hermanos**
5. From where you live, what number would you call to make reservations?
6. What words are used to describe the following?
   a. the food
   b. the musical revue
   c. the cruise itself

D Now look more closely at the ad and choose the most likely definition of the following words and expressions.

1. **ida y regreso**
   a. **rápido**   b. **ir y regresar**   c. **a todas horas**
2. **tarifas especiales**
   a. **descuentos**   b. **reservas**   c. **actividades**

E Write a note to a classmate inviting him or her to go with you. Tell him or her all the things you two can do on the cruise. Your classmate will write back either accepting or rejecting your invitation and give reasons.

Lectura **485**

Actividades

Actividad A Answers
Answers will vary but may include the following:
price and length of trip, available activities, points of departure.

Actividad B Answers
Answers will vary.

Actividad C Answers
1. Disfrute de 3 deliciosas comidas, baile, tome baños de sol, diviértase con la revista musical.
2. Un crucero por un día, un día fantástico.
3. a. $99.
   b. $79
   c. $79.
4. a,c,d,e (f depends on age of student's family members)
5. Answers will vary.
6. a. deliciosas
   b. estilo cabaret
   c. Toda la emoción de un crucero por más días en un día fantástico.

Actividad D Answers
1. b
2. a

Actividad E Answers
Answers will vary.

Bell Ringer Review

Directions to students: Rita saw two very strange animals at the zoo today. Draw them, using the following directions:

1. In the bottom left corner draw a fairly large elephant.
2. In the upper right corner draw a smaller gorilla, showing the perspective that distance creates.

Now, add each of the following items to the correct animal, depending on whether it is the closer one (**este**) or the one farther away (**ese**).

este gorro
esos anteojos de sol
este monopatín
este traje de baño
esos esquís acuáticos
esta bufanda
esos tenis
esos shorts
estas sandalias
esa revista romántica

Repaso Resources
1. Workbook, p. 211–214
2. Cassette 6.6
3. Student Tape Manual, pp. 179–181
4. Video Cassette
5. Cumulative Test, p. 117–125

¿Recuerdas?

Presentation

To review Chapter 6, call on individual students to give an example for each communicative function listed for Lecciones 1–3 and Lecciones 4–6, page 486. The number in parentheses on page 486 refers to the actual page(s) in Chapter 6 where each function was presented and practiced. You may wish to have

Capítulo 6 Repaso

¿Recuerdas?

Do you remember how to do the following things, which you learned in **Capítulo 6**?

LECCIONES 1-3
1. identify articles of clothing (pp. 408–409)
2. say what you do for others (p. 412)
3. tell what you and someone else did at one point in the past (p. 415)
4. describe articles of clothing (pp. 420–421)
5. describe what people do for you and others ("us") (p. 424)
6. tell what you and others like and dislike (p. 424)
7. write about the past (p. 427)
8. tell what means of transportation you and others use (p. 433)
9. give and get directions (pp. 432–433)
10. tell how far away something is (p. 432)
11. say that someone is coming (p. 437)
12. tell what someone did in the past (p. 440)

LECCIONES 4-6
1. describe the weather (pp. 446–447)
2. tell what others did in the past (p. 451)
3. refer to people and things already mentioned (p. 454)
4. describe how you feel (p. 460)
5. compare and contrast people and things (pp. 463, 467)
6. give weights, measurements, and distances (pp. 472–473)
7. distinguish one thing from another (p. 477)

Actividades

A **Lo bueno y lo malo.** Tell three good things and three bad things about the season you are in now.

Por ejemplo:

verano
Lo bueno: Puedo ir a la playa.
Lo malo: Hace mucho calor.

B **Por teléfono.** Carmen is speaking to her friend Bárbara on the phone. You can hear only Carmen's side of the conversation. What do you think Bárbara is saying in each case?

BÁRBARA	CARMEN
1. _____	Bien, bien, ¿y tú?
2. _____	Son casi las tres. Voy a ver mi telenovela favorita.
3. _____	Sí que me permite, pero dice que uso demasiado el teléfono.
4. _____	Mi mamá no está. Fue de compras con mi primo.
5. _____	Sí, mi primo nos visita.
6. _____	De Buenos Aires.
7. _____	En la Argentina, chica. ¿No estudias geografía?
8. _____	Dos semanas. Está aquí con su papá desde el 20 de abril.
9. _____	Muy simpático pero no habla mucho inglés.
10. _____	Sí, pero no me molesta. Me gusta el español pero necesito practicar más. Ya viene mi mamá. Te llamo más tarde.

"¿Sólo dijiste AT&T Español?..."

Repaso 487

your students go back to these pages for additional review and practice before continuing on to the Actividades, pages 487–489.

Lecciones 1–3 Answers

The following words and phrase are examples for each of the 12 functions listed under Lecciones 1–3. These words and phrases should be included in the students' response to each function listed.

1. El abrigo, la blusa, las botas, etc.
2. Les...
3. Jugamos, comimos, etc.
4. Ropa de invierno, ropa de manga corta, etc.
5. Nos...
6. Nos gusta, no nos gusta
7. Toqué, saqué, practiqué, expliqué, busqué, llegué, jugué, pagué, empecé
8. A pie, el autobús, el avión, el barco, la camioneta, el tren
9. Al lado de, cerca de, derecho, detrás de, enfrente de, entre, lejos de
10. Está a...
11. Vengo, vienes, viene, venimos, vienen
12. Compró, fue, dio, vio, hizo, etc.

Lecciones 4–6 Answers

The following words and phrases are examples for each of the seven functions listed under Lecciones 4–6. These words and phrases should be included in the students' response to each function listed.

1. Está nublado, hace buen tiempo, frío, etc.
2. Terminaron, fueron, dieron, etc.
3. Lo, los, la , las
4. Tengo calor, frío, hambre, miedo, prisa, sed, sueño.
5. Más/menos... que, tanto... como, tan... como
6. La libra, la milla, la onza, el pie, la pulgada
7. Este/ese

Actividades

Presentation

Each practice activity in this Chapter 6 review combines several of the language functions listed on page 486. Students are asked to use the language they have learned at a higher, more integrated level, compared to the individual practice activities in Lecciones 1–6 of Chapter 6.

Actividad A Answers

Answers will vary.

Actividad B Answers

Answers will vary but may include the following:

1. ¿Cómo estás?
2. ¿Qué piensas hacer? (¿Qué haces?)
3. ¿Tú mamá te permite ver las telenovelas?
4. ¿Por qué lo puedes usar ahora?
5. ¿Dices, tu primo?
6. ¿De dónde es?
7. ¿Dónde está Buenos Aires?
8. ¿Cuántos días va a estar con ustedes?
9. ¿Cómo es?
10. ¿Tienes que hablar (en) español con él?

Actividad C Answers

Answers will vary but may include the following:

1. El tío Samuel dice que vienen pero no pueden llegar hasta el sábado por la noche.
2. El doctor Sotelo dice que no viene porque tiene que trabajar.
3. Jorge dice que no viene porque sus padres no le permiten salir.
4. La tía Ana dice que no viene porque el niño está enfermo.
5. La tía Lourdes dice que viene y trae el postre.
6. Victoria dice que no viene porque tiene que estudiar.
7. Los abuelos dicen que vienen el sábado a las cinco y cuarto.

Actividad D Answers

Answers will vary.

Actividad E Answers

Answer will vary but may include the following:

C ¿Vienen o no vienen? Carmen's family is having a party on Saturday afternoon to welcome Tío Lucas and Rafael. Carmen calls everyone to see if he or she is planning to come. Based on the responses below, tell whether each person is coming and summarize any other messages.

Por ejemplo:

> Tío Juan: Sí, cómo no. ¿Me das la dirección?
> El tío Juan dice que viene pero necesita la dirección.

1. Tío Samuel: Sí, pero no podemos venir hasta el sábado por la noche.
2. el doctor Sotelo: Tengo que trabajar todo el fin de semana.
3. Jorge: No puedo. Mis padres están enojados conmigo. No me permiten salir.
4. Tía Ana: No puedo porque el niño está enfermo.
5. Tía Lourdes: Sí, les llevamos el postre.
6. Victoria: ¡Ay, qué pena! Tengo exámenes.
7. los abuelos: Llegamos el sábado a las cinco y cuarto.

D **El detective.** Bring an unusual object to class in a paper bag. In groups of three or four, try to guess what's in each person's bag by asking questions such as those below. Think of other helpful questions of your own.

Por ejemplo:

> ¿De qué es? ¿Cómo es? ¿Para qué sirve? ¿De qué color es? ¿Cuánto pesa?

E **¡Qué horror!** Tell what you did—or didn't do—in the following situations.

Por ejemplo:

> En el restaurante cuando te sirvieron el plato que pediste, ¡viste insectos en la comida! ¿Qué hiciste?
> *Pedí otro plato. No pagué.*

1. Cuando saliste del restaurante, recordaste que dejaste (you left) tu billetera en la mesa. ¿Qué hiciste?
2. Tú y tus amigos fueron al cine pero parece que todos dejaron las billeteras en casa. ¿Qué hicieron?
3. Cuando pediste permiso para salir con tus amigos el viernes por la noche, tu mamá te contestó: "Si no limpias tu habitación y haces todas tus tareas, no puedes salir". ¿Qué hiciste?
4. Nadie estudió para el examen de biología. Cuando tú y los compañeros llegaron a clase, ¿qué hicieron?

F **Los quehaceres de la casa.** The members of Carmen's family take turns doing the chores. Below is last week's schedule. How would Carmen describe everyone's chores for each day last week?

Por ejemplo:

El lunes pasado, mi papá _____. Mi mamá _____. Yo_____.

	lunes	martes	miércoles	jueves	viernes	sábado	domingo
preparar la comida							
	m	p	C	m	C	p	m
limpiar los baños							
	C					m	
dar de comer al conejo							
	C	C	C	m	m	p	p
barrer la terraza							
	m	m	m	p	p	C	C
cuidar al gato del vecino							
	C	C	C	C	p	p	m

1. Regresé al restaurante. Busqué mi billetera.
2. Regresamos a casa. No fuimos al cine.
3. Limpié mi habitación y después hice mis tareas.
4. Tomamos el examen pero sacamos malas notas.

Actividad F Answers
1. El lunes pasado, mi mamá preparó la comida y barrió la terraza. Yo limpié los baños, di de comer al conejo y cuidé al gato del vecino.
2. El martes pasado, mi papá preparó... , mi mamá barrió... y yo di... y cuidé...
3. El miércoles pasado, mi mamá barrió... y yo preparé... y cuidé...
4. El jueves pasado, mi mamá preparó... y dio... , mi papá barrió... y yo cuidé...
5. El viernes pasado, mi mamá dio... , mi papá barrió... y cuidó... , y yo preparé...
6. El sábado pasado, mi papá preparó... , dio y cuidó... Mi mamá limpió... y yo barrí...
7. El domingo pasado, mi mamá preparó... y cuidó... Mi papá dio... y yo barrí...

Verb Charts

Present Tense

REGULAR VERBS

-ar		-er		-ir	
hablar		comer		escribir	
hablo	hablamos	como	comemos	escribo	escribimos
hablas	habláis*	comes	coméis*	escribes	escribís*
habla	hablan	come	comen	escribe	escriben

STEM-CHANGING VERBS

e—ie		o—ue; u—ue		e—i	
querer		poder		pedir	
quiero	queremos	puedo	podemos	pido	pedimos
quieres	queréis*	puedes	podéis*	pides	pedís*
quiere	quieren	puede	pueden	pide	piden

Other stem-changing verbs like querer: empezar, entender, pensar, perder, preferir.

Other stem-changing verbs like poder: dormir, jugar, recordar.

IRREGULAR VERBS

decir		estar		ir		oír	
digo	decimos	estoy	estamos	voy	vamos	oigo	oímos
dices	decís*	estás	estáis*	vas	vais*	oyes	oís
dice	dicen	está	están	va	van	oye	oyen

ser		tener		venir	
soy	somos	tengo	tenemos	vengo	venimos
eres	sois*	tienes	tenéis*	vienes	venís*
es	son	tiene	tienen	viene	vienen

THE FOLLOWING VERBS ARE FORMED REGULARLY WITH THE EXCEPTION OF THE YO FORM.

conocer	conozco	pertenecer	pertenezco	salir	salgo
dar	doy	poner	pongo	traer	traigo
hacer	hago	saber	sé	ver	veo

*This form is rarely used, except for Spain.

Preterit Tense

REGULAR VERBS

-ar		-er, -ir				
hablar		comer			escribir	
hablé	hablamos	comí	comimos		escribí	escribimos
hablaste	hablasteis*	comiste	comisteis*		escribiste	escribisteis*
habló	hablaron	comió	comieron		escribió	escribieron

IRREGULAR VERBS

dar		hacer		ir		leer	
di	dimos	hice	hicimos	fui	fuimos	leí	leímos
diste	disteis*	hiciste	hicisteis*	fuiste	fuisteis*	leíste	leísteis*
dio	dieron	hizo	hicieron	fue	fueron	leyó	leyeron

oír		pedir		ver	
oí	oímos	pedí	pedimos	vi	vimos
oíste	oísteis*	pediste	pedisteis*	viste	visteis*
oyó	oyeron	pidió	pidieron	vio	vieron

VERBS ENDING IN -AR WITH SPELLING CHANGES IN THE YO FORM

buscar	busqué	jugar	jugué
explicar	expliqué	llegar	llegué
practicar	practiqué	pagar	pagué
sacar	saqué	empezar	empecé
tocar	toqué		

*This form is rarely used, except for Spain.

Vocabulario Español-Inglés

The **Vocabulario Español-Inglés** contains all productive and receptive vocabulary from the text.

The numbers following each productive entry indicate the chapter and lesson in which the word is introduced.

The following are abbreviations used in this glossary.

adv.	adverb
com.	command
f.	feminine
fam.	familiar
inf.	infinitive
m.	masculine
pers.	personal
pl.	plural
prep.	preposition; prepositional
pron.	pronoun
sing.	singular
subj.	subjunctive

A

a at, 1.3; to, 1.5
  a causa de due to
  ¡a comenzar! Let's
    begin!
  a la izquierda to the
    left, 3.3
  a la una at one
    o'clock, 1.3
  a las (dos) at (two)
    o'clock, 1.3
  a medida made-to-
    order
  a menudo often
  a mí me gusta I like,
    4.1
  a pie on foot, 6.3
  ¿A qué hora es . . .? At
    what time is . . .?,
    1.3
  a ti te gusta you like,
    4.1
  a veces sometimes,
    2.4
  a ver let's see, 1.6
abajo downstairs, 3.3
el / la **abogado(a)** lawyer, 4.2
el **abrazo** embrace, hug
  un abrazo fuerte a
    strong embrace
abreviado(a) abbre-
    viated
el **abrigo** overcoat, 6.1
abril April, 4.6
abrir to open, 5.2
la **abuela** grandmother, 4.1
el **abuelo** grandfather, 4.1
los **abuelos** grandparents,
  4.1
aburrido(a) boring, 2.2;
  bored, 3.4
  ¡Qué aburrido! How
    boring!, 1.6
las **aceitunas** olives
acompañado(a)
  accompanied
acompañar to
  accompany
la **actitud** attitude

la **actividad** activity
el **actor** actor, 2.1
la **actriz** actress, 2.1
el **acueducto** aqueduct
  el **Acueducto Romano**
    Roman Aqueduct
    (Spain)
adaptarse to adapt
  oneself
adecuado(a) adequate
los **ademanes** gestures
adentro indoors; inside,
  3.3
adiós good-bye, 1.4
adivinar to guess
el / la **adivinador / a** guesser
¿adónde? (to) where?,
  1.5
  ¿Adónde quieres ir?
    Where do you want
    to go?, 1.5
  ¿Adónde vas? Where
    are you going?, 2.3
las **aerolíneas** airlines
el **aeropuerto** airport
afectar to affect
afectuoso(a)
  affectionate
los **aficionados** fans
africano(a) African
afuera outside, 3.3
las **afueras** outskirts
la **agencia** agency
  la **agencia de servicios**
    sociales social ser-
    vice agency
  la **agencia de viajes**
    travel agency
el / la **agente** agent
  el **agente de pro-**
    piedades real es-
    tate agent
agosto August, 4.6
el / la **agricultor / a** farmer, 4.2
el **agua** (f.) water, 2.5
ahora now, 2.3
ahorrar to save, 3.1
el **aire** air
  al aire libre outdoors
el **ajedrez** chess, 4.5

el **ají** bell pepper
al (a + el) to the, 1.5
  al aire libre outdoors,
    6.4
  al final at / in the end
  al lado de next to, be-
    side, 6.3
  al máximo to the
    maximum
  al sur to the south
alarmarse: se alarman
  they become alarmed
la **alberca** swimming pool
  (Mexico)
el **álbum** album
el **alemán** German (language), 5.3
alemán(ana) German,
  5.3
Alemania Germany
la **alfombra** rug, 3.6
el **álgebra** algebra, 1.4
algo something, 1.2
el **algodón** cotton, 5.2
algunos(as) some
los **alimentos** food
allí there, 3.3
el **almacén** department
  store
el **almuerzo** lunch, 2.5
alrededor around
alto(a) tall, 2.2
el / la **alumno(a)** student
el **ama de casa** (f.) homemaker, 4.2
amable kind, 2.1
amarillo(a) yellow, 3.6
la **América Central** Central
  America
la **América del Norte**
  North America
la **América del Sur** South
  America
las **Américas** the Americas
el / la **amigo(a)** friend, 2.3
anaranjado(a) orange,
  3.6
andar: andar en mono-
  patín to skateboard,
  1.2

los **Andes** Andes (Mountains)

el **anillo** ring, **6.1**

el **animal** animal, **4.3**

anoche last night, **5.3**

ante before, in front of (prep.)

anteayer the day before yesterday, **5.3**

los **anteojos** eyeglasses, **4.4**

los **anteojos de sol** sunglasses, **6.1**

antes before (adv.)

antes de before (time), **3.1**

antiguo(a) old (object), **3.5**

antipático(a) unpleasant (person), **2.2**

el **anuncio** advertisement, **5.1**

el **anuncio comercial** commercial

el **año** year, **4.6**

el **año pasado** last year, **5.3**

el **año que viene** next year, **4.6**

¿En qué año naciste? What year were you born?, **5.3**

el **aparato** gadget, machine, **5.2**

la **apariencia** appearance

el **apartamento** apartment, **3.2**

el **apellido** last name

la **apendicitis** appendicitis

aplicado(a) industrious, studious, **2.2**

aprender to learn, **1.4**

aprender a + inf. to learn (how) to, **4.5**

aprobado passing

no aprobado failing

aprovechar to take advantage (of)

aquí here, **1.1**

árabe Arab

el **área** (f.) area

el **arete** earring, **6.1**

argentino(a) Argentinian, **5.3**

el **armario** dresser, **3.6**

la **armería** armory, gunsmith

el / la **arquitecto(a)** arquitect, **4.2**

arreglar to arrange, organize

arriba up, upstairs, **3.3**

arrogante arrogant, **2.1**

el **arroz** rice, **2.5**

el **arte** art, **1.4**

las **artes marciales** martial arts

las **artesanías** crafts

los **artículos** articles

los **artículos de viajes** travel needs

el / la **artista** artist, **2.1**

artístico(a) artistic

el **ascensor** elevator, **3.3**

así so; this way

así como just like

asistir a to attend, **5.4**

la **asociación** association

la **aspiradora** vacuum cleaner, **5.6**

atraer to attract

los **audífonos** headphones

auditivo: el sistema auditivo hearing

el **auditorio** auditorium

aunque although

austral southern

el **auto** automobile, car

la **autobiografía** autobiography

el **autobús** bus, **6.3**

autorizado(a) authorized

avanzado(a) advanced

la **avenida** avenue, **3.2**

la **aventura** adventure, **4.5**

el **programa de aventuras** adventure program, **4.5**

la **aviación** aviation

la **compañía de aviación** aviation (airline) company

el **avión** airplane, **6.3**

ayer yesterday, **5.3**

el **ayudante** aide, assistant

ayudar to help, **5.1**

el **ayuntamiento** city hall

azul blue, **3.6**

B

la **bahía** bay

bailar to dance, **1.2**

el / la **bailarín(ina)** dancer, **2.1**

el **baile** dance, **1.5**

bajar to go down

bajo(a) short (person), **2.2**

el **baloncesto** basketball, **1.2**

el **banco** bank, **2.6**

el **baño** bathroom, **3.6**

barato(a) inexpensive, cheap, **3.5**

la **barba** beard, **4.4**

el **barco** boat, ship, **6.3**

barrer to sweep, **5.6**

el **barrio** neighborhood

la **base** base, foundation

básico(a) basic

basta it's enough

bastante fairly; enough, **2.2**

la **basura** trash, **3.3**

la **bebida** beverage, **2.5**

el **béisbol** baseball, **1.2**

la **belleza** beauty

el **beso** kiss

la **biblioteca** library, **1.5**

la **bicicleta** bicycle, **1.2**

montar en bicicleta to ride a bicycle, **1.2**

bien fine, well, **1.1**

bienvenido(a) welcome

el **bigote** mustache, **4.4**

bilingüe bilingual

el **billete** ticket

la **billetera** billfold, wallet, **5.2**

la **biografía** biography

la **biología** biology, **1.4**

los **bisabuelos** great-grandparents

la **bisutería** costume jewelry

blanco(a) white, **3.6**

la **blusa** blouse, **6.1**

la **bodega** grocery store

las **boleadoras** hunting slings (Argentina)

el **boletín de evaluación** report card

el **boliche** bowling, **2.6**

jugar boliche to bowl, **2.6**

el **bolígrafo** ballpoint pen, **1.4**

boliviano(a) Bolivian, **5.3**

la **bolsa** handbag, **6.1**

el **bolsillo** pocket, **5.2**

el **bolso** handbag

el / la **bombero(a)** firefighter, **4.2**

la **bombonería** candy and chocolate shop

bonito(a) pretty, **3.5**

boreal northern

el **bosque** forest, woods, **6.4**

las **botas** boots, **6.1**

el **bouffett** buffet

las **boutiques** boutiques

bucear to skin-dive, **5.4**

buen: ¡Buen viaje! Have a good trip!

bueno(a) good, **1.6**

buenas noches good evening, good night, **1.3**

buenas tardes good afternoon, **1.3**

buenos días good morning, **1.3**

¡Qué bueno! That's great!, **1.6**

bueno: lo bueno the good thing

la **bufanda** scarf, **6.1**

buscar to look for, **2.3**

C

el **caballero** gentleman, man, **6.2**

la **ropa de caballeros** men's clothing, **6.2**

el **caballo** horse, **4.3**

montar a caballo to ride horseback, **1.5**

la **cabeza** head

cada each

cada uno(a) each one

cada vez más more and more

el **café** coffee, **2.5**; coffee shop

café brown, **4.4**

la **cafetería** cafeteria, **1.5**

los **calcetines** socks, **6.1**

la **calculadora** calculator, **1.4**

el **calendario** calendar

la **calle** street, **3.1**

el **calor** heat, **6.5**

hace calor it's hot, **6.4**

tener calor to be hot, **6.5**

la **cama** bed, **3.6**

la **cámara** camera, **3.1**

cambiar to change, **3.1**

el **camello** camel, **4.3**

la **caminata** hike, **6.4**

hacer una caminata to take a hike, **6.4**

el **camión** bus (Mexico)

la **camioneta** pick-up truck, **6.3**

la **camisa** shirt, **6.1**

la **camiseta** T-shirt, **3.5**

el **campo** countryside, **1.5**

canadiense Canadian, **5.3**

el **canal** channel (TV)

el **canario** canary, **4.3**

cansado(a) tired, **3.4**

el / la **cantante** singer, **2.1**

cantar to sing, **1.5**

la **cantidad** quantity

la **capital** capital

el **capítulo** chapter

el **Caribe** the Caribbean (Sea)

el **cariño** affection

cariños (with) love

el **carnaval** carnival

la **carne** meat, **2.5**

caro(a) expensive, **3.5**

el / la **carpintero(a)** carpenter, **4.2**

el **carro** car

la **carta** letter, **3.1**

la **carta de presentación** letter of introduction

las **cartas** playing cards, **4.5**

jugar cartas to play cards, **4.5**

el **cartel** poster, **3.5**

el **cartucho** cartridge

la **casa** house, home, **2.6**

la **casa de cambio** money exchange office

ir a casa to go home, **1.2**

casado(a) married

el **casete** cassette, **3.5**

casi almost, **5.5**

el **catálogo** catalogue

la **catedral** cathedral

católico(a) Catholic

catorce fourteen, **1.3**

la **caza** hunting, **6.4**

ir de caza to go hunting

la **celebración** celebration

celebrar to celebrate

celeste sky-blue

la **cena** supper, dinner, **2.5**

cenar to eat supper

centígrado(a) centigrade (degrees)

el **centro** downtown, **2.3**

el **centro comercial** shopping center, **1.5**

cerca de   near, **6.3**
el **cereal**   cereal, **2.5**
cero   zero, **1.3**
cerrado(a)   closed
el **césped**   lawn, **5.6**
el **ciclismo**   cycling
los **ciegos**   blind persons
cien   one hundred, **3.3**
ciento   one hundred,
   4.2
ciento uno (dos)   one
   hundred one (two),
   4.2
la **ciencia ficción**   science
   fiction, **4.5**
el **programa de ciencia
   ficción**   science fiction program, **4.5**
las **ciencias**   science(s), **1.4**
   las **ciencias domésticas**
      home economics
cierto   true; certain
cinco   five, **1.3**
cincuenta   fifty, **3.3**
el **cine**   movie theater, **1.5**
el **cinto**   belt
el **cinturón**   belt, **6.1**
el **circo**   circus
la **cita**   appointment
la **ciudad**   city, **1.5**
el / la **ciudadano(a)**   citizen
claro(a)   light, bright
la **clase**   class, **1.4**; kind,
   4.5
   ¿Qué clase de . . .?
      What kind of . . . ?,
      4.5
el / la **cliente**   client
el **clima**   climate
la **clínica**   clinic
el **club**   club, **5.5**
cobrar   to charge
el **coche**   car, **1.5**
el **cochinillo asado**   roast
   suckling pig
la **cocina**   kitchen, **3.6**;
   cuisine
cocinar   to cook, **1.5**

la **cola**   line, **5.5**
   hacer cola   to stand in
      line, **5.5**
la **colección**   collection, **3.5**
el / la **coleccionista**   collector
el **collar**   necklace, **6.1**
colombiano(a)   Colombian, **5.3**
colonial   colonial
la **combinación**
   combination
el **comedor**   dining room,
   3.6
comer   to eat, **1.2**
   dar de comer   to feed,
      5.6
comercial   commercial
el **comercio**   commerce,
   business
cómico(a)   funny, **4.5**
el **programa cómico**
   comedy (program),
   4.5
la **comida**   food, **2.5**; meal
la **comisión**   commission
como   as, like, **6.5**
   así como   just like
   como siempre   as
      always
   tan . . . como   as . . .
      as, **6.5**
¿cómo?   what?; how?,
   1.4
   ¿Cómo es . . .?   What is
      he / she / it like?;
      What are you (for-
      mal) like?, **2.1**
   ¿Cómo está usted?
      How are you (for-
      mal)?, **1.3**
   ¿Cómo estás?   How
      are you (fam.)?, **1.3**
   ¿Cómo se dice . . .?
      How do you
      say . . .?, **5.2**
   ¿Cómo son?   What are
      they like?, **2.1**
   ¿Cómo te llamas?
      What is your name
      (fam.)?, **1.1**

¡cómo!: ¡Cómo no!   Of
   course!, **1.2**
la **comodidad**   comfort
cómodo(a)   comfortable,
   3.1
el / la **compañero(a) de clase**
   classmate, **2.1**
la **compañía**   company, **4.2**
la **compañía de avia-
   ción**   aviation (airline) company
los **complementos**
   accessories
completamente
   completely
la **composición**   composition, **1.4**
los **compradores**   buyers
comprar   to buy, **1.2**
las **compras**   the shopping
   ir de compras   to go
      shopping
comprender   to
   understand
la **computación**   computer
   class
la **computadora**   computer,
   1.5
   usar la computadora
      to use the computer,
      1.5
común   common
con   with, **1.2**
   con el tiempo
      eventually
   con permiso   excuse
      me, **2.3**
   conmigo   with me, **5.4**
   contigo   with you
      (fam.), **5.4**
el **concierto**   concert, **2.3**
el **concurso**   game show,
   4.5
el **condominio**
   condominium
el **conejillo de Indias**
   guinea pig
el **conejo**   rabbit, **4.3**
la **confección**   sewing

la **confección deportiva** athletic wear
la **confusión** confusion
la **conga** popular Cuban music and dance
el **conjunto** musical group, **2.3**
conocer (zco) to know, be familiar with a person or place, **5.5**
el **consejo** piece of advice, **5.6**
   dar consejos a to give advice to, **5.6**
construido(a) built
el **consulado** consulate
el **contacto** contact
contar (ue) to count
contemplar to look at
contemporáneo(a) contemporary
contento(a) happy, **3.4**
contestar to answer, **1.4**
contener to contain
contra against
las **contribuciones** contributions
el **control** control
controlar to control
la **conversación** conversation
conversar to talk, chat
el **corazón** heart
la **corbata** necktie, **6.1**
la **correa** belt
el **correo** post office, **5.1**
   el **correo aéreo** air mail
correr to run, to jog, **1.2**
la **corsetería** corset shop
cortar to cut, **5.6**
las **cortes** courts (of law)
corto(a) short (object), **4.4**
la **cosa** thing, **5.2**
la **cosmética** cosmetics
la **costa** coast
costarricense Costa Rican, **5.3**
la **costumbre** custom

creo: creo que I think that, **4.2**
cruzar to cross
el **cuaderno** notebook, **1.4**
la **cuadra** city block, **6.3**
cuadrado(a) square, **5.2**
el **cuadro: de cuadros** plaid, **6.2**
¿cuál? which (one); what?, **4.5**
   ¿Cuál es tu número de teléfono? What is your telephone number? (fam.), **3.3**
¿cuándo? when?, **2.4**
¿cuánto(a)? how much?, **3.3**
   ¿Cuánto mide(s)? How tall are you (is he / she / it)?, **6.6**
   ¿Cuánto pesa(s)? How much do you (does he / she / it) weigh?, **6.6**
   ¿Cuánto tiempo? How long?, How much time?, **5.4**
   ¿Cuánto tiempo hace que . . .? How long has (have) . . . ?, **5.5**
   ¿Cuánto vale? How much does it cost?, **4.2**
¿cuántos(as)? how many?, **3.3**
   ¿Cuántos años tiene(s)? How old are you (is he / she / it)?, **4.2**
cuarenta forty, **3.3**
el **cuarto** room (of a house), **3.6**
cuarto(a) fourth, **3.2**
cuatrocientos(as) four hundred, **4.2**
cubano(a) Cuban, **5.3**
el **cuero** leather, **5.2**
cuesta it costs
cuidar to take care of, **4.3**
la **cultura** culture

el **cumpleaños** birthday, **4.6**
la **curiosidad** curiosity
el **curso** course

CH

el **chachachá** popular Latin American dance
la **chaqueta** jacket, **6.1**
el **cheque** check, **5.1**
   el **cheque de viajero** traveler's check, **3.1**
   hacer un cheque to write a check, **5.1**
chileno(a) Chilean, **5.3**
el **chino** Chinese (language), **5.3**
chino(a) Chinese, **5.3**
el **choclo** ear of corn (Andes)
el **chorizo** Spanish sausage
los **churros** fritters, crullers

D

las **damas** ladies, **6.2**
   para damas for ladies, **6.2**
dar to give, **5.1**
   dar consejos a to give advice to, **5.6**
   dar de comer a to feed, **5.6**
   dar un paseo to go for a walk, **1.2**
de of, from, **2.3**
   de acuerdo OK, **2.6**
   de antigüedad of antiquity
   de compras shopping
   de cuadros plaid, **6.2**
   de flores flowered (print), **6.2**
   de habla española Spanish-speaking
   de invierno winter (clothes), **6.2**
   de la mañana in the morning, **1.3**

de la noche in the evening, at night, **1.3**

de la tarde in the afternoon, **1.3**

de lunares polka-dotted, **6.2**

de manga corta short-sleeved, **6.2**

de manga larga long-sleeved, **6.2**

de medicina medical

de moda in fashion, **6.2**

de nada you're welcome, **2.1**

de otoño autumn (clothes), **6.2**

de primavera spring (clothes), **6.2**

¿De qué es? What's it made of?, **5.2**

¿De qué marca es? What's the brand name?, **3.5**

¿De quién es / son? Whose is it / are they?, **2.3**

de rayas striped, **6.2**

de un solo color solid (color), **6.2**

de verano summer (clothes), **6.2**

debe he / she / it / you (formal) must (probability)

deber should, ought, **3.1**

décimo(a) tenth, **3.2**

decir to say, to tell, **5.5**

la **decisión** decision

los **defensores** defenders

del (de + el) from the, of the, **2.3**

delgado(a) thin, **2.2**

delicioso(a) delicious

demasiado(a) too, too much, **2.2**

el / la **dentista** dentist, **4.2**

depender to depend

dependiente dependent

el **deporte** sport, **1.2**

el / la **deportista** athlete, **2.1**

deportivo(a) casual, sports, **6.2**

el programa deportivo sports program, **4.5**

deprimente depressing, **2.1**

deprimido(a) depressed, **3.4**

la **derecha** right, **3.3**

a la derecha to the right, **3.3**

derecho(a) straight ahead, **6.3**

sigue derecho go straight ahead (fam. sing. com.), **6.3**

el **desastre: ¡Qué desastre!** What a disaster!, **1.6**

el **desayuno** breakfast, **2.5**

descansar to rest, **1.2**

el **descuento** discount

desde since, **5.3**

el **desfile** parade

el **desierto** desert, **6.4**

despacio slow

las **despedidas** farewells

después afterwards, **2.3**

después de after, **3.1**

detrás de behind, **6.3**

el **día** day, **2.6**

buenos días good morning, **1.3**

el **día de fiesta** holiday

el **Día de la Raza** Hispanic Pride Day

el **dialecto** dialect

diariamente daily

el **diario** diary

dibujar to draw, **1.5**

el **dibujo** drawing

el **dibujo técnico** drafting

el **diccionario** dictionary

dice he / she / it says, you (formal) say, **4.5**

dices you (fam.) say, **5.5**

diciembre December, **4.6**

los **dientes** teeth, **4.4**

los **frenos en los dientes** (dental) braces, **4.4**

diez ten, **1.3**

diez y nueve nineteen, **1.3**

diez y ocho eighteen, **1.3**

diez y seis sixteen, **1.3**

diez y siete seventeen, **1.3**

la **diferencia** difference

diferente different, **2.1**

difícil difficult, **1.6**

digo I say; I mean, **5.5**

los **diminutivos** diminutives

el **dinero** money, **2.3**

la **dirección** address, **3.2**

el / la **director / a** director

el **disco** record, **1.2**

las **discotecas** discotheques

la **distancia** distance

la **larga distancia** long distance

distinguido excellent

divertido(a) fun, **2.2**

¡Qué divertido! What fun!, **1.6**

doblar to turn, **6.3**

doce twelve, **1.3**

el / la **doctor / a** doctor, **4.2**

el **dólar** dollar, **1.3**

el **domingo** Sunday, **2.6**

dominicano(a) Dominican, **5.3**

el **dominó** dominoes (game)

don title of respect used with a man's first name

donde where

¿dónde?: ¿Dónde está? Where is it?, **3.2**

doña title of respect used with a woman's first name

dormir (ue) to sleep, **3.1**

el **dormitorio** bedroom

dos two, **1.3**

doscientos(as) two hundred, **4.2**

doy I give

el **drama** drama (class)

el / la **dueño(a)** owner, **4.2**

durante during

E

la **economía** economy

ecuatoriano(a) Ecuadorian, **5.3**

la **edad** age

el **edificio** building, **3.2**

la **educación física** physical education, **1.4**

educativo(a) educational, **4.5**

el **programa educativo** educational program, **4.5**

el **efecto** effect, result

el **ejercicio** exercise, **2.3**

hacer ejercicio to exercise, **2.3**

el the (m.), **1.4**

él he, **3.1**

el / la **electricista** electrician, **4.2**

el **elefante** elephant, **4.3**

elegante elegant, **2.1**

ella she, her, **3.1**

ellas they, them (f.), **3.1**

ellos they, them (m.), **3.1**

el **elote** ear of corn (Mexico)

emocionado(a) excited, **3.4**

emocionante exciting, **2.1**

empezar (ie) to start, **4.5**

el / la **empleado(a)** employee, **4.2**

en at; in; on, **3.2**

en fin in all

en punto on the dot, **2.6**

¿En qué año naciste? What year were you (fam.) born?, **5.3**

¿En qué piso está? What floor is it on?, **3.2**

en realidad in reality

en vez de instead of

enamorado(a) in love, **3.4**

encanta: le encanta he / she / it loves, you (formal) love

encontrar (ue) to find

la **encuesta** survey

enero January, **4.6**

la **enfermería** infirmary, hospital

el / la **enfermero(a)** nurse, **4.2**

enfermo(a) sick, **3.4**

enfrente de in front of, **6.3**

enojado(a) mad, angry, **3.4**

enorme enormous

la **ensalada** salad, **2.5**

enseñar to show, **5.1**

enseñar a to teach how to, **5.4**

entender (ie) to understand, **2.6**

entero(a) whole

entiendes you (fam.) understand, **2.6**

entiendo I understand, **2.6**

entonces then, **2.3**

la **entrada** admission ticket, **5.5**

entrar to enter

entre between, **6.3**

la **época** period

el **equipo** team, **5.5**; equipment

equivocado(a) mistaken, **3.4**

eres you are, **2.1**

¿Eres de aquí? Are you from here?, **1.1**

es he / she / it is, you (formal) are, **2.1**

es controlado(a) is controlled

es decir that is to say

es formado(a) is formed

¿Es usted . . .? Are you (formal) . . . ?, **2.1**

esa that (f.), **6.6**

esas those (f.), **6.6**

la **escala** scale

la **escalera** stairs, **3.3**

escribir to write, **1.4**

el / la **escritor / a** writer, **2.1**

el **escritorio** desk, **3.6**

escúchame listen to me (fam. sing. com.)

escuchar to listen to, **1.2**

la **escuela** school, **1.5**

ese that (m.), **6.6**

eso that

esos those (m.), **6.6**

España Spain

el **español** Spanish (language), **1.4**

español / a Spanish, **5.3**

especial special

especialmente especially

las **especias** spices

el **espejo** mirror, **3.6**

los **espejuelos** eyeglasses

esperar to await

esperar to wait for, **5.5**

el **esquí acuático** water skiing, **5.4**

practicar el esquí acuático to water-ski, **5.4**

esquiar to ski, **1.5**

la **esquina** street corner, **6.3**

esta this (f.), **6.6**

esta mañana this morning, **2.4**

esta noche tonight, **2.4**

esta tarde this afternoon, **2.4**
estacionar to park
la **estación** season, **6.2;** radio station
el **estadio** stadium, **1.5**
el **estado** state
los **Estados Unidos** the United States
estadounidense from the United States, **5.3**
estar to be, **3.2**
  está nublado it's cloudy, **6.4**
  estar a + distance to be + distance from, **6.3**
  estar casado(a) to be married
  estar en to be in (at, on), **3.2**
  estás en tu casa make yourself at home
estas these (f.), **6.6**
este this (m.), **6.6**
el **estéreo** stereo, **3.5**
estimado(a) dear
estimar to estimate
estos these (m.), **6.6**
estricto(a) strict
estridente noisy
la **estructura** structure (grammar)
el / la **estudiante** student, **2.1**
estudiar to study, **1.2**
  estudiar para to study to be a, **4.2**
  estudiar para un examen to study for an exam, **1.4**
la **estufa** stove, **3.6**
estupendo(a) terrific, **5.4**
Europa Europe
evidente evident
exacto correct, right
el **examen** exam, test, **1.4**
excelente excellent, **2.1**
el **exceso** excess
la **excusa** excuse

la **exhibición** exhibition
exigente demanding
existían they existed
el **éxito** success
la **experiencia** experience
experimentado(a) experienced
el / la **experto(a)** expert
explicar to explain, **5.6**
expresar to express
el **expreso** express (train)
exquisito(a) exquisite
extranjero(a) foreign, **4.5**
la **película extranjera** foreign film, **4.5**

F

la **fábrica** factory, **4.2**
fácil easy, **1.6**
la **falda** skirt, **6.1**
la **familia** family, **3.1**
los **familiares** relatives
famoso(a) famous
fantástico(a) fantastic
el **favor** favor, **5.1**
  favor de please
favorito(a) favorite, **2.3**
febrero February, **4.6**
la **fecha** date
  la **fecha de vencimiento** expiration date
fenomenal phenomenal, terrific
feo(a) ugly, **2.2**
la **feria** fair
el **festival** festival
la **fiesta** party, **1.5**
fíjate look (fam. sing. com.)
fijo(a) fixed
el **fin** end
  el **fin de semana** weekend, **2.6**
  en fin in all
  por fin finally
final: al final at / in the end
finalmente finally

financiero(a) finance
la **revista financiera** finance magazine
la **firma** signature
formado(a) formed
  es formado is formed
formal formal
formar to form
formidable terrific, great, **2.1**
la **fórmula** formula
el **formulario** form (document), **2.1**
la **fotografía** photography
el / la **fotógrafo(a)** photographer
la **foto** picture, photograph
  sacar fotos to take pictures, **1.5**
frágil fragile
el **francés** French (language), **1.4**
francés(esa) French, **5.3**
los **frenos: los frenos en los dientes** dental braces, **4.4**
el **fresco** coolness, **6.4**
  hace fresco it's cool, **6.4**
los **frijoles** beans, **2.5**
el **frío** cold, **6.5**
  hace frío it's cold, **6.4**
  tener frío to be cold, **6.5**
la **fruta** fruit, **2.5**
fuerte strong
  un fuerte abrazo a strong embrace
el / la **fumador / a** smoker, one who smokes
fumar to smoke
el **fútbol** soccer, **1.2**
el **fútbol americano** football, **1.2**
el **futuro** future
futuro(a): la futura mamá future mom

G

las **gambas** shrimp (Spain)

el / la **ganador(a)** winner

las **ganancias** revenues

ganar to earn money, **2.3**; to win, **4.5**

la **gaseosa** soft drink, soda, **2.5**

la **gasolinera** gasoline station

gastar to spend money, **5.4**

el **gato** cat, **4.3**

los **gauchos** Argentinian cowboys

la **gaveta** locker, **1.4**

los **gemelos** twins

la **generación** generation

general: por lo general in general

generalmente generally

generoso(a) generous, **2.2**

la **gente** people

la **geometría** geometry, **1.4**

el **gimnasio** gymnasium, **2.3**

el **giro postal** money order

el **gobernador** governor

gobernar to rule

el **gobierno** government

el **golfo** gulf

la **goma** rubber, **5.2**

gordo(a) fat, **2.2**

el **gorila** gorilla, **4.3**

el **gorro** cap, **6.1**

el **gourmet** gourmet

la **grabadora** tape recorder, **3.5**

gracias thank you, thanks, **1.2**

gracias por . . . thank you for . . . , **2.1**

el **grado** grade

los **grados** degrees

gran great

grande big, **2.2**

gris gray, **3.6**

el **grupo** group

la **guagua** bus (Caribbean)

la **guanábana** soursop, tropical fruit

los **guantes** gloves, **6.1**

guapo(a) good-looking, **2.2**

guardar to keep, store, **5.2**

guatemalteco(a) Guatemalan, **5.3**

la **guayabera** loose-fitting men's shirt

la **guerra** war

la **guitarra** guitar, **5.3**

tocar la guitarra to play the guitar, **1.5**

el / la **guitarrista** guitar player, **2.1**

gusta: ¿Le gusta . . .? Do you (formal) / does he / she / it like . . . ?, **4.1**

me gusta I like, **1.4**

¿Qué te gusta más? What do you (fam.) like best?, **1.4**

te gusta you like, **1.4**

¿Te gusta . . .? Do you like . . . ?, **1.6**

gustan: ¿Les gustan . . .? Do you (pl.) / they like . . . ?, **4.1**

te gustan you like (pl.), **1.4**

¿Te gustan . . .? Do you (fam.) like (pl.) . . . ?, **1.6**

el **gusto** taste

H

la **habitación** bedroom, **2.3**

hablar to speak, talk, **1.2**

hablar con to speak with, talk to, **1.2**

hablar por teléfono to talk on the telephone, **1.2**

hace: hace buen tiempo the weather is nice, **6.4**

hace calor it's hot, **6.4**

hace fresco it's cool, **6.4**

hace frío it's cold, **6.4**

hace mal tiempo the weather is bad, **6.4**

hace . . . que it has been . . . since, **5.5**

hace sol it's sunny, **6.4**

hace un tiempo regular the weather is so-so, **6.4**

hace viento it's windy, **6.4**

hacer to do, **1.2**

hacer cola to stand in line, **5.5**

hacer ejercicio to exercise, **2.3**

hacer la tarea to do homework, **1.2**

hacer las maletas to pack (suitcases), **3.1**

hacer un cheque to write a check, **5.1**

hacer un favor to do a favor, **5.1**

hacer una caminata to hike, **6.4**

hacer una pregunta to ask a question, **1.4**

las **haciendas** ranches

el **hambre** (f.) hunger, **6.5**

tener hambre to be hungry, **6.5**

la **hamburguesa** hamburger, **2.5**

hasta until, **2.6**; as far as, **6.3**; even

hasta entonces until then

hasta luego see you later, **1.4**

hasta pronto see you soon

hay there is, there are, **3.3**
hebreo(a) Hebrew
hecho(a) made
el **helado** ice cream, **2.5**
el **hemisferio** hemisphere
la **herencia** heritage
la **hermana** sister, **4.1**
el **hermano** brother, **4.1**
los **hermanos** siblings (brothers and sisters), **4.1**
el **hielo** ice, **1.5**
la **hija** daughter, **4.1**
el **hijo** son, **4.1**
los **hijos** children (sons and daughters), **4.1**
hispano(a) Hispanic
los **hispanohablantes** Spanish-speakers
los **hispanos** Hispanics
la **historia** history, **1.4**
histórica historic; historical
la **historieta** comic strip, **4.5**
hola hi, hello, **1.1**
el **hombre** man, **4.2**
el **hombre de negocios** businessman, **4.2**
hondureño(a) Honduran, **5.3**
la **hora** hour, **5.5**
a toda hora at all hours
el **horario** schedule
horrible horrible, awful, **2.1**
el **horror: ¡Qué horror!** How horrible!, **1.6**
el **hospital** hospital
el **hostal** hostel
hoy today, **2.4**
hoy día nowadays
el **huevo** egg, **2.5**

I

la **idea** idea
ideal ideal

el **idioma** language, **1.4**
la **iglesia** church, **2.6**
la **imagen** image
impaciente impatient, **2.1**
el **impermeable** raincoat, **6.1**
importa: no importa it doesn't matter, **2.4**
importante important
imposible impossible
la **impresión** impression
incluir to include
incluso including
incluyo I include
increíble incredible, **2.1**
la **independencia** independence
independiente independent
indicar to indicate
indio(a) Indian
la **información** information
informal casual (clothes)
el / la **ingeniero(a)** engineer, **4.2**
el **inglés** English (language), **1.4**
inglés(esa) English, **5.3**
el **ingrediente** ingredient
el **inmigrante** immigrant
la **institución** institution
el **instrumento** instrument
inteligente intelligent, **2.1**
intercambio exchange
interesante interesting, **2.1**
los **intereses** interests
internacional international
el **invierno** winter, **6.2**
la **invitación** invitation
los **invitados** guests
invitar to invite, **5.1**
ir to go, **1.2**
ir a casa to go home, **1.2**
ir a pie to go on foot, walk, **6.3**

ir de pesca to go fishing, **5.4**
ir de vacaciones to go on vacation, **2.3**
la **isla** island
el **italiano** Italian (language), **5.3**
italiano(a) Italian, **5.3**
la **izquierda** left, **3.3**
a la izquierda to (on) the left, **3.3**

J

el **jamón** ham, **2.5**
el **japonés** Japanese (language), **5.3**
japonés(esa) Japanese, **5.3**
joven young, **2.2**
los **jóvenes** young people, **4.3**
la **joya** jewel, pl. jewelry, **6.1**
la **joyería** jewelry store
juegas you (fam.) play, **2.4**
juego I play, **2.4**
el **juego** game, **4.5**
el **juego de mesa** board game, **4.5**
el **jueves** Thursday, **2.6**
jugar (ue) to play, **1.2**
el **jugo** juice, **2.5**
julio July, **4.6**
justo(a) fair
la **juventud** young people; youth

L

la the (f.), **1.4**
el **laboratorio** laboratory
lacio straight (hair), **4.4**
el **lado** side, **6.3**
al lado de next to; beside, **6.3**
el **lago** lake, **6.4**
la **lámpara** lamp, **3.6**
la **lana** wool, **6.2**

el **lápiz**   pencil, **1.4**
los **lápices: los lápices de co-
    lores**   colored pencils
  largo(a)   long, **4.4**
  la **larga distancia**   long
      distance
el **latín**   Latin (language)
  latino(a)   Latin
  lavar   to wash, **2.6**
la **lección**   lesson
la **leche**   milk, **2.5**
la **lechuga**   lettuce, **2.5**
la **lectura**   reading
  leer   to read, **1.2**
  legal   legal
las **legumbres**   vegetables, **2.5**
  lejos   far, **6.3**
    lejos de   far from, **6.3**
la **lencería**   linen shop
la **lengua**   language
el **lenguaje**   language
los **lentes**   lenses, eyeglasses
  los **lentes de contacto**
      contact lenses, **4.4**
el **león**   lion, **4.3**
la **libra**   pound, **6.6**
  libre   free, **4.5**
    al aire libre   outdoors,
        6.4
  los **ratos libres**   free
      time, **4.5**
la **librería**   bookstore
el **libro**   book, **1.2**
  ligero(a)   light (wind)
  limpiar   to clean, **2.3**
  lindo(a)   pretty
la **línea**   line
la **línea del ecuador**
      equator
el **lío: ¡Qué lío!**   What a
      mess!
la **liquidación**   clearance
      (sale), **6.1**
  listo(a)   smart, **2.2**
  liviano(a)   light (weight),
      6.6
  local   local
la **lotería**   lottery
  luego   later, **2.3**
el **lugar**   place, **1.5**

el **lunes**   Monday, **2.6**

LL

la **llama**   llama, **4.3**
  llamar   to call, **3.1**
  llamo: me llamo . . .   my
      name is . . . , **1.1**
la **llave**   key, **5.2**
  llegar   to arrive, **2.4**
    llegar a   to arrive at, **2.4**
  llenar   to fill
  lleno(a)   full
  llevar   to take, **3.1**; to
      carry, **5.2**; to wear, **6.1**
  llueve   it's raining, **6.4**
la **lluvia**   rain

M

la **madera**   wood, **5.2**
la **madre**   mother, **4.1**
el / la **madrileño(a)**   native of
        Madrid
el / la **maestro(a)**   teacher, **1.2**
  la **maleta**   suitcase, **3.1**
    hacer las maletas   to
        pack (suitcases), **3.1**
    malo(a)   bad, **2.2**
  la **mamá**   mom, **4.1**
  el **mamey**   mamey, tropical
      fruit
    mandar   to send, **5.1**
    manejar   to drive, **1.5**
  la **manera**   manner, way
  la **manga**   sleeve, **6.2**
    de manga corta   short-
        sleeved, **6.2**
    de manga larga   long-
        sleeved, **6.2**
    sin mangas   sleeveless,
        6.2
    mantener (ie)   to main-
        tain, to support
  la **mantequilla**   butter, **2.5**
  la **mañana**   morning, **2.4**
    de la mañana   in the
        morning, **1.3**
    esta mañana   this
        morning, **2.4**

  por la mañana   in the
      morning, **2.4**
  mañana   tomorrow, **2.3**
el **mapa**   map, **3.1**
la **máquina**   car (Caribbean)
el **mar**   sea, **5.4**
  **maravillarse: se mara-
      villan**   they marvel
      (at)
  maravilloso(a)   mar-
      velous, wonderful
la **marca**   brand name, **3.5**
las **marcas: marcas interna-
      cionales**   inter-
      national brands
  marcar   to dial
el **marido**   husband
la **marroquinería**   Moroc-
      can leatherwork
el **martes**   Tuesday, **2.6**
  marzo   March, **4.6**
  más   more, **6.5**
    más o menos   more or
        less, **6.6**
    más que   more than,
        6.5
las **matemáticas**   mathemat-
      ics, **1.4**
las **materias**   subjects
  materno(a)   maternal
  máximo(a)   maximum
    al máximo   to the
        maximum
  mayo   May, **4.6**
  mayor   older, **4.1**
el / la **mayor**   the oldest
los **mayores**   older people;
      adults
la **mayoría**   majority
la **mazorca**   ear of corn
la **mecánica**   mechanics
el / la **mecánico(a)**   mechanic,
        4.2
  la **media**   half, **1.3**
    mediano(a)   medium
  las **medias**   stockings, **6.1**
    medievales   medieval
    medir(i)   to measure
    mejor   better, **6.5**
  la **memoria**   memory

menor younger, **4.1**
el / la **menor** the youngest
menos less, **6.5**
   menos que less than, **6.5**
el **mensaje** message
el **mercado** market
la **mermelada** jam, preserves, **2.5**
el **mes** month, **4.6**
   el **mes pasado** last month, **5.3**
   el **mes que viene** next month, **4.6**
la **mesa** table, **3.6**
el **metal** metal, **5.2**
el **metro** subway
metropolitano(a) metropolitan
mexicano(a) Mexican, **5.3**
mi my, **3.6**
mí me (prep. pron.)
   a mí me gusta I like, **4.1**
   para mí for me
la **microinformática** computerware
el **miedo: tener miedo** to be scared, **6.5**
el **miembro** member
mientras while
el **miércoles** Wednesday, **2.6**
mil one thousand, **4.3**
la **milla** mile, **6.6**
el **millón (de)** million, **5.3**
mimado(a) spoiled
mínimo(a) minimum
el **minuto** minute, **5.5**
mira look (fam. sing. com.)
la **misión** mission
el / la **mismo(a)** the same
   lo mismo the same thing
misterioso(a) mysterious
la **mochila** bookbag, knapsack, **1.4**

la **moda** fashion, **4.5**
   de moda in fashion, **6.2**
el **modelo** model
moderno(a) modern, **3.5**
el **monasterio** monastery
la **moneda** coin, **3.5**
el **mono** monkey, **4.3**
el **monopatín** skateboard, **1.2**
   andar en monopatín to skateboard, **1.2**
la **montaña** mountain, **6.4**
montar to ride, **1.2**
   montar a caballo to ride horseback, **1.5**
   montar en bicicleta to ride a bicycle, **1.2**
morado(a) purple, **3.6**
moreno(a) dark (hair, complexion), **4.4**
los **moros** Moors
el **mostrador** counter (in a shop)
la **moto** motorcycle, **3.5**
la **motocicleta** motorcycle
el **motor** engine
la **muchacha** girl, **2.2**
el **muchacho** boy, **2.2**
muchísimos(as) many
mucho a lot, **1.4**; a lot (of), many, **4.2**
   mucho gusto nice to meet you, **1.1**
   muchos(as) a lot, many, **4.2**
los **muebles** furniture, **3.6**
la **mujer** woman, **4.2**
   la **mujer de negocios** businesswoman, **4.2**
   la **mujer policía** police officer, **4.2**
el **mundo** world
   todo el mundo everybody, everyone
la **muralla** city wall
el **museo** museum
la **música** music, **1.4**
el / la **músico(a)** musician, **2.1**

muy very, **1.1**
   muy bien very well, **1.1**

N

nací I was born, **5.3**
el **nacimiento** birth
nacional national
   el **sistema nacional** national system
nada nothing, **1.2**
nadar to swim, **1.2**
natural natural
la **naturaleza** nature
la **Navidad** Christmas
necesario(a) necessary
necesitar to need, **1.4**
los **negocios** business(es)
negro(a) black, **3.6**
nervioso(a) nervous, **3.4**
ni nor
   ni . . . ni neither . . . nor
nicaragüense Nicaraguan, **5.3**
los **nietos** grandchildren
nieva it's snowing, **6.4**
ningún(una) not any, any, **1.5**
   no quiero ir a ningún lugar I don't want to go anywhere, **1.5**
el / la **niño(a)** child, **4.3**
no no, not, **1.2**
   ¿no? no?, **1.4**
   no aprobado failing
   no importa it doesn't matter, **2.4**
   ¡No me digas! You don't say!, **1.6**
   no muy bien not too well, **1.1**
   no sólo not only
la **noche** night, **2.4**
   de la noche at night, **1.3**
   esta noche tonight, **2.4**

por la noche at night, **2.4**
el **nombre** name, **5.1**
el **norte** North
   norteamericano(a)
    North American, **5.3**
   nosotros(as) we, us, **3.1**
la **nota** grade, **1.4**; note
   sacar buenas notas to
    get good grades, **1.4**
las **noticias** news, **4.5**
el **noticiero** newscast
   novecientos(as) nine
    hundred, **4.3**
la **novela** novel, **4.5**
   noveno(a) ninth, **3.2**
   noventa ninety, **3.3**
   noviembre November,
    4.6
   nuestro(a) our, **5.4**
   nueve nine, **1.3**
   nuevo(a) new, **3.5**
el **número** number, **3.1**
el **número de teléfono**
    telephone number, **3.1**
   nunca never, **2.4**

O

   o or, **1.4**
el **objeto** object
la **obra** work (artistic)
   ochenta eighty, **3.3**
   ocho eight, **1.3**
   ochocientos(as) eight
    hundred, **4.3**
   octavo(a) eighth, **3.2**
   octubre October, **4.6**
la **ocupación** occupation
   ocupado(a) busy, **3.4**
   ocurre it occurs, it
    happens
la **oferta** offer
la **oficina** office, **3.3**
   ofrecer to offer
   oír to hear, **5.5**
el **ojo** eye, **4.4**
las **olas** waves (ocean), **5.4**
   correr las olas to surf,
    5.4

   olvidar to forget, **3.1**
   once eleven, **1.3**
la **onza** ounce, **6.6**
la **opinión** opinion
la **opinión pública** pub-
    lic opinion
la **oportunidad** opportunity
la **óptica** optical store
el **origen** origin
   original original
el **oro** gold, **5.2**
el **oso** bear, **4.3**
el **otoño** autumn, **6.2**
   otro(a) another, other,
    4.5
   oye: ¡oye! hey!, listen!,
    2.4
   oyes you (fam.) hear, **5.5**

P

la **paciencia** patience
   paciente patient
los **pacientes** patients
el **padre** father, **4.1**
los **padres** parents, **4.1**
la **paella** Spanish rice dish
    with chicken, seafood,
    etc., seasoned with
    saffron
   pagar to pay, **5.6**
la **página** page, **1.4**
el **país** country
la **palabra** word, **1.4**
la **pampa** extensive plain
    in Argentina
el **pan** bread, **2.5**
   el **pan tostado** toast, **2.5**
   panameño(a) Panama-
    nian, **5.3**
los **pantalones** pants, **6.1**
el **papá** dad, **4.1**
los **papás** mom and dad, **4.1**
las **papas fritas** french fries,
    2.5
el **papel** paper, **1.4**
la **papelería** stationery
    store
   para for, **2.5**; to; in order
    to, **5.2**

   para caballeros for
    gentlemen, **6.2**
   para damas for ladies,
    6.2
   para el desayuno (el
    amuerzo, la cena)
    for breakfast (lunch,
    dinner), **2.5**
   para mí for me
   ¿Para qué sirve? What
    is it used for?, **5.2**
   para ti for you
   para todos for all
la **parada** bus stop
el **paraguas** umbrella, **6.1**
   paraguayo(a) Para-
    guayan, **5.3**
   parece seems, looks
    like, **4.1**
   parece que . . . it
    seems that . . . , **4.3**
la **pared** wall, **3.6**
el / la **pariente(ta)** relative, **4.1**
el **parque** park, **1.5**
   el **parque zoológico**
    zoo, **4.3**
la **parte** place; part
   particulares private
el **partido** game, match,
    1.2
   pasado(a) last, **5.3**
   el **año pasado** last year,
    5.3
   pasado mañana the
    day after tomorrow,
    4.6
la **semana pasada** last
    week, **5.3**
el **pasaporte** passport, **3.1**
   pasar to spend (time),
    5.4
   pasar la aspiradora to
    vacuum, **5.6**
   pasar to pass
   pasa come in (fam.
    sing. com.)
   pasa: ¿Qué pasa?
    What's wrong?,
    What's going on?

pasar por to pass by, stop by
pasear to go for a ride
  pasear en bote to go for a boat ride
  pasear en velero to go sailing, **5.4**
el **paseo** stroll, walk, **1.2;** boulevard, promenade, **3.2**
  dar un paseo to go for a walk, **1.2**
el **pastel** pie, pastry, **2.5**
los **pastores** shepherds
patinar to skate, **1.5**
  patinar sobre hielo to ice-skate, **1.5**
pedir (i) to ask for, **5.6**
  pedir permiso to ask for permission, **5.6**
peleados: están peleados they are not on speaking terms
la **peletería** fur shop
la **película** movie, film, **1.2**
  la **película extranjera** foreign film, **4.5**
  la **película policial** detective movie, **4.5**
  la **película de terror** horror movie, **4.5**
pelirrojo(a) red-headed, **4.4**
el **pelo** hair, **4.4**
la **pena: ¡Qué pena!** What a shame!, **1.6**
pensar (ie) to intend, to plan, **2.2**
peor worse, **6.5**
el / la **pequeñito(a)** little one
pequeño(a) small, **2.2**
la **percusión** percussion
perder(ie) to lose, **4.5**
perdón excuse me, **1.4**
perezoso(a) lazy, **2.2**
perfectamente perfectly
la **perfumería** perfumery
el **periódico** newspaper, **2.3**
el / la **periodista** journalist, **4.2**

el **periquito** parakeet, **4.3**
el **permiso** permission, **5.6**
  con permiso excuse me, **2.3**
  pedir permiso to ask for permission, **5.6**
permitir to allow, permit, **5.6**
pero but, **1.6**
el **perro** dog, **4.3**
las **personas** persons
pertenecer (zco) a to belong to, **5.5**
peruano(a) Peruvian, **5.3**
pesado(a) heavy, **6.6**
la **pesca** fishing, **5.4**
  ir de pesca to go fishing, **5.4**
el **pescado** fish, **2.5**
la **peseta** monetary unit of Spain
el **pez** fish, **4.3**
  el **pez dorado** goldfish, **4.3**
picante spicy
el **picnic** picnic
el **pie** foot (measurement), **6.6**
  ir a pie to go on foot, to walk, **6.3**
la **piel** leather; fur
piensan they think
piensas you (fam.) plan, intend, **2.2**
pienso I plan, intend, **2.2**
la **pileta** swimming pool (Argentina)
el **pingüino** penguin, **4.3**
pintar to paint
el / la **pintor(a)** painter
la **pintura** painting
la **piñata** hanging papier-mâché figure filled with candy and gifts
la **piscina** swimming pool, **1.5**
el **piso** story, floor (of a building), **3.2;** floor, **3.6**

la **pizzería** pizzeria
planchar to iron, **5.6**
planear to plan, **5.4**
el **plano** plan; map
la **planta** floor
  la **planta baja** ground floor
el **plástico** plastic, **5.2**
la **plata** silver, **5.2**
el **plátano** banana
el **plato** dish, **5.6**
la **playa** beach, **1.5**
la **plaza** plaza, (public) square, **3.2**
la **población** population
pobre poor
poco(a) little, **4.2**
  un poco a little, **2.2**
pocos(as) few, **4.2**
poder (ue) to be able, **4.6**
el **policía** police officer, **4.2**
la **policía** police (department)
policial: la película policial detective movie, **4.5**
la **política** politics
político(a) political
el / la **político(a)** politician, **2.1**
el **pollo** chicken, **2.5**
poner: poner la mesa to set the table, **5.6**
popular popular, **2.1**
por for; by
  por ciento percent
  ¡Por Dios! For goodness sake!
  por ejemplo for example
  por eso therefore, that's why, **5.6**
  por favor please, **5.1**
  por fin finally
  por la mañana in the morning, **2.4**
  por la noche at night, **2.4**
  por la tarde in the afternoon, **2.4**

por lo general in general

¿Por qué no . . . ? Why not . . . ?, **2.5**

por todas partes everywhere

porque because, **1.5**

portátil portable

la **portería** custodian's quarters or office

el / la **portero(a)** custodian

posible possible

la **postal** postcard

el **postre** dessert, **2.5**

practicar to play, to practice, **1.2**

practicar deportes to play sports, **1.2**

practicar el esquí acuático to water-ski, **5.4**

el **precio** price

precioso(a) beautiful

la **preferencia** preference

preferible preferable

preferir (ie) to prefer, **4.5**

la **pregunta** question, **1.4**

hacer una pregunta to ask a question, **1.4**

preliminar preliminary

preocupado(a) worried, **3.4**

preparado(a) prepared, ready

preparar to prepare, to get ready, **2.5**

la **presentación** introduction

la **carta de presentación** letter of introduction

presentar to introduce, **5.6**

el **presente** present

el **préstamo** loan

prestar to lend, **5.1**

la **primavera** spring, **6.4**

primero(a) first, **2.3**

el / la **primo(a)** cousin, **4.1**

principales main

principalmente mainly

la **prisa: tener prisa** to be in a hurry, **6.5**

privado(a) private

la **probabilidad** probability

el **problema** problem, **5.6**

el **producto** product

profesional professional

el / la **profesor / a** teacher, professor, **4.2**

el **programa** program, **4.5**

el **programa de aventuras** adventure program, **4.5**

el **programa de ciencia ficción** science fiction program, **4.5**

el **programa de terror** horror program, **4.5**

el **programa deportivo** sports program, **4.5**

el **programa educativo** educational program, **4.5**

el **programa extranjero** foreign program, **4.5**

el **programa policial** detective program, **4.5**

el **programa romántico** love story, **4.5**

la **programación** programming

prohibido(a) prohibited

prohibir to prohibit

prometer to promise, **5.6**

propio(a) one's own

la **protección** protection

el **proyecto** project

público(a) public

la **opinión pública** public opinion

el **pueblo** town, **2.3**

puedes you (fam.) can, **4.6**

puedo I can, **4.6**

el **puente de observación** observation deck

el **puerco** pork

la **puerta** door, **3.6**

el **puerto** port

puertorriqueño(a) Puerto Rican, **5.3**

pues well, **1.6**; because

la **pulgada** inch, **6.6**

la **pulsera** bracelet, **6.1**

el **punto: los puntos de reunión** gathering places

puntual punctual, **2.1**

Q

que that

que le dé that it goes to

qué what, **1.2**; how, **1.6**

¡Qué aburrido! How boring!, **1.6**

¿Qué clase de . . . ? What kind of . . . ?, **4.5**

¡Qué divertido! What fun!, **1.6**

¡Qué horror! How horrible!, **1.6**

¡Qué lío! What a mess!

¡Qué maravilla! How wonderful!

¡Qué raro! How strange!, **1.6**

¡Qué suerte! What luck!, **1.6**

¿Qué tal? How are you?, **1.1**

¿Qué tiempo hace? What's the weather like?, **6.4**

¡Qué va! No way!, **1.6**

el **quehacer** chore, task, **5.6**

querer (ie) to want

querido(a) dear

el **queso** cheese, **2.5**

quién who, **2.2**

quiere: te quiere he / she loves you

quieres you (fam.) want, 1.2
quiero I want, 1.2
la **química** chemistry, 1.4
quince fifteen, 1.3
quinientos(as) five hundred, 4.2
quinto(a) fifth, 3.2
quisiera I would like, 3.4
quitar to remove, 5.6

R

el **radio** radio (instrument, set), 3.5
la **radio** radio (broadcasting, as a medium), 1.4
rápidamente rapidly
rápido fast
la **raqueta:** la **raqueta de tenis** tennis racket
raro: ¡Qué raro! How strange!, 1.6
el **ratoncito** mouse, 4.3
el **rato:** los **ratos libres** free time, 4.5
la **razón** reason
la **reacción** reaction
la **realidad: en realidad** in reality
rebajar to lower (the price)
la **rebaja** (price) reduction
la **recámara** bedroom (Mexico)
recibir to receive, 3.1
la **recomendación** recommendation
recordar (ue) to remember, 3.1
rectangular rectangular, 5.2
recuerdas you (fam.) remember, 3.1
recuerdo I remember, 3.1
el **recuerdo** souvenir, 3.5
los **recuerdos** memories
la **red** network
redondo(a) round, 5.2
el **refresco** noncarbonated soft drink, 2.5
el **refrigerador** refrigerator, 3.6
el **regalo** gift, 2.3
regatear to bargain
la **región** region
regresar to return, 4.6
regular so-so, fair, 1.1
el **reloj** clock, 5.2
la **relojería** watch and clock store
el **repaso** review
el **reportero(a)** reporter
representar to represent
la **República Dominicana** the Dominican Republic
la **reservación** reservation
la **resolución** resolution
respetar to respect
responsable responsible
el **restaurante** restaurant, 1.5
el **resto** the rest
la **reunión** meeting, reunion, 5.5
la **revista** magazine, 1.2
rico(a) tasty
el **río** river, 6.4
riquísimo(a) very tasty
el **ritmo** rhythm
rizado(a) curly, 4.4
rodeado(a) surrounded
rojo(a) red, 3.6
romano(a) Roman
romántico(a) romantic, 4.5
el **programa romántico** love story, 4.5
la **ropa** clothes, clothing, 3.1
la **ropa para caballeros** men's clothing, 6.2
la **ropa para damas** ladies' clothing, 6.2
la **ropa interior** underwear
rosado(a) pink, 3.6
rubio(a) blonde, 4.4
la **rumba** Cuban dance
el **ruso** Russian (language), 5.3
ruso(a) Russian, 5.3

S

S.A. abbreviation of **Sociedad Anónima,** Incorporated
el **sábado** Saturday, 2.6
saber to know, 1.5
sacar to take out, 5.6
sacar buenas notas to get good grades, 1.4
sacar fotos to take pictures, 1.5
la **sala** living room, 3.6
el **salario** salary
salgo I go out, 3.1
la **salida** departure
salir to go out, 3.1
la **salsa** Caribbean rhythm and dance
saltar las olas to jump, ride the waves, 5.4
los **saludos** greetings; regards
salvadoreño(a) Salvadoran, 5.3
las **sandalias** sandals, 6.1
el **sandwich** sandwich, 2.5
Santo Tomás Saint Thomas
las **sardinas** sardines
la **sastrería** tailor's shop
se: Se dice . . . It's said . . . , 5.2
se solicita is wanted, is requested
sé I know, 1.5
la **sed** thirst, 6.5
tener sed to be thirsty, 6.5
la **seda** silk, 6.2
según according (to)
segundo(a) second, 3.2
seguro(a) sure, certain, 3.4

seis six, **1.3**

seiscientos(as) six hundred, **4.3**

el **sello** stamp, **3.5**

la **semana** week, **2.6**

  la **semana pasada** last week, **5.3**

  la **semana que viene** next week, **4.6**

sensacional sensational

el **señor** Mr., sir, **1.3**

la **señora** Mrs., ma'am, **1.3**

las **señoras** women

la **señorita** Miss, **1.3**

septiembre September, **4.6**

séptimo(a) seventh, **3.2**

ser to be, **2.1**

la **serpiente** snake, **4.3**

el **servicio** restroom, **3.3**; service

servir (i) to serve

sesenta sixty, **3.3**

setecientos(as) seven hundred, **4.3**

setenta seventy, **3.3**

sexto(a) sixth, **3.2**

los **shorts** shorts (pants), **6.1**

si if, **3.1**

sí yes, **1.1**

siempre always, **2.4**

sienten they feel

siete seven, **1.3**

sigue go on, continue (fam. sing. com.), **6.3**; he / she / it continues; you (formal) continue

sigue derecho go straight (fam. sing. com.), **6.3**

siguen you (pl.) go on, **6.3**

sigues you (fam.) go on, **6.3**

el **silencio** silence

la **silla** chair, **3.6**

similar similar

simpático(a) nice, pleasant, **2.2**

sin without, **6.2**

  sin embargo nevertheless

  sin mangas sleeveless, **6.2**

la **sinagoga** synagogue, **2.6**

sincero(a) sincere

sino que but also

sirve: sirve para . . . it's used for . . . , **5.2**

  ¿Para qué sirve? What is it used for?, **5.2**

el **sistema** system

el **sistema auditivo** hearing

el **sistema nacional** national system

la **situación** situation

sobre about

el **sobre** envelope, **5.1**

sobresaliente outstanding

sociable sociable, friendly

el **sofá** sofa, **3.6**

el **sol** sun, **6.4**

solicita: se solicita is wanted, is requested

solicito I want

solo(a) alone

sólo only

somos we are, **2.1**

son they are, **2.1**

el **sonido** sound

la **sopa** soup, **2.5**

el / la **sospechoso(a)** suspect

el **sótano** basement (of a house), **3.3**

soy I am, **2.1**

  soy de . . . I'm from . . . , **1.1**

su(s) his, her, your (formal), their, **4.1**

la **sucursal** branch of a department store

Sudamérica South America

el **sueño** sleep, **6.5**; dream

  tener sueño to be sleepy, **6.5**

la **suerte** luck, **1.6**

  ¡Qué suerte! What luck!, **1.6**

el **suéter** sweater, **6.1**

suficiente sufficient

el **supermercado** supermarket, **2.6**

supervisar to supervise

el / la **supervisor / a** supervisor, **4.2**

el **sur** South

  al sur to the south

el **suroeste** Southwest

T

tacaño(a) stingy, **2.2**

la **talla** size (of clothing)

  las **tallas especiales** special (clothing) sizes

el **tamaño** size

también also, too, **1.6**

tampoco neither

tan: tan . . . como as . . . as, **6.5**

tanto: tanto como . . . as much as . . . , **6.5**

tantos(as): tantos(as) como . . . as many as . . . , **6.5**

las **tapas** hors d'oeuvres (Spain)

tardar: tardar en . . . to take time . . . , **6.6**

la **tarde** afternoon, **2.4**

  de la tarde in the afternoon, **1.3**

  esta tarde this afternoon, **2.4**

  por la tarde in the afternoon, **2.4**

tarde late, **2.4**

la **tarea** homework, **1.2**

la **tarjeta**   card, **5.1**
la **tarjeta de crédito**   credit card, **5.1**
   la **tarjeta joven**   special student card for Spain's train system
   la **tarjeta postal**   postcard, **3.5**
el **té**   tea, **2.5**
el **teatro**   theater
la **tele**   TV, **1.2**
   ver la tele   to watch TV, **1.2**
el **teléfono**   telephone, **3.1**
   hablar por teléfono   to talk on the phone, **1.2**
   el **número de teléfono**   telephone number, **3.1**
la **telenovela**   soap opera, **4.5**
el **televisor**   television (set), **3.5**
la **temperatura**   temperature
la **temporada**   season
temprano   early, **2.4**
tener   to have, **3.5**
   tener calor   to be hot, **6.5**
   tener frío   to be cold, **6.5**
   tener hambre   to be hungry, **6.5**
   tener miedo   to be scared, **6.5**
   tener prisa   to be in a hurry, **6.5**
   tener que   + inf. to have to, **4.4**
   tener sed   to be thirsty, **6.5**
   tener sueño   to be sleepy, **6.5**
   tengo   I have, **3.5**
el **tenis**   tennis, **1.2**
los **tenis**   sneakers, **6.1**
   tercero(a)   third, **3.2**

terminar   to end, finish, **4.5**
el **territorio**   territory
el **terror**   horror, **4.5**
   la **película de terror**   horror movie, **4.5**
el **tesoro**   treasure
ti   you, yourself (prep. pron.)
   a ti te gusta   you like, **4.1**
   para ti   for you
la **tía**   aunt, **4.1**
el **tiempo**   time, **5.5**; weather, **6.4**
   con el tiempo   eventually
la **tienda**   store, **1.5**
   la **tienda vaquera**   jeans store
   tienden   they tend to
   tienes   you (fam.) have, **3.5**
la **tierra**   land, country
el **tigre**   tiger, **4.3**
   tímido(a)   timid, shy
el **tío**   uncle, **4.1**
los **tíos**   aunt(s) and uncle(s), **4.1**
   típicamente   typically
   típico(a)   typical
   tirar   to throw
los **títulos**   titles
   tocar   to play (an instrument), **1.5**; to touch
   todavía   still
      todavía no   not yet
   todo   everything
      todo lo que . . .   everything that . . .
   todo(a)   every, all, **4.2**; whole
      para todos   for all
      todas las horas   all the time
      todo el mundo   everybody, everyone
      todos los días   every day, **2.6**

tomar   to take, **3.2**
   tomar algo   to drink something, **1.2**
   tomar sol   to sunbathe, **5.4**
el **tomate**   tomato, **2.5**
   tonto(a)   silly, foolish, **2.2**
la **torre**   tower
la **tortilla**   omelet (Spain)
la **tortuga**   turtle, **4.3**
el **total**   total
   trabajar   to work, **1.4**
el **trabajo**   work, job, **2.3**
   traer   to bring, **5.1**
el **tráfico**   traffic
   traigo   I bring, **5.2**
el **traje: el traje de baño**   bathing suit, **6.1**
   el **traje para caballero**   gentleman's suit, **6.1**
   el **traje para dama**   lady's suit, **6.1**
   tranquilo(a)   calm, relaxed, **3.4**
   transmitir   to transmit, to broadcast
el **transporte**   transportation
el **tranvía**   local train (Spain)
   trece   thirteen, **1.3**
   treinta   thirty, **3.3**
el **tren**   train, **6.3**
   tres   three, **1.3**
   triste   sad, **3.4**
el **trofeo**   trophy, **3.5**
   tropical   tropical
   tu   your, **3.6**
   tú   you, **3.1**
el **turismo**   tourism
el / la **turista**   tourist

U

un   a, **3.5**
una   a, **3.5**
la **universidad**   university
uno   one, **1.3**

la **urgencia médica**   medical emergency
uruguayo(a)   Uruguayan, 5.3
usado(a)   used
usar   to use, 1.4
usted   you (formal), 1.3
ustedes   you (pl.), 3.1
utilizar   to use

V

va   he / she / it goes, you (formal) go, 2.3
las **vacaciones**   vacation, 2.3
  ir de vacaciones   to go on vacation, 2.3
el **valle**   valley
vamos   we go, 2.3
  ¡Vamos!   Let's go! (pl. com.)
van   they go, 2.3
el **vaquero**   cowboy
las **variedades**   varieties
el **programa de variedades**   variety show
varios(as)   various, 5.5
los **varones**   boys
vas   you (fam.) go, 2.3
las **veces**   times
  a veces   sometimes, 2.4
el / la **vecino(a)**   neighbor, 5.5
veinte   twenty, 1.3
el **velero**   sailboat, 5.4
  pasear en velero   to go sailing, 5.4

los **vendedores**   salespeople, vendors
vender   to sell, 5.6
venezolano(a)   Venezuelan, 5.3
vengo   I come, 6.3
venir (ie)   to come, 6.3
la **ventana**   window, 3.6
ver   to watch, to see, 1.2
  ver la tele   to watch TV, 1.2
el **verano**   summer, 6.2
verdad: ¿verdad?   right?, 2.5
verde   green, 4.4
las **verduras**   vegetables
el **vestíbulo**   entryway
el **vestido**   dress, 6.1
vestido(a)   dressed
los **veteranos**   veterans
el / la **veterinario(a)**   veterinarian, 4.2
viajar   to travel, 3.1
el **viaje**   trip
la **vida**   life
el **vídeo**   video, 3.5
  el **vídeo musical**   music video
la **videocasetera**   videocassette player
el **videojuego**   video game, 2.1
el **vidrio**   glass (material), 5.2
viejo(a)   old, 2.2
vienes   you (fam.) come, 6.3
el **viento**   wind, 6.4
  hace viento   it's windy, 6.4
el **viernes**   Friday, 2.6

vino   he / she / it / you (formal) came
la **visita**   visit
los **visitantes**   visitors
visitar   to visit, 1.2
la **vista**   view
la **viuda**   widow
vivir   to live, 3.1
vivo(a)   alive; live
el **vocabulario**   vocabulary
el **volumen**   volume
  a todo volumen   at its loudest (volume)
vosotros(as)   you (fam. pl.), 3.1
voy   I go, 2.3
el **vuelo**   flight

Y

y   and, 1.6
  y media   half past the hour, 1.3
ya   already, 1.5
  ya no   no longer
yo   I, 3.1

Z

la **zapatería**   shoe store
la **zapatería deportiva**   sport shoe store
los **zapatos**   shoes, 3.5
la **zoología**   zoology

Vocabulario Inglés-Español

The **Vocabulario Inglés-Español** contains all productive vocabulary from the text.

The numbers following each productive entry indicate the chapter and lesson in which the word is first introduced.

The following are abbreviations used in this glossary.

adv.	adverb
com.	command
dir. obj.	direct object
f.	feminine
fam.	familiar
ind. obj.	indirect object
inf.	infinitive
m.	masculine
obj. of prep.	object of the preposition
pers.	personal
pl.	plural
prep.	preposition; prepositional
pron.	pronoun
sing.	singular
subj.	subjunctive

A

a un(una), 3.5
  a lot mucho, 1.4
  a lot of mucho(a), 4.2
actor el actor, 2.1
actress la actriz, 2.1
address la dirección, 3.2
admission: admission ticket la entrada, 5.5
adventure la aventura, 4.5
  adventure program el programa de aventuras, 4.5
advertisement el anuncio, 5.1
advice el consejo, 5.6
to advise dar consejos a, 5.6
after después de, 3.1
afternoon la tarde, 2.4
  in the afternoon de la tarde, 1.3; por la tarde, 2.4
  this afternoon esta tarde, 2.4
afterwards después, 2.3
airplane el avión, 6.3
algebra el álgebra, 1.4
all todo(a), 4.2
to allow permitir, 5.6
almost casi, 5.5
already ya, 1.5
also también, 1.6
always siempre, 2.4
and y, 1.6
angry enojado(a), 3.4
animal el animal, 4.3
another otro(a), 4.5
to answer contestar, 1.4
anything: I don't want to do anything no quiero hacer nada, 1.2
anywhere: I don't want to go anywhere no quiero ir a ningún lugar, 1.5
apartment el apartamento, 3.2

April abril, 4.6
Argentinian argentino(a), 5.3
arquitect el / la arquitecto(a), 4.2
to arrive llegar, 2.4
  to arrive at llegar a, 2.4
arrogant arrogante, 2.1
art el arte, 1.4
artist el / la artista, 2.1
as . . . as tan . . . como, 6.5
  as far as hasta, 6.3
  as many as . . . tantos(as) como . . . , 6.5
  as much as . . . tanto(a) como . . . , 6.5
to ask for pedir (i), 5.6
  to ask for permission pedir permiso, 5.6
  to ask a question hacer una pregunta, 1.4
at a, 1.3; en, 3.2
athlete el / la deportista, 2.1
to attend asistir a, 5.4
August agosto, 4.1
aunt la tía, 4.1
  aunt(s) and uncle(s) los tíos, 4.1
autumn el otoño, 6.2
avenue la avenida, 3.2

B

bad malo(a), 2.2; mal, 6.4
  the weather is bad hace mal tiempo, 6.4
ballpoint pen el bolígrafo, 1.4
bank el banco, 2.6
baseball el béisbol, 1.2
basement (of a house) el sótano, 3.3

basketball el baloncesto, 1.2
bathing suit el traje de baño, 6.1
bathroom el baño, 3.6
to be estar, 3.2; ser, 2.1
  to be in / at / on estar en, 3.2
to be able to poder (ue), 4.6
beach la playa, 1.5
beans los frijoles, 2.5
bear el oso, 4.3
beard la barba, 4.4
because porque, 1.5
bed la cama, 3.6
bedroom la habitación, 2.3
been: it has been . . . since hace . . . que, 5.5
before antes de, 3.1
behind detrás de, 6.3
to belong to pertenecer (zco) a, 5.5
below abajo, 3.3
belt el cinturón, 6.1
best: What do you [fam.] like best? ¿Qué te gusta más?, 1.4
better mejor, 6.5
between entre, 6.3
beverage la bebida, 2.5
bicycle la bicicleta, 1.2
  to ride a bicycle montar en bicicleta, 1.2
big grande, 2.2
biology la biología, 1.4
birthday el cumpleaños, 4.6
black negro(a), 3.6
block: city block la cuadra, 6.3
blond rubio(a), 4.4
blouse la blusa, 6.1
blue azul, 3.6
board: board game el juego de mesa, 4.5
boat el barco, 6.3

Bolivian boliviano(a), 5.3
book el libro, 1.2
boots las botas, 6.1
bored aburrido(a), 3.4
boring aburrido(a), 2.2
  How boring! ¡Qué aburrido!, 1.6
born: I was born nací (nacer), 5.3
boulevard el paseo, 3.2
to **bowl** jugar boliche (m.), 2.6
boy el muchacho, 2.2
bracelet la pulsera, 6.1
braces (dental) los frenos de los dientes, 4.4
brand: brand name la marca, 3.5
  What's the brand name? ¿De qué marca es?, 2.3
bread el pan, 2.5
breakfast el desayuno, 2.5
to **bring** traer, 5.1
  I bring traigo, 5.2
brother el hermano, 4.1
  brother(s) and sister(s) los hermanos, 4.1
brown de color café, 4.4
building el edificio, 3.2
bus el autobús, 6.3
businessman el hombre de negocios, 4.2
businesswoman la mujer de negocios, 4.2
busy ocupado(a), 3.4
but pero, 1.6
butter la mantequilla, 2.5
to **buy** comprar, 1.2

C

cafeteria la cafetería, 1.5

calculator la calculadora, 1.4
to **call** llamar, 3.1
calm tranquilo(a), 3.4
camel el camello, 4.3
camera la cámara, 3.1
Canadian canadiense, 5.3
canary el canario, 4.3
cap el gorro, 6.1
car el coche, 1.5
card tarjeta, 5.1
  credit card la tarjeta de crédito, 5.1
carpenter el carpintero(a), 4.2
to **carry** llevar, 5.2
cassette el casete, 3.5
cat el gato, 4.3
cereal el cereal, 2.5
chair la silla, 3.6
to **change** cambiar, 3.1
check el cheque, 5.1
  traveler's check el cheque de viajero, 3.1
cheese el queso, 2.5
chess el ajedrez, 4.5
chicken el pollo, 2.5
child el / la niño(a), 4.3
children (sons and daughters) los hijos, 4.1
Chilean chileno(a), 5.3
Chinese chino(a), 5.3; (language) el chino, 5.3
chore el quehacer, 5.6
church la iglesia, 2.6
city la ciudad, 1.5
class la clase, 1.4
classmate el / la compañero(a) de clase, 2.1
to **clean** limpiar, 2.3
clearance (sale) la liquidación, 6.1
clock el reloj, 5.2
clothing la ropa, 3.1
cloudy: it's cloudy está nublado, 6.4

club el club, 5.5
coffee el café, 2.5
coin la moneda, 3.5
cold el frío, 6.5
  it's cold hace frío, 6.4
  to be cold tener frío, 6.5
collection la colección, 3.5
Colombian colombiano(a), 5.3
to **come** venir (ie), 6.3
  I come vengo, 6.3
comedy (program) el programa cómico, 4.5
comfortable cómodo(a), 3.1
comic (strip) la historieta, 4.5
company la compañía, 4.2
composition la composición, 1.4
computer la computadora, 1.5
concert el concierto, 2.3
to **continue:**
  you [fam.] **continue** sigues, 6.3
  you [pl.] **continue** siguen, 6.3
to **cook** cocinar, 1.5
cool: it's cool hace fresco, 6.4
corner: street corner la esquina, 6.3
to **cost** valer, 4.2
Costa Rican costarricense, 5.3
cotton el algodón, 5.2
countryside el campo, 1.5
course: Of course! ¡Cómo no!, 1.2
cousin el / la primo(a), 4.1
credit card la tarjeta de crédito, 5.1
Cuban cubano(a), 5.3

curly (hair) rizado(a), 4.4

to **cut** cortar, 5.6

D

dad el papá, 4.1

to **dance** bailar, 1.2

dance el baile, 1.5

dancer el / la bailarín(ina), 2.1

dark (hair, complexion) moreno(a), 4.4

daughter la hija, 4.1

December diciembre, 4.6

dentist el / la dentista, 4.2

depressed deprimido(a), 3.4

depressing deprimente, 2.1

desert el desierto, 6.4

desk el escritorio, 3.6

dessert el postre, 2.5

detective: detective movie la película policial, 4.5

different diferente, 2.1

difficult difícil, 1.6

disaster: What a disaster! ¡Qué desastre!, 1.6

dish el plato, 5.6

to **do** hacer, 1.2

doctor el / la doctor / a, 4.2

dog el perro, 4.3

dollar el dólar, 1.3

Dominican dominicano(a), 5.3

door la puerta, 3.6

dot: on the dot en punto, 2.6

downtown el centro, 2.3

to **draw** dibujar, 1.5

dress el vestido, 6.1

dresser el armario, 3.6

to **drink** tomar, 1.2

to **drive** manejar, 1.5

E

early temprano, 2.4

to **earn (money)** ganar, 2.3

earring el arete, 6.1

easy fácil, 1.6

to **eat** comer, 1.2

Ecuadorian ecuatoriano(a), 5.3

education: physical education la educación física, 1.4

educational educativo(a), 4.5

egg el huevo, 2.5

eight ocho, 1.2

eight hundred ochocientos(as), 4.3

eighteen diez y ocho, 1.3

eighth octavo(a), 3.2

eighty ochenta, 3.3

electrician el / la electricista, 4.2

elegant elegante, 2.1

elephant el elefante, 4.3

elevator el ascensor, 3.3

eleven once, 1.3

employee el / la empleado(a), 4.2

engineer el / la ingeniero(a), 4.2

English inglés(esa), 5.3; **(language)** el inglés, 1.4

enough bastante, 2.2

envelope el sobre, 5.1

evening noche, 1.3 **in the evening** de la noche, 1.3; por la noche, 2.4

every todo(a), 4.2 **every day** todos los días, 2.6

exam el examen, 1.4 **to study for an exam** estudiar para un examen, 1.4

excellent excelente, 2.1

excited emocionado(a), 3.4

exciting emocionante, 2.1

excuse: excuse me con permiso, 1.4; perdón, 1.4

to **exercise** hacer ejercicio, 2.3

expensive caro(a), 3.5

to **explain** explicar, 5.6

eye el ojo, 4.4

eyeglasses los anteojos, 4.4

F

factory la fábrica, 4.2

family la familia, 3.1

far: far from lejos de, 6.3

farmer el / la agricultor / a, 4.2

fashion la moda, 4.5 **in fashion** de moda, 6.2

fat gordo(a), 2.2

father el padre, 4.1

favor el favor, 5.1 **to do a favor** hacer un favor, 5.1

favorite favorito(a), 2.3

fear el miedo, 3.6

February febrero, 4.6

to **feed** dar de comer a, 5.6

few pocos(as), 4.2

fifteen quince, 1.3

fifth quinto(a), 3.2

fifty cincuenta, 3.3

film la película, 1.2

to **finish** terminar, 4.5

firefighter el / la bombero(a), 4.2

first primero(a), 2.3

fish el pescado, 2.5; el pez, 4.3

fishing la pesca, 5.4 **to go fishing** ir de pesca, 5.4

five cinco, **1.3**
  five hundred quinientos(as), **4.2**
floor el piso, **3.6**
  What floor is it on? ¿En qué piso está?, **3.2**
flowered (print) de flores, **6.2**
food la comida, **2.5**
foot (measurement) el pie, **6.6**
  on foot a pie, **6.3**
football el fútbol americano, **1.2**
for para, **5.2**
  What is it used for? ¿Para qué sirve?, **5.2**
foreign extranjero(a), **4.5**
  foreign film la película extranjera, **4.5**
forest el bosque, **6.4**
to **forget** olvidar, **3.1**
form (document) el formulario, **2.1**
forty cuarenta, **3.3**
  four hundred cuatrocientos(as), **4.2**
fourteen catorce, **1.3**
fourth cuarto(a), **3.2**
free libre, **4.5**
  free time los ratos libres, **4.5**
French francés(esa), **5.3**; **(language)** el francés, **1.4**
french fries las papas fritas, **2.5**
Friday el viernes, **2.6**
friend el / la amigo(a), **2.3**
from de, **2.3**
  Are you [fam.] **from here?** ¿Eres de aquí?, **1.1**
  from the del (de + el), de la, **2.3**
  I'm from . . . soy de . . . , **1.1**

front: in front of enfrente de, **6.3**
fruit la fruta, **2.5**
fun divertido(a), **2.2**
  What fun! ¡Qué divertido!, **1.6**
funny cómico(a), **4.5**

G

gadget el aparato, **5.2**
game el partido, **1.2**
  game show el concurso, **4.5**
garbage la basura, **3.3**
generous generoso(a), **2.2**
gentleman el caballero, **6.2**
  for gentlemen para caballeros, **6.2**
geometry la geometría, **1.4**
German alemán(ana), **5.3; (language)** el alemán, **5.3**
to **get: to get good grades** sacar buenas notas, **1.4**
gift el regalo, **2.3**
girl la muchacha, **2.2**
to **give** dar, **5.1**
  to give advice to dar consejos a, **5.6**
  I give doy, **5.2**
glass (material) el vidrio, **5.2**
gloves los guantes, **6.1**
to **go** ir, **1.2**
  he / she / it goes, you [formal] **go** va, **2.3**
  I go voy, **2.3**
  they go van, **2.3**
  we go vamos, **2.3**
  you [fam.] **go** vas, **2.3**
to **go out** salir, **3.1**
  I go out salgo, **3.1**
gold el oro, **5.2**
goldfish el pez dorado, **4.3**
good bueno, **1.6**

good afternoon buenas tardes, **1.3**
good evening buenas noches, **1.3**
good morning buenos días, **1.3**
good night buenas noches, **1.3**
good-looking guapo(a), **2.2**
good-bye adiós, **1.4**
gorilla el gorila, **4.3**
grade la nota, **1.4**
grandfather el abuelo, **4.1**
grandmother la abuela, **4.1**
grandparents los abuelos, **4.1**
gray gris, **3.6**
great: That's great! ¡Qué bueno!, **1.6**
green verde, **4.4**
group: musical group el conjunto, **2.3**
Guatemalan guatemalteco(a), **5.3**
guitar la guitarra, **5.3**
  guitar player el / la guitarrista, **2.1**
  to play the guitar tocar la guitarra, **1.5**
gymnasium el gimnasio, **2.3**

H

hair el pelo, **4.4**
half: half an hour la media hora, **1.3**
  half past the hour y media, **1.3**
ham el jamón, **2.5**
hamburger la hamburguesa, **2.5**
handbag la bolsa, **6.1**
happy contento(a), **3.4**
to **have** tener (ie), **3.5**
  to have to tener que + inf., **4.4**

I have tengo, **3.5**
he él, **3.1**
to **hear** oír, **5.5**
heat el calor, **6.5**
heavy pesado(a), **6.6**
hello hola, **1.1**
to **help** ayudar, **5.1**
her su(s) [poss.], **4.1**
her ella [obj. of prep.], **3.1**; la [dir. obj.], **6.4**; le [ind. obj.], **4.1**
here aquí, **1.1**
to **hike** dar una caminata, **6.4**
him le [ind. obj.], **4.1**; lo [dir. object], **6.4**
his su(s), **4.1**; de él, **2.3**
history la historia, **1.4**
home casa, **1.2**
  to go home ir a casa, **1.2**
homemaker el ama (f.) de casa, **4.2**
homework la tarea, **1.2**
  to do homework hacer la tarea, **1.2**
Honduran hondureño(a), **5.3**
horrible horrible, **2.1**
  How horrible! ¡Qué horrible!, **1.6**
horror el terror, **4.5**
  horror program el programa de terror, **4.5**
horse el caballo, **4.3**
horseback: to ride horseback montar a caballo, **1.5**
hot: it's hot hace calor, **6.4**
hour la hora, **5.5**
house la casa, **2.6**
How . . . ! ¡Qué . . . !, **1.6**
how? ¿cómo?, **1.4**
  How are you [fam.]? ¿Cómo estás?, **1.3**; ¿Qué tal?, **1.1**

How are you [formal]? ¿Cómo está usted?, **1.3**
How do you say . . . ? ¿Cómo se dice . . . ?, **5.2**
How long? ¿Cuánto tiempo?, **5.4**
How long has it been since . . . ? ¿Cuánto tiempo hace que . . . ?, **5.5**
how many? ¿cuántos(as)?, **3.3**
how much? ¿cuánto(a)?, **3.3**
How much do you (does he / she) weigh? ¿Cuánto pesa(s)?, **6.6**
How much does it cost? ¿Cuánto vale?, **4.2**
How old are you (is he / she)? ¿Cuántos años tiene(s)?, **4.2**
How tall are you (is he / she)? ¿Cuánto mide(s)?, **6.6**
hundred: one hundred cien, **3.3**; ciento, **4.2**
  one hundred one (two) ciento uno (dos), **4.2**
hungry: to be hungry tener hambre(f.), **6.5**
hurry: to be in a hurry tener prisa, **6.5**

I

I yo, **3.1**
ice el hielo, **1.5**
ice cream el helado, **2.5**
to **ice-skate** patinar sobre hielo, **1.5**
if si, **3.1**
impatient impaciente, **2.1**

in en, **3.2**
  in love enamorado(a), **3.4**
inch la pulgada, **6.6**
incredible increíble, **2.1**
industrious aplicado(a), **2.2**
inexpensive barato(a), **3.5**
inside adentro, **3.3**
intelligent inteligente, **2.1**
interesting interesante, **2.1**
to **introduce** presentar, **5.6**
to **iron** planchar, **5.6**
it lo [dir. obj. pron.], **6.4**
  it is + distance **from** está a + distance, **6.3**
its su(s), **4.1**
Italian italiano(a), **5.3**; **(language)** el italiano, **5.3**

J

jacket la chaqueta, **6.1**
jam la mermelada, **2.5**
January enero, **4.6**
Japanese japonés(esa), **5.3**; **(language)** el japonés, **5.3**
jewel la joya, **6.1**
job el trabajo, **2.3**
journalist el / la periodista, **4.2**
juice el jugo, **2.5**
July julio, **4.6**
jump saltar, **5.4**
jump the waves satlas las olas

K

to **keep** guardar, **5.2**
key la llave, **5.2**
kind amable, **2.1**; la clase, **4.5**

What kind of . . . ?
¿Qué clase de . . . ?,
4.5
kitchen la cocina, **3.6**
knapsack la mochila,
1.4
to **know** saber, **1.5; (a person or place)** conocer (zco), **5.5**
I know sé, **1.5**

L

ladies las damas, **6.2**
for ladies para damas,
6.2
ladies' clothing ropa
para damas, **6.2**
lake el lago, **6.4**
lamp la lámpara, **3.6**
language el idioma, **1.4**
last pasado(a), **5.3**
last month el mes pasado, **5.3**
last night anoche, **5.3**
last week la semana
pasada, **5.3**
last year el año pasado, **5.3**
late tarde, **2.4**
later luego, **2.3**
see you later hasta
luego, **1.4**
lawn el césped, **5.6**
lawyer el / la abogado(a), **4.2**
lazy perezoso(a), **2.2**
to **learn** aprender, **1.4**
to learn how to aprender a + inf., **4.5**
leather el cuero, **5.2**
left la izquierda, **3.3**
(on) to the left a la izquierda, **3.3**
to **lend** prestar, **5.1**
lenses: contact lenses
los lentes de contacto,
4.4
less menos, **6.5**

less than menos que,
6.5
more or less más o
menos, **6.6**
letter la carta, **3.1**
lettuce la lechuga, **2.5**
library la biblioteca, **1.5**
light (weight) liviano(a),
6.6
like como, **6.5**
to **like: Do you like . . . ?**
¿Te gusta . . . ?, **1.6**
Do you [fam.] **like**
[pl.] **. . . ?** ¿Te
gustan . . . ?, **1.6**
Do you [formal] **(does
he / she) like . . . ?**
¿Le gusta . . . ?, **4.1**
Do you [pl.] **(do they)
like . . . ?** ¿Les
gustan . . . ?, **4.1**
I like me gusta, **1.4;** a
mí me gusta, **4.1**
I would like quisiera,
3.4
What do you [fam.] **like
best?** ¿Qué te
gusta más?, **1.4**
you like te gusta, **1.4;**
a ti te gusta, **4.1**
you like [pl.] te gustan,
1.4
line la cola, **5.5**
to stand in line hacer
cola,
lion el león, **4.3**
to **listen (to)** escuchar, **1.2**
Listen! ¡Oye!, **2.4**
little: a little un poco,
2.2
to **live** vivir, **3.1**
llama la llama, **4.3**
locker la gaveta, **1.4**
long largo(a), **4.4**
long-sleeved de
manga larga, **6.2**
to **look for** buscar, **2.3**
to **lose** perder (ie), **4.5**
love: in love enamorado(a), **3.4**

love story el programa
romántico, **4.5**
luck la suerte, **1.6**
What luck! ¡Qué
suerte!, **1.6**
lunch el almuerzo, **2.5**

M

ma'am señora (abbreviation Sra.), **1.3**
magazine la revista, **1.2**
man el hombre, **4.2**
many muchos(as), **4.2**
map el mapa, **3.1**
March marzo, **4.6**
mathematics las
matemáticas, **1.4**
matter: it doesn't matter no importa, **2.4**
May mayo, **4.6**
me me [obj. pron.], **5.1**
meat la carne, **2.5**
mechanic el / la
mecánico(a), **4.2**
meeting la reunión, **5.5**
men los caballeros, **6.2**
men's clothing ropa
para caballeros, **6.2**
metal el metal, **5.2**
Mexican mexicano(a),
5.3
mile la milla, **6.6**
milk la leche, **2.5**
million el millón (de),
5.3
minute el minuto, **5.5**
mirror el espejo, **3.6**
Miss señorita (abbreviation Srta.), **1.3**
mistaken equivocado(a),
3.4
modern moderno(a), **3.5**
mom la mamá, **4.1**
mom and dad los
papás, **4.1**
Monday el lunes, **2.6**
money el dinero, **2.3**
monkey el mono, **4.3**

month   el mes, 4.6
  last month   el mes pasado, 5.3
more   más, 6.5
  more or less   más o menos, 6.6
  more than   más que, 6.5
morning   la mañana, 2.4
  in the morning   por la mañana, 2.4; de la mañana, 6.2
  this morning   esta mañana, 2.4
mother   la madre, 4.1
motorcycle   la moto, 3.5
mountain   la montaña, 6.4
mouse   el ratoncito, 4.3
movie   la película, 1.2
movies   el cine, 1.5
Mr.   señor (abbreviation Sr.), 1.3
Mrs.   señora (abbreviation Sra.), 1.3
music   la música, 1.4
musician   el / la músico(a), 2.1
mustache   el bigote, 4.4
my   mi(s), 3.6

N

name   el nombre, 5.1
  my name is . . .   me llamo . . . , 1.1
  What is your name [fam.] ?   ¿Cómo te llamas?, 1.1
near   cerca de, 6.3
necklace   el collar, 6.1
necktie   la corbata, 6.1
to need   necesitar, 1.4
  neighbor   el / la vecino(a), 5.5
nervous   nervioso(a), 3.4
never   nunca, 2.4
new   nuevo(a), 3.5
news   las noticias, 4.5

newspaper   el periódico, 2.3
next   que viene, 4.6
  next month   el mes que viene, 4.6
  next year   el año que viene, 4.6
  next to   al lado de, 6.3
Nicaraguan   nicaragüense, 5.3
nice   simpático(a), 2.2
  nice to meet you   mucho gusto, 1.1
  the weather is nice   hace buen tiempo, 6.4
night   la noche, 2.4
  at night   de la noche, 1.3; por la noche, 2.4
  last night   anoche, 5.3
nine   nueve, 1.3
  nine hundred   novecientos(as), 4.3
nineteen   diez y nueve, 1.3
ninety   noventa, 3.3
ninth   noveno(a), 3.2
no   no, 1.2
North American   norteamericano(a), 5.3
not   no, 1.2
notebook   el cuaderno, 1.4
nothing   nada, 1.2
November   noviembre, 4.6
now   ahora, 2.3
number   número, 3.1
  telephone number   el número de teléfono, 3.1
nurse   el / la enfermero(a), 4.2

O

o'clock: at one o'clock   a la una, 1.3

  at (two) o'clock   a las (dos), 1.3
October   octubre, 4.6
of   de, 2.3
  of the   del (de + el), de la, 2.3
office   la oficina, 3.3
OK   de acuerdo, 2.6
old   viejo(a), 2.2; (object) antiguo(a), 3.5
older   mayor, 4.1
on   en, 3.2
one   uno, 1.3
  one hundred   cien, 3.3; ciento, 4.2
to open   abrir, 5.2
or   o, 1.4
orange   anaranjado(a), 3.6
ounce   la onza, 6.6
our   nuestro(a), 5.4
outdoors   al aire libre, 6.4
outside   afuera, 3.3
overcoat   el abrigo, 6.1
owner   el / la dueño(a), 4.2

P

to pack (suitcases)   hacer las maletas, 3.1
page   la página, 1.4
Panamanian   panameño(a), 5.3
pants   los pantalones, 6.1
panty hose   las pantimedias, 6.1
paper   el papel, 1.4
Paraguayan   paraguayo(a), 5.3
parakeet   el periquito, 4.3
parents   los padres, 4.1
park   el parque, 1.5
party   la fiesta, 1.5
passport   el pasaporte, 3.1
pastry   el pastel, 2.5

to **pay**   pagar, **5.6**
  pencil   el lápiz, **1.4**
  penguin   el pingüino, **4.3**
  permission   el permiso, **5.6**
  Peruvian   peruano(a), **5.3**
  physical: physical educa-
    tion   la educación
    física, **1.4**
  pick-up truck   la ca-
    mioneta, **6.3**
  picture   la foto, **1.5**
  pink   rosado(a), **3.6**
  place   el lugar, **1.5**
  plaid   de cuadros, **6.2**
to **plan**   pensar (ie), **2.6**
  planear, **5.4**
  plastic   el plástico, **5.2**
to **play**   jugar (ue) **(game),**
  1.2; tocar **(instru-**
  ment), 1.5
  playing: playing cards
    las cartas, **4.5**
  plaza   la plaza, **3.2**
  please   por favor, **5.1**
  pocket   el bolsillo, **5.2**
  police officer   el / la mu-
    jer policía, **4.2**
  politician   el / la polí-
    tico(a), **2.1**
  polka-dotted   de lunares, **6.2**
  popular   popular, **2.1**
  post office   el correo, **5.1**
  postcard   la tarjeta
    postal, **3.5**
  poster   el cartel, **3.5**
  pound   la libra, **6.6**
to **practice**   practicar, **1.2**
to **prefer**   preferir (ie), **4.5**
to **prepare**   preparar, **2.5**
  pretty   bonito(a), **3.5**
  problem   el problema, **5.6**
  professor   el / la pro-
    fesor / a, **4.2**
  program   el programa, **4.5**
to **promise**   prometer, **5.6**
  Puerto Rican   puertorri-
    queño(a), **5.3**
  punctual   puntual, **2.1**
  purple   morado(a), **3.6**

Q

  question   la pregunta, **1.4**
  to ask a question
    hacer una pregunta, **1.4**

R

  rabbit   el conejo, **4.3**
  radio (as a medium)   la
    radio, **1.4; (set)** el ra-
    dio, **3.5**
  raincoat   el impermea-
    ble, **6.1**
  raining: it's raining
    llueve, **6.4**
to **read**   leer, **1.2**
to **receive**   recibir, **3.1**
  record   el disco, **1.2**
  rectangular   rectangular, **5.2**
  red   rojo(a), **3.6**
  refrigerator   el re-
    frigerador, **3.6**
  relative   el / la parien-
    te(ta), **4.1**
to **remember**   recordar (ue), **3.1**
to **remove**   quitar, **5.6**
to **rest**   descansar, **1.2**
  restaurant   el restau-
    rante, **1.5**
  restroom   el servicio, **3.3**
to **return**   regresar, **4.6**
  rice   el arroz, **2.5**
to **ride**   montar, **1.2**
  to ride a bicycle   mon-
    tar en bicicleta, **1.2**
  to ride horseback
    montar a caballo, **1.5**
  right   la derecha, **3.3**
  to the right   a la de-
    recha, **3.3**
  right?   ¿verdad?, **2.5**
  ring   el anillo, **6.1**
  river   el río, **6.4**
  room (of a house)   el
    cuarto, **3.6**
  bathroom   el baño, **3.6**
    dining room   el co-
      medor, **3.6**
    living room   la sala, **3.6**
  round   redondo(a), **5.2**

  rubber   la goma, **5.2**
  rug   la alfombra, **3.6**
to **run**   correr, **1.2**
  Russian   ruso(a), **5.3;**
    (language) el ruso, **5.3**

S

  sad   triste, **3.4**
  sailboat   el velero, **5.4**
  sailing: to go sailing
    pasear en velero, **5.4**
  salad   la ensalada, **2.5**
  Salvadoran   sal-
    vadoreño(a), **5.3**
  sandals   las sandalias, **6.1**
  sandwich   el sandwich, **2.5**
  Saturday   el sábado, **2.6**
to **save**   ahorrar, **3.1**
to **say**   decir (i), **5.5**
  I say   digo, **5.5**
  it's said   se dice, **5.2**
  You don't say!   ¡No me
    digas!, **1.6**
  scared: to be scared
    tener miedo, **6.5**
  scarf   la bufanda, **6.1**
  school   la escuela, **1.5**
  science(s)   las ciencias, **1.4**
  science fiction   la ciencia
    ficción, **4.5**
    science fiction pro-
      gram   el programa
      de ciencia ficción, **4.5**
  sea   el mar, **5.4**
  second   segundo(a), **3.2**
to **see**   ver, **1.2**
  let's see   a ver, **1.6**
to **seem: seems**   parece, **4.1**
  it seems that . . .   pa-
    rece que . . . , **4.3**
to **sell**   vender, **5.6**
to **send**   mandar, **5.1**
  September   septiembre, **4.6**
to **set: to set the table**
    poner la mesa, **5.6**
  seven   siete, **1.3**
    seven hundred   sete-
      cientos(as), **4.3**
  seventeen   diez y siete, **1.3**
  seventh   séptimo(a), **3.2**

seventy   setenta, 3.3
several   varios(as), 5.5
shame: What a shame!
   ¡Qué pena!, 1.6
she   ella, 3.1
shirt   la camisa, 6.1
shoes   los zapatos, 3.5
shopping center   el centro comercial, 1.5
short (object)   corto(a), 4.4; (person) bajo(a), 2.2
short-sleeved   de manga corta, 6.2
shorts (pants)   los shorts, 6.1
should   deber, 3.1
to show   enseñar, 5.1
   game show   el concurso, 4.5
siblings   los hermanos, 4.1
sick   enfermo(a), 3.4
side   el lado, 6.3
silk   la seda, 6.2
silly   tonto(a), 2.2
silver   la plata, 5.2
since   desde, 5.3
to sing   cantar, 1.5
singer   el / la cantante, 2.1
sir   señor (abbreviation Sr.), 1.3
sister   la hermana, 4.1
six   seis, 1.3
   six hundred   seiscientos(as), 4.3
sixteen   diez y seis, 1.3
sixth   sexto(a), 3.2
sixty   sesenta, 3.3
to skate   patinar, 1.5
to skateboard   andar en monopatín (m.), 1.2
to ski   esquiar, 1.5
to skin-dive   bucear, 5.4
skirt   la falda, 6.1
to sleep   dormir (ue), 3.1
   to sleep outdoors   dormir al aire libre, 6.4
sleepy: to be sleepy   tener sueño, 6.5
sleeve   la manga, 6.2
   sleeveless   sin mangas, 6.2

small   pequeño(a), 2.2
smart   listo(a), 2.2
snake   la serpiente, 4.3
sneakers   los tenis, 6.1
snowing: it's snowing   nieva, 6.4
so-so   regular, 1.1
   the weather is so-so   hace un tiempo regular, 6.4
soap opera   la telenovela, 4.5
soccer   el fútbol, 1.2
sociable   sociable, 2.1
socks   los calcetines, 6.1
soda   la gaseosa, 2.5
sofa   el sofá, 3.6
soft drink (noncarbonated)   el refresco, 2.5
solid (color)   de un solo color, 6.2
something   algo, 1.2
sometimes   a veces, 2.4
son   el hijo, 4.1
soup   la sopa, 2.5
souvenir   el recuerdo, 3.5
Spanish   español / a, 5.3; (language) el español, 1.4
to spend (time)   pasar, 5.4; (money) gastar, 5.4
sport   el deporte, 1.2
   to play sports   practicar deportes, 1.2
sports   deportivo(a), 6.2
   sports program   el programa deportivo, 4.5
spring   la primavera, 6.2
square   cuadrado(a), 5.2
stadium   el estadio, 1.5
stairs   la escalera, 3.3
stamp   el sello, 3.5
to stand in line   hacer cola, 5.5
to start   empezar (ie), 4.5
stereo   el estéreo, 3.5
stingy   tacaño(a), 2.2
store   la tienda, 1.5
story (of a building)   el piso, 3.2
stove   la estufa, 3.6

straight   derecho(a), 6.3
   go straight   sigues derecho [fam. sing.], 6.3
straight (hair)   lacio, 4.4
strange: How strange!
   ¡Qué raro!, 1.6
street   la calle, 3.1
striped   de rayas, 6.2
stroll: to go for a stroll
   dar un paseo, 1.2
student   el / la estudiante, 2.1
to study   estudiar, 1.2
   to study for an exam   estudiar para un examen, 1.4
   to study to be a   estudiar para, 4.2
suit   el traje, 6.1
   gentleman's suit   el traje para caballero, 6.1
   lady's suit   el traje de dama, 6.1
suitcase   la maleta, 3.1
summer   el verano, 6.2
sun   el sol, 6.4
to sunbathe   tomar sol, 5.4
Sunday   el domingo, 2.6
sunglasses   los anteojos de sol, 6.1
sunny: it's sunny   hace sol, 6.4
supermarket   el supermercado, 2.6
supervisor   el / la supervisor / a, 4.2
supper   la cena, 2.5
sure   seguro(a), 3.4
sweater   el suéter, 6.1
to sweep   barrer, 5.6
to swim   nadar, 1.2
   swimming pool   la piscina, 1.5
synagogue   la sinagoga, 2.6

T

T-shirt   la camiseta, 3.5
table   la mesa, 3.6
to take   llevar, 3.1; tomar, 3.2

to take care of cuidar (a), **4.3**
to take a long time tardar en, **6.6**
to take out sacar, **5.6**
to take pictures sacar fotos, **1.5**
to **talk** hablar, **1.2**
  to talk on the telephone hablar por teléfono, **1.2**
  to talk to hablar con, **1.2**
tall alto(a), **2.2**
tape recorder la grabadora, **3.5**
tea el té, **2.5**
to **teach how to** enseñar a, **5.4**
teacher el / la maestro(a), **1.2**
team el equipo, **5.5**
teeth los dientes, **4.4**
telephone el teléfono, **3.1**
  to talk on the telephone hablar por teléfono, **1.2**
television (set) el televisor, **3.5**
ten diez, **1.3**
tennis el tenis, **1.2**
tenth décimo(a), **3.2**
terrific formidable, **2.1**; estupendo(a), **5.4**
thank: thank you gracias, **1.2**
  thank you for . . . gracias por . . . , **2.1**
thanks: no, thanks no, gracias, **1.2**
that ese (m.), esa (f.), **6.6**
the el (m.), la (f.), **1.4**; los (m.), **1.4**; las (f.), **1.4**
theater: movie theater el cine, **1.5**
their su(s), **4.1**
them ellos (m.); ellas (f.), **3.1**; les [ind. obj. pron.], **4.1**; los [m., dir. obj. pron.], **6.4**; las [f., dir. obj. pron.], **6.4**
then entonces, **2.3**

there allí, **3.3**
there: there is, there are hay, **3.3**
therefore por eso, **5.6**
these estos (m.), estas (f.), **6.6**
they ellos (m.); ellas (f.), **3.1**
thin delgado(a), **2.2**
thing la cosa, **5.2**
to **think: I think that** creo que, **4.2**
third tercero(a), **3.2**
thirsty: to be thirsty tener sed (f.), **6.5**
thirteen trece, **1.3**
thirty treinta, **3.3**
this este (m.), esta (f.), **6.6**
those esos (m.), esas (f.), **6.6**
thousand: one thousand mil, **4.3**
three tres, **1.3**
Thursday el jueves, **2.6**
ticket (admission) la entrada, **5.5**
tiger el tigre, **4.3**
time la hora, **1.3**; el tiempo, **5.5**
  At what time is . . . ? ¿A qué hora es . . . ?, **1.3**
  free time los ratos libres, **4.5**
tired cansado(a), **3.4**
to a, **1.5**
  to the al (a + el), a la, **1.5**
toast el pan tostado, **2.5**
today hoy, **2.4**
tomato el tomate, **2.5**
tomorrow mañana, **2.3**
  the day after tomorrow pasado mañana, **4.6**
tonight esta noche, **2.4**
too también, **1.6**
  too much demasiado, **2.2**
town el pueblo, **2.3**
train el tren, **6.3**
to **travel** viajar, **3.1**
trophy el trofeo, **3.5**
Tuesday el martes, **2.6**
to **turn** doblar, **6.3**

turtle la tortuga, **4.3**
TV la tele, **1.2**
twelve doce, **1.3**
twenty veinte, **1.3**
two dos, **1.3**
  two hundred doscientos(as), **4.2**

U

ugly feo(a), **2.2**
umbrella el paraguas, **6.1**
uncle el tío, **4.1**
to **understand** entender (ie), **2.6**
United States: from the United States estadounidense, **5.3**
unpleasant (person) antipático(a), **2.2**
until hasta, **2.6**
upstairs arriba, **3.3**
Uruguayan uruguayo(a), **5.3**
us nos [obj. pron.], **6.2**
to **use** usar, **1.4**
  to use the computer usar la computadora, **1.5**
  used: it's used for . . . sirve para . . . , **5.2**

V

vacation las vacaciones, **2.3**
  to go on vacation ir de vacaciones, **2.3**
to **vacuum** pasar la aspiradora, **5.6**
vacuum cleaner la aspiradora, **5.6**
vegetables las legumbres, **2.5**
Venezuelan venezolano(a), **5.3**
very muy, **1.1**
  very well muy bien, **1.1**
veterinarian el / la veterinario(a), **4.2**
video el vídeo, **3.5**

video game   el video-
    juego, **2.1**
visit   la visita, **5.4**
to **visit**   visitar, **1.2**
volleyball   el vóleibol, **5.5**

W

to **wait for**   esperar, **5.5**
walk: to go for a walk
    dar un paseo, **1.2**
to **walk**   ir a pie, **6.3**
wall   la pared, **3.6**
wallet   la billetera, **5.2**
to **want**   querer (ie), **1.2**
    I want   quiero, **1.2**
    I don't want to do any-
      thing   no quiero
      hacer nada, **1.2**
    I don't want to go any-
      where   no quiero ir
      a ningún lugar, **1.5**
    you [fam.] **want**
      quieres, **1.2**
to **wash**   lavar, **2.6**
to **watch: to watch TV**   ver
    la tele, **1.2**
water   el agua, **2.5**
    to water ski   practicar
      el esquí acuático, **5.4**
waves (ocean)   las olas, **5.4**
way: No way!   ¡Qué va!, **1.6**
we   nosotros(as), **3.1**
to **wear**   llevar, **6.1**
weather   el tiempo, **6.4**
    What's the weather
      like?   ¿Qué tiempo
      hace?, **6.4**
Wednesday   el miércoles, **2.6**
week   la semana, **2.6**
    last week   la semana
      pasada, **5.3**
weekend   el fin de se-
    mana, **2.6**
welcome: you're wel-
    come   de nada, **2.1**
well   bien, **1.1**; pues, **1.6**
    not too well   no muy
      bien, **1.1**
    very well   muy bien, **1.1**

what?   ¿qué?, **1.2**;
    ¿cómo?, **1.4**
What is he / she / it
    like?   ¿Cómo es
    . . . ?, **2.1**
What is it used for?
    ¿Para qué sirve?, **5.2**
What's it made of?   ¿De
    qué es?, **5.2**
What's your phone
    number?   ¿Cuál es
    tu número de telé-
    fono?, **3.3**
when?   ¿cuándo?, **2.4**
where: to where?
    ¿adónde?, **1.5**
    Where are you going?
    ¿Adónde vas?, **2.3**
    Where is it?   ¿Dónde
    está?, **3.2**
which: which (one)?
    ¿cuál?, **4.5**
white   blanco(a), **3.6**
who?   ¿quién?, **2.2**
whose: Whose is it / are
    they?   ¿De quién
    es / son?, **2.3**
why: Why not . . . ?   ¿Por
    qué no . . . ?, **2.5**
to **win**   ganar, **4.5**
wind: It's windy   Hace
    viento, **6.4**
window   la ventana, **3.6**
winter   el invierno, **6.2**
with   con, **1.2**
    with me   conmigo, **5.4**
    with you [fam.] con-
      tigo, **5.4**
without   sin, **6.2**
woman   la mujer, **4.2**
wood   la madera, **5.2**
wool   la lana, **6.2**
word   la palabra, **1.4**
work   el trabajo, **2.3**
to **work**   trabajar, **1.4**
worried   preocupado(a), **3.4**
worse   peor, **6.5**
to **write**   escribir, **1.4**
    to write a check   hacer
      un cheque, **5.1**

writer   el / la escritor / a,
    2.1

Y

year   el año, **4.6**
    last year   el año pa-
      sado, **5.3**
    next year   el año que
      viene, **4.6**
    What year were you
      [fam.] **born?**   ¿En
      qué año naciste?,
      5.3
yellow   amarillo(a), **3.6**
yes   sí, **1.1**
yesterday   ayer, **5.3**
    the day before yester-
      day   anteayer, **5.3**
you [fam.] tú, **3.1**; [fam.
    pl.] vosotros(as), **3.1**;
    [formal] usted, **1.3**;
    [pl.] ustedes, **3.1**
young   joven, **2.2**
    young people   los
      jóvenes, **4.3**
younger   menor, **4.1**
your   tu, **3.6**; [formal]
    su(s), **4.1**

Z

zero   cero, **1.3**
zoo   el parque zoológico,
    4.3

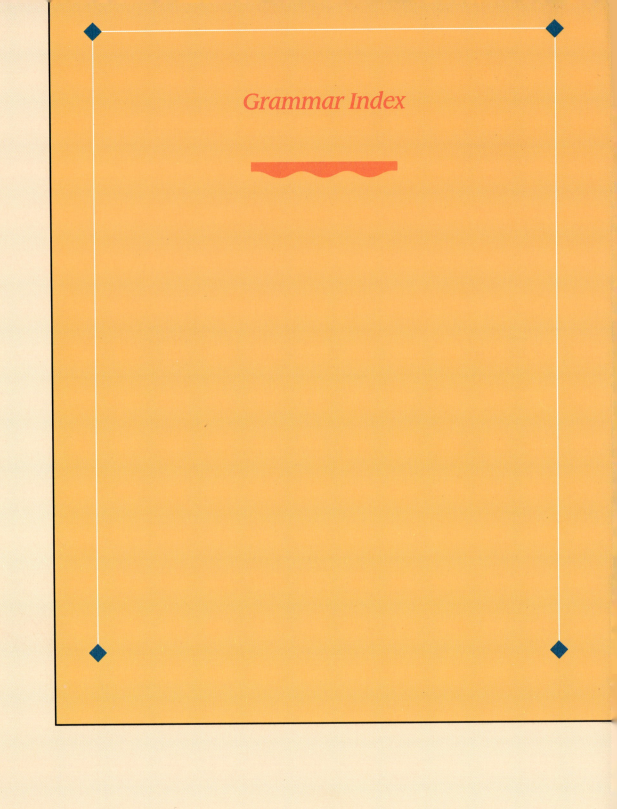

Grammar Index